EMERGENCE OF THE STATE

Compiled & Edited
by
Dr. R.K. Pruthi

DISCOVERY PUBLISHING HOUSE
NEW DELHI-110002

First Published-2005

ISBN 81-7141-998-4

Published by

DISCOVERY PUBLISHING HOUSE
4831/24, Ansari Road, Prahlad Street,
Darya Ganj, New Delhi-110002 (India)
Phone: 23279245 • Fax: 91-11-23253475
E-mail:dphtemp@indiatimes.com

Printed at:
Arora Offset Press
Laxmi Nagar, Delhi 110 092.

Preface

Why did state originate? How did it evolve? What were its aims, nature, function and its relation with the society? In this book attempt has been to seek answers to the above questions.

Aim is to make available to our readers material on the eastern and western classical concepts of the various aspects of the state. Chapters on the crisis of political theory and history and sources of the science of polity, to provide sound background and research orientation have been included. Effort has been made to select useful essays for students and teachers.

In preparing this work, we have been influenced by the authorities on the subject. We record our respectful acknowledgements to them.

We have received every possible co-operation and help from librarians and their staff members. We thank them.

My publisher and his staff members have worked hard. Our readers satisfaction will be our best reward.

R.K. Pruthi

Contents

1

The State

What is a State? That is the question to which we must try to find an answer to-day. Let us begin with suggested and accepted definitions, and test them, so as to eliminate anything which we consider to be either superfluous or erroneous. The shorter a definition the better, provided its terseness does not mar its clarity and sufficiency. It should contain the essentials of the term defined, and also its differentia or specialties, so as to separate it from cognate and allied terms. Where the thing defined is complex, as is the case with the thing we call the State, the difficulty of reconciling adequacy and terseness is obvious.

THE EAST

India

We turn first to India, as indicated in the last lecture, in our search for the definition of a State. We have to fact here the difficulty, that, as Bernouf—I think it was—said of Egypt, there are no "beginnings" in the modern sense; the State "springs forth on the stage of history complete, as Minerva from the head of Jove".

Nor is there anything surprising or unlikely in this if the traditions of Egypt and India are true, for in each case tradition tells of Divine Dynasties, of a superhuman Legislator, and in India the latter, named Manu, was literally the Father of his people. Thus the race began in his Family, multiplied and spread for unknown periods of time in Central Asia, ultimately invading India, conquering it and settling down therein, while other branches from the same Patriarchal Family went westwards in successive waves, and spreading over and settling in Europe, and carrying with them the early simple Āryan polity of self-governing village communities, their ineradicable love of liberty, and the genius for democratic institutions so characteristic of the Āryan race. After explaining the Teutonic Mark (*Village communities.* Lecture), or Township as:

> An organized self-acting group of Teutonic families, exercising a common proprietorship over a definite tract of land, its Mark, cultivating its domain on a common system and sustaining itself by the produce.

Maine points out that similar groups were "the political unit of the earliest English society," existed in Scandinavia, were observed in the Orkney and Shetland Islands by Walter Scott, and in England were later absorbed in larger aggregations. The "larger groups, in which Families are found to have been primitively combined for the purposes of ownership of land", make the Village, living on its land, which can be fully studied in India. He speaks of the individual property in land as disengaging itself from collective holdings, as shown in Teutonic and Scandinavian villages, and even in England, and notes that "these primitive European tenures and this primitive European tillage constitute that actual working system of the Indian village communities, and that they determine the whole course of Anglo-Indian administration". These villages lived under customary law; the:

> Council of village elders does not command anything; it merely declares what has always been... Their antiquity is by itself assumed to be a sufficient reason for obeying them... a person aggrieved complains not of an individual wrong, but of the disturbance of the order of the entire little society. More than all, customary law is not enforced by a sanction. In the almost inconceivable case of disobedience to the award of the Village Council, the sole punishment, or the sole certain punishment, would appear to be universal disapprobation.

The importance of this to us is that we find in the West the view that the function of the Government of a State is to give "command under penalty," but in this early Village State there is no command, and no penalty save disapprobation.

Maine once more, compelled by his study of law, remarks on the ignorance of Eastern phenomena shown by the Western writers on this subject, and says:

> The Village Community of India exhibits resemblances to the Teutonic Township which are much too strong and numerous to be accidental; where it differs from the township, the difference may be at least plausibly explained. It has the same double aspect of a group of families united by the assumption of common kinship, and of a company of persons exercising joint ownership over land. The domain which it occupies is distributed, it not in the same manner, upon the same principles, and the ideas which prevail within the group of the relations and duties of its members to one another appear to be substantially the same. But the Indian Village Community is a living and not a dead institution. The causes which transformed the Mark into the Manor, though they may be traced in India, have operated very feebly; and over the greatest part of the country the Village-Community have not been absorbed in any larger collection of men, or lost in a territorial area of wider extent. For fiscal and legal purposes it is the proprietary unit of large and populous Provinces. It is under constant and careful observation, and the doubtful points which it exhibits are the subject of the most earnest discussion and of the most vehement controversy. No better example could therefore be given of the new material which the East, and especially India, furnishes to the juridical enquirer.... [India] is the great repository of verifiable phenomena of ancient usage and ancient juridical thought.

Sir Henry Maine refers to two-books, one by Sir John Lubbock and the other by Mr. McLennan, who "conceive them selves to have shown that the first steps of mankind towards civilization were taken from a condition in which assemblages of men followed practices which are not found to occur universally even in animal nature". These he observes, may be found in India in some aboriginal tribes, driven into inaccessible recesses in mountainous districts, but some of these usages, referred to immemorial antiquity, "have been described to me as having been for the first time resorted to in our own days through the mere pressure of external circumstances or novel temptations". This view agrees, we shall see presently, with that of Dr. Wilson.

We are on safer ground when, following the most ancient Indian literature, we see society originating in the Patriarchal Family, which is a "group of men and women, children and slaves, of animate and inanimate property, all connected together by common subjection to the Paternal Power of the chief of the household". Such families growing up in Central Asia, forming villages and cities and spreading thence, would when once settled in India, while keeping the original type in the villages, readily develop into cities and kingdoms in the course of many generations, multiplying "for untold centuries," as Vincent Smith says, and becoming the highly civilized communities we read of three thousand years before the Christian era.

There are thousands of years for their growth before the books on polity, now in our possession, were written, during which the history of the then existing States is at present lacking. Dr Sayce, in his Hibbert lectures of 1887, mentions Indian trade with Babylon nearly five thousand years ago, in 3000 B.C., India being then a congeries of wealthy, highly civilized, and trading States. Vincent Smith speaks of sixteen States between the Himalayas and the Nerbudda river, some monarchical, more aristocratic-republican, separated by forests, jungles, and unsettled lands.

Forms of Government were very various. Agatashatru, hereditary king of Magadha, was contemporary with Darius, King of Persia in the sixth century B.C. On the other hand, Dr. Radhakumud Mukerji, writing on the "Republics of Ancient India" (*The commonweal,* June 20th, 1918) quotes Megasthenes as speaking of five Nations by name, as peoples "Which are free, have no Kings and occupy mountain heights where they have built many cities". Curtius gives the name of "a powerful Indian people whose form of Government was democratic and not regal, who had no kings, but were led by three Generals". Arrian mentions others who preserved their autonomy intact for a long time before Alexander's invasion. He also mentions Nysa, a City-State, such as we shall find described in Aristotle, ruled by three hundred wise men, forming a Council with a President. When Alexander asked that one hundred men should be sent to him from the governing body, the President answered: "How, O King, can a single city, if deprived of a hundred of its best men, continue to be well governed?"

Not only do we find in India these manifold types of government, but we find also the State organism of a higher order the Empire over many kingdoms. Chandragupta Maurya, 321-297 B.C., ruled from the Hindu Khush to the Nerbudda, from the Arabian Sea to the Bay of Bengal. Bindusara extended his father's Empire to the south of Madras. Ashoka extended it still further, and had four Viceroys under his for administrative purposes. The Empire lasted from 321 B.C to 232 B.C. Other such Empires arose, earlier and later; I select this one, because it was the first reckoned in the West as historical. The Chakravarti, or Overlord, was a well-recognised figure in Ancient India, and was proclaimed with special ceremonial, as all readers of Indian literature know. The last "horse-sacrifice," the recognition of the Overlordship of the Lord Paramount of India, was offered in the seventh century A.D., by Ādityasena.

The literature we have belongs naturally to the more advanced and complex conditions, the "full-grown 'State' from the head of Jove". The polity is laid down by authority, if we accept the literature concerned, and this, so far as known, deals with kingdoms, castes, classes, kings, councillors, officials, etc., among the movables, villages, towns, districts, forts, etc., among the immovables, all in full working order, or with directions how to create the villages, etc., where the did not exist, as when population was too dense, or additional territory was acquired, new villages had to be formed. Fragments of history in the early days are available, from travellers mostly, which show us many forms of government over areas of varying size, from a city to a large district and on to great kingdoms and empires. In these we have descriptions of States, not definitions of "the State," and the word State as used in modern days is applicable to each of these areas. Thus we arrive at eliminating any special kind of government, and see only a Government, not a form of government, as essential to the idea of a State; moreover, it is a Government over an organized people, settled in a definite territory.

The *Arthashastra* of Kautilya (translated by R. Shamasastry, Mysore Government Oriental Library Series, Government Press, Bangalore, 1915), known also as Vishnugupta and Chanakya, the great Minister of Chandragupta Maurya, who began to reign six years before Alexander invaded Afghanistan, deals with a complicated and hug Empire, highly organized.

I am not concerned with any details of these Governments any more than of the villages—that will come later—and mention the existence of them in our search for definitions, merely to show that, as said, while a State implies a Government of same sort, the form of the Government is non-essential. In the time of Kautilya the Science of Government had been much discussed, and in Book I, chap. ii, after mentioning that there were four sciences, of which Danda Niti, the science of Government, was one, Kautilya mentions the schools of Manu, Brihaspati, Ushanas, as all dealing with the Science of Government, on which, says Kautilya, the other three sciences depend (Book I, chap. iv, I, p. 10).

We do not find either in Manu or in Kautilya and discussions as to the nature of a State. But we are told that a kingdom have seven limbs, or constituent parts: "The King, his Minister, his capital, his realm, his treasury, his army and his ally" (Manu's *Institutes*. (Chap. ix, v. 294, p. 395).

Kautilya gives them as "The King, the minister, the country, the fort, the treasury, the army and the friend" as "the elements of sovereignty". (Book VI, Chapter i, p. 318). But this does not help us to a definition of the State. Manu's laws are concerned with the inhabitants of a kingdom, their relationships, their offices, their functions, their duties, etc. The Family is the unit; "To be mothers were women created and to be fathers men"; "Let mutual fidelity continue until death; this may be considered as the summary of the highest law for husband and wife". "he only is a perfect man who consists of his wife, (Chap. ix, shl. 96, 101). himself and his offspring.... The husband is declared to be one with the wife"

(*Ibid.*, shl.45)—a far nobler conception, as we shall find, than that of Aristotle, the Greek.

It is the duty of the King to unite Families into Villages. "Villages," says Kautilya,

> consisting each of not less than a hundred families, and of not more than five hundred families of agricultural people of Shudra caste, with boundaries extending as far as a krosha or two and capable of protecting each other shall be formed. Boundaries shall be denoted by a river, a mountain, forests, bulbous plants, caves, artificial buildings, or by trees. (Book II, chap. i, para. 46).

Every aggregation of ten villages is to be protected by a sangrahana; in the centres of 200, 400 and 800 villages, fortresses of different kinds are to be erected, and strong forts with boundary guards on the frontiers of the kingdom, which is also to have a fortified capital in its center. (chap. iii, 51).

Manu directs that soldiers, commanded by a trusty officer, should be placed in the midst of groups of villages to protect the people, and each village is to have its ruler, and there are rulers also for groups of villages, 10, 20, 100, 1000 (chap. vii, 114, 115).

The details of organisation, once more, will be studied later. Here, as I said, we are seeking for definition of the State.

The *Shukraniti* (translated by Professor Benoy Kumar Sarkar, Panini Office, Allahabed), contains minute details for the discharge of the respective duties of the various classes of the people, and is purely practical. The State is the Kingdom, "an organism of seven limbs" (chap. i, 121), the same as already mentioned; it is composed of "*gramana, purana, deshan*", (*ibid.*, 751) villages cities and districts; the villages may be arranged in groups of 10, 100, 1,000, 10,000 for the purposes of government. The word indicating the State is Rashtran, equally used for kingdom, district, or region; it includes all immovable and movable objects within its area, and "belongs to him under whose submission it comes"—its ruler. The ten requisites in the administration of justice are the King, officers, councillors, Smrti Shastras, accountant, clerk, gold, fire, water and one's own men. (chap. iv, § v, 72).

A court of justice is that place where the study of the social, economic and political interests of man takes place according to the dictates of Dharma Shastras (*Ibid.*, 82). For definition these books yield:

"The State is an organism of seven limbs, under a Ruler and Council; it consists of villages, cities and districts, and has a body of laws and customs."

No form of government except this, apparently, is contemplated. It is obvious from the language used that we are in the presence of highly organized kingdoms, and this idea, arising from the most superficial glance, will become absolutely established in our later study. Summing up the general results from the facts available in ancient India we see a ladder of ascent. We have the rungs of Family, Village, Groups of villages, becoming larger and larger integrations, living in definite areas with their rulers, reaching the Kingdom, or the Republic. Eliminating differences, we find in all these four common factors: they are aggregations of human beings, of varied occupations, living on a fixed territory, with a government over each; that is, each is an organized community, a community with organs for the discharge of definite functions, and from a study of these we must form our Indian definition:

A State is an organized community of human beings settled in a definite area, and directed by a Government.

We see a family-State, a Village-State, a Multiple-Village-State, a Country-State.

To Manu we owe the luminous idea that all human societies like a family, consist of elders, equals, and youngers, to each of whom special duties should be rendered, reverence to the elders, friendship to the equals, protection to the youngers, and on the due discharge of these, the happiness of all States depends. The State should be founded on the Family, and State obligations are enlarged family obligations. The profound principle which emerges from this fundamental idea that man only becomes man in the family, that Man, the truly *human* being, is not a separate man, a husband-wife-child, raises Duty above Rights, obligations, above claims; it substitutes mutual helpfulness for competition, the law of sacrifice for the law of the struggle for existence. It is the recognition that man is a social, not an isolated being, and that the State should be moulded in accordance with this natural law. You will see the importance of this conception when you come to study the State, as conceived in modern Europe, until modern science reinforced ancient teaching, and thus gave birth to Socialism.

The Hebrews

In the Hebrew Nation we see the sequential development of the State from a patriarch, Abraham, the head of a Family from his twelve great-grandsons the multiplication into twelve Tribes, recognizing a descent from a common ancestor; the welding of these Tribes into a Nation, and the establishment of the Nation on a Territory. The story is probably true in the main outline, and if so offers a case of the gradual building up of the successive types of the State. In addition to this, the Hebrews become a Theocracy, after the multiplication of the Families into Tribes, and the theocratic element is dominant through the monarchies that succeed. It also gives an interesting illustration, I think unique, of the perishing of the Nation-State, by the destruction of its Government and the loss of its Territory and the survival of the Nation without country or ruler, preserving its National characteristics through its adherence to its National religion. It is a fact in favour of the view of a Nation, as being an Individual, a Spiritual Entity, a fragment of the Divine, able to live and preserve its individuality, without some of the organs which normally constitute parts of its form, and are generally regard as essentials of National life.

THE WEST

Greece

Let us now turn away from the East to the West, and again seek for a definition of the State as conceived in Greece and Rom. In the western world Plato with his *Republic*, Aristotle with his *Politics*, are the commanding figures as regards the idea of the State Bluntschli says of the last:

> His *Politics*, although written in that youthful period of the world's history which preceded the more advance development of the State,

> has yet remained for two thousand years one of the purest sources of political wisdom. (Chap. ii, p. 7).

Plato's essential idea of the State was that it was an organism, not merely an artificial compound. It should follow the Law of Nature, and be, as it were, the Ideal Man:

> The best State is that which approaches most nearly to the condition of the individual. If a part of the body suffers, the whole body feels the hurt and sympathises altogether with the part affected. (*Republic*, quoted by Bluntschli. (Book I, chap. iii, p. 36).

The idea of the unit of the State as a solitary individual merely, not as in the Indian view, a family lies at the root of many errors in practice, for it is man as isolated, not man as a Family, and leads to combat rather than to co-operation. The value of the Greek idea lies in recognizing the State as an Organism. Bluntschli well sums up his teaching:

> The State, according to Plato, is the highest revelation of human virtue, the harmonious manifestation of the powers of the human soul, humanity perfected. As the soul of man consists of a rational, a spirited, and a desiring element, and as reason and spirit ought to rule the desires, so in the Platonic ideal, the wise ought to rule, the brave warriors should protect the community, and the classes which are occupied with material acquisition and bodily work should obey the two higher orders. In the Body Politic, justice requires that each part should do its own work. (Book I, chap. iii, p. 36).

Aristotle does not in so many words give a definition of the State, but he identifies it with the City; he says that the best possible Society is City, "and the society thereof a political society". (Book I, chap. i, p. 9). As a definition this is hardly satisfactory, since it comes to the statement that "the society of a City is a City society," "political" being a derivative of *polis*, a city; but the meaning is clear, that only men who live in a city form a society worthy of the name, a city-man society. Such a "Political," or City-State, has a Government adapted to the nature of free men, and "is the government of free men and equals" (Book I, chap. vii, p. 20).

Aristotle does not ignore the fact that the family exists apart from the City, and that "Hesiod is right when he says, 'first a house, then a wife, then an ox for the plough,'" but this society "which Nature has established for daily support is the domestic"; also he remarks that "the society of many families, which was first instituted for their lasting mutual advantage, is called a village, and a village is most naturally composed of the descendants of one family," whence village government is the government of elders. But these, he does not regard as States, since States are governed by men who are free and equal. A City only arises as follows:

> When many villages so entirely join themselves together as in every respect to form but one society, that Society is a City, and contains in itself, if I may so speak, the end and perfection of government, first founded that we might live, but continued that we may live happily. (Book I, chap. ii, pp. 10-12).

Also he has said: "A City is a community of free men" (Book III, chap. vii, p. 92). "A City, in one word, is a collective body of such persons, sufficient in themselves to all the purposes of life," "such persons" being "citizens," or those who have a right to "share in the judicial and executive part of Government" (Book III, chap. i, p. 81).—that being his very useful, if not complete, definition of a citizen. Again he says:

> A City is a Society of people joining together with their families and their children to live agreeable, for the sake of having their lives as happy and independent as possible; and for this purpose it is necessary that they should live in one place and intermarry with each other; hence in all cities there are family meetings, clubs, sacrifices, and public entertainments to promote friendship, for a love of sociability is friendship itself; so that the end then for which a City is established is that the inhabitants of it may live happy, and these things are conducive to that end; for it is a community of families and villages, for the sake of a perfect independent life, that is, as we have already said, for the sake of living well and happily. It is not therefore founded for the purpose of men merely living together, but for their living as men ought (Book III, chap. ix, p. 98).

The last words recall those lately spoken by President Wilson: "To make the world fit for free men to live in". Aristotle's purpose is ethical; the ideal City is a place in which the free man can develop to his highest possibility; the motive is to live "as men ought," for "with us," he says, "reason and intelligence are the end of Nature" (Book VII, chap. xvi, p. 262). To him, outside the City, the State, therefore, did not exist, and nearly all his treatise deals with Government, its type and its duties—a matter, once more, that you will have to study in detail presently. We find, then, in Aristotle, no clear definition of the State as a concept, and we can only make a definition out of the conditions he postulates. I suggest for his idea:

"A State is a Society of men inhabiting a City, with a Government composed of men who are free and equal, and are capable of filling an office in the Government."

It will be noticed that this definition does not include within the State women, children, or slaves, all of whom lived in the City. Women were under Domestic Government, as being by nature inferior to men, but were to be treated as citizens of a free State—though not coming within the definition of a citizen, that he must be able to fill an office in the State; children were under Domestic Government as being young and imperfect (Book I, chap. xii, p. 31); slaves as being "a particular species of property" (Book I, chap. viii, p. 21). The confining of the State to men was the natural and logical outgrowth of Aristotle's view of the Family, as consisting of three aspects united in one man, who filled the "three parts of Domestic Government," as master—of the slaves; as father—of the children; as husband—of the wife. This view of the State colours European thought, the subjection of women being characteristic of European systems and as we shall see it comes out strongly in Bluntschli's view of the State as a masculine entity. Shakspere said truly that

The evil which men do lives after them.

Even in India it has degraded the higher view of the Family as the unit of the State, with all the network of ideas of which the Family is the center. It has made the man everything, and in the household all gives way to his convenience and comfort, thus making selfishness instead of sacrifice the pivot of Family life. Only in the woman is the old ideal preserved, and her utter sacrifice to husband and son is apt to increase masculine selfishness. None the less, in her self-sacrifice lies the salvation of India. The future welfare of the Indian State depends on the re-establishment of the old ideal of the Family, with its mutual sacrifice, and mutual service, and mutual helpfulness, conditioned, in their form not in their essence, by the "elder, equal, and younger".

Rome

The Roman idea of the State was based on the Greek, but laid more stress on law; the Greek saw as the purpose of the State that men might have Happiness; the Roman made predominant the protective power of the State, and saw as its purpose that men might have Justice. Bluntschli says of the Greeks:

> They base the State upon human nature, and hold that only in the State can man attain his perfection and find true satisfaction. "The State is for them the moral order of the world, in which human nature fulfils its end....
>
> The Romans first distinguished law from morality, and gave it a definite form, and thus they brought out more distinctly the legal nature of the State. Thereby they limited the State, and gave it greater firmness and power. It no longer summed up for them the ethical ordering of the world, but was primarily a common legal organisation. (Book I, chap. iii, pp. 35, 38, 39).

Moreover, in the Roman State, the masses were given a more distinctly recognized place than among the Greeks, though I am not forgetting the meetings of the Athenian people in the Agora, or the laws of Draco, or the reforms of Solon. The Patricians, like the Greek Aristocrats, stood high in the State, the descendants of the Gens, or Family. The Gentes included no plebeian.

> The history of the city of Rome shows us that the nucleus of its was composed of a number of primitive clans living each in its separate settlement, but side by side, for the oldest districts of the city have the names of the ancient patrician gentes. In short, a number of indications concur to show that Rome—though in the time of Cicero the fact had been quite forgotten—first took shape as a League of cognate but distinct clans, each clan being a conventional family, into which admission could only be procured through the fiction of adoption.

But Cicero points out that when the people were organized they were part of the State; this does not include all men, but only those who are organized into a society; then, but only then, the Popular Organism became the source of law; "Vox populi, vox Dei"—"The voice of the people is the voice of God". The proud Roman would have had supreme contempt for the idea that any shouting mob was the voice of God, though the phrase is so used occasionally in modern days. For the ignorant mob, "Bread and Games" was his prescription. For the Organised People, respect. For organisation is only possible with individual self-control. "Salus populi supreme lex," "The welfare of the people is the supreme law." The struggle of the people to assert and organize themselves is full of interest, and they gradually became a recognized Order in the State.

A further addition to the idea of the State, as existing in the West, was made by the Romans—its extension over many Nations, thus carrying it into a higher order of Individual. The Roman Eagles flew over the Western World, and invaded the Eastern, and Roman citizenship was extended to the borders of the Empire, and was obtainable both by birth and by purchase.

The Roman view of the State maybe summarized:

The State is the People Organised, governed by its own assemblies and its elected officers; with its citizenship extended to persons and families belonging to other Nations, over whom the authority of the central City was exercised.

The Social Contract

For our purpose we need not delay over medishval Europe, and need only pause very shortly on the new idea which emerges in the seventeenth century, and is discussed through the eighteenth. Hooker, Hobbes and Locke in the seventeenth century, and Rousseau in the eighteenth, are its typical exponents. Briefly outlined, the theory is: that the natural condition of men was one of war; to obtain order and security, men surrendered some of their personal inherent rights, and formed by contract a State in which they vested them, this State being an absolute Power, monarchical or other, responsible to none. This supposed contract is the origin of the State.

Grotius: The complete union of free men, who join themselves together for the purpose of enjoying law, and for the sake of public welfare.

Hobbes: The State, therefore, is a single person, for whose acts a great multitude by mutual covenants, one with another, have made themselves every one the author, to the end he may use the means and strength of them all as he shall think expedient for their peace and common defence.

Rousseau: To find a form of association which defends and protects the person and property of every associate with the common power of all, and by which each, uniting himself with all, only obeys himself and remains as free as before; such is the fundamental problem resolved in the *Contrat Social.*

In all these the State is not the Nation organized, but the Government. So also in the *Encyclopaedia Britannica*, which has some interesting definitions:

> As currently employed in that department of Political Science which concerns itself, not with relations of separate political entities, but with the political composition of society as a whole, the word State expresses the abstract idea of government in general, or the governing authority as opposed to the governed, and is thus used by Herbert Spencer in all his discussions of government and society. Louis XIV's "l' état moi," Rousseau's theory of the "contrat social," Bastiat's "donne a l'état le strict nécessaire et garde le reste pour toi," all imply this opposition.

Yet this is the very idea we need to oppose. Again:

> "In constitutional law, the State," says a leading English authority, "is the power by which rights are created and maintained, by which the acts and forbearances necessary for their maintenance are habitually enforced" (Anson, *Law and Custom of the Constitution* pt. i, p. 2). In France, where the State embraces a hierarchy of bodies and authorities culminating in the President of the Republic, whose acts are the final form of a series of incomplete acts of the

members of the hierarchy, it come nearer to the theoretical meaning of the word....

Hence a general definition:

The State is a human corporation resting on contract, which defends its members against aggression and preserves order by law.

In this the idea of the State as an evolving organism has wholly disappeared, and it becomes an apparatus, manufactured by man in Society for his security and order, exercising the rights vested in its by him, and restricted within as narrow limits as are consistent with the purpose of its manufacture. Under these conditions, the State and the People are separate entities and are in a condition of vigilant and armed truce, the individual guarding against any invasion of the rights he has retained, and the Government, as the embodied Power of the State, tending to become a tyranny. It is a veiled condition of War between the Government and the Individual, the Government resenting resistance, the Individual fearing encroachment.

We thus continually find the State and the Liberty of the Individual regarded as in conflict, for the more the State does, the less it leaves to the Individual. Hence the value of the State as a collective organisation largely disappears, and ownership by the State is looked on as an interference with individual enterprise and initiative; collective help is regarded as a destruction of independence, and as a pauperization of the Individual. The idea of the Family as the fundamental unit of the State is renounced, and the isolated man becomes the unit; combat, competition, struggle, form the recognized conditions of the people, and society becomes an anarchy within a circle of laws; the exploiter of human labour and the proletarian, the land-holder and the landless, the capitalist and the wage-earner, the millionaire and the pauper, appcar, over against each other, and the extremes of luxury and of poverty, divided by an unbridgeable gulf, are the typical productions of modern civilization. Had it not crashed down in a World War, it would have been torn into pieces in class convulsions. A return to the ideal of the Family as the unit of the State has reappeared in modern thought, and Political Science is re-establishing on a scientific basis the higher Ideal. That Ideal, enlarged from the Family to the Nation, is what is called Socialism, and is the analogue, in the State, of Ethic or Morality in Society. As Ethic resides in making universal and normal the love-emotion, as revealed in the harmonious Family, so is Socialism the extension to the State of the principles of mutual helpfulness and sacrifice found in the happy and prosperous family. It has, as its axiom: "From every one according to his capacities; to every one according to his needs" (Proudhon).

Modern Views

In the nineteenth century began an effort to construct a true Political Science out of the facts recorded in History, and in the first quarter of the twentieth century we find Professor Seeley complaining of the want of a text-book. He pointed out that:

> As a matter of course human beings like other animals are united together in families, and we might be prepared to find the family tie stronger and the family organisation somewhat more developed than in inferior animals. But we observe something more... very surprising and unexpected. We find that men have another bond of union beyond that of the family, and another higher organisation... Almost in any place, in any circumstances where a human being might be found, if you questioned him you would find that he considered himself to belong to some large corporation which imposed duties and conferred rights upon him.... The English State may be held together in some degree by a common interest, still it is not a mere company composed of voluntary shareholders, but a union which has its root in the family and which has grown, and not merely been arranged, to be what it is. Now, it is surely impossible not to admit that this phenomenon, vast and highly developed as it now appears, is in its large features similar to the most primitive and barbarous tribe. That, too, is a great association, to which its members are attached for life and death. For that, too, its members fight; about its interests they debate. In the tribe, too, we can often discover that individuals may have no attachment by kindred to the whole; they may have come in as slaves and received emancipation, or as foreigners by adoption. In short, compare the most advanced State with the most primitive tribe, and you will see the same features, though the proportions

> are different. In the State there is more of mind; in the tribe more of nature. Free-will and intelligent contrivance have more play in the former; blood and kinship rule in the latter. Still the State has not ceased to be a tribe; kinship still counts for much in it, as the Nationality-movement of the present century has strikingly proved (Lecture i, p. 14, Lecture ii, pp. 35, 36).

The Professor regards the principle of Government as essential to the State, and he regards the fact of Government as that on which "depends almost everything important in human history." (p. 37). This Government is to him the main characteristic of the State, and it is universal. "Everywhere the human being belongs to something which may be called a polity, and is subject to something which may be called a Government." (p. 38) It is the making "use of the arrangement or contrivance called Government", (lecture i, p. 17) which distinguishes the State, and so to him Political Science is concerned with Government, "as political economy deals with wealth, as biology deals with life, as algebra deals with numbers, as geometry deals with space and magnitude" (p. 18). Government he defines as "command enforced by penalty" (Lecture iii, p. 75) a curiously narrow conception, for surely if the State be an organized community, and the Government the executive of its will, then every purpose that the organized community desires to carry out collectively becomes a duty of the State to be carried out by its Executive. The organism specializes organs, for the discharge of its functions, its life-activities. For the better exercise of its function of Justice, it specializes an organ composed of judges and lawyers; for its function of healing, it specializes an organ composed of doctors and nurses; for its function of commerce, it specializes an organ or merchants, and accountants, and sailors; and so on, as it becomes more and more specialized and complex. Our illustration of the body and its organs is more than a metaphor—it is a reality. The "contrivance called Government," or as I should prefer to call it, the Organ of Government, is perhaps the first organ specialized in the organism named the State. The State should not be though of as over against the Nation, but as the Nation organized to perform all that is done more efficiently by it collectively than individually. If the State takes over, as in many countries, the management of railways, it is the Government that will manage them and collect their revenue, but its proceedings hardly come within "commands enforced by penalty". Moreover we have seen the Village State in the East, untroubled by commands and free from penalties. But then Professor Seeley knew nothing of the East.

We saw last week that the Professor considers the State as an organism not a machine, as a growth not a manufacture. We may then embody his view of the State in such a definition as the following:

The State is an Organism, consisting of human beings, evolved from the Family through the Tribe, and controlled by a Government.

Characteristically, the Professor will not say that the State exists for any object. "We do not speak of the object of a tree or an animal" (Lecture ii, p. 40). He wishes to study facts and leave purposes alone—again an unwise narrowing of view.

Dr. Woodrow Wilson begins by remarking that it would be desirable to include all tribes, Hottentot or Iroquois, Finn or Turk, in a general survey, but that it is enough to study the " Aryan and Semitic races which have played the chief parts in the history of the European world" (chap. i, § 2). It is not clear what he means by Aryan; it does not apparently include Indians, for he goes on to say:

> In order to trace the lineage of the European and American Governments, which have constituted the order of social life for those stronger and nobler races which have made the most notable progress in civilization, it is essential to know the political history of the Greeks, the Latins, the Teutons and the Celts principally, if not only, and the original and political habits and ideas of the Aryan and Semitic races alone. The existing Governments of Europe and America furnish the dominating types of to-day. To know other systems which are defeated or dead would aid only indirectly towards an understanding of those which are alive and triumphant. (Chapter i, § 2).

India is apparently swept away with the Hottentots and their similars.

Dr. Wilson sees in Kinship the origin of social organisation, and in the Paternal Authority the origin of Government. He contrasts the Patriarchal Family, as the original type institution in humanity, with the view that it emerged from an earlier condition of polyandry and polygyny, which were preceded by promiscuity. But he excludes these, because such conditions were not found in the European field. The Romans and the Greeks descended from the Patriarchal Family.' Sir William Maine, as we have seen, gives a better reason. Says Dr. Wilson:

> No belief is more deeply fixed in the traditions of the great peoples who have made modern history, than the belief in direct common descent, through males, from a common male ancestor, human or divine; and nothing could well be more numerous or distinct than the traces inhering in the very heart of their polity of an original Patriarchal organisation of the family as the archetype of their political order (Chap. i, §§ 5, 6).

It is curious that Dr. Wilson states the Indian view, while ignoring India. Promiscuity belongs, he thinks, to "times of decadence, rather than to the origins of the race," polyandry where "women were fewer than the men, ploygyny among the wealthy (§ 7). Hence the Family ruled by the Father is the earliest unit, showing "that clear authority and close organisation which was to serve in fullness of time as the prototype and model of the State" *(Ibid)*. In the Patriarchal Family sons and grandsons swelled the number, but "there was no majority for them while the father lived"; this group broadened into the Gens, and the Gentes into the Tribe, and "Tribes at length united to form a State" (§ 7). This State might be nomadic, "a travelling political organisation, a State without territorial boundaries or the need of them" (§ 7). In this view of the State, Dr. Wilson remarks, that modern definitions do not concur with him; he says: " 'A State,' runs the modern definition, 'is a People organized by law within a definite territory'". Dr. Wilson will not have this. He says: "The first builders of Government" saw no reason "why they might not move their whole people, 'bag and baggage' to other lands (§ 7). Dr. Wilson supports this novel view by the fact that the Franks were not confined to any Frank-land, and their Kings were "Kings of the Franks," not of a territory. So there were "Kings of the English" for centuries, and John was the first who took the title of "Kind of England". Indian Kings preserved this idea as to towns and villages, we may note. We find new towns, some miles from ruined or semi-ruined ones, whence the inhabitants had been bodily removed, not "bag and baggage," but bundles and pots. Dr. Wilson urges:

> The original Governments were knit together by bonds closer than those of geography, more real than the bonds of mere contiguity. They were bound together by real or assumed kinship. They had a corporate existence which they recognized as inhering in their blood, and as expressed in all their daily relations with each other. They lived together because of these relations; they were not related because they lived together. (§§ 11, 12).

Not by Contract, Dr. Wilson decides, after glancing at that theory, but from the Family, arises the State. "The Family was the primal unit of political society, and the seed-bed of all larger growths of Government" (§ 22). Dr. Wilson quotes and agrees with John Morley's standpoint in his criticism of Rousseau. In view of:

> The observed and recorded experience of mankind, the ground and origin of society is not a compact; that never existed in any known case, and never was a condition of obligation either in primitive or developed societies, either between subjects and sovereign, or between the equal members of a sovereign body. The true ground is the acceptance of conditions which came into existence by the sociability inherent in man, and were developed by man's spontaneous search after convenience. (*Rousseau.* John Morley Vol. ii p. 183).

Man dislikes loneliness, seeks his mate and his fellows. "Kinship and Religion operated as the two chief formative influence" thinks Dr. Wilson (§ 25). Adoption into the Family admitted into the Family religious mysteries:

And so too, Houses could grow by the adoption of families, through the engrafting of the alien branches into this same sacred stock of the esoteric of religion of the kindred. Whether naturally, therefore, or artificially, Houses widened into tribes, and tribes into commonwealths, without loss of that kinship in the absence of which, to the thinking of primitive men, there could be no communion, and therefore no community at all (§ 24).

The Ancestors were worshipped as the Gods of the Family and were accepted by the adopted member. In India this adoption survives, and the Family Pitris are the Pitris of the adopted son.

As Tribes grew, lines of descent became obscured, and family government and race government became differentiated. The State continued to be conceived as a Family; but the headship of this huge and complex Family ceased to be natural and became political (§ 41).

Dr. Wilson's definition of the State would seem to be:

The State is a body of persons descended from a common ancestor, and with a common Government.

Sir Henry Maine, in his *Ancient Law*, remarks that "the *Unit* of an ancient society was the Family, of a modern society the Individual" (Seventeenth impression. Chap. v, p. 126. John Murray, London).

> The elementary group is the Family, connected by common subjection to the highest male ascendant. The aggregation of Families forms the Gens, or House. The aggregation of Houses makes the Tribe. The aggregation of Tribes constitutes the Commonwealth. Are we at liberty to follow these indications, and to lay down that the Commonwealth is a collection of persons united by common descent from the progenitor of an original family? (Chap. v, p. 128).

That was the view of Antiquity, an Maine accepts it, at least as a Legal Fiction, which permitted the useful practice of adoption. In later times, came in the principle of local contiguity, which has driven out the earlier.

Bluntschli develops the idea of a descent from the common masculine ancestor into the unusual proposition that the State is masculine. And in this he is thorough and logical. To this the view of Aristotle distinctly leads; the citizen of the State is the man. Bluntschli says distinctly that a family, a clan, may become the nucleus round which a State may in time form; but neither a family nor a horde is a State: "Without a Tribe, or, at a higher stage of civilization, without a Nation, there is no State" (Book I, chap. i,

p. 16). He is no way denies the line of evolution, Family, Tribe, etc.; but he refuses the use of the word "State" of anything less than a Nation, and thus somewhat departs from his principle of reaching from historical facts to the conception of a State, since he bids us survey the many actual States in the world's history and discover "their common characteristics" (p. 15). But when those are found and isolated, their presence in any aggregation of people should assign to that aggregation the name of State.

His speciality lies in the restriction of the State to masculinity. You will remember his fine description of the State, quoted last week on p. 19 of my lecture. I recall only the points which I now need to emphasise:

The State is in no way a lifeless instrument, a dead machine; it is a living and therefore organized being.... In the State spirit and body, will and active organs, are necessarily bound together in one life. The one National Spirit, which is something different from the average sum of the contemporary spirit of all citizens, is the Spirit of the State; the one National Will, which is different from the average will of the multitude, is the Will of the State.... It is a moral and spiritual organism, a great body which is capable of taking up into itself the feelings and thoughts of the Nation, of uttering them in laws, and realising them in acts; we are informed of moral qualities and of the character of each State. History ascribes to the State a personality which, having spirit and body, possesses and manifests a will of its own.... The State is, par excellence, a Person, in the sense of public law. The purpose of the whole constitution is to enable the Person of the State to express and realize its will, which is different from the individual wills of all individuals, and different from the sum of them. (Book I, chap. i, pp. 18, 19, 20, 22).

He then proceeds to point out that:

> the personality of the State is, however, only recognized by free people, and only in the civilized Nation-State has it attained to full efficacy.... The same is true with regard to the masculine character of the modern State. This becomes first apparent in contrast with the feminine character of the Church." (Book I, chap. i, pp. 22, 23).

Hence he defines the State, after describing its factors:

> To put together the result of this historical consideration, the general conception of the State may be determined as follows: "The State is a combination or association of men, in the form of government and governed, on a definite territory, united together into a moral, organized, masculine personality; or, more shortly—the State is the politically organized National Person of a definite country." (Book I, chap. i, p. 23).

Now, the danger of this conception of the State, we have seen in the Germany of to-day. The State becomes the highest entity recognized by the People, and Power becomes its chief characteristic. Whether the Power be embodied in a Person, as in the German "All-Highest," the representative of God on earth, or whether it be embodied in the Government of a Republic, or of a Parliament, it matters very little. For safety, we must resort to the Indian view, that above the sceptre of Government authority, there is Dharma, the Law, establishing Righteousness, Justice, and Liberty, the fundamental principles on which the stability of the State itself is based. They must be recognized as essential to the unfolding of the Divine Nature in man, of the human Spirit. Brahman is free, righteous and just, and these qualities inhere in the Self, the Spirit, in man.

Bluntschli looks forward to the Universal State, and points out that time is "bringing the Nations nearer to one another, and awakening the universal consciousness of the community of mankind". (Book I, chap. ii, p. 31). Each State, he says, feels any disturbance in another State as an evil affecting itself. The European Nations, who "know their superiority over other Nations well enough," but "have not yet come to a clear understanding among themselves" as to how they shall "manage the world" must gain knowledge. Until this has been done,

> the Universal Empire will be an idea after which many strive, which none can fulfil. But as an idea of the future, the general theory of the State cannot overlook it. Only in the Universal Empire will be true human State be revealed, and in it international law will attain a higher form and an assured existence. To the Universal Empire the particular States are related, as the Nations to

> Humanity...The highest conception of the State—which, however, has not yet been realised—is thus: the State is Humanity organised, but Humanity as masculine, not feminine : the State is the Man (*ibid.*, p. 32).

A rather curious and simple definition is that of Bodin:

> A right Government, with sovereign power of several households and their common possessions.

This would take us from a group of Families up to the Universal State.

The *Encyclopaedia Britannica* remarks:

> In England, we may say, the notion of State, from the constitutional point of view, is still inchoate, but the play of international intercourse seems to be gradually leading to a clearer conception of the fact that an increasing national responsibility requires a corresponding increase in the power of co-ordinate State control....

> Much has been written on the "science" of the State, or, as we prefer, in Anglo-Saxon lands, to call it, "Political Science." In Germany the subject is dealt with as an independent branch of university education. Several of her universities have a *staatswissenschaftliche Facultät*, granting a special degree in the subject. In consequence of the great attention paid to the subject in Germany, her State polity has been largely the work of her political writers. The result has not unnaturally tended to a system bearing some resemblance to that of the American Union, with this very important difference, however, that whereas in the United States the federal power is derived from the democratic forces of the individual States, in Germany it is derived from their aristocratic and absolutist force. German political thinkers, in fact, have worked out *Staatsrecht* as a comparative study, in which arguments in favour of absolute government have received as much careful consideration as those in favour of democratic institutions, and the German State has developed upon lines based on the best theoretical arguments of these thinkers. There is, therefore, no anomaly in its practically absolutist government working out the most democratic reforms as yet put into legislative form. It follows, however, that German theories are of little use in the consideration of the State problems with which British and American political thinkers have to deal. Anglo-Saxon institutions are following their

independent development, and if the influence of foreign institutions is felt at all, it is probably that of the clear logical detail and cohesion of French institutions.

It is for you to study, to think over, to decide what "the State" should mean to you, how you mean to work out the State in India. Make some definitions for yourselves.

I suggest the following as a fairly inclusive definition:

A State is a multi-human organism, embodying a Life, inhabiting a definite Territory, with a Government as its executive, specializing organs for its activities, and shaping its evolution to achieve a common end.

If we test this by each larger State successively we find it true. In the Family we have several persons, elders, contemporaries, youngers, living together as an organized unit; it lives in a house; it has a Family Life, with the parents as ruler, and the various members specialize their work, to achieve the common end of Family happiness. This is equally true of the Village-State, the Tribe-State, the City-State, the Nation-State, the Commonwealth-State, the World-State, and each point is true in each.

But why not try to better it?

—Annie Besant

2

The Origins of the State

Of the numerous organized groups that constitute society, the state is the special concern of the student of politics. As with all human associations, the state emerges and exists within society. The taproots of government reach down into the same soil that nurtures the family and the church, the corporation and the trade union, the school and the club. But what is it that stimulates the state to grow in its own particular manner? What are the seeds of the political process? Why the need for government and where does it originate? These are some of the questions that this chapter will explore.

Their phrasing, however, reveals a problem which confronts every analysis of this subject. The difficulty is partly conceptual and partly verbal. Our topic involves three basic terms: *politics, state, and government.* Frequently, these are used as synonyms, and many definitions employ them interchangeably. But the facts we have to explain, and the ideas they incorporate, imply some genuine distinctions, for which we need different words if the meaning is to be clear. Hence, this discussion will differentiate between politics, state, and government so as to clarify the facts. Society was defined earlier as the broadest possible concept, embracing all human relationships and groups. If we proceed from the broad to the narrow, the concept the comes next is politics.

More limited than politics is the concept of the state. This is the institution through which the dynamics of politics are organized and for malized. The state consists of citizens with their

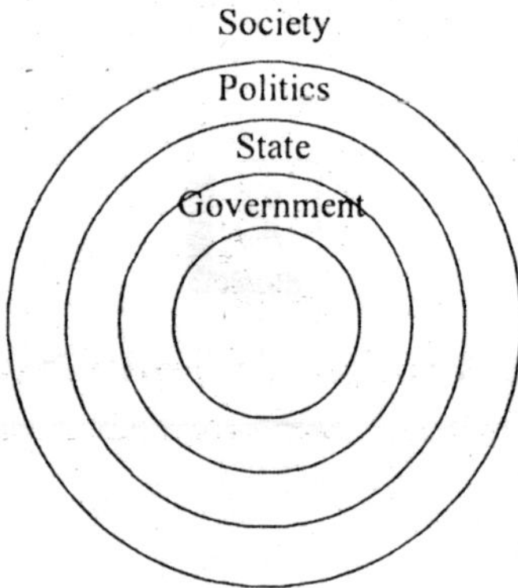

FIGURE 1

rights and duties, institutions and jurisdictions, principles and powers. It is a network of structured relationships. The point that politics is broader than the state can be easily demonstrated. Wherever the state exists, there is also politics. But the converse is not true—that wherever politics exist, so does the state. We can speak of international politics, but as yet there is no supranational state. We can talk of politics within churches or corporations or trade unions, although none of those is a state. The state, however, comprises another and narrower concept—that of government. Every state has its government, and the latter signifies those specific persons who hold official positions and wield authority on behalf of the state. Governments in this sense will change while the same state continues. Government, therefore, implies a distinction within the state between rulers and ruled. We can visualize this series of concepts as concentric circles, where society is the outermost and government, the innermost (see Figure 1).

The Primary Function of the State

If all groups are organized in response to some social need, the state, being a universal institution, must correspond to needs that are universal. Hence, it should be possible to infer the need to which the state responds by studying the functions it undertakes. Anybody who surveys the vast complex of activities undertaken by the state in different periods and places must wonder why they are conducted by this particular association. We know that certain functions were conducted by the state long ago, while others were added more recently. There is wide agreement that some duties are appropriate for the state to undertake and controversy about the suitability of others. Consequently we begin to ask whether the functions of government can be classified into primary and secondary, original and derivative, essential and optional. To answer such questions, it would help to identify one function and say, "this without dispute is the function of the state." Or, approaching the same point from another direction, we should ask, "What is the minimum indispensable function the state must perform in order to be a state? Is there any activity of the state so vital that, were it performed by another association, the latter in effect would be or become a state?"

The Universal Drive for Protection

To these questions the facts of government disclose an answer. Among the common concerns of all human beings is the desire for security of life and limb. Everywhere people seek guarantees of protection from physical harm. But though the urge to ward off bodily threats is universal, different means of protection have been employed. It has not been uncommon, for example, for human beings to rely primarily on themselves. In most historical periods—and almost certainly in the prehistoric—weapons were kept in the home and were carried on journeys. The first line of defence against attack upon one's person or possessions was also, in a sense, the last. It lay in one's own strong arm, since the help of others, even if offered, might arrive too late. But under certain circumstances self-reliance would be inadequate. This was so when the likelihood of attack was constant; when the techniques available to an aggressor placed the defence at a disadvantage; and when the chief disturbance to one's peace came, not from within the group, but from the strength of another organized group outside. Security, therefore, to be effective, had to bc collective. The protection that people could not obtain singly had to be found by cooperating as a group. But when a need, like this for protection, remains constant, the method by which the group satisfies it is to develop practices and procedures which must be continually repeated. At some stage, by virtue of repetition, these become accepted. They are then endowed with formal organization. In a word, they are institutionalized. What we call an "institution" is the outgrowth in structured form of the repetitive practices with which a group fulfills a common need. The nucleus of the state is formed when a group of persons has institutionalized its own protection.

So far, however, this analysis of the need for protection has consisted more of assertions than proof. Is there evidence to show that protection is the original function of the state? The answer can be drawn from various sources, including historical data and the analysis of present-day governmental functions. The historical evidence, though fragmentary, is sufficient to justify some highly probable conclusions. Since about 3000 B.C. enough is known to warrant the use of the term *history* by contrast with earlier *prehistory*. At the dawn of history, however, the institution of government already existed. It was born, therefore, in the prehistoric night before the dawn. Hence any assertion about the origins of the state must repose mainly on conjecture.

Nevertheless there is testimony to show that an intimate connection has always existed between the organization a group adopts for its defence and for its government. When human beings lived as nomads, hunting or herding their food supply, their mobility necessitated a military organization since they transported their families and possessions with them. The able-bodied males on their mounts were a cavalry; the wagons of a caravan made a defensive post. The change from nomadism to a settled habitat, associated with the shift from hunting or tending animals to planting crops, altered the tactics of protection because the objects to be defended—the home and its source of food—were stationary, and a person who planted a seed had to remain there until the crop ripened. Consequently, though people who became agriculturists preferred the plains which were easier to sow and reap, they also required a defensible frontier on the rim of the plain and some fortress in the interior. Out of this need, and the institutions occasioned by it, the primary function of government was founded.

Cities began when people clustered together for social and economic reasons, and a government was needed to give organization and security. The world's oldest known city is Jericho, for it has been occupied continuously since about 7800 B.C. From early times, Jericho was strongly fortified with a watchtower and its famous walls. Archaeological inquiries into the beginnings of civilization in Mesopotamia have explained the circumstances in which the state emerged. In the area watered by the Tigris and the Euphrates, urban centers evolved to control a river-borne commerce and an expanse of fertile fields. The social order of Akkad and Sumer and Babylon was a combination of temple officials, merchants, craftsmen, and landowners, competing for influence. The scattered cities, all independent, struggled for control of the land and water. What happened under these conditions is thus described: "A new institution was needed to restrain these conflicts. By the beginning of historical times the State had emerged, but it was embodied in the single person of the *City-governor* or king, who may be just 'corn-king' and war-chief amalgamated and writ large." The Greek *Polis,* ancestor of the term *Politics,* signified the strong point where scattered farmers and villagers could gather, where the women and children would be secure, and where the defence had military advantages. The center of Athenian civic life, and the dominating feature of its topography, was its "high polis," or Acropolis. The city of Rome likewise commenced its history as the rallying point for scattered rural settlements in the Latin plain whose inhabitants could find protection on the seven hills beside the River Tiber.

Elsewhere in early times, not only has the duty of protecting the group devolved upon its able-bodied males, but often the privilege and responsibility of government have been entrusted to the same hands that bear or once bore the burden of defence. Under the Athenian constitution of the seventh century B.C. prior to Solon's reforms, the citizen body was divided into three classes, each having different rights. The classes were determined by property qualifications, but they were also distinguished by their military functions. A parallel to this Athenian example is provided by Rome, where one of the citizens' assemblies was known as the *Comitia Centuriata.* Its organization reproduced the "centuries," of "hundreds," which were the basic units in the formation of the Roman army.

Similarly in the Teutonic world the same carry-over form war to government may be observed. The roman historian Tacitus published in A.D. 97 the earliest known literary study of the Germans and says this of their tribal organization:

> On minor matters their chief men consult alone; on more important business they all meet....Their love of liberty makes them independent to a fault: They do not assemble all at once or as though they were under orders: but two or three days are wasted by their delay in arriving. They take their seats as they come, all in full armour... if the opinion expressed displeases them, their murmurs reject it: if they approve they clash their spears.

On this point modern experience confirms ancient history. What happens in the twentieth century to a state which engages in a major war? When the safety and existence of the entire community are imperiled, everything is subordinated to the struggle for survival. The need to organize for defence and attack takes priority over all other activities. Centers of production are guarded and expanded. Huge military establishments are thrown together. The whole economy is diverted to the equipment and supply of the armed forces. Abruptly and compulsorily the rhythms and patterns of daily life are changed to a new design. The cells that make up the family group are plucked apart, and some are killed. The home itself may suffer destruction. Citizens respond to new stimuli. They dress in uniforms; they drive toward a goal which they call victory. And to accomplish this result, the state assumes the responsibility. Its functions are enlarged to embrace all aspects of society with military relevance—which in the total warfare of this century means practically everything. Not only was protection the *raison d'êter* of the state in ancient times; but whenever a modern people is momentarily preoccupied with protecting itself and destroying an enemy, the state literally "takes over." Furthermore, the defeated state falls under the control of the victors, as happened after World War II in the military occupation of Germany, Italy, and Japan. In other words, the government of the state, which cannot protect itself for the time being, ceases in effect to be a government.

It is not only form outside, however, that the security of the group can be menaced. One's safety may be disturbed by individuals who belong in the same group. Thus the outlaw or gangster is in the group, but places himself "out of its law." Furthermore it is possible for conflict between groups—between a corporation and a trade union, for instance—to be carried to lengths where other interests are prejudiced and where thee unity of the society to which they belong may be jeopardized. Government must therefore guard against the internal aggressor as well as the external. As this is phrased in the preamble to the Constitution of the United States, while on governmental function is "to provide for the common defence," another is "to insure domestic tranquility." How does the state meet this need? What principles are implied in its solution? And what problems then arise?

The Nucleus of the State

For a starting point, consider this account by Herodotus of an actual event, the consolidation of the ancient kingdom of Media. According to "the Father of History," the Medes were living in anarchy and suffered form insecurity. Their need presented an opportunity which a far-seeing individual was ready to grasp:

> Among the Medes, there was a wise man named Deioces, the son of Phraortes. Deioces coveted absolute power and this was what he did. The Medes, at that time, were living in separate villages and there was much lawlessness throughout the whole land. Being already a person of repute in his own village, and knowing that the just is the enemy of the unjust, he became even more zealous to practice justice. His fellow-villagers, seeing how he behaved, used to choose him to judge their quarrels. In his ambition for power, he gave them just and straightforward decisions and this conduct brought him great praise from the citizen body. Consequently when residents of other villages, who formerly had met with unfair judgments, learned that Deioces was the only man whose decisions conformed to justice, they gladly frequented his

> home so that they too could have him for their judge. Finally they would go to no one else. As more and more litigants kept on appearing when they learned that suits were always settled with fairness, Deioces knew that everything was falling into his lap. Whereupon he announced his unwillingness to hold sessions where he had done so previously, or to continue adjudicating. For, as he put it, it was not profitable to him to settle his neighbours' disputes day after day and neglect his own business. Then when looting and lawlessness broke out among the villages to an extent even greater than before, the Medes assembled and discussed what had taken place, most of the speakers, in my estimate, being friends of Deioces. "since we cannot live in the country in its present state," they said, "come, let us constitute somebody as our king. Thus the land will be well governed and we shall conduct our affairs without being uprooted by lawlessness." By these arguments they persuaded themselves in favour of a monarchy; and as soon as they began proposing candidates for the kingship, Deioces was the one most proposed and praised by all. So they agreed upon him for their king.

This passage is worth quoting—not for its historical truth, but for the insight into the fundamentals of organizing state. When people conflict in their dealings, they need an orderly process to compose their differences, and a recognized tribunal to give decisions whose binding character they will accept. To promote cooperation and confine competition within limits that are not injurious, society erects protective ramparts. The duties of the mediator, arbitrator, judge, and ruler are like steps on an ascending ladder of government. But the ascent is only possible under two conditions. There must be a widespread understanding that the restraints imposed through law and order are less irksome than the disturbances that erupt in their absence. Further, the tribunal to which disputing parties resort must inspire confidence on the grounds that its procedures are fair and its decisions just. In the Herodotean story, Deioces fulfilled these requirements. He was therefore able to found a state and become its king.

A celebrated episode in the history of Switzerland also illustrates the role of the honest arbitrator in cementing the foundations of the state. During the fifteenth century the Swiss Confederation was at the height of its military power, since its citizens were then the finest foot soldiers in Europe. The country was expanding through pressure on its neighbours, some of whom became its subjects, while others joined the confederation or were associated as allies. The change in Swiss power and the enlargement of the state provoked internal tensions between urban and rural centers. The original members were principally rural, while some of the new adherents contained strong cities with manufacturing and mercantile interests. In 1481 a controversy erupted about raising Solothurn and Fribourg from the status of allies to that of full confederates. The opposition of the rural cantons was voiced so strongly that there was a risk of the confederation splitting apart. At this point during a meeting of the Diet at Stans, Nicholas von der Flue, an eminent man who had retired form political life, suddenly intervened in the discussions and by sheer weight of argument, force of personality, and disinterested patriotism, composed the rivalries and achieved an acceptable settlement. Acting as arbitrator and conciliator he brought to both sides an awareness of their common interest in staying united and in making reasonable concessions to one another. The understandings thus reached strengthened the state, while enlarging its membership, and thereby saved Switzerland.

More recent history confirms these observations. Whenever human beings are uprooted form their established ways and exposed to the hazards of a new environment, a social bond has to develop anew. Their prime political need is then to organize in common for protection and physical security. The settlement of the United States by European immigrants contains many incidents of this nature. The pioneers who peopled an unmapped continent were exposed to risks at one another's hands and to the hostility of the Indians whose lands they seized. Life on the frontier was not far removed form Hobbes's characterization of the state of nature—solitary, poor, nasty, and brutish. At times it was also short. A man who rode within sight of another on a backwoods trail did not know whether to trust the stranger; both had their guns ready for the draw. Wherever something essential was in short supply, such as water in the West, men fought for its control. Like medieval barons with retainers, ranchers armed their employees to protect boundary stakes and cattle from neighbouring rustlers. The conflict between an agriculture based on slaves and one employing free labour brought violence and bloodshed, as in Kansas, and ultimately a civil war. An event like the discovery of gold in California attracted an inrush of adventurers, whose aggressive individualism raised the temperature of the economic order to a fever while that of the social order dropped to zero.

In newly settled territories, if people came to work and stay, rather than to loot and depart, they wanted that minimum stability and security without which progress is impossible. Hence they were forced simultaneously to construct a community out of a mosaic of individuals who previously had no connecting ties, and to found a state by establishing law and enforcing order. It was necessary for state and community to grow together, since, until and unless political institutions were created, the soft tissue of society lacking a skeleton was formless and flabby. A state was born in the West when scattered individuals banded together and established the sheriff's office. The state did not grow up, however, until his authority was generally obeyed. Only then was a framework of security organized within which other social institutions—such as economic, religious, educational—could proceed about their respective tasks.

This can also be seen happening in reverse whenever a settled and organized community breaks down into civil war. As the state disintegrates and rival parties seek to capture its machinery, ordinary people may be reduced to presocial and prepolitical savagery. The Russian author Boris Pasternak alluded to this in his account of the events that accompanied the Bolshevik Revolution and the subsequent civil war between Reds and Whites. "That period," he wrote, "confirmed the ancient proverb, "Man is a wolf to man.' Traveller turned off the road at the sight of traveller, stranger meeting stranger killed for fear of being killed. There were isolated cases of cannibalism. The laws of human civilization were suspended. The jungle law was in force. Man dreamed the prehistoric dreams of the cave dweller." A still grimmer example is the case of the Congo after the Belgians gave up their rule in the early 1960s. Rapidly, as tribe turned savagely against tribe, the edifice of central authority disintegrated. With anarchy substituted for order, nothing was secure and nobody was safe.

Yet more recently, the tragedy of disintegration has been reenacted in Lebanon. Only a few decades ago that small state was being compared to Switzerland—as an oasis of sanity and stability in a turbulent region. The Lebanese had emerged form World War II with an agreement among its major communities to share political power and coexist in peace. Thus a Christian served as president, a Sunni Muslim as prime minister, a Shiite Muslim as speaker of the parliament. This *Modus vivendi* was challenged when the Muslims, perceiving that their numbers had increased faster than the Christians, began demanding a larger share in the legislative representation. Then from the outside, the apple of discord was hurled which drove the communities apart. The Palestine Liberation Organization, ejected from Jordan by king Hussein's army, sought refuge in Lebanon and there proceeded to construct a state within a state. Unable to absorb the intruder, the Lebanese turned on each other in civil war so violent that the Arab league intervened. Soon, the Syrians, who had always claimed parts of Lebanon as theirs, occupied much of the country. Subsequently the Israelis mounted an invasion form the south in order to destroy the bases form which the PLO was launching attacks upon their people. Lebanon thereafter plunged into anarchy. The numerous communities—Maronites, Sunnis, Shiites, Druzes, Palestinians, and others—had their own militias commanded by their own warlords, supported or opposed by Syria, Israel, or Iran. Beirut itself, the sometime capital of a nonfunctioning state, was divided by an internal frontier, the "green line" demarcating the Muslim and Christian sections. Kidnappings, assassinations, gunfire, and warfare; treachery, intrigue, and broken agreements—those were the tragic spectacle which Lebanon presented to the world in the 1970s and 1980s. Under such conditions, the "state" was fiction; its "government," a tragic farce; its politics, a process of murder. No superstructure of law, justice, and basic services can hold together when its foundations have been swept away and violence stalks the land.

Protection, Order, and Justice

What are the implications of this analysis? First, it demonstrates that what began as protection broadened out. Human beings expect more than physical safety. To conduct their ordinary daily dealings with their fellow creatures, they require a minimum of stability which depends on mutual trust. Furthermore, people acquire relationships with material goods. Through their labours they accumulate possessions which they wish to preserve as property. Hence the function of safeguarding life and limb is expanded to throw a general framework of security around the relations of person to person and of persons to things. The best term to describe this is *order*. Order is only able to grow after protection is assured, and an orderly way of life is what government nurtures. This is what the traditional phrases signify that ascribe to government the provision of "law and order" or "peace and good order." In other words, if order is to give peace, it must rest upon law and upon agencies capable of enforcing it. Order is the product of common rules effectively applied through common institutions.

But that is not all. There is order in a barracks as there is in a prison. In fact, the most orderly place on earth is a cemetery. Yet a barracks, a prison, or a cemetery is not a state—even though the modern dictatorship with its police state has features that resemble all three. Something more than order is required for the fully developed state. Just as order grows out of protection, so a further goal grows out of order. A clue to its nature may be discovered in this passage by Augustine:

> Set justice aside, then, and what are kingdoms but great robberies? Because what are robberies but little kingdoms? For in thefts, the hands of the underlings are directed by the commander, the confederacy of them is sworn together, and the pillage is shared by the law amongst them. And if those ragamuffins grow up but to be able enough to keep forts, build habitations, possess cities, and conquer adjoining nations, then their government is no more called thievish, but graced with the eminent name of a kingdom, given and gotten, not because they have left their practices, but because that now they must use them without danger of law.

History ineed confirms the accusation that kingdoms are great robberies. Monarchs have traditionally used their opportunities for self-enrichment, like birds of prey feathering their own nests. Witness the wealth of the Hapsburgs, Bourbons, and Romanovs. Queen Elizabeth II of Great Britain is often described as "the world's wealthiest woman." How did her ancestors acquire so much in Nicaragua, the Somozas are said to have accumulated assets worth between 400 and 500 million dollars in just over four decades. In Iran, the Pahlavis reportedly amassed billions of dollars in only two generations. The speed record, however, in this disreputable history of personal enrichment from political power probably belongs to Ferdinand Marcos, the dictator of the Philippines until he was deposed in 1986. His ill-gotten gains from a decade of cronyism corruption, and assassination of opponents have been estimated at several billions of dollars. Under these circumstances, what happens to justice?

Society may arrive at the stage of order based on law. It may eliminate anarchy and be systematically organized. But merely to establish order is not enough. Order must embody what people consider just. A system organized to ensure protection, but where people are not persuaded that they are justly treated, may gain obedience, but never allegiance. Justice consists in both a method and a result. The method is fair dealing. The result is to recognize equally the basic interests of all individuals and groups and promote a harmony between them. People will feel that they have justice when their community accords them all an equal chance and safeguards their fundamental interests in a manner proportionate to the like interests of others. As Herodotus shows, a government can originate under two conditions. The understanding must be widespread that the restraints imposed through order and its law are less irksome than the disturbances which erupt in their absence. In addition, the tribunal to which disputants resort must inspite confidence in the fairness of its procedures and the justice of its decisions. Deioces fulfilled these requirements. He was therefore able to found a state and become its king. But, as Augustine reminds us, if you remove justice, what distinguishes a state form a band of robbers?

The Use and Monopoly of Force

The next questions are: By what methods and through what institutions are these results achieved? What happens when a community mobilizes to protect itself, then founds a system of order, and finally establishes justice? Every association must employ the methods that are indispensable, or best fitted, for performing its primary function. If the state originates in the need for protection, to it belong initially any techniques which insure attainment of that objective; and if the state is to progress toward broader goals, the techniques of government must evolve in the process. Granted that protection, order, and justice are successive ends to which the state aspires, what are the means for obtaining each?

Since an institution must possess the means appropriate to its function, it follows that, if it is to give protection, the state must have force at its disposal. Protection against attacks form outside cannot be provided unless the group can repel force with force. Likewise, protection against attack from within calls for agencies—for example, police, militia, army, courts, and prisons—capable of applying coercion to the disorderly and the lawless. The tribunals that are supposed to settle disputes must be able to enforce their decisions. Otherwise none of us will have assurance that the rules we obey will be observed by others. it is therefore the special purpose for which the state originates, namely to afford protection, which imposes on the state the necessity of employing force. Many of the problems that distinguish the state from other associations flow from the simple yet fundamental fact that the state must use force or it cannot even begin to be a state.

Let us consider what some of these problems are. First, because it must employ force, the state inevitably seeks to monopolize it. Any force not controlled by the state represents a potential source of resistance and a limit to what the state can do. In order to be unchallenged in performing its protective function, the state seeks to be the sole possessor of coercive techniques. Conversely, whenever force is available for use by associations other than the state or by persons other than the government, there exist in embryo the potential makings of a substitute state and government. An incident which illustrates this fact is cited by Augustine in the sequel to the passage quoted earlier:

> For elegant and excellent was that pirate's answer to the great Macedonian Alexander, who had taken him: the king asking him

> how he durst molest the sea so, he replied with a free spirit, "How darest thou molest the whole world? But because I do it with a little ship only, I am called a thief: thou, doing it with a great navy, art called an emperor."

Alexander could not tolerate the pirate because the state, to maintain itself, must be a monopolist of force; the state then attempts to moralize this monopoly by serving the ideal of the public good. The little gang appears antisocial because it preys upon the larger community and puts its special advantage before the general interest.

History exemplifies the danger that threatens the state when any force is organized within its midst to break its monopoly. During the sixth century B.C. Peisistratus usurped power in Athens and established a dictatorial regime. He accomplished a coup d' etat by employing a bodyguard that had been assigned to him by his fellow citizens after he had feigned attacks upon his life. The closing century of the Roman Republic from 133 B.C. to 31 B.C. witnessed a cumulative series of futile efforts by the Senate to control its armies in the field. At the end of victorious campaigns abroad, successive generals—such as Marius or Sulla, Pompey or Caesar, Antony or Augustus—were able to bend the government to their will or make themselves masters of the state. There were even periods when the Senate could not keep order in the streets of Rome and lay at the mercy of the vicissitudes of violence between rival gangs like those of Clodius and Milo. Then when the republic, which could not rule an empire, gave way to emperors who could , the latter, too, were at times made or unmade by the captains of the Praetorian Guard who garrisoned the capital city, or by army commanders in a distant province. In the Middle Ages when feudal regimes in Western Europe were highly localized, the kings of England or France found it difficult to exercise authority over powerful nobles who were secure in their castles and could place in the field a body of retainers and vassals wearing their livery. If medieval monarchs could not control what the historian Fortescue called their "overmighty subjects," it was because the latter were backed by private armies.

Essentially the same has been true of the modern state. When would be dictators emerge in the midst of weak regimes, they seek to subvert the armed forces and organize militias of their own. In Italy between 1920 and 1922, Mussolini overawed and paralyzed the government by mobilizing his Black Shirts and obtaining the passive connivance of the army. Hitler organized thugs to capture the city streets and ended up molesting the whole world. Elsewhere, it is by launching a military rebellion that a politically ambitious officer overturns the civilian authorities and installs himself in power. This is what Franco did in Spain in the 1930s; thereafter, for a third of a century his brutal regime relied on repression by the police and the army. Until mid-1974, the Greek army also put up a fair imitation of the Spanish. And there have been scores of such military dictators, long-lasting or short-lived, in recent decades. Many of the governments in the Middle East, southeast Asia, and Latin America now belong or have recently belonged in this category. The rule of the gunmen, in uniform or not, is indeed a phenomenon as widespread as it is depressing. Even the gangs that flourished in various cities of the United States during the Prohibition era form an aspect of the same story. When Capone dominated the Chicago underworld in the 1920s and conduced illegal rackets on a vast scale, was it no in his gunmen that a major portion of the city's power was located? Nor is it without significance that what the gangster offers to the victims of his blackmail he calls "protection." In the same category are the terrorists, or urban guerrillas, who have become so ubiquitous since the 1960s. These groups—as in Germany and Italy, in Argentina or throughout the Middle East—are unlike old-style brigands or gangs whose rationale was economic. Contemporary terrorists are politically motivated and devote themselves with fanaticism to some cause or mission. Their actions demonstrate how a mere handful, who are ready to die and utterly ruthless, can produce chaos in an orderly society. Similar to this was the chaos caused in several countries of Asia and Latin America by the worldwide spread of the drug traffic in the 1980s. In Colombia, perhaps the worst case on a bad list, the drug dealers controlled the city of Medellin as their power base and thence proceeded to assassinate leading politicians, judges, officials and journalists, as well as to dynamite public buildings. "We declare total and absolute war on the Government on the industrial and political oligarchy...," they announced in 1989. How is one to describe the institution of the state in Colombia at that time? The lesson is obvious. The state must either monopolize the force of the community or risk surrender to whoever can muster counterforce for its overthrow. The logic of coercion dictates monopoly.

Officials and the Public

When one speaks, however, of force being monopolized by the state, what exactly is meant? The state is an abstraction. In practice, acts of government are done by a few on behalf of everybody. Those who act may be variously described as representatives, agents, deputies, officials, or, simply, the government. It is characteristic of the state to entrust its use of force to persons who are recognized by the whole community as acting on their behalf. In this sense a distinction can be drawn between public and private, official and unofficial, government and governed; and a different social significance attaches to the same action according to the persons who perform it and the methods they employ. Thus it is one thing for a mob to track down and lynch a suspect; another, for a sheriff to conduct an arrest. It is one thing to carry on a personal vendetta, and another to seek remedies for a wrong through a judicial process. When law enforcement reposes in the police rather than in a mob, when defence is secured by a standing army and not by guerrilla bands, the trained professional acting under public orders is substituted for the unauthorized acts of private individuals. Save under the extreme necessity of self-defence, citizens may no longer take the law into their own hands once it has been entrusted to officials. If they do, their actions lack the character of law and they then become "outlaws."

This latter truth was brought home to the American people in the period from 1963 to 1968 when four men of national prominence were assassinated by gunshot. These were President John F. Kennedy, his brother Senator Robert F. Kennedy, the Black Muslim Leader Malcolm X, and the Reverend Martin Luther King, the campaigner for civil rights who was an apostle of non-violence and had received the Nobel Peace Prize. Such well-known victims belong within the broader context of a people with an appallingly high rate of deaths from shooting. Some 200 million firearms are estimated to be in private hands in this country—more than in the armed forces of the United States, the republics of the former USSR, and the NATO countries combined. Is it any wonder that, with guns so easily accessible, too many are used and persons in public life become targets?

On the other hand, an emergency may arise whose dimensions lie beyond the ordinary resources of officialdom. In those cases, the principle that the official is the agent of the community is reinforced by invoking the aid of the citizens themselves. Under English common law if a policeman blows his whistle when he is attacked or is trying to make an arrest, any able-bodied citizen within earshot must go to his assistance. Similarly, the sheriff in western territories in an earlier day would call out the posse to help him track an outlaw. The theory is that the policeman is the agent of all the citizens. When the latter go to his aid, therefore, they are momentarily doing for themselves what he does ordinarily on their behalf. For similar reasons, under extraordinary conditions threatening the whole community, reinforcements may be mobilized by doctors fighting an epidemic, by firemen extinguishing a conflagration, of by engineers trying to contain a flood. Finally, in the ultimate case of total warfare, the professional army is expanded through universal conscription, and all fit persons are enlisted.

Force and Consent

How then does the government come to exercise the coercive force of the whole? What is it that enables a few to wield the force of many? The answer can be found if one remembers that, though the functions of government begin with protection, they evolve beyond their starting point. Protection grows into order and order seeks to blossom into justice. Something similar happens with the techniques of government, since a method that was adequate at one stage of development ceases to be so at the next. Force may be sufficient for protection. But to create order. more is required. This extra is *Power*. What is power? It is simply force with some consent added. How large a volume of consent is debatable. Indeed the quantity may vary, with consequential differences of great importance.

Let us examine more closely this relation between force and consent. All governments in the world use force, and even the most dictatorial is supported by some minimal measure of consent. People always want certain results from their government, and they are willing that their officials have the means of bringing those results to fruition. Therefore, they give their consent to the general body of law which prescribes the order they desire; and, along with law, they approve coercive enforcement against those who would infringe it. The nature of this relationship has been well stated by A. D. Lindsay:

> Many people think that the state's use of force gives the lie to the doctrine that government can rest on consent, yet it is also clear that without some sort of consent the government's force would not exist. These puzzles confound more people than should be so confounded. Men have been accustomed so much to think of the law as restraining other people than their respectable selves that they easily think of the state's force as necessary to enable some people to restrain others.... But a little consideration will show us that we need and desire the power of the state to restrain ourselves. Consider a simple example form traffic control. We most of us think there ought to be laws regulating traffic, compelling us to light our lamps at a certain time and so on. Such rules have our consent and approval. Yet most of us, if we are honest, know that we are likely to break those laws on occasion and that we are often restrained form breaking them by the sanctions of the law. Most laws are like that. They will work and can be enforced because most people want usually to keep them. The state can have and use organized force because most people usually want common rules and most people want those rules to be universally observed; there must be force because there are rules which have little value unless everyone keeps them, and force is needed to fill up the gap between most people usually and all people always obeying.

Power and Authority

Power is an ability to achieve results through concerted action. It is the product of the mobilization of support and involves a relationship between a group and its agents. The latter may be described as delegates or representatives, in the sense that they follow the group; or as leaders, if the group follows them. The building of consent may depend on the capacity of a group to organize itself coherently, formulate its programme, and instruct its representatives; or alternatively on the capacity of a leader to attract adherents and win a following. The support elicited will thus be reciprocal. A group supports its agents, while they support the group. Franklin D. Roosevelt, in a critical period of domestic economic breakdown and aggressive international militarism, confidently offered programmes that gave people new hope. Thus he was the first to be elected president four times.

But the evolution of governmental techniques does not terminate with power. As order, to be securely stabilized, attempts to gain acceptance as justice, so does power aspire toward a concept yet more advanced. If protection is sustained by force and order by power, justice requires authority. What does authority mean, and how is it distinguished from power? To understand the contrast, one must introduce a further refinement into the distinction between the government and the governed. In fact, the governed subdivide into two parts—the supporters of the government and its opponents. This means that the citizens who compose the state are actually made up of three groups:

1. Representatives (or leaders) and their official subordinates.
2. Those who support the representatives.
3. Those who dissent and oppose the representatives.

Power consists in the fusion of items 1 and 2. It is able to include that ingredient of force which makes government ultimately effective, because of the support mobilized in its favour. But the claims of power to hold sway are, by definition, valid only for those who consent. Likewise, the rightness of its force is justified only in the eyes of those who render it support. The force that power may deploy will be resented, and may be resisted, by those who disagree. Opponents may have to submit to the decisions of power; but submission is different form acquiescence. The imperatives of power may secure compliance; but this is not the same as allegiance.

What demarcates authority form power is that the former is power recognized as rightful. Authority is a rule which all accept as valid. Its exercise is therefore sanctioned by those who approve the particular act or agent and is tolerated by those who disapprove. Confronted with power, the citizen has a choice: whether to support or oppose. Confronted with authority, it is one's duty to obey. Resistance to power is lawful; resistance to authority, unlawful. Power is naked; authority is power clothed in the garments of legitimacy.

How this transformation takes place can be illustrated in two episodes, one ancient and one modern. The first is the sequel, as Herodotus relates it, to the rise of Deioces to the kingship.

> Deioces ordered them to build him a palace worthy of a king and to guard it with spearmen. This the Medes did. They built him a large, strong palace on a site that he picked, and authorized him to select any of the Medes for his bodyguard. Once established in authority, he compelled the Medes to build a single capital city and equip and adorn it, devoting less care henceforth to other towns. In this, too, the Medes obeyed him, and thus he built the great strong fortress called Agbatana with its girdle of walls rising one above the other.... These fortifications Deioces built for himself—especially round his own palace—but the rest of the people he ordered to live outside the walls. When all was completed, Deioces instituted a ceremonial, the first of its kind. Nobody form outside could enter the royal quarters or see the king. All business was transacted by messengers. No one, moreover, could laugh or spit in the king's presence. The reason for surrounding himself with this solemn etiquette was to keep out of sight of his former companions who had been brought up with him, who belonged to equally good families, and who were as brave as he. For seeing him, they might resent his position and plot against him; but if he were unseen, they might think of him as being of more than common clay. With this protocol arranged and his

> absolutism established, he was a stern watchdog for justice.... If he learned of anyone waxing insolent, he would send for them and punish them according to their offence. For he kept his spies and informers up and down the country that he ruled.

Mush political science is compressed into this narrative. A number of human beings, suffering from anarchy, sought to improve their lot. They wished to resolve their disputes by a method that would be fair to the antagonists and by conditions that could be accepted as just. Voluntarily, they turned to one of their members, their need dovetailing with his capacity and ambitions. After repeated experience with him, they found the results they wanted. Continued acceptance of his verdicts created the strongest presumption that they were binding. In order to formalize its newfound security, the group became supporters of Deioces. By these steps the influence he had acquired was converted into power. The later, once it was recognized and sanctioned, became authority. After this, he was entitled to enforce the law that he expounded. His decisions, compliance with which was formerly optional, were thenceforth compulsory. Resistance or disobedience was visited with coercion.

A comparable modern case—the birth of a state and the erection of the authority to govern it—is described by one who saw it happen and contributed his share. In the *Seven Pillars of Wisdom,* T. E. Lawrence describes his experience during the first World War when he was attempting in conjunction with Feisal to instigate a revolt of the Arabs against the Turks. A major obstacle was to overcome the ancient tribal jealousies and feuds between the respective Arab chieftains and their followers. So that they would combine and not bicker at cross-purposes, they had to be persuaded to adjust their animosities, to merge themselves into a whole larger than the tribe, and accept a superior authority as binding. This was Feisal's occasion and his challenge. Lawrence thus relates it:

> Except that all its events were happy, this day was not essentially unlike Feisal's every day.... The roads to Wejh swarmed with envoys and volunteers and great sheikhs riding in to swear allegiance... Feisal swore new adherents solemnly on the Koran

> between his hands "to wait while he waited, march when he marched, to yield obedience to no Turk, to deal kindly with all who spoke Arabic (whether Bagdadi, Aleppine, Syrian, or pure-blooded) and to put independence above life, family and goods." He also began to confront them at once, in his presence, with their tribal enemies, and to compose their feuds. An account of profit and loss would be struck between the parties, with Feisal modulating and interceding between them, and often paying the balance, or contributing towards it form his own funds, to hurry on the pact. During two years Feisal so laboured daily, putting together and arranging in their natural order the innumerable tiny pieces, which made up Arabian society, and combining them into his one design of war against the Turks. There was no blood feud left active in any of the districts through which he had passed, and he was Court of Appeal, ultimate and unchallenged, for western Arabia. He showed himself worthy of this achievement. He never gave a partial decision, nor a decision so impracticably just that it must lead to disorder. No Arab ever impugned his judgments of questioned his wisdom and competence in tribal business. By patiently sifting out right and wrong, by his tact, his wonderful memory, he gained authority over the Nomads form Medina to Damascus and beyond. He was recognized as a force transcending tribe, superseding blood chiefs, greater than jealousies. The Arab movement became, in the best sense, national, since within it, all Arabs were at one, and for it, private interests must be set aside.

There then is a picture of the growth of authority rendered possible because it was being founded on consent, with force at its disposal. Feisal met the need of the Arab tribes for a wider system of order, into which he infused his concepts of justice. Thereby his power became authority; and thereby he made history.

The Evolution of Political Ends and Governmental Means

What I am arguing is that both the ends of the state and the means of government undergo a progression. Because protection, though necessary, is not enough, human beings construct a system of order; and form order they strive for justice, because the most durable order is that which people deem just. A similar progression occurs with the techniques which government employs to fulfill these ends. The prerequisite for protection is force. But since the latter alone cannot sustain a system of order, power is generated by the admixture of force and consent. Finally, if order is to culminate in justice, power must be transmuted into authority.

Each stage, therefore, builds on, and develops beyond, the one preceding. Authority is a shell without a filling if it lacks power, and power may be flouted with impunity unless it can wield force. Justice enhances, yet depends upon, order, without which men could have no confidence or trust in each other; while order itself must be based on the protection that makes them secure. These relationships and sequences are expressed diagrammatically in figure 2.

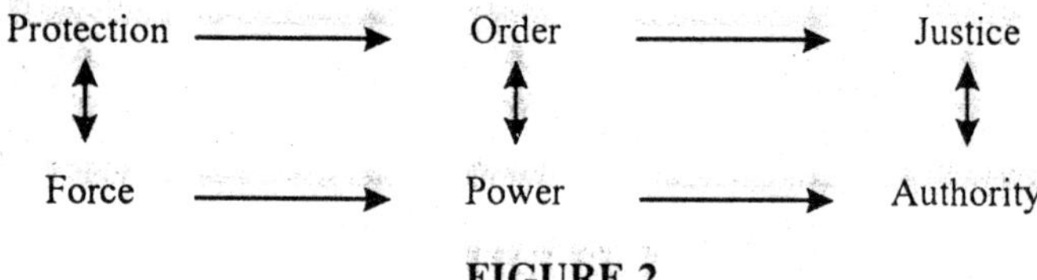

FIGURE 2

The foregoing account outlines the historical origins of government and sketches an ideal development which some states subsequently realize in practice. Manifestly it does not describe what all states are actually like or what they succeed in becoming. Many states never reach the level of justice. Some establish it for the majority only. In that case, what the majority regards as justice the minority views as a system of "law and order" imposed unjustly by majority power; the minority may then resort to force of its own, which by definition is illegal, to resist that power. Other states advance little beyond protection. Many governments are unable to convert power, into authority. In others again, the blend that produces power consists of more force and less consent. How does this happen and what are the political consequences?

Abuse of Force

The ends of the state—protection, order, justice—are achieved by the means of government—force, power, or authority. It has been said that the end justifies the means. But this is untrue, because some means are so immoral that no end can justify them. The truth is rather the contrary. Because we pass moral judgements on methods and goals alike, the means can stultify the end. In the field of statecraft, especially the implications of this are far-reaching. Perhaps more than any other institution, the state is peculiarly affected by the nature of the means it employs, and their abuse may fatally vitiate its ends. The possibility of this occurring arises form two facts already mentioned: the claim of the state to monopolize force, and the choice of representatives and officials to perform the functions of government. When these facts are combined, the result is to place this monopoly in the hands of officialdom. Thus the rest of the community may be at the mercy, or under the grip, of their own officials, since the latter have means of coercion at their fingertips. Because protection depends on the opposition of force to force, a group which has institutionalized its protection cannot avoid entrusting to officials the means of physical compulsion. But what guarantee is there that the force, which is intended to be used for the group, may not be used against it?

Plato expounded this problem in a memorable passage of the *Republic:*

> "Then we are quite clear as to what must be the bodily characteristics of our guardians?"
>
> "Yes."
>
> "And as to their mental qualities, we know they must be spirited.
>
> "Certainly."
>
> "Then, Glaucon," I said, "with such natures as these how are they to be prevented form behaving savagely towards one another and the other citizens?"
>
> "By Zeus," he said, " that will not be easy."
>
> "Still, we must have them gentle to their fellows and fierce to their enemies.
>
> If we can't effect that, they will prevent the enemy form destroying the city by doing it first themselves.

More pungently, the Roman satirist Juvenal inquired in words that have become proverbial: "But who will guard the guardians themselves? Force, like fire, can be a useful servant of mankind. But it is a dangerous master; and like fire, once out of control, it has vast potentialities for destruction. This perennial truth, had any doubted it, was proven once again when mass protests and demonstrations were organized during the late 1960s. The same scenario was reenacted with horrifying similarity in Chicago and New York, Paris and Tokyo, Mexico City and Berlin. Once violence is unleashed—be this the revolutionary stratagem of dissident groups or the repressive force of established authority, or both—restraints vanish and brutality prevails. The resort to violence be private group can never be justified, morally or politically, when it is directed against a system which offers a regular and effective constitutional procedure for encompassing change by peaceful means. But when the powers that be react by unleashing what one American report described as "a police riot," the result for the individual citizen is even worse. The police are there for the public's protection against private lawbreakers. Against police excesses, how shall we protect ourselves?

Many governments are so widely detested that they can stay in office only by policing the people under their control. This truth is borne out by the language we use in political discussion, since our words express concepts that summarize our experience. The term *Police-state* signifies a regime in which coercive force prediominates, where the government functions as a gendarmerie, and where it is no coincidence that the words *executive and executioner* stem from the same root. The regimes which fell in Teheran and Managua in 1979 had long seemed unassailable because the rulers could count on a loyal and well-equipped army. But when the power base of the Shah and Somoza crumbled, military force could not sustain them. Their opponents succeeded in massing such a counter-force, as power tilted to their side, that the Iranian Army and the Nicaraguan National Guard disintegrated. Similarly when marcos was overthrown in 1986, the climactic events which forced him to flee the country he had pillaged were the mass demonstrations in Manila by people supporting Corazon Aquino, the widow of his political opponent whom his supporters had murdered. What finall enabled Aquino's supporters to control the streets was the split in the army, both in the leadership and among the soldiers, enough of whom switched sides for a popular uprising to triumph. The same political truth has been reinforced in eastern Europe and in the Soviet Union itself. In the late 1980s, it was masses of people in the streets who were the decisive factor in overthrowing the police states of East Germany, Czechoslovakia, and Romania. Likewise in the Soviet Union, when a coup was launched against President Gorbachev in August, 1991, it failed for three reasons: divisions within the military and the security forces, the courageous defiance of Boris Yeltsin, the President of the Russian Republic, and the resistance of ordinary citizens by the tens of thousands who had lost both their confidence in the Communist Party and their fear of the KGB. But what finally enabled them to control the streets was the split in the army, both in the leadership and among the soldiery. Enough switched sides for a popular uprising to succeed.

The Paradox of Power

Because power consists of force plus consent, the difficulties attending the use of naked force are still present when the latter is buttressed by consent to generate power. Those in power can abuse the force at their command by seeking to impose their order on the recalcitrant, and the means lie at their disposal when they are so minded. Hence the existence of force and the construction of power, which are the inescapable products of our need for protection and order, are the root-cause of government's perennial dilemma. Force and power there must be. Otherwise there can be no government; nor can some basic ends of the state be attained. But such means permit restraints upon the opponents of government, which can be extended to the point where freedom is endangered. Power is susceptible to abuse by those who possess it and is then convertible into tyranny. What originates as an instrument of service can culminate in a weapon of enslavement. Hence many of the controversies concerning the organization and functions of the state revolve around the problem of fixing limits within which power may usefully be employed and beyond which it cannot safely be increased.

As applied to power these considerations are more complex than as applied to force. That is because power includes that quota of consent which, by definition, is absent form force. If the state consisted only of a simple bisection into government and governed, its problems would at least be more clear-cut. In fact, however, all governments are an eternal triangle, whose three angles are those in office, their supporters, and their opponents. Power flows from the supporters to the government, which then exercises it over both its supporters and the opposition. But what makes a vital difference in these relationships is the amount of consent that goes into power, as compared with the volume of dissent. Every government uses force and, initially at least, is supported by some consent. This is true of dictatorships as well as democracies. Lenin, Stalin, Hitler, Mussolini, and their brethren today could not have gained power or stayed on top without the support of like-minded persons who were content to do their bidding. There is an enormous difference, however, in the respective quantities of force and consent that combine into power, and in the relative importance of each. As a general rule, the broader and stronger the consent, the fewer the occasions to employ force. Conversely, wherever the apparatus of force bulks large in the machinery of government and is in constant use, it is reasonalble to suppose that the supporters of government are not strong enough to control their opponents by other means: Every police state relies heavily on methods of coercion, because its rulers are not backed by enough consent and therefore have not sufficiently transformed their power into authority.

Nor should one overlook the effect on government of the lapse of time. Power, and even authority, may initially be built on a foundation of consent that is wide and deep. But as the years pass, these foundations can crack. A Deioces wins a kingdom with willing acclaim. Yet he himself in later years, or his successor, may lose support through tyrannical acts. The authority, which was once legitimate and just, can then be perverted into despotism. Temporarily, a ruler of ruling group may continue to wield power with waning consent. They succeed for a while because people at large are imbued with obedient habits, are paralyzed by inertia, and severally are inferior to the force mobilized by the ruler. Once rooted, power is not easily shaken. But having consumed its initial capital of consent, it falls into the bankruptcy of despotism. Then, when the sustaining conditions of government are removed, when justice vanishes and order has to be imposed, people start inquiring into the purposes that justify the acts of government, at which point the insolvency of political pretensions is laid bare. For if the state requires force, or power, or authority to perform a service, it is the continuation of the service, and this alone, that warrants the continuation of the means.

Thus force enables a regime to outlive the consent with which it was formerly endowed. In erecting the force to serve them, people also create a technique for dominating over them. Mobilized because of their wish, that force may later be directed against their wish. This possibility reaches the extreme point when a government uses force, not to protect the governed, but to protect itself against them. In that case the rulers reveal the truth about their political situation in the architectural style of their governmental buildings. When a regime is on guard not only against external foes, but against some of its own people, it houses itself within a fortress for safety from its domestic opponents. Thus in medieval Italian cities, the ruling faction would shelter behind stout walls and equip itself with lofty watch-towers, at the same time prohibiting others from doing likewise. Observe the exterior of the famous Signoria in Florence, and what you see—allowing for the sculptural embellishment—is not a city hall but a citadel, and designed with that end in view. So have the despots of Russia and Germany dwelled in their Kremlins and their Berchtesgadens, as if in a constant state of seige. The perils of their position were understood and are described by Plato:

> "It seems to be that in our inquiry on this matter (a good and an evil life) we must get light from the following sources."
>
> "From which?"
>
> "By examining each of those rich individuals in cities who own a great number of slaves; for they have this point of similarity with tyrants, that they are rulers of many. No doubt the tyrant has the best of it in point of numbers?"
>
> "He has."
>
> "You know, I suppose, that they live unconcernedly, and are not afraid of their servants?"

"Well, is there anything for them to fear?"

"Nothing," I said; "but do you see why that is?"

"Yes. The whole city gives assistance to each individual."

"Excellent," I said, "But supposing one of the Gods were to take a man who possesses fifty slaves or even more and were to lift him and his wife and children out of the city and put him down with all his property and his slaves, in a desert place where there would be no free men to come to his assistance, do you not suppose that he would be in the most terrible fright in apprehension lest he and his children and his wife should be killed by their servants?"

"In the worst of frights," he answered.

"Would he not then be compelled to pay court to some of those his slaves, to make them many promises, and to set them free, quite against his desire, and stand revealed as his own servants' today?"

"He would certainly have to do so or die," he said.

Plato's insight should give us pause to reflect when we observe the spectacle of governments in the present day. We take it for granted that such conditions prevailed under totalitarian regimes, whether in Berlin or Moscow. But it has been a revelation and a shock to discover what happened in the federal government of the United States since the 1960s, a discovery made possible by investigations into the misdeeds of the Johnson, Nixon, and Reagan administrations both at home and abroad. Anybody elected President of the United States is walled off nowadays from ordinary contacts and is guarded in the White House and other encampments. One reason for this is the genuine possibility of assassination by psychotics or terrorists. Another is the psychological or political twist which happens to some incumbents so that they identify their personal survival with the national security and fortify their position by cultivating the mystique of the presidency among the public at large. At any rate, it is now known that under the Johnson and Nixon administrations the surveillance employed at home and abroad by the FBI and CIA against those whom they dubbed enemies was used domestically against political opponents, conscientious objectors, and intellectual dissenters. When those in office use such methods to stay there, democracy is being killed from within.

The Philosophy of Anarchism

The state's resort to force has often evoked an ethical revulsion that generates political consequences. Many persons of high moral ideals are so affronted by the raw brutality of the coercive apparatus of governments—of the police, prisons, and army—that they veer around to a completely antithetical position. Any violence, they argue, used by one human being against another is not only morally wrong, but makes morality impossible. Ethical behaviour has to flow freely and spontaneously; it cannot be externally imposed. Consequently, they say, an institution which insists it cannot perform its task without at times employing force is *ipso facto* immoral. The only thing to do with the state, therefore, is to abolish it along with its whole apparatus of coercion.

That, of course, is a summary of the philosophy of anarchism. It is a viewpoint that students of politics should note because it raises the question that logically comes first: Is government necessary? Anarchism, as the word signifies, is a philosophy that argues for a society without government. Its ethical values are of the highest. It prefers cooperation to competition, freedom to power, spontaneity to coercion. Assuming that human beings are naturally good, it asserts that we are driven into bad habits by our institutions and by the powerful who control them.

These doctrines commended themselves to some distinguished thinkers in the nineteenth century—for example, Godwin in Great Britain, Proudhon in France, and Thoreau in the United States. But it is significant that Russians paid the most attention to this theory and produced three of its best-known exponents: Bakunin, Tolstoi, and Kropotkin. These men had much in common. All were born of noble families; all served as young officers in the Czarist army. Form this experience they emerged thoroughly alienated form their country's government. It is indeed no accident that the most repressive regime in Europe should have produced such outspoken anarchists. Contrary to what the behaviourists assume, conditioning can provoke the opposite reaction.

The anarchist philosophy is at its best in stressing the basic goodness of human nature and in advocating voluntary cooperation among free individuals. It is at its weakest, however, in deciding how much order such a society would require and how to treat those who break whatever rules it adopts. Communities based on anarchist principles have functioned in small group whose members were highly motivated and idealistic and whose technology was fairly simple. Anarchism has yet to be tried in a large society with a complex technology and organization.

Confusion of Politics with Power

Because force is brutal and power, once acquired, may be transformed by abuse, the essence of the state and the nature of the governmental process are often misunderstood. Every student of the state observes that it controls the organized force of the group, and we know that those who monopolize force misuse it at times and on occasion with success. These indisputable facts have led to conflicting interpretations. Because the state wields force in order to provide protection, and because force, to be effective, must be amassed as a monopoly, many regard this force not merely as the instrument by which the state operates, but as its principal characteristic. Seen from this viewpoint, the state is differentiated from other associations and is definable by virtue of its being the sole rightful monopolist of the force available within society. Max Weber, for example, wrote:

> Ultimately, one can define the modern state sociologically only in terms of the specific *Means* peculiar to it, as to every political association, namely, the use of physical force. Of course, force is certainly not the normal or the only means of the state—nobody says that—but force is a means specific to the state. Today the relation between the state and violence is an especially intimate one.

When so much stress is placed upon the state's exercise of force, this feature is no longer treated as a tool incidental to performing the function of protection. Instead, force is placed in the center of the analysis of the state, and the latter is then discussed in terms not to the needs it serves but of the specific method it employs. The emphasis is moved form ends to means with the result that they are reversed. What once was considered the instrument is now conceived to be the master. Instead of using force to carry out its protective function, the government is pictured as performing that function so as to maintain its coerce.

Next, the logic is extended from the narrow concept of force to the broader one of power. Because government is energized through power, the central problem of the state on this view is how to accumulate it. Politics is then considered the arena where the struggle for power is conducted; and power is no longer regarded as the tool through which other results may be accomplished, but as if it were itself the objective to be attained. Under those circumstances, the reversal of means and ends is complete. Arguments that once interpreted the state in terms of the functions it undertakes are twisted into justifications of the power it must employ. Gorge Orwell has thus stated the point: "Power is not a means, it is an end.... The object of persecution is persecution. The object of torture is torture. The object of power is power." The practices that follow from this attitude raise some crucial questions about the relation between power and ethics. If the political process is in truth a battle for might, what is its relevance to choices between right and wrong or evaluations of good and bad?

The Ethics of Power

Three views are possible, each of which has its exponents. First, power may be clothed with moral approval and upheld as good. When the accumulation of power is viewed as the goal of the state, the next step is to argue that what conduces to might is right and then to conclude that might is right. Second, power may be thought to be unconnected with moral choice. The sphere of the state and the processes of politics are deemed amoral, as having no concern with matters of right or wrong. The latter belong to a different order of inquiry, much as art is often held to exist for art's sake exempt from moral connotation. In this case it makes no sense to pass judgment on the state, except in terms of whether it succeeds in maintaining power. The third possibility is that power may be condemned as evil, on the ground that its control of force involves coercion which is morally wrong. If the state, then, is preeminently a power-wielding institution that employs force, condemnation of force leads to condemnation of the state as immoral. This value judgment is reinforced empirically by the knowledge that power is often abused and is employed in ways and for ends that affront a civilized conscience.

The three views lead to different deductions. The first results in glorifying power and the state that employs it. The second carves out spheres of interest, assigning politics to a separate compartment of life. The third seeks to combat the evils of power either by adopting the extreme position of the anarchist, who says that all coercion is morally wrong and that consequently the state must be abolished; or by upholding the less drastic view that the functions of the state had better be confined to a minimum, since the fewer they are, the less power will exist. Such divergent conclusions are made possible by the ambiguity in the concept of power. Since power combines some force with some consent, people's opinion of power will vary according to whether it is the force or the consent which appears uppermost in the compound. But divergent though they be, the various conclusions share a common origin and derive from the same premises. They spring from a preoccupation with the techniques which the state uses rather than the end it pursues, and they substitute the means for the ends as the essential criterion of the state.

Nothing has given rise to more misconceptions about the activities of government and the place of the state in society than this false emphasis with its gratuitous switching of priorities. Numerous political scientists sanction this distortion of the truth by equating politics with power and professing that their picture of it is "value-free." Such a claim is pure fantasy since no inquiry into human society by a human being can wholly eliminate the subjective element. Nevertheless, much of the research and writing by political scientists since 1950 has been dominated by categories drawn from behavioural psychologists and Weberian sociologists. Power and politics were treated as synonymous; the study of government was the analysis of " the decision-making process";

its human participants were portrayed in terms of a fictional model of a "Political Man" competing aggressively for larger amounts of Power. The result of this one-sided bias has been a caricature of the subject, exaggerating some of its features and omitting others. power and politics are, of course, related, but the correct view of the relationship is this: Policy is what politics is about, and policy decisions always involve a choice among values. Power comes into politics, necessarily but secondarily, because without it no policy can take effect.

To clarify the substance of politics and view it undistorted is the purpose of this book. Thus far, I have inquired into the why and wherefore of social groups and have traced the genesis and growth of the state and its government. Now begins the analysis of politics in terms of the five permanent issues which make it what it is. The next ten chapters, in pairs, will examine these issues and the would-be solutions, both classic and contemporary, which humanity has tried in the quest for civilization.

3

Nature and Functions of the State

We saw in the last chapter how the state came into existence in ancient India and what were the different theories advocated about its origin. Let us now see what according to the ancient Indians were to be the nature, aims and functions of the state.

While discussing the origin of the state in the last chapter, we have passingly referred to the conception of ancient Indians about the nature of the state. They regarded it as essentially a beneficent institution evolved in prehistoric times for the efficient protection of human life and for the better realization of its higher ideals. The idea that it was a necessary evil to be tolerated, as there as a no other alternative, was not subscribed to by any ancient Indian thinker.

State was no doubt an unwelcome institution to evil-doers, but they had no right to expect that their convenience and feelings should be respected by society, which they were out to disorganize and destroy.

It is owing to the presence of this anti-social element that *daṇḍa* or force becomes the ultimate sanction of government. Ancient Indian thinkers do not desire that *daṇḍa* should make its appearance, every now and then; on the other hand they regard that state as an ideal one where its exercise is rendered almost unnecessary by the willingness of the people to accept the scheme of a righteous life, determined by the code given to humanity by God. This code was binding alike upon the people and the king. If the people were to be guilty of its breach, they were to be punished by the king. If the latter contravened its provisions, he would forfeit his subjects' allegiance, who would be at liberty even to kill him if necessary. In the ideal state both the king and the subjects were expected to follow the provisions of the divine code for peace and prosperity both here and in the life to come.

The historic method being then unknown, the evolution of the state through various stages is not discussed by ancient Indian writers. The available evidence, however, shows that the state in the early Vedic period was still tribal. The Yadus, the Turvaśas and the Bharatas, for instancd, who played a prominent part in the Vedic history, had for a long time no permanent territorial basis for their states; the latter moved along with the peoples of their tribes and had thus only a tribal basis. In the later Vedic period, however, the state became territorial; we have clear references to the different tribes settling down in the different parts of the country, and to kings becoming masters both of their people as well as their country *(rāshṭra).* In the later Vedic period the emperor is described as one who rules over the earth bounded by the oceans. The different stages, however, by which the state gradually became territorial cannot be clearly visualized from the scanty evidence available to us at present.

What are to be the constituents of a territorial state and how are they inter-related and held together is the question that we have to consider next.

Vedic literature does not enable us to get an idea of what were the contemporary notions about this topic; we, however, begin to get welcome light from c. 4th century B.C., when the political thought had become fairly developed. Both Kauṭilya and Manu held that the state was not a loose assemblage of parts, each having its own interests and moving at its own will; it was characterized by an organic unity. The king, the ministry, the territory, the resources, the forts, the military forces and the allies constitute, according to these writers, the seven constituents of the state. Later writers like Kāmandaka and Śukra regard this as a self-evident truth, and epigraphs also often describe how the kingdoms acquired by the heroes, whom they eulogise, possessed all the seven constituents.

Let us now compare these constituents of the ancient Indian state with those postulated by modern thinkers. According to the latter territory population and central governmental having a juristic personality, a common will and sovereign powers, are the main constituents of the state.

Let us now see how far any of these constituents find their counterpart in ancient Indian list of the seven constituents, given above.

Of the seven constituents, *svāmin* (king) and *amātyas* (ministers) constituted the central government, which exercised the sovereign powers and imparted the central unity. *RČshṭra* (territory), *durgas* (forts), *bala* (army) and *kosha* (treasury) constituted the resources of the state. The stage of the tribal state had long passed, and so territory was regarded as an essential element of the state. Forts and armed forces were vitally necessary to defend the every existence of the state and so are regarded as its essential constituents. The defence of the country and the proper discharge of the constituents and ministrant functions of the state required ample resources, and so *kosha* (treasury) is also regarded as indispensable to the very existence of the state. The inclusion of its allies among the constituents of a state strikes us as rather strange. The existence of a state, however, depends, as contemporary history has been showing in a forcible manner, upon its securing a proper balance of power by making suitable alliances. A large number or small states existed in the Indian sub-continent, and our political thinkers felt that the existence of none could be guaranteed for a long time unless a proper balance of power was secured by wise alliances. It is a little surprising to note that population as such is not mentioned as one of the constituents of the state; that was probably because it was realized that it was too evident a truth to be specifically mentioned.

The seven constituents of the state are regarded as the limbs *(aṅgas)* of the body politic by the Indian thinkers. Some of them like the king and the ministers may be more prominent than others like the forts and the allies. Each limb, however, though by itself it may look unimportant, is indispensable to the body politic, for its functions cannot be efficiently discharged by any other. The state can exist and function properly only if all the limbs of its body politic become mutually integrated and cooperate with each other. No limb of the body politic can strictly be regarded as more important than any other. The body politic cannot stand if one of them is missing, just as three sticks poised properly against one another will collapse, it one of them is taken away.

It is thus clear that ancient Indian thinkers regarded the state as an organic whole. They no doubt regarded the king and the government as the most important limbs of the organism, but others, if less important, were also indispensable for the proper functioning of the body politic. We should not also forget to note that the organic conception of the state is only partially true. The cells and limbs of an organism have no separate existence of their own and cannot function independently. Such is obviously not the case with at least some of the constituents of the state. Forts and resources can exist independently and may be wielded into a new state by some groups of the subjects, who may not be able to see eye to eye with the old government.

Out authorities devote considerable space to describe the seven constituents of the state referred to above, and the excellences and strong points that should be developed in each. Of these the forts and the armed forces need not detain us as, they are constitutionally unimportant. The king, the ministry, the resources and the allies will be discussed in later chapters dealings with the Kinghsip the Ministry, Income and Expenditure and Interestate Relations respectively. As far as the territory is concerned, our authorities point out that the prosperity of a state will to a great extent depend upon the natural resources of its territory and the case with which it can be defended. It must of course be populated by an energetic and industrious population, for the character of its people determines the destiny of a state more than any other fact or consideration. The territorial size of an ideal state is not discussed by our authorities. They, however, regarded the whole country from the Himalayas to the sea as the proper sphere for the activity of an emperor. As far as the smaller kingdoms were concerned, there were no natural boundaries in India to separate them in most cases; they were usually small enough to be well-governed and large enough to be self-sufficient.

Whether an ideal state should consist of people of exclusively one nationality, having the same race, religion and language, or whether it can be a composite political unit of people of different nationalities, belonging to diverse races, professing many creeds and speaking several languages is a question which as not been discussed by ancient Indian thinkers. This need not surprise us, because it did not arise at all in the ancient period. It is true that a number of foreigners like the Greeks, the Parthians, the Scythians, the Kushāṅas and the Hūṅas invaded and conquered the country and settled down in it as its governors. But they did not remain foreign nationals with a different language, religion and culture for a long time. Within a generation or two all of them used to become completely Indianised and converted into Hinduism or Buddhism. They did not create any problems for the Indian states. The latter used to repose implicit confidence in their new Indianised subjects, who also used to entertain no extra-territorial loyalties.

A state no doubt becomes homogenous if there is unity of language, race and religion among its subjects. Ancient Indian writers have not emphasized upon this point, because there was no necessity whatsoever to do so. Most of the states in ancient India did not differ from their neighbours, either in race or in language or in religion. Hindus, Buddhists and Jains lived in all states peacefully and harmoniously. Sanskrit was the international language and Prakrits had not differentiated from one another to such a degree as to become mutually unintelligible. All the foreigners who were coming into the country, used to be rapidly Indianised and completely absorbed into the Hindu community. Thus the different states in ancient India did not at all differ in race, language or religion. Most of them had developed into separate entities primarily owing to individual ambition, administrative convenience or geographical considerations. It did not, therefore occur to our thinkers that they should emphasises upon the advisability of racial, linguistic or religious uniformity in the population of a state.

The Aims of the State

The Vedic literature does not specifically discuss the aims or ideals of the state. Incidental observations made therein, however, enable us to gather that peace, order, society and justice were regarded as the fundamental aims of the state. The king or the head of the state was to be like god Varuṅa, the upholder of the law and order *(dhṛitavrata);* he was to punish the wicked and help the virtuous. Religion was to be promoted, morality was to be encouraged and education was to be patronized. The state, however, was to secure not only the moral but also the material well-being of its citizens. The kingdom of king Parīkshit, idealized in the *Atharvaveda* (XX. 127), flowed with milk and honey. All round welfare of the public was clearly regarded as the chief aim of the state during the Vedic and Upanishadic ages, i.e. down to c. 600 B.C.

When the literature on politics proper began to be developed, we find that promotion of *dharma, artha* and *kāma* are usually mentioned as the aims of the state. The state was to promote *dharma,* not by championing any particular sect or religion, but by fostering a feeling of piety and religiousness, by encouraging virtue and morality, by extending help to the establishments belonging to all religions and sects, by maintaining free hospitals and feeding houses for the poor and the decrepits and last but not least, by extending patronage to literature and sciences. The promotion of *artha* was to be procured by encouraging trade, industry and agriculture, by developing national resources, by bringing fresh land under cultivation, by building dams and canals to make agriculture independent of rain, and by encouraging extensive and systematic working of mines. The state was to promote *kāma* by ensuring peace and order, so that each individual many enjoy life undisturbed, and by offering encouragement to fine arts like music, dancing, painting, sculpture and architecture in order to promote aesthetic culture. The state was thus expected to maintain peace and order and promote moral, material and aesthetic progress of society.

Our writers have thus practically recognized the ideal of perfect development of the individual to the full development of the society, when they laid down that it was the business of the state of promote Dharma, Artha, Kāma and Moksha; only they have not used the modern terminology. The ideal of *sarvabhūtahita*, which is emphasized in several places, refers not only to the spiritual but also to the mundane sphere.

The inclusion of the promotion of *dharma* among the aims of the state has given rise to a considerable misunderstanding in modern times, which has been to some extent caused by the habit of later writers of describing the king as the champion of *varṇas* and *āśramas*. It is contended that *varṇadharma* or the caste-system in particular is based upon iniquitous principles; it exhalts the Brāhmaṇa and confers almost divine honours upon him, while it reduces the Śūdras and Chāṇḍālas almost to the position of slaves, denying them the most elementary rights of ordinary citizenship. The Śūdras were prevented from holding property and were subjected to more heavier punishments than those meted out to the Brāhmaṇas for identical offences. The Chāṇḍālas were treated worse than dogs. When the state become a champion of *varṇas* and *āśramas*, it became a party to all these iniquities. It enforced the iniquitous *varṇāśrma-dharma* at the point of the sword to the detriment of the lower classes. It was thus based upon social injustice. It confounded *dharma* with the existing iniquitous social order. It idealized the actual instead of trying to actualise the ideal.

The above criticism is mostly based upon a misunderstanding of the factors that have promoted the development of the Hindu social institutions. Customs and traditions changed in ancient India by the silent operation of social approval or disapproval and not by the noisy process of a legislative enactment or repeal. The state only enforced what had been previously approved by the social conscience. When society in early period was sancioning intercaste dinners and marriages, the state had no objection to them. When later on it disapproved both these practices, the state did not propose to encourage them. In early days widows had no right of inheritance; the property of a person having no heir other than a widow escheated to the state. Later on society decided to recognize widow as an heir of her deceased husband, and though this change adversely affected the interest of the excheqor, the state cheerfully sanctioned it. The recognition of the promotion of *dharma* as one of the duties of the state did not result in the apotheosis of the *status quo;* every student of Hindu social institution will concede that changes were gradually and continuously taking place in them. Levirate (*niyoga*), once approved, was later stamped out of existence; not only the proprietary rights of women, but also those of the Śūdras were being constantly enlarged in spite of the opposition of the earlier writers.

It would, therefore, be unfair to attribute the existence of certain inquities in the Hindu social order to *dharma* being considered as one of the aims of the Hindu state. The state no doubt claimed to be the champion of *varṇadharma,* but it did not support the Brāhmaṇas' claim to their exemption from the taxation and the capital punishment. It is extremely doubtful whether many cases had occurred in ancient India of the state punishing the Śūdras and Brāhmaṇa women for presuming to study the Vedas. The prohibition was regarded by the society, including the Śūdras, as divinely ordained, and as there was no material benefit whatsoever to be gained by its violation, there was no incentive to break it. The number of Brāhamaṇas themselves, who studied the Vedas, was microscopically small and provision was made to meet the needs of the religiously minded persons among the Śūdras and Brāhmaṇa women by throwing open the epics, the *Gitā* and the Purāṇas to the.

There is no doubt that some iniquities existed in the Hindu social order and their number increased in the first millennium of the Christian era. But that was due to the narrow-mindedness of the Hindu society of that age and not to the state's making *dharma* as one of its aims. Of course it can be argued that the state should have given a lead in the matter by encouraging a more liberal policy. We should, however, not forget that legislation did not come within the normal activities of the state. Recent experience in our country about the Sharda Act also shows that legislation, far in advance of the social views on the point, tends to remain dead later. The state was not interested in enforcing caste iniquities; if any cases actually arose, they must have been decided by the caste or the village Panchāyats, which where purely non-official bodies. The state sought to encourage *dharma* by promoting piety and religiousness, by extending equal patronage to all sects and religions and their establishments and by financing works of public utility like tanks, canals, wells, poor houses and hospitals, and not by becoming an instrument in the hands of the church or the priests.

WAS THE ANCIENT INDIAN STATE THEOCRATIC?

It would be convenient here to examine how far the ancient Indian state was under the influence of technology and to what extent it can be described as theocratic. A theocracy may arise when a king usurps the functions of the Church, as the case with the Khalifas, or when the head of the Church becomes the king as is the case with the Dalai Lama of Tibet and the Pope of the Vatican kingdom. Or, the king may be a mere agent or instrument of the church, as was the case for some time in Europe during the 8th and the 9th centuries A.D. The Pope and the bishops at this time claimed the right to punish the king, if he was not ruling according to the will of God. Some rulers like Charles the Bold admitted the right and even the duty of the prelates to suspend the execution of the orders of the state regarded as objectionable by them. Orders of the Pope were to be regarded as of greater moment and validity than those of the Emperor, as they had the authority over the soul as well. Of course, the majority of the emperors were not disposed to recognize this claim and the early medieval European history presents an interesting tussle between the Church and the State.

Faint echoes of a similar conflict between the king and the church can be heard in the early Indian literature. *Gautama-Dharmasūtra* (c. 500 B.C.) claims that the royal authority does not touch the priest and reminds the king that he can prosper only if supported by the latter. If he does not employ a qualified Brāhmaṇa priest, says the *Aitareya Brāhmaṇa,* gods will not at all accept his oblations. At the time of the coronation, the king three times bows before the Brāhamaṇa; he thereby accepts his subordinate position, and as long as he does so he will prosper. Priests like Vasishṭha exercised profound influence of the royal court. Rituals were also devised to ensure the subordination of the Kshatriyas and the Vaiśyas to the Brāhmaṇas. In the *Rigveda* there is a clear passage to show that a king, who honoured his chaplain properly, could secure an easy mastery over his subjects and a smashing defeat over his enemies. In Europe the Pope claimed the right to confirm the election of the emperor made by the nobles; we do not know whether such a right was advanced in ancient India.

The above evidence shows that down to the end of the Brāhmaṇa period (c. 1000 B.C.) the priests tried to extend their sway over the monarch and through him over the state. It is natural that many kings, should have opposed this tendency; the bitter curses that are pronounced against the rulers who confiscate the cows, i.e. the wealth of the Brāhmaṇa, seem to be directed against those monarchs who were opposing the efforts of the priests to forge a theocratic state, where their voice was to reign supreme. Unfortunately we have no detailed information about any specific and individual cases, as we have in the case of early medieval Europe.

In the course of time, however, the church and the state or the Brāhmaṇas and the Kshatriyas made up their quarrel. It was realized that the two could prosper only if they cooperated with each other. Each conceded a qualified divinity to the other, as both realized that they could prosper only if there was a complete harmony between them. It is interesting to note that this view agrees closely with the of Gregory VII, who maintained that the kingship and the Popedom were both divine, their position being comparable to that to the two eyes of the human body.

The general trend of the evidence of the Brahmanical literature is to show that the prince or the state was under the leading strings of the Brāhmaṇas or the church. The royal chaplain (*purohita*) knew rituals which could either promote or retard the welfare of the king and the state. The aim of the government, as shown already, was to promote *dharma*, and the laws which it enforced were regarded as divine in origin or inspiration. *Varṇāśramadharma,* which the state had to enforce, was largely moulded by the priests, who were the writers of the books on the subject. They not only claimed to be above the state, but they also put forth the right for exemption from taxation and capital punishment. The punishments that could be given to them were to be milder than those to be inflicted upon others. The appointment of the *dharmamahāmātras* by the Mauryas and the *vinayasthitisthāpakas* by the Guptas to regulate religious practices and moral conduct of the population would be a natural corollary of the swing towards theocracy.

There is, therefore, a considerable force in the view that the ancient Indian state was theocratic to a great extent. We should, however, note the limits to the theocracy and the period during which it was operative. The claims that have been put forth on behalf of the Brāhamaṇas in the Brahmanical literature are to a great extent exaggerated. They represent the wish more than the reality. There is no doubt that the influence of the royal chaplain over the king was great during the age of the Vedas and the Brāhamaṇas. Its extent, however, should not be judged merely by the implications of the passages referred to above. For there are other passages in the Brāhamaṇa literature itself, which give the other side of the picture. A passage in the *Taittirīya Brāhamaṇa* confesses that a king, at his sweet will, can lord it over the Brāhmaṇas. Another in the *Aitareya Brāhmaṇa* admits that a king can expel the Brāhmaṇas at will. The *Bṛihadāraṇyaka Upanishad* states that it is the Kshatriya or the king who enjoys the highest status in society; the Brāhamaṇa sits lower than and next to him. When princes Śarmishṭhā suspected that Devāyanī, the daughter of the royal chaplain, was assuming an air of superiority, she sharply reprimanded her: 'Enough of presumptuousness. Sitting in a humbler place your father goes on flattering may father day and night. You are the daughter of him who begs and flatters, I am the daughter of him who donates and is praised.

It would, therefore, be wrong to suppose that even in the Vedic period, the king or the state was under the leading strings of the Brāhmaṇa or the Church. Generally speaking the priest was treated with decorum; the spiritual help offered by his rituals and sacrifices was welcome. But the king was far from becoming a mere instrument in the hands of the priest; he could show him his proper place or even expel him, if he tended to become presumptuous. Brāhmaṇas no doubt claimed a number of privileges including exemption from the taxation and the capital punishment. In the course of time, the divinity of the king was recognized. This, however, did not make the king infallible or even the sole interpreter of the divine will. Laws, though regarded as divine, were really based upon social customs and traditions. By sanctioning their operation, the state did not become an instrument in the hands of the Church or the priests; it rather became the mouthpiece of the social will.

From about the 4th century B.C. the influence of technology on the state began to decline further. The Vedic sacrifices themselves fell into disgrace and disuse, which naturally undermined the influence of the chaplain. Politics developed into a special science and princes naturally studied it assiduously in preference to the Vedic lore or the Upanishadic philosophy. Positive law began to be differentiated from religious rituals and traditional customs; and the school of politics began to aver that the former was more important than the latter. Hindu polity thus succeeded in emancipating itself from the leading strings of theology by the beginning of the Christian era. The king was no doubt regarded as the protector and enforcer of Dharma, but we have shown already how this did not make the state theocratic. His duty was to promote piety and religiousness by extending equal patronage to all sects and religions and to enforce customary laws approved by the social conscience; he discharged this function through officers like the *dharmamahāmātras* and the *vinayasthitisāpakas*. He was not to be an agent of a particular religion or sect working to promote its interests or seeking to carry out its commands. The crusade of a Hindu state against Bauddhism or Jainism is rarely met with in ancient Indian history.

The Influence of Religious Concepts on Polity

The influence of technological, religious and philosophical concepts on Hindu polity may be briefly noticed here. The concept of Dharma, the ultimate and supreme power was responsible for the king being struck by the Dharmadaṇda thrice on the occasion of his coronation; it was also responsible for the exhortation to him to lead his whole life as dedicated to duty, *dhṛitavrata*. The duties of the king were conceived as Rājadharma. The violation of Dharma was ultimately punishable by God. So the king became ultimately accountable to God, who was to punish him in a suitable manner; our political writers therefore usually did not encourage the subjects to seek to punish the king for his delinquencies. This concept of the supremacy of Dharma prevented the development of a reasoned philosophy of the rights of the people or opposition to tyranny.

The doctrine of Karman also has left some influence on the polity. At one stage of its development this doctrine believed in the possibility of an individual's *karman* being transferable to another; the political thinkers therefore regarded it as possible for the sages to pay off their dues to the state by transferring one sixth of their *puṇya* or merit to it. The threat that was held out to the king that if he misgoverned, the siṇ fo the crimes of the subjects would be visited on him was also another corollary of the same doctrine. The usual view however was that a person reaps as he sows; this was responsible for the threat of a long sojourn in hell held before a vicious king or a false witness. Three days' respite that Aśoka has granted to condemned criminals was for the purpose of enabling them or their relations to undertake pious acts, so that the criminals may benefit by them after their execution.

The theory of the supremacy of the moral order suggested the ideal of a moral state which should have no sinners or thieves among its subjects. It was also responsible for the enunciation of the code of righteous war, *dharma-yuddha*, which was followed to some extent at one stage of our history. The state was to strive for the realization of the moral and religious ideals along with those in the spheres of social and economic life. It was thus to secure both the moral and material development of the people and the country.

The theory that God is omnipresent and is the giver of all good things has left its own influence here and there on the polity.

The *Gita* preaches that whatever is preeminent, striking or brilliant is particularly surcharged with the Divine Presence and illustrates the point by recognizing the divinity in the king.

Alternatively the king began to be regarded as Diving Guardian. When the theory of incarnation became popular, the king was regarded as an incarnation of Vishnu. Some kings (e.g. king Gautamiputra of the Bhita seal, c. 1st century A.D.) regarded their kingdom as a gift from God; other states like the republic of the Yaudheyas regarded themselves as presided over by their favourite deity like Kartikeya, though there is no evidence to show that the rulers in these cases regarded themselves as agents of God. All this was a natural consequence of regarding God as the giver of all good things and protector of all good persons or states.

The gospel of *Aparigrahá* is responsible for the ideal of self-denial placed before the king. The freedom from taxation that was conceded to pious and poor Brahmanas was due to the view that those who practised *aparigraha* should not be made to bear avoidable economic burdens.

The Vedāntic doctrine that soul is identical with or similar to God should have led to the spread of the doctrine of social economic and legal equality. Strangely enough this did not happen. The theory that everything here is Brahman was effectively counterpoised by the gospel of the caste system, which permitted social and economic inequalities. Buddhism is sometimes assumed (though quite wrongly) to be opposed to the caste system; but in the Lichchhavi republic which was under marked Buddhist influence, there were sharp economic and political inequalities.

To conclude, we have to admit that religious and philosophical dogmas and concepts did not deeply influence the Hindu political thought, practice or institutions.

FUNCTIONS OF THE STATE

Having finished our discussion of the nature and aims of the state, let us now consider its functions.

Modern writers usually divide the functions of the state into two categories, constituent and ministrant. Under the former class fall those functions of the state which are absolutely necessary for the orderly organization of society, viz., defence against foreign aggression, protection of person and property, preservation of peace and order and adjudication. Under the latter class fall those activities of the state which it undertakes to promote the welfare of the people, to increase their wealth by a cooperative effort, and to add to their amenities of life. Education, sanitation, postal services, trade regulations, roads and communications, development of mines and forest, care of the poor and invalid, etc. would come under the ministrant functions of the state. The modern tendency of the state is to increase its ministrant functions.

The available evidence shows that for a long time the state in ancient India confined itself only to the constituent functions. The Vedic state protected citizens from foreign aggression. It also maintained internal order by enforcing respect for the traditional law. Like Varuna, the celestial king, the Vedic monarch was *dharmapati,* the protector and enforcer of law, morality and *dhrama*. Even the civil and criminal cases were decided by popular bodies (*sabhas*); whether they were presided over by a royal officer is not definitely known.

With the development of the political literature from c. 4th century B.C., we begin to get greater information about the functions of the state. The evidence of the *Mahabharata* and the *Arthasastra* shows that the sphere of the state activity was very extensively extended between the Vedic and the Mauryan age; we, however, are unable to trace the different stages of this development owing to the lack of evidence.

The activity of the state, as envisaged by the *Mahabharat* and the *Arthasastra,* relates to all the aspects of human life,—social, economic and religious. The state was not regarded as a necessary evil, whose coercive activities were to be reduced to the minimum. The *laissez faire* theory, which advocates that the sphere of the state activity should be reduced to the narrowest functions consistent with the preservation of law and order, was not at all popular. The activity of the state was to embrace the whole of human life, both here and hereafter. The state was to offer facilities to religions and sects to develop on their own lines and foster and inculcate piety, morality and righteousness. It was to improve the social order and to encourage learning, education and art by subsidising learned academies and extending patronage to scholars and artists. It was to establish and maintain rest houses, charity halls and hospital and relieve the distress due to floods, locusts, famines, pestilences and earthquakes. It was to see that the population is evenly distributed and encourage colonization of fresh lands. It was to enrich the resources of the country by developing forests, working mines and constructing dams and canals in order to make agriculture independent of rain as far as possible. It was to offer active help to trade and industry, but also to protect the population against capitalistic selfishness, if merchant princes sought to corner the market and raise the prices. It was to regulate the vices of the community by appointing its own officers to supervise over wine booths, gambling houses and prostitutes.

The well-organised governments in ancient India like those under the Mauryas and the Guptas discharged most of the above functions. It is, however, possible that the smaller states may have confined themselves to a restricted sphere of state activities, especially in troubled times.

The jurisdiction of the state in ancient India thus extended over almost all the spheres of life. Did it not interfere with individual liberty? Did it become possible because the very conception of liberty was not properly developed or because people were disposed to accept the state's claim to omniscience or infallibility?

State in ancient India was regarded as the center of society and the chief instrument for its welfare, and hence it was permitted to have a wide sphere to activity. Individual liberty did not appreciably suffer in consequence, primarily because the state discharged its multifarious functions not exclusively through its own bureaucracy. The market superintendents and trade officers belonged to the state bureaucracy, as also the superintendents of morality, but these worked in close co-operation with trade guilds and Brahmana or Sramana assemblies, where the voice of the people had the upper hand. The state and its officers only tried to harmonise the divergent interests after full consultation with the guilds and local assemblies, which were more stable institutions than the state itself and, therefore, enjoyed very considerable prestige and confidence. It encouraged education by liberal grants to colleges and universities, but never thought of controlling these institutions by its own Director of Public Instruction and his subordinate staff. It made liberal grants to Hindu temples and Buddhists monasteries, but never cared to dictate the dogmas or tenets that were to be encouraged under their auspices. The principle of decentralisation was carried to a very great extent and extensive powers were delegated to the village *Panchayats,* city councils ad trade guilds; and the state carried on its socialistic activities with the active cooperation of these popular bodies. There was hardly any encroachment on the individual liberty. Ancient Indians permitted the state a wide sphere of activity, not because they did not value individual liberty, but because they felt that state could organize them best by reconciling conflicting interests, if its bureaucracy worked in closer co-operation with well-established popular bodies like the trade guilds and village councils.

DISTRIBUTION OF FUNCTIONS

In the modern state, the executive, the legislative and the judicial powers and functions are usually distributed in different bodies. In theory the king in ancient India was like the President of the new Indian Republic, the final source of all the executive, legislative and judicial powers. In actual practice, however, the situation differed from age to age. In Vedic age, it would appear that the Samiti or the Parliament shared the executive powers with the king; in some cases it could over-rule him also. The king was the supreme judicial functionary in ancient India from the post-Vedic period; but in actual practice considerable powers were delegated to the local popular courts or Panchayats. Kings and Government officers usually declined to entertain a suit at first instance. The Parliament or the popular assembly disappeared as an effective body in the post-Vedic period; this led to the increase in the influence and authority of the king in executive and administrative matters. Legislation in the modern sense of the term was not the function of the Samiti in ancient India; laws, if secular, were sanctioned by custom and if religious, by the sacred texts. For a very long time the Ancient Indian State used to enforce laws which were not formally approved by any limb of its body politic. The scheme of taxation also was usually the one approved by the usage of the land, as codified in the Smṛitis. The Smṛitis however permitted a considerable variation in the incidence of taxation; the land tax could be anything between 12 to 33 per cent. The actual amount of the tax could thus be varied by the executive, which usually meant the king and the officers appointed by him and holding office during his pleasure. There is sufficient evidence to show that kings soon began to claim the power to make ordinance if not laws; Sukra expressly concedes this power to the king. With the disappearance to the Parliament or Samiti, the executive, the judicial and the legislative powers (as far as they could be exercised by the state) tended to be concentrated in the hands of the king and the ministry nominated by him. The village councils and town corporations, which were largely poplar bodies, could successfully contest with king to some extent in the exercise of the judicial, executive and taxation powers in the limited sphere of their jurisdiction, during the Gupta and post-Gupta period.

VESTING OF THE SOVEREIGNTY IN ANCIENT INDIAN STATE

It would be convenient to make a few observations about the vesting of sovereignty in the Ancient Indian State. It has first to be noted that the modern conception of sovereignty was probably not fully developed. There is no Sanskrit term exactly corresponding to it, though *svamitva* in the *Arthasastra* may be partly approaching its meaning. In the Vedic period sovereignty was probably vested jointly in the king and the Samiti; in the republican states it was vested in the Central Executive, which worked under the general superintendence of the republican Parliament, where however only the aristocracy was usually represented. When Samitis or Parliaments disappeared, the sovereignty became vested in the king alone. In the republican state, the presidents tended to become more and more powerful; their posts often became hereditary and they began to enjoy royal titles also. Republics however disappeared from India at c. 400 A.D.; and the king's position became very strong from this time.

One school held that the king was not above the law or Dharma; but that the latter constituted the essence of kingship. Dharma was the sovereign over the sovereign and it may therefore be said that the sovereignty vested in it.

But though the king was below the Dharma and was bound by it, though it was the law (Dharma) which made the king, the ancient Indian polity provided no constitutional means or checks to call the king to account if he transgressed the law.

Another school however pronounced the king to be *adaṇḍya* or above punishment. If he broke the law, the punishment was left to God. In extreme cases extra-constitutional remedies like, the rebellion or regicide were suggested; but they were usually impracticable. Village councils and town corporations often enjoyed almost complete freedom in their local affairs; the courts, whether royal or popular, usually administered the traditional law as embodied in the *jātidharma* (caste rules), *śreṇidharma* (guild rules) and *janapadadharma* (local customs). But a willful king could set all these at naught and rule in a tyrannical way, as is shown by the pages of the *Rajatarangiṇi* dealing with the history of medieval Kashmir. From c. 400 A.D. the sovereignty was vested in the king and it was not controlled by constitutional checks of the modern types. Of course it should not be forgotten that most of these checks were evolved in Europe only in the post-Reformation period.

Manu no doubt pronounces that a king was to pay a fine of a thousand coins when an ordinary man had to pay that of one coin only, but he does not specify the offence, nor indicate the agency which was to try the king. The commentator Kullūka says that the fine was to be self-imposed and was to be given to Brahmanas or to be thrown into water in the name of Varuṇa. It is thus clear that Manu's statement is a merely idealistic one and hardly provides any real and practicable constitutional check.

4

The Evolution of the State

We have dealt with the definition of a State, and, for the purpose of these lectures, the definition given in the last lecture will govern the use of the word. That definition was:

A State is a multi-human organism embodying a Life, inhabiting a definite Territory, with a Government as its executive, specialising organs for its activities, and shaping its evolution to achieve a common end.

Wherever we find the whole of these characteristics, we have a State; wherever we do not find them, there is no State.

In this lecture, I propose to trace the Evolution of the State from the Family to the Commonwealth or Empire, in a general way, from the simple to the complex, defining the term used in each case, and thus making a framework for our future study, into which we shall have to fit a large number of details. Such an outline is necessary for clear comprehension and orderly thinking, and by your later reading, when your time for technical studentship is over, you will be able, by intensive study of any part of it, to acquire as much more of detail as you like, without "losing sight of the forest because of the trees".

We begin then with the need for definitions, and proceed to the supplying of that need, showing also the place of the thing defined in the evolution of the State.

DEFINITIONS

Now there are certain terms used in Political Science which need careful and exact definition, for they are connected with the idea of the State, sometimes form constituents of the State, but are not identical with it. Hence, for useful discussion, we must define each of them, for half the controversies which are carried on among us tend to be futile, because of the misunderstandings which arise from the lack of a common meaning attached to the terms used. One of the objects of Education is to substitute clear for confused thinking, and clear thinking demands the use of a word to denote one thought and one thought only; for this we need accurate perception of the similarities and the differences between things. Similarities show the relation between two or more things, uniting them; differences show the peculiar characteristics of two or more things, separating them. Thus the term Biped marks a similarity, a uniting relation, between birds and men; both are two-legged. The beak, wings and feathers of the bird, to name but three differences, mark it off as compared with the lips, arms and skin of the man, into a smaller group, a subdivision of Biped. Science classifies by similarities, and separates its main divisions into smaller and smaller groups by differences, thus reducing into ordered relations and separations the confused masses of individuals of all sorts, sizes, and shapes. The theory of evolution is based on a discovery of hidden similarities under patent differences, as the fore-limbs of the bird and the man have a common fundamental structure, modified into a wing in the one, into an arm in the other. So also in our subject, since it is a Science—Political Science—we must use the scientific method with its admirable clarity, and therefore we must define the meaning of our terms. This lucidity in the use of words is one of the characteristics of the Keltic branch of the widely spread Aryan root-stock, the artistic type of the Aryan; the Kelts are artists in words, as in colour and form—words being verily the form of thoughts. As was said of the French: "Ce qui n'est pas clair, n'est pas francais"; "That which is not clear—or, better, lucid—is not French."

There are a number of words: Family, Tribe, Nation, Empire or Commonwealth, Society, Government, Race, Society, people, all of which have something in common—they are aggregations of human beings, the last being so vague that it needs some additional words to mark the sense in which the speaker is using it. These terms, down to the term "Society" preceding "Government" have a common characteristic, they all have a Government; but the term "Society" is used in two senses, hence it is repeated after "Race". Let us now try to define each, and mark its passage into the next, and thereby its place in the evolution of the State.

FAMILY

Husband-wife-child—the latter born or legally adopted. The Family subsequently includes younger generations, grandchildren, great-grandchildren, etc. Intermarriage is normally forbidden in each generation between children of the same parents, bust the rule varies as to intermarriage between later generations. Descent is normally recognised along the male line, the daughter of a family married into another family becomes a member of the latter. The Government resides in the Father; as generations, the eldest male ancestor is the common Father, then styled Patriarch, and the rule remains in his eldest male descendant. The Family House is the Territory. Separation into allied Families comes with multiplication of members, but the common Ancestor remains as a tie, rendered the more binding by Ancestor-worship, or commemoration of Ancestors by religious ceremonies as the family Piṭṛs, or Fathers. These separated Families when aggregated, are sometimes called a Clan, or, as in Rome, a Gens.

It is worthy of notice that the recognition of obligations is, at this early stage, restricted within the limits of the Family. There is a Family Dharma, a Family Duty. There must, for Family peace and comfort, be no cheating, no robbery, no rape, no murder, within the Family limits. The stronger must not deprive the weaker of his share in the common possessions and comforts of the Family. These obligations do not hold with regard to other Families. Morality is within the Family.

As multiplication increased the numbers in the Family, and they outgrew the Family House, other houses would be built, more land would be brought under cultivation, and the Family territory would cover a larger area. As numbers continued to grow and territory to spread, a stronger Family would come into touch with a smaller and therefore weaker one, or one of about equal strength, with the same or a different Patriarch. If intermarriages had taken place, with the exchange of daughters within family memory, i.e., tradition, and convenience of contiguity pointed that way, as increasing defensive power, the Families might amalgamate peaceably for mutual benefit, forming a Clan, or a Tribe. If there were no recognised alliances, the stronger Family—Family Morality not including any duty, any obligation, to another Family—might attack the weaker, rob it of its territory and other possessions, reduce the inhabitants to slavery, and thus obliterate it as an independent Family, and strengthen itself. Thus by peaceable amalgamation or by conquest, Families became joined into a Clan, and Clans into Tribes. The difference between Clan and Tribe is vague; in the Clan a common ancestor is recognised, as a rule, while in the Tribe this may or may not be. I am not sure that the use of the term is not largely influenced by the number of the aggregation. In any case, it does not form a regular and inevitable stage. Later we shall see how in India the orders of the Patriarch because Laws, quickening the evolution of the Moral Sense, and how kinship and contiguity and common law bound into a Nation the descendants of the original Patriarch, with many accretions from outside, with invasions of a land already civilised, with conquests and amalgamations, and the suffering of invasions in turn. But here, in following the general evolution of the State from the Family through more complex sages to the Empire or the Commonwealth, we cannot delay on the story of the Aryan root-stock. We shall return to it.

Meanwhile we have our definition of the Family:

A group, originally consisting of husband-wife-child, and developing by multiplication and adoption into a group of men, women and children, with common movable and immovable property, all united in obedience to the eldest male descendant of a common paternal ancestor, dividing the family work for the promotion of family happiness and prosperity.

We have here the State in its simplest form, becoming more complex by increase of numbers, but preserving recognisably the Family Idea.

THE TRIBE

The Tribe is formed of aggregations of Families, who may, or may not have formed the earlier aggregations termed Clans. It is an interesting speculation, but one which has not been tested, much less verified, by any research into the matter, whether monarchic forms of Government may not have appeared in Tribes which were formed out of Families looking back to a common Patriarch, in which the idea of authority from above, descending from an elder Ancestor, would be familiar. Perhaps we might regard China as such an instance; it is, indeed, spoken of as a Patriarchal State, and Bluntschli writes of it as holding "to the fiction that the Head of the State is Father of his people," and he quotes Gobineau, "who has shown grounds for believing that the State was first founded by Aryans," and who "ascribes the patriarchal idea to their suggestion".

Dr. Woodrow Wilson regards the early Greek monarchies as "Patriarchal Presidencies," the Kings being

> chief nobles rather, the 'first among equals,' presidents of councils of peers..., I have called this presidency of the King in State affairs a 'patriarchal' presidency, because it belonged to him by hereditary right as chief elder by direct descent...., He was the high priest of his people, performing all those sacrifices and leading in all those ceremonials which spoke the family oneness of the Nation. He was the representative of the Nation in its relations with the Gods. He was also commander-in-chief in War, here again representing the unity of the people over whom he presided. But here the Kingly prerogatives ended. These presidential and representative functions of the early Greek King contained the sum of his powers.

Secondly, Conquest—by making the new distinction between conqueror and conquered, giving rise to the classes of propertied and unpropertied, landlord and slave-labourer, aristocrat and plebeian, alien from the Family Idea—might produce, in common with the peaceful amalgamation of Families with different Patriarchs, a Government of equal Elders, presumably of the Best, the Aristocrats, over the general body of the youngers of the Families, who would be equal citizens, with the conquered classes below them as slaves. Or, thirdly, the Families, as equals, might give rise to democratic, republican, institutions. This would be most likely to happen where Tribes were isolated, and where therefore conquests had not occurred. It would be the outcome of undisturbed and peaceful lives.

In India we find traces of all these three types.

The Patriarchal form gave rise in India to Monarchies, the originals, in the Aryan rootstock, of the Kingships described by Dr. Wilson in one of its Keltic branches, the early Greek. There also we have a King, surrounded by a Council, for as Manu says of a King:

[The Law] cannot be properly enforced without a Ministry for he [the King] may be greedy, inexperienced and attached to worldly desires.

The Ministry varied in number; a typical constitution is given in the Mahabharata: 4 Brahmanas, 8 Kshattriyas, 21 Vaishyas, 3 Sudras and one Suta. The "Sutas" were classes born of mixed marriages, and included such persons as carpenters, singers, etc.

The Aristocratic and Republican forms are generally mentioned as Governments of Tribes, but this will be dealt with more fully later. Professor Radhakumud Mukerji mentions from Greek and Latin historians the Maltecorae, Singhae, Marohae, Rarungae, Moruni, Sabarcae, Gedrosii, Siboi, Agalassoi, Yandheyas, Malloi, Oxydrakai, Adrastai, Kathaioi and Sudrakas. One of these, the Sabarcae, do not, however, appear to have been peaceful, since they were ruled by three Generals. Curtius describes them as "a powerful Indian people, whose form of government was democratic and not regal, who had no Kings but were led by three Generals". He speaks also of "the Gedrosii as a free people with a Council for discussing important matters of State". The city of Nysa, with its Council of three hundred "best men," was clearly aristocratic, while the Empires and Kingdoms, of which so many details are given, are clear descendants of the Patriarchal Family, with Monarchs bound by the Law which originated in the Patriarch, and surrounded by a Council composed of the four castes. We read in ancient literature of a condition in which all were equal, India's Golden Age, and of the institution of Kingship to correct abuses, as the children of the Family developed the passions of youth. The Purāṇas tell of this Golden Age, when there were no castes, and when Nature supplied the simple wants of a simple united people. And they tell how gradually "egoism and a sense of mindness" appeared, "and the trees which had given them all they needed, dwelling, food and raiment, died out because of that sin"; and how the people began to make "the first artificial dwellings... and they also began to work for food," and there grew up "trees, bearing various kinds of fruit at fixed seasons, and wild careals of fourteen kinds". "But loves and hates and jealousies and mutual hurting increased yet more among them, and the stronger took possession of the trees and careals, excluding the weaker; for inequalities of mind and body had appeared." Then came "industry and agriculture and horticulture.... laws and conventions, differentiating the people gradually, more and more, into castes and colours, according to their different capacities and tendencies". (*Markandeya Purana,* as translated by Bhagavan Das, in his *Science of Social organisation,* Theosophical Publishing Society, Benares and London, and *Theosophist* Office, Adyar, Ed. 1910.) The Vishnu-Bhagavata tells of the first King, Pṛṭhu, who taught the people agriculture, and buildings and the working of mines and quarries. A very interesting account is also given in the Yoga-Vasishtha, in which the Sage, addressing Shri Ramachandra, tells of the ending of the Golden Age, "the Age when infant humanity simply moved and acted always and as bidden by the Elders of the Race, and so grew towards maturity—then, because the growing egoism struggled with the old innocent obedience, humanity suffered confusion, as does the child passing into youth. Then as I was sent, so were other Sages.... these Sages then established Kings in various regions of the earth to guide the perplexed people, and formulated many Laws and Sciences". These admirable accounts trace out the emergence of the Aryans from the simple Family life onwards into Tribes and Nations, and the reason for the arising of Kingship out of the Patriarchate. We may further note that the warrior Tribe, often engaged in War, would necessarily for the most part range itself under its most capable fighter as Chief, as indeed happened even as late as the decadent days of the Roman Empire in the election of Emperors by the army.

In Tribes remaining to-day there are traces of old Family origins. Each of the Hebrew Tribes—two of which remain—traced its origin to one of the twelve sons of the Patriarch Jacob—the descendants of one son were omitted from the territorial Tribes, and two grandsons of Jacob made up the twelve, but this is immaterial—and this, gives an interesting case of single Families multiplying into Tribes. As a Family becomes more and more numerous, family ties weaken; a seventeenth cousin, several times removed, is but a shadow relative, and the blood tie has worn very thin. In fact, the difference between Families and Tribes is largely one of number, and though there may be a common Ancestor of Families that have forgotten him, the non-recognition of him makes the separation of the Family into Families, and their union makes the Tribe.

A noticeable trace of consanguinity is found in some so-called savage Tribes, really the decaying relics of long-past great civilizations. Just as certain degrees of consanguinity bar intermarriage, so does the totem.

> The real social unit of the Australians is not the tribe; but the *totem* group.... The *totem group* is primarily a body of persons distinguished by the sign of some natural object such as an animal or a tree, who may not intermarry with one another. "Snake may not marry Snake. Emu may not marry Emu." This is the first rule of savage social organisation. (History of Politics. E. Jenks. Edition 1900. Quoted by Stephen Leacock, B.A., Ph.D., Elements of Political Science, Part I chap. iii, p. 42, Revised Edition. Constable & Co., London.)

On the connection between the Family, the Tribe, the Nation and the State, Bluntschli introduces confusion, probably due to his desire to make the State a "masculine personality"; this he could not do, if he started with the Family. Hence he refuses to include the Family and the Tribe as States. He remarks:

> Ancients and moderns alike have found in the family the pattern of the State. The State, they say, is an extension of the family, the head of the State being the father, the people his children. The comparison is only true in a limited sense; it only applies to the patriarchal State, not to the higher forms of the State, which are based on Nationality or humanity.

To say that the Family is the foundation, the beginning of the State, is not to say that it is its highest form, any more than to say that the roots of a tree are its branches, flowers and fruits. The argument that the State consists rather of individuals than of families, lies at the basis of the warring civilisation of Europe. However, he gives away his contention by saying:

> Even in the Aryan Nations the beginnings of the State are connected with the head of the family and the tribe. It was here that the first leaders, judges and magistrates found the necessary support for their authority: and it was only gradually that a political order arose which outgrew these limits. The tribal constitution served as a bridge between the family and the State, and fell away as soon as the State was assured.

I pointed to this refusal in Lecture II, and he also rejects the Clan and the Horde. He says:

We cannot talk of a State until we get beyond the circle of a single family, and until a multitude of men (i.e., families, men, women and children) are united together. A family, a clan like the house of the Hebrew Patriarch, Jacob, can become the nucleus round which, in time, a greater number gathers, but a real State cannot be formed until that has happened, until the single family has broken up into a series of families, and kindred has become extended to the race. The horde is not yet a Tribe. Without a Tribe, or, at a higher stage of civilisation, without a Nation, there is no State.

But this distinction is arbitrary. If a Family, a Clan, a Tribe, has a fixed territory and a Government, it is a State. He may exclude the nomadic horde, for that has no fixed territory.

Bluntschli, however, gives a useful suggestion on the Tribe, and gains it, curiously enough, by looking at a Tribe as a division of a "People". Trib, he says, "express the inner differences of a people," and they "are the product of history, which tends to develop and bring to light internal differences"; "they are only fractions of a people... expressions, variously coloured or accentuated, of the common national spirit. They thus perpetuate their separate existence, and keep alive the inner differences which influence the character of the people". He points out that the ancient constitution of the Germans "was nothing but an organisation of tribes," and that "even now the opponents of German unity make use of tribal prejudices to embarrass, if they cannot prevent, the national development." He also remarks that a Tribe " may furnish the starting point for the formation of a new nation," may "become a nation, and form a new State, however small".

This method of studying the modified portion in a later structure, its entry into which has caused the modifications, is somewhat peculiar. It is more usual to study the portion when it was independent and self-contained, before it was modified by becoming a part of a larger whole. In that way it is more clearly understood, and the later modifications are seen as results of the interplay between the whole and its part.

In seeking for the reason of the "inner differences" which mark the Tribe, may we not reasonably look for them in the types of the Families that united to form any particular Tribe? These are innate, the persistence of Family peculiarities, and when we see the qualities of Families reappearing in the Tribe, and the qualities of the Tribes in the Nation, we do not speak of history developing and bringing to light inner differences, but of inner Family qualities persisting in the Tribe which has been formed by their union, and in the Nation which has been formed by the union of Tribes. It seems to me to be a mistake to say that " as the races of mankind divide into peoples, so peoples divide into tribes". It is historically true that races divide into peoples—a People to him being the depositary of an " accumulated culture" handed down "from generation to generation," implanting hereditary characteristics—but it is historically false that peoples divide into Tribes, seeing that Tribes are united into Nations and Peoples—terms that we have yet to define.

Again it is worthy of notice that Tribal obligations are restricted within the limits of the Tribe, but transcend the Family, since the Tribe include many Families. A Tribesman must not cheat, rob, rape, nor murder within his Tribe; if he does, the Tribe will punish him. These obligations do not hold with regard to other Tribes. Morality is Tribal.

Let us now define our Tribe:

A group composed of the descendants of a Family or Families, under any form of Government, completely united together, organised for existence and defence, within a definite area.

We must note that this excludes nomadic hordes, to whom the term "Tribe" is often assigned. But it is better to restrict the term to those who are settled, just as we do not include wolves among social animals, though they hunt in packs.

THE NATION

The word Nation, from *nascere* to be born, indicates a unity of birth, an ethnic unity, and thus it is naturally used in the ascending series of larger and larger aggregations of human beings in a settled order, Families merging into Tribes, Tribes into Nations. Primarily, a Nation descends from a common ancestor, but into this main stream of descent flow, in the course of time, many other contributory streams, which swell the river of National Life. A common religion, in the early days of an evolving Nation, is a large factor in forming its unity, so large, indeed, that even in comparatively modern times, rejection of the National Religion was regarded and punished as treason to the State. Just as there were Family Deities, so there were Tribal Deities, and National Deities: these are recognised in the Hebrew Testament as the celestial rulers of the Nations against whom the Hebrews and their National Deity battled, with varying success: they are the Devas, or Shining Ones, of the Hindu and the Buddhist, the Archangels of the Christian, with their subordinate hosts. The early members of the National root-stock of the Aaryan Race were united by their Aryan birth and by their Vaidik religion, and when they migrated from Central Asia into India, and spread over it by conquest, subduing its inhabitants of an earlier Race, these two strong ties, the ethnic and the religious, bound them together as a Nation. The civilisation they found and that which they brought with them interpenetrated each other, the latter finally dominating; intermarriage played its part, especially in Southern India, only a minority of families preserving jealously the pure Aryan blood; the earlier religion took on the Aryan form; the slow process of amalgamation enriched, instead of destroying, the National Life. Gradually, from the Himalayas to Cape Comorin the same manṭrams were chanted, effacing differences and intensifying likenesses. Many were the invasions: Assyrians, Egyptians, Persians, Greeks—they all came and went away, leaving traces of their blood, their thought, their art, to enrich the growing culture of the Indian Nation. Then came the great stream of the Muhammadan invaders, bringing new elements into India, but as the great rivers of Jumnā and Gaṅgā flow into each other at Prāyāg, and run side by side, distinguished by their colours, yet forming one mightier river, so did the invaders settle down and become Indians, an integral part of the Indian Nation. This unifying force, the Spirit of the Nation, assimilates the elements congruous with itself, enriching its own Life, and casts forth the unassailable; it takes the gold, stamps it with its own image and superscription, and sends it out into the National currency, casting forth the dross.

The Nation forms organs for the discharge of its life-functions, executive, legislative, judicial, educational, commercial, industrial, agricultural, and has its corporate Life, harmonising all. Only one difference sometimes separates it from a State: it may be without a territory. The Nation of the Franks, before-mentioned, migrated into France and there became a State.

Let us consider the various conditions which are often said to be essential parts of the Nation, and see whether they are really essential. These are: a geographical area, or territory; a common language; a Government; organisation; a common religion; a common ethnic type; all these, by different authors have been regarded as necessary for a Nation. But is it so?

The Hebrew State was lost in the Babylonian Captivity, rose again on the return of the Nation to Palestine, fell with the fall of

Jerusalem, but the Hebrew Nation survived all changes and still survives. A Nation then can exist without a territory. Nor need it have a common language, though such a language is necessary in the early stages of its growth, and is later a binding tie, as with the Hebrews; witness the Bretons and Basques, who are parts of the French Nation, yet keep their own tongues; the Swiss, who have French, German and Italian languages, and no Swiss language. Again on the the hand, the Canadians and the citizens of the United States are two Nations, thought their language is the same. Nor is even a Government necessary, as is seen in the widely scattered Hebrew Nation. This therefore lacks two of the essential factors of the State, territory and government, and is viable without them; but if it lost three of the binding ties, territory, language, government, it is doubtful if the Nation would not become weak, and if it lost a fourth, organisation, and a fifth, religion, it seems to me that it would inevitably pass away. Moreover, for the Nation to preserve its individuality, the religion must forbid intermarriage with other Nations, otherwise the sixth strong tie, ethnic unity, would go. In the United States, intermarriage is destroying the ethnic type of the Hebrews, and many are becoming Americans. It is true that there are Nations composed of many ethnic types, as the English Nation, in which are still recognisable Saxon, Dane, Norman, and perhaps other types; but they are subsidiary to the English type which has grown out of their intermingling, and which now dominates them. In the Republic of the United States are Finnish, German, Dutch, Italian, English, Irish, and other ethnic types, but they are gradually changing into a common American ethnic type, the beginning of a new Race. But if a Nation loses all its binding ties, territory, language, organisation, government, religion, ethnic type, it seems as though its Spirit would be compelled to leave a body so mutilated, and seek reincarnation elsewhere.

What is it then that makes a Nation? It is, as with other Individuals, a fragment of God Himself, a Jīvāṭmā, a living Self, with innate qualities which gradually appear and form its *Character*. Contrast the Indian and the Englishman, and you will see the difference in the National Character: the Indian, spiritual, courteous, polished, keenly intellectual, inclined to philosophy and poetry, with an acute sense of duty, of obligation, to his surroundings; the Englishman, somewhat blunt and abrupt, strong mentality scientific and practical, public-spirited. Climate, environment, social customs, all act on physical peculiarities, and through them on character also. A Nation is distinctly an Individual with a Character, and that character depends on the nature of the Spirit at its core, and its gradual unfolding to play its part in humanity as a whole. It draws into itself and assimilates all that its congruous with its inner Self, is Spirit, and it is the Spirit that unites, that harmonises, that evolves the Nationality which embodies it. Anything special may go, only mutilating the National body, but it all goes, the Spirit must find another home.

Therefore have Nations died in the past, as other Individuals have died, and die. Where is Egypt, where Assyria, where ancient Greece, where ancient Persia? In the hybrid modern peoples who bear some of the ancient names, the Spirit of the ancient Nation does not dwell. The fellaheen of Egypt show the ethnic type of the Egyptian in the days of his glory. The Pārsīs of India show much of the ethnic type of Irān, ancient Persia. And if India still survive all who were her contemporaries five thousand years ago, it is because the same Spirit lives in her National body as lived in it then; she has passed through many valleys of humiliation, but never has she entered the valley of the shadow of death; she has been invaded, and has assimilated her invaders; her ethnic type, the Āryan, still survives in a minority, through she has wrought into it many others; her ancient language is still living, although it has given birth to many dialects which have become great languages; her Governments have changed their forms, and she has passed through periods of local, but only local, anarchy, and to-day she is renewing her youth like the phonix, and from the pyre of temporary subjection she is arising, the same Nation, but purified, enriched, to a future greater than her past.

Once more, I must call your attention to the fact that National obligations are restricted within the limits of the Nation; a man must not cheat, rob, rape, nor murder his country folk; if he does, the Nation will punish him. But he may cheat man of other countries, calling it diplomacy; he may rob them, calling it annexation; he may rape and he may murder, calling it war. Morality is now National, and is beginning to grope outwards towards other Nations, and to become International. But still the less evolved praise as manly virtues in relation to other Nations that which they punish as crimes within their own.

For our definition of a Nation we have:

A grouped composed of a much-multiplied Tribe, or of Tribes, closely united in a common Life, with organs developed for the discharge of its life-functions, ready to become a State by the addition of a fixed territory and a Government, where either, or both, are wanting.

AN EMPIRE OR COMMONWEALTH

On this we need not delay; it is enough to define it, and to point to such examples as the British Empire and the Republic of the United States. The first includes Self-Governing States, and autocratically ruled Dependencies and Colonies, the Imperial authority resident in the hereditary King, the Lords and Commons of Great Britain. The second consists of a number of States, federated together under a common Government, the Federal authority residing in the President, the Congress, and the Supreme Court.

These are therefore the next higher State Individual, the first comprising free States and subject dependencies, the second comprising free States federated together. we need, therefore, two definitions:

An Empire is an assemblage of free and subject Nations, with a common Government, which may be autocratic, or partly democratic.

A Commonwealth is an assemblage of free States, federated together under a democratic Government.

SOCIETY

This word is used in such different meanings that I insert it here, before Government, as I shall have to insert it again later, merely to avoid confusion. We need not delay on its narrow meaning. In this narrow sense it is merely:

A voluntary group of human beings associated together for a common purpose, with its own Government and Laws, exercising no authority except over its own members. It may, or may not, be recognised and partially controlled by the Government of the country in which it exists.

GOVERNMENT

An essential organ in every state is a Government, in which resides the sovereignty, or supreme power, of the State. It is the organ through which is expressed and carried out the Will of the State, which directs the forces of the State, and supplies the machinery for doing all those things which can be better performed by the Nation collectively, than by voluntary societies within it, or by individual activities. Aristotle deals fully with forms of Government, and classifies them:

> It is evident that every form of Government or administration, for the words are of the same import, must contain a supreme power over the whole State and this supreme power must necessarily be in the hands of one person, or a few, or many.

These are monarchic, aristocratic, and "the citizens at large," and these "may degenerate into a tyranny, an oligarchy, and a democracy," of which the first seeks only the good of one man, the second considers "only the rich," and the third "only the poor".

This matter of Government we shall have to study; meanwhile I had better say that I include under the term Government the three great Departments which must exist in it, the Legislature which makes the laws, the Judiciary, which interprets the laws, and the Executive, which administers the laws.

We have, then, as the definition of Government:

A tripartite group, legislative, judicial and executive, in which resides the supreme power of the State.

RACE

A Race descends from common Ancestor, and Races form the great successive divisions of Humanity, markets off from each other by broad physiological and psychological peculiarities. As they multiply, they divide into branches, or Sub-Races, and these again subdivide as they migrate, and are largely evolved, differentiated and moulded by climate and environment generally, while preserving the fundamental type.

As definition we have:

An ethnic type, distinguished by marked physical, mental, emotional, and spiritual characteristics, consisting of a root-stock and, later, of branches.

SOCIETY

Society, in the large sense of the term, is rooted in the nature of man, and is, as before pointed out, necessary to his evolution. The study of it includes all human inter-relations, customs, habits, traditions, institutions, religions, and cultures, subdivisions into classes, castes, communities, all of which are included under the head of Social Science.

All the groupings we have seen are included in Society in this large sense; it is co-extensive with organised Humanity, but also includes all organised subdivisions within any of these groupings. It is therefore vague as a term, but is useful as drawing out the idea of the ties which unite human beings together and specialising these for study, men as men. Leacock says:

> The term Society has no reference to territorial occupation; it refers to man alone, and not to his environment.... It applies to all human communities, whether organised to unorganised. It suggests not only the political relations by which men are bound together, but the whole range of human relations and collective activities. The study of society involves the study of man's religion, of domestic institutions, industrial activities, education, crime, etc.

The description is a good one, but I quarrel with the phrase "to man alone and not to his environment"; it is inaccurate though intelligible as emphasizing the human not the spatial relations. And surely there cannot exist an unorganised *community*.

We may take as definition.

All relations of human beings is an organised association with each other.

PEOPLE

In normal use this is the most indefinite of terms, and yet we need it. It requires an affix or suffix of some sort to render it precise. "The people" of a town, a country, a race, a nation, that we understand, and in this sense it means "persons belonging to". Bluntschli deals very clearly with the conception which to him is implied in the term. It "implies a civilisation, not a political idea":

> To form a People, the experiences and fortunes of several generations must co-operate, and its permanence is never secured until a succession of families, handing down its accumulated culture from generation to generation, has made its characteristics hereditary.

A People, he says, must have "common spirit, common interests, and common customs".

> The essence of a People lies in its civilisation (Kultur): its inner cohesion and its separation from foreign People spring mainly from development in civilisation, and express themselves chiefly in influencing its conditions. It can only be understood from a psychological point of view: its essence is to be seen in the common spirit and common character which inspire it.

Giving to the word this specific sense, it becomes a valuable term. Persons of the same People would understand each other; persons of the same Nation very often would not. For a People may be scattered among different Nations, as the Slaves, the Germans, the Greeks. The term thus used becomes a subtle psychological tie.

We may define it:

A psychological entity, which may or may not be ethnically or politically one, united by a common spirit, common interests, and aspirations.

Although you may find this lecture of terms and definitions somewhat irksome, I would strongly advise you to study and master it, for it will mean to you, if mastered, greatly increased accuracy and clarity of thought and expression.

— Annie Besant

5

Types of the State

Modern works on polity devote considerable space to the discussion of the question of the origin of the State. No contemporary evidence is available or is ever likely to be available to enlighten us on the point. While we possess ample evidence to show how some particular states originated among people already accustomed to political life, we have only the uncertain light of legends and mythology to visualize the circumstances under which men for the first time associated themselves into a political organisation. We are, therefore, left more or less to speculate on the problem. The modern speculation, however, is largely influenced by the scientific method and the theory of evolution, and seeks to fortify its conclusions by such analogies as can be drawn from the known condition of societies, which are more or less in an uncivilized condition at the present time. We should not forget that this line of approach was unknown to the ancients, whether of the East or the West. Most institutions were regard in ancient India as due to divine agency or inspiration and the State was no exception to this rule.

We have occasional speculations on the origin of the State in the *Mahābhārata* and the *Digghanikāya*, and though these works belong to different centuries and religions, their version shows a marked similarity. They both aver that for a long time after the creation of society, there prevailed a golden age of harmony and happiness, when people led happy and peaceful lives on account of their innate virtuous disposition, though there existed no government to see that the laws of nature were respected and followed. Popular imagination has dreamt of a golden age in the dim and distant past not only in the East but also in the West. Plato's Republic may well be regarded as the idealisation of such a Golden Age; the actual state could be only a faint copy of the ideal one delineated by him. As late as the 18th century, Rousseau held that the era of the Golden Age had disappeared many centuries ago; the utmost that men could do today was to try to realise it to some extent in the present imperfect society.

The Sāntiparavan goes to narrate that society flourished without a king or law court for a long time, but later somehow there was a moral degeneration. People fell from rectitude; greed, selfishness and cupidity began to sway their mind and the earthly paradise which they had been enjoying was soon converted into a veritable hell. The law of the jungle began to prevail; the strong devoured the weak, as is the order of the day among the fish (*mātsyanyāya*). Gods then became alarmed and decided to remedy the situation, when men went out in a deputation to pray for relief. Brahmadeva, the chief god, thought over the matter and came to the conclusion that human society can survive only if a code of law was framed and enforced through the instrumentality of a king. He composed a comprehensive code, created an asexual son named Virajas, appointed him king and men agreed to obey his orders.

Elsewhere in the Sāntiparvan we have a slightly divergent account of the origin of the state, which seems to refer to an unsuccessful contract at one stage. People were tired of the law of the jungle which prevailed for a long time, and entered into a mutual contract that persons guilty of unsocial acts like misappropriation and adultery would be expelled from society. We are expressly told that in order to inspire mutual confidence, they entered into a universal social contract to guarantee the agreement. We are however told that people still continued to be unhappy, probably because there was no king or government to enforce the contract. They then approached the Creator with a request to appoint a king, who on the one hand, should be worth the reverence of the community and on the other, should be able to protect the people. The Creator straightway appointed Manu as the king. To rule over a refractory populace was however distasteful to him and he did not like to undertake the job. Here the epic does not refer to the Creator solving the difficulty by composing a law code; containing the atmosphere of the theory of Social Contract it states that people themselves assured Manu that law would be followed and the sin would go the law-breakers and not to the king for punishing them. They further agreed to pay the necessary taxes.

These divergent theories would show that the Great Epic is merely specualting about the origin of the state. According to both the theories God helped the humanity to escape from the law of the jungle by giving it a king. But one of theories refers to an apparently unfructuous earlier social contract, which however failed to put an end to anarchy before a God-appointed king appeared on the scene to restore law and order.

The accounts in the Mahabharata show that the state was regarded as a divine institution; king's right to govern was partly due to his divine creation and partly due to the agreement of the subjects to be governed by him in order to terminate the anarchy.

We may passingly note that the theory of the divine origin of State was widely held in Europe under the influence of the Christian dogma, especially in the Middle Ages, when the king was regarded as the annointed representative of God, ruling by divine right. Islam also shared a similar view, for it regarded king as the shadow of God.

The version of the *Dīghanikāya* resembles the above account to a great extent. Buddhists did not believe in God and so Brahmadeva as the creator of the first king and code does naturally not figure in it. But we are told that in the dim and distant past, there was a golden age, when men who had ethereal and refulgent bodies, lived in virtue and happiness. Somehow there was a fall from this ideal state; there arose anarchy and chaos, and people wondered how to put an end to it. Eventually there arose on the scene a person named Mahājanasammata (lit. one acceptable to the great community), who was born asexually. He was wise, virtuous and able and the public requested him to become their king and to put an end to the prevailing chaos. He acceded to their request and people then elected him to be their king, agreeing to give him a part of their paddy in return for his services.

Jinasena, a Jain author of the 9th century, also holds that the earth was a paradise (*bhogabhūmi*) in the distant past, when all human wants were satisfied by desire-yielding trees (*kalpavṛikshas*). These latter, however, gradually disappeared and there was a chaos. But order was soon restored by the first Tirthankara, Rishabhanātha, who introduced kings officers castes and professions.

Let us now take a review of the opinions of other writers on politics. Kautilya refers to the problem of the origin of the state only incidentally during a discussion of spies among themselves. One party there argues that government came into existence to counteract the law of the jungle that prevailed in society. People themselves selected Manu as their king and agreed to pay him the necessary taxes. The work does not make any reference to any Golden Age existing in prehistoric times. Nārada and Brihaspati postualte the original existence of a Golden Age and point out that it soon came to an end and was succeeded by a social chaos. Government came into existence to put an end to it. They do not enter into any detailed discussion of the problem. Śukra has no useful observations to make about the origin of the state. He recognises a quasidivinity in the case of a virtuous king; this may suggest that he was not much inclined to believe in the theory of Golden age or social contract.

A survey of the above passages shows that whatever may be the state of affairs in the mythical past, Hindu thinkers held that state was an indispensable institution for the orderly existence and progress of society in the imperfect world as known to us in historic times; a country without government cannot even exist. The idea of a primeval Golden Age is accepted only in some sections of the *Mahābhārata* and Buddhist literature. Writes on polity only toy with it for some time and hasten to point out that it was soon succeeded by a social chaos, which was terminated only when God gave a king to society. They thus regarded State as a divine institution, implying thereby that it is as old as society and owed its origin to that socio-political instinct which is twin-born with man.

The *Mahābhārata* implies that people accepted Virajas as king; the *Digghanikāya* expressly states that Mahājanasammata accepted the people's request to put an end to anarchy and thereupon people elected him to be their king. There is no doubt a notion here of government coming into existence as a result of some implied contract. Some such idea seems to have been also in the mind of the Dharmasūtra writers, when they aver that the king is a servant of the people charged with the duty of protection, 16 per cent tax being his wage. Hindu writers, however, do not further develop the theory of contract, as was done in the West. Probably they had realised that it could not be fully applicable to the origin of government and society. These come into existence out of conditions primarily arising from the sociability inherent in human nature.

It is now generally recognised that the contract theory of the origin of government is bad history and worse logic; it can no doubt explain the origin of a particular form of state among people who have already developed governmental institutions, but it cannot explain how the first agreement took place among the members of a community, which was still in the state of nature. Contract is possible only in a society where mutual rights and obligations are respected, and this is obviously impossible in a society where the law of the jungle prevails.

It would be, however, interesting to compare ancient Indian theory of contract with similar theories advanced in the west. The theory is rarely referred to by ancient thinkers of Greece and Rome; it is worked out in detail only in the post-Reformation period. Hobbes and Locke are its important advocates.

Like most of the ancient Indian thinkers, Hobbes held that there was a state of anarchy in the beginning, the hand of each being against all. Tired of this state, people eventually agreed to surrender part of their rights to the sovereign. It was not, however, a contract between the sovereign on one side and the people on the other. It was merely an agreement among the people, which imposed no obligation upon the sovereign; who however got unlimited and irrevocable rights under it. Hindu writers also, like Hobbes, have presupposed a contract, which eventually put an end to the law of the jungle; but it was not a contract which imposed obligations only on the people. The first king Virajas got no unlimited rights under it; his powers were restricted by the Code of Law prepared by Brahmadeva for him. The same was the case with his son Kardama and grandson Anaṅga. The latter's son Vena was a tyrant, but the sages destroyed him by their supernatural powers. Vena's son Pṛithu was however brave and law-abiding and he willingly took the vow to rule righteously, as requried by the sages. It would be thus seen that the king who came into power after the agreement among the people and at the intervention of divine power, was far from being a law unto himself, as was the case with the king as conceived by Hobbes.

According to Locke, the state of Nature in the pre-government period was more or less analogous to the Golden Age of the Hindu mythology. People as a general rule obeyed the laws of reason and nature, and respected one another's person and property. Society had thus come into existence, but not government. When, however, occasional breaches of law occurred, each individual could act both as a judge and executor of his own decrees, which created certain inconveniences. Though the law of Nature was known to all, still owing to difference of intelligence and conflicts of interests disputes arose as to the method of its enforcement, which gave rise to confusion and uncertainty in life. To put an end to it people entered into a convenant, surrendered their right to enforce the law of Nature and organised a government which was also bound by the terms of the original contract. Hindu writers vaguely suggest that somehow there was a fall from the Golden Age of the primeval period, owing to greed getting the upper hand in human nature. How the greed once absent from human nature began to warp it, they cannot explain, just as Locke cannot explain how in a society where the laws of reason prevailed, there were occasional breaches of its provisions and how, when they occurred, every party in the transaction could act both as the judge and the executor. Locke makes the provisions of the original contract binding on the king. Hindu writers seek to regulate his powers by the provisions of the original divine code.

It will thus be seen that the desire to put an end to anarchy and evolve a better type of society and government are stated to be the chief grounds for people entering into the original contract, that brought government into existence. Western thinkers, however, looked at the problem from a purely secular point of view; it is well-known how the views of some of them were unconsciously influenced by people's struggle against autocracy that was then in full swing in some countries. They, therefore, are anxious to thrash the idea of contract threadbare, initiate fundamental principles of political association, define the authority of the sovereign and prescribe the conditions under which popular obedience would be expected, and discuss whether the transfer of power by the people to the sovereign is irrevocable or otherwise. Ancient Indian writers did not live in an age of rationalism like Locke and Rousseau; they looked at the question from a semi-religious and semi-sociological point of view. They have, therefore, neither gone deep into the fundamentals of the problem, nor defined precisely the limits of the powers of the state and the people. They observe, the instance, that people offer obedience and taxation in return for the protection and services they expect from the government. If the king's government fails in its duty, they permit the people to remove the king, and even to kill him. But what precisely will constitute a breach of the contract on the part of government, and what is the secular constitutional machinery by which people can enforce the performance of the terms of the original contract is nowhere clearly described. The permission to remove a tyrant or to kill him no doubt assumes the ultimate sovereignty of the people and invests them with supreme authority. This remedy, however, is drastic and difficult; it would have been more useful if our authorities had recommended a less extreme but more practicable remedy in the form of an everyday constitutional check. We should not, however, forget that such a remedy has been perfected even in the West only in the modern age.

There are various other theories advocated about the origin of State by modern writers. It is argued that people in the distant past willingly entrusted government powers to an individual, either because he was a priest who could ensure divine help and favours, or because he was a magician who could command rain, or because he was a doctor who could cure patients. It is suggested that individuals who thus happened to gain ascendancy over the minds of their contemporaries, managed to retain it by the use of force, which they could exercise with ease owing to their pre-eminent position, already recognised on a large scale. It is quite possible that in some primitive societies government may have actually arisen owing to the operation of the above factors. But as far as the Indo-European communities are concerned, the institution of the patriarchal joint family seems to have been the germ out of which State was gradually evolved. The evidence of the comparative philology shows that even when the Aryans were in their original home, they were living in joint families consisting of the grandfather, father, uncles, nephews, sons and daughters-in-law. The evidence of Homer shows that these joint families were sometimes so big as to include two or three hundred persons. The patriarch of the joint family wielded very wide powers over its members; he could pledge, sell, amputate and even kill any person under his potestas for an offence committed by him. The Roman patriarch possessed these powers; some Vedic legends also show that the father could blind or sell a guilty son by virtue of his patriarchal authority. The position of the patriarch in prehistoric times was more or less like that of a king amongst all the Indo-European communities. His jurisdiction increased, though perhaps his powers diminished, as the joint family expanded into a big federation of several natural families, springing from a common ancestor, real or imaginary, and living in the same village. The senior member of the senior-most family in such a village was regarded with great reverence by the whole community and used to be entrusted with most of the governmental functions to be discharged, no doubt, in consultation with other elder persons of the locality. The Rigvedic evidence shows that the Aryan society in that early period was divided into families, *janmans*, *vśasi* and *janas*. *Janmans* seen to have corresponded to a village consisting of people claiming a common descent, and a number of such villages joined together by a bond of kinship seem to have constituted a vis; its chief was known as a *vispati*. *Visas* were closely knit together, and on the battle fields battalions were often arranged as per viś from which they had been recruited (R.V.X, 84, 4). Several *viśas* made a *jana* or tribe, which had its own *janapati* or the king. The organisation among the Vedic Aryans shows a striking resemblance to the condition prevailing in Rome in early days. There the smallest unit, gens, consisted of a small number of families descended from a common ancestor; a number of these gens constituted a curia and ten curiae made a tribe. Vedic *jana* probably corresponded with the tribe, *viś* with the curia and *janman* with the gen.

The available evidence thus shows that as among other Indo-Aryan communities, State was evolved in India also in pre-historic times out of the institution of the joint family. The patriarch of the family was instinctively reversed and obeyed; and social traditions and atmosphere inspired a similar respect for, and evoked a similar obedience to the head of the village and tribe, who generally acquired the status of chiefs and kings. The power of the kings gradually became more and more extensive as states became larger and larger.

The institution of the joint family thus gradually led to the evolution of kingship. It also presupposed the rise and acceptance of the notion of family property, and also of the inviolability of the sacred family ties and relationships, especially connected with the institution of marriage. Molestation of women had to be stopped and the peaceful enjoyment of property had to be ensured. This could be guaranteed only by the rise of the Institution of State. The institution of the family with the notion of the family property thus played its own part in the origin of the State.

TYPE OF STATES

Let us now see what were the different types of states existing an-ancient India. Ancient constitutional writers hardly discuss this problem. This is probably due to their having flourished in an age when monarchy had become the prevailing type of State. Had a book on *daṇḍanīti* been written by a citizen of an aristocratic or republican state, we might have got some interesting discussion about the nature and types of different states like monarchy, aristocracy and republics and their relative merits and defects. But curiously enough this does not seem to have happened.

Our writers again and again revolve round the same type of state, viz., monarchy; only a few of them passingly refer to the *Saṅgha* (republian) state. We have shown already how for a long time the state was tribal. Apart from the frequent references to *viśpatis* and *janapatis* the *Rigveda* (c. 2500 B.C.) frequently refers to specific tribes like the Yadus, the Purus, the Anus, the Turvaśas, etc. Viśvāmitra's prayers are said to have protected the Bharata people; in the Rājasūya sacrifice, the king is announced as the ruler of the Bharatas or the Kuru-Panchālas and not as the sovereign of a particular province or kingdom. The notion of a *rāshṭra* or a territorial state, however, was being gradually evolved in the later Vedic period; we find it clearly refers to in the *Atharvaveda*. The *Taittīriya Saṁhitā* refers to a ritual a partial performance of which could secure a king the over-lordship over his tribe (*viś*), but not over the country (*rāshtra*). The Brāhmaṇa literature frequently refers to the emperors as the rulers not over all the tribes but over the whole earth bounded by the sea. It is clear that the notion of the territorial state was fully established at this time (c. 1000 B.C.)

Monarchy was the normal form of the State in the Vedic period, *rājā* (a king), *mahārāja* (a great king), *samrāṭ* (an emperor) are the different terms by which kings were designated according to their power and prestige. Some of them were also called *svarājas* and *bhojas;* probably they were feudatories and zemindars.

In the description of the coronation, the ritual is sometimes described as securing *rājya, svarājya, bhaujya, vairjyya, mahārājya* and *sāmrājya* to one and the same individual. A doubt, therefore, naturally arises as to whether these terms really denoted different types of states or monarchies. It is, however, not unlikely that it is the desire to emphasise the omnipotence of the ritual that is responsible for the priest claiming that the king who is receiving the holy coronation from him, can attain to all the different positions referred to above. This conjecture becomes more probable when we remember that a passage in the *Aitareya Brāhmaṇa* states that the different types of States like *rājya bhaujya, vairājya,* and *sāmrājya* flourished in different provinces of the country.

In the later Indian history we always come across a large number of kings, enjoying different degrees of autonomy and ruling as feudatories of an emperor (*samrāṭ*). It is not unlikely that such feudatories existed in the Vedic period as well; they may have been known as *bhojas* and *svarājas* and their feudal lords as *samrāṭs.* The territorial extent of the dominion of a *samrāt,* as compared to that of *svarāṭ,* cannot be definitely determined. Most of the states in Vedic period were small; it is doubtful whether there was a state big enough to extend over a quarter of the Punjab. The dominion of a *samrāṭ* was perhaps not much bigger than that of a ordinary king. Military glory and achievements were probably more responsible for his higher title than the extent of his dominion. Rājya probably denoted a smaller but independent kingdom. The statement in the *Aitareya Brāhmaṇa* that kings were common in the Madhyadesa and emperors in Eastern India would support our interpretation. *Vairājya* denoted a republic, a state which had no king.

States where the principal executive authority was vested in two rulers as in ancient Sparta were not unknown in ancient India. One such state existed at Paṭala in Sindh in Alexander's days, where the sovereignty was vested in two different kings hailing from different houses. The *Arthaśāstra* also refers to such a state; probably it used to come into existence when two brothers or cousins, being claimants to the same kingdom, preferred to rule it jointly instead of dividing it into two parts. But just as two swords cannot remain in the same scabbard, two kings can hardly rule in harmony, when the power of each is unlimited and extends over the same kingdom. Such a state must have been often torn by factions and parties supporting the power of each ruler; one can, therefore, well understand why the *Arthaśāstra* does not approve of it, and why a Jain monk is advised not to travel through or stay in it. To avoid discord, very often the brother or cousin rulers of a *dvairājya* state would divide the kingdom between them, as was done in the *dvairājya* kingdom, created in Vidarbha by the Sungas. It would appear that though the kingdom was divided, the two rulers would hold joint consultations on all important matters. When the two kings were ruling in harmony, the state was called a two-kings-state (*darajja* in Prakrit and *dvirājaka* in Sanskrit); when they were pulling in opposite directions, it was called a self-fighting state (*virudharajja* in Prakrit and *viruddharājya* in Sanskrit).

The Vedic literature sometimes refers to *kings* meeting together in an assembly; we are also told that person alone can become a *king* who is permitted to become one by other kings. These passages probably refer to the existence of an oligarchy, where power was vested in a council of nobles, each member of which was entitled to call himself a kin and had a right to elect the chief of the state, who also was called a king. We shall see later how this type of the state continued to exist down to the 6th century B.C. in some parts of North-Eastern India.

Side by side with monarchical and oligarchical states, there also existed republican governments in ancient India as early as the Vedic age. A passage in the *Aitareya Brāhmana* states that the people in the vicinity of the Himalayas like the Uttarakurus and the Uttaramadras have a *virāṭ* (kingless) type of the state and are, therefore, called *vi-rāṭ* or kingless. When it is remembered how the same passage earlier refers to the *kings* of the easterners and the southerners and the titles that were borne by them, and how it carefully states that it is the *people* among the Uttarakurus and Uttaramadras,—not their kings,—who were called *virāṭ,* it becomes quite certain that these people had a non-monarchical or republican form of government. This conclusion is further strengthened when we remember how Greek authorities tell us that in the territory above referred to, republican types of states were the order of the day as late as the time of Alexander the Great. Whether the non-monarchical states of ancient India were also republican will be discussed later in.

The city state was another feature of the political life in the early period. We get some account of its constitution and administration from the Greek writers. Arrian describes Nyasa as a free city state flourishing at the time of the invasion of Alexander the Great; its President, when out to meet the Macedonian hero with thirty deputies, said, 'How Oh king, can a single city, if deprived of a hundred of its best men, continue to be well governed? It is thus clear that Nyasa was not the capital of a kingdom, but a city state, almost entirely dependent upon its own resources. When Diodorus describes how the citizens from the sibi state offered their submission, upon which Alexander permitted them to retain their freedom, he is obviously referring to the city state of the tribe. Several other city states are referred to by Greek writers; among them we may mention Pimprama of the Adraisti and Sangala of the Kathaians and Patala in Sindh. When the *Mahābhārata* refers to the powerful *grāmas* on the bank of the Indus, it is obviously referring to the powerful city states, some of which are mentioned by the Greek historians. Coins issued by a number of cities like Tripuri, Mādhyamikā, Ujjayini, Vārānasī Kauśāmbī etc. have come to light. It is quite probable that at some periods of their history they were city states, rather than capitals, issuing coins on their own authority. It was but natural that the city states should have brought under their control some of the outlying villages; but the government was usually carried on by the aristocratic classes in the city itself.

Composite and confederate states were not unknown to ancient India. The Kurupanchalas in the later Vedic period seem to have formed one composite state, ruled by a common king. The Kshudrakas and the Mālavas were separate states in the days of Pānini, but are very frequently mentioned together in the *Mahābhārata*. They had formed a confederation to meet the invasion of Alexander the Great, and it seems to have lasted for about a century. The alliance had been cemented by 10,000 intermarriages. The Yaudheya republican state seems to have comprised three sub-states. These confederations often lasted for short periods; in the life-time of the Buddha and Mahāvīra, the Lichchhavis had formed a confederation, once with the Mallas and once with the Videhas. The Lichchhavi-Malla federal council consisted of 18 members, nine being elected by each of the confederating state. We do not, however, possess sufficient information to indicate how these composite or confederate states were functioning,—what powers were retained by the federating units and what authority was delegated to the federal centre. It, however, seems very probable that the jurisdiction of the central government of the confederating states was confined only to foreign policy and the declaration and prosecution of war. Otherwise each state retained its sovereignty. The general for the joint army in a particular campaign was elected by the confederating states; in the campaign against Alexander the Great, Kshudrakas and Mālavas had elected at Kashudraka generalissimo, who was famous for his skill and bravery.

Normally, however, states in ancient India were unitary in character. King was the fountain source from which the ministers and provincial governors derived their power. Village Panchayats, town-councils and trade-guilds also were under the general supervision and control of the central government. Long established tradition had, however, limited the state's intervention in the autonomy of these bodies only to those rare occasions when they were guilty of a breach of their traditional rules and constitutions. The unitary character of the state in ancient India was, therefore, to a great extent modified by the presence of these autonomous bodies, which used to function on their own lines, though revolutions occurred at the centre.

—A.S. Aetekar

6

Individuals, Groups and Society

When we study ourselves as social creatures, all the relations between human beings are relevant. The name we give to the entirety of these relations is society. Politics is one such relationship, and that fact has two implications. First, politics can only be fully understood within its complete social context. Second, any facet of our social life may at one time or another acquire a political relevance. To understand politics, therefore, we must start with a picture of society as a whole, and then observe the genesis of politics within the social matrix. These are the topics of this chapter and the next. Here, I shall discuss the conditions which give rise to society and its component groupings. Chapter 3 will explore the emergence of a political function and, with it, the birth of the state and its government.

We know that our political attitudes are so closely connected to the rest of our social life that even the most exact analyses cannot completely disentangle one from the other. The outlook we display on political issues and the judgments we express on governmental actions are shaped by the whole social amalgam, any one of whose aspects may assume a temporary prominence. All of us are influenced, for example, by the manner in which we earn a livelihood and by the monetary return that this brings. Teachers, farmers, trade unionists, business people, and civil servants cannot be expected to hold identical views on economic matters. They produce differently, render different services, respond to different social demands, are vulnerable to different risks, and are differently rewarded. Thus, for example, one can understand why in Denmark the pluralism of economic life is reflected in the politics of a multiparty system. There is or has been a party for industrial wage earners, another for urban business business people, a third for small farmers, and a fourth for large farmers. Elsewhere, the principal bond of social cohesion is religious belief and the organization that sustains it. In this case, Protestants may group together because they are Protestants, and Catholics because they are Catholics, a fact directly relevant to politics in Switzerland and the Netherlands. Religious division may even provoke animosities which lead to political separation, as occurred in Ireland, India, and Palestine. Differences of language, too, create communities of speech and culture that complicate a wider union; witness the problems of Canada, Spain, and Belgium. Likewise, where the population contains more than one race, politics will develop in their relationships. Miscegenation may be accepted, as in Hawaii or Brazil; or some type of coexistence may be worked out with a tendency toward mutual tolerance; or official policy may segregate and discriminate, as was done in South Africa.

These examples could be multiplied manifold. But they suffice to show that politics is deeply embedded in the fundamentals of the social order and draws content from its characteristics. Any of these factors may explain why people are liberals or conservatives; why they vote for a certain candidate, if indeed they vote at all; why they advocate a foreign policy of toughness or conciliation. Hence the analysis of politics should begin where society itself begins—that is, with the formation of groups. Society is a cluster of groups, and these are the breeding ground for politics.

Since all human beings live in groups and the state is one organized grouping among many, some initial questions arise whose answers throw light on the issues of politics. For what purposes do groups exist? How do their members relate to one another and to the whole group? What unites the various groupings?

The Social Character of Human Beings

A virtually universal truth—such as the fact that ours is a social species—must stem from circumstances deeply rooted in human nature. Indeed, the rare exceptions (those who lead a hermit existence) serve to prove the rule. Their psychology and mode of living have been described by the literary imagination, as in *Timon of Athens or Robinson Crusoe*, and by philosophers, presenting various pictures of how we would behave if there were no bonds uniting us. Perhaps the grimmest picture is the one drawn by a seventeenth-century Englishman, Thomas Hobbes. Having sought security in France while civil war between Royalists and Parliamentarians was ravaging his native land, he proceeded, during the 1640s, to write his celebrated *Leviathan*. In somber hues he sketches the outline of a presocial stage. Hobbesian creatures are driven by their "natural passions," of which fear is uppermost, to preserve themselves against attack. Because of their all-pervading suspicions and distrust, they are unable to combine. They search for security in isolation or by getting their blow in first. Thence ensues "a warre of every man against every man... In such condition," he writes, "there is no place for industry; because the fruit thereof is uncertain: and consequently no culture of the Earth, no navigation, nor use of the commodities that may be imported by sea... no arts; no letters; no society; and which is worst of all, continuall feare, and danger of violent death; and the life of man, solitary, poore, nasty, brutish, and short." Hobbes concedes that such a state of affairs " was never generally so, over all the world," but he asserts " that there are many places, where they live so now." As evidence he mentions " the savage people in many places of America," who "except the government of small families.... have no government at all"—an erroneous view of the nature of Indian tribal structure, but one that was widespread in the seventeenth and eighteenth centuries. Hobbes claims to see other analogies in the dissolution of authority through civil war and in the international relations of independent states, though in such cases he confuses the absence or breakdown of the state with the absence or breakdown of society. No doubt, Hobbes's intellect is carried away by his imagination, but he underlines the truth that we all require association with our fellows. Human life is accurately described as life in groups.

The reasons for this are elemental. In early years we depend on parents and other adults for life, sustenance, and upbringing; as we mature, we act with others in order to accomplish what we cannot do alone. Because our needs compel us to be interdependent, groups are rooted in human nature, and in this sense they are natural. The history of our species is a continuing evolution from bare subsistence to broadening choices. This ceaseless quest for improvement results in civilization.

The needs we satisfy by cooperation with our fellow creatures are not only the necessities of food, shelter, and clothing, but also the widening demands that mark a progressive civilization. There are large areas of the world—the periphery of the Sahara, for example—where it is still idle to speak of achieving the good life, since life itself is precarious and hazardous. However, in communities where people have eliminated the perils of death from hunger or exposure, the social order is directed to many objects not necessary for subsistence, but which may contribute to a better or at least a more comfortable life. As society evolves from a preoccupation with necessities to the satisfaction of a vast range of desires, people undergo a profound psychological as well as material change. This is expressed in the enlargement of their field of choice and the exercise of critical judgment. A necessity is both predetermined and inescapable. In order to stay alive, for instance, we must have food. Within limits, we can choose what to eat and when; where to find our food, or how. But the goal is fixed without our willing it, since eat we must.

With wants in the broader sense, however, the area of selection extends both to the means and to the formulation of ends that can be altered, expanded, and ranked in order of priority. The structure that was adequate to provide a rough shelter from wind and rain later evolves into a house with an architectural style. Those who dwell in it develop the institution of the family, and, living together, infuse into a building the emotional attachments of a home. Food and drink acquire the sophisticated and selective character of dining or diet. Clothing is designed for comfort or fashion. In a culture where people can decide how much to raise in taxes and where to spend their money, they can choose between having more policemen on patrol or a job-training programme for the unemployed, improving the schools or the sewage-disposal, encouraging high-rise buildings or beautifying the parks.

A preoccupation with bare existence belongs to a level of thought and discussion less complex than a concern about a standard of living, for a standard involves comparisons and consequent valuations. A modern community relearns this basic truth whenever it undergoes the experience of a major war. Its concern immediately switches from bettering its living standards to preserving life itself. Those whose wants have reached the stage of inquiry about a standard of living are making intellectual comparisons and ethical choices. When we select a pattern of life from the available alternatives, our preferences are transmuted into terms of good and bad, of right and wrong—in a word, of values.

This is the distinguishing mark of our species, for what makes us preeminently human is that we are value-selecting animals. On the foundation of necessities, we build an elaborate structure of choices which stamp us as rational and moral beings. And whatever values we choose to adopt, we incorporate into our lives by group action. In large measure this evolving process through which we formulate and attain our wants is social in character. "The gains of commonwealths," as Charles E. Merriam has written, "are essentially mass gains." Without associating in groups, we would never have become humanized, nor could we long remain so. Cooperation is truly the source of civilization.

Self-Development and Selfishness

But there are other relationships between human beings beside the cooperative. We are not all altruists; we do not always cooperate. To be more accurate, some persons behave selfishly most of the time; the rest of us—except for a few saintly individuals—are selfish on occasion. What consequences follow from actions whose primary focus of interest is the self? Some can be good. Each person is a unique creation. The use of our capacities, the development of our individuality, is a worthwhile goal that everyone has the right to seek and society has the duty to encourage. Humanistic psychologists, such as Abraham Maslow, refer to self-actualization as the process through which our humanness finds expression. But self-development changes its character when it impinges on others, at which point the results become socially relevant. The consequences of an action may be intended or unforeseen. In either case, they spread out, like the ripples from a stone flung into water. Anybody who is affected by someone else's acts has an interest in what he or she does. If the results are beneficial, no one is likely to object. This optimistic possibility was the basic assumption of Adam Smith, the Scottish founder of laissez-faire economic, who had been a professor of moral philosophy. He thought that, while pursuing our own self-interest, we may, without knowing or intending it, be "led by an invisible hand" to promote simultaneously the interest of society. How these good effects are produced or whose is the invisible hand, he did not explain.

But what if the results are harmful? An individual can harm others in thousands of ways. When too many persons are smoking in a crowded room, the air becomes filthy for everybody—nonsmokers included. When we drive our automobiles, we pollute the air and contribute to smog. However well meaning we are individually, when too many do the same thing at the same time in the same place we can produce a collective disaster. In the common interest, therefore, we must protect ourselves, which is possible only when we regulate or prohibit certain types of behaviour. Thus, as John Stuart Mill and John Dewey agree, some restraints on individual liberty become justifiable and necessary.

The need for restraint is even greater when individuals act competitively and aggressively. This happens when two or more persons wish to possess the same object or enjoy some limited resource whose use is then denied to others. Competition occcurs when the interests of the self dominate over one's concern for other people. This is the situation when each seeks to gain an advantage over any rivals who stand in the way. Inherently, competition sets individuals and groups against each other in a hostile relationship. It is, therefore, destructive and, if carried to its ultimate conclusion, self-destructive. For the aim of competition is to eliminate the opponent, in which case competition ceases. Wherever it is unrestrained, competition tends in the direction of monopoly until it eventually destroys the conditions of its own existence. When competition is utterly cutthroat, the throat that gets cut is its own.

What is a society to do about the results of competition? Three possibilities suggest themselves. The competitors may be left to battle it out. Or people may organize into groups and determine by an agreed procedure what settlement is just for all parties concerned. Third, as an intermediate course, the group may refuse to decide the outcome, but, like a referee, may prescribe the rules of conducting the contest. The first of these possibilities is merely Hobbes's "warre of every man against every man" all over again. Its results are so destructive that people generally prefer a more orderly solution. The two latter methods (though one is confined to the regulation of means and the other regulates both means and ends) are alike in employing group authority to mitigate the destructive results of unrestrained competition.

The Alternatives of Cooperation or Competition

Paradoxically, although human society presupposes cooperation, many persons behave in the opposite manner and believe that competition is superior. In fact, the literature of social thought abounds with instances of this contradiction between the two principles. Some examples will illustrate how philosophies and their ethical conclusions differ, according to where the priority is placed.

In ethical theory, many doctrines emphasize the cooperative side of human relations and prescribe a course of conduct based on our need for one another. Witness the injunction of the Gospels to "love thy neighbour as thyself," or the Golden Rule to " do unto others as you would have others do unto you." In similar vein are these eloquent words of John Donne: "No man is an *iland,* intire of it selfe; every man is a piece of the *continent*, a part of the *maine;* if a clod be washed away by the sea, *Europe* is the lesse, as well as if a *promontorie* were, as well as if a *mannor* of thy *friends* or of thine owne were; any man's *death* diminishes *me* because I am involved in *Mankinde;* and therefore never send to know for whom the *bell* tolls; it toils for *thee.*

Some readers may consider such statements to be noble precepts, but impractical. We pay lip service to ideals of this kind, but nobody really lives by them. If that is your feeling,. It would be well to remember some saintly persons who demonstrated in recent practice that such principles are possible—think of Eleanor Roosevelt, Pope John XXIII, Martin Luther King, Mahatma Gandhi, Albert Schweitzer. All these were inspired by a common faith in a universal human family. All tried to change the world around them and to reform its governing institutions. All encountered opposition, of course, and two were assassinated—one in India, the other in the United States. As Emerson wrote: "The power of love, as the basis of a State, has never been tried."

Opposed to universal benevolence are dogmas of universal selfishness. In one passage, Niccolo Machiavelli thus summarized his view of humanity: "For it may be said of men in general that they are ungrateful, voluble, dissemblers, anxious to avoid danger, and covetous of gain; so long as you benefit them they are entirely yours; they offer you their blood, their goods, their life, and their children, as I have before said, when the necessity is remote; but when it approaches, they revolt." No less self-centered was the characterization offered by Hobbes, who considered that "of the voluntary acts of every man, the object is some *good to himself.*" He even goes to the length of arguing that pity "ariseth from the imagination that the like calamity (of another) may befall himselfe," which is as clear a case as may be found of twisting the truth to save a theory.

In economic thought and the policies based thereon, some further instances of the same tendency occur. During the nineteenth century the economic theory prevailing in Britain and the United States assumed that the principle of competition constituted the strongest stimulus to work, and even that it produced the greatest good for society as a whole and for its members severally. Adam Smith, who initiated this doctrine, believed the most potent motivation to be "the natural effort of every individual to better his own condition, when suffered to exert itself with freedom and security." When this belief is harnessed to the principle of the division of labour, which forms the opening theme of the *Wealth of Nations.* There arises that peculiar linkage, the economic relation, in which each pursues and satisfies a particular interest and yet simultaneously satisfies some interest of others. Smith recognized that "man has almost constant occasion for the help of his brethren." But he goes on to say that it is in vain for a man to expect that others will help him "from their benevolence only.... He will be more likely to prevail," runs the argument, "if he can interest their self-love in his favour, and shew them that it is for their own advantage to do for him what he requires of them. Whoever offers to another a bargain of any kind, proposes to do this; Give me that which I want, and you shall have this which you want." That is selfishness developed to a high degree, but tempered by some qualifications. For Smith concedes that even self-lovers must cooperate. This he is bound to admit, since, once the division of labour is chosen as a starting point, it follows that specialists are interdependent.

The State of Nature and the Nature of Society

The gratuitous assumption of the classical theorists was that universal egoism determines economic behaviour and permeates our social relations. This was aided in the nineteenth century by inferences drawn from biology. The concept of evolution envisaged human beings as linked with other animals in a continuous chain of being. The nature of other species thus seemed to suggest analogies for understanding ourselves on the assumption that the basic requirements of "nature" may be modified within society but cannot be wholly eradicated or permanently transformed. The question then arose: What was the nature of "nature"? What lessons did it teach? As is often the case, people looked at the same phenomena, selected different data, and arrived at opposite conclusions.

One line of argument consisted of variations on the theme of the Greek philosopher Herachlitus, who pronounced that "strife is the parent of all things." The world was seen as a jungle, and the jungle as a battleground. Nature's law was to use your claw. It was the lot of the weak to be dominated or exterminated by the strong or the cunning. Such doctrines were applied by Herbert Spencer to social theory in combination with the other "natural laws" of Smith's economics. The outcome was simple: Let dog eat dog. Which side then did morality take? Ethics followed nature, siding with the eater, not the eaten.

On this Point Let Spencer Speak for Himself:

> Pervading all nature we may see at work a stern discipline, which is a little cruel that it may be very kind. That state of universal warfare maintained throughout the lower creation, to the great perplexity of many worthy people, is at bottom the most merciful provision which the circumstances admit of. It is much better that the ruminant animal, when deprived by age of the vigour which make its existence a pleasure, should be killed by some beast of prey, than that it should linger out a life made painful by infirmities, and eventually die of starvation.... Meanwhile the well-being of existing humanity, and the unfolding of it into this ultimate perfection, are both secured by the same beneficent, though severe discipline, to which the animate creation at large is subject.... The poverty of the incapable, the distresses that come upon the imprudent, the starvation of the idle, and those shouldering aside of the weak by the strong, which leaves so many "in shallows and in miseries," are the decrees of a large, far-seeing benevolence.... Nevertheless, when regarded not separately, but in connection with the interests of universal humanity, these harsh fatalities are seen to be full of the highest beneficence...which brings to early graves the children of diseased parents, and singles out the low-spirited, the intemperate, and the debilitated as the victims of an epidemic.

Such ideas were reinforced when Charles Darwin, nine years after the *Social Statics* had appeared, published his epochal *Origin of species*. If humans and monkeys were descended from a common ancestor, whatever conditions promoted the survival of the latter must also be relevant to the former. Darwin, moreover, offered clues to such analogies in his hypotheses of " the struggle for existence" and "the survival of the fittest." Biological species had evolved by success in combat and by adaptation to environment. Mankind must, therefore, subdue or be subdued, destroy or be destroyed.

Opposite inferences, however, were drawn by the Russian anarchist, Prince Kropotkin. Serving for five years in Siberia as a young cavalry officer, he used his opportunity to study the behaviour of wild animals in their natural habitats. Observation led him to conclude that the Darwinians were misrepresenting the facts.

A murderous struggle for existence was not what he discovered among the higher animals, even among the carnivorous. Insufficient attention had been given, in his view, to the evidence of cooperation which exists on all rungs of the ladder of evolution, and increases among the more advanced species. What he had read in zoology and anthropology, along with what he had observed, brought him to the following conclusion:

"Don't compete!—competition is always injurious to the species, and you have plenty of reasons to avoid it!" that is the tendency of nature, not always realized in full, but always present. That is the watchword which comes to us from the bush, the forest, the river, the ocean "therefore combine—practice mutual aid! That is the surest means for giving to each and all the greatest safety, the best guarantee of existence and progress, bodily, intellectual, and moral." That is what nature teachers us; and that is what all those animals which have attained the highest position in their respective classes have done. That is also what man—the most primitive man-has been doing; and that is why man has reached the position upon which we stand now...."

The contrast is indeed vivid. There could hardly be a sharper antithesis than that between Kropotkin's ideas and Spencer's. And the lives of certain individuals bear this out. Could any two human beings be more unlike than, say, Hitler and Pope John? Or could the impact of two lives on humanity in general be more dissimilar? The questions, then, to consider are these: what are the implications for society of competition and cooperation? Since their results differ so, which is better? Can we have a community in which people are able both to compete and to cooperate? If not, which of the two should we practice ourselves and encourage in others?

When we look around, we find that our social system contains institutions grounded in contrary ideals and manifesting opposite tendencies. Cooperation is generally at its highest in the family, even though rivalry and tension divide some families, and some marriages terminate in desertion or divorce. The business world. On the other hand, generally functions with a high degree of competition. As for government, contrast domestic with international politics. In countries where most people feel a common identity and purpose, domestic policy is marked by a substantial amount of cooperation (or consensus, as it is also called). The opposite is true for relations between states. There it is competition that predominates and power in the pursuit of self-interest, not justice, that prevails—so much so that humanity still wrestles with the problem of how to restrain national policies that hurt others and promote active cooperation in matters of mutual interest. Thus in the family, and within the nation, the emphasis is on cooperation; in business and in international relations, it is on competition.

These differences demand evaluation by moral standards. Are the relations between the members of a family normally superior in ethical terms to those of business? Is there normally less destructive hostility in domestic politics than in the international arena? The answers are self-evident, and I take them as further proof that cooperation is superior to competition, both for the individuals who practice it and for society at large.

This is necessarily the case because competition divides, whereas cooperation unites; competition is destructive, cooperation is constructive. Competition develops the self in rivalry with others, whereas cooperation develops the self in harmony with others. It would be possible for a society to function solely through cooperation, without any competition; the reverse is impossible. In fact, even groups which are constituted around the intention to attack others have a measure of internal cooperation. Thus, the requirements of competition, but the latter never brings people into competition. So for society and its politics, the paramount need is to act cooperatively.

Relations Among People in a Group

Reality is always influenced by our thoughts of what it ought to be. If people think that cooperation has beneficial results, then their conduct will follow accordingly, as will the pattern of their social relationships. When we emphasize cooperation, we are giving priority to matters of common interest, to whatever binds us together. It is the reverse, of course, when we stress competition. In that case, each person is preoccupied with the self; we focus on differences and uniqueness.

Can we understand such opposites? Which picture of our relationships with our fellow creatures is valid? Can they be equally true? There are various ways of asking this fundamental question: What is a group and what are the relations among the people who comprise it? The answers to this question are many and varied because the situation is complex.

When we try to understand something as intricate as human society, we seek to make the problem intelligible by dividing it into parts and observing how they are connected. The question then arises: Which is to be regarded as the whole, and which are the parts? What, in other words, is the unit whose unity has significance? One may approach the group from the standpoint of the individuals who comprise it, or the individuals from the standpoint of the group to which they belong. In the latter case, we refer to human beings as associated in a group. In the former, a group is said to consist of its members. Which is the prior reality to be explained, the group or the individual? And, whichever of these we take as the primary unit, how do we explain the other?

As might be expected, both possibilities have found support. Some argue that the unit is the group and that we individuals are its vulgar fractions. Others say that the unit is the single human being. Each view has been defended by analogies that supposedly illustrate the nature of a social group by comparisons with other associations. For those who hold that the group is the unit, a favourite parallel is the biological organism. The members of a social body are then though to resemble the members of an animal body, wherein all parts are functionally related and none can exist in separation from the rest. On this theory, just as the body has a natural unity, so has a social group. It then becomes a false abstraction to conceive of the individual as a person divorced from relationships with others. An arm lives only as part of an organic whole. Amputated from the body, it dies. An opposite conception results when the individual is believed to be the unit. It is then the single human being who is viewed as a natural unity and the group that appears artificial. Society is considered an aggregate, not an organism. A human group is thought to resemble a heap of stones. They are associated, yet separable. A stone may be removed from the heap, but it remains a stone.

The first comment to be made on these contrasts is that their opposition itself needs explaining. If opinions so contrary have been formulated, each may contain some elements of truth and correspond to certain facts. Plainly there is a sense in which every human being is unique and has a distinct existence, physically and psychically. When the bell tolls for John Jones, John Donne may say that it tolls for me also. But at that moment I can hear it and John Jones cannot—and that is no small difference! Moreover, although a characteristic is attributed to a group, a group as such does not exist, or feel and move, or act and suffer. It is what its members are. It does only what they do. In speaking about it in the singular, one is generalizing about them in the plural. Yet in another sense, a group is an intelligible and describable fact and has a kind of meaning that single human beings do not. John Jones may have died, but the group of which he was a member continues to exist with virtually the same characteristics it possessed in his lifetime. People are united by an intricate network of connections. They do not all move in one direction, like traffic on a one-way street. At countless crossroads they react and interact. They cannot separate themselves from the relationships that arise from their cooperation or their competition, their needs and their deeds. Each such relation is a projection from one's personality, and, like a shadow, belongs both to the person who casts it and to the place where it falls. Unless the projections are included, their source cannot be properly understood.

To explain the character of this relationship between individuals in a group is a perennial question of social thought. Being subtle, the essence of the relationship has eluded precise description. Consequently, from Plato to the present, theorists have resorted to analogies as an explanatory device. Groups have been variously depicted as if they were the same as an organism, a contract, a system, the physical universe, and so on. Such comparisons are helpful up to a point; but beyond that they cease to correspond to the facts. When pressed too far, analogies become misleading.

A clear inference may be drawn from all these attempts. Let us comprehend a human grouping as it is, and not as if it were something else. The truth is that a group of human beings is unique. It forms a class by itself, and the best way to understand it is to see it in its own true colours. The unique quality that all human associations possess can be thus described: A group is composed of individual members who must become parts of a whole since, unless associated, they are unable to develop themselves. Yet it is the parts, and only these, that possess a consciousness both of the self and of the whole, and are thereby capable of contributing to the whole its purpose and organization. In a paradoxical manner, human beings exist separately but are inseparably united.

The Variety of Groups

That statement, however, does not complete the analysis of groups, for there are further facts to note. One reason why it is difficult to fathom the nature of a group is that we are tempted to regard it as existing by itself, and to consider the relations among its members as circumscribed within its borders. But that is not the case. In truth, we belong to many groups. So varied are the relationships created by human needs that the same persons, like the pieces in a kaleidoscope, form and reform, combine and recombine, into numerous associations with myriad patterns. Groups are as prolific as the causes of cooperation; many groups coexist because our needs vary so much.

The best way to describe and classify groups is by the purpose they seek to fulfill. Many associations, for example, are created in response to material necessities and wants. Such "economic" groups correspond to the innumerable phases of the process of production, distribution, and consumption. To lift a weight takes the strength of two; to repair a fence between two farms, the neighbours work together. These instances may seem a far cry from the intricate structures of a modern economy. But just as the symphonies of Beethoven presuppose the simpler harmonics of a birdcall or tom-

tom, so do underlying similarities of principle persist through the evolution of social organization, from rudimentary to complex. A business firm is an organization of persons engaged in supplying some commodity or service on terms profitable to themselves. The joint stock company, the corporation, a banking or insurance system, and a cooperative store are familiar instruments by which people pool their resources and accomplish on a larger scale results otherwise unattainable. The trade union, once treated as a criminal conspiracy, has become a recognized and generally a conservative part of the established order. Nowadays, like the medieval guild, it seeks to promote the security of its members both by providing a standard of skill and by eliminating mutually ruinous undercutting in the competition for jobs.

As a need like the economic, which is common to all mankind, has produced our economic associations, so have other universal or widespread needs evoked their counterparts. All of us are curious about ourselves and our environment. We learn, we teach; we wonder and ponder; we wish to know and to understand. As a reasoning animal, whose mind communicates its thoughts through the faculty of speech, the human being has a need for education which can be satisfied only by a cooperative endeavour. Our store of knowledge was transmitted through the generations and is bequeathed to the human race as our common intellectual heritage. To encompass its vast dimensions requires the meeting of many minds in a fellowship of learning. Hence a network of institutions provides an organized response to our desire to know. Similarly, but without labouring the point, we may cite other familiar instances where a felt need stimulates association. Belief in a Supreme Being and the wish to worship have produced the world's religions. The family group gives companionship to adults and an upbringing to children. The cultural interests of like-minded people find a medium in operas,. Theaters, art galleries, libraries, symphony orchestras, the ballet, and so on, just as fondness for recreation and physical exercise results in sporting and athletic clubs.

Components of Groups

These comparisons permit us to subdivide a group into its components and then, as in table, 6.1, to analyze the features it

Table 6.1. The Components of Groups

Elements Common To all Groups	*Elements of Religious Groups*	*Elements of Educational Groups*	*Elements of Family Groups*	*Elements of Business Firms**	*Elements of the State*
1. Members	Congregation The Faithful	Teachers Students	Parents Children	Owners, Managers, Employees	Citizens, Subjects, Officials
(*a*) How they join	Initiation Baptism Conversion	Appointment Admission	Marriage Birth Adoption	Purchase of shares Hiring for job	Birth Naturalization Residence
(*b*) How they leave	Nonattendance Excommunication	Retirement Resignation Graduation Expulsion	Desertion Death Divorce	Sale of shares Resignation Dismissal	Renunciation Deportation Deprivation of citizenship
2. Functions†	Worship	Teaching Learning	Cohabitation Propagation	Manufacturing Sales	Protection, Justice, Welfare
3. Institutions	Church, Temple, Mosque, Synagogue	School, College, University	The Home	Firm Corporation	The State
4. Rules	Canon Law, Ritual, Mosaic law, Koran	Regulations Classroom discipline	Marriage Fidelity	Articles of incorporation Shop rules, etc.	Law Custom
5. Governing authority	Congregation Clergy	Teachers Administrators	Parents	Management Foreman	Government Officials
6. Revenue	Donations Tithes	Grants Fees	Income	Profits	Taxes, loans, etc.
7. Ideas	Theology Creed	Pedagogy Curriculum	Monogamy Polygamy Polyandry	Property, Private ownership, Contract, Competition	Political theory

* The business firm is, selected as an example, of one type of economic grouping.

† The functions listed in the table are not intended to be complete and exhaustive. Those stated in each case are the central and primary ones, not those that are secondary and derivative. All groups tend to acquire additional functions.

shares with others and those specific to each kind. Of what elements is a group composed? The first is necessarily the membership, since without this there would be no group. Members are variously named and related according to the nature of their association. In a church, they are the congregation or, in terms of the belief they profess, the faithful. In a family, they are parents, children, uncles, cousins—or, all inclusively, relatives. In a business firm, they are owners, managers, employees. A state has citizens or subjects, rulers and officials. How is membership acquired in the group? Sometimes by the voluntary choice of the person who seeks admission and of the existing members who decide to admit. Thus a person may undergo conversion and then be initiated into a religious faith, or may apply and be accepted at a school or university. One may be appointed to a job in a business firm, be naturalized as a citizen, marry and start a family. Sometimes the act of joining a group is involuntary, as when an infant is born into a family, is baptized into a church, and automatically receives the citizenship of the country of its birth. Similarly, membership in the group may be terminated by voluntary act of the individual or under compulsion from the group. You may sever your link with an organized religion by non-attendance, or it may excommunicate you. You may graduate from school or college, or drop out or be expelled; resign your job or be fired; renounce your allegiance or be stripped of citizenship.

If the members constitute the original element in any group, its functions form the second. Members associate to fulfill a purpose by carrying on a function. The chief function of the family is to propagate and live together; that of the religious group, to worship; of the firm, to conduct a business; of the state, to protect. Functions such as these cannot be performed without organization, structure, and system. In other words, every organization that maintains its identity and retains its continuity begets a progeny of institutions. Though variously named, the latter are fundamentally alike in the role they perform. Education is institutionalized through schools, colleges, and universities. Religion is organized by temples, mosques, synagogues, or churches. Business is carried on by the firm or corporation. The family clusters round the home. Likewise the state acts through government and its specialized agencies—the legislature, law court, administrative department, and civil service.

When an institution is organized, three further elements appear: a body of rules, a governing authority, and revenue. Every association produces rules that define the relations of its members, allot their rights and responsibilities, and prescribe its operating procedures. In a church, this takes the form of canon law and ritual. In the family, the law of marital relations reinforces the moral code of fidelity. A business firm not only has internal regulations but also conforms to general trade practices and operates inside the framework of laws of contract, property, corporations, and so on. The state is both creator of law and creature of custom. To enforce its rules and give general guidance to the group is the task of its governing authority. This appears under different guises, depending on the nature of the association—as the management, clergy, parents, teachers, or government. Similarly, in every group an essential ingredient is its revenue—if that term is understood to comprise the physical and material resources by which the group accomplishes its purposes. Thus a school or university is maintained by public funds or private fees and endowments; a business, by its profits; the state, by taxes and frees, the family, by its property and income.

Finally, there is one more component. Every group is both producer and product of the ideas concerning it which exist in its members minds. These ideas are an integral part of the life of the group since they embody the hopes and aspirations of its members, expressing their conception of the group's purpose and their understanding of its processes. The ideas that sustain the group are not always explicitly formulated. In certain cases they are inarticulate, and are divined rather than defined. Even if expressed, they may not always be systematized into a coherent philosophy. For example, family systems are numerous and various, as are the types of political systems. But while political theories are many, theories of the family are few. This does not mean, however, that the family group lacks its ideology. Nor, for that matter, can religions fulfill its purposes without a theological creed; a university, without an educational philosophy; or a business firm, without a theory of economic behaviour.

The Unity of Society

This analysis shows that human groups are many in number and different in purpose. It also reveals how complex is the sum total of associations, i.e., society, comprising all relationships and organized groups. But just as society consists of many groups, every human being also has numerous memberships. By nature, we are joiners. Each person belongs to a collection of groups, no one of which can embrace every interest. Not only is society a pluralistic union of groups, but the ways in which individuals associate are also plural.

The numerous groupings into which all people enter bring them sometimes into relations with the same persons, but more usually with different ones. Thus, as a partner in a business firm, *A* may be associated with *B, C, D,* and *E;* as a university alumnus, with *C, D, L,* and *M;* as a worshipper in a church, with *W, X, Y,* and *Z;* and so on. As the purposes for combination vary, so all of us find ourselves associated with different samples of our fellow creatures. Neither in function nor5 in membership are the groups identical.

These obvious facts produce most controversial implications. In the first place, the use of the singular term *society* to describe the sum total of relationships and groups involves a major assumption. One should raise, rather than beg, these fundamental questions: Is society truly a unity? Is there anything that embraces the plurality of groups? If so, what makes it a whole? Does this oneness occur only subjectively in our minds and attitudes, or does it also manifest itself in some external structure and organization? A second difficulty arises from the first. It can be readily seen that the processes of cooperation create social relations, and that these relations receive an orderly character through the formation of groups. But once the groups have been formed, what regulates the relations between groups themselves? How is the grouping of groups arranged? Human needs and interests cannot be so demarcated as to prevent all contact or overlap. When one speaks of the economic need, the educational need, or the cultural need, these are not a string of airtight compartments but rather the many facets of a community that functions as a whole. Human needs interlock; we pursue objectives that conflict. So it is with the resulting groups, as some examples will indicate.

Divided Loyalties of the Individual

Business practices, backed by economic theory, sanction the lending of capital for interest. But religion may condemn this as the sin of usury. Painters interpret the world as they see it and insist that they pursue their art for its own sake. Yet a critic may charge that they offend the moral susceptibilities of others, and assert the subordination of art to ethics. Parents wish their children to be educated so that their opportunities may be broadened. But the poverty of the home makes it necessary to increase the family earnings by sending children into early employment. A man and a woman wish to marry. But the church to which one of them belongs forbids the union on the grounds that the other party belongs to a different church or has been divorced. An industrial firm wants to erect a factory that will employ many workers on a desirable piece of land in a city of expanding population. The same area is sought by educational authorities for a school and playground, by a building contractor for a housing project, by a movie exhibitor for a theater. How are such conflicts resolved? Who arbitrates the merits of the contending claims? On what principles is a just decision based?

Such cases are not imaginary. They are scenes from actual life. If they possess drama, it is because any situation of conflict is inherently dramatic. Nor is this conflict one that exists solely between groups. It goes deeper, since within each human being and inside each group a struggle develops between contrary sentiments, attitudes, habits and ideas. All of us belong to a number of systems that correspond with our respective interests and needs. But these interests overlap, the needs crisscross, the systems clash. A father of a family has an obligation to his wife and children which may be at variance with his financial circumstances. The adherents of a religious faith accept dogmas, which, as participants in an educational programme, they may be expected to question. An artist may seek to portray a person or a situation truthfully as these appear. But to do so may be running counter to the conventions of the social order. Each of these systems—the economic, religious, cultural, and familial—lays claim to the loyalty of its members. Since each system, however, covers only a segment of our total needs and interests, the allegiance that each can exact must itself be partial. How then can a person come to a decision when faced with antagonistic demands? Amid so many claims, how is one to know which to respect?

The Search for Social Harmony

Two answers to these questions are possible. The competition of loyalties could be resolved by compromise. Strictly understood, this means that neither of the rival claims is completely satisfied. Instead, an agreement is reached at some intermediate position. Each side succeeds on some points, and concedes on others. But if this is done, one naturally inquires: Who acts as intermediary? Who negotiates the compromise? On what principles is it based? How are these determined? Even these queries, however, do not apply to conflicts whose nature permits no compromise whatsoever. Take, for example, the demand of Roman emperors that they and they deified predecessors be worshiped as divinities by inhabitants of their empire. Between this demand and the religious beliefs of their Christian subjects, no compromise was possible. Or consider the implications of the most divisive domestic issue that has erupted in the United States since the achievement of independence: the institution of slavery. There was no mid-way point for settlement between one who upheld the principle that human beings may be bought, owned, and sold as the legal property of other human beings, and one who asserted that they may not. The two views could not be reconciled or harmonized. As the judgment of Solomon indicated when two women claimed the same child, the price of compromise was to kill the baby. The outcome of the slavery question was in fact left to the arbitrament of war; and arms decided not which view was better, but which in practice would prevail.

As a second possibility of resolving conflict between groups, when compromise is impracticable or inadmissible, the loyalty to one group must bow before the loyalty to another. But how is this achieved? Who decides which group shall predominate and by what means it shall triumph? One method is to use force, with the consequent suppression or overpowering of the unsuccessful side. A second is the voluntary submission of one side after peaceful persuasion. A third is to appeal to some larger association which will choose between opposing claims in the light of a still wider union. Thus the difficulty of harmonizing cooperation with competition, of groups with individuals, is viewed in broader focus when it is treated not simply as a matter of relations between persons within a single group but as a complex of interrelations between numerous groups whose members are associated and reassociated in diverse ways.

Consequently it is necessary to reframe the earlier question, of how to describe the relation of the group to the individual. This can now be more accurately expressed as the problem of organizing many multimembered groups of human beings into one multigroup society. Can the principles of social theory and the practices of social organization devise a rationale of uniting the various groups with their many members and the various members with their many groupings? The search for this union can end only with the discovery of an interest sufficiently broad to absorb all partial, lesser interests and of an association wide enough to embrace the lesser, limited associations., It is time, therefore, to turn to the origins of the state and the contribution of government.

State and Society

An Historical View of the Relation of State and Society and of Theories About Their Relation

Burke, in his *Reflections on the Revolution in France,* laid down the proposition, 'society is indeed a contract ... but the State ought not to be considered nothing better than a partnership agreement in a trade... it is a partnership in all science; a partnership agreement in all art; a partnership in every virtue, and in all perfection'. The proposition suggests two reflections. The first is that Burke, sliding unconsciously from a mention of 'society' into a mention of 'the Sate', implies that the two are one. The second is that he views this single and unitary system (which we may call a 'society-state') as a total and all-inclusive partnership which is competent for every purpose: not only the legal purpose of enunciating and enforcing a scheme of law and order (a purpose which he does not mention, because it may be assumed as self-evident), but also the economic purpose of 'trade', the cultural purpose of 'science' and 'art', and the moral and religious purpose of 'every virtue' and 'all perfection'. What then, we may ask, of the Church? Is it not also a partnership, a separate partnership, directed to a religious purpose which involves and includes connected purposes such as the promotion of education? Burke would reply that by virtue of 'a state religious establishment' the Church is welded into the State to form one consecrated commonwealth which embraces both church and state. But what, we may also ask, of bodies such as trade unions? Are they not also partnerships, separate partnerships, which beginning from economic 'agreement in a trade' may rise to wider charitable and even cultural purposes? In 1790, when Burke was writing his *Reflections,* trade unions were sparse and struggling bodies, already illegal (or at any rate of dubious legality) under the common law, as being 'conspiracies in restraint of trade' and therefore contrary to 'public policy', but made more illegal still, only a few years later, by the Combination Acts of 1799-1800, which added the force of statute and legislative prohibition to the disabilities already imposed by the rules of the common law. The state thus seemed (but only *seemed,* as we shall see later) to stand alone in conservative Britain at the end of the eighteenth century; alone, and all-comprehensive.

But it seemed to be equally solitary, and no less comprehensive, in revolutionary Fance. Article (*3*) of the *Déclaration des droits de l'homme et du citoyen,* promulgated in 1789 and prefixed to the Constitution of 1791, laid it down that 'le principe de toute souveraineté réside essentiellement dans la nation [that is to say, in the national state]; null corps, nul individu ne peut exercer d' autorité qui n'en emane expressement'. This principle of national sovereignty was carried into effect for the Church by the 'Civil Constitution of the Clergy', which turned the Catholic Church in France at once into a branch and a copy of the new revolutionary State, deriving authority from that State and modelled upon it, point by point, in its organisation. The principle was equally, or even more stringently, applied in the same year (1790) to trade unions, by a law which declared combinations of workers to be 'inconstitutionnelles, attentatoiries a la liberté et à la Déclaration des droits de l'homme et du citoyen, et de nul effet'.

IDEAS TODAY

Today we generally distinguish between Society and the State. Our starting-point, when we use either term, is the given and historical fact of the nation. We assume, as the basis of our thought, a distinctive space, or territory, inhabited by a distinctive human stock (racially mixed, as a rule, but none the less distinctive), which is engaged in a nexus of co-operative activity. We then go on to the further assumption that this unit or nation—this amalgam of space and stock, with its nexus of co-operative activity—behaves in two ways, or as two orders, and does so concurrently and simultaneously. It acts in a social or voluntary way, as a social order or Society. It acts in a legal or compulsory way, as a legal order or State.

(a) By 'Society' we mean the whole sum of voluntary bodies, or associations, contained in the nation (and even ramifying beyond it by the connexions which they establish with similar bodies in other nations), with all their various purposes and with all their institutions. Taken together, and regarded as a whole, these associations form the social substance which goes by the general and comprehensive name of 'Society'. Taken separately, and regarded in themselves, they generally show and share two features: first, they are essentially *voluntary* in origin: secondly, they are essentially *specific* in purpose, each existing for some one purpose—religious, economic, educational, charitable, or 'social' in that narrower sense in which we speak of any of the purposes of our ordinary human intercourse (such as the common enjoyment of sport or the common cultivation of leisure) as being a 'social purpose'. But if each, taken separately, thus exists for a specific purpose, all taken together exist for a number and a variety of purposes. In view of the many and various purposes of its parts, we may accordingly say that Society does, in Burke's words, constitute 'a partnership in *all* science,. . . . in *all* art, ... in *every* virtue and in *all* perfection'; and we may even say that, so conceived, Society is in a sense total or 'totalitarian'. But to say that is not to say—indeed it is a very different thing from saying—that the State, which has its own separate basis and its own peculiar character, is also 'totalitarian'.

(b) What, then, is the separate basis and the peculiar character of the State? By 'the State' we mean a particular and special association, existing for the

special purpose of maintaining a compulsory scheme of legal order, and acting therefore through laws enforced by prescribed and definite sanctions. The State, as a rule, is national in its scope (though a given State may be multi-national), just as Society also is national: in other words, most States are what we call 'national States'. But if, on this point, the State agrees with Society—or, more exactly, is coextensive with Society—it also differs (and differs profoundly) from the associations other than itself which we call, in their sum, by the name of 'Society'. It differs in two respects. First, it includes *all* the members of the stock which inhabits its space or territory, and it includes them all as a matter of necessity: other associations include only *some* (though a national church, in Sweden for instance, may include nearly all), and they include these on a voluntary basis. Secondly, the State has the power of using legal cocercion, the power of enforcing obedience, under the sanction of punishment, to ordained rules of behaviour; other associations, in virtue of their voluntary basis, can apply only social discipline, and can expect only voluntary obedience to agreeds ways of behaviour, obedience enforced in the last resort by the sanction of exclusion from membership We may therefore say of the State that while it is an association like other associations, in the sense of being a union of men for the purpose of acting as *socii* or partners in the realization of a common purpose, it is also an association which is unlike other associations, in the sense of having a unique *purpose* (the purpose of maintaining a compulsory scheme of legal order) which gives it the unique *scope* of including compulsorily all the persons resident in a given territory and the unique *power* of making law and using legal coercion.

The distinction here stated is a problem, or rather a cause of problems, as well as a distinction. On the argument which has been followed a nation is simultaneously, and coextensively, two things in one. It is a social substance, or Society, constituted of and by a sum of voluntary associations, which have mainly grown of themselves—in the sense that they have been formed by voluntary and spontaneous combination—and which desire to act and to realize their purposes as far as possible by themselves. That is one side of the nation. The other side (which we may call either the reverse or the obverse, according to our preference) is that it is a political, or, as it is perhaps better called, a legal substance; a single compulsory association including all, and competent, in all cases where it sees fit, to make and enforce rules for all. This double nature of the nation—this simultaneity and coextension of its social and its legal aspect—raises a threefold problem. (1) What are the thing which belong to the nation in its legal aspect, as an organized State? (2) What are the things which belong to the nation in its social aspect, as a sum of voluntary associations? (3) What control should the nation, as organized in a State (and therefore competent to deal with all persons and judge in all cases *in the elgal sphere),* exercise over itself as organized in a society of voluntary associations acting *in the social sphere?*

The totalitarian states which have appeared—and disappeared—in recent years (if indeed they have disappeared, and if communism be not a new incarnation of their spirit) gave a simple answer to all these problems. They denied the distinction between State and Society and shelved the questions which it raises. They integrated the nation in the State, and made the State the solitary and total expression of the nation. This was not a revolution: it was rather a reversion. The history of the past can furnish us with many examples of totalitarianism. But it can also furnish us with examples of divergencies from, or reactions against, the theory of the solitary and total State. We may, therefore, attempt an historical retrospect, and seek to attain an historical view both of the relation between State and Society in the past and of the theories of the past about their relation.

THE GREEK CITY-STATE

The Greek city-state is still of importance, and a living part of the living past, because it has left us a theory, expressed in the writings of Plato and Aristotle, which still lives in our minds and colours our thoughts. Though it bore the name of 'Polis', which we naturally associate with politics, the city-state was something more than a political system; and it went far beyond the legal purpose of declaring and enforcing a body of rules for the control of legal relations. it was State and Society in one, without distinction or differentiation; it was a single system of order, or fused 'society-state', of the type unconsciously assumed by Burke in the theory of his *Reflections.* Because the Polis was more than a state—because it was also, over and above that, a religious confession and an ethical society; because it was also, into the bargain, an economic concern for the purpose of production and trade; because it was also, in addition to that, a cultural association for the common pursuit of beauty and truth—because it was all these things, Plato expects it in his *Republic,* to formulate the true idea of God and the rules of moral behaviour, to regulate economic life, and to control all art and science by its system of education. Aristotle is less far-reaching: he is even willing to recognize the Polis as an 'association of associations'. But even to Aristotle the political association is sovereign and all-inclusive, embracing and regulating all the others; and the science of this association—the science of politics—is a master-science which 'determines what other sciences should be studied in states, which of them should be learned by each group of citizens, and to what extent they should be learned'. When he speaks of man as being by his nature a *politikon zōon,* he does not mean that 'man is by nature a political animal', in the sense of having a natural interest in what we call politics and a natural instinct for indulging that interest. He means that man is a being who is intended by the capacities of his nature for life in a Polis, as bees are intended by their capacities for life in a hive: a being who *must* live in a Polis if he is to develop his capacities, for the simple reason that those capacities can only grow from 'potency' to 'act' in a general and generous environment which includes not only what we call politics, but also art and science and 'every virtue and all perfection'.

But the very fact that the Polis was something more than a State is a reason why we should approach with caution the lessons of Greek political theory. They are noble lessons; but they are the lessons of a theory which was something more than political. It was a theory, we may say, of an omnicompetent 'Society-State'. Our modern theory, based on our own experience of life, which is different from that of the Greeks, is more in a single dimension. It is simply a theory of the competent State—that is to say, of a State which is competent simply and solely for its specific purposes, which are essentially legal purposes. The State, in our experience, is a guarantor of rights and duties. It has in its hands the instrument of law; and it does whatever can be done by the use of that instrument. Its strength is as the strength of law; and it can avail no more, and no farther, than law. The State of our theory is accordingly a State which legally declares and legally guarantees the rights and duties of its members, whether those members are individuals or societies of individuals. It can declare and guarantee the rights and duties of authors, teachers, and all other persons who are engaged in the creation and transmission of culture; but it is not itself the creator and inculcator of culture. It can declare and guarantee the rights and duties of all agents engaged in the area of economic production and distribution: indeed it can even become itself an agent in that area, if a due guarantee of the rights of the labouring classes and the duties of their employers cannot be otherwise provided; but it offends against its own nature, and it injures its own primary legal function, if it loads itself with any large burden of direct economic activity. It is the supervisor of activity, and not the generator. It is the author of a framework of rights and duties, but not itself the whole framework of life.

THE IMPACT OF CHRISTIANITY

The rise and spread of the Christian religion made a great break in the antique system of ideas: the system enshrined in the Greek Polis (and still visible in the Parthenon), and similarly enshrined in the parallel *civitar Romana*, which beginning on the Tiber (and still visible in the Roman Forum and on the Capitol) gradually made the whole of the Mediterranean world on 'city' and styled it the *imperium Romanum.* Beneath the ancient city state there grew the catacombs; and from the catacombs there emerged an authority—the authority of the Church—which stood distinct from and over against, the authority of a city-state now magnified into a city-empire. There is dynamite in the text, 'Render... unto

Caesar the things which are Caesar's; and unto God the things that are God's (Matthew xxii.21). Ultimately, it meant the sundering of the sphere of Society from the sphere of the state; and we may even say that in the field of social and political theory (though that is only one field, and the explosive emergence of the Christian religion was felt in other and wider fields) this was the great result of the teaching of Christ. Immediately, and indeed for long centuries, which begin with the recognition of Christianity as a *religio licita* by Constantine, and extend into and through the Middle Ages, the effect of Christianity was the emergence of the doctrine of the two ends—the temporal and, which alone belongs to the State, and the eternal end which belongs to, and is the prerogative of, the Church.

What was the Christian doctrine of the nature of the temporal end? It was eventually formulated, like so much else, by St. Thomas Aquinas in the thirteenth century. His theory is that it involves four things, which thus belong to the State—all else, as a matter of the eternal end, belonging to the Church. The first of these four things is security and sufficiency of life: in other words, freedom from the threat of death and freedom from the threat of starvation. The second thing, in the scale, is a legal scheme of order and justice: a scheme of law, proceeding from the people or from a competent authority acting on their behalf, with a correlative scheme of administrative order. The third thing, rising still further in the scale, is what may be called the promotion of a minimum standard of morality, in aid of, and subsidiary to, the major moral activity of the Church, which has the general custody of moral life *sub specie aeternitatis:* the State, which acts in the order or time and in temporal society, being thus concerned, and only concerned, with immoral acts which excite repulsion in the majority of the members of such a society or undermine the every foundations of its existence. The further and last thing, at the top of the scale, is the protection of religion, as a function ancillary to the life of the Church: the State being bound, by a due respect for the eternal end, to secure for its members the conditions in which they can exercise the faculty of contemplating eternal truth under the wing and guidance of the Church.

Corresponding to the doctrine of the two ends, there is the paralleled doctrine of the two powers (*duo fines, ergo duae potestates*). The doctrine of the two powers is first clearly expressed by Pope Gelasius I, when he writes of 'Duo...quibus principaliter mundus hic regitur: auctoritas sacrata pontificum, et regalis potestas'. In the development of this doctrine the authority of the State (*regalis potestas*) becomes a specifically *legal* authority, with a subsidiary moral and an ancillary religious function; and on the other hand the authority of the Church, while primarily religious, becomes in addition a moral and an educational (or cultural) authority. The scope of the authority of the Church is indicated by the triple power regarded as inherent in the clergy—the religious *potestas ordinis,* in all matters concerning the sacraments; the moral *potestas jurisdictionis* (though, as we shall have occasion to notice, clerical jurisdiction came also to cover outside the category of morals); and the educational *potestas docendi.* Armed with this triple power, the Church divides the regimen of the world with the State on a system of dyarchy. In the original theory of Gelasius, that system is still regarded as a system of parity: the Popes in Rome have still some deference for the imperial authority, though that authority has come to reside beyond the seas in Constantinople; and their idea is still an idea of equality, parity, or parallelism. Each authority is equal to the other in its own sphere. Not only so, but each authority is dependent on the other when once it enters the sphere of the other; the clergy depending as much on the governors of the State in temporal matters as the governors of the State depend on the clergy in matters spiritual. It is a nice balance—each equal to the other when acting in its own sphere: each equally dependent on the other when acting in the sphere of the other. But there is already a shadow of coming disturbance, and a certain oscillation of the nicely adjusted balance. Gelasius notes that the burden of the clergy is the heavier of the two, inasmuch as they have to render account even for the rulers of the State at the final day of judgement. The 'heavier burden' may easily become a 'greater power'.

There are two further things to be noted. The first is that though, in the new conception, there are two *authorities*, there is still a single *community*. The two authorities rule simultaneously the same community. That community—Rome having achieved an oecumenical unity of the Mediterranean world—is a universal community of all Christian men, *respublica Christiana,* which is at one and the same time a Church and a State, with coextensive and identical membership: a Church, when regarded as pursuing the eternal end: a State, when regarded as pursuing the end which is an end in time. One community, but two governments—two governments corresponding to the two ends of the community—this is the first thing to be noted. The second, in logic at any rate, is consequential on the first. If there was one community, it was natural that one of the two governments should attempt, in spite of theories of dyarchy, to make itself supreme, by reducing 'government' as well as 'community' to the sovereign principle of unity: and it was further natural that the clerical government, as being charged with the greater end and bearing the heavier burden, should be the government which made this attempt. Accordingly, from Pope Gregory VII to Pope Boniface VIII (or, roughly, from 1150 to 1300), the clergy begin to enter the sphere of the end which is an end in time, and to take over temporal causes from the authority of the State. Legalizing itself in the process, the Church moves into the area of legal order and justice. In matters civil, for instance, it attempts to stop usury, and to enforce just prices on traders, by its courts and their canon law: in matters criminal it attempts to control the perennial feuds of fighting nobles by the institution of the 'truce' or 'peace' of God; in matters international, it attempts to bring even kings, and their wars and policies and treaties, under the jurisdiction of the papal *curia*. The Church is the judge of sin (*peccatum*); and what are the bounds of sin? When a king, for instance, has broken a treaty, has he not committed the *peccatum* of perjury (this was the argument of Innocent III), and must he not therefore be judged for his sins by the Church? Sin thus becomes an engulfing conception. It absorbs breaches of contract, breaches of the peace, and other contraventions of the general scheme of law. The boundary between morality and legality beings to fade; and the guardian of morality thus becomes the general guardian even of law.

This is a return, on a far larger scale and under far different auspices, of the old totality of the city-state. The Church, which had begun with a division of spheres, and had taught the doctrine of the two ends and the correlative doctrine of the two powers, had ended by the time of Boniface VIII in a new junction of spheres and an implicit rejection of any division. Indeed Boniface VIII had *explicitly* rejected division. The terrene power, he had said in the Bull *Unam Sanctam Ecclesiam* of 1302, shall be judged by the spiritual; but the supreme spiritual power shall be judged by God alone. It is a *divina potestas,* given by the word of God to St. Peter and his successors; and whoever therefore resists this power, thus ordained of God, resists the ordinance of God, 'nisi duo, sicut Manichaeus, fingit esse principia, quod falsum et haereticum esse judicamus'. Here dyarchy has gone; and here, we may even say, Gelasianism has been turned into and condemned as Manichaeism, or a recognition that the principle of evil is equal to the principle of good. Thus the policy of the medieval church, at its apogee or rather its extremity of logic, would bring all human life under a single *lex divina* enforced in the last resort by the supreme authority of the Papacy, acting through an array of ecclesiastical courts and institutions. (The registrar of the Roman chancery headed the Bull of Boniface VIII with the rubric 'Declaratio quod subesse Romano pontifici est omni humanae creaturae de necessitate salutis', which is a summary of its concluding words.) This may fairly be called the return of the omnicompetent 'Society-State', with its undifferentiated unity and its single controlling authority. But the Greek and Roman city-state had really controlled all life with an integrated authority. The medieval polity of which the Popes dreamed—a polity with supreme authority integrated in a theocracy—might claim a similar authority. But it could only claim; and the claim was confronted by facts of life and factors of power before which it collapsed in the moment of its statement. A medieval king, Philip IV of France, showed by the success of the measures which he took against Boniface VIII that the power of territorial kingship, however limited its area, was greater than the claims of the Universal Church, however wide its scope.

MEDIEVAL KINGDOMS AND ESTATES

The Middle Ages proper—the 'middle' Middle Ages, from

the eleventh to the thirteenth century—were a period of turbulence and germination. They contained, and developed, other facts and factors besides the theoretical polity of a single *res-publica Christiana*, whether that polity was conceived as conducted on the principle of dyarchy or viewed as reduced to unity under the supreme power of a theocracy. Two of these facts demand special notice for their bearing on the future development of Europe.

The first is the *regnum*. Though theory (which was mainly or even exclusively a theory expounded by the clergy), basing itself on the ancient fact of a universal Roman Empire, proclaimed the existence of a single universal community, which in its temporal aspect was a single *Regnum* or empire, as in its spiritual aspect it was a single *Ecclesia* or church—though theory ran in this channel of unity, life itself ran in the channels of diversity. Actually there were many *regna*, territorial or regional *regna*, at any rate in the West. Soon after the end of the thirteenth century the lawyers were even beginning to claim that each territorial king was the emperor of his kingdom (*rex in regno suo est imperator regni sui*): in other words, they held that the territorial or regional *Rex* excluded the 'emperor' of the would-be universal *Regnum* from the bounds of his own particular *regnum*, and was himself (as his lawyers styled our Richard II) 'the entire emperor of his realm'. Externally the claim might have some force, as a rebuttal of imperial claims of sovereignty; internally, in view of domestic turbulence, it was as yet an idle claim. It is true that the territorial or regional *regnum* was the area in which, with the development of nationalism and the rise of powerful national monarchies during the course of the sixteenth century, new national States would arise, and modern history (which is the history of such States) would take its beginning. But there was little of a national State—indeed there was little of any sort of State—in the territorial *regnum* o the Middle Ages. It was a paradise of Estates rather than the pattern of a State.

The second fact which demands our notice is this fact of Estates. Whatever the lawyers might say about his being 'the entire emperor of his realm', the king of each *regnum* had to face three serious competitors within his realm. In the first palce there was the territorial branch of the Church Universal (the *ecclesia Anglicana,* or the *eclesia Gallicana*), claiming for itself the privilege of immunity from the royal courts in a range of cases both civil and criminal, and able to appeal to the authority of the Papacy if its claim were challenged. (Not that the position was simple, or that a king might not sometimes be allied with the church of his territory to defend its liberties against the Papacy, or sometimes, again, with the Papacy to defend—and share—the lucrative prerogatives of patronage and taxation which the Popes sought to exercise over each territorial church.) In the second place, there were the feudal nobles, who individually acted as sovereigns, so far as they could, in their local fiefs, and collectively formed a baronage ready to dispute authority at the centre as a body of rival kings. Finally, there were the *communitates,* the local communities or 'commons', particularly in the towns, which locally sought autonomy for their municipal governments and their various merchant and craft guilds, and centrally, if they were joined together in an assembly of 'the Commons', might join the baronage in challenging the king—or the king in challenging the baronage.

These three competitors of the king (some of whom, however, might on occasion act as his interested allies)—the clergy, the baronage, and the commons—were loosely organized, and came to be known, as Estates. As they took shape, the medieval kingdom became an 'Estates-State': a State of the three Estates. Such a State, because by its nature its authority was disputed, or we may even say divided, was hardly competent, as it stood, for the specific purpose which any form of State must fulfill if it is to be worthy of the name; the purpose of making and enforcing a single scheme of law and order. In brief, there was an abundance of 'Society' in the territorial kingdoms, or 'Estates-States', of the Middle Ages; but there was very little 'State' Associations in various forms—clerical, baronial, municipal: whether based on religion or class or calling—became so many factotums, each making its own law and order in a time of general self-help; and the authority of the State, as represented by the king and his courts, was penned into a corner.

THE SIXTEENTH CENTURY AND THE NATIONAL STATE

The later centuries of the Middle Ages presented a sharp antithesis, or even self-contradiction: on the one hand, the ideal, or the theory, of a universal society under the regimen of a single theocracy: on the other, the fact of a number of quasi-national, or potentially national, kingdoms, all seeming to be disintegrated into so many polyarchies. In the age of the Renaissance, Reformation, and Reception—one of the great turning-points in the course of human history—a movement emerges, and gathers weight, towards the formation of unified national States. These states not only vindicate for themselves the province of law and order: they also annex, so far as they can, the province of religion; they assert a protectorate over the sphere of education and culture; and they gradually invade, under the banner of mercantilism, the territory of economics. The State reacts against the medieval invasion of its province by Society: it proceeds, in turn, to invade Society. Such is the swing of the pendulum, and such the recurrence of thesis in the face of anti-thesis.

Various causes contributed to foster the movement towards the formation of unified national States. There was a political cause: the rise of national feeling (particularly in the Western Kingdoms), partly in reaction against the divisions and miseries of civil war, partly in response to the challenge of foreign adventures and expansion; a feeling which demanded some centre of stability and loyalty, and was content to find that centre in the absolutism of a new monarchy ready to play on the strings of a feeling which suited its aims. There was an economic cause: the new development of trade and commerce fostered by the great discoveries (in Africa, America, and Asia), and the demand of traders and merchants for an effective central system of law and administration as the necessary condition of their economic success. There was an intellectual cause: the recovery of classical ideas, and especially the vogue and spread (the Reception as it is called) of the civil law of Rome, which its traditions of the sovereign city-state and the sovereign 'majesty' of the *princeps*. Finally there was a religious cause: the Reformation, which allying itself, or drawn into alliance, with the other tendencies of the time produced in England, and in some of the principalities of Germany, the system of the State-Church, independent of Rome and the Papacy, but dependent on the State and its prince, who thus added to his headship of the State a headship of the Church under the style of 'supreme governor' or *sumus episcopus.*

By the action of these causes the medieval Estates-State was turned into a national monarchical State; and a return was made to the classical unity of the Greek city-state and the Roman Empire, with their integration of human life in a single embracing and compelling community. The State now becomes, at any rate in the area of the Anglican and the Lutheran Reformation (but not, or not to the same extent, in the area of Calvinism), a Church as well as a State: it may even be said to become Society as well as the State, the one and total organisation of human life. A new emphasis on the notion of sovereignty—the old *majestas* of the Romans—accompanies this development. In contradistinction from the medieval Estates State, the national monarchical State of the sixteenth century gravitates towards autocracy and a system of absolutism: it is a 'Prince State'. It is true that the notion of sovereignty had already been apprehended and emphasized by medieval Popes. Bodin said of Innocent III that 'he knew best of all men the rights of sovereignty', and we have already seen that Boniface VIII could proclaim those rights in resounding terms. But this was a proclamation of the rights of a spiritual autocracy; and it was a new thing when Machiavelli and Bodin proclaimed the rights of secular sovereignty. Machiavelli was a 'statist', in the sixteenth-and seventeenth-century sense of the word; and for 'reason of State' he preached in his *Prince* (composed in 1515) the doctrine that 'the prince'—though he was thinking especially and mainly of a *nuovo principe,* seeking to create a new unity and order in a disordered Italy—may go to work against religion and morals in order to establish the absolute executive sovereignty which is the supreme end of the State, or rather the supreme means to its end of unity and order. Bodin was rather the legist; and in his *Republique* (first published in 1577) he lays it down that in every State there must exist a legislative sovereignty, or *majesté,* which may be defined as 'a supreme power over citizens and subjects, free from the laws' (though itself the author of laws)—except, he adds, 'fundamental laws' such as the Salic Law of France. Machiavelli may be said to arm the executive sovereign, and Bodin the legislative; but armed by both the sovereignty of the State is clad in full panoply, so far as concerns the temporal sphere of which they were both mainly thinking.

But what of the spiritual sphere? In his *Ecclesiastical Polity* (of which the first four books were published in 1594) Hooker enunciates two propositions. The first is that 'in a ... Christian State or Kingdom. . . . one and the self-same people are the Church and the Commonwealth'. In other words a *populus*, or nation, is at once an *ecclesia* and a *respublica:* all the members of the *respublica* are *ipso facto* members of the *ecclesia*, and citizenship and churchmanship are therefore coextensive: there is only one community, which is both a Church and a State, and which is both simultaneously and in one. This, as has already been noted, had also been the view of the Middle Ages; but Hooker's one community, instead of being universal, as the Middle Ages had thought, was a national body or *populus* living in a national State or kingdom. If this first proposition marks one great change, Hooker's second also marks another. 'It is expedient', he states, 'that their sovereign... in causes civil have also in ecclesiastical affairs a supreme powerful'. The supreme power of the civil sovereign is thus extended to the ecclesiastical sphere; and though we may think of 'a personal union' (as when one king rules two different kingdoms under two separate titles), the result remains that the same authority controls the Church and the State.

The sixteenth century thus issues in a sovereignty which, besides possessing an absolute executive and an equally absolute legislative authority in the temporal sphere, is also possessed of 'a supreme power', if not in 'the religious sphere' at any rate in 'ecclesiastical affairs' (it would be a nice distinction to determine the difference between the two, as it would equally be to determine the difference between the nature of supreme power in 'civil' and its nature in 'ecclesiastical' affairs). The idea grows of the State as the one form of human grouping, and of that State as controlled and determined by an absolute sovereignty which is its essence. But the idea did not go unchallenged; and indeed a number of challenges appeared. In England, although the Tudor commonwealth was largely shaped by its royal masters in the new pattern, there was always Parliament, to which Sir Thomas Smith, in his *De Republica Anglorum* (published in 1583), ascribes 'the most high and absolute power of the realm'; and during the course of the seventeenth century the power of this Parliament grew and grew, as there also grew along with it a system of local government, almost of a voluntary type, in the hands of unpaid Justices of the Peace. Again, in the area of the Roman Church the idea began to be developed, to meet the case of a Protestant sovereign (though it was not confined to that case), that the Church was a separate society with rights of its own inherent in its own distinctive nature. This idea attained its most notable expression in the theory of the Spanish Jesuit Suarez; and even in the days when the Spanish Inquisition was still serving as the instrument of Spanish monarchical policy, he was already teaching (in his *Tractatus* of 1611) a doctrine of 'Community' which not only made the church a *communitas politica vel mystica,* based on divine foundation and on that basis transcending communities of human invention, but also ranked some secular groups, such as knightly orders and local communities, in the category of 'perfect communities capable of political government', and thus placed them on an equal footing with the State. Last, but not least, in the area of Calvinism there was an abundance of dissidence from the idea of the all-conclusive State. Triumphant Calvinism might indeed proclaim the no less rigorous idea of the all-inclusive Church, answering the claims of autocracy by the similar claims of theocracy, and seeking to make kings 'God's silly vassals'. But Calvinism was seldom, or long, triumphant: it was generally the faith of minorities: and it gradually came into line with the 'sects' (Congregationalists, Baptists, and others) who stood for the cause of minorities and the rights of the 'gathered' Free Church based upon voluntary compact. This is a development which mainly belongs to the seventeenth century; but even earlier, in the latter half of the sixteenth, the struggling Calvinists of France had already challenged any idea of the all-inclusive State. The *Vindicaie Contra Tyrannos* of 1579 is a Huguenot argument against the *Machiavellani* of absolutism, and a plea for the contracted rights of the people; and the Huguenots were even ready to all themselves with old ideas of the 'Estates' State', alleging against the King of France the ancient rights both of the nobility of the provinces and of the commons of the cities, in the knowledge that Huguenot nobles and townsfolk were the necessary stay and support of their cause.

THE FRENCH REVOLUTION

The idea of the all-inclusive monarchical State, which had emerged in the sixteenth century, was still active in the eighteenth; and indeed it may seem to have attained its crown and consummation in the enlightened despots of the latter half of that century. The French Revolution, at the first blush, appears as a great reaction and a swing of the pendulum to the opposite extreme. It was a reaction and a swing of the pendulum, but by no means a reaction to the opposite extreme. It rejected the adjective 'monarchical'; but it retained the more crucial adjective 'all-inclusive'. National sovereignty (*la souveraineté nationale*) was a cardinal tenet of the Revolution; and national sovereignty meant the absolute might of the nation, acting through its representatives, or even through a single plebiscitary first consul or emperor, to do whatever it thought fit to do—regulating the Church; suppressing guilds and annulling combinations of workers; annihilating ancient provinces; controlling all education; in a word, omnicompetent.

From this point of view the Revolution was at one with enlightened despotism; and indeed it issued in the most enlightened (and the most despotic) of all the despots. But it had also its other side. It was based on the democratic idea that the nation should make, or any rate approve, a government representative of itself; and not only that, but that it should also make, or at any rate approve, its own constitution or permanent scheme of political life. (Not that the schemes proved permanent; but their very impermanence meant a renewal, again and again, of national making or national approval.) This was a genuine revolution. Moreover, the Revolution produced, as the very first of its fruits, a Declaration of the Rights of Man; and that declaration too was destined to repeated renewal. On the other hand, the Declaration of the Rights of Man may also be said to be little more than a catalogue of exceptions to the action of an otherwise absolute State. Nor is that all. The exceptions are only in favour of individuals, and not of groups or associations. It is possible to exaggerate the significance of article 10 of the Declaration, that 'nul ne doit être inquiété pour sees opinions, même religieuses, pourvu que leur manifestation ne trouble pas l'ordre public, établi par la loi'. But this article, at the best, can hardly be said to be a recognition of religious liberty. It is not so much the proviso or *pourvu* that matters: religious liberty must always make its account with the demands of public order. It is rather that the word *nul* is an individualistic word, and that religious liberty is not only, or even mainly, a liberty of individuals. It is indeed that; but it is also the liberty of religious *societies*—and not merely their liberty to worship, but also their liberty to educate, to persuade, and to conduct their mission. The French Revolution, not only in its immediate but also in its long-time effects, which have lasted into the twentieth century, has not been tender to religious societies; and if it has not disquieted the individual for his opinions, *mêmes religieuses,* it has not always left the group in peace. The revolutionary theory of France has generally remained a theory which, if it professes to be democratic, and to respect the rights of man, is still a theory of the State as the one organization—and the only organizer.

GERMAN ROMANTICISM AND IDEALISM

Different as is the German theory of the early nineteenth century from that of the French Revolution, it has some fundamental similarities; and indeed it was partly drawn from Rousseau (the prophet not of rights of man, but of the sovereignty of the general will) and from the spirit of the Revolution. But German theory has its own genius; and that genius may perhaps be expressed in the word 'romanticism'. It was the tendency of German thinkers to make a romance or *Märchen* out of the State and the *Volk* or Folk (which is something different from *la nation*) that stood behind the State. They were in the mood depicted by Heine: 'Ich weiß nicht was soll es bedeuten' (there generally *was* a haze about their thought), but

Ein Märchen aus altern Zeiten

Das kommt mir nicht aus dem Sinn

The romantic thought of Germany began by idealizing the Folk, primarily the early Teutonic folk 'of old times', and then, by a natural extension (the more natural in view of national reaction against the French Empire) the German Folk of the present. It regarded the Folk as a maker of folk-lore, of folk-songs and folk-music, of folk-law, and of a general folk-intution-into-the-world-and-life (*Weltanschauung*): it made the Folk an entity, a being, even a person, which sang, made ballads, created law, and directed the march of history. Well and good, we may say—so long as the Folk is not also the State, or still retains some being apart and distinct from the State; so long as Folk is another word (which we may not like, but may allow to serve) for what we prefer to call 'Society'—the community acting for itself in its own general social way, and as such distinct from the State with its particular and legal way of action. But this was not the line which was followed by German thought. The romanticized Folk, just because it is made an entity, a being, and even a person, can readily be identified (at any rate by the synthetic mind) with the entity, being, or person of the State—that is to say with the Government—that is to say, when we come to the last resort, with the person of the Governor (*der Herrscher)*. This is what actually happened: this is Hegelianism, on its political side; and here the political romanticism of Germany touches one of the trends of the political realism of France—the trend towards *souveraineté nationale* and the vesting of that sovereignty in a single plebiscitary ruler called first consul or emperor. (But there were other trends also in France.)

The political philosophy of Hegelianism, an outcome of German romanticism, may be summarily regarded from two different but complementary points of view. It lifts the Folk up into being a Mind, and not only a Mind, but also and incarnation of the Eternal Mind. It pulls the Folk down into being a State, and not only a State, but also a monarchical State of the Prussian type. From the first point of view we may see the eternal consciousness expressing itself. in the course of its eternal process of movement or 'becoming', through Folk-minds which are the operative organs of God in time and space, and indeed are God Himself as He operates in time and space. These Minds are therefore divine: as such, they cover the whole range of life; as such, again, they are final and right, within their space and time, for everything which they cover. From the second point of view we see the Folk-mind, while still remaining an organ and expression of the Eternal Mind, identified first with the general being and action of *the* State, and then, by a further extension, with the particular being and action of *a* State, a particular form of State, a monarchical State of the Prussian type.

To understand the first of the two identifications just made—the identification of the Folk-mind (or *volksgeist*) with the general being and action of the State—we must turn to the Hegelian method, which is a method that goes, as it were, in threes: first the thesis, then the antithesis, and then the synthesis of both in a higher unity. In the sphere of moral and political philosophy the thesis is Law, or the external realization of Right; in other words. it is a system of rules for controlling outward relations—partly in the field of family-life, with its rules of marriage and the descent of property, but mainly in the greater field of 'bourgeois' relationship (*die bürgerliche Gesellschaft*) the field of industry and commerce, with its nexus of economic interests and all the rules implied in the nexus. This Law, or external realization of Right, is the mark and constituent force of the State in the lower and cruder form in which it first appears: indeed we may even say that, apart from the field of family-life, the State in its lower and cruder form is simply the system of 'bourgeois' relationships *regarded as producing law* (from and through the necessities of its nexus of interests) *and as controlling itself by the law which it produces.* So far of the thesis of Law. The antithesis is Morality, or the internal realization of Right: in other words, it is the system of rules made by the individual conscience for the control of its inward self. The divergence between the thesis of outward Law and the antithesis of inward Morality demands a synthesis and reconciliation. This is to be found in a third conception: that of Social Ethics (*Sittlichkeit*), which consists of the whole system of rules, disciplines, and influences—the union of the legal and the moral—controlling in harmony the whole of life both inward and outward. The vehicle of this system of rules, disciplines, and influences is the fully developed State; and thus the State, in its lower form the vehicle of Law, becomes in its higher form the vehicle of a system of Social Ethics. But if the developed State is the vehicle of such a system, so transcending Law and Morality, and so uniting them both in a single spiritual texture, this State may be regarded as merged in, and may be identified with, the Folk which is the operative organ of the eternal consciousness; or vice versa (and this is perhaps the better mode of expression) the Folk may be regarded as merged in, and may thus be identified with, the general being of the developed State.

This is the first identification. The second follows; and by this second identification the Mind of the Folk, already merged in the general being of the State (in its higher and developed form), is further merged in the particular being of a particular form of State, the Prussian monarchical form; which means, in effect, the identification of the Mind of the Folk with the mind of a Prussian King. How was this second merger achieved? The answer is that the essence of the higher form of State consists in its being a higher and reconciling unity, and that such unity is best secured in 'an active individual, in the will of a decreeing individual, in monarchy'. The King stands above the play of 'bourgeois' relationships and outside the nexus of economic interests: he is the organ of impartiality—but above all he is the focus of unity.

If this summary account is just, it follows that Hegelianism is a version, and possibly the extremist version, of the unified 'Society-State'. Hegelianism make the State the vehicle of a system of social ethics, which is law and morality in one; and by making it the vehicle of such a system it makes it all-inclusive. It identifies the State, so regarded and so conceived, with the Folk which is an operative organ of God; and it then proceeds to identify this Folk-State with the monarch, who thus becomes an organ of God in his turn. Finally, by deifying this Folk-State-Monarch—by making the Folk-State God's organ, and the Monarch, through it, God's commissary—it makes the amalgam absolute: absolute both within and without. The amalgam is absolute within, because it admits no democratic rights of the collective people and no civil rights of the individual man and citizen: the collective people is absorbed in and contained by the Monarch, and the individual man and citizen is absorbed in and contained by the State's system of Social Ethics. Absolute within, the amalgam is equally absolute without, and it is so because—being deified, and therefore infinite and unlimited—it knows no international society of States and none of the rules and duties imposed by such a society upon its constituent members. There is just the solitude of the State; and the State is all in all.

None the less, there are elements in Hegelianism which look in other directions, and may be pleaded in aid of other causes, than that of the absolute State. There is, for instance, the idea of the system of 'bourgeois' relationships (*die bürgerliche Gesellschaft*); the idea of the play and counterplay of its economic interests; the idea of its connexion with the development of law. This, as we shall have occasion to notice, was a starting-point of Marxian theory; and indeed it is a commonplace that Marx built on Hegelian foundations—even though, as he said himself, he had first turned them 'upside down' by substituting the process of Matter, and the conception of dialectical materialism, for Hegel's process of Mind, and his conception of dialectical idealism. But however it might be modified or turned 'upside down' for the purpose, Hegelianism could certainly be used to support not only the cause of absolutism, but also that of socialism. Perhaps this could be done the more easily because there is, after all, some measure of kinship between the two, and because, in some of its forms, socialism tends to the absolute. On the other hand, there are also elements in Hegelianism which may be pleaded in aid of the cause of liberalism; and here there can be no question of any kinship with absolutism. The *political* theory of Hegel is indeed inimical to liberalism; but his general *philosophical* theory is none the less not wholly unfavourable to liberal ideas. His conception of the eternal debate of thesis and antithesis, and of the opposition of thought to thought in the operation of Mind, involves the necessary conclusion that debate and discussion must always be at work in any society of minds, now emphasizing *this* idea, and now emphasizing *that*, but always seeking to achieve a synthesis, or, as we also say, in one of our common English terms, 'to find a compromise'. If we think of political parties as representing thesis and antithesis, and of Parliament as seeking to find a reconciling synthesis, we can defend parliamentary democracy in terms of Hegelian ideas. We can even argue that Hegel himself was untrue to his own ideas when he became a political absolutist. He failed to see that the sovereign thing in political thought, as in all the thought of the world, is the *process* of thought itself, as it works its way between the clashing rocks of thesis and antithesis. Distrusting, or rather forgetting, the *process* (and the essence of liberalism is reliance upon it), he turned instead to an *organ* or instrument; and for the natural synthesis of debate he substituted the artificial synthesis of 'a decreeing individual'.

ENGLISH INDIVIDUALISM

In the course of the argument there have appeared a variety of expressions of the unified and all-inclusive 'Society-State': first the classical City-State; then the theocratic Church-State of the dreams of Boniface VIII; then the Prince-State of the sixteenth century; then the Nation-State of the French Revolution, with its assertion of national sovereignty; and then the monarchical Folk-State of German romanticism. All along—from the first explosive emergence of Christianity to the Jesuit and Calvinist thinkers of the seventeenth century, and from them to our own days—all along there has been at work a leaven of Christian thought; and that leaven has been a cause of constant fermentation. 'Render... unto Caesar the things which are Caesar's; and unto God the things that are God's.' Sometimes, it is true, the leaven has ceased to be true to its nature: it has been a rennet that curdles rather than a leaven of fermentation: it has sought to bind Church and State together in one inclusive whole, either, at one extreme, by making the Church also a State, and thus instituting some form of theocracy, or, at the other extreme, by making the State also a Church, and thus arming the ruler of the State with a final and supreme power in affairs ecclesiastical. On the whole, however, and in the main, the influence of Christian thought, in its long-time operation, has been the influence of a solvent, which has made for the opening of any 'closed' system of social organization; and this is true not only of the reformed branches of Christianity, but also (and this in spite of the Inquisition and the Index) of the general spirit and tendency of the Roman Catholic Church since the age of the Reformation and the Counter-Reformation.

But there is also a secular factor which must be taken into the reckoning when we seek to trace the development of the relation between State and Society and the growth of men's ideas about the nature of their relation. That factor is the individualism (but it is something more than individualism, and the name is really a misnomer, for there is something more in question than individuals and their rights) which for the last three centuries and more has inspired so much of English life, not only 'within the realm', but also in the many settlements planted 'overseas' on the continent of America and under the southern stars. The matter is not only a matter of Britain: it is also a matter of the whole British Commonwealth: it is even a matter of the United States of America, which was cradled in the Commonwealth. Here, however, we must restrict our scope to Britain, and even to England, for it was in the conditions of English life in the seventeenth century that the temper of life and the method of action of Anglo-Saxon 'individualism' began to develop.

The England of the sixteenth century had cherished the conception of the one undivided commonwealth ('the very and true commonweal', as one writer calls it)—with religious life under a State-Church; with economic life regulated by a system of State-protection at the ports, and by a State labour code (the Statute of Artificers of 1563) in the towns and shires; and even with moral life supervised by the courts of the State-Church, which, punished sexual immorality and other moral offences. 'This realm of England', so runs the beginning of the Statute for the Restraint of Appeals (1533), 'is...governed by one supreme head and king,...unto whom a body politic, compact of all sorts and degrees of people divided in terms and by names of spirituality and temporalty, be bounded and ought to bear, next to God, a natural and humble obedience.' Some of the lawyers went even farther: instead of soaking of a body politic annexed to (but yet distinct from) the King, they spoke of the King himself as having, or being, a body politic, of which the 'members' were his subjects, and in which he and they were so united that they formed one corporation. We already begin to see the Leviathan of Hobbes when we read in Plowden's reports (about the year 1550) that 'he and his subjects together compose the corporation,...and he is incorporated with them, and they with him, and he is the head and they are the members, and he has the sole government of them'.

English history in the seventeenth century is the history of the disintegration of this inclusive corporation, or rather of the progressive differentiation, and the progressive liberation, of bodies of opinion and bodies of men which move outside the orbit of the 'body politic'. But the inclusive 'commonwealth', the single 'body politic' the one 'corporation', had never been so united as it is assumed to be in the statutes and law reports of the sixteenth century. There were two inheritances from the Middle Ages which could not be absorbed in the body of Levia than. The first was the system of the common low, and the legal profession behind that system. The system of the common law was a firm deposit of rules and processes largely intended, and generally effective, for the protection of the rights of the subject: a deposit too hard, and too unmalleable, to be dissolved by any new absolutism. The legal profession, pivoted on the Bar, and on barristers who had long been organized in their own voluntary Inns of Court, was largely an autonomous profession, engaged (along with judges who had themselves been barristers in their day) in developing rules of law and methods of legal procedure on its own professional lines, and confronting the King and his ministers with the collective weight of its professional opinion. But there were also a second inheritance. This was a 300-year-old Parliament, with its own deposited procedure and its own system of ideas (largely, it is true, derived from the lawyers, who had always played a large part in Parliament from the earliest days of that 'High Court'); and this too confronted the King and his ministers with its collective weight.

This legal and political basis of the common law and the high court of Parliament provided the ground and the opportunity for the new developments which began to appear in the seventeenth century. They are developments which are partly religious and partly economic; but the two are interconnected. Between them they achieved, gradually and almost unconsciously, a progressive differentiation of the unified common wealth and a progressive liberation of social groups.

The great religious fact is the existence and growth of the 'free churches'. It is true that the free churches, as groups or societies, only achieved recognition of their right to exist, and to assemble for worship, by the Toleration Act of 1689: it is true that their members, as individuals, only won the right to full citizenship by the repeal of the Test and Corporation Acts in 1828, and only gained admission to the two old Universities by the Universities Tests Act of 1871: it is true that it was a long slow process, covering almost the whole of three centuries, which at last established the equality of the members of the free churches with the members of the State-Church. But the thing that matters is the struggle itself, even more than the achievement. From the reign of Elizabeth onwards the free churches were always there, and always seeking to vindicate the principle of the freedom of the religious group against the idea and practice of the inclusive 'body politic'. Nonconformity was to the English national state what early Christianity was to the Roman imperial state: indeed we may even say that, never having been adopted by the English State, as early Christianity was by the Roman empire, it was even more. It steadily stood for the principle that the State had nothing to do with religion, so far as churches other than the State-Church were concerned: it vindicated the conception of religion as something apart from, and independent of, the State: and it thus prepared the way for the general principle and practice of the distinction between State and Society. Nonconformity is wrongly judged as a religion of individualism, and as a simple plea for the individual right of the solitary conscience. It had indeed a solitary quality and a tough fibre of individualism; but it had also something more, and something at least as great. It was a religion of 'the society' (Baptist, Quaker, or Methodist), and a plea for the collective right of the freely 'gathered' group. Here, as else where, what is called individualism is something more than individualism; and if the obverse side is the unit, the reverse side is the group.

If religious developments thus followed the banner of Free Religion, economic development similarly followed the banners of Free Trade and Free Labour—free trade, as against the old State-protectionism: free labour, as against the old State labour-code. Nonconformity prepared the way for this trend of economic development, partly in virtue of the simple fact that it was vindicating a parallel cause in its own field of religion, and partly because it was Nonconformists who largley constituted the trading class which demanded free and were that back-bone of the working class which later demanded free labour. Free Trade—which is here to be understood not in its narrow sense of freedom from the imposition of traffis, but in the broad sense in which it means the freedom of trade and industry to develop themselves, without state-regulation by means of exclusively chartered companies and restrictive monopolies—Free Trade in this broader sense is anterior to the repeal of the Corn Laws in 1846. It is a cause as old as the parliaments of the reign of Charles I: it won some triumphs after the Restoration of 1660: it may be said to have consolidated itself with the Revolution of 1688. It may seem to be pure individualism, and indeed it is more individualistic than the parallel cause of Free Labour; but at any rate it encouraged the action of social (and not merely private) enterprise, and it promoted the formation of voluntary social groups, or companies, for the conduct of such enterprise. (Lloyd's and the London Stock Exchange, both originally associations based on the social life of city coffee-houses in the eighteenth century, may serve as examples of these groups.) The cause of Free Labour, struggling for existence in the eighteenth century, emerged to light in 1824-5, with the repeal or drastic modification of the Combination Laws of 1799-1800; and here, especially in the subsequent growth of trade unions and their organization, the collective side of a demand which begins with a claim of the rights of men is obvious to every eye. Free Labour means the claim of a right for organized labour groups to bargain collectively and in the last resort to strike collectively; and Free Labour doubles its group production when it creates, by way of reaction and answer, organized employer-groups on the other side. Taken together, Free Trade and Free Labour mark another large development of Society, paralleled to the religious development, and another stage in the process of differentiation between Society and the State.

Such was the general process which began its course in the conditions of English life in the seventeenth century, and such were the results towards which it moved. We may therefore agree with a modern historian that 'the main feature of British history since the seventeenth century has been the remoulding of a State by a powerful Society', which has at once differentiated itself from the State and then acted upon it and even in it. (Parties, after all, are social formations: the Whig party began its life in a city inn, just as Lloyd's and the Stock Exchange began in coffee-houses; and the social formations called parties, though they belong to the area of society, act in and upon the State.) We may also agree, when we reflect on the Virginia and Massachusetts 'Companies' which laid the foundations of what is now the United States of America, that 'the expansion of England in the seventeenth century was an expansion of Society, and not of the State'. The general process, at home and abroad, was a process by which Society grew round the State—surrounded it indeed, with growths—and yet left it as the hard core and legal substance of organization, affecting all the growths, and affected by all the growths, in a constant interaction.

MARXIAN SOSIALISM: HEGEL TO LENIN

The very term 'socialism' would seem to suggest another and perhaps alternative way of the disengagement of society. But does the theory of Marxian socialism, as it was developed in Germany during the nineteenth century, and afterwards amplified and exemplified in Russia during the first half of the twentieth, correspond to the suggestion of the term? Names and terms can be veils as well as mirrors; and we shall do well to study the actual evolution of socialism before we attach any credence to the suggestion of its name.

The evolution begins in the theory of Hegel's *Philosophy of Right*, and especially, as has already been noticed, in Hegel's conception of 'burgess' or bourgeois society. It was on this theory and this conception that Marx and Engels built, as Lenin, in his turn, built again on the structure which they had raised. According to Hegel's theory the system of 'bourgeois society'—or, as we may also call it, the 'nexus of economic relationship', or the 'community of economic interests'—was something which supervened, in the course of the dialectic of history, on the original and natural kin-group for the purpose of providing more abundant means of subsistence than the kin-group was able to provide, and of doing so by means of the institutions of private property and accumulation of capital. The ways of providing the means of subsistence being various, bourgeois society accordingly became a various system of different classes, or orders, or estates. Hegel distinguishes three of these classes: the class of those engaged in dealing with the immediate products of nature; the class of those engaged in the further manufacture of such products, and in the general operations of distribution; and the class of those concerned in securing the general interests of the whole society. Tracing the development of this system of classes, Hegel proceeds to argue that it turns itself, in the process of its development, into what may be called the first or lower form of the State, and does so by the process of evolving a body of laws. These laws, however, represent only the *de facto* rules of the actual proceeding of the society: they follow the lines of the natural course of social development, which, if it is natural, is not necessarily just: they solidify and sanction, rather than elevate and control, the existing system of order. Along with this body of laws, and in order to give it support, the system of classes or orders—turning itself still further into a form of State—also develops an organized police, and with it adds a further sanction and a firmer solidity to the existing order. Laws and police—these are the State, and these are the foundations and pillars of 'bourgeois society'.

So far, and if he had stopped at this point, Hegel was handing the keys of the State to the impending siege of the marxians. He had spoken of bourgeois society turning itself into a form of a State, and buttressing itself by a body of laws and an organized police in order to consecrate an existing system of economic order which was a system of private property and the accumulation of capital. But Hegel's argument went farther; and it reached a higher stage. He argued that in the later and developed form of State (which would seem to be identical with the Prussia of his day) two further things were added; one of them from above, and the other from below. From above there came the reconciling and the humanizing force of a system of State protection and a system of State education, the one regulating the clashes and the other supplementing the defects of the bourgeois system of classes. From below there came the development of corporations or guilds, each inspired by a sense of honour and a pride in good workmanship; each, accordingly, moved by a disposition to do its best for the benefit of the whole; and all thus concurring to provide a new moral root of the State and the foundation of a system of 'Social Ethics' (Incidentally, it should be noted that in his view of the nature and functions of corporations Hegel may be regarded as a parent of the corporative State of Italian Fascism as well as of the socialist State of the Russian Soviet system; and it should be noted that, just as in Italy a century later, his corporations are all to be authorized or chartered—for 'no association has existence and place in society, except such as are legally constituted and acknowledged'.) It follows that from above and below the original bourgeois society is endowed with a new moral character; and on this basis the true State, the State in its developed and rational form, can build that system of social ethics which, as has already been noted, is the synthesis of the external rules of bourgeois society with the inner morality of conscience. Elsewhere, Hegel argues (he means elsewhere than in Prussia, and he refers in particular to England), the mere play of Society is left to its unchecked action, with no true State for its guidance, but merely with a parliament which, if it is called representative, is representative only of social factors and economic interests; and here there ensues, on the one hand, an unregulated accumulation of wealth, and on the other, the depression of a rabble (*Pöbel,* or proletariate) below any decent standard of subsistence. It follows that a society of this order does not possess, for all its accumulation of capital, the means of preventing the miseries of poverty: it is accordingly driven to colonization and commerce with backward territories, and it slides into what, in the language of a later day, is styled by the name of 'imperialism'. The moral is that a bourgeois society which fails to rise to the level of a true State, by attaining a system of social ethics, is a poor thing likely to perish, weakened by its own abundance.

Omit Hegel's theory of the 'true State' (but that is a large omission), and you have here the essential elements of Marxianism. The nature of the building which can be constructed from these elements is clear from the argument of Lenin's pamphlet on 'the State and Revolution'. That argument may be resumed in some five propositions. (1) Society, in the sense of economic society, is driven by the collision of its opposing interests to institute a State, *seemingly* above itself, which will moderate the force of collision by keeping it within the bounds of a form of law and order; and professional armed forces, serving in lieu of a 'self-acting armed organization of the population', are attached by it to that State. (2) But since this State is the result of collision, it is *actually,* and as a matter of fact, no more—and no less—than the strongest of the colliding interests, the interest of the class engaged in manipulating accumulated capital; and thus, instead of standing above society, a State of this order is really immersed in the play society and dominated by its dominant interest—being, in effect, the organized domination of the strongest class, which is that of the capitalists, for the purpose of exploiting the weakest class, which is that of the manual workers. (3) Even the democratic Republic, with its system of universal suffrage, is still a means of capitalist domination: indeed, it is 'the best possible political form for capitalism', since it enables the omnipotence of wealth to assert itself indirectly—but all the more effectively—through the bribery of officials and representatives, the control of the Press, and the influence of the Stock Exchange on the policy of government. (4) On the other hand, the process of economic development, as it expands the range of its operations and multiplies the number of its operatives, is steadily tending to lift the proletariate—that is to say, the manual workers in urban industries—into the position of the strongest class, closely knit together by propinquity and solibly organized in their own unions; and thus, though the memocratic

Republic is 'the best possible political form the capitalism', it is also 'the best form of the State for the proletariate under capitalism', since it gives its members the best opportunity of organizing themselves for political objects. (5) So organized, the urban proletariate, in the day when it is the strongest and conscious of its own strength, will capture the State from capitalism by revolution and the use of force, as capitalism in its day had captured the State from the other interests and classes of society by the same method and the same means. It is all a matter of collision. The grinding of collision is the process of history; and the results of the grinding are at once inevitable and right.

So far the argument of Lenin is an analysis of the historical process and an interpretation of the past. But history does not stop; and the past flows into the future. What does Lenin see when he puts his hand to his brow and under it scans the horizon of the future? He sees no perpetuity of the proletarian State of the workers. The proletariate will maintain the State for a time, but only for a time. It will maintain it temporarily for the two necessary—but also transitory—purposes of suppressing the capitalist class and guiding the semi-proletariate (the peasant and the lower middle classes) along the path of reconstruction. These two purposes once achieved, the State—even the proletarian State, which will now have done its work and exhausted its mission—will 'wither away'. In the new era there will be no classes; and since the State, by its nature, is an organ of class (this class or that, but always *some* class) there will be no State. There will be nothing but society, community, communism—a society, community, communism destitute of classes and free from even the shadow of force; a society, community, communism where there are neither lions nor lambs, and all are 'accustomed to observing the elementary conditions of social existence without force and without subjection'. Thus the proletarian State—the State of 'socialism'—is only a phase. The consummation of history, on the horizon of the future, is the negation of the State, even in its socialist form, and the emergence of a pure society no longer vexed by collision, but knit together in the spontaneous harmony of a natural and unforced communism. The end of socialism, is, we may say, the ending of socialism (for even socialism presupposes the State), and the inauguration in its place—if also by its means—of a perpetual reign of pure society under the style of communism.

It may thus be said that Marxian Socialism, in Lenin's interpretation, means the use of the categories of 'State' and 'Society' for the purpose of argument; but the argument which they serve is an argument (1) that there has never been any real distinction of State and Society during the centuries of struggle (on the contrary the State has always been, and must always be, the organ of a social interest), and (2) that in the final millennium there will be no distinction at all, because there will be no State. In neither phase, the pre-millennial or the millennial, is there any room for distinction between Society and the State. *Omnia reducuntur ad unum*: it would be Manichaeism, as Pope Boniface VIII said in 1302, to allege two principles. In the pre-millennial phase the State is immersed in Society, and is indeed a function of Society—capitalistic when Society is capitalistic and under the dominance of the capitalist class; proletarian when Society is proletarian and under the dominance of the proletariat; but always a function of Society and indistinguishable from Society. In the millennial phase the State has gone: unity drops the disguise (which was never more than a disguise) of its Janus mask: there is one organization of human life, and only one.

But it is not always easy to distinguish the millennial from the pre-millennial in the theory of Marxian Socialism. There pre-millennial, in its last stage of the socialist State or proletarian dictatorship, has a way of becoming itself millennial. (The future will come, and will be better than the present; but meanwhile the present is good.) If we stop our inquiry, as perhaps we may, at the stage of the socialist State, it would appear that Marxianism, like the doctrine of Hegel, combines and confuses State and Society in a single and total organization of all human life. It only differs from the doctrine of Hegel in abandoning the idea of a controlling system of social ethics in favour of the idea of a controlling system of social economics—which means, in effect, that Marxianism stops short at Hegel's first or lower form of State, and refuses to proceed to the true or higher State, in its developed and rational form. Apart from this difference—and it is great difference—Marxianism and Hegelianism both repeat the idea of the unified Society-State which is already apparent in the Greek *polis* and has continued to recur through subsequent ages. Marxianism, or Leninism, as it confronts us today, presents again the picture of an omnicompetent Society-State, which embraces the whole of life; and just as Plato would have had his 'republic' control theology and aesthetics, as well as economics, so the Union of Socialist Soviet Republics aims at providing a new form of faith and a new style of worker's art and literature, in addition to regulating all economic life, agricultural as well as industrial.

FRENCH SYNDICALISM AND ITS TREND

The theory of French syndicalism has generally followed a different line. Here there has been a genuine revolt against the revolutionary doctrine of 1789—the doctrine of the national State, entirely controlled by a single *souveraineté nationale*, as the one organization and sole organizer of life. It is true that a form of syndicalist theory first appeared in England, during the period of the Reform Bill of 1832; partly in the pacific teaching of Robert Owen, who advocated the organization of trades in associations and the union of these associations, through their representatives, in a central national council; and partly in the more militant doctrine of William Benbow and other extremists, who preached a general, strike or 'holiday month' and founded (but failed to establish) a Grand National Consolidated Trades Union for the purpose. But the general theory of syndicalism, in the course of its development, became specifically French; and its first clear prophet, who may also be said to have remained the chief of its prophets, was Proudhon (1809-65).

A printer and proof-reader by profession, but turning also in his later years to the career of a journalist and author, Proudhon expounded the doctrine, first that the economic order was anterior in time and superior in importance to the political, and secondly that *droit économique*, based upon and constituted by the principal of *mutulité*, was similarly anterior and superior to *droit politique*, which ought to be deduced from, and should be a reflection of, the economic principle of mutuality. The essence of the economic order, in his view (as that view was expounded in his work *Du Principe fédératif* of 1863), was federal essence: the order, he held, was by its nature *une fédération mutualiste,* composed of occupational groups freely formed for the purpose of production and exchange and freely cohering in virtue of their mutual service and benefit. (Proudhon was thus attracted to the idea of the social contract, which, he wrote, 'should become in reality, and not merely in Rousseauist abstraction, the basis of society'.) Such an economic order—federative and 'mutualist'—issued by its nature in an economic rule of right, or *droit économique,* of reciprocal service and proportionate exchange between its constituent groups; and it was, with its correlative rule of right, the major substance and inner core of human interest. True, indeed, there had also developed, in the course of time, a political order, which represented 'the social body in its unity and in its relations with the world outside': true, again, this political order had its own *droit politique,* or political rule of right, for the regulation of the social body in its unity and its relations. But the functions of the political order were subordinate, and might even be called sub-functions; and the political rule of right should be derived from, and should correspond to, the principles of the economic rule—with the citizens of the political order voting according to their occupational divisions, and with a system of political federation (here Proudhon thought in terms of 'autonomous' communes and 'sovereign' provinces) as the proper corollary of the natural and spontaneous federalism of the economic order.

This is all a clear reaction against the revolutionary principle of a single and indivisible France. A division is made between the economic order and the political: the political is relegated to a lower plane, in which it is a reflection of and a derivation from the economic; and within both orders a plural system of federalism is enthroned. But the simple and cardinal principle of Proudhon is the division between the economic and the political order. He makes things 'two and two, one against another': he sets the economic order and its *droit économique* over against the political order and its *droit politique*. The late theory of syndicalism, as it has since developed in France from the seed sown by Proudhon, and as it appears in the polemics of Georges Sorel's *Réflexions sur la Violence* (1908) and the legal argument of Duguit's *Traité de droit constitutionnel* (1911), has proceeded, consciously or unconsciously, on the lines already traced by Proudhon in his doctrine of the economic order and its *droit économique*. The syndicalists, opposing themselves to the revolutionary idea of the single and sovereign nation, have preferred and championed the idea of a prior and higher economic society; and they have conceived this society not, like the German Marxists, in terms of colliding classes, but in terms of occupational groups, complementary to one another and knit together in a federal union by the fact of mutual need and the bond of mutual service. Syndicalists and Marxists might have the same goal: Proudhon might speak of *une souveraineté effective des masses travailleuses*, as Marx and his followers spoke of a proletarian dictatorship; and French syndicalists of the twentieth century (repeating Benbow's scheme of 1834) might proclaim the 'myth', or even embrace the policy, of the general strike, as the Marxists embraced a similar policy of revolution. But there is still a world of difference between the general climate of syndicalism and the general climate of Marxianism—the difference between a federal society of complementary occupations and a warring society (which is *not* a society) of colliding classes. The difference shows itself clearly when we turn to the notion of *droit économique* propounded by Proudhon and elaborated by Duguit. The very word *droit* is significant: there is right in question as well as the might of conflicting opposites; and the theory of syndicalism—the theory of *mutualité*, with each autonomous group of producers freely exchanging its products for those of other groups on a just basis of reciprocal equality—has been an influence in the development of juridical thought in France.

There remains, however, a dualism, or more exactly a scheme of dyarchy, at the root of syndicalist theory. The political order and its *droit politique* stand by the side of the economic order and its system of *droit économique* with no clear delimitation. It is easy to begin with the simple postulate of 'two and two' one against another'. On the one hand, you assume a federal economic order of *syndicats ouvriers,* based on a primary *droit économique,* and you suppose that in this order each of the units will be autonomous, though you also suppose the existence of some central federal organ—even if it be only a statistical committee—competent to suggest how much each unit is to produce, and for how much of the product of other units it should exchange its product. On the other hand you assume a political order (also federal, as far as possible—but you admit that the degree of federalism will be less than it is in the economic order), based on the secondary *droit politique,* and dealing with the same society of men regarded as a *corps social* or unity; and you suppose that the agents of this order will handle the things which belong to unity, such as education within and foreign relations without. But what is to follow on this beginning? Some may wish to move boldly ahead; to extend the range of economic federalism almost to the extinction of the unitary State, or indeed of any form of State; to urge, as the great means of that extension, the preaching and the waging of a general strike for the paralysis of the political order. Their policy will be, 'Let the coercive machinery of the State be made to disappear, and let its place be taken by the mutual and freely co-operating services of workers, traders, teachers, and the rest'. Others, less radical or more cautious, may refuse even to peach, and still more to practice, the general strike; and instead of seeking to extinguish the State in favour of a self-acting society of services, they may content themselves with an attempt to reconcile and unite the political order with the economic. Their policy will be, 'Let us introduce elements from the economic order into the political; let us base the political parliament on electorates composed of *syndicates owriers,* or at any rate let us institute an economic parliament (which may conveniently be called an economic council, and be vested at the least with consultative powers) by the side of the political parliament'.

But whatever its forms and its oscillations, the ideas and trends of French Syndicalism have exerted an influence not only in France but also in England and Italy. Distinguishing the economic order from the political, and emphasizing its federal nature and the autonomy of its federated units, syndicalism has partly challenged, and partly even modified, the regours of Marxian Socialism. In England the syndicalist leaven may be said to have had two effects. One, which has now disappeared, was the philosophy of 'Guild Socialism'—a sort of Franco-German mixture: German in its 'socialism', and in vesting the State with the ownership of the means of production; French in remitting to the 'Guild', or rather to a number of guilds, the management of those means, and French again, though with some modifications, in its theory of the two Parliaments, an economic parliament based on guilds for the affairs of economic society, and a political parliament based on local constituencies for the affairs of the State. The other effect—if indeed it be an effect, and not a native and independent development (we have to remember that syndicalist ideas appeared in England as early as 1834, and that an organized system of powerful trade unions is an old and indigenous growth)—is the crossing and modification of the Socialist or Labour party and programme by ideas and policies of a sysndicalist character. The Socialist or Labour party is largely based on the adherence and subscription of trade unions: by its side stands the Trades Union Congress as a central federal organ, economic in character, but also interested in politics (just as, conversely, the Labour party is political in character, but also interested, and deeply interested, in economics); and there is thus a criss-cross and interfusion which is confusing in theory and yet works in practice. As with the party, so with the programme. The programme has been, and still remains, a programme of the nationalization of industries and their final control by representatives of the community; but it has also been, and still is, a programme of the association of the various grades of the workers, both managerial and manual, in the conduct and the administration of their respective industries. There is thus accommodation and compromise—there is even what may be called a 'margin of impression'—in the English adjustment between socialism and syndicalism.

The influence of syndicalism in Italy has been of a different character. It may be said to have followed two main directions, affecting, on the one hand, the Vatican and the policy of the Papacy, and, on the other, the Quirinal and the policy of the Italian

State from 1922 to 1939. The two directions differed: indeed they differed profoundly; but they were united by one common feature. Alike in the Papal Encyclical *Quadragesimo Anno* (1931) and in the various and multifarious secular laws of the Fascist period there is a common use of the idea of 'corporativism'. Corporativism may be defined as syndicalism writ double. It is a philosophy of the economic group as consisting not only of workers, but also of employers, both of them acting together, in a double organization which is somehow also single, to render the service and enjoy the benefits of their particular branch of economic activity. As such a philosophy it has pitted itself against the two extremes of *laissez-faire* individualism and 'regulatory socialism'. But corporativism itself has its own extremes and oppositions. At one end of the scale is the *ordo* of the Papal Encyclical, with the employers and employed of each *ordo* freely collaborating in the production of goods and the rendering of services, and with all the *ordines* freely joined in concord for the promotion of the common good; and here the keynote is freedom—freedom for the members of each *ordo* to choose whatever form they prefer; freedom, too, tor the whole society to recover the riches of an articulated system of social groups, *per diversi generis consociationes composite evoluta,* which in 'an earlier age' (apparently the Middle Age) was interposed between the individual and the State, easing and smoothing their relations and contacts. At the other end of the scale is—or was—the *corporazione* of the Fascist system: an institution, it is true, which similarly embraced employers and employed, but an institution created by the State, controlled by the State, and intended, by definition, to serve as 'an organ of the administration of the State'. The corporativism of the Fascist régime was a pseudo-syndicalist stucco hastily applied and superficially attached to a structure of *étatisme*; and all its paraphernalia of vocational groups and vocational representation, Proudhonist as it might appear, was at the antipodes from Proudhon. The history of ideas may be a history of their degradation. Few ideas, in any country, have been so degraded as the idea of syndicalism was in Fascist Italy.

In itself, and apart from its 'corporative' transformations whether Catholic or Fascist, syndicalism has made its contribution to the development of human thought. It has been a force which has made for the disengaging of the concept of Society from the concept of the State. But it has also done more—or less—and this in two ways. In the first place, it has tended to confine the idea of Society to one of its aspects or fields, and to make it essentially, or even solely, a matter of economics. Society is wider than that. It *is* a matter of economics; but it is also a matter of religion, of education, science, and culture, of charity in its broadest sense, of the play of the faculties in amusement or the enjoyment of leisure, and of all the activities which the mind of man proposes for the various purposes of its own free exercise. In the second place, syndicalism has sometimes tended, in its extremer forms, to push its conception of Society almost to the length of denying and destroying the State. There is room for both State and Society; and as long as human nature remains the same, and men are men, the State will always be with us. The political order has its necessity: it is at least as natural as the economic; and it may even be said to be prior, in the sense that it is the necessary condition of the existence of any form of economic order. There were States before there were guilds: and there could not have been any guilds—or, for that matter, any property, or any production, or any exchange—unless there had been a rule-making State in terms of whose rules such things could develop.

8

The Study of Politics

Understanding is the beginning of freedom. To be free is to control one's own life. There are two sides to freedom: the negative, which is freedom from restraint; and the positive, which is freedom to act. We enjoy the former whenever we are not subject to another person's compulsion. Only then can we exercise positive freedom. The latter is the opportunity to choose between alternatives and to act on our choice. Through this freedom we develop our potentialities, and therewith our individuality.

Wisdom is not the whole means to this end, but it is the most important. Our feeling—such as hope or fear or courage—enter into our decisions, as does strength or weakness of character. But motivations, as the word implies, are the driving forces, supplying power so that we propel ourselves to act. Understanding is different, because it is an intellectual process. It is like the driver who decides where to go and selects the route. To choose the good, we must form some idea of what it is.

Freedom or coercion are concepts which apply to an individual or to a group. The criteria for judging freedom are the same for both. But an individual differs from a group in the capacity to exercise a choice and in the influences that lead to a decision. It is these contrasts, this mix of similarities and differences, that make the study of human society and its politics so extraordinarily complex. As we try to understand what freedoms we have or could have, great issues arise.

These statements already imply certain assumptions—and they are assumptions about human nature. Since politics is produced by human action, political inquiry always implies an image of human nature. The image which I consider valid will permeate the following discussion and colour my conclusions. Here, I shall be explicit at the outset, so that the reader will discern how the argument is constructed and where it leads.

This notion of freedom presupposes a special view of what it means to be human. It implies, first, that we can and do make choices which are not necessarily predetermined or predictable; and second, that having freedom of choice is good, so that the freer we are the better. Both assumptions are rejected by some thinkers. The former, they say, is an illusion; the latter, spurious.

Those who argue that freedom is illusory are determinists or, in the form some moderns have given this doctrine, behaviourists. In their view, everything we do is settled without our consciously willing it by stimuli that shape us, whether we like it or not. Freud, Pavlov, Watson, and Skinner have been leading exponents of this doctrine—which must mean that their own formulations of it, if it be true, were predetermined for them.

Both those who theorize about the psychology of the individual and those who speculate on the sociology of the community often reach the same conclusion that authoritarianism is inevitable. Freud envisaged the individual as driven by forces deeply embedded in the unconscious, which leave their permanent imprint on the embryo in the womb and the infant in the cradle. Behaviourists from J. B. Watson to B. F. Skinner have held that all of a person's attitudes and actions are patterned from birth onward by external stimuli and can therefore be determined if the environment is sufficiently controlled. Marx argues that broad classes of people, which in different periods the defines as free men and slaves, lords and serfs, or bourgeoisie and proletariat, behave as they do because of compulsions arising from their positions within the "relations of production." Similarly many sociologists since the time of Auguste Comte, along with today's systems analysts, regard individuals as puppets going through the motions and performing the roles prescribed by the social order.

Although the textures of these doctrines vary, they are of one design. They explain how we behave in terms of the influences exerted upon us, emphasizing what the environment does to us and minimizing what we can do to it. Above all, they deny that we could choose to act otherwise than we do. How we behave is how we must.

Others take a different tack. They concede that freedom may be possible, but they consider its value dubious at best or bogus at worst. What matters, they insist, is how freedom is used. If you are ignorant, foolish, ormalicious, your freedom to act can harm others besides yourself. Many people, they go on to say, are deficient in moral maturity or intellectual capacity. For them, the wisest course is to submit to those who know better how to guide them in the right direction. The outcome of such reasoning is plain. The bias being elitist, the conclusion is antidemocratic.

Everybody who seeks to understand politics must face the implications of such beliefs. If that image of humanity is correct, our conception of politics and of the art of government can only be authoritarian. But if such beliefs are false, politics—and social action generally—will be conceived in the opposite manner. It makes all the difference, therefore, whether we see ourselves as the creatures of our institutions or as their creators, as flotsam adrift upon the stream of events or as regulations able to direct their flow.

Where the Determinists Go Wrong

My own view is the reverse of determinism. That psychology has exaggerated its elements of truth out of all proportion. In consequence, its image of human nature is distorted. Not only do determinists make false assumptions, but they fail to account for certain facts which are clear beyond doubt.

To begin with, the concept of determinism is a fuzzy one. It hovers ambiguously between causation and necessity. Perhaps this explains why so many are confused about its meaning and accept it uncritically. One could plausible argue that every human action has a cause (in the sense that action *Y* is the consequence of circumstance *X*). But it does not follow that every action is necessitated (in the sense that, because of *X*, only *Y* could ensue, and not *W* or *Z*). Causation admits of alternatives; necessity does not. What produces a human personality is a complex interaction between nature and nurture, between genetic and environmental factors. But the mystery that confounds the determinists and behaviourists is that the influences of the two sets of factors cannot be wholly known. Nor, *a fortiori*, can their intermixture. Hence, if the amount of each factor and its strength can never be measured exactly, it follows that no programming can guarantee its results with certainty.

The portion of our nature that we inherit is not derived solely from our parents or other immediate progenitors. In fact, the genetic pool, which supplies the building components of the individual, includes the contributions from remote ancestors whom we never knew but whose traits can surface in some generation centuries afterward. No computer can correlate all this because the information fed into it will always be incomplete. Nor can any amount of selective breeding wholly eradicate the latent genes of which we are unaware.

What holds true of genetics applies equally to the environment, which can never be so thoroughly controlled as to yield a fully regimented pattern of behaviour. The totalitarian system which governed the Soviet Union for seven decades sought to indoctrinate its citizens with officially oppressed opinions and to limit their exposure to different ideas. This continued unremittingly for two generations. Yet there was abundant evidence in the 1980s that many Russian intellectuals—artists, writers, scientists, and others—were in dissent, and the revolutionary events of 1991 demonstrated how widespread was the opposition to the Communist Party and its dogmas. Similarly, one can think of persons who trained and indoctrinated in carefully controlled environments where the pressures to conform are very strong (for example, the priesthood or the military), but who later rebel and reject what was forced upon them. We see children of the same parents, brought up in the same household, who differ markedly in abilities and personality. This can even be the case with twins. Abraham Lincoln, born to a family of no known distinction and raised in the backwoods of Kentucky and southern Illinois, developed utterly differently from others in his neighbourhood exposed to similar influences.

Can one avoid the conclusion that those behaviourists who think that human action can be predetermined are chasing fantasies? Environment alone is never the whole explanation of how a person develops. Surely there is an irreducible, unfathomable, and unpredictable core of human free will which the methods of science, whether biological or social, are incapable of explaining. Indeed, if anyone can have insight into these matters, it is likely to be the poets and the artists. They come closer to the hidden springs of human conduct through intuitions that leap beyond empirical data and rational calculus.

This discussion of freedom in the individual carries implications for social conduct and, thereby, for politics. Here, too, the determinists claim to detect the operation of vast impersonal forces, or so-called laws of the historical process, to which necessarily, albeit unknowingly, our individual actions conform. On that view, freedom is twisted inside out; it becomes a species of compulsion and degenerates into bowing to necessity, exactly as Hobbes conceived it. Political scientists who teach along that line—and in recent years they have been the majority—compose textbooks which are commentaries on power, on the conflicts between those who compete for it, and on the necessity of our submitting to those who win it.

This book is founded on other assumptions. I reject the behaviourists' approach because I believe in the capacity and desirability of human beings for independent action, singly and collectively. Politics is a branch of social conduct, where nothing is predetermined beyond our power to change. Nothing that we have inherited or are now doing is exempt from our capacity to keep or later. All social actions, social organization, and social institutions are the product of human activities, past and present. Being made wholly by human beings, they are not necessitated for us by external forces or impersonal laws. Rather they are molded through causes that originate in ourselves and therefore can be changed by human will. Whatever blessings we enjoy in civilization are the fruits of our own work. By the same logic, so too are many of the curses. Poverty, ignorance, unemployment, despotism, and war—the worst scourges that afflict humanity—generally wreak more disaster than do hurricanes, earthquakes, or volcanoes. But, whereas the latter are not of our making, the causes of the former lie within humanity's power when our own doings become our undoing. A *fortiori,* therefore, where the causes spring, resides the cure. Human beings can change what human beings have made.

All this implies that society can be made intelligible and that politics is a sphere of purposeful behaviour which we could live better than we do now. Treated as a subject of study, the events of politics can be clarified by rational analysis. Conducted as a practical art, the substance of politics may be improved by the values we choose to apply. When the results of understanding enlarge our powers, the use of reason can bring self liberation. Before there can be action, however, there must be decision; before decision, a choice among alternative values; before choice, deliberation; before deliberation, knowledge. The mind must analyze before the will decides.

The Ant's-Eye View of Society

But this is a picture of politics as it ought to be, not as it normally is. Indeed there are times when we seem, not masters of our social fate, but slaves of circumstance, when the paths of rationality and freedom are blocked by obstacles; when politics, far from yielding inspiration and betterment, bears all the stigmata of corruption or chaos. For various reasons we are less successful than we might be in treating the maladies of a disordered world. First, a mass inertia arises from widespread passivity. Because many fear the disturbances that accompany innovation and doubt their ability to control its course, they acquiesce in known evils rather than risk the unpredictable chances of change. Second, we are all, to some extent, creatures of habit and imitators of the past; and though it is to the past that we also owe whatever freedoms we enjoy, the sanction of age has the effect of prolonging many practices that restrict the opportunity to invent and improve. Most adults are conservative much of the time. When the philosopher Diderot proposed his ideas for governmental reform, the Empress Catherine of Russia responded: "Ah, my dear friend, you write upon paper, the smooth surface of which presents no obstacle to your pen. But I, poor Empress that I am, must write on the skins of my subjects which are sensitive and ticklish to an extraordinary degree."

Nor is the paralysis of the will that stems from habit or timidity the only impediment to progress. Action can also be inhibited by paralysis of the intellect. Before we act, most of us want to be reasonably sure about what we are doing or whither we hope to move. Not only do we disagree about our objectives and the means of realizing them, but we cannot always be sure about our diagnosis of current ills and their causes. We may be dedicated to ideals that we call democracy, freedom, justice, welfare. But we dispute their definition because each can mean different things to different people, and the applicability of an abstract notion to particular circumstances is always arguable. We dislike depressions. We condemn injustice. We hate wars. We want to prevent them from starting; or, when they begin, we want to end them. But do we know what their causes are? Can we confidently prescribe how to avoid them in the future? Considering that so much is at stake in the policies that governments choose, how high is the probability that our answers will be correct?

Many of the puzzles that confront us when we face the problems of our social system and seek to remedy them have a common source in this fact: human society is composed of millions of persons, and social processes are the sum-product of numberless individual actions. In order to decipher this confusing network of contacts among people, we study the past; we note contemporary events; we look at our fellow creatures and at ourselves. But seeing is not the same as having insight. Sometimes we feel as bewildered as if we gazed, uncomprehendingly, at an ant heap and saw a swarm of movements whose meaning we could not fathom. It is hard to obtain an overall view of a complex society, to detect the significant details and relate together those that are causally connected. It is even hard for individuals to recognize what quota they contribute, however infinitesimal, to a general social mosaic which all have helped to piece together but none has planned. When the economy undergoes inflation, the majority seek to protect themselves by boosting prices, pressing for higher wages, charging bigger fees. Yet, if too many behave alike, the net effect is that nobody benefits. The same can happen in an armaments race, where governments that distrust one another pursue security severally by methods that yield collective insecurity. Rather than act blindly, we search for a rationale, a principal of cause and effect, a set of laws perhaps that will make the relationships plain. Failing that, the behaviour of a mass of people often reenacts the tragedy of Hamlet. For our doubts bring indecision and lead to postponement and delay.

> And thus the native hue of resolution
> Is sicklied o'er with the pale cast of thought,
> And enterprises of great pith and moment
> With this regard their currents turn awry
> And lose the name of action.

The World Prospect

Never was it more urgent than now to look at politics afresh, to reassess the government and misgovernment of humanity, and take stock, worldwide, of the direction in which we are drifting or being led. Without doubt, we live in a revolutionary age. Before the year 2000, the human race must confront a number of related problems that together contain higher risks of global catastrophe than ever in the past; paradoxically, we also have greater opportunity than heretofore to improve our lives as individuals and communities.

The clear and present dangers we confront consist of both new and ancient ills. The rate of population growth is a new threat. For hundreds of thousands of years, the human population of our planet increased very slowly. In fact, we did not reach one billion until about 1830. The second billion, however, was added within one century (1830-1930), and the third in only three decades (1930-1960). In 1986, we passed the figure of five billion. Hereafter, unless deliberate measures are adopted to restrict the number of births, our numbers will double every 20 years or so. When one contemplates the implications of these figures—the certainty of overcrowding and of struggles for ever scarcer resources, the likelihood of mass poverty, famine, and war—can one avoid the conclusion that those governments and churches which oppose birth control are sinning against humanity?

A related trend which aggravates these dangers is that we are so rapidly using up, and even willfully destroying, the irreplaceable resources of our plannet. Everywhere we are poisoning the soil and polluting the air and water on which our lives depend. The rate of deterioration and destruction is most rapid, of course, in the vicinity of the huge urban and industrial concentration that increasingly dominate our modern society. There are two major reasons, in addition to population growth, why this is taking place. One is the psychology which urges us constantly to acquire new possessions and to consume ever more material goods. This attitude is encouraged by business people, who make a profit from what they sell; by advertisers, who stimulate demand with a mix of truth, half-truth, and untruth; and by economists, who engage in growth worship and measure a people's achievement on the graph of the gross national product. The second, and connected, reason in the technological development which feeds the desire to accumulate and is nourished by it. Today's technology is both a blessing and a curse. Infinitely resourceful and ingenious, and drastically revolutionary in the changes it offers, it transforms the physical environment and reshapes human relation without sufficient foresight or concern for consequence. For each problem it "solves," technology generates new ones. Its innovations spawn a network of systems, ever more complex; and this occurs so rapidly that we have scant occasion to adapt. In its application, too much of our technology is ruled by this reckless attitude: If it's feasible and profitable, we'll do it.

The disregard of science and technology for human values is at its worst in the proliferation of military weapons. The arms race of recent decades—to which we and the Russians were the contributors, with the French, British, and Chinese following in our wake—has led to a situation where the means of offense have completely outstripped the means of defence. Such is the accumulation of unclear bombs in Russia and the Untied States.

and such the capacity to deliver them with rockets, that not only could each government destroy the other's population several times over, but together they could exterminate all human life on this planet. Power of that kind ought not to be lodged in human hands. What is more, the bigger producers give or sell their armaments of smaller governments—many of them unstable and unsavory—thus providing the means to begin local conflicts that could easily spread. And, if we ask why this has come about, the answer is: because the pursuit of scientific knowledge and technical innovation has too often been directed by aggressive politics and economic greed.

Serious as these dangers are, they are further compounded by evils inherited from the past. Society has been based traditionally on a double standard. The commonest from of government has been some species of oligarchy, wherein a small number of privileged persons lord it over the rest. The same pattern has generally prevailed throughout the social system. Wealth has always been distributed unequally, with a handful living in luxury while the masses exist in poverty. This situation persists today in most parts of the world and is intensified by the disparities between the more developed economies and the underdeveloped. In fact, the gap between richer and poorer is growing. Meanwhile, other established forms of discrimination continue to perpetuate inequality and provoke a sense of injustice. Scarcely anywhere in the world do people of different races consort together in the same community under genuinely equal conditions. Religious prejudice, reinforced by differences of culture, foments dislike and even hatred—witness the conflicts in Ulster and Cyprus, between Arabs and Israelis, between Indians and Pakistanis, between Tamils and Sinhalese. And most pervasive of all—because it has lasted the longest and is the most widespread—the male half of the human race kept the female half in a position of legal, economic, and social dependency amounting in some places to actual servitude.

Whether these conditions will continue depends wholly on our awareness and our attitudes. Such situations will remain unchanged or will worsen if we do not care about them. If we care enough, they could all be altered. There are, in fact, some signs that give modest, but genuine, grounds for hope. In the last two decades a rising chorus of voices has been protesting these new dangers and ancient degradations, bringing them to the forefront of consciousness and thereby awakening our consciences. The underprivileged have made some definite gains—small in comparison with what is needed, but large in relation to the past. Since the late sixties, public opinion has been aroused by the threats to our environment—threats we daily see, hear, taste, and smell—and television has literally brought home the atrocities of war to millions who formerly were oblivious to its effects. The future does not have to be what power-seeking government or profit-seeking corporations would decree. The future could be humanized and become humane. Or it could be the reverse. However we act or fail to act, the moral responsibility will be ours.

Information and Understanding

If "the proper study of mankind is man," as Alexander Pope has written, our primary duty as citizens is to learn about the state. This is something that we owe to ourselves because government touches everybody, and consequently all of us have common interest in its actions. The price we pay for not understanding politics is servitude to others or to circumstance. Several thousand years ago a revolutionary change occurred when law was first committed to writing, instead of being deposited in the memory of a few and passed on from mouth to mouth. Once written, it could more easily be known and studied, its interpretation debated, and officials punished for not adhering to the text. The significance of that change is shown by the example of contemporary states where the decisions of government continue to be shrouded in mystery and ordinary people are in the grip of tyranny. There is no way of knowing how much stupidity, how many mistakes, what evil acts, are regularly concealed in the various dictatorships that continue to dominate the majority of the human race. Nor have the modern democracies been immune from this disease. During the period when the United States was conducting war in southeast Asia, three presidents (Kennedy, Johnson, and Nixon) deliberately covered up activities they had ordered, then publicly lied about them—as did a succession of secretaries of state and defence and presidential advisors. Secrecy and falsification are part of the regular stock-in trade of modern governments. Understandably, former Senator Fulbright, when asked for his reflections on the Vietnam experience, responded: "The biggest lesson I learned from Vietnam is not to trust government statements." His point is underscored by the evidence, made public in 1987, of untruths by President Reagan and various high officials in his administration. Their deception was designed to conceal the secret sales of weapons to Iran and the subsequent diversion of the proceeds, in defiance of congressional legislation, so as to finance military operations against the leftist government of Nicaragua. What Alexander Solzhenitsyn said of the Soviet Union applies to countless regimes, both past and contemporary, both democratic and dictatorial: "In our country the lie has become not just a moral category, but a pillar of the state."

Even in states which make a virtue of publicity and expect their citizens to participate in politics, the difficulties in the path of understanding, and thus controlling, a modern government are truly formidable. Not only are its operations obscured by their vastness and complexity, but the information about it is now so detailed and voluminous as well-night to baffle an inquiring intellect. Anybody who wants visual proof of this fact has only to observe the size of the catalog at the Library of Congress or visit the collections of public archives or scan the corridors of records in the filing division of a big department. The ningle epsiode of General Mac-Arthur's dismissal by President Truman in 1951 occasioned a Congressional iniquiy whose hearings and testimony filled over 8000 pages of print. The assassination of President Kennedy was exhaustively investigated for 10 months by a commission that set forth its findings in a report of 300,000 words and in 26 bulky volumes of testimony. The reelection of President Nixon in 1972 was accompanied by so many illegal acts and unethical practices that in 1974 he resigned in disgrace. This occurred after tearings before a Senate committee and the House Judiciary Committee, which extended to many thousands of pages of testimony and questioning, as well as grand jury indictments and trials in the courts of law whose proceedings fill yet more thousands. All the paperwork of the federal government was estimated by the General Accounting Office in 1973 to occupy nearly 30 million cubic feet of space. The footage of federal files alone would stretch from Washington to Cairo, from the Oval Office in the White House to the tombs of the Pharaohs. Year by year, the task of digesting these enormous amounts of material—all the statutes and statistics, bebates and directives, opinions and orders—becomes increasingly difficult. Our civilization sinks neck-deep in paper, and those who would think about its problems risk being crushed by the weight of documentation.

In the field of technology, necessity has been called the mother of invention. In politics, necessity is the mother of absolutism. Rousseau's political classic *The Social Contract* opens with the words: "Man is born free, yet everywhere he is in irons." He would have been nearer the truth had he written: "People are born helpless, but everywhere they have the capacity to become free." Also, one should add, they have the capacity to conduct their lives better they do now. In politics, everything can be found that is contained with the individual. Love, will passion, and hattred play their parts, along with memory, knowledge, and logical thought. Kindness and mercy are present, but so are cruelty and evil. The differences between he various political systems are attributable in large to the relative infiuence which each of these exerts.

Up to a point, our understanding of politics can be susceptible to rational analysis. But reason alone does not encompass everything, nor does it possess a monopoly of truth. The deeper insights in this branch of learning, as in all others, do not derive from the collection and classification of empirical data, necessary though these are. They come from feats of imagination, from the audacity that takes a lead in the dark. Our ultimate assumptions about humanity, especially about our potential for creative growth and ethical advance, will always be a blend of reason and intuition.

Since the state is wholly constructed of, by, and for human beings, its study is a form of self-analysis. Hence, complete detachment is impossible. To understand politics is somewhat like being both spectator and critic of a play when one is also acting in the cast. This means, of course, that all political inquiry includes a subjective element. There is no way to get around this and no need to explain it away. Quite the contrary. If we are aware of how we respond as individuals to war, taxes, elections, the flag, and so on, and if we are honest in recognizing our own attitudes, this is to our advantage. Such awareness can help us interpret the responses of others and see meanings in what otherwise would appear a chaos.

Without interpretation, the factual data of politics are devoid of significance. An event in the history of art may help us understand this point. In 1501 the government of Florence invited sculptors to submit their designs for using a 17-foot block of Carrara marble that had lain in the cathedral courtyard for 70 years. An earlier sculptor had begun working on it, but had given up. Subsequent artists had judged the marble to have been gouged so deeply as to be ruined. The winning design was Michelangelo's. He carved for three years; the result was the statue of *David.* Asked how he found the solution for the problem of the "ruined" marble, Michelangelo said simply that he had seen the figure imprisoned and set it free.

My point is that, where others only looked with sight, Michelangelo looked with insight. Can this suggest something to a student of politics? Meanings and interpretations are not taken from thin air or pulled out of a hat like the conjuror's rabbit. When we, as critic-spectators, judge the drama in which we also play a role, our judgment is based on certain principles or criteria. Which ones are appropriate? From what angle of vision do we view the action? How do we disentangle the plot?

Permanent Problems, Changing Solutions

Philosophical inquiry always asks two basic questions: What is reality, and how do we know it? In studying politics the same questions arise. We must know what politics consists of and how we can best understand it. Since intelligent choices are impossible unless we discover what the alternatives are, where can we find them? Two sources suggest themselves—historical experience and imaginative speculation. In order to understand before acting, we need the equivalents of a map and compass. We should know the terrain and topography, the main routes and distances. Without these, we cannot compare early practices with modern, or detect the similarities and differences in the present, or decide our preferences for the future.

The purpose of this book is to provide such a map and compass, without which we would have no idea what routes are open and where they take us. This is a book about politics—and its accompanying institutions, the state and government—because, if we are to plan our course, we need to be clear about the values we prefer and the organizations most likely to put them into effect. Politics is central to this process because it is essentially a choice between values. States and governments are involved because these are the structures through which we work toward the values we have chosen.

The fact that alternatives exist suggests a way to analyze the state and understand its politics. This book expresses the belief that political history and contemporary government exhibit certain patterns which render them meaningful. When the patterns are clear, events that otherwise appear chaotic can be seen in significant relationships. Because our lives are spent amid flux, we are acutely aware of a continual need to adjust, individually and collectively, to technological invention, social innovation, rapidity of movement, economic instability, threats of war, and doubts concerning long-held ethical values. While recognizing the urgent compulsions of change, we need—in order to adapt intelligently—to discover any relevant parallels between our times and the past in terms of factors which do not change.

The analysis offered here attempts to fill these two requirements. It interprets in terms of fundamentals which remain constant and reveals the rhythms in their variations and mutations. To put it briefly, all governments face certain basic issues which they must somehow settle. The issues form the substance of politics. They are permanent. They cannot be evaded. However, they permit alternative solutions that leave mankind with the possibility of choosing or of substituting one preference for another. Because changes occur in the context within which these problems are tackled, change itself is as constant a factor as the issues. Conditions, techniques, methods, and institutions are highly variable. Political systems resemble one another—or differ—according to their respective preferences for solving each issue singly and for combining the solutions. In this way we can distinguish intelligibly between the political characteristics of broad historical periods, such as classical antiquity, the Middle Ages, the modern nation-state; and of contrasted systems, such as dictatorship or democracy, class rule or equalitarianism, nationalism or international organization.

The Great Issues

The core of politics consists of five basic issues. The first of these arises from the fact that, because we are associated within the state, we must have some relation to one another. What form is that to take? Should all of us stand on an equal footing? Or are some to be superior to the rest? The same point may be phrased differently: Is citizenship exclusive or all-inclusive? If the former, then the people who make up a state are divided into two groups, one having rights of full citizenship and other treated as inferiors or subjects. If citizenship is all-inclusive, however, then everybody will have the same basic status without discrimination or limitation. The governing principle is a regime of privilege in one case, of equality in the other.

A second issue arises from controversy over the functions which a state performs for its members. Originating for mutual protection,16 the state has traditionally widened its sphere of action. Thus, the inevitable questions are presented: Is there a limit to what the state is justified in undertaking? Are there some things in cannot do well? If a limit is necessary, where should it be set? On this point schools of philosophy, as well as the practices of political, have been opposed from times ancient to the present. Some have held that no social activity and no group can, or should, be exempt from the jurisdiction of the state. Others maintain that somewhere a boundary line must be set within which the state may move freely, but outside of which it is trespassing.

The third and fourth issues revolve around the authority which enables the state to perform its functions, but they are occupied with separate aspects of it. One problem is to determine the source from authority is derived. This question has become acute because, in order to provide services to its citizens, the state needs to acquire and exercise power. Since its powers are funnelled into the hands of the government, and since the officials who staff the latter are far fewer than the rest of the community, the relation of government to governed becomes a debatable issue. Those who govern, besides claiming authority, seek to justify using it; the governed, however, may be try to retain the ultimate control over political power. If the distribution of power within the state is visualized as a pyramid, the government can be likened to the apex, and the remainder of the people to the base. Authority can then be imagined either to stem from the base and travel up to the apex or to originate in the apex and flow down to the base. Under the first view, the government is controlled by, and is responsible to, the people. Under the second, the people are subjects to those who govern and are obliged to obey their commands.

Nor is the query about its source the only fundamental issue raised by the existence and establishment of authority. Irrespective of whether it originated from the base of the pyramid or its apex, another issue concerns the manner in which that authority is subsequently organized. One possibility is for power to be concentrated at a single focal point. Alternatively, it can be subdivided into powers that are then diffused. These can be parcelled out among separate branches of the government and distributed among different levels. Checks and balances may be either introduced or removed. Whichever happens, the machinery of government will vary accordingly.

The fifth basic issue is that of magnitude—both of the area the state covers and the population it contains—and the connected problem of relations between separate states. How large should the unit of government be? It there an optimum size for a state? Are there limits to its dimensions? How are independent states related? Must their relations be hostile? Can they be peaceful? These are vexing questions in the cogitation's of political theorists and the calculations of statecraft. Since the Western world has already experimented with units as divers as the city-state; nation-state, and empire-state and continues to experiment with new forms of international organization, much can be learned from comparing government of small, middle, large, and mammoth scale and tracing the patterns of inter-state politics.

Analysis of the Great Issues

These five issues can be summarized as follows:

1. The coverage of citizenship: Should it be exclusive or all-inclusive?

2. The functions of the state: Should its sphere of activity be limited or unlimited?

3. The source of authority: Should it originate in the people or the government?

4. The structure of authority: Should power be concentrated or dispersed?

5. The magnitude of the state and its external relations: What unit of government is preferable? What interstate order is desirable?

Logically, each of these topics is distinct from the rest. Each, moreover, can be analyzed alone because it pivots on a unique problem. The first issue deals with the reciprocal rights and duties of members of the state; the second, with the scope of governmental functions; the third, with the birthplace and legitimizing of authority; the fourth, with the institutionalizing of power; and the last, with the size of territory and population. All these issues; present an opportunity to choose between at least two possibilities. This is self-evident in a sense, because the factor of choice marks the essence of the problem. If there were no room to choose, there could be no issue.

The breadth of the choice presented under the various issues can be envisaged in the series of contrasts:

> The first issue is the choice between equality and inequality.
>
> The second issue is the choice between a pluralist and a monistic state.
>
> The third issue is the choice between freedom and dictatorship.
>
> The fourth issue is the choice between a dispersion of powers and their unification.
>
> The fifth issue is the choice between a multitude of states and a universal state.

Thus described, the choice in every case appears to lie between two alternatives. In actuality, however, more than two possibilities present themselves, because every issue may be resolved at intermediate stages between the opposite poles. Thus, the functions undertaken by government can be more or less limited. Powers can be more or less dispersed. There may be more or less freedom, and so on . Theory conceives of absolutes; practice is always a matter of degree.

Here then is a way to make the political process intelligible. The key is that five basic issues are involved, and that all admit a choice. The types of government and the consequent character of the state vary with the respective decisions. Since there are so many issues, and at least two solutions for each, numerous permutation and combinations of political patterns are possible. This variety constitutes the fascination and the challenge both to those who practice the art of politics and to those who systematize its study into a body of organized knowledge. No people can establish a government without confronting these five issues, nor can they avoid including some decision about each in the pattern of whatever state they choose. Every state institutionalizes its answer to the basic problems with which the five issues are concerned. A student of politics cannot find any government system of nonnomadic peoples in any place or period that does not contain its solutions of these issues. Wherever the great issues are present, there is politics. Wherever politics is found, there are these issue. Such an analysis, moreover, interprets the political process in dynamic terms, for no solution can ever be fixed on final.

All governments has a touch of the temporary and the tentative. We change our preferences. We oscillate from one pole to another. Ceaselessly, we alter the edifice of government, remodelling its floor plan and facade.

Synthesis of the Great Issues

Such changes are conditioned, however, by another fact. It was suggested above that each issue is unique and can be distinctly analyzed. That is true only in logic. Reality never corresponds perfectly to logic; neither, therefore, can our analysis. To elucidate the nature of politics, one could take a cue from the comment of Marc Chagall on the painting he executed for the ceiling of the Paris Opera: "There is nothing precise in it. One cannot be precise and still be true." In political practice, the issues are not entirely separate. Rather, they are connected and interact. Nobody can say precisely where one stops and another begins. Their edges are ragged, not sharp. Analysis of political complexities into five issues, each having its varying solutions, is an aid in simplification. Yet it would be oversimplification, and hence distortion, if politics were finally presented as an amalgam of five mutually exclusive categories, somehow glued together.

The analogy of a watch may help to explain this. We divide the dial arbitrarily into 12 hours and 60 minutes. Such intervals show us the time at the moment we are looking. But time itself is a continuum. It is a ceaseless, unbroken flow. And so it is with politics. When the analyses are done, the need remains for resynthesis. As governments operate in reality, the five issues act upon and interact with each other, just as the minute hand moves simultaneously with the hour hand. Indeed, whatever choice is adopted in politics under the heading of any issue can scarcely fail to have some effect on the decisions concerning all or some of the others. Thus a change anywhere tends to promote accompanying changes elsewhere. The history of politics, briefly stated, consists of trying alternative solutions for the basic issues in new combinations.

The Method and Its Implications

This approach to the subject involves both a picture of the matter of politics and a method of studying it. As between matter and method, the relative priority is not in doubt. In any field of learning the substance to be understood must control the methodology. That order should not be reversed, nor should a commitment to a particular method dictate one's view on the subject. In this particular case, the characterization of politics as an arena of debatable choices in five substantive topics invites an appropriate method.

To begin with, if we are to comprehend the nature of politics, we should not confine our attention to the contemporary period or to events of recent memory. One cannot properly grasp the meaning of the present—still less, chart a course of action for the future-without delving into the past. There is a valid point in the response of General de Gaulle to a historian who suggested that the problems of contemporary France dated back to 1936. "Why not to 1513," said be Gaulle, "or, if you prefer, to 1425?" In more general terms, the relation between the study of politics and history was thus expressed by a British historian, J.R. Seeley, who helped to develop the discipline of political science late in the nineteenth century:

> History without political science has no fruit;
>
> Political science without history has no root.

Such an approach to politics supplies a corrective to an undue concentration on the more pressing problems of the moment. Otherwise we tend to forget that what may seem a major problem to us (for example, the relation of the state to the economy) was not always so, and that controversies over which our ancestors shed blood (such as the relations of church and state) do not move all peoples to acts of violence today. To understand politics, it is necessary to step, as it were, outside our immediate context in space and time, to see our world as a whole and in Spinoza's phrase, "under the guise of eternity," Many persons usually take for granted the prevailing ideas, the dominant institutions, of their period and place; and if on the whole these serve our needs, we judge them good. But does this mean that what we are familiar with and accept is right and good only for ourselves, and only here and now? Are our practices and principles equally appropriate for contemporary peoples elsewhere? How does our particular system of government resemble those of the past? Does it exhibit any features that are distinctive or unique? In either case, how do we explain both the continuation of the old and the invention of the new?

The logic contained in these questions also suggests the wisdom of using comparisons to find the answer. If it is unwise to restrict our scrutiny to our own century, so would we be at fault in failing to look beyond our own country. To learn about the government of a single state at a particular phase of its history is not the same as analyzing the political process. For politics is a seamless web, woven continuously from past to present and retracing its design from state to state. The fundamental issues which form its content must therefore be observed from the perspective of space as well as time. This requires that governments be studied by a comparative method. The politics of a particular country may sometimes be best understood by comparisons with its own politics in earlier periods; sometimes, however, by comparisons with the government of other peoples, past or present. This helps us to distinguish between what is accidental or transitory and what is fundamental or permanent. In this way, too, the causes of political phenomena may be more accurately divined than if no such comparisons were attempted. For example, anyone who wishes to know why the United States is a federal union may obtain clues from the United States alone. But, since Switzerland, Canada, India, and Australia are also federal unions, a study of the reasons why they are similarly governed will be likely to lead to valid generalizations about the causes of federalism; and these will be more securely founded by resting on a broader base. Hence, the comparative method is employed throughout this book, and the nature of politics is illustrated by examples drawn from any era or area whose experience is relevant to the issue. We can learn about government not only by observing modern America or Britain or Russia or Japan but also by studying the lessons of the birth of the nation-state, the medieval experiment in church-state dualism, the growth and collapse of the Roman Empire or that of the Incas, and the legacy of ancient Athens.

But that is not all. The reference to earlier periods and the use of comparisons contribute to a more intelligent understanding by means of classification and clarification. Since the core of politics consists of choice, the orderly analysis of data forms the prelude to an act of judgment. In politics we are perennially arguing pro and con, debating the merits and demerits of alternative policies, disputing the wisdom of ultimate goals, and weighing the efficacy of possible means. In short, we are engaged in a search for values. The politics process—not only as discussed in philosophical treatises but also as actually conducted in daily life—abounds with invocations of ideals. People dedicate their government to life, liberty, and the pursuit of happiness; to equality, justice, peace and good order; to the eradication of class divisions, and similar noble purposes. But how are these defined? How is democracy itself to be interpreted so that we shall know when we have it? What happens, moreover, if one ideal appears to conflict with a second? Life is sometimes sacrificed for liberty. Liberties can be lessened for the sake of equality. The public safety may clash with the rights of the individual. At one stage of their history, people are embattled for private enterprise; at another, for the general welfare. At one time they prize their freedom from the state; at another, their security through the state. It may be their wider union that they hold most dear, or states' rights and local autonomy. Concepts and abstractions have their place in politics because human beings identify their particular interests with these broad symbols; then, since beliefs influence conduct, the choice of the symbol and its definition and future application affect the course of history.

Theorizing about values, itself a speculative activity, is not independent of reality. Quite the contrary. The idealizations of philosophy have a habit of becoming the currency of the marketplace. Conversely, ideas grow out of experience; and when they are developed into a coherent whole—which is what philosophy aims at—they are signposts to further experience. Thus Rousseau, repelled by French society in Paris and Versailles in the mid-eighteenth century, wrote a doctrine of protest to which some of the architects of the French Revolution appealed for their justification. The men who framed to Constitution of the United States two centuries ago retained many principles from the English tradition of constitutionalism and the structure of colonial governemnt. But they went further and hammered out the new design of a federal union, containing governments of limited jurisdiction, which has provided the model for extensive imitation and further experiment. Political doctrines do not hover weightless in a sealed chamber removed from the everyday world. They are a working part of the living reality of society and its governance. Consequently, they help us understand the state and render it intelligible. Theory serves, in part, as a form of mental shorthand, compressing innumerable facts into a few short symbols; in part, it is an aspiration for a future that we should like to see realized. "The beginning of all practicality in politics," wrote Hubert Humphrey, "is a vision of things as they ought to be."

Politics and Ethics

The formulation of political ideals is thus central to the conduct of politics, and the study of the subject embraces the concepts of political philosophy. As Bismark defined it, politics is "the art of the possible." As here conceived, however, politics is the art of selecting the most worthwhile among whatever policies are possible. The essence of politics is choice, which involves a deliberate preference for one set of values over another. The values themselves are not taken for granted, nor are they somehow determined apart from the political process. Politics is a search for ends as well as means. Through practical politics, values are disputed, their relevance is tried, and their validity is tested. Likewise, the striving for values injects into politics a purpose and a rationale. That indeed is the significance of the issues which this book presents. For these are the focal points in the controversies between rival values whose adoption or rejection, fulfillment or failure, make up the core of politics.

But if the issues present a choice between opposing values, and if every value aspires to ideal, how does the ideal relate to the actual? What kind of alternatives do these issues present? Do they enlighten us about what actually occurs, or do they guide us toward what ideally should occur? Or can they help in both respects?

Though many aspects of these questions are perplexing, some points are clear. Starting with what is, the five issues reach out to what ought to be. We can think of them as yardsticks which measure the gap between what we have and should have, or as signposts that point the direction and tell the mileage from where we are to where we should like to be. This does not mean, however, that the world of reality every can or will conform exactly to dreams of the ideal. The laws of logic are not the laws of politics or ethics. In pure thought, ideas can be developed beyond the point that practice can attain. Moreover, one ideal is sure to come into conflict with another at some point. An example is the contrast between liberty and order, either of which, if fully developed, would destroy the other. Practical considerations require that the two be mixed in limited amounts.

The formulation of ideals nevertheless serves an indispensable purpose. Such Euclidean definitions as a point having position but no magnitude, or a line having length but no breadth, are concepts which no actual line or point can match. Yet it is the ideal that sets the standard whereby we test and judge the real. The same could be said about the markings on a compass. In reality, the captain of a ship of airplane very rarely sets a course due south or due north. But by such points on the compass, one can fix other directions. Th great issues occupy a similar role in politics. They constitute direction-points or ultimate goals that are ideally conceivable. They serve, therefore, as a measuring stick for testing reality. Thus we may judge how closely we approximate the ideal or, conversely, how far we are falling short. Pure and perfect equality or liberty cannot be realized in practice. But to envisage such concepts gives policy and action their meaning. By contemplating what should be, we illuminate what is.

Humanism and Politics

During its long history as a field of intellectual inquiry, the study of politics has fluctuated between two tendencies which may be inferred from the preceding discussion. In the first systematic political theory written in Europe, the Greek philosopher Plato expressed the contrast through his two protagonists in the *Republic*—Socrates and Thrasymachus—and the debate has continued ever since. It has proceeded with vigour and plausibility, because each position contains its element of truth.

Some have thought that the political process derives its character from permanent traits in human nature. Faced with similar situations, people are supposed to react similarly. If enough instances are observed, they can be gathered into generalizations enabling us to describe how people ordinarily behave and thus predict their future behaviour with reasonable probability. Such generalizations are the laws of politics. The formulate them is political science; to apply them is the art of government. On this view, both the content of politics and the categories of analysis are rooted in the actual, and speculation about them confines itself to the possible or the probable. So conceived and so practised, politics is independent of morals. Ethics, therefore, is irrelevant to the inquiry. as Machiavelli put it: "For how we live is so far removed from how we ought to live, that he who abandons what is done for what ought to be done, will rather learn to bring about his own ruin than his preservation."

Others, by contrast, affirm the union of politics with ethics. They argue that politics is the intentional pursuit of human betterment by organized public means, just as ethics seeks the same end by private means. It is true that in politics we see individuals struggling for power, groups mobilized to press for special interests, systems at times tyrannically managed, and institutions deflected from their proper purposes. Nobody would gainsay these facts. But it is any less true that politics also involves the judgment on them? People observe and then evaluate in terms of right and wrong. The Watergate affair is a case in point. The udnerwood of *realpolitik* comes eventually before the higher court of moral judgment. Ethical values are central to actual political bebaviour. Moreover, can one deny that there is more to politics than its seamy side? Altruism and benevolence, self-sacrifice, dedication to the public good, a solicitude for human welfare—these too are manifest in political history as well as the pathology which is the stock-in-trade of self-styled realistic writers. Hence, if ethical elements are part of the substance of politics, how can ethical appraisal be exclused from its understanding?

Students of politics have sometimes pursued their disagreements over methodology with a vehemence similar to the controversies about politics itself. Conflicts between opposing political systems and their supporting philosophies were hotly conducted in the wake of the major revolutions of the last 300 years—the English, American, French, Russian, and Chinese. People have justified the existing order or have risen in revolt, they have defended their privileges or argued for reform, generalizing their points of view in terms of an array of doctrines—conservatism or liberalism, capitalism or socialism, racism or integration, autocracy or democracy. These rivalries were continued in the recent competition between democratic and communist systems, as well as between different types of democracy and different brands of communism, and similarly between the Chinese and Indian methods of engrafting Western innovations upon Asian traditions. it is as true now as in the past that politics forms the arena where people choose the values for organizing their societies. hence the nature of the subject indicates the method of its study. if politics is the search of a society for public ethics, the study of politics is a research into the results, ethically judged.

The Values in Politics

It follows that the word *science* in the title *political science* should not be taken too literally. The study of politics can be considered "scientific" to the extent that, in the search for truth, we seek to ascertain facts with accuracy and to relate causes to consequences. Beyond that, the methods conventionally attributed to the physical sciences—i.e., forming generalizations inductively from empirical observations or from experiments conducted under controlled conditions—have only limited use in social inquiry. For that matter, their sometimes paramountancy is now questioned in the physical sciences themselves. In the history of science, many of the revolutionary discoveries and revealing insights did not result from using the method as postulated from the seventeenth century to the nineteenth. On the contrary, they were the products of a leap in the dark, of audacious guesswork, of creative imagination. Experimentation normally comes into use afterward to test the validity of the original institution. This has been convincingly argued by Karl Popper in his seminal work on the scientific method and is attested by scientists who recognize that a restrictive method, too slavishly followed, will not lead to truth. Nor are the conclusions of the physical scientists endowed with that degree of certainty to which the determinists of psychology and sociology so irrationally aspire. Such, for example, is the element of uncertainty in the measurable behaviour of wave and particle, that the physicist Heisenberg formulated an "indeterminacy principle" to admit a range of related variations that elude precision.

A *fortiori,* what is true for physical science is truer still when the subject of study is humanity or the works of human creativity. With the aid of modern instruments, a student of art can learn many facts about a painting by Rembrandt or Michelangelo. One can test the pigment, photograph the brush technique, and conduct microscopic analysis of the materials and their use. But what does this add up to? Such data do not reach the core of the painting. They cannot explain the sensibilities and intuition of the artist or tell us why a canvas covered by an old wrinkled face or a scene such as *The Creation of Adam* stirs our emotions.

And it is the same with politics. The measurements and models, systems and statistics, games and other gimmicks, so much in vogue in contemporary "scientific" research, yield some information and suggest some clues. But do they touch the heart of the subject? There is more to politics than can be reduced to a linear flow from the id to the IBM. All the complexities of human nature, with its many-sidedness, its good and evil, attractiveness and repulsiveness, are present in actual politics. Of this, the techniques of science can explain only so much. The rest—in fact, the most important part of the subject—consists of human interpretation which necessarily contains a subjective element. Thus in any political study we must employ many categories, not only true or false, but also good or bad, right or wrong, wise or foolish.

Out chief preoccupation is with choices, priorities, values, and issues—to which institutions procedures, and power, though important, are secondary. Politics, so viewed, is a continuing adventure in the question for civilization, and its study a perennial inquiry into human backwardness or betterment.

—A Lipson

9

Classical Greek View of the State

We shall deal with the classical Greek view of the state. We shall examine the definition of the state developed by Plato (427-347 B.C.) and Aristotle (384-322 B.C.), which formed part of the basis for later theories of the state in Western political theory. Plato's famous work 'Republic' completed when he was about 40 years of age, is widely considered to be the first work of Western political science in that it is a systematic and critical enquiry into political ideas and institutions.

The Greek view of the state has been conditioned and shaped by the experiences of the Greek city state. In other words, the concepts developed by Plato and Aristotle were a product of their times. Thus the concepts of the good life, justice and the nature of the state reflect the realities of the Greek city state or polis.

The ancient city state, as compared with modern states, was extremely small both in area and population. The population of Athens, the city-state where Plato's Academy was located, was just slightly over three hundred thousand. This population was divided into three main classes. At the bottom of the social scale were the slaves who were about one third of the population. Consequently, slavery was characteristic of the city-state economy. However, the slave had absolutely no political rights, and in Greek political theory his existence was taken for granted.

The second main class in a Greek city state was of the resident foreigners or metics. Foreigners could not legally become citizens even if they had been residents for generations. They, like the slaves had no place in the city's political life.

The third class of people were the citizens or privilege of birth, a Greek became a citizen of the city to which his parents belonged. All citizens participated, though not equally, in public affairs. Since political rights were based on a person's class background and birth, the political problem for the Greek thinkers was to discover what place each class deserved in a state. This will be clear in the following discussion on Plato and Aristotle.

BASIS OF PLATO'S REPUBLIC

The Republic which is the most important of Plato's works cannot be easily classified. It deals with the whole of human life and thought, including philosophy, history, political, economics and the theory of education. In fact, the famous French philosopher Rousseau claimed: "the Republic is not a work upon politics but the finest treatise on education that was ever written". But Plato's work was so all-inclusive precisely because all these subjects were at that time, more than two thousand years ago, still one. Knowledge had not been systematically divided into separate subjects. Yet, the Republic, as title suggests is a dialogue with politics as its central theme.

Virtue is Knowledge

A key concept in Plato's Republic is that "virtue is knowledge". This is based on Plato's definition of what is good. There is an objective good which exists and can be known. This objective good exists even if the people in general may not realise what is good for them, because they are subjective about it. This good can be understood through rational or logical investigation. It cannot be discovered through intuition or guesswork. This good is real and must be achieved and realised, even though men may not want it. It is important to realise because it is good.

Plato's focus on the good and his identification of goodness with knowledge leads to his belief that the philosopher or scholar/ scientist should have decisive power in government because his knowledge entitles him to this.

Plato argues that knowledge cannot be useful unless the purpose for which it has to be used is known clearly. Thus 'master knowledge' is when one knows the proper use of knowledge to any particular field or branch of activity. Plato shows that only statesmen who possess this master knowledge can know the true or objective good which gives men happiness.

This leads Plato to a theory of a state controlled by perfect knowledge, which has a final purpose which is 'the good life' based on the objective good.

Therefore every human activity should serve the desired end: the state. The statesmen who possess such a knowledge must communicate it to others, who in turn must serve according to their own capacities. The main element in knowledge is that each person has a specific function and must work according to that. The specific function of the individual who possess master knowledge is rule. Therefore Plato supports the rule of the philosopher king in the Republic.

Plato's Theory of Justice

Plato is best known for his ideas on justice. The importance given by him to the idea of justice is indicated by the fact that Plato's Republic is sub-titled 'a treatise concerning justice'.

Plato discusses in a form of a dialogue. During Plato's time there were various existing ideas on justice which contained certain errors and problems. What Plato does is to put forward these views and argue against them so as to arrive at a true theory of justice.

The first common view of justice which Plato examines is that justice was " speaking the truth and paying one's debts". This view also includes the belief that justice is an art, that it is an art which gives good to friends and evil to enemies. Plato rejects this traditional view of justice because if it is just an art, then it can do two opposite things: both good and bad.

Moreover, if justice is doing good to friends and evil to enemies then a person may only appear to be a friend but really be an enemy. Plato therefore argues that this traditional view should be given up. According to him, the correct view on justice cannot be acquired just through experience but instead must be based on great knowledge.

The second common view of justice that Plato critically examines is the belief that justice is 'the interest of the stronger', or that, 'might is right'. This leads to the acceptance of the will of the ruler. Plato however argues that the individual in society is not an isolated unit but part of a larger order. Each individual has a place in that order. Therefore, justice requires that the individual should do his duty according to his position in that order.

The third common view of justice that Plato rejects is similar to the second. In this view justice is an artificial thing and a product of convention i.e. tradition.

Plato, while rejecting these positions, emphasises that justice is not something external like chance or convention, but is something internal because it is part of the human soul. Thus justice is not based on chance or convention but is part of man's nature and is therefore everything.

For Plato, justice consists of a man performing the role that society lays down for him. Thus, justice is linked to man's specialised role or position in the social structure. It is logical, therefore, for Plato to propose that justice exists both in the individual and the state. It exists on a small scale in the individual and on a large scale, and thus in a more clear way, in the state. In this view of justice, therefore, the individual is supposed not to please himself, but to play the role assigned to him in the social order. This means that an individual should perform the tasks that the state lays down for him and the class that he belongs to. Thus, basic to Plato's theory of justice is the idea the particular classes have particular duties that they should unquestioningly perform.

CLASSES IN PLATO'S REPUBLIC

While studying the state Plato draws parallels between it and the individual. He believes that the characteristics of the citizens and the social classes are reflected in the state. For example, the courage of a state is the combined courage of its individuals. Similarly, as we have seen above, the spirit of justice that exists in the individual is reflected in the state. Since for Plato states arise and are based on the character of their citizens, he logically considers it necessary to study the character of men along with the essence of the state. Plato examines three basic human characteristics which contribute to the making of a state. These three basic characteristics of the human soul are: (a) appetite, (b) spirit, and (c) reason.

Appetite: The Producing Class

The most basic element in the human soul according to Plato, is 'appetite' taken to mean desire with which are associated pleasure and satisfaction. From this arise hunger, thirst, love and other appetites. To satisfy these appetites, people combined together for food, clothing, warmth and shelter. These economic necessities led to the specialisation of economic tasks or what is called a division of labour. This division of labour and the association of men in a community led to the formation of a state. Plato shows that the economy has an important role in the formation and maintenance of the state. The economy makes the state into a self-centred and self-sufficient unit. It is, thus, an important basic element. To this basic element of appetite there corresponds a class of people, whom Plato calls the 'farmers', who are the economic or producing class.

Spirit: The Soldiers

Plato knows that men cannot be satisfied by these basic physical necessities alone. They have certain cultural needs, including fine arts, fashionable dress, etc. A large population and territory to support this population is also necessary. To defend the territory, or to acquire more, soldiers are necessary. Here Plato discusses the element of 'spirit' which is necessary to inspire men to fight. Therefore, corresponding to this second element of the human soul, there is a class of warriors or soldiers who form the military.

Reason: The Guardians and the Philosopher-King

Plato emphasises the importance of the highest human element of reason. Reason expresses itself most clearly in the governing of a state. Corresponding to this element of reason is the guardian class. However, on the basis of what is the dominant element, this guardian class is divided into two sections. These are the military guardians whose dominant characteristic is spirit and the philosopher guardians, whose dominant characteristic is reason.

The philosophic guardian or philosopher-king is the key element in Plato's ideal state. He describes this ruler as being unselfish, wise and loving. This is because only those men can govern the state who care for it most. And this care can only be possible if they consider the state's welfare to be their own. Reason, thus, holds the state together. Because though appetite may have drawn men together through economic ties, and spirit added the military bond, it is ultimately reason that holds men together by teaching them to understand and love.

In this way, Plato distinguishes a ruling class which is distinct and specialised. Everyone cannot be a philosopher, as the ability to reason is restricted to a few rare souls. The philosopher-king must know the idea of the good'. He must be clear about the reason for existence and the purpose of all he does.

Plato's ideal state clearly implies the division of men into three main classes: the governmental, the military and the producers. While the governmental and military classes have the special gifts of reason and spirit, the producing class does not have these gifts in any large amount. But just as the rulers and military have a specialised function, so does this producing class. Its single function is to satisfy the ends of the community. The Platonic ideal state is thus clearly marked by a division of labour between the rulers, soldiers and producers.

Here, once again, we can see the parallel Plato draws with the human soul. Each individual as a part of the state must perform his specific role by developing that aspect of the soul for which he has been designated. Only then will be the perfect harmony necessary for the ideal state be achieved. Similarly, Plato outlines the virtues of the state to be wisdom, courage and temperance or self-control. While wisdom is the virtue of the ruling class, courage is that of the soldiers and self control is a virtue that belongs not only to the producers but to all the classes. From this it follows that justice, as we have shown earlier, is the necessary to do what one has to because of one's position in society. Thus, justice is in the mind of every citizen who does his duty in his appointed place.

The ideal state is ruled by philosopher-kings who get their training through the state. For Plato, the state itself is an educational system because it must be guided by knowledge. And since the only true knowledge is philosophy, the state must be guided by philosophers. The rule of the philosopher-kings is absolute, in that they are not restricted by any written law. But these philosopher-kings are not tyrants, since Plato, like most Greeks of his time, opposed tyranny. The rulers powers were limited, by the need to preserve what we may call the basic structure or features of the constitution.

This meant that the state could not be moved, and changed as the philosopher wished. The state was to be preserved in a state of rest, as a static body, in accordance with four basic principles. These were: (i) the rulers have to guard against either poverty or wealth coming into the state: (ii) they have to limit the size of the state, making sure that it is neither too large nor too small, so that it remains united and self-sufficient; (iii) they must maintain the rule of justice and see that every citizen is occupied according to his specific function in the state; and (iv) most important of all, they must ensure that there is no change in the system of education.

By placing these restrictions on the philosopher-kings, Plato, as Barker notes, is like other Greek theorists ensuring an unchanging social order.

PLATO'S THEORIES OF EDUCATION AND COMMUNISM

In the Republic Plato develops his theories of education and communism. These two great institutions are the basis for the building of the type of ideal state that he proposes.

Education

In Plato's theory, education is the first of the two great institutions by means of which the ideal state can be built. Plato proposes a system of education which is intended to train the citizens for the special work they are to perform in keeping with their role in society. Through the system of education he shows how the soul can be trained to achieve the growth best suited both for it and the state. Plato's emphasis on education follows from his overall theories of virtue being knowledge and of justice, and is meant to create the ideal state.

Plato suggests two main stages in education. During the first stage there is a system of common education for the youth of the two upper classes. Until the age of twenty years, there is training in gymnastics and music (including poetry and the arts). Through this values such as courage, chivalry would be developed, in order to produce the necessary 'spirit' requried by a soldier. Most of the youth only go through the first stage of education, which equips them for the military functions.

The second stage is only for those who are fit to be in the governing class i.e. the philosopher-kings. At this stage Plato proposes the study of mathematics, science, philosophy, literature, etc. He emphasises the importance of mathematics which he believes would help the students to understand the common principles of all the subjects they have studied. These studies should last for at least ten years still the age of thirty. The best of these students would then study dialectic (philosophy) so that they could get knowledge of the idea of the good, which is the final object of thought.

During this period, these mature students are tested and those who are successful become the philosopher-kings and perfect guardians. Then for the next fifteen years, from the age of thirty-five to fifty, they will gain experience through serving the state. From these ranks will come the philosopher-kings who are fit to rule the ideal state: the Republic.

Communism

Plato proposes a social order of communism as the second of the two great institutions necessary for an ideal state. Under Platonic communism, the guardian class will give up both family life and private property. This is very much a part of his other ideas on justice, education, etc.

In the ideal state, the philosophers and soldiers will own everything in common. The guardians will eat at common tables and live in common barracks. They will also have common wives and children. The philosopher-kings will arrange temporary marriages with a view to produce the best citizens for the state. There will be no discrimination against the women who could also become guardians.

Since there will be no family and no property for the guardians, they will be unselfish and identify their own interests with those of the state. They will not be concerned with the economic tasks or the element of appetite and therefore can develop the elements of spirit and reason in keeping with the functions assigned to them by the state. The third class of producers or farmers, on the other hand, will not be part of this system of Platonic communism. But even in their case, the state will ensure that producers become neither too rich nor too poor.

We can see, therefore, that through this form of communism, Plato seeks to ensure the necessary conditions for his ideal state. Through Platonic communism the unity and the stability of this state is ensured.

Criticism

Starting with Aristotle, critics have sharply criticised Platonic communism as a totalitarian and dehumanizing theory. Modern critics have called Plato an enemy of an 'Open Society' (i.e. a free and democratic society). They have even accused him of being a forerunner of Fascism.

To some extent these criticisms may be true. But to evaluate Plato's theory objectively we must look at it is its proper historical context. The Greek theorists, based on their own experiences of the city-state, were not always admirers of democracy. After all, it was a democratic government in Athens which had put Plato's teacher Socrates to death. The aristocratic or elitist rule that Plato proposes, is in a broad sense, similar to that proposed by Aristotle, and to the one which existed in Sparta.

Platonic communism has little in common with modern communist theory (Marxism) apart from its name. Unlike Plato, Marxists seek to abolish private property for all, not just for the ruling class. In contrast to Plato's enlightened despot or philosopher king, Marxists consider the communist party to be the guiding force. While Plato's rule is elitist, with governance being the activity only of the guardian class; in Marxist theory there should be participative rule with the people participating in government through bodies like Soviets, etc. The emphasis in modern communist theory is on the role of the working class which is absent in Plato's theory. In Plato's time no working class (as we define it today) existed. Similarly, Plato's theories about the family and the communism of wives are not part of modern communism. Therefore, despite the use of the same term, Platonic communism should not be confused with Marxism.

Plato, was therefore neither a Fascist nor a totalitarian as we understand these terms today. He believed in the rule of reason and the vision of the good. The philosopher-kings was not supposed to be a tyrant but an enlightened, selfless and far-sighted ruler.

PLATO'S LATER WRITINGS

Plato himself realised in later life that the political system proposed in the Republic may not be possible in this world. In his later writings, especially the "Statesman and the Laws", he considerably changes his ideas. Here he advocates 'mixed' states and 'mixed' constitutions rather than the Ideal state. In the Laws he restores the supremacy of the law. He classifies the actual states on the basic of the number of rulers and the legitimacy of governments. He allows for the existence of private property and the family though with great restrictions and control. He also reintroduces the main political institutions of the Greek polis like the town-meeting. Council and Magistrates. In fact it is the state described in the Laws, in which he tries to balance property interests and democratic interests, that is the source of Aristotle's ideas. But the state described in the Laws is only the second best, a concession to human weaknesses. The best is still the ideal state of the Republic.

ARISTOTLE

Aristotle (384-322 B.C.), the second of the major Greek theorists was Plato's most famous student as well as his most famous critic. He was Plato's student for 20 years. He had a great influence on later European philosophy which is why he was later called "the father of the who know".

In the history of political thought no one has perhaps equalled Aristotle's encyclopaedic knowledge and interests. His work ranged from zoology, physics and the natural sciences in general, to philosophy, aesthetics, history and politics. His book Politics does not have the style or force of the Republic, but it is more systematic and analytical, and after twenty-three hundred years, it is still widely considered an introductory textbook to Political Science.

Aristotle's father was the court physician to the king of Macedonia and both his parents were Ionian. Aristotle's scientific interests may be due to his parentage because of the Ionians' interest in the scientific study of nature. Similarly, his inclination towards biological sciences may be due to the influence of his father's profession. In fact, Aristotle classification of constitutions, his study of the structure and arrangement of their parts as well as their progressive deterioration, are similar to the methods of a doctor who studies different types of living organisms and the symptoms of their disease and prescribes remedies for them.

For a period after Plato's death. Aristotle was the instructor of Prince Alexander of Macedonia who later became famous as Alexander the Great. However, Aristotle does not seem to have recognised the revolutionary importance of Alexander's conquest of the East, which had led to the decline of the city-state. In Aristotle's thought, as in Plato's before him, the polis is central to political life.

ARISTOTLE'S CONCEPT OF STATE

Aristotle examines the state in its relationship to other associations like the family and the village. He then classifies the various types of states and constitutions. In his analysis, Aristotle sees the need for mixed constitutions in order to ensure the stability of the state.

State: Natural to Man

Aristotle says that man is by nature a political animal. He therefore joins together with other men and women into associations to achieve a common good through joint action. All associations are political. The family is the first form of association, followed by the second form which is the village. The state is the third form of association.

According to Aristotle: (1) the state is an association, and (2) it is the highest of all associations. He argues that the state is a "natural" organism with all the characteristics of a living being.

It is "natural" in two ways. Firstly, in the historical sense the state is the final stage in the natural growth of association from the family through the village to the polis. Secondly, the state is "natural" in a logical and philosophical sense. The state is the whole of which the other associations and the individual are a part. Therefore, says Aristotle, the state must naturally come before the family and the individual as the whole comes before its parts.

Aristotle shows the state to be the highest association in terms of social and historical evolution, values and purpose. The family is the first and lowest association which is necessary for the supply of man's every wants. The village is a second more developed association, in which men get some companionship and community. The polis is the third and highest association in all ways; while the family and village exist to preserve life and to provide companionship, the "state exists for the sake of a good life and not for the sake of life only." and "political society exists for the state of noble actions, and not of mere companionship" Thus the purpose of the state becomes moral.

Since the state is viewed as a "natural' body with the characteristics of a living being, it also, like the other lower associations, reflects man's own nature. Aristotle sees man as a compound of qualities that are reflected in forms of association.

Man's material appetites and biological urges are reflected in the family. His social sentiment is shown in the village and his moral nature, his highest, most human qualities, is fulfilled in the state.

It is for these reasons that Aristotle views the state as the highest association of all, representing as it does the highest good and most moral action. Therefore, in both Aristotle, and in Plato, the dominance of the polis or city-state is accepted as basic. This is typical of the Greek theorists.

Types of State

In order to arrive at a definition of in ideal state. Aristotle studied one hundred and fifty-eight constitutions and governments. He also examined what other writers had written on this subject. In contrast to Plato, Aristotle says that we "should consider, not only what form of government is best, but also what is possible and what is easily attainable by all".

While Plato in the 'Republic' first constructed the ideal state and then his later works (Statesman Laws) showed how existing states deviated from the ideals, Aristotle does the opposite. He first examines actual states and then constructs an ideal state on the basis of that analysis. But he too uses ideal principles to criticize and classify real states.

Classification of States

Aristotle classified states on the basis of their constitutions and governments. He examined the ends of the state (i.e. what the state's actions are ultimately based on) as a principle of classification. The second principle was whether a government acts in the interests of people in general or serves the private interest of the one, few or of the many. Eased on these principles. Aristotle divides constitutions into two types: normal and perverted. A normal government is one where the end is virtue and the government acts in the interests of the people in general, whereas a perverted government is one where a false end is aimed at and power is used in the interest of the ruling class alone. Under these two broad divisions there is a sub-division based on the number of rulers: monarchy, aristocracy and polity in the normal forms: with tyranny, oligarchy and democracy in the perverted ones.

Monarchy or kingship is a government of the virtuous one in the interest of the people and when it degenerates it becomes tyranny.

Aristocracy is a government by the virtuous few in the general interest and its perverted form is obligachy which means the government of the rich few in their own interest. Polity is the government of the many if it works in the common interest but it becomes its perverted form democracy, when it acts against the interests of the people.

Types of Government—1

No. of Rulers	*Normal/True Form*	*Perverted Form*
One	Monarchy/Kingship	Tyranny
Few	Aristocracy	Oligarchy
Many	Policy	Democracy

Aristotle, however, takes the real basis of the constitution not to be the number of people but the social classes to which they belong. Thus oligarchy is really a government by the wealthy class and democracy is the rule of the poor. This classification is also based on Aristotle's theory of justice.

Since the constitution is defined as the arrangement of offices, the difference between two types of constitutions can be explained by the principle according to which they award offices. Therefore, the principle of distributive justice becomes the basis of classification.

Thus, democracy awards offices on the principle of free birth and oligarchy on the basis of wealth. By using this principle we may not only classify constitutions but also grade them in order of merit.

Aristotle considered monarchy to be the best of the normal of true constitutions because it aims at supreme virtue, followed by aristocracy with polity coming last. Similarly, among the perverted forms of government, democracy is considered the least harmful, followed by oligarchy and then by tyranny.

Aristotle in other words, is classifying constitutions based on whether the basis of rule is the common good of all or the sectional good of the ruler or rulers. The first type is normal or true form whereas the second type is the perverted form.

Types of Government-2

No. of Rulers		*Aim*	*Type*	*Form*
1.	One	Common Good	Monarchy/Kingship	Normal/True
2.	Few	Common Good	Aristocracy	Normal/True
3.	Many	Common Good	Polity	Normal/True
4.	Many	Good of Majority	Democracy	Perverted
5.	Few	Good of Rulers	Oligarchy	Perverted
6.	One	Good of Ruler	Tyranny	Perverted

As you can see from the above table, for Aristotle though the rule of democracy is in the interest of the majority against the minority but because it is not in the interest of all it is therefore, a perverted constitution.

Aristotle's deep sympathy for monarchy can be explained by his own relations with the rising Macedonian monarchy which was trying to conquer the Greek city-states intellectually as well as politically and militarily. In Athens, the leader of the anti-Macedonian and democratic movement. Demosthenes, considered all monarchy to be "un-Athenian", and, thus, the dominant conservative classes were generally pro-Macedonian and received intellectual support from Plato's Academy and Aristotle's school of philosophy.

The Mixed Constitutions

Aristotle is aware that for the stability of the state it is necessary to have mixed constitutions. These are constitutions which have elements of two different types of systems and are therefore mixed. The term 'polity' is used by Aristotle in two senses: the true form and the mixed form.

For example, polity or constitutional government, in its mixed form, is based on a compromise between the two principles of freedom and wealth. It is an attempt, in Aristotle's own words, to "unite the freedom of the poor and the wealth of the rich", without giving either of the two principles priority. This, he realises is essential because "a state in which many poor men are excluded from office will necessarily be full of enemies."

Aristotle's emphasis on a compromise between these two principles of freedom and wealth leads him to stress the importance of the middle class. He argues "that the best political community is formed by the middle class." In fact, he expects those states to be well administered where the middle class is large, and at least stronger than either of the other two classes of the rich and the poor. The middle classes therefore provide the balance and equilibrium necessary for the continued existence of the constitution.

It is because of this realisation that political stability is based on a large middle class, that Aristotle opposes selfish class rule either by an excessively rich oligarchy or by the mass of the poor.

ARISTOTLE ON RULE OF LAW AND THEORY OF JUSTICE

Aristotle, following from Plato's later work 'Laws', says that in a good state there should be a rule of law and not of a person. He emphasises the importance of constitutional rule as opposed to despotic rule, including the rule of the philospher-king. Since, according to him, customary law or customs are based on the collective wisdom of the people and are therefore better than the knowledge of the wisest ruler. Aristotle does not find written law as important as custom or convention; but it is one of the three main elements of constitutional rule. These are: (1) rule in public interest as opposed to rule in the interest of a single class or individual; (2) lawful rule based on general regulations, customs and conventions of the constitution and not by arbitrary decrees; and (3) constitutional government means a government of willing subjects which is different from a despotic government based on force.

Like his reachier Plato, Aristotle emphasis the ethical purpose as the major end of a state. The purpose of the state is to bring about the highest moral development of its citizens. And like Plato before him, Aristotle's ideal was the Greek city-state.

Aristotle, however, never constituted his ideal state and Aristotle's Politics unlike Plato's Republic is not a book on an ideal state but upon the ideals of the state.

Aristotle had a theory of distributive justice based on proportionate equality. Offices of the state are distributed in proportion to the contribution an individual makes to the well-being of a state.

The question is: how should the contribution of individuals be judged. The answer, according to Aristotle is, that aristocracy will measure contribution through virtue. oligarchy on the basis of wealth, and democracy simply through free birth. Though the only true standard of distributive justice is virtue or education, in actual practice. Aristotle takes into account several considerations, particularly those or wealth and birth.

This theory of disrubutive justice means that honours, rewards or punishment are given on the basis of the individuals's contribution. In other words, the rights of citizens should be proportionate to their contributions to the state.

REVOLUTIONS

Causes and Prevention

Aristotle examines both the general causes of revolution and the particular causes that relate to specific types of constitution. The most general cause of revolution, according to him, is a passion for some concept of equality, which is involved in the idea of justice. If any group feels it does not enjoy the share of constitutional rights that it feels entitled to, on the basis of its conception of justice, it will revolt. This will lead either to complete change in the constitution or to a partial modification in its character.

In dealing with the general causes of revolution. Aristotle takes into account: (i) psychological motives; (Aristotle's) the objects at stake; and (iii) the occasions and origins of disturbances.

Psychological

These include inferiority and superiority complexes. Some revolt because they have not got their fair share or that others equal to them have got an unfair advantage. Others stir up sedition.

because they believe that they get no advantage over others although they consider themselves more than equal to the rest.

Objects at Stake

While the above state of mind creates sedition, the objects at stake are profit and honour, or their opposites, loss and disgrace. People revolt because they feel they have not got their fair share of profit or honour, or because they or their friends have unjustly suffered some loss or disgrace.

The Occasions and Origins of Disturbances

According to Aristotle, there are seven major occasions which may encourage the attitude of mind and lead to the pursuit of objects listed above. These are insolence, profit making, questions of honour, presence of some form of superiority, fear, contempt, and the disproportionate increase of one or the other element in the state. There are also four other reasons for dissent and revolution which may accidentally lead to revolution. These are election intrigues, willful neglect, the overlooking of trifling changes on the part of the ruling class, and the dissensions within the ruling class.

In aristocracies, jealously and mutual suspicion leads to the downfall of the ruling group. A defective balance of different elements of the constitution generally leads to the collapse of aristocracies and polities. Tyrannies are destroyed by the hate and contempt the tyrants arouse, as well as by the influence of neighbouring states. In monarchies revolutions are usually caused by fear, by contempt, by desire for fame or by the resentment of the people of their insult by the king. All constitutions can also be overthrown by external influences, including the actions of neighbouring states.

How to Avoid Revolutions?

After discussing the general and particular causes of revolution, Aristotle also prescribes methods for ensuring constitutional stability. The most major means for ensuring the stability of constitutions, according to him, is the education of the citizens in the spirit of their constitution. Through this education the citizens will carry out the actions necessary for the survival of the constitution. This method introduced by Aristotle for the necessary political education of citizens is now-a-days termed 'political socialization'.

Once the citizens accept the spirit of the constitution and act accordingly, respect for the law and constitution will be maintained. The rulers should generally be fair. Offices or posts in government should be distributed to deserving people and relations between the officers and the public should be good. Steps should be taken to prevent offices from being made a source of profiteering.

In democracies the rich should not be oppressed and in oligarchies the poor should be protected. In monarchies or kingships the policy of moderation should be followed. For the preservation of tyrannies, Aristotle prescribes two methods. The first is the policy of repression towards the subjects. The second is to mix kingship with self-restraint.

PLATO AND ARISTOTLE: A COMPARISON

Aristotle has been called the father of political science. This is because he was the first to examine politics in an empirical and scientific manner. He did this through his systematic collection and analysis of all the available information. By doing this he laid the basis for later developments in political science. By his comparative study of all the then known constitutions and political systems, he laid the foundations of an important subject in political science, comparative government and politics.

Aristotle's emphasis on constitutional government and the rule of law is considered by some to be his most major contribution. It became a dominant political idea during the Middle Ages in Europe. In the modern period it is considered to be the basis of democratic government.

Plato, as we have seen, in the Republic first constructs his ideal state: and then in later work analyses existing state as distortions or corruptions of the ideal. In other words, he arrives at certain conclusions about existing states on the basis of his earlier theory of the ideal state. This method of logically drawing conclusions from other things already known or considered to be true, is known as the deductive method. Plato's method, therefore is deductive. Aristotle follows the opposite procedure. He first critically examines existing states, and on the basis of this examination arrives at some conclusions about the ideal qualities of a state, even though he never actually describes an ideal state. In other words, on the basis of his study of particular constitutions. Aristotle arrives at general conclusions. This method adopted by Aristotle is known as the inductive method.

According to Plato the eternal ideas or 'idea' of the good should be the guiding principle of a ruler. In Republic, he, therefore, has no place for law. Aristotle, on the other hand, stresses the importance of law. While Plato argues for rule by a philosopher king, Aristotle considers the rule of law preferable to the rule of a single individual.

The idea of an ideal state, the Republic, is part of Plato's view that what is essentially good of natural is unchanging and unchangeable. Aristotle has a more dynamic and relativist attitude. He is able to appreciate mixed forms of government or mixed constitutions, which combine differing proportions of the ideal and the real.

Aristotle is sharply critical of Plato's theory of communism. Of course, Plato, advocates communism only for the guardian class, not for the entire polity. This is a detail that Aristotle overlooks. But he emphasises the importance for citizens of private property and family life as these are natural as well as necessary for the moral life of a state.

Aristotle is also less critical of democracy. But he wants the principle of popular rule balanced by the principle of wealth. But like Plato, Aristotle can only imagine democracy as it exists in the polis. In a polis or city-state as we have discussed above, only a minority of the population were citizens with full democratic rights.

Both Plato and Aristotle in their theories reflect the ideas and conditions of their time. Both theories are based on the model of the polis, which already was in decline. Because of their elite, upper class backgrounds, both are critical of democracy and favour monarchy or aristocracy, which in effect means the rule of the propertied classes.

The limitations, and others are a product of the social and historical situation in which the Greek political theorists developed their theories. But despite this, Plato and Aristotle have made major and enduring contributions to political philosophy and political science. The contributions make the study of the Greek political theorists relevant. By studying them we can understand the origins or basis of concepts and theories.

OTHER CONTRIBUTIONS OF THE GREEKS TO POLITICAL THEORY

The scientific methods used by Plato and Aristotle, i.e. the deductive and inductive methods are now widely used in social sciences. The emphasis by these two theorists on the need for rule by 'superior' or more talented persons is the basis of the theories of elite rule. The elite theorists have also based themselves on Aristotle's defence of private property. In fact, the recognition of the need for the continued existence of private property is accepted by liberal and conservative theorists. Similarly, the idea of the moral end of the state is now a part of modern political theory. Aristotle's study of revolutions and recognition of the need for political socialization have also been developed further by modern political theorists. The important role of the middle class stressed by Aristotle is now widely accepted.

The classical Greek theorists in not distinguishing between state and the society, and between the interests of the state and that of the individual, provided some of the ideological justification for modern totalitarian theorists. Similarly, Plato and Aristotle's distrust of democracy have been taken up by conservative and totalitarian theorists.

10

The Crisis of Political Theory

Political theory has a long and rich tradition extending over more than two thousand years. Ever since its beginning, it has been practised in the style evolved by the Greek thinkers. Perhaps nothing more eloquently testifies to the vitality of the traditional style of theorizing about politics than that a large number of thinkers of vastly different tempers and philosophical outlooks adopted it. But in recent years there has been a general disenchantment with the traditional style of theorizing about politics. In fact, the traditional approach to the study of politics has been sharply criticized and, under the impetus of contemporary intellectual movements, new approaches have been developed. An inquiry into contemporary political thought would show that in the English-speaking countries the condition of political theory is far from happy.

I

As already noted, there has been much concern about the state of political theory in our times. In the 1950s and 1960s especially, a large number of students of politics argued that politial theory had declined. Whether this view was accepted or rejected, supported or disputed, the state of political theory became a subject of intense discussion. It was perhaps Leo Strauss who in 1946 initiated the discussion on the state of political theory in our times when he discussed the 'present crisis in political philosophy'. A number of scholars and commentators on political theory followed him by variously referring to the 'dearth', 'poverty', 'decline', 'decay', and even 'death' of political theory. The view that political theory had declined spread with amazing swiftness. Even those who disagreed with the 'decline' thesis recognized that there was a widespread feeling among students of politics that political theory had entered upon bad times.

In the 1950s, students of contemporary political thought by and large tended to accept the diagnosis that political theory had declined or was dead. An index of the extent ot which the fact of decline was accepted is that, in general, scholars and commentators were more interested in studying the causes of the decline than in establishing that the decline had in fact taken place. In course of time a more critical attitude developed. In the 1960s, many scholars challenged the 'decline' thesis and argued that political theory was not dead or dying.

The decline or death of a tradition which has had a history of nearly twenty-five hundred years would be a phenomenal development. Before such a claim is advanced, it should be clarified as to what would constitute the decline of political theory. But it is surprising that most of the commentators and scholars who wrote on the decline of political theory did not clarify how one could show that political theory had in fact declined. This was clearly reflected in the writings of commentators like Laslett, who first declared political philosophy 'dead' and then within a few years claimed its 'revival'. Partridge summed up the prevailing confusion when he admitted that he did not know the 'kind or amount of evidence [that] is necessary to prove that political theory has declined'. He himself reflected the confusion when he said, on the one hand, that 'it is not hard to construct a case against' the view that 'there has been a "slackening" of the "moral urge"' and, on the other hand, that in contemporary political thought there is 'a skepticism concerning general speculation about the moral issues of politics'.

The main evidence cited in support of the view that political theory is dead or dying is that no major theoretical work on politics has been produced for quite some time. An inquiry into the history of political thought would show that long patches of routine intellectual activity have been punctuated with major works on political theory. But, as Cobban, an exponent of the 'decline' thesis, points out, 'there has been rather a long interval since there was last any original political thinking'. In fact, the feeling is widespread among students of politics that no major work on political theory has been produced in our times. Most historians close the history of political theory with a study of the political ideas of Marx and Mill. But one may wonder whether this could provide an adequate basis for claiming the decline or death of political theory. One reason is that there is no agreement on how a great work on politics is to be defined. There has also been a feeling that it is arbitrary to conclude the history of political theory with Marx and Mill. It has, in fact, been argued that significant theoretical work has been done in recent times. In his study of past political theories, Hacker, for example, says: 'To close with John Stuart Mill is not to suggest that there have been no significant contributions to political theory since 1861.' In fact, he has 'no doubt that there are currently in our midst writers who will one day have the standing of Hobbes, Locke, and Hegel. But he also joins scholars like Easton in complaining about some of those very trends in recent political thought on the basis of which the decline of political theory has been proclaimed. He does not clarify as to what he is complaining about if, as he says, great thinkers are writing on politics today. But other scholars have sought to refute the view that political theory is dead by referring to the works of such writers as Rawls, Strauss, Popper, Oakeshott, and others in evidence of the vitality of political theory today.

In any case, it is doubtful whether even the absence of a major work on politics could be regarded as conclusive evidence in favour of the claim that political theory is dead of dying. As Cobban himself points out, a great political thinker 'cannot be produced to order'. The death of political theory can be claimed not so much by showing that no major work on politics has been produced as by showing that none can in fact be produced. In other words, it has to be shown that it is no longer logically possible to theorize about politics in the traditional style. If it is not possible to theorize on the basis of the assumptions which past thinkers had accepted, it is doubtful whether works written in the traditional style could be cited to show that political theory is in good shape.

This is the point which Berlin makes in his well-known article, 'Does Political Theory Still Exist?' And in criticizing the claim that political theory is dead, he relies mainly on the argument that it remains a legitimate pursuit. According to him, political theory, as traditionally conceived, is essentially a normative inquiry. And questions of ends in politics which form 'the core of traditional political theory' are philosophical questions. Whereas we can obtain clear answers to empirical and formal questions, he believes, 'there is no automatic technique, no universally recognized expertise, for dealing with [philosophical] questions'. In the history of human thought, he says, there has been a gradual shuffling of the basic questions into the empirical and the formal. But numerous attempts to reduce questions of value to questions of fact have not succeeded. This has led some scholars to doubt the legitimacy of these questions. But, Berlin argues, they are not wrong questions. If we are not able to obtain clear answers to them, that is because these are philosophical questions. Indeed, it would be 'a gratuitous abdication of our powers of reasoning' if we cease to be concerned with these questions. Thus, so long as there is 'rational curiosity', Berlin believes, 'political theory will not wholly perish from the earth'. But, then, Berlin admits that political theory is leading a 'shadowy' existence today. This creates an anomalous situation, particularly 'at a time when, for the first time in history, literally the whole of mankind is violently divided by issues the reality of which is, and has always been, the sole *raison d'etre* of this branch of study'. Berlin is aware that this is 'a strange paradox'. But there is nothing in his analysis to account for it.

The point is that it is not enough to argue that political theory continues to be a legitimate pursuit. The question of the state of political theory could not be disposed of merely by arguing that its basic assumptions have not been shown to be erroneous. For there is still the possibility that students of politics may give up the approach developed by traditional theorists in favour of new approaches to the study of politics. Were such a tendency to develop, it would surely mean that political theory is languishing. Moreover, if the basic assumptions of political theory have fallen into disuse, it would once again be doubtful whether we could claim that the condition of political theory is satisfactory by merely referring to some writers who have adopted the traditional approach to the study of politics. In fact, even the exponents of the 'decline' thesis have admitted that some thinkers in our times have followed the traditional style. Cobban, for example, refers to Laski; Easton refers to Dewey, Barker, and others. In this context, the names of de Jouvenel, Voegelin, Strauss, Oakeshott, and others have also been mentioned. But if there has been a general tendency to cease thinking about politics in the style adopted by political theorists in the past, those who write on politics in the traditional style today are likely to be ignored. It is therefore not surprising that a scholar like Germino, who seeks to show that the 'decline' thesis is 'seriously in error' by referring to the works of scholars like Strauss and Voegelin, finds himself in a difficult situation. For he is compelled to recognize that the vast majority of the students of politics have hardly taken notice of their work. It is, of course, possible to argue that contemporary political scientists 'are incapable of recognizing genuine political theory when they see it'. Since they define theory as 'behaviourist methodology or value-laden ideology', they are unable to see that we are on the verge of 'a truly creative flowering', indeed a 'renaissance of political theory in the grand manner'. But, then, this also raises doubts about the success of the attempts to revive political theory. Thus, it is not surprising that after exhorting us to 'joyously' commemorate the revival of political theory, Germino cautions us against actually beginning the celebrations. For the fears that the 'success of the restorative movement is by no means guaranteed.

Thus, to apprehend the state of political theory today it is necessary to examine the nature of contemporary political thought. Such an inquiry will show whether the assumptions accepted by traditional political theorists have continued to provide the basis for the study of politics in recent times or not. If contemporary students have developed new approaches to the study of politics, this will indicate whether the assumptions of traditional political theory have been shown to be erroneous or whether they have simply fallen into disuse.

II

As conceived by traditional thinkers, political theory was an all embracing study of human society. It included not only a study of the political aspects of society, empirical and normative, but also a study of its social, economic and other aspects. Aristotle's *Politics*, for example, included his views on the nature of justice, descriptive accounts of the actual working of political organizations, generalizations regarding causal relations between the economic structure and political power, an inquiry into the structure and composition of different social classes, an account of the exchange of goods and the role of money in exchange, and so on. Since the late eighteenth and the early nineteenth centuries, however, studies of various aspects of society, which formed part of political theory, have tended to drift away from the parent body. The study of economic aspects was the first to move away from the parent body. Under the impetus provided by Adam Smith it began to acquire a separate identity. It progressed rapidly and, in course of time acquired the reputation of being a scientific discipline which is the envy of most social sciences. Similarly, under the impetus provided by thinkers like Comte and Durkheim, the study of society also began to separate itself from the study of politics. With a number of thinkers contributing to its development, the study of society grew into the independent discipline of sociology. In fact, students of politics are finding it difficult to preserve the separate identity of the study of politics. It has been argued by sociologists like Parsons that politics does not constitute a distinctive field of inquiry like economics. Though students of politics may claim a separate identity for their field of inquiry, they have begun to borrow concepts, categories and models from other social sciences. We have come a long way from the days when the studies of various aspects of social life were included in the study of politics.

Though economics and sociology may be disciplines of recent origin, they have acquired great importance in our times. We have increasingly begun to look to them for the solution of our problems. It is to Keynes, for example, that we have turned in recent years. With the development of the welfare state and economic planning, the economist has found himself in a sew role.

Economics has thus begun to take over the function which earlier belonged to politics. In recent years, sociologists have also begun to carve out a bigger role for themselves. In fact, ever since its inception, sociologists had visualized a grandiose role for sociology in social and political life. Comte, for example thought of sociology as essentially a scientific remedy for the long-standing social, political, and cultural crisis of Europe. Later, Mannheim, who believed that all social and political thought had an ideological character, argued that in our age 'unattached intellectuals' could synthesize the prevailing 'partial views' and develop a unified perspective which would be free from 'existential determination'. Thus, he thought that the sociologist was more suited to perform the sort of task which traditionally political philosophers had performed. In fact, according to Lipset, in the years following the Second World War sociological analysis has tended to take the place of ideological thinking. It can hardly be denied that governmental and non-governmental agencies are today increasingly turning to sociologists for advice. But questions regarding the kind of life prevailing in society today, which Lipset claims to be essentially sociological, have traditionally belonged to the study of politics. What Lipset is really saying is that sociologists are better equipped to tackle the kind of questions which have traditionally preoccupied political thinkers.

Supporters of the classical tradition may lament that the emancipation of large segments which formerly belonged to it has left political theory a 'pitiable rump'. But social scientists have in general welcomed the development of new disciplines. It is pointed out that this is not the first time that new disciplines have been carved out of a larger body of thought. Thought the ages a number of areas of study drifted away from the main body of philosophy and acquired independent status with recognizable structures of their own. This is how, it is argued, disciplines such as physics and astronomy, for example, came into existence. What is interesting, however, is that even political scientists have welcomed the disintegration of the area which has traditionally been theirs. Indeed, they believe they are making a positive contribution to this process. It is pointed out that the attempt to separate the study of the empirical aspect of politics from the normative aspect is a continuation of the process of the disintegration of political theory which began in the late eighteenth century.

Contemporary social scientists have justified the development of new disciplines on grounds of the growing need for specialization. It is suggested that past students of society were seekers of general wisdom. If the knowledge of society is to grow, it is argued, specialization is necessary. This may be so. But it has generally been ignored that traditional political thinkers sought to solve the problems confronting society and these problems cut across the borders of academic disciplines. Today a sociologist like Lipset may reared a certain social problem at once concerns different aspects of society. This is the reason why traditional thinkers did not distinguish between those aspects of society which have in recent times been separated for purposes of academic inquiry. And they conducted their discussion under the rubric of political theory. It has been commonly thought that the study of society was included in the study of politics because for ancient Greek thinkers the political almost coincided with the social. But what has been ignored is that they were primarily concerned with the problems confronting society. An effort to solve these problems inevitably raises questions regarding the way the social and political life of society is organized. And these questions are essentially political questions. This is the reason why studies of various aspects of society have traditionally been included in the study of politics.

There has, of course, been some concern among students of society about the separatist tendencies in the social sciences. In recent years sociologists have, in fact, begun to question 'the idea of a sociology as a separate discipline'. Birnbaum, for example, attributes the 'lack of intellectual substance which is so troubling' about sociology to its 'recent self-containment. And he argues that 'instead of persisting in the attempt to construct a solipsistic universe of discourse', sociologists should devote themselves to the study of society. If the work is 'interesting', it matters little if it could not be classified in 'the conventional academic categories'. After all, as students we are 'primarily interested in society and secondarily in sociology. These observations could justifiably be applied to the study of any other aspect of society such as politics. The reason is that various aspects of society which can be analytically separated are in fact interconnected. A study of one aspect of social life is likely to involve other aspects too. It is of course possible to isolate and systematize a social or a political theory from a larger system of thought. It may also be possible to work out the implications of a certain theory. It is here that specialization may prove useful. But it is doubtful if we can theorize meaningfully about an aspect of social life in isolation from other aspects.

But the fact remains that social scientists have made break with the approach adopted by social and political thinkers through the ages. Whereas traditional thinkers were concerned with the social and political problems confronting society, social scientists today have come to regard themselves as essentially students of a subject called political science or a subject called sociology. A point has come when students of politics can be forbidden from tackling serious problems confronting society on the plea that these are social rather than political problems. The assumption is that the study of a discipline should proceed from a definition of its own subject matter. One no longer visualizes the concern of students of politics in terms of problems confronting society. In such an intellectual climate political theory in the classical style could hardly flourish.

III

A traditional political theory was, as discussed above, a blend of normative and empirical theories. Concerned with the solution of problems confronting society, a traditional political theorist simultaneously inquired into the normative and empirical aspects of politics. This has been an essential feature of the traditional approach to the study of politics. In recent times, however, there has been much interest in the study of the empirical aspect of politics and a concerted effort has been made to make it 'scientific'. The new approach has come to exercise an extraordinary sway over political science, particularly in America in the post-Second World War period.

It has been suggested that the 'behavioural approach to politics', as it is popularly called, owes its development to a general 'dissatisfaction with the achievements of conventional political science, particularly through historical, philosophical, and the descriptive-institutional approaches'. For this reason, Dahl describes it as 'a protest movement'. Eulau does not accept Dahl's description. According to him, the behavioural approach owes its development to 'a realization that the problems encountered in concrete research required new theoretical and methodological departures. In any case, dissatisfaction with 'conventional approaches' to the study of politics had been brewing for quite some time. It found manifestation in the works of Graham Wallas, A.F. Bentley, Charles E. Merriam and others, who sought to find alternative approaches to the study of politics. The Second World War provided an impetus to the intellectual tendencies which had been at work for some time. The new approach—called variously 'the new science of politics', 'the scientific study of politics', or, more often, the 'behavioural approach to politics'—crystallized in the 1950s.

In spite of the growing hegemony of this school, there is no unanimity even among political behaviouralists in defining their approach. Even in 1969, when Easton claimed that a psot-behavioural revolution had occurred in political science, he pointed out: 'The behavioural revolution has never been fully understood... we are still grappling with its meaning'. The ambiguity about the nature of the behavioural approach seems to have led some scholars like de Grazia to propose that the term itself be dropped. Dahl, however, thinks that this ambiguity is 'perhaps the most striking characteristic' of the behavioural approach to politics. But it is doubtful whether the uncertainty about its meaning could be considered a peculiarity of the behavioural approach. For it is often difficult to precisely define a school of thought. However, one difficulty in defining the behavioural approach to politics is that a number of its leading practitioners define it by saying what it is not, instead of by saying what it is. Thus, it has been pointed out, it does not include philosophical speculation, historiography, legal studies or moral considerations. Another difficulty is that some of the practitioners of this approach, like Dahl, do not think that there are definite beliefs, assumptions, methods, or topics that could be identified as constituting the behavioural approach. He describes it as a 'mood'—a mood that seeks 'to make the empirical component of the discipline more scientific'.

Be that as it may, a number of students of politics believe that the behavioural approach stands for a study of the individual, rather than larger political units, as the focal point for political research.

Truman, however, does not think it desirable to contrast behavioural analysis with institutional analysis. In his opinion, what is new in political science is the tendency to utilize new kinds of date from the hard core social sciences, namely, psychology, sociology, and anthropology, in the study of politics. But it has been argued that this view fails to place the changes in the study of politics in the context of 'a deeper shift taking place in the social sciences as a whole'. According to Easton, in recent years the social sciences have experienced 'an intellectual upheaval... that has.., been identified as the behavioural approach'. The behavioural approach to politics is an 'integral part' of the 'movement of the social sciences' in our times. According to him, the behavioural approach has two aspects. One is the commitment 'to use the most advanced methods of the social sciences'. A number of scholars and practitioners of the behavioural approach tend to view it as essentially an effort to introduce 'scientific' methods and techniques to the study of politics. But Easton thinks it inadequate to define the behavioural approach in terms of methods and techniques alone because, in his view, it has a theoretical aspect also. According to him, 'the construction of empirically oriented theory' is the goal of political science. But a number of exponents of the behavioural approach do not take 'for granted' the need for such a theory. According to Eulau, for example, 'to search for a comprehensive schema is to chase a phantom'. Of course, Eulau accepts the need to provide 'theoretical directions' to empirical research. But when he says that behavioural research should be cast in 'some theoretical frame of reference', what he has in mind is not a general theory but 'theorizing carried out in the context of empirical research. In this way, the exponents of the behavioural approach have continued to disagree about the nature of the approach they have developed. In spite of the differences, however, they have been united by the goal of making the study of politics scientific.

But this is not the first time that an attempt has been made to make the study of politics scientific. An inquiry into the history of political theory would show that a number of such attempts have been made—in fact, Plato and Aristotle were the first to strive to do so. What is distinctive about the contemporary attempt is that it challenges the assumptions of the traditional style of studying politics. Past political theorists placed the study of normative questions at the center of the study of politics. They believed that it was possible to discuss rationally the normative question which arise in politics. But contemporary political scientists have adopted a thoroughly relativistic view of values. They do not think it possible for science to judge the moral worth of ends in politics. Science could help in acquitting knowledge which may be useful in realizing ends, but not in deciding which ends to pursue. Today it is widely believed that one reason why classical politics theorists were unable to develop a reliable knowledge of politics is that they placed the study of values at the centre of the study of politics. Following this, political scientists have developed the notion of a value-free science of politics. They have south to ban the study of values from the scientific study of politics which, they believe, ought to concentrate on facts.

It is common to regard the relativistic approach to values as 'the logical implication of Scientific Method'. It is believed that there are no reasonably acceptable scientific methods whereby one could attain 'intersubjectively transmissible' knowledge of any objective standard of value. The methodological argument has been derived from a philosophical position whose roots can be traced to Hume. The 'chief technical ground' for the withdrawal of science from the study of values, as Brecht points out, is the logical difference between 'is' and 'ought'. Following this difference, it is argued that one cannot logically derive a value judgment from a consideration of facts. It should, however, be realized that the distinction between 'is' and 'ought' is only a logical distinction.

And it is not at all certain whether logical relationship is all that there is to the relationship between facts and values. Indeed, there is a strong feeling that 'the fact that one cannot find equivalences, make valid deductive argument, and so on, may show nothing about' the relationship between facts and values. Thus, one may wonder whether logical considerations alone could provide an adequate support to the relativistic view of values.

Contemporary political scientists have, however, gone ahead with the task of making the study of politics 'scientific'. The result is that in recent years immense work has been done on the empirical aspects of politics. But in the course of empirical inquiry it has been realized that 'whatever effort is exerted, in undertaking research we cannot shed our values in the way we remove our coats'. And the presence of values in empirical research is far from innocuous. Not only do values play a role in the selection of an empirical problem, they also influence one in selecting facts and even in establishing interconnections among them. American political scientists have, thus, found it necessary to estimate the implications of values which may underlie empirical research. They have emphasized that a student of politics should state his value position in detail before embarking on the main empirical inquiry They have, in fact, begun to feel the need for developing a value theory for the purpose of overcoming the deficiencies of research in political science. Political science has thus come a long way from the hey-day of a value-free science of politics.

But the belief in the fact-value dichotomy has only partially been undermined. Political scientists may have realized that values have implications for facts. But they continue to hold that factual investigations do not influence values. The view prevails that values can ultimately be reduced to emotional responses conditioned by the individual's total life-experience. The implication of reducing values to emotional responses is that it is not possible to support or undermine a value position by empirical investigation. Emotional responses can be explained by life-experience but not justified by facts about society. In the words of a political scientist: "The moral aspect of a proposition... expresses only the emotional response of an individual to a state of real or presumed facts. It indicates whether and the extent to which an individual desires a particular state of affairs to exist. Although we can say that the aspect of a proposition referring to a fact can be true or false, it is meaningless to characterize the value aspect of a proposition in this way.'

However, considerations of fact may have a bearing on questions of value. In recent years, doubts have been raised about the view that we are free to adopt an indefinite number of value positions before a given set of facts. Indeed, in a critical examination of some of the popular empirical theories of politics, Taylor has shown that a 'value-slope' is implicit in an empirical theory. If facts have implications for values, empirical considerations would be relevant in the study of questions of value which arise in politics. It may not be possible to derive values from facts, but factual considerations could be adduced in favour of or against a normative position. An example could be the attempt by theorists like Schumpeter to undermine Rousseau's model of democratic society, in which power was equally shared among all people, by bringing forward evidence in favour of the elite model. It can, thus, be argued that questions of value are not independent of questions of act. Indeed, scholars have begun to emphasize the importance of sociological evidence in the study of normative questions. The grip of the fact-value dichotomy, which had strangulated the study of politics for a long time, is beginning to loosen. The possibility of a reasoned discussion on questions of value which arise in politics seems to be slowly emerging.

But it is still doubtful whether we can say that political philosophy is alive again. It is true that doubts have been raised about the relativistic view of values. It is also true that philosophers have started taking an interest in questions of value. But it remains true that students of politics, especially in America, have not yet abandoned the relativistic view of values. The notion of political inquiry which dominates political thought, thus, continues to derive inspiration from the relativistic view. The reason could be that developments in philosophy have not yet percolated to the study of politics. But it is also not clear how these could be utilized by political scientists. It is perhaps no longer possible to dismiss questions of value summarily. But it is not clear how this could lead those interested mainly in making the study of politics scientific to the study of values. The point is that it is not enough to show that we can rationally study questions of value. For political science has gone so far away from the traditional approach to the study of politics that this alone can hardly persuade political scientists to take an interest in the study of values. What has to be shown is that the study of normative questions is central to the study of politics.

Thus, in recent years the nature of political inquiry has been redefined. But there is no agreement among students of politics concerning the significance of the change. According to Dahl, the behavioural approach has brought about a revolution in the study of politics. Eulau does not agree with Dahl's assessment which he finds 'unduly optimistic'. He argues that Dahl's view amounts to saying that 'the old political science' is dead. But, he points out, traditional ways of doing things have a tendency to survive in the social science. Development in the social sciences is not as linear and cumulative as it is in the natural and physical sciences. Eulau sees 'the behavioural movement more as a successful renaissance than as a successful revolution'. According to him, the behavioural approach has not displaced the more traditional approaches; rather, it has joined them as one more approach to the study of politics. But Easton endorses Dahl's interpretation of the nature of the changes taking place. According to him, the behavioural approach has brought about a 'revolution' in political science. The result of a 'revolt against tradition', it foreshadows ' the beginning of a fundamentally new direction of development'. In 'the context of the whole historical movement of the social sciences', it represents, according to Easton, the latest stage 'in a truly linear movement in the nature and assumptions about our understanding of man in society'.

Whether the behavioural approach represents an advance in our understanding of politics or not, it is difficult to deny that it makes a sharp break with the traditional approach. Whereas traditional political theorists inquired simultaneously into the empirical and normative aspects of politics, contemporary political scientists have sought to concentrate on the study of the empirical aspect alone. They do not think it possible to develop reliable knowledge of normative questions. In fact, they hold the preoccupation of past thinkers with normative issues responsible for keeping them from developing a reliable knowledge of politics. Even when the difficulties in conduction value-free inquiry into politics were reveled, they continued to believe that we should study the empirical aspect alone. For them there was no going back to the traditional approach. They sought rather to overcome these difficulties by other means.

The new approach to the study of politics, which emerged in the years following the Second World War, came to dominate the study of politics in America and influence it in other countries also within a few years. So complete has been its dominance that students of politics have begun talking of it as the new 'orthodoxy' and of 'the behaviouralists as members of an "establishment" within the discipline'. Though some exponents of the behavioural approach like Eulau may insist that it has not become a 'new establishment', it is difficult to deny that it holds tremendous sway over the study of politics. The traditional approach to the study of politics has not been altogether forgotten, but it does not carry the aura of legitimacy which surrounds the behavioural approach. So powerful is the dominance of the behavioural approach that even outstanding scholars who have not succumbed to its mystique tend to be ignored. Thus, the development of the behavioural approach to politics has had far-reaching consequences for the study of politics in the classical style.

IV

In the twentieth century, philosophy in England as elsewhere in the English-speaking countries has tended to become analytical, the analytical movement began when Moore and Russell rebelled against the idealist position which had dominated English philosophy in the latter half of the nineteenth century. The conception of analysis has not, of course, remained static. It has undergone important changes as a result of successive movements in philosophy. The conception of analysis which has dominated

English philosophy since the Second World War has strongly influenced the study of politics. Under the impetus of linguistic philosophy, political philosophy too has tended to become analytical.

The conception of political philosophy developed in the early 1950s makes a radical break with the traditional conception of political philosophy. The purpose of philosophy, it has been argued, is 'to expose and elucidate. linguistic muddles'. It is not the job of philosophy 'to provide new information'. For philosophical problems are second order problems. They are 'generated by the language in which facts are described and explained'. In particular, it has been pointed out that political philosophy does not have substantive implications for politics. For it is not concerned 'with the establishment and the demolition of political principles'. In sum, philosophy 'has done its job when it has revealed the confusions which have occurred and are likely to recur in inquiries into matter of fact'.

Linguistic philosophers are aware that this is not how traditionally political philosophy has been conceived. But they have argued that the traditional conception is misconceived. The thrust of the argument is that the questions which political philosophers have traditionally asked are wrong questions. Margaret Macdonald, who mounts this criticism in her well-known article, 'The Language of Political Theory', argues that we search in vain for general answers to the eternal questions of political theory. Take, for example, the question of political obligation which has been one of the perennial questions of political philosophy. Macdonald examines some of the theories of politics, like the social contract theory and the organic theory, and argues that they do not provide satisfactory answers to this question. In fact, she claims that it is not even possible to provide a universal rule of obedience to sate power. Political theorists want an answer to the question of political obligation which is 'always and infallibly right', but, she argues, this is a 'senseless' request, for it results from 'stretching language beyond the bounds of significance'. We know what would be relevant in deciding on the merits of a particular item of legislation or even in embarking on illegal resistance to a particular government. But when we move from 'Why should I obey the Conscription Act?' to 'Why should I obey any law?', the specific context which gives meaning to the former is by definition removed by the latter. Any answer to a general question is, therefore, bound to be so vague as to be useless.

Weldon follows Macdonald in maintaining that the questions which political philosophers have traditionally asked are 'wrongly posed. In the form in which they normally occur they cannot be answered but can be shown to be unprofitable'. According to him, most well-known political philosophers form Plato onwards have taken for granted that 'What is the proper relation between the State and the Individual?' is a legitimate question. And they have sought to answer it with different sets of axioms and definitions involving political words like 'state', 'law', and 'right'. But Weldon does not think this to be a legitimate question. It is a meaningless question and so attempts to answer it are necessarily worthless. His argument is that a meaningful discussion in politics could take place only in the context of concrete social and political situation and not 'in the abstract'. But traditional political philosophers have asked 'general questions to which no answers can be given because they lack any precise meaning', such questions as 'What is the proper relation between the Individual and the State?' or 'Why should I obey the law?' are not difficult but empty questions. This according to Weldon is why no progress has been made in answering the questions which Greek philosophers formulated about politics, though a number of philosophers have sought to solve them.

According to Weldon, traditional political philosophers were interested in making appraisals in politics. And they believed that the task of political philosophy was to provide the criteria with which to make appraisals. This led them to ask general questions. They believed that 'if we can discover what is the right or proper relation of the State to the Individual', it would be possible to determine 'whether, or how far, any set of actual institutions satisfies this condition'. It was assumed that the answer to a general question would yield 'a sort of standard or measuring rod' with which to 'conclusively' make an appraisal. In other words, traditional political philosophers sought to derive appraisals from general principles rather than to base them on empirical evidence. According to Weldon, they seem to have assumed that theoretical reasoning can yield axioms from which it is possible to deduce judgments in politics. But Weldon does not think that politics is amenable to mathematical calculations. In fact, it is so complex that no simple formula can cover all circumstances. Similarly, he argues that the 'foundations' of democracy, fascism, and communism are useless because they are too vague to be of any use. The conclusions to which a principle leads are 'either vacuous or highly disputable and not at all self-evident'. Thus 'foundations' like 'Men are always to be treated as ends and never as means' do not and, in fact, cannot 'serve as axioms, from which practical conclusions can be derived'.

The thrust of the argument is that the traditional quest for general political standard is misconceived. It is conceded that we make rational appraisals in politics, but it is stressed that they are not derived from general standards. The idea is that a given social and political situation provides the criteria with which to make valid appraisals. Now there is no doubt that we make contextual judgments in politics. It is also difficult ot deny that there has been a tendency to derive judgments in politics from 'pure reason' while wholly ignoring the context. In emphasizing the importance of the context in making political judgments, this argument contains as element of truth. But it still does not follow that political institutions, practices, etc., have to be judged only contextually and that non-contextual criteria are never called for. The context may provide a criterion for appraisal but it is not the only criterion, nor necessarily a valid criterion. Macdonald and Weldon, however, do not think it legitimate to inquire into the validity of the contextual criteria. But this amounts to assuming the validity of the prevailing criteria, which is open to question. Traditional political philosophers considered it essential to discuss the question of the validity of the criteria of appraisal and to provide non-contextual criteria if they did not find the prevailing criteria acceptable. It is also not correct to say that they were discussing these questions 'in the abstract'. They discussed these questions in the context of concrete social and political problems which they were trying to solve. On the other hand, the logical positivists who divide sensible discourse into empirical and analytical realms, do not think that the study of moral and political questions constitutes sensible discourse. But linguistic philosophers do not agree with them. In fact, they criticize logical positivists for denying that one could sensibly talk about moral and political questions. But, then, they too do not think that that philosophers could legitimately make an inquiry into the worth of the criteria of appraisal.

Under the influence of linguistic philosophy the 'mistake' of traditional political philosophy is attributed to 'carelessness over the implications of language'. It arises from 'the primitive and generally unquestioned belief' that words have 'intrinsic or essential meanings'. Thus, according to Weldon, classical political philosophers believed that the difficulties in making appraisals arise only because the meaning of such words as 'justice' and 'liberty' is not clear to us and that once their meaning is discovered, it will not be difficult to make judgments in politics. But, he points out, an inquiry into the meaning of words is 'doomed to sterility because words do not have meanings in the required sense at all; they simply have uses'. Words like 'justice' and 'liberty' are 'only part of the verbal apparatus we make use of for describing and criticizing certain types of human conduct'. 'To know their meaning is to know how to use them correctly'. However, according to Weldon, this 'radical mistuned-standing' regarding the meaning of words has given rise to a whole family of 'illusions' which make up the greater part of what is known as 'metaphysics'. Three of the illusions which are especially pervasive in discussion on politics are the illusion of real essences, absolute standards, and geometrical method.

Though it may be generally true that political philosophers have not been very particular about linguistic considerations and that their arguments suffer form linguistic confusions, it is far from correct to say that political philosophy is simply theorizing about pointless and unanswerable problems due to verbal confusion and misunderstanding regarding the logic of language. In any case, this view has not been substantiated with an inquiry into the history of political thought. On the other hand, linguistic philosophers like

Macdonald have conceded that it is not merely 'philosophical discomfort about language' which induces people to ask certain questions about their social life and accept certain answers. While she insists that problems of philosophy, such as those of epistemology, are 'mainly academic' and have a 'predominantly linguistic character', she does not think this to be true of the problems of political theory. The language employed by political theorists may appear 'peculiar', but the fact is that 'it has some use' in social and political life. This is why, she thinks, for understanding theories of politics more than linguistic considerations are required. And what she has in mind is the need to relate political theories to the historical conditions in which they were produced!

Thus, by 1950 developments in the field of philosophy began to percolate to the study of politics. In general, the effect of linguistic philosophy was to undermine traditional political philosophy. It led scholars to doubt the legitimacy of questions which political philosophers had traditionally asked and to think it futile to strive to answer them. The result was the development of a mood of skepticism regarding the traditional style of theorizing about politics. The criticism of traditional political philosophy was hardly legitimate. In any case, linguistic philosophers had not succeeded in showing that the question which political philosophers had traditionally asked were wrong. Nevertheless, the criticism of traditional political philosophy made by Macdonald, Weldon, and other played an important role in the development of 'dissatisfaction with the traditional type of political theory'. Weldon especially is regarded as one of the 'most widely influential authors' who wrote on politics in the 1950s. But it is doubtful whether he had many disciples in the English-speaking countries. One may also wonder whether his *Vocabulary of Politics* was a particularly 'powerful work'. What is perhaps true is that it remains the only comprehensive treatment of political philosophy from the point of view of linguistic philosophy. This, however, does not mean that it is a 'classic' even of analytical political philosophy. Indeed, it is hardly the sort of work to expound a new conception of political philosophy. Its chief merit lies in being the first to apply the insights of contemporary philosophy to the study of politics. But this is not to deny the influence which Weldon has had on students of politics, as also on the general public. Indeed, his work 'was above all responsible for engendering the popular impression... that all substantive social and political theory had died'.

In the initial stages few linguistic philosophers turned to the study of politics. It was widely believed that there was little philosophers could do except reveal the conceptual errors and confusions of those who had philosophized about politics. Weldon's *Vocabulary* was an example of this attitude which dominated English philosophy in the 1950s. But then the mood changed. In the 1960s, philosophers began to take an interest in concepts which had been central to the concerns of traditional political philosophy. And a tendency to apply the techniques of linguistic analysis to such concepts as justice, law, rights, and obligation, developed. This led some scholars to claim the revival of political philosophy. Now there is no doubt that philosophers have turned 'linguistic analysis to positive use'. But it is difficult to see how this could be interpreted as a revival of political philosophy. It is true that past political theorists made conceptual investigations. But they were primarily interested in substantive issues in politics. And they made conceptual investigations while they were grappling with these issues. Contemporary philosophers, on the other hand, are primarily interested in making analytical investigations. They have not addressed themselves to the kind of questions political philosophers have traditionally asked. But why they are not concerned with these questions is far from clear. For they no longer say that these are wrong questions. In spite of the increasing interest philosophers are taking in the study of politics, these issues have not been clarified. Indeed, it is hard to find a work in which the prevailing approach to the study of politics has been authoritatively expounded or defended.

With the publication of A *Theory of Justice* by John Rawls, however, the situation seems to have undergone a change. This work has not only been acclaimed for the substantive theories it offers. It has also been welcomed for showing how the techniques of analysis developed in recent times could be effectively employed in the study of substantive issues. Thus, Rawls makes a break with the trend that has dominated philosophy in recent times. Unlike philosophers who have been interested essentially in analyzing concepts, Rawls is primarily concerned with developing ' a substantive theory of justice'. The task, as he conceives it, is to develop a theory which describes our sense of justice. The principles of justice should, therefore, accord with our considered judgments about what is just. We may, of course, have to adjust our principles and judgments in order to achieve the best fit. This he calls 'reflective equilibrium'. The difficulties in anchoring values in facts have, thus, led scholars like Rawls to anchor them in prevailing moral and political opinion. But the trouble is that there may be no agreement of moral and political questions. And so if we rely on our considered judgments for checking our moral theories, we may fall a prey to relativism. In any case, this is to make the validity of a theory depend on its agreement with the prevailing view. But one may wonder whether we can justify a normative theory simply by showing that it can give an account of our moral convictions, even extend them 'in an acceptable way'. Perhaps all we can legitimately claim is that it has systematized the prevailing view. We can claim to have justified it only on the assumption that the prevailing view is valid. And it is not at all certain that such an assumption can be made.

A *Theory of justice* has proved to be a very popular work. One reason for its popularity could be that it is in general agreement with the attitudes and beliefs prevailing in the West today. It has been commonly noted that what Rawls has developed is essentially a liberal theory. He has even been reproached for this. But the difficulty with Rawls's theory is not that it is a liberal theory. The difficulty is that it could not claim objective validity. The philosophical basis of Rawls's theory is rather fragile. We have reached a situation in which it has become difficult to rationally study normative issues. Even when it has been realized that normative discussion is not meaningless, little has been done to provide a basis on which a value theory could be developed. Though some philosophers like Nozick have not hesitated from offering normative theories, the difficulties in proving the validity of a normative theory have led some scholars to 'conclude that we shall have to make do with more modest results'. It thus been argued that students of politics should confine themselves to analyzing concepts.

But it should be realized that concepts like justice and equality ar e part of political theories. Even if it is difficult ot prove the truth of a political theory, it is doubtful whether we can understand the meaning of a term without relation it to the theory in which it occurs. It is therefore not at all certain if linguistic analysis can help us in fully understanding political ideas. This has been realized by scholars in the course of analyzing concepts of politics. A plea for an inquiry into the intellectual context of concept has thus been advanced by them. They have, of course, continued to insist that linguistic analysis plays a useful role in understanding political ideas. Now there is no doubt that recent philosophers have provided students of politics with useful techniques of analysis. But if a concept acquires its meaning form its place in a theory, it is not at all certain whether we can rely on linguistic analysis to determine 'the uses to which [a concept] may legitimately be put'. An inquiry into the history of political theory would show that concepts like justice and freedom have been given new meanings by political thinkers. But if we rely on linguistic analysis to determine 'the range and limits' of the use of a concept, we would be tempted to reject new meanings as illegitimate.

The point is that a concept does not have an independent existence of its own. For not only does the meaning of a concept depend on its place in a political theory. It can be justified only in terms of the theory in which it occurs. One may wonder how adequate is the notion of political theory which connected with the theory in which it occurs that it could hardly be the object of independent inquiry. We should rather concern ourselves with problems connected with theorizing about politics. And if concepts are not objects of inquiry, we can hardly regard linguistic analysis 'indispensable as a starting-point'. We can regard it only as a technique that could be utilized in the study of politics. We may not know how to validate theory. But it is not at all clear how this could lead us to study concepts. Rather, this should lead us to ask how a theory could be validated. The problems connected with the validation of theory are serious and difficult problems which we must not evade.

The rise of linguistic philosophy had far-reaching consequences for the study of ploitcs and led to the development of an animus against the traditional style of approaching politics. It is true that students of politics no longer think it the task of political philosophy to expose the errors and confusions of those who philosophized about politics. It is alos true that they have begun to be keenly interested in the study of concepts which occur in political discourse. They have even turned to works on traditional political philosophy in which these concepts have been discussed. But the fact remains that they are not interested in substantive political issues. They are interested in analytifal investigations. There is no denying that recent philosophy has provided students of politics with new techniques of analysis. That these can be usefully employed in the study of normative issues has also been effectively demonstrated by Rawls. But contemporary students of politics have given up the traditional concerns of political theory. They tend to regard analysis as the chief end of political philosophy. The model provided by linguistic analysis has, thus, deeply influenced the study of politics in the English-speaking countries. A student of politics may not formally deny the possibility or usefulness of 'comprehensive syntheses' such as those produced by past political thinkers, but he believes that 'they should follow analysis rather than precede it!

V

Interest in traditional political theory has, of course, not completely disappeared. Universities continue to offer courses in the subject and books continue to be written on it. But the interest in political theory has taken a new form: it has become primarily historical. A large number of students of politics have turned to the study of past political ideas. The tone of this kind of research was set by Dunning, Allen, McIlwain, Sabine, and others. it speaks volumes for their influence that an enormous literature has been produced on the history of political ideas. Innumerable books have been written on specific thinkers, on the thought of different historical periods, on the origin and development of various political concepts, and so on. Little did Dunning, who, writing at the start of the twentieth century, found it difficult 'to understand why the history of political theories has attracted but little attention' in the English-speaking countries, realize that he was initiating a trend which was to become very popular.

In recent years, it has been widely pointed out that historians of ideas have not taken much interest in defining the nature of their inquiry into past political ideas . But an effort can still be made to elicit some of the principles which have guided them. An inquiry would show that historians have been primarily interested in giving a descriptive account of past ideas. In this task they have relied on an analysis of the work of the thinker whose ideas they wished to elucidate. As a part of the inquiry into the meaning of political ideas, historians and commentators have also inquired into the consistency and the implications of the political ideas examined by them. They have moreover attempted to relate political ideas to their specific social and intellectual context. It has been widely assumed that political ideas are so closely connected with the historical conditions in which they are produced that an inquiry into these conditions would help in understanding their meaning. Historians of ideas have, therefore, emphasized the importance of acquiring 'a thorough knowledge of the conditions, social, political, and economic', in which a thinker wrote.

It is, of course, true that historians have not been particularly conscious of methodological issues involved in the study of political thought. The absence of methodological awareness has even been considered, 'on the whole, a sign of health'. Though it has generally been assumed by historians that political ideas are related to the conditions in which they are produced, few have seriously asked how an inquiry into their social and political contexts could help elucidate ideas. There has also been a tendency among historians to assume that social and political conditions 'determine' political ideas. Therefore, instead of elucidating political ideas by referring to the context, historians have inquired into the social and political conditions with a view to providing an 'explanation' for what a thinker is believed to have said. In spite of the prevailing confusion, however, it is difficult to deny that there has been wide agreement that ideas are so closely connected with the conditions in which they originate that, in order to understand them, it is necessary to place them in their specific context. It is, therefore, difficult to agree with those like Skinner who believe that in general historians have failed to appreciate the importance of the context in the study of political thought.

In the 1950s, research into the history of political thought came in for sharp criticism particularly at the hands of those political scientists who were interested in making the study of politics scientific. They wondered how past ideas could have any relevance today and questioned the interest which students of politics had taken in the study of political thought. Students of political thought, however, defended it by claiming the 'perennial' importance of the political theories of Plato, Aristotle, and others. It was argued that these theories were as relevant today as they were when first formulated. The dominant approach to the study of political thought was criticized for limiting their relevance. By seeking to understand ideas in their specific social and political context, it had shown them to be essentially related to the conditions in which they originated. But, students of political thought argued, we do 'injustice' to past thinkers if we see them 'only... as products of their times'. They insisted that what past thinkers 'have to say has meaning and application far beyond the peculiar historical environment they knew'. This had serious implications for the approach to the study of political thought. It led scholars like Plamenatz to emphasize the need to study past thinkers 'without attention to the particular conditions which surrounded them at the time they wrote'. It was argued that we learn more about the meaning of past ideas by 'a close study' of the texts, by reading them 'over and over again' rather than by relating them to the conditions in which the were written. In this way, students of political thought sought to make 'a sharp break' with the 'traditional method' of studying past political ideas.

In emphasizing the need to relate the study of political thought to the study of politics today, scholars like Plamenatz made a significant point. But it is doubtful whether we can correctly question the legitimacy of elucidating political thought by relating it to its social and political context. Since political thinkers have written with the purpose of solving the problems of their own times, we can understand the ideas of a thinker only in the context of the problems in response to which he wrote. If we view a political theory as a response to problems confronting society, it not only helps us understand why it is necessary to relate political thought to historical conditions, but also in reconstructing the context. Social and political reality is extremely complex and it is not clear how we could reconstruct the context in which a thinker wrote. But if we perceive social and political reality in terms of problems confronting society, it would help us in apprehending more meaningfully the historical situation in which a thinker wrote. In any case, those who wished to make a break with the 'traditional method' remained ambivalent. They conceded that a reference to social and political conditions 'may contribute' to understanding the political ideas of a thinker. They also continued to preface the inquiry into a political theory with a description of the historical conditions in which it was produced.

It is therefore difficult to find fault with historians for trying to elucidate political ideas by placing them in their historical context. But the point remains that they have not related their inquiry to the study of politics today. This led scholars like Plamenatz to propose changes in the style of studying the history of political thought. Though attempts to make the study of political thought relevant have been embroiled in methodological difficulties, the importance of the question these scholars have raised cannot be denied. But students of political thought have in general not addressed themselves to this question. The nature of interest in past ideas remains largely historical. In fact, in recent years the tendency to study political thought from a purely historical point of view has been on the ascendancy. Scholars like Skinner have exposed the errors and confusions prevailing in the literature on the history of political ideas to show that historians have not paid sufficient attention to methodological questions. And they have sought to develop new approaches to apprehend past political ideas. In other words, these scholars have been primarily interested in methodological questions involved in the study of political thought. The question raised in the 1950s regarding the relevance of the history of political ideas for the study of politics today has gradually receded to the background. The style of writing the history of political ideas which has dominated contemporary political thought, thus, reflects the ethos of an age in which political theory is languishing.

Nevertheless it would seem that at a time when there has been little theorizing about politics, studies in the history of political ideas have at least kept alive the interest in political theory. But there is a feeling that 'historical research' has in fact 'driven from [political theory] its only unique function, that of constructively approaching a valuational frame of reference'. This is what Easton has in mind when he argues that political theory has declined into 'historicism'. Now historicism is a term which has assumed a variety of meanings in contemporary thought. Easton is aware of this, but, he thinks, he must 'unfortunately' give it yet another meaning. When he accuses 'contemporary research in political theory' of being 'historicist', he means that 'it believes that very little more can be said about values except that they are a product of certain historical conditions and that they have played a given role in the historical process'. According to him, 'political theorists' like Dunning, Sabine, and others are preoccupied with 'problems of history, rather than with problems of reflection about the desirability of alternative goals'.

There is no doubt that students of politics have been greatly interested in the history of political ideas. What is doubtful is that writers like Dunning or Sabine are 'political theorists' who have defined political theory as the study of the history of political ideas. They are properly historians interested in the history of political ideas and have visualized themselves as such. It is true that in his well-known work entitled *The Modern Democratic State Lindsay* defined political theory as a form of historical inquiry. But it is not at all certain if this is how writers like Sabine have conceived the nature of their work. In particular, they have not been concerned with making an inquiry into ideals which are 'operative' today. Nor have they undertaken an inquiry into the history of political ideas with a view to making 'men understand what their purposes and will regarding the state actually are'. Whether Lindsay has 'unwittingly' articulated the conception of political theory which has dominated contemporary political thought is, therefore, not at all certain. Thus, it is difficult to accept the diagnosis that political theory has declined into historicism. In any case, a conception of political theory as the history of political ideas would surely require a his toricist theory of knowledge to support it. But Easton denies that research in the history of political ideas in connected with historicist thinking. Therefore, the point is not, as Easton has sought to make, that political theorists of today are concerned with problems of history. It is that students of past political ideas are not concerned with the problems of politics.

But Easton is not alone in equating the history of political theory with political theory. In recent years, a number of scholars have tended to do so. It is believed that, as the history of political ideas, political theory 'has as its subject matter the historical texts and the conditions which surrounded their writing'. The confusion is so pervasive that, in compiling its *Biographical Directory,* the American Political Science Association distributed a questionnaire in which 'Political Theory and Philosophy (Historical)' is mentioned along with 'Political Theory and Philosophy (Normative)' and 'Political Theory and Philosophy (Empirical)'. The result is that the history of political ideas has tended to become a substitute for political theory. Far from keeping interest in political theory alive, the study of past political ideas has tended to divert attention from it.

An inquiry into the contemporary political thought of the English-speaking countries, thus, shows that students of politics have sought to make a break with the traditional style of theorizing about politics. They do not think that the assumptions adopted by traditional political thinkers provide an adequate basis for approaching the study of politics. And so they have sought to develop new approaches. If this were a complete account of the situation, one could perhaps agree with Strauss when he says that 'the very possibility of political philosophy' has been 'finally' destroyed. If one cannot quite do so, it is because the attack on the assumptions of political theory has not been fully justified. Nor has it gone entirely unchallenged. The attempts to develop new approaches too have not proved very satisfactory. Yet the fact remains that these approaches have exercised great sway over the study of politics. This does not mean that interest in the traditional style of theorizing about politics has completely disappeared. But this does mean that the traditional style no longer carries an aura of legitimacy. The result is that those who have approached the study of politics in the traditional style have largely been ignored by the vast majority of contemporary students of politics. A number of writers have used the word 'decline' to describe the state of political theory today. Whether we prefer the word 'decline' or not, it is difficult to deny that the condition of political theory is far from satisfactory.

History and Sources of the Science of Polity

THE NAME OF THE SCIENCE

Political science in India was known by several terms like the Rājadharma, Rājyaśāstra, Daṇḍanīti Nītiśāsta and Arthaśāstra. Some of these terms like the Rājadharma 'Duties of the king' and Rājyaśāstra, 'Science of the state' require no explanation. Monarchy was the normal form of the state and the science of politics and government was therefore naturally called Rājadharma or Rājyaśāstra. The term Daṇḍanīti also is self-edxplanatory.

Like many thinkers of the modern time, some Indian writers like Manu held that the ultimate sanction behind the state is force. If it is not used, the alternative is the law of the jungle (*mātsyanyāa*). It is Daṇḍa (physical force or physical punishment) which rules over all the subjects, it is Daṇḍa which protects them; when all else are sleeping, Daṇḍa keeps awake; law is nothing but Daṇḍa itself.

Daṇḍa however, must be wielded with discretion. If it is used too harshly, the subjects are distressed; if it is used too lightly, the king will not be held in awe; if it is used in the proper manner, the subjects are happy and the realm progresses.

Some writers like Kauṭilya, however, do not understand Daṇḍa in a narrow sense. They point out that punishment or threat of punishment is not to be viewed only in its prohibitive aspect. It establishes law and order in society and thus indirectly brings about a natural tendency in the average individual to obey the law of the land, which renders the frequent use of force unnecessary. It ultimately secures proper progress in religion, philosophy and economic well-being, so necessary for social stability. Daṇḍa enables the individual and the state to have new achievements to their credit, to protect and increase what has been acquired and to distribute the gains properly as between the state and the individuals, as also among the individuals themselves. The entire social well-being is thus dependent upon it. Daṇḍanīti thus deals with the totality of social, political and economic relationships and indicates how they are to be properly organised and integrated with one another. All relationship, says, Uśanas, is rooted in the Daṇḍanīti (*Mbh.* XII. 62, 28-9).

Manu goes to the extent of declaring that it is Daṇḍa who is the real king, the real leader and the real protector. The rules about the functions and duties of the king and the welfare of the state were therefore naturally called Daṇḍanīti.

The works on the science of politics written by Usanas and Prajāpati were known as Daṇdanīti; it will be soon shown (p. 4) how the *Arthaśāstra* of Kauṭilya also was known by that term.

The next term we have to consider is Nītiśāstra. Nīti is derived from the root *ni* to lead; Nīti therefore, means proper guidance or direction. It was held that this would become possible by following the ethical course of conduct and therefore, one connotation of the term Nitiśāstra was the science of ethics. Proper guidance or direction usually presupposes propriety; prudence and wisdom; so Nītiśāstra also came to denote the science of wisdom and right course. Bhartṛihari used the term in this sense when he described one of his books as Nītiśāstra. Greatest propriety, wisdom and circumspection have, however, to be shown in shaping and guiding the internal and foreign policy of the State, and so the term Nītiśāstra became very popular to designate the science of government from about the 5th century A.D. Kāmandaka and Śukra prefer to call their works as books on Niti and not on Daṇdanīti or Arthaśāstra. Lakshmīdhara (1150 A.D.), Annambhaṭta (1200 A.D.) Chaṇḍeśvara (1350 A.D.), Nilakaṇṭha and Mitramiśra (1625

A.D.) call the relevant books of their digests as Nītikalpataru, Nītichandrikā, Nītiratnākara, Nītimayūkha and Nītiprakāśa respectively, and not as Arthaśāstra-Kalpataru or Rājadharma-ratnākara, Rājyaśāstra-mayūkha or Daṇḍanītiprakāśa. The aim of the government is to secure all round progress and prosperity of society and the same was taken to be the scope of Nītiśāstra. Śukra points out how Nītiśāstra is a *sine qua non* for the stability and progress of society in all directions and how it enables the realisation of the four-fold goals connected with Dharma. Artha, Kāma and Moksha.

Arthaśāstra is the next term for the science of politics which we have now to consider. The usual meaning of the term Artha is money or wealth and so the term Arthaśāstra should connote the science of wealth or economics, and not the science of government. While conceding that Artha denotes the avocations of men, Kauṭilya contends that the term also can denote the territory where the people live together. Arthaśāstra, therefore, says Kauṭilya, is the science which deals with the acquisition and protection or governance of territory. This explanation to justify the use of the term Arthaśāstra for the science of politics appears to be rather forced and far-fetched. But posterity has acquiesced in the term primarily because the most important book on the science of politics is known as Arthaśāstra. Thus the *Śukranīthśāra* states that the *Arthaśāstra* discusses instructions about the government along with the acquisition of wealth (IV. 5.56). A perusal of the opening chapter of Kauṭilya's *Arthaśāstra* would show that the author had originally intended to Christian his book as a Daṇdanīti; later on he seems to have changed his mind and decided to call it as Arthaśāstra. The explanation and justification of the term Arthaśāstra occurs only in the last chapter of the work. In its colophon the work is called simply as Śāstra; it can be an abbreviation of Arthaśāstra as well as of Daṇḍanītiśāstra. It is interesting to note that the work was known to Daṇḍin as Daṇdanīti and not as Arthaśāstra. The *Amarakosha* also equates Daṇdanīti with Arthaśāstra as also the *Mitākshar*ā on Yājñavalkya I, 311 and 313.

To conclude, in the early stages of the development of the science, it was known as Rājadharma; Daṇdanīti became a more popular term a little later, and Arthaśāstra was suggested as an alternative to it. In course of time, however, the word Rājanīti-śāstra, abridged into Nītiśāstra became most popular and gradually supplanted the other terms.

THE HISTORY OF NITIŚĀSTRA

We shall now proceed to describe the origin and development of the Nītiśāstra in ancient India. This will incidentally enable the reader to get an idea of the main sources available for reconstructing the picture of ancient Indian Polity and Administration and of the difficulties and limitations under which we have to work while engaged in this task.

Systematic literature on what we may call the Science of Polity does not go back to a time earlier than c. 500 B.C. This is but natural. Even semi-secular and semi-religious subjects like grammar, etymology and astronomy began to develop as independent treatises only from about the 8th century B.C. The science of polity, therefore, cannot be expected to have acquired an independent existence much before the sixth century B.C.

Though there was no systematic literature on the political science composed in the earlier period, usually called the Age of the Vedas and the Brāhmaṇas, there are scattered passages in the Vedic literature, which throw considerable light, sometimes dim, sometimes clear, on the theory and practice of government in the contemporary times. The material in the *Rigveda* is very scanty, but that in the *Atharvaveda* is relatively more copious; it however mostly refers to the institution of the kingship. In the different Saṁhitās of the Yajurveda and in the Brāhmaṇa literature, we frequently come across the description of the coronation ceremony and of the different sacrifices laid down for the king either at the time of his accession or at some later time in his career. These give us valuable glimpses into the position of the king, the prestige he enjoyed, the taxes he collected and the entourage that surrounded him. There are numerous passages in this literature which discuss the relative position and privileges of the different castes, especially the Brāhmaṇas and the Kshatriyas, which also are valuable to the student of the political institutions.

From about the 8th century B.C. an age of specialisation commenced and the specialists in grammar and etymology, prosody and astronomy began to form separate schools and compose special manuals for the beginners as well as the advanced scholars. The beginning of a school of politics, properly so-called, has to be ascribed to this age of specialisation; it is however certain that it was somewhat later in origin than the above sciences and probably contemporaneous with the school of the Dharma-śāstra. The earliest works on polity, which unfortunately have all been lost, were probably composed in *c.* 7th century B.C.

It is also but natural that in about the 7th century B.C. the science of politics should have begun to develop. The country was studded with small kingdoms and the advisers of kings, who were sages and scholars of mature judgement, were naturally expected to discuss problems of administration with them. It is interesting to note that in the Śāntiparvan of the *Mahābhārata*, while answering to some of the questions of Yudhishṭhira, Bhīshma does not give his own opinion, but suggests it by referring to the dialogues between kings and sages of hoary antiquity, who had discussed similar problems. While discussing the divinity of the king, Bhīshma refers to a dialogue between Māndhātā and Indra (chap 65); while emphasisting the importance of Daṇḍa he draws attention to a dialogue between king Vasuhoma and Māndhātā, (chapters 68, 122); while exhorting the king to be righteous, Bhishma quotes from a dialogue between Yauvanāśva and Māndhātā (chapter 90); while emphasising the importance of the priest, he draws attention to a dialogue between king Aila and Kāśyapa (chaps 73); while warning a king against depletion of treasury, he refers to a dialogue between sage Kālakavriksha and Kośala king (chaps. 82, 164); while referring to the problems of the republic, he quotes from a dialogue between Krishṇa and Nārada (chap. 81). It is quite obvious that these dialogues must not have been hanging in the air or in oral traditions only; some of them must have formed part of books on political science. The science of polity must have had a pretty number of books by about the 7th or the 6th century B.C.

Politics attained the status of an independent science in the west a couple of centuries later, when Aristotle composed his famous work, *Politics*, disentangling politics from ethics for the first-time.

We are indebted to the *Mahābhārata* and the *Arthaśāstra* of Kauṭilya for an account of the works written and theories propounded by the pioneer writers in the field. It is interesting and important to note that these two works, which represent independent traditions and sources, agree with each other as far as the names of the early writers and concerned. The *Mahābharata* account is semi-legendary and semi-historical. It states that a huge work on the science of polity extending over a lakh of verses was originally composed by Brahmadeva, the Creator, when he put an end to the prevailing anarchy and re-established the social order. It was then successively abridged by Śiva-Viśālāksha, Indra, Brhaspati and Śukra. Manu, Bhāradvāja and Gauraśiras are also mentioned by the epic as other authors on the science of polity.

The names of well-known works like the *Manusmriti*, the *Yājñavalkyasmṛiti*, the *Parāśarasmṛti* and the *Śukranīti* show that in ancient India authors often preferred to remain incognito and attributed their works to divine or semi-divine persons. We need not therefore suppose that works on polity attributed to Brahmadeva, Manu, Siva or Indra existed only in the imagination of a Kauṭilya or the author of the *Mahābhārata*.

This conclusion is supported by the data of the *Arthaśāstra* of Kauṭilya; for in numerous places it refers to and discusses the various views of Viśāslāksha, Indra (Bahudanta), Bòihaspati, Śukra, Manu, Bhāradvāja, Gauraśiras, Parāśara, Piśuna-Kauṇapadanta, Vātavyādhi, Ghoṭamukha, Kātyāyana, Charāyaṇa and other scholars of the Science of Polity that are referred to in the *Arthaśāstra* (Bk. VI chap. 5).

As was the case with the other branches of knowledge, there were several schools among the students of the Science of Polity as well; some of them claimed Manu (the father of the human race) as their founder, others Bṛihaspati, the teacher of the gods and others still Śukra or Uśanas, the rival teacher of the Asuras. Some chose to affiliate themselves to Brahmā, some to Indira and some to Śiva. In the beginning very probably handbooks for the use of the beginners were composed, which were later developed into comprehensives works. It is these books, written by human scholars but ascribed to super-human authors, which are referred to by the *Mahābhārat* and the *Arthaśāstra*.

Unfortunately none of these books have survived to our times. It appears that the material contained in some of them was incorporated in the Rājadharma section of the Śāntiparvan of the *Mahābhārata* and that the others were superseded and thrown into the background by the masterly work of Kautilya. Some of them, however, existed down to the 9th century; for a verse of Viśālāksha has been quoted in the *Bālakrīdā*, a 9th century commentary of the *Yāñavalkyasmṛiti* by Sureśvarāchārya.

The references to the views of these authors made in the *Athaśāstra*, however, enable us to get a fair idea of their contents. The science of polity was a new one at this time and therefore many of these writers seem to have started their works with a discussion of its relative importance as compared to the Vedas, the philosophy and the economics. One of them, named Uśanas, went to the extent of advocating the extreme view that politics was the only science worth study. The polity which these writers were discussing was obviously a monarchical one, and they seem to have devoted considerable space to the discussion of the training of the prince and the qualifications of an ideal ruler. The relative importance that he should attach of an ideal ruler. The relative importance that he should attach to the difficulties and calamities in connection with the treasury, forts and army were also exhaustively discussed. The constitution and functions of the ministry were described at length by most of them and they widely differed from one another about the number of the ministers and their qualifications. Principles of foreign policy also were debated upon, Bhāradvāja advocating submission to the strong when there is no alternative and Viśālāksha recommending a fight to the finish, even if it meant annihilation. Vātavyādhi did not subscribe to the theory of *Shāḍguṇya* but advocated that of *Dvaiguṇya*. Problems connected with taxation do not seem to have been discussed by these writers; at any rate the *Arthaśāstra* has no quotations from them bearing on that topic. The questions of the control over revenue and provincial officers were discussed, but the local government seems to have been left untouched. On the other hand these early works contained important sections dealing with civil and criminal law and laid down a scheme of fines and punishments for theft, robbery, misappropriation, etc. We would not be far wrong in concluding that the treatises of most of these writers were the precursors of the *Arthaśāstra* of Kauṭilya but dealing, of course in a much less exhaustive way, only with those topics dealt with in its books I, II, III, IV, VI and VII.

If the questions from the works of his predecessors given by Kauṭilya can be taken as representative of their contents, we may well conclude that there was a fairly strong school of politics in India from c. 500 B.C. This school would be the counterpart of the Dharmsūtra school, which existed at this period. Whether the one school was Brahmanical and the other Kshatriya, it is difficult to state. It is, however, quite likely that some of the writers of the Niti school may well have belonged to the class of the administrators of the age.

The *Mahābhāraa* is an important source to the student of the science of polity. The Śāntiparvan has an extensive section devoted to the Rājadharma or the duties of the king and the government. It discusses the importance of the science of politics (Chaps. 63-64) and advocates its own theories about the origin of the state and kingship (Chaps. 56, 66, 67). The duties and responsibilities of the king are discussed at length in several chapters (Chaps. 55-57, 70, 76, 94, 96, 120), as also those of the different ministers (Chaps. 73, 82, 83, 85, 115, 118). Taxation is discussed in half a dozen chapters (Chaps. 71, 76, 87, 88, 120, 130), but the duties of the different officers are not laid down in detail as in Book II of the *Arthaśāstra*. Internal administration is briefly described only in one chapter (87). Problems connected with the foreign policy and peace and war naturally occupy a good deal of space (Chaps. 80, 87, 99, 100-103, 110 and 113). There is no doubt that the Rājadharma section represents a further advance over the works of the writers mentioned in it and in the *Arthaśāstra;* it is not unlikely that it incorporates some of their theories and chapters.

Apart from the Rājadharma section of the Śāntiparvan, there are some other chapters in the work where problems of government are discussed Sabhāparvan Chap. 5 gives us a very good idea of the ideal administration. Ādiparvan Chap. 142 contains a justification of Machiavellianism under certain circumstances. Sabhāparvan Chap. 32 and Vanaparvan Chaps. 25, 32, 33 and 150 contain interesting discussions on the emergency policy.

As the *Mahābhārata* has undergone several recessions, it is not easy to fix the time of the above chapters. The treatment of the topics however suggests that the above chapters may be belonging to a period earlier than that of the *Manusmriti,* i e. to about the 4th century B.C.

The next important source is the famous *Arthaśāstra* of Kauṭilya. It belongs to the same category as the above works, but discusses the old topics with a remarkable thoroughness. referring to the views of the earlier writers and advancing its own theories. The setting of the work is secular. In Dharmasūtra works, Rājadharma forms but one section. Here on the other hand the study of the state is the main topic, though the king is expected to master the Vedas and philosophy. After discussing in Book I the various problems connected with the kingship, it gives an exhaustive picture of the civil administration in Book. II. The next two books deal with the civil, criminal and personal law. The Book V deals with the duties and responsibilities of the courtiers and retainers of the king and Book VI describes the nature and functions of the seven *prakṛitis* of the State. Then the work devotes its last nine Books to an exhaustive discussion of the problems connected with the foreign policy, the 'circles' of kings and the policy to be followed in connection with its different members, the ways and means by which to establish one's ascendancy among them, the occasions suitable for war and peace, the manner in which the warfare was to be carried on or dissensions were to be sown among the enemies, etc.

The *Arthaśāstra* is more a manual for the administrator than a theoretical work on polity discussing the philosophy and fundamental principles of administration or of the political science.

It is mainly concerned with the practical problems of government and describes its machinery and functions, both in peace and war, with an exhaustiveness not seen in any later work, with the possible exception of the *Śukranīti*.

Tere is a great controversy about the date of the *Arthaśāstra*. Messrs. Shamasastri, Ganapatishastri, N.N. Law, Smith, Fleet and Jayaswal hold that the work proceeds from the pen of the famous minister of Chandragupta Maurya, while Messrs. Winternitz, Jolly, Keith and D.R. Bhandarkar hold that the work is a much later one, written in the early centuries of the Christian era. Conclusive evidence supporting either view is lacking and the question has become complicated owing to the work being occasionally retouched in later times. The second school points out that if the book was really written by Kauṭilya, the Mauryan premier, it is strange that it should not contain some references to the Mauryan empire and its administrative machinery, so well known to us from Greek sources. It ignores the boards of town officials, and lays down no rules for the care of foreigners, for escorting them to the border and looking after their effects if deceased. The fact that the views of Kauṭilya himself are quoted in the 3rd person would suggest that the real writer of the work was different from him.

Shamasastri and Jayaswal demur to these conclusions. They point out that the colophon of the work distinctly states that it was written by Kauṭilya, who had rescued the country from the Nandas. To say that the author was not acquainted with a wide empire is incorrect, for he states (at p. 340) that the sphere of the jurisdiction of a *chakravartin* extends from the Himalayas to the ocean. The aim of the book is to describe the machinery of a normal state; the organisation of a big empire which was only an occasional phenomenon in Indian history is not, therefore, discussed in detail. The *Arthaśāstra* no doubt refers only to the superintendents of the different departments; the boards of five may have been omitted because they were mainly non-official in character. it is quite a common practice among Indian authors to refer to themselves by their own name in the third person singular, rather than in the first person plural; so the references to Kauṭilya in the third person need not necessarily show that he was not himself the author of the book.

It is true that the name Kauṭilya is not very complimentary; we need not however on that account doubt his historicity, because a number of his predecessors like Vātavyādhi and Kauṇapadanta had equally unflattering names. Nor can it be argued that Kauṭilya is later than Bhāsa, because the verse *Nawaṁ śarāvaṁ* etc. occurring in Book X Chap, 2 of the *Arthaśāstra* is to be seen in *Pratijñā-Yaugandharāyaṇa* of Bhāsa. Kauṭilya never fails to mention the names of his sources; he has mentioned by name a number of earliest writers on polity; had he borrowed the above verse from Bhāsa, he would also have mentioned his name. The *Arthaśāstra* introduces this verse along with another with the remark '*Apīha ślokau bhavatah*', 'There are these two verses', showing clearly that they were traditional ones; both Kauṭilya and Bhāsa have obviously borrowed from the mass of floating popular verses. To argue that Kauṭilya was not a historical figure because his name is not mentioned by Megasthenes would have had some force, if the entire work of the Greek ambassador had come down to us; as only fragments of the book are available, it is quite possible to presume that the name may have been mentioned in some of the lost chapters. Similarly Patañjali's silence about Kauṭilya cannot go against his historicity. It is true that he mentions Mauryas and also the *ṣabhā* of Chandragupta. But the point at issue is where there was an occasion for Pataāñjali to refer to Kauṭilya and whether he is still silent. No *sūtra* of Pāṇini or *vārtika* of Kātyāyana called for such a reference in the commentary. It may be pointed out that Patañjali is also silent about Aśoka and Bindusāra. Are we to conclude that they did not exist because of this silence? The argument that the chemical and metallurgical knowledge presupposed by Book. II Chap. 12 of the *Arthaśāstra* is too advanced for the 3rd century B.C. will hardly carry any conviction when it is remembered how our knowledge of the development of these subjects in ancient India is very meagre.

The society depicted by Kauṭilya permits levirate and remarriages of widows, as also post-puberty marriages and divorces (pp. 151-159). This was the state of affairs in the Mauryan age. Scant respect is shown to the Buddhists (p. 199) and persons are prohibited from becoming recluses without providing for their families (p. 48). This would indicate that the work was written at a time when Buddhism had not yet become strong enough to induce people to leave their families and join the order. The work frequently uses the word *yukta* in the sense of an official, as is done in the edicts of Aśoka. In later centuries this term went out of vogue.

The reference to the Madras, the Kambojas, the Lichchhavis and the Mallas as republics in Bk. XI, Chap. I of the *Arthaśāstra* would also support the view that the book belongs to the early Mauryan times, when these republics are known to have been flourishing. In the 4th century A.D. very few knew of their existence as republics. Like Yāska, who was a predecessor of Pāṇini, the *Arthaśāstra* refers to only four parts of speech, and not to eight as has been done by the great grammarian. This would suggest that Pāṇini's grammar had not yet become very authoritative in the days of Kauṭilya. He should therefore be placed in the 4th century B.C. rather than in the 4th century A.D.

It is worth noting that there are several striking points of resemblance between the *Arthaśāstra* and the extant fragments of Megasthenes. Like Megasthenes, the *Arthaśāstra* refers to the royal procession at the time of hunting and religious ceremonies (Bk. I, chap. 20) and to the necessity of guarding the road on the occasion (Bk. I, Chap. 18). Both authorities refer to female body guards of the king and to his habit of shampooing (Bk. I, Chap 1 19). Megasthenes' account of irrigation canals and sluices reminds us of the observations on the *setubandha* in the *Arthaśāstra* (Bk. VII, Chap. 14). Megasthenes' overseers moving up and down and reporting to the king are obviously the spices of the *Arthaśāstra*.

Megasthenes' officials for the measurement of the land belong to the same service of which the *gopa* of the *Arthaśāstra* was a subordinate member. The great officers in charge of the markets and rivers, of cities and arts and crafts, mentioned by the Greek ambassador, remind us of some of the *adhyakshas* of the Bk. II of the *Arthaśāstra* .

There are no doubt some serious discrepancies between Kauṭilya and Megasthenes; but in most cases it can be shown that the Greek ambassador's account is unreliable. The latter is, for some reasons unknwn to us, drawing too rosy a picture of the Indian society when he states that theft, drinking and slavery were unknown in India. The data in the *Arthaśāstra* are not consistent with these statements, but are supported by the evidence of the Dharmasūtras written at about the 4th century B.C.; we can therefore well place him in the Mauryan period, though his picture differs from that of Megasthenes. Megasthenes' statements that Indians did not know the art of writing and administered the laws from memory is now universally accepted as incorrect. His statement that the horses and elephants were the monopoly of the king is contradicted by Strabo and Arrian, who agree with *Kauṭilya* in recognising private ownership of these animals. When Megasthenes states that the state was the owner of land, he probably refers to the crown lands. Patañjali agrees with Kauṭilya in recognising the private ownership of arable land. The non-reference in the *Arthaśāstra* to the boards of five in the city and the military administration may be due to the fact that Kauṭilya perhaps wanted to refer to only the heads of the offices and not to their advisory councils.

All things considered, it has to be admitted that there is a substantial agreement between the administrative and social picture as given by Kauṭilya and Megasthenes and we may well conclude that they were not far removed from each other in time.

The above facts as well as the colophon of the work would suggest that its kernel at any rate belongs to the Mauryan age and embodies the views of Kauṭilya. It was, however, retouched here and there in later times. Thus the reference to China could not have been in the original work, as the country was not known by that name in c. 300 B.C. It is probable that passages containing the term *suraṅga,* derived from the Greek term syrinx, may be later. At p. 255 the view of Bhāradvāja is placed after that of Kauṭilya. This may be an instance of opposite views being placed side by side in an impartial manner. But if it suggests that the view of Bhāradvāja was to be preferred to that of Kauṭilya, the passage would be a later addition.

Apart from a few such passages, the work seems to be substantially of the Mauryan age and may be taken to embody the views of the great minister of Chandragupta.

Kauṭilya was not only a famous statesman but also the founder of a school of politics; hence the great respect in which his name and work have been held by the subsequent centuries. Both Bāṇa and Daṇdin refer to the study of this work especially by the princes, and the Jain tradition, as recorded in the *Nandīsūtra* (p. 391) enumerates the work among the heretical books along with the *Rāmāyaṇa* and the *Bhārata*. Even south Indian epigraphs describe skilled administraos and diplomats like king Durvinīta (9th century) and Mārashimha (10th century) of the Ganga dynasty as incranations of Vishṇugupta or Kauṭilya or as well versed in his statecraft.

The position of the *Arthaśāstra* in the realm of the literature of politics is analogous to that of Pāṇini's *Ashṭādhyāyī* in the field of grammar. Like Pāṇini, Kauṭilya superseded all his predecessors; their works were, therefore, lost in the course of time. The excellence of Pāṇini's work was so great that very few among the later grammarians thought it possible to supersede the great master. The same apparently was the view of the later scholars in the realm of the political science. That seems to be one of the reasons for the relative dearth of original works in the later history of the science.

There were also some other reasons for this phenomenon. The Smṛitis written during c. 200 B.C. to 200 A.D. like those of Manu (Chaps. VII-IX), Vishnu (Chap. III) and Yājñavalkya (Chap. I, 304-67) took over the discussion of the topics like the duties of the king, the functions of the different offices, the rules of civil and criminal law and the different theories concerning the foreign policy. Of course their treatment of these subjects was not as comprehensive or systematic as that of the *Arthaśāstra* , but it was quite sufficient for every day purposes. They possessed the additional advantage of including a discussion of the rules of *varṇa, āśrama* and *prāyaśchitta* and thus appeared as more useful manuals to the public than the books on the pure *Arthaśāstra*, as they dealt with a number of religious, social and philosophical topics also, in which the age was more interested than in the pure discussion of the details of political theories or the problems of Government administration.

The Smṛiti works referred to above deal with the administrative problems in a general way. Their treatment would have been found inadequate and new books would have come into the field, had there been intense activity in the realm of the political thought. But there was no such activity. The general form of the works of the political science was determined by the *Arthaśāstra* and a few other manuals of similar nature. New political theories were not adumbrated in later centuries. The semireligious and semi-moral outlook of the writers of the time was responsible for this. Our writers, for instance, concede the principle that the king is the servant of the people and there is no sin in killing a tyrant. A good many theories and books could have come in the field, if the problem of regicide had been viewed purely from the secular point of view. What are the duties of the king in his capacity as the servant of the people, what are the secular remedies for the people, if the king begins to behave autocratically, under what circumstances would people be justified in withholding allegiance or the payment of taxes, how public opinion was to make itself felt, what were the different milder remeides that people could adopt before they had recourse to regicide, how were they to be made effective in the face of the police and military forces of the king,—these and similar questions would have given rise to a number of divergent theories, resulting in a rich literature extending over several centuries. But this could not happen, because our writers looked at the question from the religious and moral point of view. The king was to be a virtuous rulers, devoted heart and soul to the welfare of the people; if he was not such, then gods will punish him. The subjects had no secular remedies feasible in normal times; gods were expected to destroy a bad king. Sometimes it is stated that he should be killed like a mad dog, but how, by whom, and under what circumstances is not explained. Abstruse thinking and daring speculation which is characteristic of Hindu thought in other departments like philosophy and poetics are strategy enough conspicuous by their absence in the works on the science of polity.

Epigraphical evidence shows that there existed considerable divergence in the country in the sphere of taxation and local government. New taxes were introduced by the different states in the course of time and the local government institutions developed on different lines in the various provinces of India. New books could have been written discussing these developments. But this did not happen, probably because taxation and local government were governed by local traditions, which were not usually incorporated in the standard works on polity.

The administrative machinery of the Guptas considerably differed from that of the Mauryas; fresh developments took place in this sphere under Harsha, as also under the rule of the early medieval dynasties. Books could have been written bearing upon the changes that were taking place in the administrative machinery. But this also did not happen. Probably the students of the political science felt that these were minor changes of details which were not sufficiently important to warrant the composition of fresh books.

It has been suggested that the foreign invasion and alien rule during *c.* 200 B.C. to 300 A.D. may have been responsible for the dearth of the political literature in the post-Kauṭilya period. This, however, appears improbable; the dominions of the Greeks, the Scythians, the Parthians and the Kushāṇas did not extend beyond the Punjab for any appreciable time. Madhyadeśa and Bihar, which were the centre of Aryan culture from *c.* 500 B.C. remained practically unaffected by the foreign conquests.

To conclude, the relative sterility in political literature in the first millennium of the Christian era seems to be due to the great sway which the classical work of Kauṭilya continued to have over the public mind and the absence of any noteworthy development in the sphere of the political thought or government machinery. A few manuals, with no particular claim to originally, were of course composed during this period and we shall briefly refer to them after a few remarks about the state of affairs in South India.

South India in the early period did not produce any important works on polity. We get only occasional references on the government of the day from such literary works as the *Tirukkural,* and the *Silappadikaram*. But they usually refer to the king and his officers and hardly throw any light either on the political theories or on the administrative structure as a whole.

The great fasciantion which Kauṭilya had over his successors is well illustrated by *Kāmandakīya Nītisāra,* composed probably in the Gupta age (*c.* 500 A.D.). This book is nothing but a metrical summary of the work of Kauṭilya. Obviously its anonymous writer felt that the best service he could render to the students of politics would be a summarise this standard work in the popular Anushṭub meter, so that it could be easily memorised by the student. The work, however, does not at all describe the administrative Machinery. The king and his courtiers dominate the picture, showing the great importance that monarchy had acquired by this time. Kauṭilya's chapter on republican states is omitted, probably because they were no longer in existence. Civil, criminal and personal law are completely left out, probably because the Smṛti writers of this period had specialised in this branch. Jayaswal attributed the work to Śikharasvāmin, a minister of Chandragupta Rājyaśāstra; his arguments however are not convincing. Vishākhadatta and Daṇdanīti do not refer to the work but Vāmana (*c.* 800 A.D.) knows it. Its time may be somewhere between 500 and 700 A.D.

The *Nītivākyāmṛita* is also a colourless summary of earlier political thought; it is somewhat interesting as it proceeds from the pen of a Jain author, Somadevasūri (*c.* 960 A.D.)

The *Śukranīti,* whose date is rather uncertain, is the next work to be considered. It is very important for the student of ancient Indian polity. Like other works of the class, it does not occupy itself with theoretical discussion of the principles of polity or government, but it gives us a more detailed and comprehensive picture of the administrative machinery than is given by any other work of the post-Kauṭilya epoch. Its polity is of course monarchical, republics having disappeared long before the date of the work.

Besides discussing the duties of the king and the functions of his ministers and officers the work describes the problems of foreign policy and methods of warfare. Civil administration is described in very great details. We get a vivid picture of the judicial administration. The four popular courts are referred to substantive law is however not dealt with. The state as envisaged by Śukra was an organisation for the welfare of the subjects. It was not only to suppress crime and disorder, but to control gambling and drinking. It was to maintain hospitals and rest-houses and encourage learning and scholarship. It was to increase the resources of the country by encouraging trade, developing mines, forests and industries and exciting schemes of irrigation.

In several respects the work supplies information not to be found in other works on polity. Interesting and minute details are given about the seating arrangements in the royal court on formal occasions (11,70-71) and about different grades of feudatories and their incomes (I, 282-83). The portfolios of different ministers are given in this work for the first time; it enables us to have a clear picture of the day to day working of ministry with the assistance of the secretaries and under the control of the king (II, 109-10). Unlike any other work, Śukra gives us the percentage of the state income to be spent on different items (I, 316-17). The section dealing with the army administration (IV, Sect. VII) gives us the most comprehensive picture of the army organisation,—how the soldiers were to be recruited, trained and paid, how martial types of elephants and horses were to be selected, how weapons were to be manufactured or procured, etc.

Widely divergent views are held about the date of the *Śukranīti*. G. Oppert placed it even in the pre-Christian period; Dr. U.N. Ghosal thinks that the work was written between 1200 and 1600 A.D. and the view of R.L. Mitra was similar. The fact is that the work is a composite one and was being retouched down to the 14th century; but its greater part has to be ascribed to the 11th or the 12th century A.D. The statement that the Mlechchhas resided in the north-west of India, the reference to Sāmantas as both feudatories and officials, (I. 189), the Information that the price of gold was 16 times that of silver (IV, 2. 92), as stated by

Bhāskarāchārya, the inclusion of Deśabhāshās (vernaculars) as topics of study (IV. 3.30), the reference to the Advaita Vedānta doctrine of Śankara (IV. 3.50), the injunction that peace should be made even with an Anārya, because otherwise he may uproot the kingdom (IV. 7.243), the enunciation of the principle that the treasury should have a reserve equal to 20 years revenue (IV. 2. 23), which was obviously followed by Hindu kings of the 11th century as shown by the accounts of the plunder obtained from their treasuries by Muslim conquerors,—all these tend to show that the book as a whole belongs to the period between 900 and 1200. The verses dealing with firearms and gunpowder (IV. 7. 195-213; I, 231; II. 95 and 195) may have been added by the end of the 14th century, when gunpowder is known to have been used by the army of Vijayanagar.

The *Bārhaspatya Arthaśstra* is a small, unimportant and late booklet, doing justice neither to its subject nor to the reputation of its supposed author. Like some of the earlier Smṛitis, a few later Smṛitis also occasionally deal with administration, but their treatment is quite perfunctory. The Purāṇas of the Gupta and post-Gupta period also deal with State and Government, but disclose no originality of thought or treatment.

From *c.* 1000 A.D. originality disappeared from most of the branches of Indian learning, and the science of polity was no exception. From *c.* 1000 A.D. to 1700 A.D. a number of compendiums were written giving a comprehensive treatment of Dharma in its different branches; *rājanīti* or politics also formed a section of most of these works. As important works of this class, we may mention *Abhilashitārthachintāmaṇi* (1st four chapters) of Someśvara, *Yuktikalpataru* of Bhoja (*c.* 1025 A.D.), *Rājanītikalpataru* of Lakshmīdhara (*c.* 1125 A.D.), *Rājanītikāṇda* of Devaṇa-bhaṭṭa (*c.* 1300 A.D.), *Rājanītiratṇākara* of Chandesvara (c. 1325 A.D.), *Amuktamālyada* of king Krishṇadevarāya of Vijayanagar dynasty, *c.* 1525 A.D. *Nitimayukha* of Nilakaṇṭha (*c.* 1625 A.D.) and *Rājanītiprakāśa* of Mitramiśra (*c.* 1650 A.D.). Most of these works are written from the theological rather than from the political point of view. Thus the *Rājanītiprakāśa* devotes as many as 100 pages to the description of the coronation ceremony.

The *Nītimayūkha* gives detailed instructions to the king as to how he should cleanse himself, shave and bathe, what he should do if there are bad dreams and omens, and what different *śāntis* he should perform to avert different calamities. We have got sections in these works dealing with ministers, forts, treasury, foreign policy, war, etc. But there is nothing new about them. We usually get only a collection of quotations from earlier writers bearing upon these and similar topics.

Of the above mentioned works, we may review in detail the *Mānasollāsa*, as a typical work of the class; it was composed by the Chālukya king Someśvara (1125-1138 A.D.). Though written by a ruler, it is most disappointing as a book on Polity. Of its hundred chapters as many as 60 deal with the kings' luxuries, amusements and pastines (*upabhogas, pramodas* and *krīḍās*) and only the first forty deal with the acquisition of a kingdom and its stabilization. But even here the viewpoint in more religious than secular. Among the best means of gaining a kingdom figure the telling of the truth, the observance of sex mortality, the offering of Śrāddha and the going on pilgrimage. The royal author is more anxious to display his knowledge of other subjects than that of the science of politics and seizes every opportunity to make unjustified digression. While dealing with the health of the king, he gives a long list of tonics; while referring to the duties of the treasurer, he gives the multiplication tables, rules of three and five, etc. (II. 99-123). The author is less anxious to give instructions about the training of war elephants and more particular to give details about their abodes and varieties (II. 172-331). While dealing with the army we have large sections on the medical treatment of horses and elephants (II. 529-674). The section on treasury gives less information about the principles of taxation and its varieties and more details about the qualities and types of pearls, diamonds, etc. (II. 361-516). While dealing with military operations, we have a very detailed discussion of good and bad omens to be inferred from the position of stars and planets and the notes and cries of crows, dogs and jackals, (II. 753-948).

As to purely political topics, the qualities of the kings, the qualifications of ministers (I, 54 ff.) and the duties of the treasurer, chamberlain and royal physician are mentioned, but there is nothing noteworthy about them. The same is the case about the discussion of the foreign policy. Occasionally however we get some interesting information. We are told that it was the duty of the foreign minister to summon feudatories at proper intervals in order to check their actions and policies (II. 128). it appears that forts were provisioned with snakes (kept in jars), tigers and other carnivorous animals, which, were let loose when the enemy besigned them (II. 555). Detailed lists are given about the weapons of the army (II. 681 ff.). The author allows destruction of crops, burning of towns and villages, imprisonment of enemy citizens, etc. during the course of the war.

The book is on the whole quite disappointing as a treatise on political science and shows that the manual-writers of this period had hardly any genuine interest in the science of politics; they were mainly occupied with the task of the describing the hobbies, luxuries and pastimes of the king. The political science in the real sense of the term had ceased to be cultivated.

The same tendency is illustrated by a few works on polity written in vernaculars at this time. For instance, a manual on political science was written in Marathi in *c.* 1680 by Ramachandra Pant Amātya, a minister of Shivāji, for the guidance of the latter's son, but it shows no originality of thought. These works, therefore, possess very little intrinsic value to the student of the political science. Original thinking had come to an end for reasons already explained.

OTHER ORIGINAL SOURCES

Apart from the works on Nītiéāstra, there are a number of other books in Sanskrit, Pali and Prākṛita literatures that incidently throw light on the science of polity. As shown already, (p. 5) a number of hymns in the *Ṛigveda* and the *Atharvaveda* and passages in the *Śātapatha, Aitareya, Taittirīya* and *Panchaviṁéa Brāhmaṇas* are very valuable to the student of the subject. The importance of these passages is considerably enhanced by the circumstance that they refer to an early period when the literature on polity and administration had not yet come into existence. The Dharmasūtras and Smṛitis have usually important sections dealing with the duties of kings and the working of administration; these, however, are usually written from the religious viewpoint. A few chapters on these topics occur in some Purāṇas; but they usually summaries the Smṛiti views and are not therefore very important. Works like the *Pratijñāyaugandharāyaṇa,* the *Raghuvaṁśa* and the *Mālavikāgnimitra,* the *Pañchatantrà,* the *Hitopadeśa,* the *Kādambarī,* the *Harshacharit,* the *Daśakumāracharit* and the *Rājataraṅgiṇī* have important though often small passages giving us a valuable glimpse into the contemporary political theory or administration.

The *Āchārāṅgasūtra* (in Prākṛita) and the *Digghanikāya,* the *Chullavagga,* the *Divyāvadāna* and the *Fātakas* in Pāli have important passages throwing light especially on the nature and working of ancient Indian republics.

Stone and copper inscriptions of ancient India are an extremely important source of information to the student of the political science, through unfortunately they have not yet been adequately utilised by the previous writers on the subject. Being, written by the court poets, they sometimes give an idealistic picture, but a discerning student can well differentiate between the courtly praise and prosaic facts. To a very great extent the inscriptions represent the actual state of affairs in the government machinery of the different administrations and enable us to ascertain facts and aspects sometimes altogether neglected in the works on Nitīśāstra. They are very useful in acquiring a correct picture of the territorial divisions and the official hierarchy of the different administrations. They give us a valuable insight into the taxation prevailing under different dynasties, when they enumerate the taxes from which he donees were exempted. They give us a graphic idea of the inter-state relations, as also of the relation between the suzerain and his feudatories. They often enunciate interesting maxims about the aims and ideals of government and the duties of kings and responsibilities of ministers.

The accounts of Greek historians, especially relating to the invasion of Alexander the Great, are very valuable for getting a glimpse into city states and republics. Megasthenes *Indica*, though fragmentary, is of very great values to the student of the Mauryan administration.

Numismatics or the science of coins is also not without some value to the student of polity. The coin legends often disclose the existence of a number of city states, not otherwise known to us. The existence of the republican constitutions of the Śibis, the Mālavas, the Arjunāyanas, the Kuṇidas, the Yaudheyas and the Lichchhavis is proved or confirmed by coin legends.

The sources above enumerated have now enabled us to fill a number of gaps in our knowledge of ancient Indian polity.

CHEMICAL THERMODYNAMICS

CHEMICAL THERMODYNAMICS

By

Dr. Praveen Tyagi

Lecturer

D.P.B.S., P.G. College

Anoopshahr; Bulandshahr

(U.P.)

DISCOVERY PUBLISHING HOUSE

NEW DELHI-110002

First Published-2006
Reprinted-2011

ISBN 81-8356-139-X

Published by
DISCOVERY PUBLISHING HOUSE PVT. LTD.
4383/4A, Ansari Road, Darya Ganj
New Delhi-110 002 (India)
Phone: +91-11-23279245, 43596064-65
Fax: +91-11-23253475
E-mail: parul.wasan@gmail.com
discoverypublishinghouse@gmail.com
web: www.discoverypublishinggroup.com

Printed at:
Dynamic Printers
Delhi

Preface

This book has been written for the students of under-graduate and post-graduate level of the various universities in India A special feature of the book is that the text has been illustrated with a large number of line diagrams and the data presented in the form of numerous tables for reference and comparison. In the preparation of text standard works and review by renowned author have been freely consulted and the reference given chapter wise. At the end of the book will be found useful by those who wish to make a more detailed study of the topics discussed.

We are extremely grateful to our respected Managing Director Shri Tilak Wasan, Discovery Publishing House, for valuable and active cooperation. We humble request our students and chemistry teachers to send us their constructive criticism and suggestions which we shall be using in the publication of the next edition.

Author

Contents

Pages

1

Chemical Thermodynamics

INTRODUCTION TO THERMODYNAMICS

Thermodynamics is that branch of natural science which deals with energy transformations accompanying the physical and chemical process. Thermodynamics shows the relation between various forms of energy and heat. The subject is of theoretical nature but have proved of immense importance in physics, chemistry and engineering. The advance physical chemistry is now after studied from the stand point of thermodynamics. If also help as to lay down the criteria for producing feasibility of a process including a chemical reaction under a given set of conditions. Thermodynamics help us to determine the extent to which a process including a chemical reaction can proceed before attainment of equilibrium.

Thermodynamics is firmly based upon three abstractions known as laws of *thermodynamics.* These laws arc evolved from observations made on the macroscopic world. They are more empirical than theoretical. One need not even admit to the existence of atoms or molecules for the laws of thermodynamics to be valid. Yet, they have been found to apply in all the areas of physics, chemistry and biology.

The predictions based on the laws of thermodynamics have been verified in most cases. However, cases are known where these laws show deviations. But the reasons for these deviations are well known.

The first law of thermodynamics is a statement of the law of conservation of energy, *i.e.*, the energy may change form, but may neither be created nor destroyed. The *second law of thermodynamics*, relates to the manner in which changes in system occur spontaneously, and the *third law of thermodynamics* relates, among other things, to the experimental approach to the absolute zero.

The science dealing with the macroscopic properties of matter is known as *classical thermodynamics*. Here the entire formulation has been developed without the knowledge that the matter is made up of atoms and molecules.

Statistical thermodynamics is a branch of science which is based on statistical mechanics and deals with the calculation of thermodynamic properties of matter from the classical or quantum mechanical behaviour of a large congregation of atoms or molecules.

Thermodynamics occupies an exalted position in chemistry. Usually if a conflict exists between theory and experiment, the error is ascribed to the theory. But we are so sure of thermodynamics that if a conflict occurs between the theory and an experiment, we immediately question the validity of the experiment. Thus, the laws of thermodynamics are the most certain aspects of chemistry.

Chemical Thermodynamics

It is the restricted branch of thermodynamics which deals with the study of the processes in which only chemical energy is involved. For example, heat is evolved when an acid is neutralized by a base, combustion of coal produces heat and light, discharge of storage battery produces electrical energy, and so on.

The science of chemical thermodynamics gives a quantitative account of the energy effects of chemical processes, and also uses such information in the prediction of chemical behaviour.

Importance of Thermodynamics

Thermodynamics is a fundamental subject of great importance in physical chemistry. Some facts discussed below illustrate the importance of thermodynamics.

(a) Fundamental Laws

Like all laws, these laws are based on experience and deal with the interconvsrsion of different forms of energy such as heat energy, mechanical energy, electrical energy, etc. No exception to these laws has been reported. Usually, if a conflict exists between theory and experiment, the error is ascribed to the theory. But we are so sure of thermodynamics that if a conflict occurs between the theory and an experimental result, we immediately question the validity of the experiment. Thus, the laws of thermodynamics are the most certain aspects of chemistry.

(b) Generalization of Experimental Results

Thermodynamics offers the means by which one can generalize the results of many different experiments; these generalizations being the aforementioned laws. For examples, with the help of these laws, equations relating to certain physical properties with the variations of temperature and pressure have been developed.

(c) Direction of a Reaction

Thermodynamics has very great predictive powers, *i.e., the laws of thermodynamics can be used to predict the direction in which a process would proceed.* Thus, the study of thermodynamics is of great importance to the chemist, since it can predict whether or not a chemical reaction will proceed spontaneously from a knowledge of the thermodynamic properties of reactants and products. If thermodynamics tells us that a prospective reaction is favourable, then we are on a safe ground to try to find out the proper experimental conditions to make the reaction proceed. For example, when H_2 and O_2 are mixed. Thermodynamics tells us that H_2O should be formed, since H_2O is more energetically stable than H, and O_2 It is a well known fact that at room temperature a mixture of H_2 and O_2 will not produce H_2O. However, if the mixture is sparked, water is produced with explosive violence, thereby, proving the prediction the thermodynamics makes concerning the reaction.

(d) Prediction of Relationship Between Directly Observable Properties

It is possible with the help of laws of thermodynamics to predict the relationship between directly observable properties of substances quantitatively. Relationship between quantities which can be derived from the other observable properties can also be predicted. For example, it is possible to derive the relationship among pressure, temperature and volume of a gas thermodynamically.

Limitations of Thermodynamics

Although the subject of thermodynamics has proved of great help and importance to the chemists, yet it has certain limitations. For chemists the most serious weaknesses are as follows :

(a) *Thermodynamics does not give any specific, direct information about the nature or structure of matter.* Although, this is a serious shortcoming, it should be noted that the methods of statistical thermodynamics indicate that the conclusions of thermodynamics are at least inconsistent with the quantum theory of matter.

(b) *Thermodynamics does not give any indication of how fast the reaction will proceed i.e.* in essence, the laws of thermodynamics do not contain time as a variable. Thus, thermodynamics is only interested in where the system was initially and where it is after the completion of the process. It does not care how the attainment of the final condition came about or how long it takes to reach this condition. For example, it is possible to show by means of thermodynamics that hydrogen and oxygen can react to form liquid water at ordinary temperature and pressure, but it is not possible to show whether the reaction will be slow or fast. We know by experience that the reaction is so slow in the absence of a catalyst that it cannot be practically detected for years. Such information is not obtainable from thermodynamics.

(c) Thermodynamics deals especially with the interconversion of the various forms of energy; *matter finds no consideration except as a carrier of energy.*

(d) Strictly speaking, mass is form of energy, the two are related by the Einstein equation $E = mc^2$. In the process with which thermodynamics is primarily concerned, there is, however, no measurable conversion of mass into energy. Hence, *the fact of mass being a form of energy is left out of consideration in thermodynamics problems.*

(e) Thermodynamic methods provide only a limiting value for the work, obtainable from a chemical or physical transformation. Thermodynamic functions predict the work that may be obtained if the reaction is carried out with infinite slowness, in a "so called" reversible manner. However, it is impossible to specify the actual work obtained in a real or natural process in which the time interval is finite but we can state that the real work will be less than the work-obtainable in a, reversible situation. For example, thermodynamic calculations will provide a value for the maximum voltage of a storage battery, *i.e.,* the voltage that is obtained When no current is drawn. When current is drawn, we can predict that the voltage will be less than the maximum value, but not how much less.

TERMINOLOGY OF THERMODYNAMICS

System and its Surroundings

A thermodynamical system is a part of the universe which is arbitrarily set off from the rest of the universe by definite boundaries for the purpose of experimental or theoretical studies. The remainder of the universe is then, in fact, the surroundings of the system. Usually, however, the surroundings are restricted to a region in the immediate vicinity of the system under study. The space separating the system from its surroundings is termed as boundary.

The choice of the system and surroundings is quite arbitrary. What might be considered as part of the surroundings of a system by one person may be considered as part of the system itself by another person.

Illustration of Terms

A cylinder containing a gas (or liquid) is placed in a thermostatic bath which is maintained at a constant temperature, say, 25°C. This is shown in Fig. 1.1. In this case the gas (or liquid) constitutes the system whereas the constant temperature bath is the surroundings. The walls of the cylinder constitute the boundaries.

As we come across various types of systems as well as walls or boundaries, it becomes essential to define some important types of walls. These are :

(a) *A rigid wall :* This is the wall whose position and shape are fixed.

(b) *An impermeable wall :* This is the wall which does not permit the passage of matter.

(c) *A permeable wall :* It is that type of wall which permits the Temperature Bath passage of matter and consequently, also of energy.

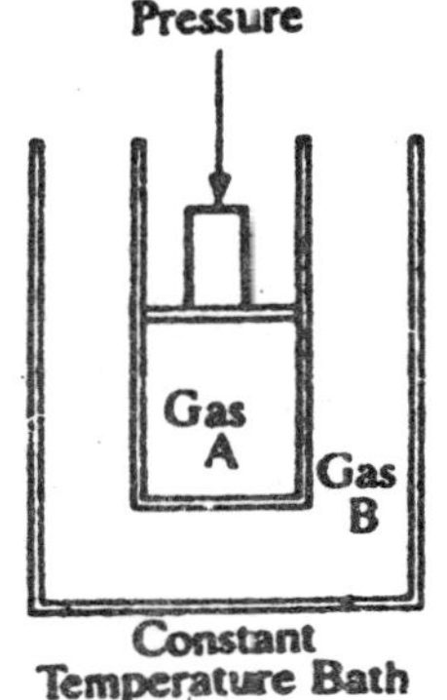

Fig. 1.1

(d) *An adiabatic wall :* It is that type of wall which when held rigid will not permit the passage of matter or energy provided no external force fields are present. An interesting example is the thermos bottle.

(e) *A diathermal or diathermic wall :* This is that type of wall which when held rigid will not permit the passage of matter but allow the passage of energy in the absence of any external force field. It means that a diathermal wall is impermeable but not adiabatic. An aluminium can is an example of a container whose walls are diathermal.

Types of Systems

The various systems arc of following types :

(a) *Real systems :* In experimental work, the system-is called real.

(b) *Ideal system :* In pencil and paper work, the system treated is called ideal. An ideal system is always considered to simplify the thermodynamic problems.

(c) *Isolated system : A system is said to be isolated when it can neither exchange energy nor matter with us surroundings.*

If the sealed tube containing liquid and vapour was thermally insulated so that heat energy could not enter or leave the liquid-vapour, system would be an isolated system. At the same time, such a tube cannot exchange matter with its surroundings. An isolated system is shown in Fig. 1.2.

(d) *Closed system : A system is said to be closed when it permits the passage of energy, but not mass, across the boundary.*

A liquid in equilibrium with its vapours in a sealed tube is an example of a closed system. Heat energy can be added to cause more liquid to vaporise, but the total amount of matter is not changed, since no more vapours can escape. This is shown in Fig. 1.3. Another example of a closed system is to consider a gaseous mixture of oxygen and hydrogen in the ratio of 1 : 2 by volume enclosed in a cylinder (Fig. 1.4). This reaction takes place in accordance with the equation

$$2H_2\,(g) + O_2\,(g) \rightarrow 2H_2O\,(l);\ AH = -68.4 \text{ Kcal.}$$

As the system can exchange energy with its surroundings, heat evolved (68 Kcal) is transferred from the system to the surroundings. Thus, the temperature of the system will remain constant. At the same time, this reaction is accompanied by decrease in volume; the piston has to move downward for allowing the pressure to remain constant. In this way, some energy in the form of mechanical work has transferred from surroundings to the system. But since the cylinder is kept closed throughout, it means that no transfer of matter occurs from the system to the surroundings or *vice-versa*. Thus, this is an example of a closed system.

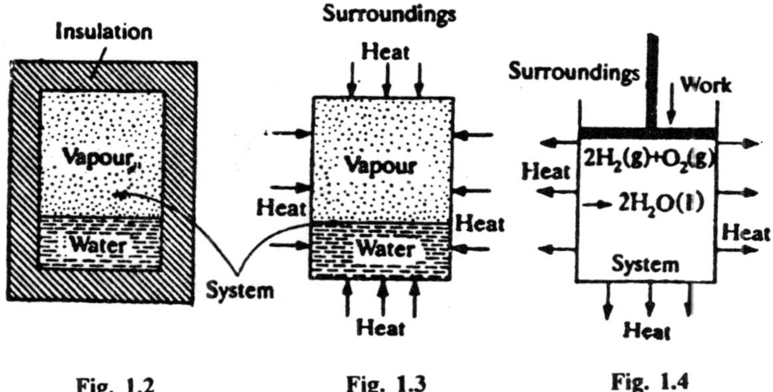

Fig. 1.2 Fig. 1.3 Fig. 1.4

(e) *Open system : An open system is one which can exchange both energy and matter with its surroundings.* For example, a beaker containing water (the system) in a thermostated water bath (the surroundings) is an open system, because the water vapour (matter) will escape into the surroundings whereas the heat (energy) required for the vaporisation will be absorbed from the surroundings. Thus, this is an example of an open system (Fig. 1.5).

Let us consider another example which involves the reaction between zinc granules and dilute hydrochloric acid taking place in an open beaker (Fig. 1.6). The hydrogen will be evolved which will pass out from the system to the surroundings. At the same time, the heat evolved in the reaction will be transferred to the surroundings by radiations, etc. Thus, this involves exchange of matter as well as energy between the system and the surroundings. It means that it is an example of open system.

(f) *Homogeneous system* : It involves only one phase and its uniformity can be revealed under high power microscope. For example, a gas, a mixture of gases, a pure liquid, two miscible liquids, etc.

(g) *Heterogeneous system* : It involves two or more phases separated from each other by interfacial boundaries. A liquid in contact with its vapour is an example of heterogeneous system because it consists of two phases. Another example is a system consisting of two or more immiscible liquids or a solid in contact with a liquid in which it does not dissolve.

(h) *Macroscopic system* : A macroscopic system is one in which there are a large number of particles (may be molecules, atoms, ions, etc.)

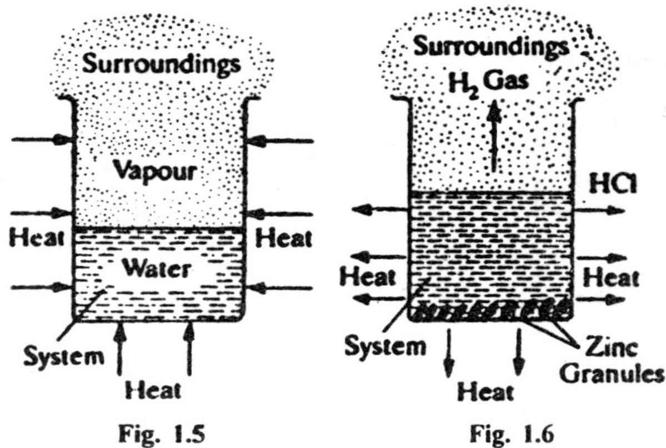

Fig. 1.5 Fig. 1.6

State of a System (State Variables)

The quantities whose values serve to describe the system completely are called the thermodynamic properties of the system. Once the properties of the system are completely specified, one says that the state of the system is specified. Thus, the defining properties are sometimes called state variables or state properties. Examples of state properties are pressure, volume, temperature and composition. The question now arises as how many variables must be determined to define the system completely. The answer to this question can be obtained by considering the following example:

A homogeneous system consists of a single substance and hence the composition is fixed automatically. The state of a homogeneous system can, therefore, be defined by .only three variables:

(i) Pressure,

(ii) Volume, and

(iii) Temperature.

For a homogeneous system of definite mass, these three properties are related to one another by a mathematical equation, PV = RT, called *equation of state*. With the help of this equation (PV = RT) the values of any one of these properties can be determined knowing the values of the other two properties.

Therefore, state of a simple homogeneous system may be completely defined by specifying only two of the three variables, *i.e.*, pressure, temperature and volume. The two variables generally specified are temperature and pressure. These are termed as independent variables. The third variable, generally volume, is called a dependent variable because its value depends upon the values of pressure and temperature.

When we are considering a closed system consisting of one or-more components, mass is not a state variable.

In order to define the state of a homogeneous system having more than one substance, one must consider and describe each of the phases of the system. For each phase, one must specify the content, *i.e.*, the amount of each substance present, and two other independent variables.

In order to define a system completely, the state variables are generally temperature (T), pressure (P), volume (V) and concentration (n). Besides these there are two more variables. Work (n) and heat (q), which are not state properties as would be proved later on. These six variables play an important role in defining chemical systems completely, especially from the view point of the thermodynamics.

Properties of a System

The observable properties of a system are of two types:

Extensive Properties

There are some properties called extensive properties whose *values are proportional to the mass of the portion of the system* or one can say that extensive properties are dependent upon the size of the system. Examples are volume, number of moles, mass, energy, internal energy, etc. The volume of ten kilogram of matter is certainly ten times the volume of one kilogram of the same matter under identical conditions arid so volume is an extensive property. The value of extensive property is equal to sum of the values for the separate parts into which the system may be subdivided.

Intensive Properties

There are some properties of a system called intensive properties, whose values are independent of the quantity of matter contained in the system. Thus, the intensive properties are characteristic of the substances present in the system. For example, refractive index, viscosity, surface tension, density, temperature, etc. are all intensive properties. Whether one considers one kilogram or ten kilograms of a given system at uniform temperature, its refractive index is the same in both the cases, and so refractive index is an intensive property.

Discussion

(i) From the above definition it follows that the extensive properties of a single pure substance will not only depend upon the number of moles (n) of the substance present but also on any two of the three variables P, V and T, known as independent variables. If n is kept fixed, the extensive property will depend only on the two out of P.V and T variables.

(ii) If a system is a solution having two or more substances, the extensive property will not only depend upon the two independent variables but also on (he number of moles n_A, n_B,......of the various constituents A, B...... present in the solution.

(iii) Any extensive property if expressed as per mole or per gram becomes an intensive property. For example, mass and volume are extensive properties, but density and specific volume, *i.e.*, the mass per unit volume and volume per unit mass respectively are intensive properties. Similarly, heat capacity is an extensive property but specific heat is an intensive property.

Some extensive and intensive properties are tabulated below:

Extensive property	*Intensive property*
volume	Molar Volume
No. of moles	Density
Mass	Refractive index
Free energy	Surface tension
Entropy	Viscosity
Enthalpy	Free energy per mole
Heat capacity	Specific heal
	Pressure
	Temperature
	Boiling point. Freezing point etc.

THERMODYNAMICAL EQUILIBRIUM

A system is said to have attained a state of thermodynamical equilibrium when it shows no further tendency to change its property with time.

For simplicity, consider a system that consists of a single homogeneous substance. If the properties of the system remain uniform throughout, then, so long as the external conditions are unaltered, the system is said to be in thermodynamic equilibrium. For example, if the pressure was not uniform, turbulence would occur until the system reaches equilibrium. It is important to mention here that the state of a given homogeneous system of given mass may be described by two state variables under equilibrium conditions only.

In the case of a heterogeneous system, consisting of a more than one phase, a thermodynamic equilibrium is said to exist in it when all of its macroscopic properties in various phases of the system do, not change with time.

The criterion for thermodynamic equilibrium requires that the following three types of equilibrium exist simultaneously in a system:

Thermal Equilibrium

If the temperature is same throughout the whole system, it is in a state of thermal equilibrium. This type of equilibrium means that the system must be at the same temperature, as its surroundings. Any temperature difference that exists will cause the heat to flow from a higher temperature to a lower one until the temperature becomes uniform throughout the system (constancy of temperature). In other words For a system to be in thermal equilibrium, there should be no temperature difference between the parts of the system or between the system and the surroundings.

Mechanical Equilibrium

It involves no flow of currents of matter within the system or at its boundaries. Mechanical equilibrium requires that there should not be any macroscopic movement within the system itself or of the system, with respect to its surroundings. If there is movement in the system, the properties cannot be constant with time. For example, consider a gas contained in a cylinder equipped with a movable piston. If the piston is pushed in rapidly, the rapid motion will set up pressure and temperature difference in the gas. Hence, no one pressure measurement will unambiguously describe the system. If enough time is allowed to elapse, these differences will level out until the pressure and temperature throughout the gas will become uniform and constant. The system is then in mechanical equilibrium (constancy of pressure). In other words, for a system to be in mechanical equilibrium, there should be no unbalanced forces acting on any part of the system or the system as a whole.

Chemical Equilibrium

If the chemical composition of a system is not spontaneously changing with time, it is in a state of chemical equilibrium.

The chemical equilibrium is a dynamic one in which the forward and reverse reactions are continually occurring at equal rates. Hence there is no net change in the concentration of reactants or products at equilibrium. If any change in chemical composition occurs in the system, it is obvious that no one composition could be found which will unambiguously describe the state of the system (constancy of composition).

In other words, for a system to be in chemical equilibrium, there should be no chemical reaction within the system and also no movement of any chemical constituent from one part of the system to the other.

When a system is in thermodynamic equilibrium and the surroundings are kept unchanged, there will be no motion and also no work will be done. On the other hand, if the sum of the external is altered, resulting in a finite unbalanced force acting on the system, the condition for mechanical equilibrium will not be satisfied any longer. This results in the following :

(i) Due to unbalanced forces within the system, turbulence, waves etc. may be set up. The system as a whole may possess an accelerated motion.

(ii) Due to turbulence, acceleration etc. the temperature distribution within the system may not be uniform. There may also exits a finite temperature difference between the system and the surroundings.

(iii) Due to the presence of unbalanced forces and difference in temperature, chemical reaction may take place or there may be movement of a chemical constituent.

From this discussion, it is clear that a finite unbalanced force may cause the system to pass through non-equilibrium states. If during a thermodynamic process, it is desired to describe every state of a system by thermodynamic coordinates referred to the system as a whole, the process should not be brought about by a finite unbalanced force.

A quasistatic process is defined as the process in which the deviation from thermodynamic equilibrium is infinitesimal and all the states through which the system passes during a quasistatic process can be considered as equilibrium states.

In actual practice, many processes closely approach a quasistatic process and may be treated as such with no significant error. Consider the expansion of a gas in a closed cylinder fitted with a piston. Initially weights are on the piston and the pressure of the gas inside the cylinder is higher than the atmospheric pressure. If the weights are small and are taken off slowly one by one, the process can be considered quasistatic. If, however, all the weights are removed at once, expansion takes place suddenly and it will be a nonequilibrium process. The system will not be in equilibrium at any time during this process.

A quasistatic process is an ideal concept that is applicable to all thermodynamic systems including electric and magnetic systems. It should be noted that conditions for such a process can never be satisfied rigorously in practice.

For attainment of complete thermodynamic equilibrium, there should be thermal, mechanical and chemical stability. When a system is in thermodynamic equilibrium, its properties have magnitudes. Whenever the system comes to that particular state of thermodynamical equilibrium, its properties will have the same magnitude, regardless of what might have occurred to the system previously. Thus, a system is said to be in thermodynamic equilibrium if,

(i) Its macroscopic properties do not alter with time..

(ii) There are no currents of matter and energy within the system or at its boundaries.

THERMODYNAMIC PROCESS

Thermodynamics deals with changes that occur in the properties of system when the system goes from one equilibrium state to another. *Such a change in the values of the properties of the system, is called a process*. Alternatively, a thermodynamic process is *the path or operation by which a system changes from one state to another.* A system can usually change from one equilibrium state to another through a variety of ways. Different types of processes connecting an initial state to a final state are :

Cyclic Process

When a system undergoes a series of slate changes in such a way that the final slate becomes identical with the initial state, if is said to have passed through a cyclic process.

If a series of changes are conducted at a constant temperature, the cycle is known as an isothermal cycle. If the changes are carried out reversibly, then the cycle is known as a reversible cycle. A well known cyclic process is Carnot's cycle.

As the internal energy of a system depends only upon its state, it means that in a cyclic process, the net change of internal energy is zero, *i.e.*,

$$\Delta E = 0 = q - w$$

or $$q = w$$

Quasistatic (or Reversible Process) : A process is said to be quasistatic if it is carried out in such a way that at every moment the system departs only infinitesimally from an equilibrium state. At every instant, the system remains virtually in a state of equilibrium and all the states through which the system passes can be described by means of thermodynamic variables referring to the system as a whole. The vanishingly slowness of the process is an essential feature of a quasistatic process.

A quasistatic process in contrast to a real process does not involve considerations of rates, velocities or times. A real process is said to be a temporal succession of equilibrium and nonequilibrium states while a quasistatic process is said to be an ordered succession of equilibrium states.

Perfect Differentials or Exact differentials

What is a Perfect Differential? Let us consider a certain quantity z depending upon two other quantities, so that z is a some single-valued function of x and y. Mathematically, we can express it as

$$z = f(x, y)$$

Let us consider two mutually perpendicular axes as the axes of co-ordinate in Fig. (1.1). Then for any particular point A of co-ordinates, x, y, the quantity z has a particular and definite value. That is, when x and y are given, the quantity z is completely determined. Then, the differential dz is called perfect differential.

Spontaneous Process

A process in which all steps cannot be retraced by themselves is called a spontaneous process, *i.e.*, a process which takes place in one direction of its own accord is a spontaneous process. If the reverse change of the spontaneous process is required, outside effort will be required. Thus, the spontaneous process is irreversible.

The processes which occur in nature are known as *natural processes*. The natural processes always try to tend towards equilibrium. The change involved in natural process is called *spontaneous change*. The *spontaneous processes* are those which take place without external interference of any kind.

Some examples of spontaneous processes are as follows:

(i) When a bar of metal, hot at one end and cold at the other end is taken, the heat will be conducted, by itself, along the bar from the hot to the cold end until the temperature becomes uniform. This process cannot reverse itself spontaneously.

(ii) The expansion of a gas into an evacuated space, or from a region of higher pressure to a region of lower pressure, takes place spontaneously, until the pressure distribution is uniform throughout.

(iii) The gas diffuses spontaneously into another gas until the mixing is complete and the system has the same composition.

(iv) A solute diffuses from a stronger to a weaker solution.

It is observed that in every spontaneous process the system approaches to a state of thermodynamic equilibrium. In the spontaneous processes, an external source is required to cause the reverse change. Thus we can say that the spontaneous processes are thermodynamically irreversible. It is remarkable to note that useful work can be obtained from the spontaneous process. The amount of work obtained from the spontaneous process is maximum when it is carried out reversibly Thus spontaneous processes take place in a direction leading to equilibrium and are thermodynamically irreversible. Work can be obtained from these processes.

Differences between a reversible process and a spontaneous process.

A reversible process is the one that can proceed in either direction with equal ease. On the other hand, a spontaneous process is unidirectional and irreversible.

None-Spontaneous Process

The reverse process of the spontaneous process is known as non-spontaneous process. These processes occur by supplying external energy to the system. For example, when water is pumped from a lower level to higher level external energy is required. Similarly, when a gas is compressed then also external energy is required.

The thermodynamic systems in engineering are gas, vapour, steam, mixture of gasoline vapour and air, ammonia vapours and its liquid. In Physics, thermodynamics includes besides the above, systems like stretched wires, thermocouples, magnetic materials, electrical condenser. electrical cells, solids and surface films.

Reversible Cell

The thermodynamic coordinates to completely describe a reversible cell are

(a) the E.M.F. of the cell

(b) the charge that flows and

(c) the temperature.

Stretched Wire

In a stretched wire, to find the Young's modulus of a wire by stretching, the complete thermodynamic co-ordinates are

(a) the stretching force F

(b) the length of the stretching wire and

(c) the temperature of the wire.

The pressure and volume are considered to be constant.

Surface Films

For liquid films, in the study of surface tension, the thermodynamic co-ordinates are

(a) the surface tension

(b) the area of the film and

(c) the temperature.

ZEROTH LAW OF THERMODYNAMICS

A thermodynamic system is said to be in thermal equilibrium if any two of it's independent thermodynamic co-ordinates X and Y remain constant as long as the external conditions remain unaltered. Consider a gas enclosed in a cylinder fitted with a piston. If the pressure and volume of the enclosed mass of gas are P and V at the temperature of the surroundings, these values of P and V will remain constant as long as the external conditions viz., temperature and pressure remain unaltered. The gas is said to be in thermal equilibrium with the surroundings.

The *zeroth law* of thermodynamics was formulated after the first and the second laws of thermodynamics have been enunciated. This law helps to define the term *temperature* of a system.

This law states that *if, of three systems. A, B and C, A and B are separately in thermal equilibrium with C, then A and B are also in thermal equilibrium with one another.* Conversely the law can be stated as follows :

If three or more systems are in thermal contact, each to each, by means of diathermal walls and are all in thermal equilibrium together, then any two systems taken separately are in thermal equilibrium with one another.

Consider three fluids A, B and C. Let P_A, F_A represent the pressure and volume of A, P_B, V_B, the pressure and volume of B, and P_C, V_C are the pressure and volume of C.

If A and B are in thermal equilibrium, then

$$\phi_1(P_A, V_A) = \phi_2(P_B, V_B)$$

or $$F_1[P_A, V_A, P_B, V_B] = 0 \quad ...(i)$$

Expression (i) can be solved, and

$$P_B = Af_1[P_A, V_A, V_B] \qquad ...(ii)$$

If B and G are in thermal equilibrium

$$\phi_2(P_B, V_B) = \phi_3(P_C, V_C)$$

or $F_2[P_B, V_B, P_C, V_C] = 0$

Also $P_B = f_2[V_B, P_C, V_C]$ ...(iii)

From equations (ii) and (iii) for A and C to be in thermal equilibrium separately,

$$f_1(P_A, V_A, V_B) = f_2[V_B, P_C, V_C) \qquad ...(iv)$$

If A and C are in thermal equilibrium with B separately, then according to the zeroth law, A and C are also in thermal equilibrium with one another.

$\therefore$ $F_3[P_A, V_A, P_C, V_C] = 0.$ ...(v)

Equation (iv) contains a variable V_B, whereas equation (v) does not contain the variable V_B. It means

$$\phi_1(P_A, V_A) = \varphi_3(P_C, V_C) \qquad ...(vi)$$

In general,

$$\phi_1(P_A, V_A) = \phi_2(P_B, V_B) = \phi_3(P_C, V_C) \qquad ...(vii)$$

These three functions have the same numerical value though the parameters (P, V) of each are different. This numerical value is termed as *temperature* (T) of the body.

$\therefore$ $\phi(P, V) = T$ ...(viii)

This is called the equation of state of the fluid.

Therefore, the temperature of a system can be defined as the property that determines whether or not the body is in thermal equilibrium with the neighbouring systems. If a number of systems are in thermal equilibrium, this common property of the system can be represented by a single numerical value called the temperature. It means that if two systems are not in thermal equilibrium, they are at different temperatures.

In a mercury in glass thermometer, the pressure above the mercury column is zero and volume of mercury measures the temperature. If a thermometer shows a constant reading in two systems A and B separately, it will show the same reading even when A and B are brought in contact.

CONCEPT OF HEAT

Heat is defined as *energy in, transit*. As it is not possible to speak of work in a body, it is also not possible to speak of heat in a body. Work is either done on a body or by a body. Similarly, heat can flow from a body or to a body. If a body is at a constant temperature, it has both mechanical and thermal energies due to the molecular agitations and it is not possible to separate them. So, in this case, we cannot talk of heat energy. It means, if the flow of heat stops, the word heat cannot be used. It is only used when there is transfer of energy between two or more systems.

Consider two systems A and B in thermal contact with one another and surrounded by adiabatic walls.

For the system A,

$$H = U_2 = U_1 + W \quad ...(i)$$

where B is the heat energy transferred, U_1 is the initial internal energy, U_2 is the final internal energy and W is the work done.

Similarly for the system B,

$$H' = U_2' = U_1' + W' \quad ...(ii)$$

Adding (i) and (ii)

$$\therefore H + H' = (U_2 - U_1) + W + (U_2' = U_1') + W'$$

$$H + H' = [(U_2 + U_2') - (U_1 + U_1')] + (W + W') \quad ...(iii)$$

The total change in the internal energy of the composite system

$$= [(U_2 + U_2') - (U_1 + U_1')]$$

The work done by the composite system = W + W'

It means that the heat transferred by the composite system = H + H'. But the composite system is surrounded by adiabatic and the net heat transferred is zero.

$$\therefore \quad H + H' = 0$$

$$H = -H' \quad ...(iv)$$

Thus, for two systems A and B in thermal contact with each and other the composite system surrounded by adiabatic walls, the heat gained by one system is equal to the heat lost by the other system.

HEAT—PATH FUNCTION

Heat is a path function. When a system changes from a state 1 to state 2, the quantity of heat transferred will depend upon the intermediate stages through which the system passes *i.e.*, its path. Hence heat is an Inexact *differential* and is written as δB.

On integrating, we get

$$\int_{1A}^{2A} \delta H = H_{1A}^{2A}$$

Here, $_1H_2$, represents the heat transferred during the process between the states 1 and 2 along a particular path A.

WORK—A PATH FUNCTION

Suppose that a system is taken from an initial equilibrium state 1 to a final equilibrium state 2 by two different paths A and B (Fig. 1.7). The processes are quasistatic.

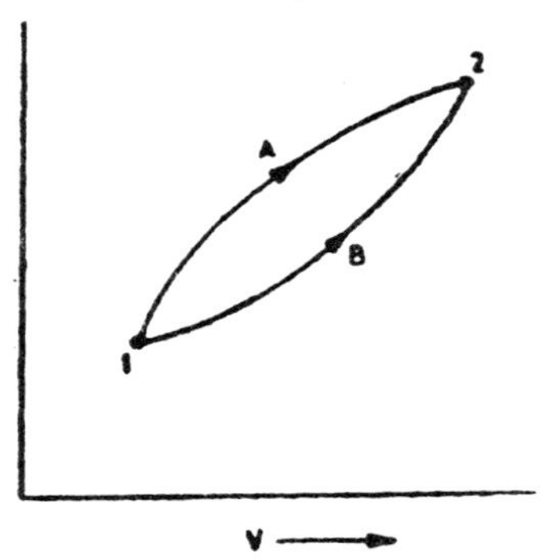

Fig. 1.7

The areas under these curves are different and hence the quantities of work done are also different.

For the path A, $W_A = \int_{1A}^{2A} \delta W = \int_{1A}^{2A} P\,dV$ ...(i)

For the path B $W_B = \int_{1B}^{2B} \delta W = \int_{1B}^{2B} P\,dV$ ...(ii)

The values of W_A and W_B are not equal. Therefore work cannot be expressed as a difference between the values of some property of the system in the two states. *Therefore,* it is not correct to represent

$$W = \int_{W_1}^{W_2} \delta W = W_2 - W_1 \qquad ...(iii)$$

It may be pointed out that it is meaningless to say "work in a system or work of a system". Work cannot be interpreted similar to temperature or pressure of a system.

In terms of calculus δW is an inexact differential. It means that W is not a property of the system and ∫ δW cannot be expressed as the difference between two quantities that depend entirely on the initial and the final states.

Hence, heat and work are *path functions* and they depend only on the process They are not point functions such as pressure or temperature. Work done in taking the system from state 1 to state 2 will be different for different paths.

COMPARISON OF HEAT AND WORK

There are many similarities between heat and work. These are:

1. Heat and work are both transient phenomena. Systems do not possess heat or work.
2. When a system undergoes a change, heat transfer or work done may occur.
3. Heat and work are boundary phenomena. They are observed at the boundary of the system.
4. Heat and work represent the energy crossing the boundary of the system.
5. Heat and work are path functions and hence they are inexact differentials. They are written as δB and δW.
6. (a) Heat is defined as the form of energy that is transferred across a boundary by virtue of difference of temperature or temperature gradient.
   (b) Work is said to be done by a system if the sole effect on things external to the system could be the raising of a weight.

It is customary to represent, work done by the system as +ve, work done on the system as –ve, heat flowing into the system as +ve, and heat flowing out of the system as –ve.

FIRST LAW OF THERMODYNAMICS

Joule's law gives the relation between the work done and the heat produced. It is true when the whole of the work done is used in producing heat or vice versa. Here, $W = JH$ where J is the Joule's mechanical equivalent of heat. But in practice, when a certain quantity of heat is supplied to a system the whole of the heat energy may not be converted into work. Part of the heat may be used in doing external work and the rest of the heat might be used in increasing the internal energy of the molecules. Let the quantity of heat supplied to a system be δH, the amount of external work done be δW and the increase in internal energy of the molecules be dU. The term U represents the internal energy of a gas due to molecular agitation as well as due to the forces of intermolecular attraction. Mathematically,

$$\delta H = dU + \delta W \qquad ...(i)$$

Equation (i) represents the first law of thermodynamics. All the quantities are measured in heat units. The first law of thermodynamics states that the amount of heat given to a system is equal to the sum of the increase in the internal energy of the system and the external work done.

For a cyclic process, the change in the internal energy of the system is zero because the system is brought back to the original condition. Therefore for a cyclic process $\oint \delta U = 0$

and $$\oint \delta H = \oint dw \qquad ...(ii)$$

[Both are expressed in heat units].

This equation represents Joule's law.

For a system carried through a cyclic process, its initial and final internal energies are equal. From the first law of thermodynamics, for a system undergoing any number of complete cycles

$$U_2 - U_1 = 0$$

$$\oint \delta H = \oint \delta W$$

$$H = W \text{ [Both are in heat units]}$$

FIRST LAW OF THERMODYNAMICS FOR A CHANGE IN STATE OF A CLOSED SYSTEM

For a closed system during a complete cycle, the first law of thermodynamics is written as

$$\oint \delta H = \oint \delta W$$

In practice, however, we are also concerned with a process rather than a cycle. Let the system undergo a cycle, changing its state from 1 to 2 along the path A and from 2 to 1 along the path B. This cyclic process is represented in the P – V diagram (Fig. 1.8).

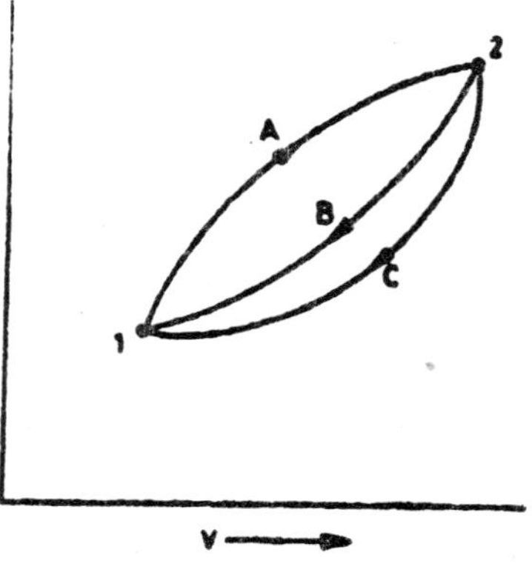

Fig. 1.8

According to the first law of thermodynamics

$$\oint \delta H = \oint \delta W$$

For the complete cyclic process

$$\int_{1A}^{2A} \delta H + \int_{2B}^{1B} \delta H = \int_{1A}^{2A} \delta W + \int_{2B}^{1B} \delta W \qquad ...(i)$$

Now, consider the second cycle in which the system changes from state 1 to state 2 along the path A and returns from state 2 to state 1 along the path C. For this cyclic process

$$\int_{1A}^{2A} \delta H + \int_{2C}^{1C} \delta H = \int_{1A}^{2A} \delta W + \int_{2C}^{1C} \delta W \qquad ...(ii)$$

Subtracting (ii) from (i)

$$\int_{2B}^{1B} \delta H - \int_{2C}^{1C} \delta H = \int_{2B}^{1B} \delta W - \int_{2C}^{1C} \delta W$$

or $$\int_{2B}^{1B} (\delta H - \delta W) = \int_{2C}^{1C} (\delta H - \delta W) \qquad ...(ii)$$

Here B and C represent arbitrary processes between the states 1 and 2. Therefore, it can be concluded that the quantity ($\delta H - \delta W$) is the same for all processes between the states 1 and 2. The quantity ($\delta H - \delta W$) depends only on the initial and the final states of the system and is independent of the path followed between the two states.

Let $dE = (\delta H - \delta W)$

From the above logic, it can be seen that

$$\int_{1}^{2} dE = \text{constant and is independent of the path.}$$

This naturally suggests that E is a point function and dE is an exact differential.

The point function E is a property of the system.

Here dE is the derivative of E and it is an exact differential.

$$\therefore \qquad \delta H - \delta W = dE \qquad ...(iv)$$

or $$\delta H = dE + \delta W \qquad ..(v)$$

Integrating equation (v), from the initial state 1 to the final state 2

$$_1H_2 = (E_2 - E_1) + {_1W_2}$$

Note: ${}_1H_2$ cannot be written as $(H_2 - H_1)$, because it depends upon the path.

Similarly, ${}_1W_2$ cannot be written as $(W_2 - W_1)$, because it also depends upon the path.

Here ${}_1H_2$ represents the heat transferred,

${}_1W_2$ represents the work done,

E_2 represents the total energy of the system in state 2,

E_1 represents the total energy of the system in state 1.

At this point, it is worthwhile discussing what this E can possibly mean. With reference to the system, the energies crossing the boundaries are all taken care of in the form of B and W. For dimensional stability of Eq. (v), this E must be energy and this must belong to the system. Therefore,

E_2 represents the energy of the system in state 2

E_1 represents the energy of the system in state 1

This energy E acquires a value at any given equilibrium condition by virtue of its thermodynamic state. The working substance, for example a gas, has molecules moving in all random fashion. The molecules have energy associated by virtue of mutual attraction and this part is similar to the potential energy of a body in macroscopic terms. They also have velocities and hence kinetic energy. This energy E therefore can be visualised as comprising of molecular potential and kinetic energies in addition to macroscopic potential and kinetic energies, The first part, which owes its existence to the thermodynamic nature is often called the internal energy which is completely dependent on the thermodynamic state and the other two depend on mechanical or physical state of the system.

E = U + KE + PE + Others which depend upon chemical nature etc.

For a closed system (non-chemical) the changes in all others except U are insignificant and

$$dE = dU$$

∴ From equation (v)

$$\delta H = dU + \delta W \qquad ...(vi)$$

Here all the quantities are in consistent units

APPLICATIONS OF FIRST LAW OF THERMODYNAMICS SPECIFIC HEAT OF A GAS (T AND V INDEPENDENT)

The internal energy of a system is a angle valued function of the state variables viz., pressure, volume, temperature etc. In the case of a gas, any two of the variables P, V, T are sufficient to define completely its state. If V and T are chosen as the independent variables.

$$U = f(V, T) \qquad \text{...(i)}$$

Differentiating equation (i)

$$dU = \left(\frac{\partial U}{\partial T}\right)_V dT + \left(\frac{\partial U}{\partial V}\right)_T dV \qquad \text{...(ii)}$$

If an amount of heat δH is supplied to a thermodynamical system, say an ideal gas and if the volume increases by dV at a constant pressure P, then according to the first law of thermodynamics

$$\delta H = dU + \delta W$$

Here $\delta W = P \,.\, dV$

$\therefore$ $\delta H = dU + P \,.\, dV$

Substituting the value of W from equation (ii)

$$\delta H = \left(\frac{\partial U}{\partial T}\right)_V dT + \left(\frac{\partial U}{\partial V}\right)_T dV + P.dV \qquad \text{...(iii)}$$

Dividing both sides by dT

$$\frac{\delta H}{dT} = \left(\frac{\partial U}{\partial T}\right)_V + \left(\frac{\partial U}{\partial V}\right)_T \frac{dV}{dT} + \frac{P.dV}{dT}$$

or

$$\left(\frac{\delta H}{dT}\right) = \left(\frac{\partial U}{\partial T}\right)_V + \left[P + \left(\frac{\partial U}{\partial V}\right)_T\right] \frac{dV}{dT} \qquad \text{...(iv)}$$

If the gas is heated at constant volume,

$$\left(\frac{\delta H}{\partial T}\right)_V = C_V \qquad \text{and} \qquad \frac{dV}{dT} = 0$$

$$\therefore \quad \left(\frac{\delta H}{\partial T}\right)_V = \left(\frac{\partial U}{\partial T}\right)_V = C_V \qquad \text{...(v)}$$

When the gas is heated at constant pressure,

$$\left(\frac{\delta H}{\partial T}\right)_P = C_P$$

∴ From equation (iv),

$$C_P = \left(\frac{\partial U}{\partial T}\right)_V + \left[P + \left(\frac{\partial U}{\partial V}\right)_T\right]\left(\frac{\partial V}{\partial T}\right)_P$$

$$\therefore \quad C_P = C_V + \left[P + \left(\frac{\partial U}{\partial V}\right)_T\right]\left(\frac{\partial V}{\partial T}\right)_P$$

or
$$C_P - C_V = \left[P + \left(\frac{\partial U}{\partial V}\right)_T\right]\left(\frac{\partial V}{\partial T}\right)_P \quad \text{...(vi)}$$

From Joule's experiment, for an ideal gas on opening the stopcock, no work was done and no heat transfer tool; place.

So $\delta H = 0 = \delta U + 0$. Therefore, $dU = 0$. Even though the volume changed while the temperature is constant, there if no change in internal energy.

$$\left(\frac{\partial V}{\partial T}\right)_P = 0$$

From the ideal gas equation

$$PV = RT$$

or
$$P\left(\frac{\partial V}{\partial T}\right)_P = R \quad \text{...(vii)}$$

$$\therefore \quad C_P - C_V = P\left(\frac{\partial V}{\partial T}\right)_P + \left(\frac{\partial U}{\partial V}\right)_T\left(\frac{\partial V}{\partial T}\right)_P$$

But
$$\left(\frac{\partial U}{\partial V}\right)_T = 0$$

$$\therefore \quad C_P - C_V = P\left(\frac{\partial V}{\partial T}\right)_P = R$$

$$\therefore \quad C_P - C_V = R \quad \text{...(viii)}$$

Here C_P, C_V and R are expressed in the same units.

From equation (iii)

$$\delta H = \left(\frac{\partial V}{\partial T}\right)_V dT + \left[P + \left(\frac{\partial U}{\partial V}\right)_T\right]dV \quad \text{...(ix)}$$

For a process at constant temperature

$$dT = 0$$

$$\therefore \quad (\delta H)_T = P(dV)_T + \left(\frac{\partial U}{\partial V}\right)_T (dV)_T \quad \text{...(x)}$$

This equation represents the amount of heat energy supplied to a system in an isothermal reversible process and is equal to the sum of the work done by the system and the increase in its internal energy.

For a reversible adiabatic process

$$\delta H = 0,$$

Therefore, from equation (ix),

$$0 = C_V\, dT + \left[P + \left(\frac{\partial U}{\partial V}\right)_T\right] dV$$

or $$C_V dT = -\left[P + \left(\frac{\partial U}{\partial V}\right)_T\right] dV$$

Dividing throughout by dV,

$$C_V \left(\frac{\partial T}{\partial V}\right) = -\left[P + \left(\frac{\partial U}{\partial V}\right)_T\right] \qquad \text{...(xii)}$$

The isobaric volume coefficient of expansion

$$\alpha = \frac{1}{V}\left(\frac{\partial V}{\partial T}\right)_P$$

$$\therefore \quad \alpha V = \left(\frac{\partial V}{\partial T}\right)_P \qquad C_P - C_V = P\left(\frac{\partial V}{\partial T}\right)_P$$

$$\therefore \quad \frac{C_P - C_V}{\alpha V} = P$$

But $$\left(\frac{\partial U}{\partial V}\right)_T = 0 = P - P$$

or $$\left(\frac{\partial U}{\partial V}\right)_T = \left(\frac{C_P - C_V}{\alpha V}\right) - P \qquad \text{...(xiii)}$$

or $$-\left(\frac{C_P - C_V}{\alpha V}\right) = \left[P + \left(\frac{\partial U}{\partial V}\right)_T\right] \qquad \text{...(xiv)}$$

From equations (xii) and (xiv)

$$C_V \left(\frac{\partial T}{\partial V}\right) = -\left(\frac{C_P - C_V}{\alpha V}\right)$$

or $$\left(\frac{\partial T}{\partial V}\right) = \frac{C_V - C_P}{\alpha V C_V} \qquad \text{...(xv)}$$

This expression holds good for an adiabatic reversible process.

THERMODYNAMIC SCALE

The empirical temperature scales depend upon the nature and properties of working substance, *e.g.*, expansion of mercury, the change in resistance of platinum, etc., with rise of temperature. Such thermometers with different working substances do not agree in scales.

The efficiency of Carnot's reversible engine does not depend upon the working substance. This property had been used by Lord Kelvin and he worked out a theory to produce a temperature scale which was not depending upon the nature of the working substance. Since the basis of this is the laws of thermodynamics, it is also known as thermodynamic scale of temperature or sometimes Kelvin's work scale as the work done by a Carnot's engine is involved.

STATEMENTS OF SECOND LAW OF THERMODYNAMICS

This law is generalisation of certain experiences about heat engines and refrigerators. It has been stated in a number of ways, but all the statements are logically equivalent to one another.

Kelvin-Planck Statement

"It is impossible to construct an engine which, operating in a complete cycle. will absorb heat from a single body, and convert it completely to work, without leaning changes in the working system."

After the completion of one cycle, the working system comes to its initial state with same coordinates so that it becomes ready for the repetition of the same processes in the second cycle. In this manner the machine continues its operation. There is nothing in the first law to prelude the possibility of converting an amount of heat completely into work. Thus second law is an independent law of nature which denies the possibility of utilising heat energy in a particular way.

The above statement is a negative statement. By this statement, it means that a single reservoir at a single temperature cannot continuously transfer heat into work. It means that there should be two reservoirs for any heat engine. One reservoir (called the source) is t ken at a higher temperature while the other reservoir (called the sink) is taken at a lower temperature.

According to this statement, zero degree absolute temperature is not attainable as no heat is rejected to the sink at zero degree Kelvin.

Suppose an engine works between any temperatures higher than zero degree Kelvin. It implies that it uses a single reservoir which contradicts the Kelvin-Planck's statement of the second law. Similarly, it can be said that no engine can be 100% efficient.

Clausius Statement

Heat flows from hot to cold body due to difference of temperature. However, in a refrigerator, heat gets absorbed from a body at lower temperature and gets rejected to a body at higher temperature. Here heat is being flown through some outer agency, *i.e.*, it is not feasible to cause heat to flow from a colder to a hotter body without absorbing from some external source. This led Clausius to state the second law of thermodynamics in the following words : *"It is impossible to transfer for a self acting machine, unaided by any external agency to convert heat continuously, from one body at lower temperature to a body at a higher temperature."*

At first sight, it appears that the statements given by Kelvin-Planck and Clausius are not at all connected to each other. But a closer analysis of the two reveals that both lead to the same meaning. To prove this, assume the Clausius statement to be false. Thus a device D\1 can extract, say Q amount of heat from a colder body and delivers it to a hotter body by itself *i.e.* without having any work done on it by any external agency. Now consider another device D_2. working between the same two bodies, extracts heat Q' from the hotter body, Q' being greater than Q, and delivers back Q amount of heat to the colder one. This is always possible since a flow of heat from a hot body to a colder one is a natural process. Now if the two devices are coupled in such a way that D_2 acts after D_1 to complete a cycle, the net result is that (i) there occurs no change in the heat content of the colder body in one complete cycle because Di extracts heat Q and Dg delivers the same quantity and (ii) the hotter body loses (Q' – Q) amount of heat in one cycle which is obviously converted into work as the colder one does not receive any extra heat. Thus, the couple Di.Dg extracts (Q' – Q) heat from a single source (hotter body) and converts it completely into work without delivering any heat to the colder one. This makes Kelvin-Planck statements to be false. Thus *falsity of Clausius-statement proves the falsity of Kelvin-Planck statement.*

Similarly, it can be proved that if Kelvin-Planck statement is assumed to be false it will prove the Clausius statement to be false. Let a device O_3 extract Q_1 amount of heat from a hot body and convert it completely into work W, violating the Kelvin-Planck's statement. Let another device D_4 extract Q_2 heat from a colder body and a work $W = (Q_1)$ be done on it and it delivers the total heat $(Q_2 + Q_1)$ to a hotter body. This process is experimentally possible. Now, if D_3 and D_4 are coupled in such a way that D_4 acts after D_3 to complete a cycle the net result is that (i) the heat content of the hotter body increases by an amount Q_2 [since D_3 extracts Q_1 and D_4 delivers $(Q_2 + Q_1)$ and (ii) the heat content of the colder body decreases by the same amount. The work done by D_3 is completely absorbed in D_4. In a nutshell, D_4, amount of heat is transferred from a colder body to a hotter one with no other effect as far as the coupled machine (D_3D_1) is concerned. This makes Clausius statement to be a false one.

Thus, as the falsity of Clausius statement implies falsity of Kelvin-Planck's and versa, the two statements may be taken as equivalent.

Planck Statement

"It is impossible to construct a device that will work in a complete cycle and convert heat into work without making any change in the surroundings".

Thomson Statement

In a heat engine, the working substance takes heat from hot body; a part of it is converted into work while remaining is given to the sink. No engine has so far been constructed which continuously takes heat from a single body and changes the whole of it to work without making any change in the system.

Hence, the presence of a cold body is a necessity for converting heat into work. This led Thomson to state that *"it is impossible to obtain a continuous supply of work by cooling a body to a temperature lower than that of coldest of its surroundings"*,

Diffusion of a gas always takes place from a region of higher to one at lower pressure, until the pressure becomes uniform.

Although the second law of thermodynamics may be stated in various ways, all the statements appear to be different from one another. But a closer look at them, reveals that they are all the modified forms of the same fundamental idea that, *"all forms of energy are convertible into heat but the heat so obtained cannot be converted into forms of energy by any process."*

PROOF OF THE SECOND LAW

No rigorous proof is available for the second law. The formulation of the second law is based upon the observations and, has yet to be disproved. No deviations to this law have so far been reported. However, the law is applicable to cyclic processes only.

IS SECOND LAW TRUE?

Suppose the second law is not true. Then, it becomes possible to drive a steam-ship across the ocean by extracting heat from the ocean or to run a power plant for extracting heat from the surrounding air. However, neither of these impossibilities violates the first law of thermodynamics. There exists nothing in the first law which preludes the possibility of converting this heat completely into work. The second law, therefore is not a deduction from the first law but is itself as a separate law of nature, referring to an aspect of nature different from that contemplated by the first law.

The continual operation of a machine which creates its own energy and thus violates the first law is known as the perpetual motion of its first kind. The continual operation of a machine that utilises the internal energy of only one heat reservoir, thus violating the second law is known as perpetual motion of the second kind.

The second law cannot be directly proved but the deductions made from this law has been reported to be in accord with experience. Besides this no machine has yet been devised which works against this law.

LIMITATIONS OF FIRST LAW OF THERMODYNAMICS NEED FOR THE SECOND LAW OF THERMODYNAMICS

There are three main limitations of first law of thermodynamics. These arc as follows:

(a) The first law of thermodynamics simply establishes equivalence between different forms of energy. However, this law fails to tell us under what conditions and to what extent it is possible to bring about conversion of one form of energy into the other. This can be understood from the following examples:

(i) Suppose that heat is flowing from a hot to cold body. First law simply reveals that the quantity of heat lost by the hot body is equal to the heat gained by the cold body. It never reveals that heat can only flow from the hot to the cold body and not in the reverse direction.

(ii) When zinc dissolves spontaneously in sulphuric acid, a definite amount of energy being liberated. The reverse process is not spontaneous. Without external influence, the reaction takes place in only one direction.

(iii) When we apply a brake to stop a wheel from rotating, the brake becomes hot owing to friction, and the internal energy of the brake increases. The reverse process is never seen, a hot brake losing its internal energy to wheel which starts rotating even though this would not violate the first law.

From the above examples it can be predicted that there must be some laws besides the first law which should be able to predict the direction of a certain reaction to occur, and, if so, and to what extent. This however, comes within the scope of the second law of thermodynamics.

(b) The first law of thermodynamics is a qualitative statement which fails to prelude the existence of either a heat engine, or a refrigerator. The first law fails to contradict the existence of a 100% efficient heat engine or a self-acting refrigerator. In practice, these two are not attainable. These phenomena are recognised and this led to the formulation of a law governing these devices called the second law of thermodynamics.

(c) The first law does not explain why chemical reactions do not proceed to completion.

For example, let us consider the reaction $CO(g) + H_2iO(g) \rightleftharpoons CO_2(g) + H_2(g)$. If originally one mole of CO and one mole of H_2O were in the reaction vessel, then, if the reaction went to completion, one mole of CO_2 and one mole of Ha would be formed. If we examine reaction vessel at equilibrium, the yield is less than 100%. However, it comes under the scope of second law of thermodynamics.

IS SECOND LAW APPLICABLE TO CYCLE PROCESS ONLY?

The second law is applicable to reversible cyclic operations only, *i.e.*, to those reversible operations in which the substance ends in the same condition as regards its temperature, pressure, etc., as it is started and which can be traced in either direction. *A process or operations due to which a system returns exactly to its original thermodynamics^ state is termed as a cyclic process.*

In other words a heat engine is chiefly concerned with the conversion of heat energy into mechanical work. A refrigerator is a device to cool a certain space below the temperature of its surroundings. The first law of thermodynamics is a qualitative statement which does not preclude the possibility of the existence of either a heat engine or a refrigerator. The first law does not contradict the existence of a 100% efficient heat engine or a self-acting refrigerator.

In practice, these two are not attainable. These phenomena are recognized and this led to the formulation of a law governing these two devices. It is called second law of thermodynamics.

A new term reservoir is used to explain the second law. A *reservoir* is a device having infinite thermal capacity and which can absorb, retain or reject unlimited quantity of heat without any change in its temperature.

Kelvin-Planck statement of the second law is as follows:

"It is impossible to get a continuous supply of work from a body (or engine) which can transfer heat with a single heat reservoir. This is a negative statement. According to this statement, a single reservoir at a single temperature cannot continuously transfer heat into work. It means that there should be two reservoirs for any heat engine. One reservoir (called the source) is taken at a higher temperature and the other reservoir (called the sink) is taken at a lower temperature.

According to this statement, zero degree absolute temperature is not attainable because no heat is rejected to the sink at zero degree Kelvin. If an engine works between any temperature higher than zero degree Kelvin and zero degree Kelvin, it means it uses a single reservoir which contradicts Kelvin-Planck's statement of the second law. Similarly, no engine can be 100% efficient.

In a heat engine, the engine draws heat from the source and after doing some external work, it rejects the remaining heat to the sink. The source and sink are of infinite thermal capacity and they maintain constant temperature.

First Part

According to Kelvin, the second law can also be stated as follows : "It is impossible to get a continuous supply of work from a body by cooling it to a temperature lower than that of its surroundings".

In a heat engine the working substance does some work and rejects the remaining heat to the *sink*. The temperature of the source must be higher than the surroundings and the engine will not work when the temperatures of the source and the sink are the same. Take the case of a steam engine. The steam (working substance) at high pressure is introduced into the cylinder of the engine. Steam expands, and it does external work. The contents remaining behind after doing work are rejected to the surroundings. The temperature of the working substance rejected to the surroundings is higher than the temperature of the surroundings.

If this working substance rejected by the first engine is used in another engine, it can do work and the temperature of the working substance will fall further.

It means that the working substance can do work only if its temperature is higher than that of the surroundings.

Second Part

According to Clausius:

"It is impossible to make heat flow from a body at a lower temperature to a body at a higher temperature without doing external work on the working substance."

This part is applicable in the case of ice plants and refrigerators. Heat itself cannot flow from a body at a lower temperature to a body at a higher temperature. But, it is possible, if some external work is done on the working substance. Take the case of ammonia ice plant. Ammonia is the working substance. Liquid ammonia at low pressure takes heat from the brine solution in the brine tank and is converted to low pressure vapour. External work is done to compress the ammonia vapours to high pressure. This ammonia at high pressure is passed through coils over which water at room temperature is poured. Ammonia vapour gives heat to water at room temperature and gets itself converted into liquid again. This high pressure liquid ammonia is throttled to low pressure liquid ammonia. In the whole process ammonia (the working substance) takes heat from brine solution (at a lower temperature) and gives heat to water at room temperature (at a higher temperature). This is possible only due to the external work done on ammonia by the piston in compressing it. The only work of electricity in the ammonia ice plant is to move the piston to do external work on ammonia. If the external work is not done, no ice plant or refrigerator will work. Hence, it is possible to make heat flow from a body at a lower temperature to a body at a higher temperature by doing external work on the working substance.

Thus, the second law of thermodynamics plays an important part for practical devices *e.g.*, heat engines and refrigerators. The first law of thermodynamics only gives the relation between the work done and the heat produced. But the second law of thermodynamics gives the conditions under which heat can be converted into work.

THIRD LAW OF THERMODYNAMICS

In all heat engines, there is always loss of heat in the form of conduction, radiation and friction. Therefore, in actual heat engines H_1/T_1 is not equal to H_2/T_2.

$\therefore \frac{H_1}{T_1} - \frac{H_2}{T_2}$ is not zero but it is a positive quantity. When cycle after cycle is repeated, the entropy of the system increases and tends to a maximum value. When the system has attained the maximum value, a stage of stagnancy is reached and no work can be done by the engine at this stage. In this universe the entropy is increasing and ultimately the universe will also reach a maximum value of entropy when no work will be possible. With the increase in entropy, the disorder of the molecules of a substance increases. The entropy is also a measure of the disorder of the system. With decrease in entropy, the disorder decreases. *At absolute zero temperature, the entropy tends to zero and the molecules of a substance or a system are in perfect order (well arranged). This is the third law of thermodynamics.*

Example:

The molecules are more free to move in the gaseous, state than in the liquid state. The entropy is more in the gaseous state than in the liquid state. The molecules are more free to move in the liquid state than in the solid state. The entropy is more in the liquid state than in the solid. Thus when a substance is converted from a solid to a liquid and then from the liquid to the solid state, the entropy increases and *vice versa*. When ice is converted into water and then into steam, the entropy and disorder of the molecules increase. When steam is converted into water and then into ice, the entropy and disorder of the molecules decrease. *Hence entropy is a measure of the disorder of the molecules of the system.*

By any ideal procedure, it is impossible to bring any system to absolute zero temperature performing a finite number of operations. This is called the principle of unattainability of absolute zero. Thus according to Fowler and Guggenheim, the unattainability principle is called the third law of thermodynamics.

ISOTHERMAL PROCESS

The process which occurs at constant temperature is called isothermal. When a gas is compressed suddenly, some heat is produced. But if the compression is slow and the heat produced is removed at once, so that the temperature remains constant, the change is isothermal. Similarly when a gas is allowed to expand suddenly, work is done by the gas and some heat is absorbed. If heat is continuously-supplied from outside so that the temperature remains constant, the change is isothermal.

From the above discussion it follows that in an isothermal change the temperature is kept constant by adding heat or taking it away from the substance. For a perfect gas, an isothermal change is represented by Boyle's law given by the following equation:

$$PV = \text{constant.}$$

The difference between isothermal and adiabatic process. In an isothermal process, the system can exchange its heat energy with its surroundings. Thus, the temperature of an isothermal process remains constant during each stage of operation. On the other hand, the temperature of an adiabatic process changes because the system cannot exchange heat with its surroundings.

The differences between isothermal and adiabatic process may be summarised as under:

Isothermal Process	*Adiabatic Process*
(i) In an isothermal process, during each operation the temperature of the system remains constant.	(i) In an adiabatic process, the temperature of the system may change according to the conditions.
(ii) In an isothermal process, the system exchanges heat with the surroundings.	(ii) In an adiabatic process, the system is completely insulated from the surroundings and thus it does not exchange heat with the surroundings.

Isothermals : The curves showing the variation in the volume of a substance when the pressure acting on it changes under isothermal conditions are called *isothermals*. In other words if a system is perfectly conducting to the surroundings and the temperature remains constant throughout the process, it is called an isothermal process. Consider a working substance at a certain pressure and temperature and having a volume represented by the point A (Fig. 1.9).

Pressure is decreased and work is done by the working substance at the cost of its internal energy and there should be fall in temperature. But, toe system is perfectly conducting to the surroundings. It absorbs heat from the surroundings and maintains a constant temperature. Thus from A to B the temperature remains constant. The curve AB a called the *isothermal* curve or *isothermal*.

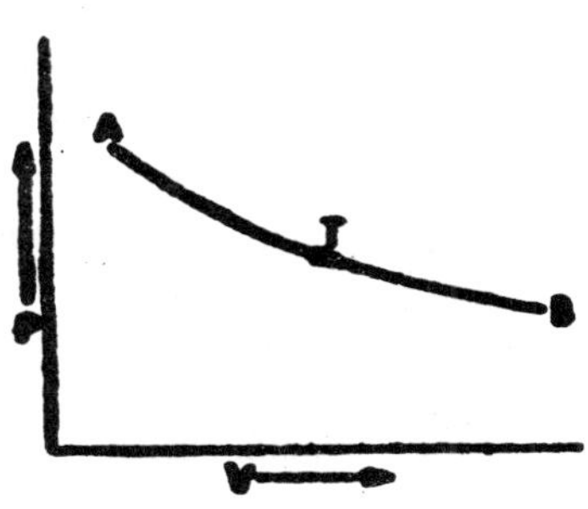

Fig. 1.9

Consider the working substance at the point B and let the pressure be increased. External work is done on the working substance and there should be rise in temperature. But the system is perfectly conducting to the surroundings. It gives extra heat to the surroundings and its temperature remains constant from B to A.

Thus, during the isothermal process, the temperature of the working substance remains constant. It can absorb heat or give heat to the surroundings. The equation far an isothermal process is

$$PV = RT = \text{constant (For one gram molecule of a gas.)}$$

For n gram molecules of a gas $PV = nRT$

ADIABATIC PROCESS

When a process is carried out under such conditions that no exchange of heat takes place between the system and its surroundings, the process is called adiabatic. Examples for this process are:

(i) The sudden bursting of a cycle tube is an adiabatic process,

(ii) The compression of the mixture of oil vapour-and-air during the compression stroke of an internal combustion engine is an adiabatic process and there is a rise of temperature.

If the process is exothermic, the heat evolved will remain in the system and, therefore, the temperature of the system rises. If, on the other hand, an adiabatic process is endothermic, the heat required to be absorbed is supplied by the system itself and hence the temperature of the system falls.

During an adiabatic process, the working substance is perfectly insulated from the surroundings. It can neither give heat nor take heat from the surroundings.

Work is done on the working substance, there is rise in temperature because the external work done on the working substance increases its internal energy. When work is done by the working substance, it is done at the cost of its internal energy. As the system is perfectly insulated from the surroundings, there is fall in temperature.

Thus, during an adiabatic process, the working substance is perfectly insulated from the surroundings. All along the process, there is change in temperature.

A curve between pressure and volume during the adiabatic process is called an *adiabatic curve* or an *adiabatic*.

1. The compression of the mixture of oil vapour and air during compression stroke of an internal combustion is an adiabatic process and there is rise in temperature.
2. The expansion of the combustion products during the working stroke of an engine is an adiabatic process and there is fall in temperature.
3. The sudden bursting of a cycle tube is an adiabatic process.

Apply the first law of thermodynamics to an adiabatic process, $\delta H = 0$.

$$\delta H = dU + \delta W$$

or $$0 = dU + \delta W \quad ...(i)$$

The processes that take place *suddenly* or *quickly* are adiabatic processes.

ISOCHORIC PROCESS

If the working substance is taken in a non-expanding chamber, the heat supplied will increase the pressure and temperature. The volume of the substance will remain constant. Such a process is called an *isochoric process*. The work done is zero because there is no change in volume. The whole of the heat supplied increased the internal energy. Therefore, during the isochoric process $\delta W = 0$.

$$\delta H = dU \quad \text{...(i)}$$

The heat transferred in such a process

$$\delta H = C_v dT$$

$$\therefore \quad C_v dT = dU \quad \text{...(ii)}$$

Hence, C_v is the specific heat for one gram-molecule of a gas at constant volume.

ISOBARIC PROCESS

If the pressure of the system remains constant during each step of the change in the state of a system, this process is said to be an isobaric process. Let us consider a mixture of hydrogen and oxygen in the ratio of 2:1 contained in a cylinder which is fitted with a weightless, frictionless, and airtight piston.

In order to initiate the reaction, an electric spark is passed through the gaseous mixture. From the chemical reaction it is evident that there is an appreciable fall in the volume of the system. Therefore, the piston will move down for allowing the pressure of system to remain constant.

$$2H_2 + O_2 \rightarrow 2H_2O$$

Let us consider another reaction of the type

$$N_2O_2(g) \rightarrow 2NO_2(g)$$

The above reaction is accompanied by the increase in volume if it is allowed to take place in the above cylinder. The piston moves up maintaining the pressure of the system constant.

From the above examples it follows that in isobaric processes change in volume may take place. In other words, a process is defined to be isobaric if the volume of the volume of the system remains constant during each step of the process. Suppose N_2O_4 is enclosed in a cylinder fitted with a weightless and frictionless piston.

$$N_2O_4(g) \rightarrow 2NO_2(g)$$

For the dissociation of every one mole of N_2O_4, two moles of NO_2 gas are produced and, thus the volume of the system will tend to increase. In order to keep the volume fixed weights are to be kept over the piston. Thus in such a case the volume of the system remains constant whereas the pressure of the gaseous system within the cylinder will increase.

Let us consider the reaction between hydrogen and oxygen.. On passing an electric spark the gases will react to form liquid water resulting in considerable decrease in volume. But if the piston is fixed, *i.e.*, not allowed to move down, the volume of the system will remain constant and there will be considerable fall in the pressure of the system.

From the above examples it follows that in isochoric processes, change of pressure may occur. In other words, if the working substance is taken in an expanding chamber kept at a constant pressure, the process is called an isobaric process.

Here, the temperature and volume change. If an amount of heat δB is given to the working substance, it is partly used in increasing the temperature of the working substance by dT and partly used in doing external work. Considering one gram of the working substance,

$$\delta H = 1 \times C_V dT + \frac{P.dV}{J} \qquad \text{...(i)}$$

But $$\delta H = C_P .dT \qquad \text{...(ii)}$$

$$P.dV = r.dT$$

$$\therefore \quad C_P dT = C_V .dT + \frac{r.dY}{J}$$

$$C_P - C_P = r/J \qquad \text{...(iii)}$$

Here C_P and C_V represent the specific beats for 1 gram of a gas and r is the ordinary gas constant

If C_P and C_V are the gram-molecular specific heats of gas, then

$$C_P - C_V = \frac{R}{J} \qquad \text{...(iv)}$$

Here A is the universal gas constant.

IRREVERSIBLE PROCESS

The thermodynamical state of a system can be defined with the help of the thermodynamical coordinates of the system. The state of a system can be changed by altering the thermodynamical coordinates. Changing from one state to the other by changing the thermodynamical coordinates is called a process.

Consider two states of a system *i.e.*, state A and state B. Change of state from A to B or vice versa is a process and the direction of the process will depend upon a new thermodynamical coordinate called entropy. All processes are not possible in the universe..

Consider the following processes :

1. Let two blocks A and B at different temperatures T_1 and T_2 ($T_1 > T_2$) be kept in contact but the system as a whole is insulated from the surroundings. Conduction of heat takes place between the blocks, the temperature of A falls and the temperature of B rises and thermodynamical equilibrium will be reached.
2. Consider a flywheel rotating with an angular velocity ω. Its initial kinetic energy is $1/2I\omega^2$. After some time the wheel comes to rest and kinetic energy is utilised in overcoming friction at the bearings. The temperature of the wheel and the bearings rises and the increase in their internal energy is equal to the original kinetic energy of the fly wheel.
3. Consider two flasks A and B connected by a glass tube provided with a stop cock. Let A contain air at high pressure and B is evacuated. The system is isolated from the surroundings. If the stop cock is opened, air rushes from A to B, the pressure in A decreases and the volume of air increases.

All the above three examples though different, are thermodynamical processes involving change in thermodynamical coordinates. Also, in accordance with the first law of thermodynamics, the principle of conservation of energy is not violated because the total energy of the system is conserved. It is also clear that, with the initial conditions described above, the three processes will take place.

Let us consider the possibility of the above three processes taking place in the reverse direction. In the first case, if the reverse process is possible, the block B should transfer heat to A and initial conditions should be restored. In the second case, if the reverse process is possible, the heat energy must again change to kinetic energy and the fly wheel should start rotating with the initial angular velocity ω. In the third case, if the reverse process is possible the air in B must flow back to A and the initial condition should be obtained.

But, it is a matter of common experience, that none of the above conditions for the reverse processes are reached. It means that the direction of the process cannot be determined by knowing the thermodynamical coordinates in the two end states. To determine the direction of the process a new thermodynamical coordinate has been devised by Clausius and this is called the entropy of the system. Similar to internal energy, entropy is also a function of the state of a system. For any possible process, the entropy of an isolated system should increase or remain constant. The process in which there is a possibility of decrease in entropy cannot take place.

If the entropy of an isolated system is maximum, any change of state will mean decrease in entropy and hence that change of state will not take place.

To conclude, *processes in which the entropy of an isolated system decreases do not take place or for all processes taking place in an isolated system the entropy of the system should increase or remain constant.* It means a process is irreversible if the entropy decreases when the direction of the process is reversed. A process is said to be irreversible if it cannot be retraced back exactly in the opposite direction. During an irreversible process, heat energy is always used to overcome friction. Energy is also dissipated in the form of conduction and radiation. This loss of energy always takes place whether the engine works in one direction or the reverse direction. Such energy cannot be regained. In actual practice all the engines are irreversible. If electric current is passed through a wire, heat is produced. If the direction of the current is reversed, heat is again produced. This is also an example of an irreversible process. All chemical reactions are irreversible. In general, all natural processes are irreversible.

REVERSIBLE PROCESS

From the thermodynamical point of view, a reversible process is one in which an infinitesimally small change in the external conditions will result in all the changes taking place in the direct process but exactly repeated in the reverse order and in the opposite sense. The process should take place at an extremely slow rate. In a reversible cycle, there should not be any loss of heat due to friction or radiation. In this process, the initial conditions of the working substance can be obtained.

Consider a cylinder, containing a gas at a certain, pressure and temperature. The cylinder is fitted with a frictionless piston. If the pressure is decreased, the gas expands slowly and maintains a constant temperature (isothermal proeess). The energy required for this expansion is continuously drawn from the source (surroundings). If the pressure on the piston is increased, the gas contracts slowly and maintains constant temperature (isothermal process). The energy liberated during compression is given to the sink (surroundings). This is also true for an adiabatic process provided the process takes place infinitely slowly.

The process will not be reversible if there is any loss of heat due to friction, radiation or conduction. If the changes take place rapidly, the process will not be reversible. The energy used in overcoming friction cannot be retraced.

The conditions of reversibility for any heat engine or process can be stated as follows:

1. The pressure and temperature of the working substance must not differ appreciably from those of the surroundings at any stage of the cycle of operation.
2. All the processes taking place in the cycle of operation must be infinitely slow.
3. The working parts of the engine must be completely free from friction.
4. There should not be any loss of energy due to conduction or radiation during the cycle of operation.

It should be remembered that the complete reversible process or cycle of operation is only an ideal case. In an actual process, there is always loss of heat due to friction, conduction or radiation. The temperature and pressure of the working substance differ appreciably from those of the surroundings.

CARNOT'S REVERSIBLE ENGINE

Heat engines are used to convert heat into mechanical work. Sadi Carnot (French) conceived a theoretical engine which is free from all the defects of practical engines. Its efficiency is maximum and it is an ideal heat engine.

For any engine, there are three essential requisites:

1. *Sink:* The sink should be at a fixed lower temperature T_2 to which any amount of heat can be rejected. It also has infinite thermal capacity and its temperature remains constant at T_2,
2. *Working Substance:* A cylinder with non-conducting sides and conducting bottom contains the perfect gas as the working substance.
3. *Source:* The source should be at a fixed high temperature T_1 from which the heat engine can draw heat. It has infinite thermal capacity and any amount of heat can be drawn from it at constant temperature T_1.

A perfect non-conducting and frictionless piston is fitted into the cylinder. The working substance undergoes a complete cyclic operation (Fig. 1.10).

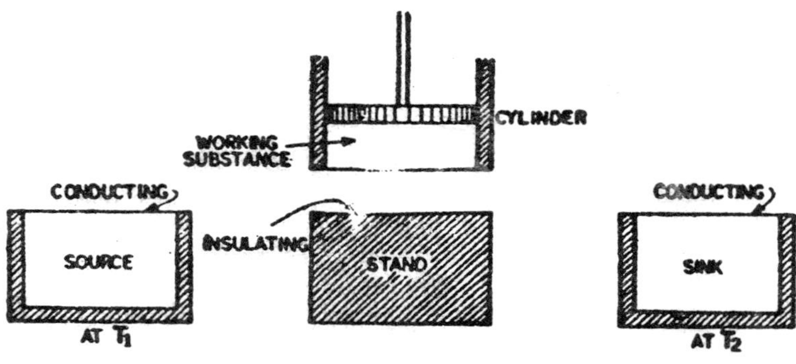

Fig. 1.10

A perfectly non-conducting stand is also provided so that the working substance can undergo adiabatic operation.

Carnot's Cycle

1. Place the engine containing the working substance over the source at temperature T_1. The working substance is also at a temperature T_1. Its pressure is Pi and volume is V_1 as shown by the point A in Fig. 1.11. Decrease the pressure. The volume

of the working substance increases. Work is done by the working substance. As the bottom is perfectly conducting to the source at temperature T_1, it absorbs heat. The process is completely isothermal. The temperature remains constant. Let the amount of heat absorbed by the working substance be H_1 at the temperature T_1. The point B is obtained.

Consider one gram molecule of the working substance.

Work done from A to B (isothermal process)

$$W_1 = \int_{V_1}^{V_2} P.dV = RT_1 \log \frac{V_2}{V_1}$$

$$= \text{area ABGE} \qquad ...(i)$$

2. Place the engine on the stand having an insulated top. Decrease the pressure on the working substance. The volume increases. The process is completely adiabatic.

   Work is done by the working substance at the cost of its internal energy. The temperature falls. The working substance undergoes adiabatic change from B to C. At C the temperature is T_2 (Fig. 1.11).

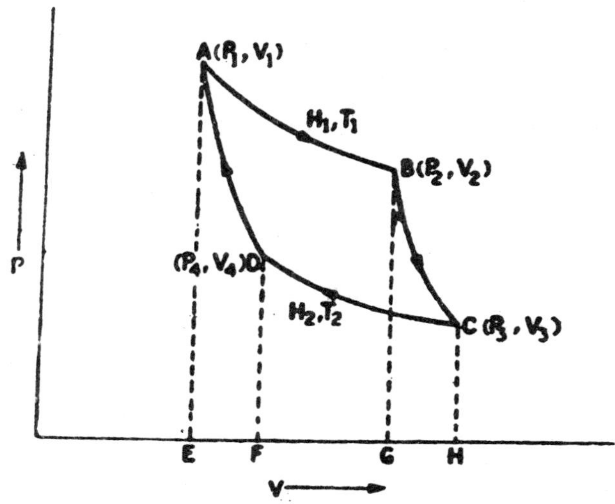

Fig. 1.11

Work done from B to C (adiabatic process)

$$W_2 = \int_{V_2}^{V_3} P.dV$$

$$= \int_{V_2}^{V_3} \frac{dV}{V^\gamma}$$

$$= \frac{KV_3^{1-\gamma} - KV_2^{1-\gamma}}{1-\gamma}$$

But PV^γ = constant = K

$$P_2V_2 = RT_1$$

$$P_3V_3 = RT_2$$

$$P_3V_3^\gamma = P_2V_2^\gamma = K$$

$$= \frac{P_3V_3 - P_2V_2}{1-\gamma}$$

$$= \frac{R[T_2 - T_1]}{1-\gamma} = \frac{R[T_1 - T_2]}{\gamma - 1}$$

W_2 = Area BCHG ...(ii)

3. Place the engine on the sink at temperature T_2. Increase the pressure. The work is done on the working substance. As the base is conducting to the sink, the process is isothermal. A quantity of heat H_2 is rejected to the sink at temperature T_1. Finally the point D is reached.

Work done from C to D (isothermal process)

$$W_3 = \int_{V_3}^{V_4} PdV$$

$$= RT_2 \log \frac{V_4}{V_3}$$

$$= -RT_2 \log \frac{V_3}{V_4}$$

W_3 = area CHFD

(The –ve sign indicates that work is done on the working substance.)

4. Place the engine on the insulating stand. Increase the pressure. The volume decreases. The process is completely adiabatic. The temperature rises and finally the point A is reached.

   Work done from D to A (adiabatic process).

$$W_4 = \int_{V_4}^{V_1} PdV$$

$$= -\frac{R(T_1 - T_2)}{\gamma - 1}$$

$$W_4 = \text{area DFEA} \qquad \text{...(iv)}$$

[W_2 and W_4 are equal and opposite and cancel each other.]

The net work done by the working substance in one complete cycle

$$= \text{Area ABGE} + \text{Area BCHG} - \text{Area CHFD} - \text{Area DFEA}$$

$$= \text{Area ABCD}$$

The net amount of heat absorbed by the working substance

$$= H_1 - H_2$$

$$\text{Network} = W_1 + W_2 + W_3 + W_4$$

$$= RT_1 \log \frac{V_2}{V_1} + \frac{R(T_1\ T_2)}{\gamma - 1} - RT_2 \log \frac{V_3}{V_4} - \frac{R[T_1 - T_2]}{\gamma - 1}$$

$$W = RT_1 \log \frac{V_2}{V_1} - RT_2 \log \frac{V_3}{V_4} \qquad \text{...(v)}$$

The points A and D are on the same adiabatic

$$T_1V_1^{\gamma-1} = T_2V_4^{\gamma-1}$$

$$\frac{T_2}{T_1} = \left(\frac{V_1}{V_4}\right)^{\gamma-1} \qquad \text{...(vi)}$$

The points B and C are on the same adiabatic

$$T_1V_2^{\gamma-1} = T_2V_3^{\gamma-1}$$

$$\frac{T_2}{T_1} = \left(\frac{V_2}{V_3}\right)^{\gamma-1} \qquad \text{...(vii)}$$

From (vi) and (vii)

$$\left(\frac{V_1}{V_4}\right)^{\gamma-1} = \left(\frac{V_2}{V_3}\right)^{\gamma-1}$$

or $$\frac{V_1}{V_4} = \frac{V_2}{V_3}$$

or $$\frac{V_2}{V_1} = \frac{V_3}{V_4}$$

From equation (v)

$$W = RT_1 \log \frac{V_2}{V_1} - RT_2 \log \frac{V_2}{V_1}$$

$$W = R\left[\log \frac{V_2}{V_1}\right][T_1 - T_2]$$

$$\therefore \quad W = H_1 - H_2$$

Efficiency $\eta = \dfrac{\text{Useful output}}{\text{Input}} = \dfrac{W}{H_1}$

Heat is supplied from the source from A to B only.

$$H_1 = RT_1 \log \frac{V_2}{V_1}$$

$$\therefore \quad \eta = \frac{W}{H_1} = \frac{H_1 - H_2}{H_1}$$

$$= \frac{R[T_1 - T_2] \log \left(\frac{V_2}{V_1}\right)}{RT_1 \log \left(\frac{V_2}{V_1}\right)}$$

or $\eta = 1 - \dfrac{H_2}{H_1}; \ \eta = 1 - \dfrac{T_2}{T_1}$ ...(viii)

The Carnot's engine is perfectly reversible. It can be operated in the reverse direction also. Then it works as a refrigerator. The heat H_2 is taken from the sink and external work is done on the working substance and heat H_1 is given to the source at a higher temperature.

The isothermal process will take place only when the piston moves very slowly to give enough time for the heat transfer to take place. The adiabatic process will take place when the piston moves extremely fast to avoid heat transfer satisfy these conditions.

All practical engines have an efficiency less than the Garnet's engine.

CARNOT'S ENGINE AND REFRIGERATOR

Carnot's cycle is perfectly reversible. It can work as a heat engine and also as a refrigerator. When it works as a heat engine, it absorbs a quantity of heat H_1 from the source at a temperature T_1, does an amount of work W and rejects an amount of heat H_2 to the sink at temperature T_2. When it works as a refrigerator, it absorbs heat H_2 from the sink at temperature T_2. W amount of work is done on it by some external means and rejects heat H_1 to the source at a temperature T_1 (Fig. 1.12). In the second case heat flows from a body at a lower temperature to a body at a higher temperature, with the help of external work done on the working substance and it works as a refrigerator. This will not be possible if the cycle is not completely reversible.

Coefficient of Performance

The amount of heat absorbed at the lower temperature is H_2. The amount of work done by the external process (input energy) = W and the amount of heat rejected = H_1. Here H_2 is the desired refrigerating effect.

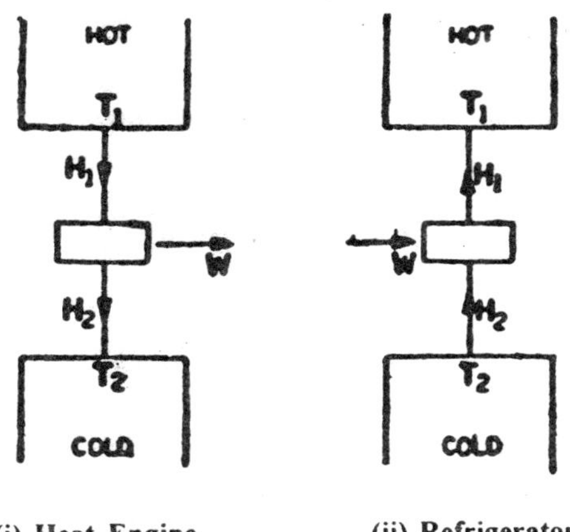

(i) Heat Engine **(ii) Refrigerator**

Fig. 1.12

Coefficient of performance

$$= \frac{H_2}{W} = \frac{H_2}{H_1 - H_2}$$

Suppose 200 joules of energy is absorbed at the lower temperature and 100 joules of work is done with external help. Then 200 + 100 = 300 joules are rejected at the higher temperature.

The coefficient of performance

$$= \frac{H_2}{W}$$

$$= \frac{H_2}{H_1 - H_2}$$

$$= \frac{200}{300 - 200} = 2$$

Therefore the coefficient of performance of a refrigerator = 2.

In the case of a heat engine, the efficiency cannot be more than 100% but in the case of a refrigerator, the coefficient of performance can be much higher than 100%.

CARNOT'S THEOREM

Efficiency of a reversible engine does not depend on the nature of the working substance. It merely depends upon the temperature limits between which the engine works. "All the reversible engines working between the same temperature limits have the same efficiency. No engine can be more efficient than a Carnot's reversible engine working between the same two temperatures." Consider two reversible engines A and B, working between the temperature limits T_1 and T_2. A and B are coupled. Suppose A is more efficient than B. The engine A works as a heat engine and B as a refrigerator.

The engine A absorbs an amount of heat H_1 from the source at a temperature T_1. It does external work W and transfers it to B. The heat rejected to the sink is H_2 at a temperature T_2. The engine B absorbs heat H_1 from the sink at temperature T_2 and W amount of work is done on the working substance. The heat given to the source at temperature T_1 is H_1'.

Suppose the engine A w more efficient than B.

Efficiency of the engine A

$$= \eta = \frac{H_1 - H_2}{H_1} = \frac{W}{H_1}$$

Efficiency of the engine B

$$= \eta' = \frac{H_1' - H_2'}{H_1'} = \frac{W}{H_1'}$$

Since $\quad \eta' > \eta'; \; H_1' > H_2'$

Also $W = H_1 - H_2 = H_1' - H_2'$

$\therefore \quad H_2' > H_2$

Thus, for the two engines A and B working as a coupled system, $(H_2' - H_2)$ is the quantity of heat taken from the sink at a temperature T_2 and $(H_1' - H_1)$ is the quantity of heat given to the source at a temperature T_1. Both $(H_2' - H_2)$ and $(H_1' - H_1)$ are positive quantities. It means heat flows from the sink at a temperature T_2 (lower temperature) to the source at a temperature T_1 (higher temperature) *i.e.*, heat flows from a body at a lower temperature to a body at a higher temperature. But, no external work has been done on the system. This is contrary to the second law of thermodynamics. Thus, η cannot be greater than η'. The two engines (reversible) working between the same two temperature limits have the same efficiency. Moreover, in the case of a Carnot's engine, there is no loss of heat due to friction, conduction or radiation (irreversible processes). Thus, the Carnot's engine has the maximum efficiency. Whatever may be the nature of the working substance, the efficiency depends only upon the two temperature limits.

In a practical engine there is always loss of energy due to friction, conduction, radiation etc. and hence its efficiency is always lower than that of a Carnot's engine.

GAS EQUATION DURING AN ADIABATIC PROCESS

Consider 1 gram of the working substance (ideal gas) perfectly insulated from the surroundings. Let the external work done by the gas be δW.

Applying the first law of thermodynamics

$$\delta H = dU + \delta W$$

But $\quad \delta H = 0$

and $\quad \delta W = P.dV$

where P is the pressure of the gas and dV is the change in volume.

$$\therefore \quad 0 = dU + \frac{P.dV}{J}$$

As the external work Is done by the gas at the cost of its internal energy, there is fall in temperature by dT.

$$dU = 1 \times C_v \times dT$$

$$C_V.dT + \frac{P.dV}{J} = 0 \quad ...(ii)$$

For an ideal gas

$$PV = rT \quad ...(iii)$$

Differentiating,

$$P.dV + V.dP = r.dT$$

Substituting the value of dT in equation (ii),

$$C_V\left[\frac{P.dV + V.dP}{r}\right] + \frac{P.dV}{J} = 0$$

$$C_V[P.dV + V.dP] + r.\frac{P.dV}{J} = 0$$

But, $\frac{r}{J} = C_P - C_V$

$$\therefore C_v.P.dV + C_v.V.dP + C_p.PdV - C_vPdV = 0$$

$$C_p.P.dV + C_v.V.dP = 0$$

Integrating, $C_v.PV$,

$$\frac{C_P}{C_V}.\frac{dV}{V} + \frac{dP}{P} = 0$$

But $\frac{C_P}{C_V} = 0$

$$\therefore \quad \frac{dP}{P} + \gamma\frac{dV}{V} = 0$$

Integrating, $\log P + \gamma \log V = \text{const.}$

or $\log PV^\gamma = \text{const.}$

$$PV^\gamma = \text{const.} \quad ...(iv)$$

This is the equation connecting pressure and volume during an adiabatic process.

Taking $PV = rT$

or $P = \frac{rT}{V}$

$$\left(\frac{rT}{V}\right).V^{\gamma} = \text{cosnt.}$$

But r is const.

$$rTV^{\gamma-1} = \text{cosnt.}$$

$$\therefore \quad rTV^{\gamma-1} = \text{const.} \qquad \text{...(v)}$$

Also $\quad V = \dfrac{rT}{P}$

$$P\left[\frac{rT}{P}\right]^{\gamma} = \text{cosnt.}$$

or $$\frac{r^{\gamma}T^{\gamma}}{P^{\gamma-1}} = \text{const.}$$

or $$\frac{P^{\gamma-1}}{T^{\gamma}} = \text{const.} \qquad \text{...(vi)}$$

Thus, during an adiabatic process

(i) PV_{γ} = const.

(ii) $TV^{\gamma-1}$ = const. and

(iii) $\dfrac{P^{\gamma-1}}{T^{\gamma}}$ = const.

SLOPES OF ADIABATICS AND ISOTHERMALS

In an isothermal process

$$PV = \text{const.}$$

Differentiating,

$$PdV + VdP = 0$$

or $$\frac{dP}{dV} = -\frac{P}{V} \qquad \text{...(i)}$$

In an adiabatic process

$$PV^{\gamma} = \text{const.}$$

Differentiating,

$$P_{\gamma}V^{\gamma-1}\,dV + VdP = 0$$

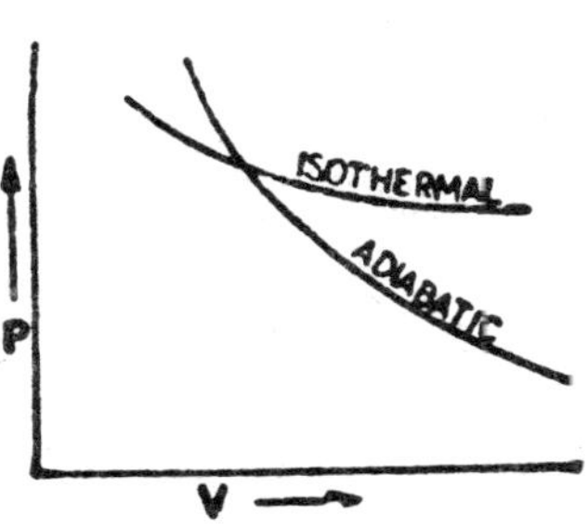

Fig. 1.13

$$\frac{dP}{dV} = -\frac{\gamma P}{V} \qquad \text{...(ii)}$$

Therefore, the slope of an adiabatic is γ times the slope of the isothermal.

Hence, the adiabatic curve is steeper than the isothermal curve (Fig. 1.13) at a point where the two curves intersect each other.

WORK DONE DURING AN ISOTHERMAL PROCESS

When a gas is allowed to expand isothermally, work is done by it. Let the initial and final volumes be V_1 and V_2 respectively. In Fig. 1.14, the area of the shaded strip represents the work done for a small change in volume dV.

When the volume changes from V_1 to V_2,

$$\text{Work done} = \int_{V_1}^{V_2} P.dV = \text{area ABba} \qquad ...(i)$$

Fig. 1.14 represents the indicator diagram. Considering one gram molecule of the gas

$$PV = BT; \; P = \frac{RT}{V}$$

$$\therefore \quad W = RT \int_{V_1}^{V_2} \frac{dV}{V}$$

$$= RT \log_e \frac{V_2}{V_1} \qquad ...(ii)$$

$$W = RT \times 2.3026 \log_{10} \frac{V_2}{V_3} \qquad ...(iii)$$

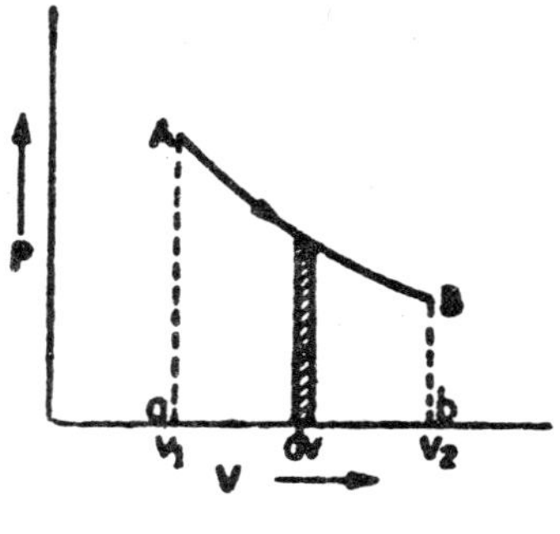

Fig. 1.14

Also $P_1V_1 = P_2V_2$

or $\frac{V_2}{V_1} = \frac{P_1}{P_2}$ $\qquad \therefore W = RT \times 2.3026 \times \log_{10} \frac{P_1}{P_2} \qquad ...(iv)$

Here, the change in the internal energy of the system is zero (because the temperature remains constant). So the heat transferred is equal to the work done.

WORK DONE DURING AN ADIABATIC PROCESS

During an adiabatic process, the gas expands from volume V_1 to V_2. As shown by the indicator the work done for an increase in volume dV = P.dV. Work done when the gas expands from V_1 to V_2 is given by,

$$W = \int_{V_1}^{V_2} PdV = \text{Area ABba}$$

During an adiabatic process,

$$PV^{\gamma} = \text{cosnt} = K \text{ or } \quad P = K/V^{\gamma}$$

$$W = K\int_{V_1}^{V_2} \frac{dV}{V^{\gamma}} = \frac{1}{1-\gamma}\left[\frac{1}{V_2^{\gamma-1}} - \frac{1}{V_1^{\gamma-1}}\right] \quad ...(i)$$

Since A and B lie on the same adiabatic

$$P_1V_1^{\gamma} = P_2V_2^{\gamma} = K$$

$$W = \frac{1}{1-\gamma}\left[\frac{1}{V_2^{\gamma-1}} - \frac{1}{V_1^{\gamma-1}}\right]$$

$$W = \frac{1}{1-\gamma}\left[\frac{P_2V_2^{\gamma}}{V_2^{\gamma-1}} - \frac{P_1V_1^{\gamma}}{V_1^{\gamma-1}}\right]$$

$$= \frac{1}{1-\gamma}\left[P_2V_2 - P_1V_1\right] \quad ...(ii)$$

Taking T_1 and T_2 as the temperatures at the points A and B respectively and considering one gram molecule of the gas

$$P_1V_1 = RT_1 \text{ and } P_2V_2 = RT_2$$

Substituting these values in equation (ii)

$$W = \frac{1}{1-\gamma}\left[RT_2 - RT_1\right] \quad ...(iii)$$

Here, heat transferred is zero because the system is thermally insulated from the surroundings. The decrease in the internal energy of the system (due to fall in temperature) is equal to the work done by the system and *vice versa*.

RELATION BETWEEN ADIABATIC AND ISOTHERMAL ELASTICITIES

1. Isothermal Elasticity

During an isothermal process

$$PV = \text{const}$$

Differentiating,

$$PdV + VdP = 0$$

or $$\frac{V.dP}{-dV} = P \qquad ...(i)$$

From the definition of elasticity of a gas

$$E_{ise} = \frac{dP}{-dV/V}$$

$$= \frac{VdP}{-dV} \qquad ...(ii)$$

From (i) and (ii)

$$E_{ise} = P$$

2. Adiabatic Elasticity

During an adiabatic process

$$PV^{\psi} = \text{const}$$

Differentiating, $P\gamma V^{\gamma-1}dV + V^{\gamma}\, dP = 0$

or $$\frac{VdP}{-dV} = \gamma P \qquad ...(iv)$$

From the definition of elasticity of a gas

$$E_{adt} = \frac{dP}{-dV/V} = \frac{V\,.\,dP}{-dV} \qquad ...(v)$$

From (iv) and (v),

$$E_{adt} = \gamma P$$

Comparing (iii) and (vi)

$$E_{adt} = \gamma E_{iso}$$

Thus, the adiabatic elasticity of a gas is γ times the isothermal elasticity.

CLEMENT AND DESORMES METHOD—DETERMINATION OF γ

Clement and Desormes in 1819 designed an experiment to find γ, the ratio between the two specific heats of a gas. The vessel A has a capacity of 20 to 30 litres and is fitted in a box containing cotton and wool. At the top end, three tubes are fitted as shown in Fig. 1.15. Through S_1, dry air is forced into the vessel A. The strip cock S_1 is closed when the pressure inside A is slightly greater than the atmospheric pressure. Let the difference in level on the two sides of the manometer be B and the atmospheric pressure be P_0. The pressure of air inside the vend is P_1. The stop-cock S is suddenly opened and closed just at the moment when the levels of the liquid on the two sides of the manometer are the same.

Some quantity of air escapes to the atmosphere. The air inside the vessel expands adiabatically. The temperature of air inside the vessel falls due to adiabatic expansion. The air inside the vessel is allowed to gain heat from the surroundings and it finally attains the temperature of the surroundings. Let the pressure at the end be P_1 and the difference in levels on the two sides of the manometer be h.

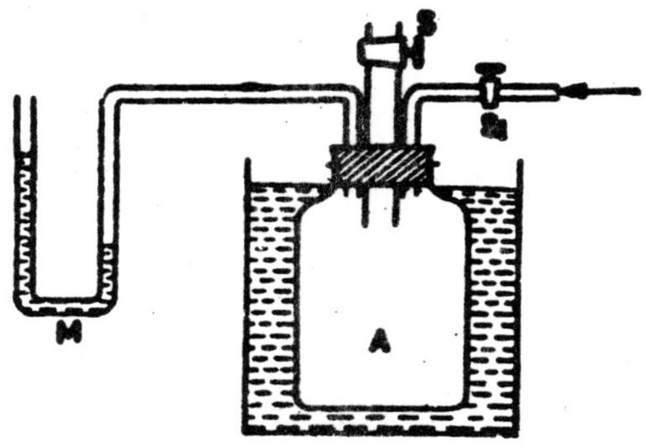

Fig. 1.15

Theory: Consider a fixed mass of air left in the vessel in the end. This mass of air has expanded from volume V_1 (less than the volume of the vessel) at pressure P_1 to volume V_2 at pressure P_0. The process is adiabatic as shown by the curve AS.

$$P_1V_1^{\gamma} = P_0V_2^{\gamma}$$

$$\frac{P_1}{P_0} = \left(\frac{V_2}{V_1}\right)^{\gamma} \qquad ...(i)$$

Finally the point C a reached. The points A and C are at the room temperature. Therefore AC can be considered as an isothermal.

$$P_1V_1 = P_2V_2$$

$$\frac{V_2}{V_1} = \frac{P_1}{P_2} \qquad \text{...(ii)}$$

Substituting the value of V_2/V_1 in equation (i),

$$\frac{P_1}{P_0} = \left(\frac{P_1}{P_2}\right)^{\gamma}$$

Taking logarithms,

$$\log P_1 - \log P_0 + \gamma[\log P_1 - \log P_2]$$

$$\gamma = \frac{\log P_1 - \log P_0}{\log P_1 - \log P_2} \qquad \text{...(iii)}$$

But $\quad P_1 = P_0 + H$ and $P_2 = P_0 + h$

$$\therefore \qquad \gamma = \frac{\log (P_0 - H) - \log P_0}{\log (P_0 - H) - \log (P_0 + h)}$$

$$\gamma = \frac{\log\left(\dfrac{P_0 + H}{P_0}\right)}{\log\left(\dfrac{P_0 + H}{P_0 + h}\right)}$$

$$= \frac{\log\left(1 + \dfrac{H}{P_0}\right)}{\log\left(1 + \dfrac{H - h}{P_0 + h}\right)}$$

Approximately, $\gamma = \dfrac{\dfrac{H}{P_0}}{\dfrac{H - h}{P_0}} = \dfrac{H}{H - h}$

Hence $\quad \gamma = \dfrac{H}{H - h}$ ...(iv)

Similarly, γ far any gas can be determined by this method.

Drawbacks

When the stop-cock is opened, a series of oscillations are set up. This is shown by the up and down movement of the liquid in the manometer. Therefore, the exact moment when the stopcock should be closed h not known. The pressure may not be equal to the atmospheric pressure when the stop-cock is closed. It may be higher or less than the atmospheric pressure. Thus the result obtained will not be accurate.

PARTINGTON'S METHOD

Fig. 1.16 represented the Lummer, Pringsheim and Partington designed an apparatus to determine the value of γ. In this method, the pressure and temperature are measured accurately before and after the adiabatic expansion.

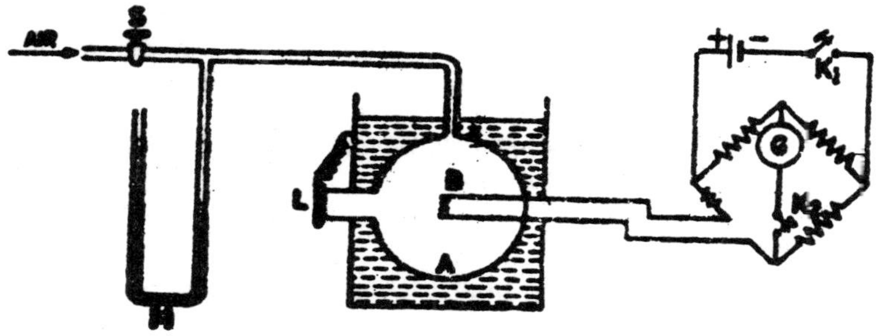

Fig. 1.16

The apparatus consists of a vessel A having a capacity between 130 and 150 litres. The value l can be opened and closed suddenly. It is controlled by a spring arrangement (Fig. 1.17). Dry air (or gas) at a pressure higher than the atmospheric pressure is forced into (he vessel A and the stop-cock S is closed. The oil manometer M is used to measure the pressure of air inside the vessel A. The bolometer B (a platinum wire) and a sensitive galvanometer are used in the Wheatstone's bridge arrangement.

The vessel is surrounded by a constant temperature bath. Let the initial pressure and temperature be P_1 and T_1 (room temperature). The bridge is kept slightly disturbed from the balanced position. The valve L is suddenly opened and closed. The Wheatstones bridge is at once adjusted for balanced position. The temperature of air inside A has decreased due to adiabatic expansion of air. Let the temperature inside be T_0 and the atmospheric pressure P_0. If the apparatus is allowed to remain as such for some time, it will gain heat from the surroundings and the balance point gets disturbed. In order that the balance point remains undisturbed, some pieces of ice are added into the water surrounding the vessel A. When the temperature of water bath is the same as that of air just after adiabatic expansion, the bridge will remain balanced.

The temperature T_0 of the bath represents the temperature of air after the adiabatic expansion.

$$\frac{P_1^{\gamma-1}}{T_1^{\gamma}} = \frac{P_0^{\gamma-1}}{T_0^{\gamma}} \quad \left(\frac{P_1}{P_0}\right)^{\gamma-1} = \left(\frac{T_1}{T_0}\right)^{\gamma}$$

$$(\gamma - 1)(\log P_1 - \log P_0) = \gamma\,[\log T_1 - \log T_0]$$

$$\gamma = \frac{\log P_1 - \log P_0}{(\log P_1 - \log P_0) - (\log T_1 - \log T_0)}$$

As P_1, P_0, T_1 and T_0 are known, γ can be calculated. The value of γ for air at 17°C is found to be 1.4034.

Drawbacks

This method cannot be used to find the value of γ at higher temperatures because it is not possible to determine the cooling correction accurately.

RUCHHARDT'S EXPERIMENT

In 1929, Ruchhardt designed an apparatus to find the value of γ. It is based on the principle of mechanics. Air (or gas) is enclosed in a big jar (Fig. 1.17). A tube of uniform area of cross section is fitted and a ball of mass m fits in the tube just like a piston. In the equilibrium position, the ball is at the point A. The pressure P of air inside the vessel, is given by

$$P = P_0 + mg/A$$

where P_0 is the atmospheric pressure and A is the area of cross-section on of the tube.

The ball is given a small downward movement through a distance y. It moves up and down and executes simple harmonic motion. Let the change in volume be dV and change in pressure be dP.

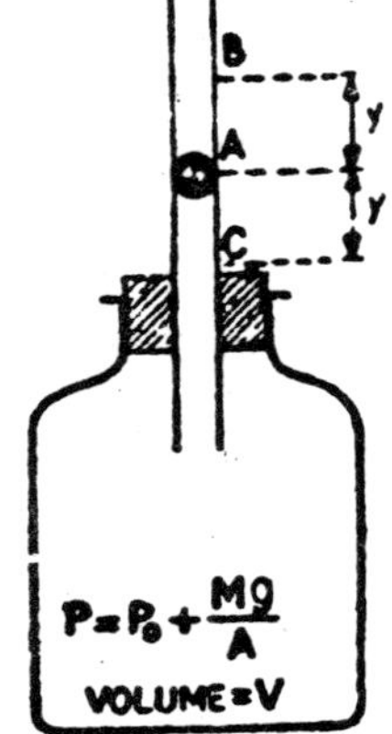

Fig. 1.17

$$dV = yA$$

and $$dP = \frac{F}{A}$$

where f is the restoring force

As the ball moves quite rapidly, the process of change in P and V is adiabatic.

$$\therefore \quad PV^{\gamma} = \text{const}$$

Differentiating, $P\gamma V^{\gamma-1}\, dV + V^{\gamma}.\, dP = 0$

$$\gamma PdV + VdP = 0$$

Substituting the values of dV and dP,

$$\gamma PyA + \frac{V.F}{A} = 0$$

But $$F = M\,.\,\frac{d^2y}{dt^2}$$

or $$F = -\frac{\gamma PA^2}{V}.y \qquad \text{...(i)}$$

$$\therefore \quad \frac{d^2y}{dt^2} + \frac{\gamma PA^2}{VM}\,.\,y = 0 \qquad \text{...(ii)}$$

Equation (ii) represents S.H.M.

Let the time period be t

$$t = 2\pi\sqrt{\frac{\text{displacement}}{\text{acceleration}}}$$

$$= 2\pi\sqrt{\frac{y}{-d^2y/dt^2}}$$

$$t = 2\pi\sqrt{\frac{VM}{\gamma PA^2}}$$

$$\gamma = 2\pi\,\frac{4\pi^2\,VM}{PA^2t^2} \qquad \text{...(iii)}$$

As F, M, P and A are already known, only the time period t is to be determined.

Hence γ can be calculated.

This experiment is not very accurate because the ball comes to rest in a short time due to friction and the time period cannot be determined accurately.

Rinkle's Modification

Rinkle suggested a modification in Ruchhardt's experiment. The ball is kept in the equilibrium position where the pressure of air (or gas) is exactly equal to the atmospheric pressure. The ball is allowed to drop and the distance L through which it drops before starting to move up again is noted. This distance is found accurately by taking a series of photographs of the moving ball.

$$\text{Work done} = \int_0^L F.dy$$

$$\text{But} \quad F = \frac{\gamma P_0 A^2 y}{V}$$

$$W = \frac{\gamma P_0 A^2}{V} \int_0^L y dy$$

$$= \frac{\gamma P_0 A^2 L^2}{2V} \quad \text{...(iv)}$$

$$\text{Work done} = MgL \quad \text{...(v)}$$

Equating (iv) and (v)

$$\frac{\gamma P_0 A^2 L^2}{2V} = MgL$$

$$\gamma = \frac{2MgV}{P_0 A^2 L} \quad \text{...(vi)}$$

As M, g, V, P_0 and A are known, L is measured from the photographic film. Hence y can be calculated. The error in the result is due to the following assumptions : (i) that there is no friction, (ii) that the gas is ideal and (iii) the process is completely adiabatic.

THERMODYNAMIC SCALE OF TEMPERATURE

The efficiency of a Carnot's engine does not depend upon the property of the working substance but it depends upon the temperature limits between which the engine works. The scale of temperature based on the working of the Carnot's engine is a standard scale and it does not depend upon the particular property of any substance, as in the case of other thermometric scales. Kelvin worked out the theory of the absolute scale called Kelvin's or thermodynamical scale and also showed that it agrees with the perfect gas scale.

Suppose an engine works between the temperatures θ_1 and θ_2. Here H_1 is the heat absorbed at θ_1 and H_2 is the heat rejected at θ_2

$$\eta = f(\theta_1, \theta_2)$$

$$h = \frac{H_1 - H_2}{H_1} = f(\theta_1, \theta_2)$$

$$\therefore \quad 1 - \frac{H_1}{H_2} = f(\theta_1, \theta_2)$$

or

$$\frac{H_1}{H_2} = \frac{1}{1 - f(\theta_1, \theta_2)} = F(\theta_1, \theta_2) \qquad \text{...(i)}$$

Similarly, if the engine works between the temperature θ_2 and θ_3. and H_2 is the heat absorbed and H_3 is the heat rejected, then

$$\frac{H_2}{H_3} = F(\theta_2, \theta_2) \qquad \text{...(ii)}$$

If the engine works between the temperatures θ_1 and θ_3 and H_1 is the heat absorbed and H_3 is the heat rejected, then

$$\frac{H_1}{H_3} = F(\theta_1, \theta_3) \qquad \text{...(iii)}$$

From (i), (ii) and (iii),

$$\frac{H_1}{H_3} = \frac{H_1}{H_2} \times \frac{H_2}{H_3}$$

$$\therefore \quad F(\theta_1, \theta_3), F(\theta_1, \theta_2) \times F(\theta_2, \theta_3)$$

$$F(\theta_1, \theta_2) = \frac{F(\theta_1, \theta_3)}{F(\theta_2, \theta_3)}$$

This temperature θ_3 is arbitrarily chosen.

This relation can be satisfied only if

$$F(\theta_1, \theta_2) = \frac{\phi(\theta_1)}{\phi(\theta_2)}$$

$$F(\theta_2, \theta_3) = \frac{\phi(\theta_2)}{\phi(\theta_3)}$$

and $$F(\theta_1, \theta_3) = \frac{\phi(\theta_1)}{\phi(\theta_3)}$$

where ϕ is another function.

$$\therefore \quad \frac{H_1}{H_2} = F(\theta_1, \theta_2) = \frac{\phi(\theta_1)}{\phi(\theta_2)}$$

This temperature θ_3 is arbitrarily chosen. This relation can be satisfied only if

$$\therefore \quad \frac{H_1}{H_2} = \frac{\theta_1}{\theta_2} \quad \text{...(iv)}$$

The expression on the right hand side represents the ratio of the two Kelvin temperatures and this can be denoted as $\frac{\theta_1}{\theta_2}$.

The relation (iv) is used to represent a new scale and this does not depend upon the property of the working substance.

$$\text{Efficiency} \quad \eta = \frac{H_1 - H_2}{H_1} = \frac{\theta_1 - \theta_2}{\theta_1} \quad \text{...(v)}$$

$$\eta = 1 - \frac{\theta_2}{\theta_1} \quad \text{....(vi)}$$

ABSOLUTE ZERO ON WORK SCALE

An engine working between the steam point and the ice point. The isothermal AB is at the steam point and the isothermal CD is at the ice point (Fig. 1.18).

$$\eta = 1 - \frac{\theta_{ice}}{\theta_{steam}}$$

$$\eta = \frac{\theta_{steam} - \theta_{ice}}{\theta_{steam}}$$

If the distance between the isothermals AB and CD is divided into 100 equal parts by drawing isothermals parallel to AB or CD, then any isothermal will be at a temperature 1° higher than the isothermal just below it.

The difference in temperature between the steam point and the ice point is 100 on this scale also. In this way, the work scale (Kelvin) of temperature is fixed. Similarly, isothermals below the ice point can be drawn and an isothermal representing absolute zero can be obtained (Fig. 1.18). The isothermal GK represents absolute zero.

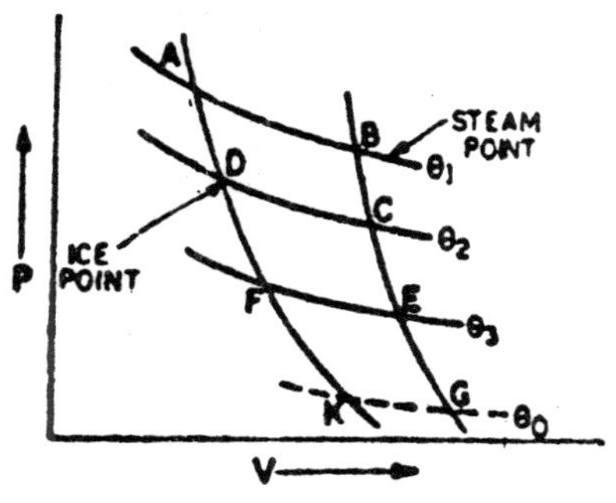

Fig. 1.18

Consider an engine working between the steam point and absolute zero ($\theta_0 = 0$).

$$\eta = 1 - \frac{\theta_0}{\theta_{steam}} = 1$$

i.e., the engine has efficiency equal to 1.

Similarly an engine working between ice point and absolute zero, will have an efficiency.

$$\eta' = 1 - \frac{\theta_0}{\theta_{ice}} = 1$$

But efficiency $\eta = \frac{H_1 - H_2}{H_1} = 1 - \frac{H_2}{H_1}$

If $\quad 1 - \frac{H_2}{H_1} = 1, \frac{H_2}{H_1} = 0$

or $\quad H_2 = 0$

It means that if the sink is at the temperature of zero degree absolute, no heat is rejected and the whole of the available energy has been used up in doing useful work and in this case the engine will have **100%** efficiency.

Thus, the absolute zero temperature on the work scale is defined as the temperature at which a system undergoes a reversible isothermal process without any transfer of heat.

Absolute zero on the work scale can also be defined as that temperature of the sink at which no heat is rejected to it.

According to Kelvin-Planck statement, no engine can have 100 per cent efficiency. Thus the absolute zero temperature is not attainable.

ENTHALPY

Enthalpy in an extensive thermodynamic property and is given the symbol A. Enthalpy is given by the equation

$$h = U + PV \qquad ...(i)$$

Enthalpy is defined as the sum of the internal energy and the product of pressure and volume.

To study the properties of this function, assume that the system undergoes an infinitesimal process from an initial equilibrium state to a final equilibrium state.

From equation (i)

$$dh = dU + PdV + VdP \qquad ...(ii)$$

Also $\delta H = dU + PdV \qquad ...(iii)$

$\therefore \quad dh = \delta H + VdP \qquad ...(iv)$

Dividing by dT

$$\frac{dh}{dT} = \frac{\delta H}{dT} + V\frac{dP}{dT} \qquad ...(V)$$

At constant pressure (isobaric process),

$$\left(\frac{\partial h}{\partial T}\right)_P = \left(\frac{\delta H}{dT}\right)_P$$

But $\left(\frac{\delta H}{dT}\right)_P = C_P$

$\therefore \quad \left(\frac{\partial h}{\partial T}\right)_P = C_P \qquad ...(vi)$

From equation (iv), during isobaric process, dP = 0

$\therefore \quad dh = \delta H$

or $\quad h_f - h_i - H \qquad ...(vii)$

Therefore change in enthalpy during an isobaric process is equal to the amount of heat transferred during the process.

In a throttling process, applying first law of thermodynamics

$$H = U_f - U_i + W$$

Here $H = 0$

and $W = P_f V_f - P_o V_i$

$\therefore \quad 0 = U_f - U_i + P_f V_f - P_i V_i$

or $U_i + P_i V_i = U_f + P_f V_f$

or $h_i = h_f$ ...(viii)

Therefore in a throttling process, there in no change in enthalpy of the system. The initial and the final enthalpies are equal.

C_P, C_V AND μ

The specific heat at constant pressure C_p, the specific heat at constant volume C_V and the Joule-Kelvin coefficient μ are defined as follows:

$$C_P = \left(\frac{\partial h}{\partial T}\right)_P \quad ...(i)$$

$$C_V = \left(\frac{\partial U}{\partial T}\right)_V \quad ....(ii)$$

$$\mu = \left(\frac{\partial T}{\partial P}\right)_h \quad ...(iii)$$

These three quantities are defined in terms of the thermodynamic properties viz. pressure, volume, temperature, internal energy and enthalpy. Hence, C_P, C_V and μ are also thermodynamic properties of a substance.

RICHARDSON'S EQUATION

Richardson derived the equation for the thermionic emission from a heated metal. He applied Clausius-Clapeyron's latent heat equation for the ejection of electrons from the surface of the metal.

Let the volume for 1 gram molecule of electrons within the metal be v_1 and outside the metal be v_2. The volume v_2 is very high as compared to v_1. The pressure of electrons under equilibrium conditions is P. The energy absorbed by N electrons during ejection from the metal surface = W. Here N is the Avogadro's number. Applying Clapeyron's latent heat equation

$$\frac{dP}{dT} = \frac{W}{T(v_2 - v_1)} \quad ...(i)$$

As $v_2 >> v_1$, v_1 can be neglected

$$\therefore \quad \frac{dP}{dT} = \frac{W}{T\, v_1}$$

$$\text{or} \quad W = T v_2 \frac{dP}{dT} \quad ...(ii)$$

The energy W consists of two parts : (i) The work function of the surface *i.e.*, energy required for ejecting N electrons just outside the metal *i.e.*, in crossing the potential barrier. This energy = Nϕ where ϕ is the work function of the surface.

(ii) The work done in admitting the ejected electrons into the electron cloud already present outside the metal. This energy is Pv_2,. For one gram molecule of electrons

$$Pv_2 + RT = N\,k\,T$$

Here k is Boltzmann's constant

$$W = N\,\phi + N\,k\,T \quad ...(iii)$$

From equations (ii) and (iii)

$$N\,(\phi + kT) = Tv_2 \frac{dP}{dT}$$

$$\text{But} \quad v_2 = \frac{NkT}{P}$$

$$\therefore N\,(\phi + kT) = T\left(\frac{NkT}{P}\right) \times \frac{dP}{dT}$$

$$(\phi + kT) = \frac{kT^2}{P} \times \frac{dP}{dT}$$

$$\frac{dP}{P} = \left(\frac{\phi + kT}{kT^2}\right) dT$$

Integrating

$$\int \frac{dP}{P} = \int \frac{\phi}{kT^2}\, dT + \int \frac{dT}{T}$$

$$\log_e P = \int \frac{\phi}{kT^2}\, dT + \log e\ T + \text{constant}$$

Let the constant be equal to $\log_e A_1$

$$\log_e P - \log_e T - \log_e A_1 = \int \frac{\phi}{kT^2}\, dT$$

$$\log_e \left(\frac{P}{A_1 T}\right) = \int \frac{\phi}{kT^2}\, dT \qquad \text{...(iv)}$$

Richardson suggested that ϕ also depends upon T. If ϕ_0 is the work function at 0 K, then

$$\phi = \phi_0 + 3/2kT$$

$$\therefore \int \frac{\phi}{kT^2}\, dT = \int \frac{\phi_0 + 3/2kT}{kT^2}$$

$$= \frac{\phi_0}{kT} + \frac{3}{2} \log_e T$$

$$= \frac{\phi_0}{kT} + \log_e T^{3/2}$$

Substituting this value in equation (iv)

$$\log_e \left(\frac{P}{A_1 T}\right) = -\frac{\phi_0}{kT} + \log_e T^{3/2}$$

$$\log_e \left(\frac{P}{A_1 T^{3/2}}\right) = -\frac{\phi_0}{kT}$$

or

$$P = A_1\, T^{3/2}\, e^{-\frac{\phi_0}{kT}} \qquad \text{...(v)}$$

If the number of electrons per unit volume = n then

$$P = n\, k\, T \qquad \text{...(vi)}$$

Equating (v) and (vi)

$$n k T = A_1 T^{3/2}\, e^{-\frac{\phi_0}{kT}}$$

$$n = \left(\frac{A_1}{k}\right) T^{3/2}\, e^{-\frac{\phi_0}{kT}} \qquad \text{...(vii)}$$

Assuming the perfect gas laws to hold good in the case of an electron cloud, the mean energy of the electron,

$$\frac{1}{2} m_0 v^2 = \frac{3}{2} kT$$

or
$$v = \left(\frac{3kT}{m_0}\right)^{1/2}$$

But Kundsen has shown that the number of electrons passing unit area in one second is,

$$n_0 = \frac{nv}{\sqrt{6\pi}}$$

$$\therefore \qquad n_0 = n \times \left(\frac{3kT}{6\pi m_0}\right)^{1/2}$$

$$= n \times \left(\frac{kT}{2\pi m_0}\right)^{1/2}$$

Substituting the value of n from equation (vii)

$$n_0 = \left[\left(\frac{A_1}{k}\right)T^{3/2}\ e^{-\frac{\phi_0}{kT}}\right]\left[nT^{1/2}\left(\frac{k}{2\pi m_0}\right)^{1/2}\right]$$

$$n_0 = \left[\frac{nA_1}{k} \times \left(\frac{k}{2\pi m_0}\right)^{1/2}\right] T^2\ e^{-\frac{\phi_0}{kT}}$$

Taking

$$\frac{nA_1}{k} \times \left(\frac{k}{2\pi m_0}\right)^{1/2} = A_2 = \text{constant}$$

$$n_0 = A_2 T^2\ e^{-\frac{\phi_0}{kT}}$$

Taking the charge on the electron = e, the current density due to electron emission,

$$I = n_0\ e = A_2\ T^2\ e^{-\frac{\phi_0}{kT}}$$

$$I = AT^2\ e^{-\frac{\phi_0}{kT}} \qquad \text{...(viii)}$$

Here $A = (A_2 e) = \text{constant}$

Equation (viii) represents the Richardson's equation for thermionic emission.

The electron emitter can be heated directly or indirectly. In the case of direct heating, the current is passed through the filament which itself serves as the cathode. Tungsten and thoriated tungsten filaments are the commonly used directly heated electron emitters. The indirectly heated electron emitter consists of a heater wire surrounded by a metal sleeve in the form of a cylinder whose surface is coated with electron emitting materials. The most commonly used cathode is the indirectly heated cathode. In both the cases, filaments can be heated either by DC or AC.

The operating temperatures for tungsten, thoriated tungsten and oxide coated emitters are given below.

Tungsten	2200 to 3000 K
Thoriated Tungsten	1900 K
Oxide coated cathode	1000 to 1150 K

Values of the Emission Constant

Material	ϕ_0 *in eV*	*A in A/m²–K*	*Melting point in K*
Carbon	4.7	–	–
Nickel	5.0	2-68 × 10^5	1725
Platinum	5.32	3.20 × 10^5	2047
Tantalum	4.1	6.02 × 10^5	3123
Tungsten	4.52	6.02 × 10^5	3655

MAXWELL'S EQUATIONS (ALTERNATIVE METHOD)

The properties of pure substances can conveniently be represented in terms of the four functions: internal energy, enthalpy, Helmholtz function and Gibb's function.

Internal energy = U

Enthalpy, A = U + PV

Helmholtz function

$$F = U - TS$$

Gibb's function 0 = h – TS

or $$G = U - TS + PV$$

All the above four quantities can be regarded as functions of

P, V, T, and S

Now, consider a system undergoing an infinitesimal reversible process from one equilibrium state to another.

(1) The internal energy changes by an amount

$$dU = \delta H - PdV$$

or $$dU + TdS - PdV \quad ...(i)$$

Here U, T and P are supposed to be functions of S and V

(2) The enthalpy changes by an amount

$$dh = dU + PdV + VdP$$

$$dh = (TdS - PdV) + P.dV + VdP$$

$$dh = TdS - VdP \quad ...(ii)$$

Here h, T and V are supposed to be functions of S and P.

(3) The Helmholtz function changes by an amount

$$dF = dU - TdS - SdT$$

or $$dF = (TdS - PdV) - TdS - SdT$$

or $$dF = -SdT - PdV \quad (iii)$$

Here F, S and P are supposed to be functions of T and V.

(4) The Gibbs function changes by an amount

$$dG = dh - TdS - SdT$$

$$dG = (TdS + VdP) - TdS - SdT$$

$$dG = -SdT + VdP \quad ...(iv)$$

Here G, S and 7 are supposed to be functions of T and P.

As U, h, F and G are actual functions, their differentials are exact.

For exact differentials

$$dZ = Mdx + Ndy \quad ...(v)$$

Here Z, M and N are all functions of x and y

$$\therefore \quad \left(\frac{\partial M}{\partial y}\right)_x = \left(\frac{\partial N}{\partial x}\right)_y \quad ...(vi)$$

To derive the Maxwell's equations, equation (vi) can be applied.

(1) From equation (i)

$$dU = TdS - PdV$$

Here $M = T, N = P, x = S, y = V$

From equation (vi)

$$\left(\frac{\partial T}{\partial V}\right)_S = -\left(\frac{\partial P}{\partial S}\right)_V \quad ...(vii)$$

(2) From equation (ii)

$$dh = TdS + VdP$$

Here $M = T, N = V, x = S, y = P$

From equation (vi)

$$\left(\frac{\partial T}{\partial P}\right)_S = \left(\frac{\partial V}{\partial S}\right)_P \quad ...(viii)$$

(3) From equation (iii)

$$dF + SdT - PdV$$

Here $M = S, N = P, x = T, y = V$

From equation (vi)

$$\left(\frac{\partial S}{\partial V}\right)_T = \left(\frac{\partial P}{\partial T}\right)_V \quad ...(ix)$$

(4) From equation (iv)

$$dG = -SdT + FdP$$

Here $M = S, - N = V, x = T, y = P$

From equation (vi)

$$\left(\frac{\partial S}{\partial P}\right)_T = \left(\frac{\partial V}{\partial T}\right)_P \quad ...(x)$$

Note: The equations for dU, dh, dF and dG can be obtained by remembering the sentence, 'Good Physicists have Studied Under Very Fine Teachers'. In this sentence, the letters, G, P, h, S, U, V, F, and T are to be used.

The diagram to be used is shown in Fig. 1.19.

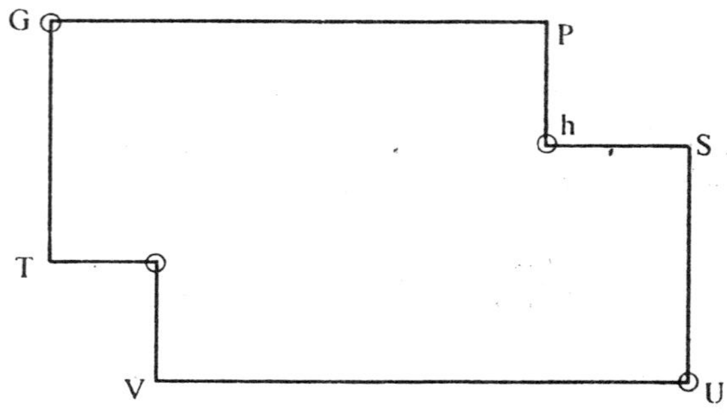

Fig. 1.19

To obtain the expression for dU, note the quantities on the two sides of U, viz. they are 8 and V. S is on the +ve direction of y-axis and V is on the –ve direction of x-axis.

$$\therefore \qquad dU = +(\quad)\,dS - (\quad)\,dV$$

The quantity associated with dS is T and with dV is P.

$$\therefore \qquad dU = TdS - PdV \qquad \text{...(i)}$$

Similarly for dh

$$dh = (\quad)\,dS + (\quad)\,dP$$

$$dh = TdS + VdP \qquad \text{...(ii)}$$

For dF

$$dF = -(\quad)\,dT - (\quad)\,dV$$

$$dF = -SdT - PdV \qquad \text{...(iii)}$$

For dG

$$dG = -(\quad)\,dT + (\;)\,dP$$

$$dG + -SdT + VdP \qquad \text{...(iv)}$$

JOULE-KELVIN COEFFICIENT

The Joule Kelvin affect was discussed in the chapter "Nature of heat".

The Joule-Kelvin coefficient is defined as the slope of the isenthalpic curve at any point on the temperature pressure curve.

$$\mu = \left(\frac{\partial T}{\partial P}\right)_h \qquad \text{...(i)}$$

From the definition of enthalpy

$$h = U + PV \quad ...(ii)$$

or $$dh = dU + PdV + PdV \quad ...(iii)$$

Also $$dU = TdS - PdV$$

$\therefore$ $dP + PdV = TdS$

$\therefore$ $$dh = TdS + VdP \quad ...(iv)$$

Also $$dS = \left(\frac{\partial S}{\partial T}\right)_P dT = \left(\frac{\partial S}{\partial P}\right)_P dP$$

$$dh = T\left(\frac{\partial S}{\partial T}\right)_P dT = \left[T\left(\frac{\partial S}{\partial P}\right)_T + V\right] dP \quad ...(v)$$

The volume coefficient a is given by

But $$T\left(\frac{\partial S}{\partial T}\right)_P = C_P \quad ...(vi)$$

The volume coefficient α is given by

$$\alpha = \frac{1}{V}\left[\frac{\partial V}{\partial T}\right]_P$$

But $$\left[\frac{\partial V}{\partial T}\right]_P = -\left[\frac{\partial S}{\partial P}\right]_T = \alpha V$$

$\therefore$ $$\left[\frac{\partial S}{\partial P}\right]_T = -\alpha V \quad ...(vii)$$

Substituting these values in equation (v),

$$dh = C_P dT + \left[V - T\left(\frac{\partial V}{\partial T}\right)_P\right] dP \quad ...(viii)$$

$$dh = \frac{1}{C_P} dh + \frac{1}{C_P}\left[T\left(\frac{\partial V}{\partial T}\right)_P - V\right] dP \quad ...(ix)$$

But $$dT = \left(\frac{\partial T}{\partial h}\right)_P dh + \left(\frac{\partial T}{\partial P}\right)_h dP \quad ..(x)$$

Comparing the coefficients of equations (iv) and (x),

$$\left(\frac{\partial T}{\partial h}\right)_{h} = \frac{1}{C_P}\left[T\left(\frac{\partial V}{\partial T}\right)_P - V\right]$$

But $$\mu = \left(\frac{\partial T}{\partial P}\right)_h$$

$\therefore$ $$\mu = \frac{1}{C_P}\left[T\left(\frac{\partial V}{\partial T}\right)_P - V\right]$$

$$\mu C_P = \left[T\left(\frac{\partial V}{\partial T}\right)_P - V\right] \quad \text{...(xi)}$$

$$\mu C_P = T^2 \frac{\partial}{\partial T}\left(\frac{V}{T}\right)_P \quad \text{...(xii)}$$

From equation (viii),

$$\left(\frac{\partial h}{\partial P}\right)_T = V - T\left(\frac{\partial V}{\partial T}\right)_P \quad \text{...(xiii)}$$

From equations (xi) and (xiii)

$$\mu C_P = -\left(\frac{\partial h}{\partial P}\right)_T \quad \text{...(xiv)}$$

The Joule-Kelvin coefficient,

$$\mu = \frac{1}{C_P}\left[T\left(\frac{\partial V}{\partial T}\right)_P - V\right] \quad \text{...(xv)}$$

$$\mu = \frac{V}{C_P}\left[T\left\{\frac{1}{V}\left(\frac{\partial V}{\partial T}\right)_P\right\} - 1\right] \quad \text{...(xvi)}$$

or $$\mu = \frac{V}{C_P}[\alpha T - 1] \quad \text{...(xvii)}$$

For a Van der Waals gas

$$\left(P + \frac{a}{V^2}\right)(V - b) = RT$$

$$PV - Pb + \frac{a}{V} - \frac{ab}{V^2} = RT$$

Differentiating, keeping P constant,

$$PdV - \frac{adV}{V^2} + \frac{2ab\,dV}{V^3} = RdT$$

or $$\frac{dV}{dT} = \frac{R}{P - \frac{a}{V^2} + \frac{2ab}{V^3}}$$

$$\left(\frac{\partial V}{\partial T}\right)_P = \frac{R}{\frac{RT}{V-b} - \frac{a}{V^2} - \frac{a}{V^2} + \frac{2ab}{V^3}}$$

$$\left(\frac{\partial V}{\partial T}\right)_P = \frac{RV^3(V-b)}{RTV^3 - 2a(V-b)^2} \quad \text{...(xviii)}$$

Substituting this value in equation (xvi)

$$\mu = \frac{V}{C_P}\left[\frac{RTV^2(V-b)}{RTV^2 - 2a(V-b)^2} - 1\right]$$

$$= \frac{V}{C_P}\left[\frac{RTV^2(V-b) - RTV^3 + 2a(V-b)^2}{RTV^3 - 2a(V-b)^2}\right]$$

$$= \frac{V}{C_P}\left[\frac{2a(V-b)^2 - RTV^2b}{RTV^3 - 2a(V-b)^2}\right] \quad \text{...(xix)}$$

From equation (xvii), as 7 and C_P are always positive, the value of μ and hence the temperature of a Van der Waals gas passing through a porous plug will depend on the value of $\alpha T - 1$.

(1) If $\alpha T > 1$, the temperature of the gas will increase.

(2) If $\alpha T < 1$, the temperature of the gas will decrease.

(3) If $\alpha T = 1$, the temperature will not change.

This temperature at which the inversion takes place is called the temperature of inversion T_i. In this case, from equation (xvii)

$\mu = 0$ and from equation (xix)

$$2a(V-b)^2 = RT_iV^2b$$

$$\therefore \quad T_i = \frac{2a(V-b)^2}{RV^2b}$$

If $V >> b$

$$T_i = \frac{2a}{Rb} \quad \text{...(xxi)}$$

Ideal Gas

From equation (xii)

$$\mu C_P = T^2 \left[\frac{\partial}{\partial T}\left(\frac{V}{T}\right)_P\right]$$

$$\therefore \qquad \mu = \frac{T^2}{C_P}\left[\frac{\partial}{\partial T}\left(\frac{V}{T}\right)_P\right]$$

For an ideal gas $\frac{V}{T} = \frac{R}{P}$

$$\therefore \qquad \mu = \frac{T^2}{C_P} \cdot \frac{\partial}{\partial T}\left[\frac{R}{P}\right]_P = 0$$

Thus the Joule-Kelvin coefficient for an ideal gas is zero and the ideal gas passing through the porous gas does not show any change in temperature.

EQUILIBRIUM BETWEEN LIQUID AND ITS VAPOUR

Applying Gibbs potential (G), it is possible to investigate the equilibrium between a liquid and its vapour or between any two phases of a substance. Consider a closed system containing a liquid in equilibrium with its saturated vapour. The temperature and pressure are equal in both the phases. As each of the phases is in equilibrium, the temperature and pressure must remain constant throughout the phase and hence the thermodynamical coordinates F, S, U and G will be equal to the product of the specific value and the mass of the substance in that phase.

Suppose m_1 and m_2 are the masses in the liquid and vapour phases and g_1 and g_2 are the specific values of the Gibbs potential in the two phases. Then, for the whole system

$$G = m_1 g_1 + m_2 g_2 \qquad \text{...(i)}$$

If a small quantity of liquid changes into vapour, differentiating equation (i)

$$\delta G = \delta m_1 g_1 + \delta m_2 \, g_2 \qquad \text{...(ii)}$$

As the change takes place at constant temperature and pressure, the process is isothermal and isobaric

$$\therefore \qquad \delta G = 0$$

From equation (ii)

$$\delta m_1 g_1 = \delta m_2 g_2 = 0$$

But $\delta m_1 = \delta m_2$

$\therefore$ $g_1 = g_2$

This shows that the thermodynamical potential per unit mass will be equal in the two phases. Equation (iii) is applicable to the processes of evaporation, fusion and sublimation.

FIRST ORDER PHASE TRANSITIONS

Consider an enclosure containing a liquid and its satur ated vapour in equilibrium. If this system undergoes an isother mal, isobaric change, then

$$g_1 = g_2 \quad \text{...(i)}$$

Let the temperature of the system be increased from T to T + dT. For equilibrium

$$g_1 + dg_1 = g_2 + dg_2 \quad \text{...(ii)}$$

or $$dg_1 = dg_2 \quad \text{...(iii)}$$

If the condition of saturation is satisfied,

$$\left(\frac{dg_1}{dT}\right)_{sat.} = \left(\frac{dg_2}{dT}\right)_{sat.} \quad \text{...(iv)}$$

The pressure also changes from p to p + dP,

$$\therefore \quad dg_1 = \left(\frac{\partial g_1}{\partial T}\right)_P dT + \left(\frac{\partial g_1}{\partial T}\right)_T dP \quad \text{...(v)}$$

or $$\left(\frac{\partial g_1}{\partial T}\right) = \left(\frac{\partial g_1}{\partial T}\right)_P + \left(\frac{\partial g_1}{\partial P}\right)_T \left(\frac{\partial P}{\partial T}\right) \quad \text{...(vi)}$$

But, for a unit mass,

$$dg = VdP - SdT \quad \text{...(vii)}$$

$$\therefore \quad \left(\frac{\partial g}{\partial P}\right)_T = V$$

and $$\left(\frac{\partial g}{\partial T}\right)_P = -S$$

Substituting these values in equation (vi)

$$\left(\frac{\partial g_1}{\partial T}\right)_{sat.} = -S_1 + V_1\left(\frac{\partial P}{\partial T}\right)_{sat.}$$

Similarly,

$$\left(\frac{\partial g_2}{\partial T}\right)_{sat.} = -S_2 + V_2\left(\frac{\partial P}{\partial T}\right)_{sat.}$$

Substituting these values is equation (iv)

$$-S_1 + V_1\left(\frac{dP}{dT}\right) = -S_2 + V_2\left(\frac{dP}{dT}\right)$$

or $$\left(\frac{dP}{dT}\right)_{sat.} = \left(\frac{S_2 - S_1}{V_2 - V_1}\right) \qquad ...(viii)$$

But $$S_2 - S_1 = \frac{\delta H}{T} = \frac{L}{T}$$

Here L is latent heat of vaporization

$$\therefore \quad \left(\frac{dP}{dT}\right) = \frac{L}{T(V_2 - V_1)} \qquad ...(ix)$$

This is Clausius-Clapeyron latent heat equation shown in Fig. 1.20.

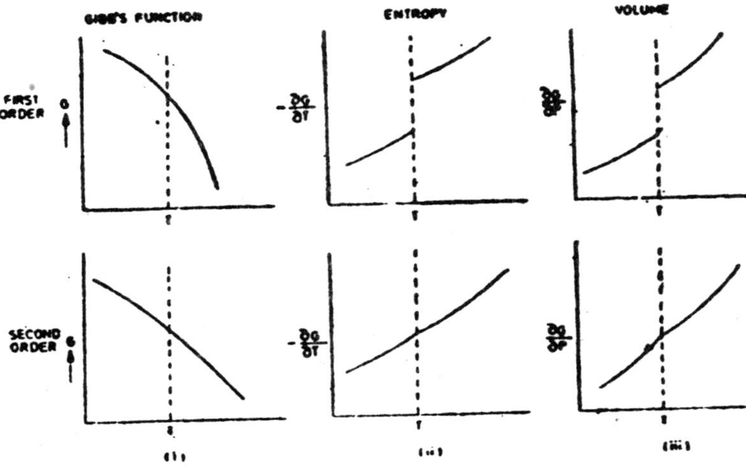

Fig. 1.20

This equation holds good in the first order phase transitions. In these processes there is transference of heat and hence there is change in entropy and volume. Therefore a first order phase transition can be defined as that one in which the Gibbs function with respect to pressure and temperature change discontinuously at the transition point. However, the value of the Gibbs function is the same in both the phases at equilibrium. These changes are represented graphically in Fig. 1.20.

THE T dS EQUATION

(1) The entropy S of a pure substance can be taken as a function of temperature and volume.

$$\therefore \quad dS = \left(\frac{\partial S}{\partial T}\right)_V = dT + \left(\frac{\partial S}{\partial V}\right)_T dV \quad \text{...(i)}$$

Multiplying both sides by T

$$T.dS = \left(\frac{\partial S}{\partial T}\right)_V dV + T\left(\frac{\partial S}{\partial V}\right)_T dV \quad \text{...(ii)}$$

$$\therefore \text{ But} \quad C_V = T\left(\frac{\partial S}{\partial T}\right)_V$$

and from Maxwell's relations

$$\left(\frac{\partial S}{\partial V}\right)_V = \left(\frac{\partial P}{\partial T}\right)_V$$

Substituting these values in equation (ii)

$$T\ dS = C_V dT + T\left(\frac{\partial P}{\partial T}\right)_V dV \quad \text{...(iii)}$$

Equation (iii) is called the first TdS equation.

(2) The entropy S of a pure substance can also be regarded as a function of temperature and pressure

$$\therefore \quad dS = \left(\frac{\partial S}{\partial T}\right)_P dT + \left(\frac{\partial S}{\partial P}\right)_T dP \quad \text{...(iv)}$$

Multiplying both sides by T

$$T.dS = T\left(\frac{\partial S}{\partial T}\right)_P dT + T\left(\frac{\partial S}{\partial P}\right)_T dP \quad \text{...(v)}$$

But $$C_P = T\left(\frac{\partial S}{\partial T}\right)_P$$

and from Maxwell's relations

$$\left(\frac{\partial S}{\partial P}\right)_T = -\left(\frac{\partial V}{\partial T}\right)_P$$

Substituting these values in equation (v)

$$T\,dS = C_P\,dT - T\left(\frac{\partial V}{\partial T}\right)_P \qquad ...(vi)$$

Equation (vi) is called the second TdS equation.

WORK SCALE AND IDEAL GAS SCALE

Consider a Carnot's reversible cycle ABCD (Fig. 1.16). The two isothermals are AB and CD. The temperature on the work scale is θ_1 and the ideal scale is T_1 for the isothermal AB and the temperature on the work scale is θ_2 and the ideal gas scale is T_2 for the isothermal CD. Let the pressure and volume for the points A, B, C and D be P_1, V_1 ; P_2, V_2 ; P_3, V_3 and P_4, V_4 respectively. Consider that 1 gram of an ideal gas is used as the working substance.

From A to B, the process is isothermal.

$$\text{Work done} = \int_{V_1}^{V_2} P\,dV$$

$$= rT_1 \int_{V_1}^{V_2} \frac{dV}{V}$$

$$\therefore \quad H_1 = rT_1 \log \frac{V_2}{V_1} \qquad ...(i)$$

Here r is expressed in heat units.

From C to D, the process is isothermal and a quantity of heat H_2 is rejected by the gas.

$$H_2 = -\int_{V_3}^{V_4} P\,dV$$

$$= -\,rT_2 \int_{V_3}^{V_4} \frac{dV}{V}$$

$$H_2 = rT_2 \log \frac{V_3}{V_4} \qquad ...(ii)$$

Dividing (i) by (ii)

$$\frac{H_1}{H_2} = \frac{rT_1 \log \frac{V_2}{V_1}}{rT_2 \log \frac{V_3}{V_4}} \qquad ...(iii)$$

Also, A and B lie on the same isothermal

$$P_1V_1 = P_2V_2$$

or $$\frac{P_2}{P_1} = \frac{V_1}{V_2} \qquad ...(iv)$$

C and D lie on the same isothermal

$$P_3V_3 = P_4V_4$$

or $$\frac{P_3}{P_4} = \frac{V_4}{V_3} \qquad ...(v)$$

B and 0 lie on the same adiabatic

$$P_2V_2^{\gamma} = P_3V_3^{\gamma} \qquad ...(vi)$$

A and D lie on the same adiabatic

$$P_1V_1^{\gamma} = P_4V_4^{\gamma} \qquad ..(vi)$$

Dividing (vi) by (vii)

$$\left(\frac{P_2}{P_1}\right)\left(\frac{V_2}{V_1}\right)^{\gamma} = \left(\frac{P_3}{P_4}\right)\left(\frac{V_3}{V_4}\right)^{\gamma}$$

or $$\left(\frac{V_1}{V_2}\right)\left(\frac{V_2}{V_1}\right)^{\gamma} = \left(\frac{V_4}{V_3}\right)\left(\frac{V_3}{V_4}\right)^{\gamma}$$

$$\left(\frac{V_2}{V_1}\right)^{\gamma-1} = \left(\frac{V_3}{V_4}\right)^{\gamma-1}$$

or $$\frac{V_2}{V_1} = \frac{V_3}{V_4} \qquad ...(viii)$$

Substituting this value in equation (iii)

$$\frac{H_1}{H_3} = \frac{T_1}{T_2} \qquad ..(ix)$$

From the work scale of temperature,

$$\frac{H_1}{H_2} = \frac{\theta_1}{\theta_2} \qquad \text{...(x)}$$

$$\therefore \qquad \frac{\theta_1}{\theta_2} = \frac{T_1}{T_2} \qquad \text{...(xi)}$$

Special Considerations

(i) If θ_1 is zero, T_1 is also zero. It means the two scales are identical at absolute zero temperature.

(ii) Consider that the Carnot's engine works between the steam point and the ice point and there are 100 degrees between the ice point and the steam point on the two scales.

$$\frac{\theta_{steam}}{\theta_{ice}} = \frac{T_{steam}}{T_{ice}}$$

$$\frac{\theta_{ice} + 100}{\theta_{ice}} = \frac{T_{ece} + 100}{T_{ice}}$$

or $\qquad \theta_{ice} = T_{ice}$

Therefore, the ice point Is the same on the two scales.

Similarly $\theta_{steam} = T_{steam}$

Hence the two scales are completely identical.

Efficiency: The efficiency of a Carnot's engine,

$$\eta = 1 - \frac{H_2}{H_1}$$

$$= 1 - \frac{\theta_2}{\theta_1} = 1 - \frac{T_2}{T_1}$$

Let the adiabatic expansion ratio be ρ

$$\rho = \frac{V_3}{V_2}$$

The points B and C lie on the same adiabatic

$$\therefore \qquad T_1 V_2^{\gamma-1} = T_2 V_3^{\gamma-1}$$

$$\frac{T_2}{T_1} = \left(\frac{V_2}{V_3}\right)^{\gamma-1}$$

$$= \left(\frac{1}{\rho}\right)^{\gamma-1}$$

$$\eta = 1 - \frac{T_2}{T_1} = 1 - \left(\frac{1}{\rho}\right)^{\gamma-1}$$

INTERNAL COMBUSTION ENGINE (PETROL ENGINE)

It consists of a cylinder with an air-tight piston. It has two valves. I is the inlet valve and O is the outlet valve. The valves are opened and closed at the proper times with a suitable mechanism. The petrol vapours and air from the *carburettor* are admitted into the cylinder through the valve I. Here S acts as a sparking plug. It is also known as a four-stroke engine.

Working Stroke

A spark is produced at the sparking plug and the compressed mixture of petrol and air ignites. The temperature rises to about 2000°C and a high pressure of about 15 atmospheres is developed inside the cylinder. The piston is pushed down and the shaft rotates. Only in this stroke, work is done by the piston.

Exhaust Stroke

The outlet valve opens and the burnt and unburnt gases are exhausted out to the atmosphere.

The cycle repeats and the engine works.

Charging Stroke

The mixture of petrol vapours and air enters the cylinder. The piston moves down.

Compression Stroke

The inlet valve closes and the piston moves up. The mixture is compressed to a high pressure and the temperature rises to about 500°C.

Engine Cooling

The internal combustion engine requires cooling, although the efficiency of the engine will be higher without cooling. Temperatures of the order of 2000°C are reached inside the cylinder, although this temperature may last only for a very short interval of time before expansion. If the engine is not cooled the following drawbacks will be present:

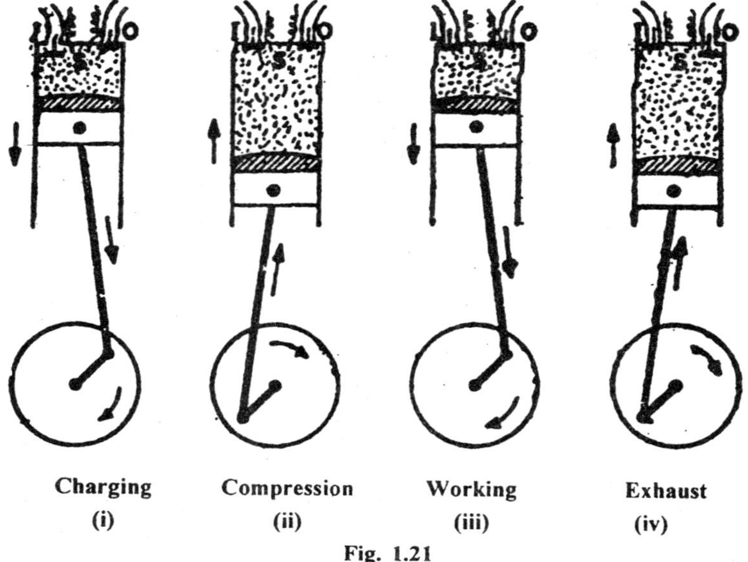

Charging (i) **Compression** (ii) **Working** (iii) **Exhaust** (iv)

Fig. 1.21

(1) Burning of the piston and exhaust valves.

(2) Irregular burning of the fuel.

(3) Seizure of the piston due to expansion.

(4) Burning of the lubricant, and

(5) Melting of the bearing material.

RANKINE CYCLE

In a steam engine, water is used as the working substance. Water is converted into steam in the boiler. The steam is super-heated above the boiling temperature. This superheated steam is introduced into the cylinder. For the first part, steam from the boiler enters the cylinder and moves the piston. The inlet valve remains open and the steam enters at a constant pressure. In the second part, the inlet valve closes and the steam expands adiabatically. The piston is moved through the rest of the working stroke. As soon as the piston reaches the end of *the stroke* the exhaust valve opens and the steam goes to the condenser. The steam gets condensed in the condenser.

This cycle of operations is known as the Rankine cycle, which is an ideal case. Its working is divided into the following parts:

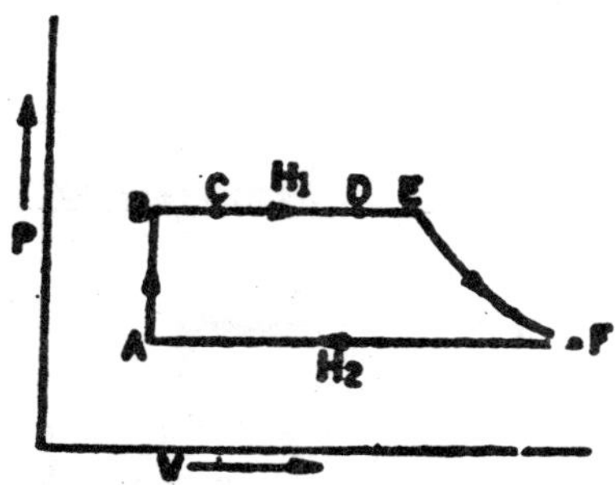

Fig. 1.22

1. A to B compression of water and the boiler pressure is reached.
2. B to C represents the heating of water in the boiler at constant pressure and the boiling point is reached.
3. C to D represents conversion of water into steam at constant pressure.
4. D to E represents superheating of steam beyond its boiling point.
5. E to f represents the adiabatic expansion of steam in doing external work. Steam is cooled and gets condensed.
6. F to A represents the rejection of steam to the condenser where the whole of the steam gets condensed. Finally, the point A is reached.

Efficiency: From B to E, the amount of heat absorbed is H_1 and from F to A, the amount of heat rejected is H_2.

$$\eta = 1 - \frac{H_2}{H_1}$$

STEAM ENGINE

It consists of a steam chest and a cylinder. These are connected by the steam ports P_1 and P_2. P is a piston that moves inside the cylinder. V is a sliding valve which can also move to and fro such that the port P_1 or P_2 is open to the steam chest. The piston and the sliding valve are connected to the main shaft eccentrically at diametrically opposite points such that when the shaft rotates they move in opposite directions. W is a flywheel attached to the main shaft. The coupling between the main rod and the piston roe is such that the linear motion of -the piston rod is converted to circular motion of the shaft. The machinery to be operated is connected to the main shaft.

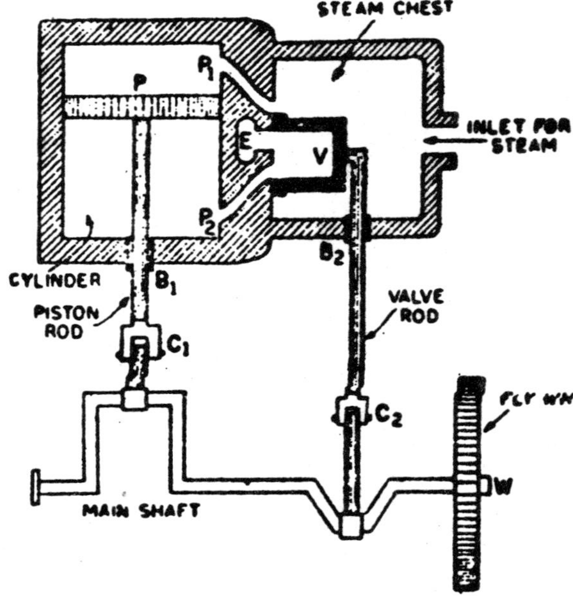

Fig. 1.23

Working

1. Steam at high pressure from the boiler enters the steam chest. The steam enters the cylinder through the port P_1. The piston P is pushed down due to the high pressure of steam (Fig. 1.18). The sliding valve moves up. Both the ports P_1 and P_2 are closed. The steam inside the cylinder expands and moves the piston further in the downward direction. At this position, the port P_1 is connected to the exhaust valve E and P_2 is opened.
2. When steam enters through the port P_3, the piston is pushed up and the sliding valve moves down.

The dead steam in the cylinder is exhausted out to the atmosphere through the exhaust valve E. Both the ports P_1 and P_2 are closed and the steam in the cylinder expands. The piston is pushed further to complete the stroke. Finally the port P_2 is closed and P_1 opens. The process is continuously repeated.

B_1 and B_2 are the stuffing boxes. These boxes allow for the free and smooth sliding of the valve rod and the piston rod. C_1 and C_2 are the cross heads. When the piston moves to and fro, the shaft is rotated and finally the machinery rotates.

Dead Centres

Twice in the rotation of the shaft, the force acts at right angles to the shaft. Theoretically a force does not produce any effect when it acts at right angles to the shaft. For this purpose *the flywheel* is used so that the momentum gained by the flywheel enables the shaft to rotate beyond the dead centre in each half rotation. Thus, the flywheel makes the motion of the shaft smooth and not jerky.

Power

Suppose the average pressure of steam = P newtons/metre^2. The length of the stroke = L metres and the area of cross section of the piston = A sq metres.

Total force on the piston = (PA) newtons.

Distance moved by the piston in a double acting steam engine = 2L

∴ Work done for one rotation of the shaft = (PA) × 2 L joules.

Let the shaft rotate N times per second.

Work done per second = (PA) × 2L × N watts

$$\therefore \text{ Power of the engine } = \frac{2PLAN}{1000} \text{ Kilowatts}$$

Efficiency

Most of the heat energy in the steam engine is wasted. Therefore, its efficiency is very low. It is of the order of 8 to 10%. Efficiency is the ratio of the useful mechanical work (W) done by the engine to the amount of heat (H) supplied by the fuel for the same time.

OTTO CYCLE

In the Otto engine (internal combustion engine), air is the working substance and petrol vapour acts as the fuel. A set of ideal conditions are assumed while discussing an Otto cycle:

1. The working substance is air all the time and it behaves as a perfect gas.

2. There is no friction.

On the basis of these assumptions, Otto cycle can be divided into the following operations:

1. E to A (Fig. 1.24) represents the *charging stroke*. The mixture of air and petrol vapour is allowed to enter at atmospheric pressure. The final volume is V_2 at temperature T_1.

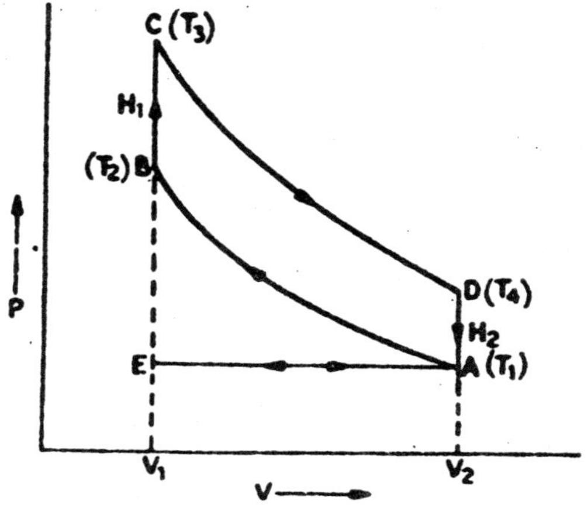

Fig. 1.24

2. A to S represents the *adiabatic compression*. There is no friction and no flow of heat through the walls of the cylinder. The volume changes from V_2 to V_1 and the temperature changes from T_1 to T_2.

   There is change in pressure also. This represents the *compression, stroke*. The compression ratio is nearly 8 *i.e.*, $V_2/V_1 = 8$ nearly. The pressure changes from one atmosphere to about 18 atmospheres.

3. B to G represents the *ignition stage*. A spark is produced and the mixture of air and petrol vapour is ignited. The pressure increases from 18 to about 80 atmospheres and the temperature changes from T_2 to T_3 (from 500°C to 2000°C).

4. C to D represents the *working stroke*. The gas expands adiabatically and the engine works. The volume changes from V_1 to V_2. The pressure and temperature decrease.

5. As the point D is reached, the exhaust valve opens. D to A represents the change of pressure to the atmospheric pressure and the temperature changes from T_4 to T_1.

6. A to E represents the *exhaust stroke*. The exhaust gases are completely discharged from the cylinder. Thus, the initial condition of the engine is restored.

Efficiency : Consider that 1 gram of the working substance is used in the process. A quantity of heat H_1 at a higher temperature is absorbed from B to C,

$$H_1 = 1 \times C_v (T_3 - T_2)$$

A quantity of heat Hy is rejected at^ lower temperature from D to A

$$H_2 = 1 \times C_v (T_4 - T_1)$$

$$\frac{H_2}{H_1} = \frac{T_4 - T_1}{T_3 - T_2} \qquad \text{...(i)}$$

$$\eta = 1 - \frac{H_2}{H_1}$$

$$= 1 - \frac{T_4 - T_1}{T_3 - T_2} \qquad \text{...(ii)}$$

The points D and C lie on the same adiabatic

$$\therefore \quad T_4 V_2^{\gamma-1} = T_3 V_1^{\gamma-1} \qquad \text{...(iii)}$$

The points A and B lie on the same adiabatic

$$T_1 V_2^{\gamma-1} = T_2 V_1^{\gamma-1} \qquad \text{...(iv)}$$

Subtracting (iv) from (iii),

$$(T_4 - T_1) V_2^{\gamma-1} = (T_3 - T_2) V_1^{\gamma-1}$$

$$\frac{T_4 - T_1}{T_2 - T_2} = \left(\frac{V_1}{V_2}\right)^{\gamma-1} \qquad \text{...(v)}$$

Substituting this value in equation (ii),

$$\eta = 1 - \left(\frac{V_1}{V_2}\right)^{\gamma-1}$$

$$= 1 - \left(\frac{1}{(V_2/V_1)}\right)^{\gamma-1}$$

$$\eta = 1 - \left(\frac{1}{\rho}\right)^{\gamma - 1} \qquad ...(vi)$$

where, ρ is the adiabatic compression ratio.

In an actual petrol engine p cannot be made greater than 10. If ρ is more than 10, the mixture gets ignited by itself due to compression much before the sparking takes place.

$$\eta = 1 - \left(\frac{1}{\rho}\right)^{\gamma - 1}$$

If $\rho = 6$ and $\gamma = 1.4$

$$\eta = 1 - \left(\frac{1}{6}\right)^{0.4}$$

$$= 0.5116 = 51.16\%$$

If $\rho = 9$ and $\gamma = 1.4$

$$\eta = 1 - \left(\frac{1}{9}\right)^{0.4} = 0.5847 = 58.47\%$$

DIESEL ENGINE

In the case of a diesel engine, air is admitted into the cylinder in the beginning. This air is compressed adiabatically so that the temperature is high enough to ignite the oil sprayed into the cylinder. The ideal conditions are assumed while discussing the complete cycle *viz.* :

(i) the working substance is air all the time and it behaves as a perfect gas, and

(ii) there is no friction. The cycle is called the *diesel cycle.*

1. E to A (Fig. 1.25) represents the intake of air and its volume changes to V_1 This is the *charging stroke.*
2. A to B represents the *compression stroke.* Air is compressed adiabatically. The temperature changes from T_1 to T_2 and the volume changes from V_1 to V_2. The temperature riles to about 1000°C and the pressure to about 40 atmospheres.
3. S to 0 represents the stage when the oil is sprayed into the cylinder. The oil burns immediately. The pressure is maintained constant. The temperature changes from T_2 to T_3 (to 2000°C) and the volume changes from V_2 to V_3.

4. C to D represents the *working stroke*. The mixture of air and diesel oil vapour expand adiabatically.

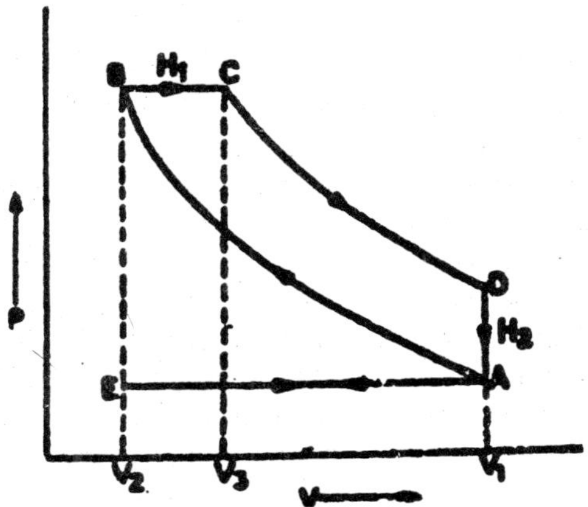

Fig. 1.25

5. As the point D is reached, the exhaust valve opens and the pressure drops to the point A. The volume remains constant but temperature and pressure decrease.

6. A to E represents the *exhaust stroke*. The unburnt vapours of the oil and the mixture of gases in the cylinder are exhausted out of the cylinder.

Efficiency: From B to C, the pressure remains constant. Considering 1 gram of the working substance, the quantity of heat absorbed,

$$H_1 = 1 \times C_P (T_3 - T_2)$$

From D to A the volume remains constant.

The quantity of heat rejected,

$$H_2 = 1 \times C_V (T_4 - T_1)$$

$$\frac{H_2}{H_1} = \frac{C_V}{C_P} \cdot \frac{(T_4 - T_1)}{(T_3 - T_2)}$$

$$= \frac{1}{\gamma} \cdot \frac{T_4 - T_1}{T_3 - T_2}$$

$$\eta = 1 - \frac{H_2}{H_1}$$

$$= 1 - \frac{1}{\gamma}\left(\frac{T_4 - T_1}{T_3 - T_2}\right) \qquad ...(1)$$

To evaluate $\left(\frac{T_4 - T_1}{T_3 - T_2}\right)$, all the temperatures are to be expressed in terms of T_2.

Let ρ be the adiabatic expansion ratio. Then $\rho = V_1/V_2$ and e the combustion expansion ratio or fuel cut off ratio $= V_3/V_2$.

(1) The points A and 5 are on the same adiabatic,

$$\therefore \quad T_1V_1^{\gamma-1} = T_2V_2^{\gamma-1}$$

$$T_1 = T_2\left[\frac{V_2}{V_1}\right]^{\gamma-1}$$

$$= T_2\left[\frac{1}{\rho}\right]^{\gamma-1} \qquad ...(2)$$

(2) The points B and C are at the same pressure

$$\therefore \quad \frac{T_3}{V_3} = \frac{T_2}{V_2}$$

or
$$T_3 = T_2\left[\frac{V_3}{V_2}\right] = T_2\,[e] \qquad ...(3)$$

(3) The points C and D are on the same adiabatic.

$$\therefore \quad T_4V_4^{\gamma-1} = T_3V_3^{\gamma-1} \quad [\text{But } V_4 = V_1]$$

$$T_4 = T_3\left[\frac{V_3}{V_1}\right]^{\gamma-1}$$

$$= T_3\left[\frac{V_3}{V_2}\times\frac{V_2}{V_1}\right]^{\gamma-1}$$

$$T_4 = T_3\left[\frac{V_3}{V_2}\right]^{\gamma-1}\left[\frac{V_2}{V_1}\right]^{\gamma-1}$$

$$T_4 = T_3 [e]^{\gamma-1} \left[\frac{1}{\rho}\right]^{\gamma-1}$$

$$T_4 = T_2 [e] [e]^{\gamma-1} \left[\frac{1}{\rho}\right]^{\gamma-1}$$

$$T_4 = T_2 [e]^{\gamma} \left[\frac{1}{\rho}\right]^{\gamma-1} \quad ...(4)$$

$$\eta = 1 - \left[\frac{T_4 - T_1}{T_3 - T_2}\right]$$

$$= 1 - \frac{1}{\gamma}\left[\frac{T_2 [e]^{\gamma} \left[\frac{1}{p}\right]^{\gamma-1} - T_2 \left[\frac{1}{p}\right]^{\gamma-1}}{T_3 [e] - T_2}\right]$$

$$\eta = 1 - \frac{1}{\gamma}\left(\frac{1}{\rho}\right)^{\gamma-1} \left[\frac{e^{\gamma-1}}{e-1}\right] \quad ...(5)$$

For the same compression ratio, the efficiency of an Otto engine is more than a diesel engine. In practice, the compression ratio for an Otto engine is from 7 to 9 and for a diesel engine it is from 15 to 20. Due tot he higher compression ratio, an actual diesel engine has higher efficiency than the Otto (Petrol) engine. The cylinder must be strong enough to withstand very high pressure.

MULTICYLINDER ENGINES

An engine having one cylinder, the engine works only during the working stroke. The piston moves during the rest of the three strokes due to the momentum of the shaft. In a multicylinder engine the four cylinders are coupled. In this way, the power of the engine increases and the shaft gets momentum during each quarter cycle.

CLAPEYRON LATENT HEAT EQUATION

Consider the isothermals FBAE at temperature T + dT and GCDH at temperature T. Here EA and HD show the liquid state of the substance. At A to B or D to C the substance is in transition from the liquid to the gaseous state and *vice versa.* At B and C the substance is purely in the gaseous state. From B to F or C to G the substance is in the gaseous state. Join A to D and B to C by dotted lines.

The cycle ABCD represents a complete cycle and Carnot's theorem can be applied. Suppose the volume at the point A is V_1 and temperature is T = dT. The pressure is just below its saturation pressure and the liquid begins to evaporate and at the point B the volume is V_2. The substance is in the vapour state. Suppose the mass of the liquid at B is one gram. The amount of heat absorbed is H_1, Here $H_1 = L + dL$, where L + dL is the latent heat of the liquid at temperature (T + dT).

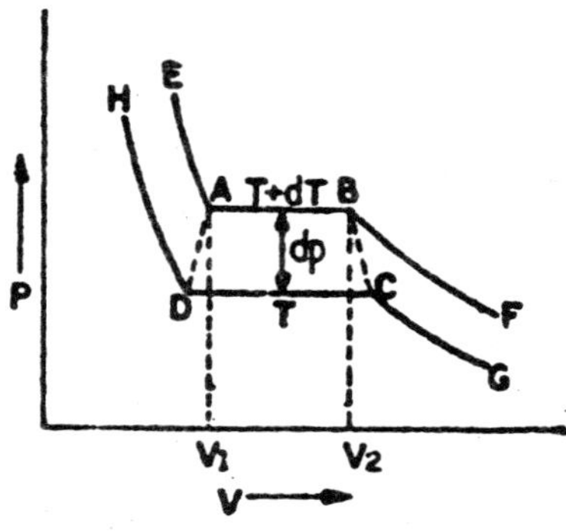

Fig. 1.26

Fig 1.26 represented the point B, the pressure is decreased by dP. The vapour will expand and its temperature falls. The temperature at C is T. As this pressure and temperature T, the gas begins to condense and is converted into the liquid state. At the point D, the substance is in the liquid state. From C to D, the amount of heat rejected (given out) is H_2 Here $H_2 = L$ where L is the latent heat at temperature T. By increasing the pressure a little, the original point A is restored. The cycle ABCDA is completely reversible. Applying the principle of the Carnot's reversible cycle

$$\frac{H_1}{T_1} = \frac{H_2}{T_2}$$

or $$\frac{H_1}{H_2} = \frac{T_1}{T_2}$$

$$\frac{H_1 - H_2}{H_2} = \frac{T_1 - T_2}{T_2}$$

Here, $H_1 = L + dL, \; H_2 = L$

$T_1 = T + dT, \; T_2 = T$

$H_1 - H_2 = L + dL - L = dL$

$T_1 - T_2 = T + dT - T = dT$

$$\therefore \quad \frac{dL}{L} = \frac{dT}{T}$$

The area of the figure

$$ABCD = H_1 - H_2 = dL$$

$$= dP(V_2 - V_1)$$

$$\therefore \quad \frac{dP\,(V_2 - V_1)}{L} = \frac{dT}{T}$$

$$\frac{dP}{dT} = \frac{L}{T\,(V_2 - V_1)} \qquad ...(i)$$

This is called the Clapeyron's latent heat equation.

Applications: (1) *Effect of change of pressure on the melting point.*

When a solid is converted into a liquid, there is change in volume.

(i) If V_2 is greater than V_1

dP/dT is a positive quantity. It means that the rate of change of pressure with respect to temperature is positive. In such cases, the melting point of the substance will increase with increase in pressure and vice versa.

(ii) If V_2 is less than V_1.

dP/dT is a negative quantity. It means that the rate of change of pressure with respect to temperature is negative. In such cases, the melting point of the substance will decrease with increase in pressure and *vice versa*. In the case of melting ice, the volume of water formed is less than the volume of ice taken. Hence $V_2 < V_1$.

Therefore, the melting point of ice decreases with increase in pressure. 'Hence ice will melt at a temperature lower than zero degree centigrade at a pressure higher than the normal pressure.

Ice melts at 0°C only at a pressure of 76 cm of Hg.

(2) *Effect of change of pressure on the boiling point.*

When a liquid is converted into a gaseous state, the volume V_2 of the gas is always greater than the corresponding volume V_1 of the liquid *i.e.* $V_2 > V_1$.

Therefore, dP/dT is a +ve quantity.

With increase in pressure, the boiling point of a substance increases and *vice versa*. The liquid will boil at a lower temperature under reduced pressure. In the case of water, the boiling point increases with increase in pressure and vice- versa. Water boils at 100°C only at 76 cm of Hg pressure. In the laboratories, while preparing steam, the boiling point is less than 100°C because the atmospheric pressure is less than 76 cm of Hg. In pressure cookers, the liquid boils at a higher temperature because the pressure inside is more than the atmospheric pressure.

THERMIONIC EMISSION

The electrical conductivity of metals is due to the free electrons present in the metal and not attached to any particular molecule. These free electrons continuously move within the metal and the velocity of the electrons increases with the increase in temperature of the metal. These electrons exert a pressure similar to that of a gas. However, the electrons cannot escape to the outer space because of the attractive forces at the surface that tend to keep the electrons within the metal. The attractive forces are much greater than the *electron gas pressure*. In order to escape from the surface, an electron has to do a certain amount of work called the work function (ϕ) of the surface and this is different for different metals. This energy is obtained from the kinetic energy of the electrons. At Ordinary temperatures the kinetic energy of the electrons is much less than the work function and hence the electrons cannot escape from the surface. With the increase in temperature of the metal surface, the kinetic energy of the electrons increases and if the kinetic energy exceeds the work function, electrons can escape from the surface of the metal. This phenomenon is called *thermionic* emission and the electrons are called *thermo-electrons* or *thermions*. The thermionic current (I) is given by the equation

$$I = AT^{e}e^{-\frac{\phi_0}{kT}}$$

where A is a constant, T is the absolute temperature of the metal, ϕ_0 is the work function of the surface at zero degree K and k is the Boltzmann's constant. I measures the thermionic current in amperes per sq cm of the emitting surface. The most commonly used emitters are *(i) tungsten (ii) thoriated tungsten and (iii) oxide coated cathodes containing barium or strontium.*

ENTROPY

A thermodynamic systems needed one more physical variable in addition to pressure?, volume V, temperature T and internal energy U, to describe completely its state. This entity, the entropy, had also a fixed value for a thermodynamic system. He showed (in 1854) that there is an integrating factor which when multiplied with δQ, gives a perfect differential, provided the change in the state of the system takes place along a reversible path. This integrating factor is the reciprocal of the thermodynamic temperature T. Thus δQ/T is a perfect differential and its integral is a state variable or a thermodynamic coordinate and is denoted by S.

It is an extensive variable (depending on n, the number of moles of the substance present) and forms a pair with T (just like V forms a pair with P). In other words the entropy is the extensive counterpart of the intensive variable, the temperature. It will be recalled that the quantity of heat absorbed or given out by a body or a system does not depend merely on its initial and final state but also on the manner in which it has passed from its initial state to final state (*i.e.*, on the path along which it passed). Whence the quantity of heat exchanged during a small step in the process is not a perfect differential hence it is to be represented by δQ (not δQ). But the differential δQ/T gives the change in the entropy, dS of a homogeneous system and is a point function. The product TdS has .the dimensions of energy and it measures the quantity of heat given to the body, (or system) at temperature Tin a quasi-static reversible process, to bring about the change in dS, in the entropy of the system.

Now, although this new quantity entropy is quite as real a physical quantity as volume, pressure and temperature yet it has something intangible about it, for there is nothing physical to represent it. It has therefore been called a ghostly quantity. But as some one has rightly remarked, 'the more shadowy the conception to be visualised, the greater the need of a material anology'. Looking, therefore for a suitable analogy, the nearest to it, we can think of is mass or inertia. We can therefore imagine entropy to be thermal inertia, which bears a relation to heat motion similar to the one that mass and moment of inertia bear to translatory and rotatory motion respectively. The meaning and significance of the term entropy will become increasingly clearer as we proceed along. Consider adiabatics L and M on the P — V indicator diagram (Fig. 1.27). All along the adiabatic L, with change in pressure there is change in volume and temperature. This shows that all along the adiabatics L or M, there is change of temperature. Consider the isothermals at temperatures T_1, T_2 and T_3. ABCD represents the Carnot's reversible cycle. From A to B, heat energy H_1 is absorbed at temperature T_1. From C to D, heat energy H_2 is rejected at temperature T_2.

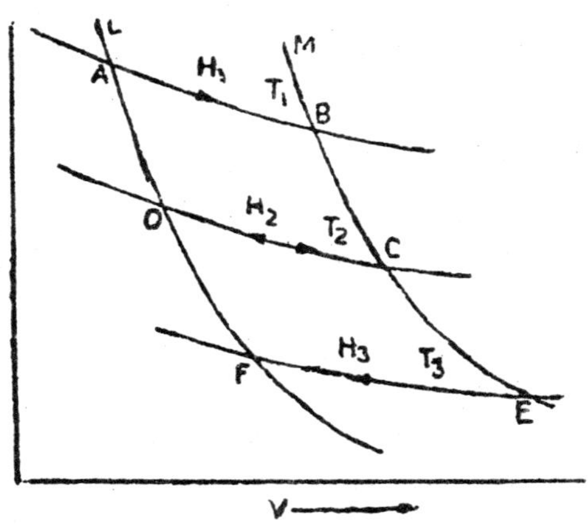

Fig. 1.27

$$\frac{H_1}{T_1} = \frac{H_2}{T_2}$$

Similarly considering the cycle DCEF

$$\frac{H_2}{T_2} = \frac{H_3}{T_3}$$

$$\therefore \quad \frac{H_1}{T_1} = \frac{H_2}{T_2} = \frac{H_3}{T_3} = \text{constant}$$

From one adiabatic to the other adiabatic, heat energy is either absorbed or rejected. The quantity of heat absorbed or rejected is not constant but it depends upon the temperature.

Higher the temperature, more is the heat energy absorbed or rejected and *vice versa*.

The quantity H/T between two adiabatics is constant and this is called the change in entropy. Let the entropy for the adiabatics L and M be S_1 and S_2 respectively.

Here S_1 and S_2 are arbitrary quantities.

$$S_2 - S_2 = \frac{H}{T} \text{ constant}$$

If the adiabatics are very close, and the heat absorbed or rejected is δH at a temperature T,

Change in entropy

$$dS = \frac{\delta H}{T} \qquad ...(1)$$

In general, the change in entropy

$$= \int_{S_1}^{S_2} dS = S_2 - S_1 = \int_A^B \frac{\delta H}{T} \qquad ...(2)$$

$\int_A^B \frac{\delta H}{T} = \int_{S_1}^{S_2} dS$ represents the thermodynamic co-ordinate of a system. This integral refers to the value of the function at the final state minus its value at the initial state. This function is called entropy and is represented by S. Moreover, dS is an exact differential since it is the differential of an actual function.

All along the adiabatic, $\delta H = 0$. Therefore, the change in entropy along an adiabatic is zero or the entropy all along the adiabatic is constant. *Thus entropy remains constant during an adiabatic reversible process. When heat is absorbed during a process there is increase in entropy and when heat is rejected during a process there is decrease in entropy.*

ENTROPY CHANGE IN A REVERSIBLE PROCESS (CARNOT'S CYCLE)

Consider a complete reversible process from A to B, heat energy H_1 is absorbed by the working substance at temperature T_1. The gain in entropy of the working substance from A to B = H_1/T_1. (H_1/T_1 is the decrease in entropy of the source from which the amount of heat H_1 is drawn at a temperature T_1). From B to C there is no change in entropy because BC is an adiabatic. From C to D, heat energy H_2 is rejected by the working substance at a temperature T_2. The loss in entropy of the working substance from C to D = H_2/T_2. (H_2/T_2 is also the gain in entropy of the sink to which the amount of heat H_2 is rejected at a temperature T_2). From D to A there is no change in entropy. Thus the total gain in entropy by the working substance in the cycle.

$$= \frac{H_1}{T_1}\frac{H_2}{T_2}$$

But for a complete reversible process

$$\frac{H_1}{T_1} = \frac{H_2}{T_2}$$

Hence the total change in entropy of the working substance in a complete reversible process

$$= \oint dS = \frac{H_1}{T_1} - \frac{H_1}{T_2} = 0$$

ENTROPY CHANGE IN AN IRREVERSIBLE PROCESS

In an irreversible process like conduction or radiation, heat is lost by a body at a higher temperature T_1 and is gained by the body at a lower temperature T_2. Here T_1 is greater than T_2.

Let the quantity of heat given out by a body at a temperature T_1 be B and the heat gained by the body at a temperature T_2 be B. Consider the hot and the cold bodies as one system.

Loss in entropy of the hot body $= H/T_1$

Gain in entropy of the cold body $= H/T_2$

Therefore, the total increase in entropy of the system

$$= \frac{H}{T_2} - \frac{H}{T_1}$$

It is a positive quantity because T_2 is less than T_1. Thus the entropy of the system increases in all irreversible processes.

ENTROPY AND ADIABATICS

Let A_1 and A_2 be two adiabatics on a P–V. Then, as we know, there is a regular change of temperature (accompanied by change in pressure and volume) along them. Let the isothermals AB, CD, EF correspond to temperatures T_1, T_2, T_3...respectively be drawn across the two adiabatics as shown. Now we have four sided figures ABDC, CDFE etc.) each representing a Carnot cycle operating between temperatures T_1, T_2; T_2,

T_3, etc. Consider first cycle ABDC If Q_1 be the quantity of heat absorbed at temperature T_1 along the isothermal AB and Q_2, the quantity of heat rejected at temperature T_2 along the isothermal DC we have

$$\frac{Q_1}{T_1} = \frac{Q_2}{T_2}$$

Similarly, considering another cycle CDFE, the quantity of heat absorbed at temperature T_1 along the isothermal CD is Q_2 and the quantity of heal rejected at temperature T_3 along the isothermal FE be Q_3, we have

$$\frac{Q_2}{T_2} = \frac{Q_3}{T_3}$$

and for vet another cycle

$$\frac{Q_3}{T_3} = \frac{Q_4}{T_4} \text{ etc.}$$

These equations read together suggest

$$\frac{Q_1}{T_1} = \frac{Q_2}{T_2} = \frac{Q_3}{T_3} = \frac{Q}{T} = \text{constant}$$

This shows that the quantity Q/T remains constant during transition between the two adiabatics along any one of the isothermals chosen. Here, as we have seen, Q is the quantity of heat absorbed or rejected at temperature T corresponding to that isothermal. Now if the adiabatics are close enough, so that the heat absorbed or liberated at temperature T of the isothermal, be δQ then $dS = \delta Q/T$ is change in entropy. It follows, therefore, that the change in entropy $S_2 - S_1$, during a finite change from the state of the system represented by A to that represented by B is

$$S_2 - S_1 = \int_A^B \delta Q/T = \int_{S_1}^{S_2} dS$$

Since during an adiabatic process, beat is neither allowed to enter not leave the system, $\delta Q = 0$ therefore the change in entropy $\delta Q/T = 0$. In other words, there is no change in entropy during an adiabatic process, *i.e.*, the entropy of a system remains constant during an adiabatic process. That is why adiabatic curves are called the isentropics or the curves of constant entropy. In the equation for entropy we have one more term the temperature. This temperature identifies the rank of an isothermal. Similarly the entropy itself identifies the rank of an adiabatic.

Definition of Entropy : In the above discussion we have considered the transition from one adiabatic to another (or from state A to state B) along an isothermal. This was, however, not necessary. All that is needed is that the change should occur along a reversible path. So let us consider that the change occurs along a reversible path AB as shown in (Fig. 1.31) where AB is not an isothermal.

Entropy is measured in joules K^{-1} and the specific entropy is measured in joules kg K^{-1}.

SOME PHYSICAL ANALOGIES OF ENTROPY

Entropy has been regarded as a function defined by an equation whence a mathematician may feel quite at home with it: But the physicist finds the conception of entropy difficult to grasp because of its intangible character. We therefore consider some analogies for this ghostly quantity for understanding its thermal manifestation. (Note—be always careful not to pursue analogies too far). Now from definition

$$dS \equiv \frac{\text{heat energy}}{\text{temperaturre}}$$

$$\therefore \text{heat energy} \equiv dS \times \text{temperature.}$$

Now compare it with

$$\text{potential energy} \equiv Mg \times h$$

$$\text{Kinetic energy} \equiv \frac{P}{2m} \times P$$

$$\text{electrical energy} \equiv C \times V$$

$$\text{thermal energy} \equiv 1/2k \times T$$

$$\text{rotational energy} \equiv 1/2I \times \omega^2$$

The quantity that follows after × is easily measurable and increase/decrease in its value gives the change in the energy level *i.e.*, h, ω, ς etc. may be taken to be level (potential) for the energy and first quantity, namely M, I may be similar to entropy. A.M. Worthington and S.G. Wheeler employed rotational motion in illustration of the properties of entropy, where rotational inertia I was not necessarily constant. It depends on arrangement of the masses. Entropy, for the purpose of analogy, was assumed to be the thermal inertia of a system. They associated it with all kinds of motion of particles of the system which measured the level of disorder.

CHANGE OF ENTROPY IN A CARNOT CYCLE

A carnot cycle consists of two isothermals and two adiabatics all of which are reversible. During the two adiabatic processes there is no change in entropy. So, changes in entropy occur only during the two isothermal processes of these, one is an isothermal expansion during which heat Q_1 is absorbed at constant temperature T_1 and the gain in entropy is therefore Q_1/T_1. The other is an isothermal compression, during which heat Q_2 is given out at a constant temperature T_2 and so the loss in entropy is Q_2/T_2. Now, since in a Carnot cycle, $Q_1/T_1 = Q_2/T_2$, it follows that the gain in entropy is equal to the loss in entropy. So the change in entropy through the cycle is zero. Mathematically,

Let us draw any arbitrary isothermal I → I' corresponding to a temperature T^1 across the two adiabatics and consider A B to be made up of a number of elements of isothermal and adiabatic curves, alternating with each other, as shown by the dotted zig-zag line. Like: ab—a small element of an isothermal curve, ab—a small element of an adiabatic curve and so on. Thus, the whole transition along AB may be supposed to be made of small transitions along these elements of isothermal and adiabatic curves.

If we produce the elementary adiabatic curves to meet the isothermal I → I', we have a number of elementary Carnot cycles like abb^1a^1, cdc^1d^1 etc. If, therefore, δQ be the quantity of heat absorbed along the isothermal ab at temperature T and δQ^1 be the quantity of heat rejected along with isothermal b^1a^1 at temperature T^1 we have $\delta Q/T = \delta Q^1/T^1$. In the limit, when Carnot cycles become infinitely small the zig-zag curve coincides with the reversible path AB and we have

$$\int_A^B \delta Q/T = \int \delta Q^1/T^1$$

Since $\delta Q^1/T^1$ represents the change in entropy between the two adiabatics A_1 and A_2 through A and B respectively, along the isothermal I → I'. It must be a constant.

$$\therefore \quad \int_A^B \delta Q/T = \text{constant}$$

i.e., the change in entropy in passing from a state A to a state B is constant irrespective of the reversible path along which the change takes place. As we have seen here, the change in entropy of a system when it passes from one state A to another state B depends upon its initial and final states only and is quite independent of the manner in which the change is brought about. This is exactly the property of an actual function of state.

Hence $\delta Q/T$ is a function of the thermodynamic coordinates or state variables of the point and 5 and its integral defines the change in entropy of the system during transition from state A to state B.

If the state A be arbitrarily chosen as the zero state of entropy, S2-S1 gives the entropy S of the system in state B relative to the arbitrarily chosen zero entropy state A.

We may thus define entropy as a single valued function of the parameters of the state (like pressure, volume) for all those states that can be reached by a reversible process from some arbitrarily chosen initial zero state.

Since we are, in general, concerned only with changes of entropy from one state to another, we need hardly bother about the standard zero state of entropy. Quite often, however, the entropy of a substance at NTP is taken to be zero.

$$\frac{Q_1}{T_1} = -\frac{Q_2}{T_2} \text{ or, } \frac{Q_1}{T_1} + \frac{Q_2}{T_2} = 0$$

for the whole cycle (negative sign indicates loss of entropy).

Thus, during a Carnot cycle, the entropy of a system remains unchanged.

CHANGE OF ENTROPY IN ANY REVERSIBLE CYCLE

The results obtained above for a Carnot cycle can be shown to be true for any reversible cycle by a method first suggested by Clausius.

Consider a reversible cycle, the indicator diagram for which is a closed curve ABCD (Fig 1.28). This may be divided into a number of Carnot cycles by drawing across the cycle a series of adiabatics A_1, A_2, A3,...close together with short isothermals ab, cd,..,.a^1b^1 introduced between them as shown. Then clearly each such

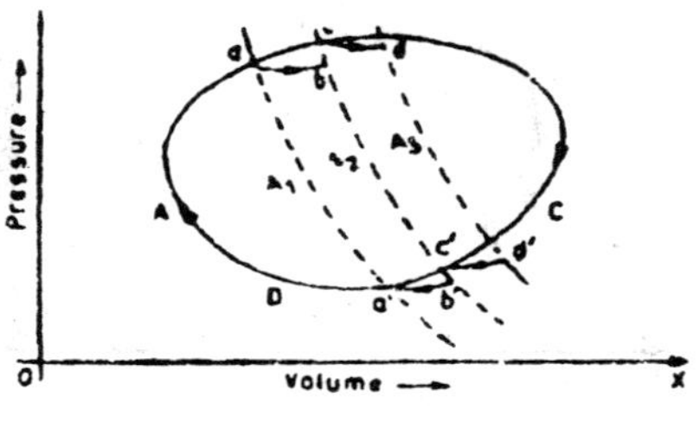

Fig. 1.28

elementary Carnot cycle formed like abb^1a^1,cdd^1c^1,...is bounded by two adiabatics and two isothermals. So that, for each one of these cycles

$$\frac{\delta Q_1 i}{T_{1i}} + \frac{\delta Q_{2i}}{T_{2i}} = 0$$

where δQ_{1i} is the heat absorbed at temperature T_{1i}, δQ_{2i} is the heat rejected at temperature T_{2i}, etc.

Summing up these results for all the elementary cycles we have

$$\sum_i \left(\frac{\delta Q_{1i}}{T_{1i}} + \frac{\delta Q_{2i}}{T_{2i}} \right) = 0$$

or, if the elementary cycles be infinitely small

$$\oint \frac{\delta Q}{T} = 0 \oint dS$$

This is known as *Clausius theorem*. It states that the charge in entropy for a complete reversible thermodynamic cycle is zero.

Corollary : We may use the above result for a reversible cycle to prove that "the entropy of a system depends upon its state only and is quite independent of the manner in which this state has been arrived at." For if the system (or the substance) be taken by a reversible path ACB, from the state represented by A to that represented by B. Clearly, difference between the entropies of the system at A and at B (or the change in entropy of the system in going from A to B) in (Fig 1.29) is

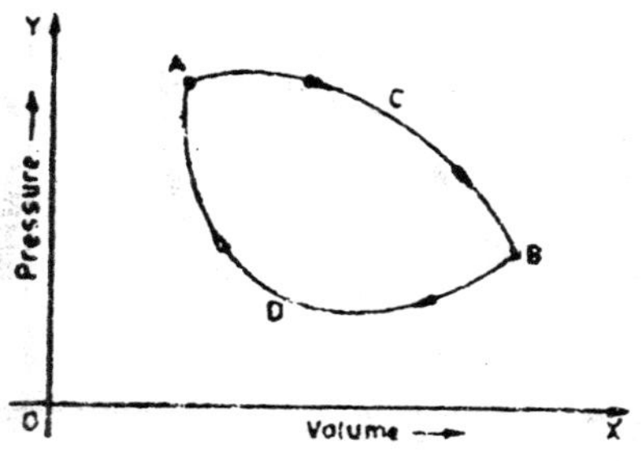

Fig. 1.29

$$\int_A^B \frac{\delta Q}{T} = \int_{S_A}^{S_B} dS = S_B - S_A$$

where S_A and S_B are the entropies of the system at A and B respectively.

If now the system be supposed to come back to its original state represented by A, along the path BDA, it will assume its original entropy and so the change in its entropy will be zero, *i.e.* change in entropy from A to B along ACB + change in entropy from B to A along BDA = 0, taking proper care of the signs. It follows, therefore, that the change in entropy of the system when taken from the state represented by A to other state represented by B is the same whether the path followed is ACB, ADB or any other. To state the same thing differently, we may say that all processes leading from a state A to a state B result in the same change in entropy—Entropy of the system is thus a point function on an indicator diagram. The entropy may be considered as an outcome of the second law of thermodynamics—a new but equally good function of state. It touches the aspect of arrangement of particles and their motions (randomness) on the body. In fact the second law of thermodynamics suggests that an ordered state tends to become disordered. "The direction which a self-sustained machine follows is that in which disorder increases."

CALCULATION OF CHANGE IN ENTROPY ALONG AN IRREVERSIBLE PATH

It has been emphasised severally that the above results apply only to a reversible process and not to an irreversible one. The expression $\int \delta Q/T$ may not give, therefore, the change in entropy in general. How then, is it possible to calculate a change in entropy if the change of state from A to B is brought about by an irreversible process? The corollary of section 9.6 gives us a clue:

We simply find some reversible process to bring the substance from state A to slate B. For this process, the change in entropy is given by $\int \delta Q/T$ and may be easily calculated. Now, since the change in entropy depends only on the initial and final states of the system, and not upon the manner of change, then entropy-change, from A to B by the irreversible process too must be the same as by the reversible process. This then, calculated as above, gives the entropy-change for the irreversible process.

Let us consider (Fig 1.30). Let the initial state of the system be A and the system follows the path AEB to attain the final state B. Furhter, let AEB be a non-reversible path. If we are to find SB-SA we may draw reversible isothermal AC and a reversible adiabetic BCN through A and B respectively. Then if the two meet at C we have, clearly, no change in entropy along BCN. Hence $S_B - S_A$ is simply $S_C - S_A$ along the reversible isothermal AC, which is given by Q/T.

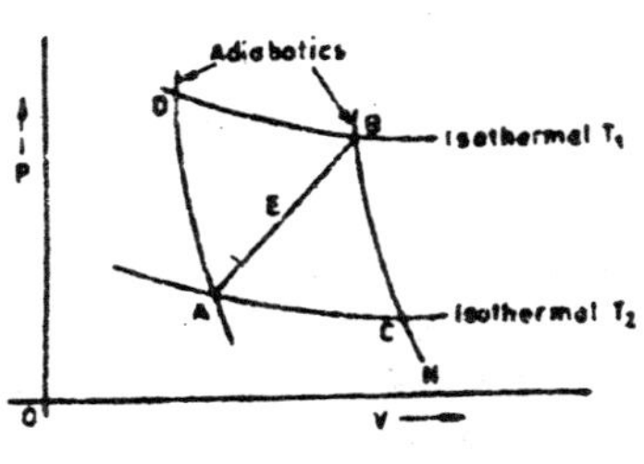

Fig. 1.30

ENTROPY OF PERFECT GAS

Consider one gram of a perfect gas at a pressure P_1 volume V and temperature T. Let the quantity of heat given to the gas be δH

$$\delta H = dU + \delta W$$

$$\delta H + 1 \times C_V \times dT + PdV/J \quad \text{...(i)}$$

$$\delta B = TdS$$

$$\therefore \quad TdS = C_V dT + PdV/J \quad \text{...(ii)}$$

Also $\quad PV = rT$

or $\quad P = \frac{rT}{V}$

$$\therefore \quad TdS = C_V dT + \frac{rT.dV}{JV}$$

$$dS = C_V \frac{dT}{T} + \frac{r}{J}\frac{dV}{V}$$

Integrating, $\int_{S_1}^{S_2} dS = C_V \int_{T_1}^{T_2} \frac{dT}{T} + \frac{r}{J}\int_{V_1}^{V_2} \frac{dV}{V}$

$$S_2 - S_1 = C_V \log_e \frac{T_2}{T_1} + \frac{r}{T} \log_e \frac{V_2}{V_1} \quad \text{...(iii)}$$

$$S_2 - S_1 = C_V \times 2.3026 \log_{10} \frac{T_2}{T_1} + \frac{r}{T} \times 2.3026 \log_{10} V_2/V_1 \quad \text{...(iv)}$$

The change in entropy can be calculated in terms of pressure also.

$$PV = rT$$

Differentiating

$$PdV + VdP = rdT$$

or $\quad PdV = rdT - VdP$

Substituting the value of PdV in equation (ii)

$$TdS = C_V \times dT + \frac{rdT}{J} - \frac{VdP}{J}$$

$$TdS = \left(C_V + \frac{r}{J}\right) dT - \frac{VdP}{J}$$

But $\quad C_V + \frac{r}{J} = C_P$

$$\therefore \quad dS = C_P \frac{dT}{T} - \frac{VdP}{JT}$$

Also $\quad PV = rT$

or $$\frac{V}{T} = \frac{r}{T}$$

$$\therefore \quad dS = C_P \frac{dT}{T} - \frac{r}{J}\frac{dP}{P}$$

Integrating

$$\int_{S_1}^{S_2} dS = C_P \int_{T_1}^{T_2} \frac{dT}{T} - \frac{r}{J}\int_{P_1}^{P_2} \frac{dP}{P}$$

$$S_2 - S_1 = C_P \log_e \frac{T_2}{T_1} - \frac{r}{T} \log_e \frac{P_2}{P_1} \quad ...(v)$$

$$S_2 - S_1 = C_P \times 2.3026 \times \log_{10} \frac{T_2}{T_1} - \frac{r}{T} \times 2.3026 \log_{10} \frac{P_2}{P_1} \quad ...(vi)$$

Note : r is the ordinary gas constant and has to be taken in units of work, C_P represents the specific beat for I gram of a gas at constant pressure.

If C_P represents gram molecular specific heat of a gas at constant pressure and 22 the universal gas constant, then

$$S_2 - S_1 = C_P \times 2.3026 \log_{10} \frac{T_2}{T_1} - \frac{r}{T} \times 2.3026 \log_{10} \frac{P_2}{P_1} \quad ...(vii)$$

TEMPERATURE—ENTROPY DIAGRAM

The temperature—entropy diagram is used in engineering and meteorology. Consider the Carnot's cycle ABCDA Fig. (1.31i). From A to B, heat energy H_1 is absorbed at temperature T_1. The- increase in entropy S_1, takes place from A to B Fig. (1.31ii). From B to C, there is no change in entropy.

The temperature decreases at constant entropy. From C to D, there is decrease in entropy (S_2) at constant temperature T_2. From D to A, there is no change in entropy but the temperature increases.

The area ABCD in the temperature-entropy diagram represents the actual amount of energy converted into work Fig. (1.31ii).

The area ABCD = $S_1 (T_1 - T_2) = S_2 (T_1 - T_2)$

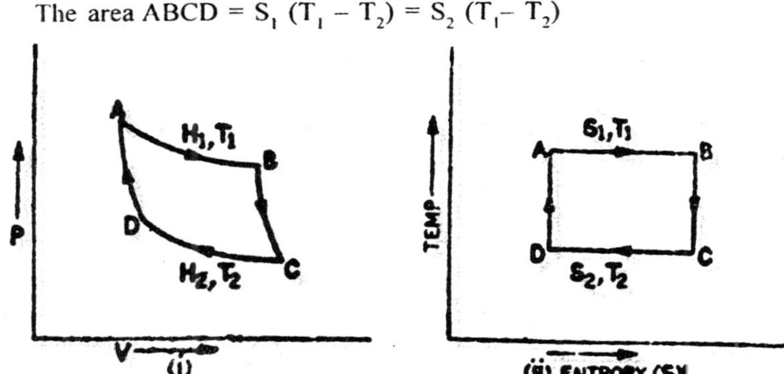

Fig. 1.31

But $$S_1 - \frac{H_1}{T_1} \text{ and } s_2 \frac{H_2}{T_2}$$

Here $$S_1 = S_2 = \frac{H_1}{T_1} = \frac{H_2}{T_2} = \frac{H_1 - H_2}{T_1 - T_2}.$$

$\therefore$ Area $$\text{ABCD} = \frac{(H_1 - H_2)}{T_1 - T_2} = H_1 = 1 - \frac{T_2}{T_1}$$

Therefore, the area ABCD represents the energy converted to work

Efficiency $$= \frac{H_1 - H_2}{H_1} = - 1 \frac{H_2}{H_1} = 1 - \frac{T_2}{T_1}$$

Here H_2 is the unavailable energy.

$$H_2 = \frac{H_1}{T_1} \times T_2 = S_1 \times T_1$$

The unavailable energy depends on the change in entropy at temperature T_1 and the temperature T_2.

ZERO POINT ENERGY

According to Kinetic theory, the energy of a system at absolute zero should be zero. It means the molecules of the system do not possess any motion. But according to the modern concept, even at absolute zero, the molecules are not completely deprived of their motion and hence possess energy. The energy of the molecules at absolute zero temperature is called zero point energy.

NEGATIVE TEMPERATURES

The specific heat of a substance decreases with increase in temperature. However, the specific heat does not tend to zero as the temperature tends to infinity. This shows that the temperature has a +ve sign only.

But recent experiments by Ramsey (1956) have shown that a part of a system *i.e.*, the nucleus of a solid, can have a negative temperature. This sub-system is considered isolated from the main system (*i.e.*, solid lattice). The specific heat of the sub-system tends to zero at high temperature. A small amount of heat energy tends to raise the temperature of the system to infinity. It is possible to add still more energy to the sub-system at infinity and it forces the sub-system into the negative, temperature region. It has been shown by microscopic statistical analysis that there is no distinction between the temperature of $+\infty$ and $-\infty$. In thermodynamics, the parameter $1/T$ is more significant than T.

The negative temperatures are hotter than the positive temperatures and minus zero (–0) is the hottest temperature and plus zero (+0) is the coldest temperature.

The negative temperature is not possible with the system as a whole and is only an exception to the rule that only positive temperatures exist. The negative temperatures are possible only for isolable sub-systems. For all normal purposes the temperatures are always positive.

HELMHOLTZ FUNCTION

Helmholtz function F, is the property of a system and is given by the equation

$$F = U - TS \qquad \text{...(i)}$$

In practice, the primary function of heat engines and other devices is to perform mechanical work. From the first law of thermodynamics, for a system working between two equilibrium states,

$$\delta H = dU + \delta W \qquad \text{...(ii)}$$

or

$$\delta W = \delta H - dU \qquad \text{...(iii)}$$

It means that the energy converted into work is provided partly by the heat reservoir with which the system is in contact and which gives up a quantity of heat δH and partly by the system whose internal energy decreases by $(-dU)$.

When a system undergoes a process between two equilibrium state, how much maximum work can be done by it? This can be derived by assuming that the system exchanges heat energy only with a single heat reservoir at a temperature T_0.

From the principle of increase of entropy, it is known that the sum of the increase in entropy of the system and that of the surroundings is equal to or greater than zero. Suppose,

Increase in entropy of the system = dS

Increase in entropy of the surroundings (reservoir) = dS_0

Heat absorbed by the system from the reservoir = δB

Temperature of the reservoir = T_0

$$\therefore \quad dS + dS_0 > 0 \qquad \text{..(iv)}$$

For a reservoir. $dS_0 = \dfrac{-\delta H}{T_0}$ [Since reservoir has given heat]

$$\therefore \quad dS - \frac{\delta H}{T_0} > 0$$

or
$$T_0 \,.\, dS > \delta H \qquad \text{..(v)}$$

From equations (iii) and (v)

$$\delta W < T_0 \,.\, dS - dU \qquad \text{...(vi)}$$

The quantities U and S are the properties of the system and T_0 is a constant. Therefore, for a finite process between state 1 to state 2, by integrating equation (vi),

$$W < T_0 (S_2 - S_1) - (U_2 - U_1) \qquad \text{...(vii)}$$

$$W < (U_1 - U_2) - T_0(S_1 - S_2) \qquad \text{...(viii)}$$

Suppose that the initial and the final temperatures are equal and are the same as that of the heat reservoir.

$$T = T_0$$

Here T is the temperature of the system.

Equation (viii) can be written as,

$$\therefore \quad W_r < (U_1 - U_2)_T - T(S_1 - S_2)_T \qquad \text{...(ix)}$$

The Helmholtz function,

$$F = U - TS$$

Therefore for two equilibrium states 1 and 2 at the same temperature T,

$$(F_1 - F_2) = (U_1 - TS_1) - (U_2 - TS_2)$$
$$= (U_1 - U_2) - T(S_1 - S_2)$$

or $$(F_1 - F_2)_T = (U_1 - U_2)_T - T(S_1 - S_2)_T \quad ...(x)$$

From (ix) and (x)

$$W_T < (F_1 - F_2)_T \quad ...(xi)$$

Thus, the maximum work that can be done in any process between two equilibrium states at the same temperature is equal to the decrease in the Helmholtz function of the system. Here the system exchanges heat with a single heat reservoir at the same temperature. Moreover maximum work is done when the process if reversible. If the process is irreversible, the work done is less than the maximum.

It is to be remembered that the maximum work that can be done is equal to the decrease in the Helmholtz function of a system but the energy converted into work is provided partly by the system and the remaining by the heat taken from the heat reservoir.

CLAUSIUS INEQUALITY

Before considering entropy, it is necessary to establish the Clausius inequality which states that

$$\oint \frac{\delta H}{T} < 0$$

This relation is between the temperatures of an arbitrary number of heat reservoirs and the amounts of heat transferred (given up or lost).

Consider three heat reservoirs at temperatures T_1, T_2 and T_0 (Fig. 1.32).

The engine C works as a heat engine. It absorbs heat H_1 from reservoir at temperature T_1 and H_2 from reservoir at temperature T_2. The system as a whole does an amount of work W and rejects a quantity of heat By to the reservoir at temperature T_0.

Carnot's engines A and B work as refrigerators. The engine A absorbs heat H_{0A} from the reservoir at temperature T_0, an amount of work W_A supplied to it and it rejects a quantity of heat H_{1A} to the reservoir at temperature T_1. The engine B absorbs heat H_{0B} from the reservoir at temperature T_0, an amount of work W_B is supplied to it and it rejects a quantity of heat H_{2B} to the reservoir at temperature T_2.

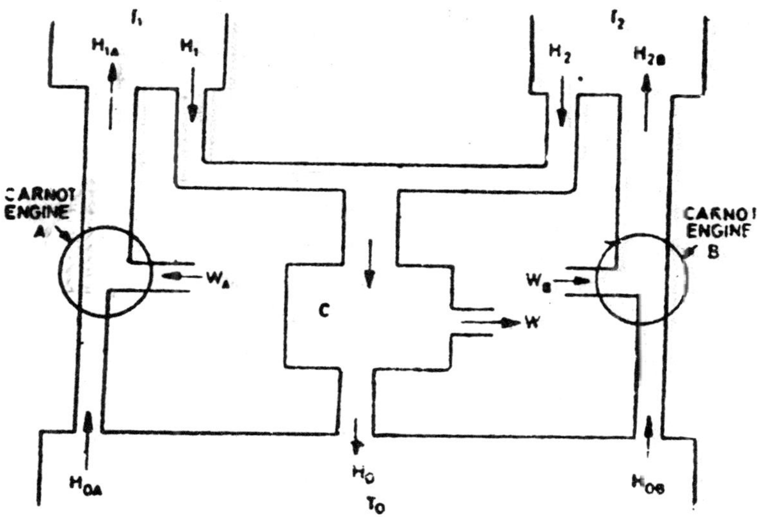

Fig. 1.32

In the general discussion given below, no restriction on the direction of interchanges of the energy is made except that the interchanges must be consistent with the first and the second laws of thermodynamics.

The engine A working as a refrigerator rejects heat H_{1A} to the reservoir at temperature T_1.

Here, $H_{1A} + H_1 = 0$ ...(i)

Similarly the engine B working as a refrigerator rejects heat H_{2B} to the reservoir. at temperature T_2.

Here $H_{2B} + H_2 = 0$ ...(ii)

It means that when the three engines work simultaneously, there is no outstanding change in the temperature of reservoirs at temperatures T_1 and T_2.

Thus, there has been no change except for the reservoir at temperature T_0 and the mechanical system that supplied or absorbed work. If H_0 is not equal to the sum of H_{0A} and H_{0B}, the reservoir at temperature T_0 must have gained or lost heat. Similarly, if W is not equal to the sum of W_A and W_B, the mechanical system must have gained or lost work. According to the first law, the net flow of heat from or to a heat reservoir must necessarily be equal to the amount of work done on or by the mechanical system. As far as the first law is concerned it is a matter of indifference whether the reservoir gains or loses heat as long as the mechanical system loses or gains the same quantity of work. The consideration is different with reference to the second law.

If the heat reservoir loses heat and the mechanical system gains an equal amount of work, it means that the whole of the heat absorbed from the reservoir is converted into work but this violates the Kelvin-Planck statement of the second law of thermodynamics.

Therefore, H_0 must always be greater than the sum of H_{0A} and H_{0B} except in the limiting case when they are equal.

For the engine A,

$$\frac{H_{1A}}{T_1} = \frac{H_{0A}}{T_0} \quad ...(ii)$$

For the engine B,

$$\frac{H_{2A}}{T_2} = \frac{H_{0B}}{T_0} \quad ...(iv)$$

Also the quantities, H_1 and H_2 are positive, H_0 is negative, H_{1A} and H_{aB} are negative, H_{0A}. and B_{0B} are positive. Mathematically we write all the quantities as positive.

From equation (iii)

$$H_{0A} \frac{T_0(H_{1A})}{T_1} = \frac{T_0(H_1)}{T_1} = T_0\left(\frac{H_1}{T_1}\right) \quad ...(v)$$

Similarly, $$H_{0B} \frac{T_0(H_{2A})}{T_2} = \frac{T_0(H_2)}{T_2} = T_0\left(\frac{H_2}{T_2}\right) \quad ...(vi)$$

The net quantity of heat drawn from the reservoir at temperature T_0 is

$$H_0 + H_{0A} + H_{0B}$$

According to the second law, this quantity should be less than or equal to zero.

i.e. $$H_0 + H_{0A} + H_{0B} < 0$$

Substituting the values of H_{0A} and H_{0B}

$$H_0 + T_0\left(\frac{H_1}{T_1}\right) + T_0\left(\frac{H_2}{T_2}\right) < 0$$

Dividing by T_0

$$\frac{H_0}{T_0} + \frac{H_1}{T_1} + \frac{H_2}{T_2} < 0 \qquad ...(vii)$$

In general, for a system using a large number of reservoirs, it can be written as,

$$\sum \frac{H}{T} < 0 \qquad ...(viii)$$

When the number of reservoirs is infinite and the heat exchanges take place by infinitesimal amounts, it can be written as

$$\int \frac{\delta H}{T} < 0 \qquad ...(ix)$$

Equations (viii) and (ix) represent the *Clausius inequality*. The relation holds goods for any cyclic process, reversible or irreversible.

Examples:

Consider two blocks at temperatures 300 K and 200 K that are in contact. The block at higher temperature conducts heat to the block at- the lower temperature. Suppose, 200 joules of heat is transferred. Here,

H_1 = 200 joules; T_1 = 300 K

H_2 = 200 joules, T_2 = 200 K

$$\therefore \quad \sum \frac{H}{T} = \frac{H_1}{T_1} + \frac{H_2}{T_2}$$

$$= \frac{200}{300} + \frac{(-200)}{200} = -\frac{1}{3}$$

$$= -0.33 \text{ joule/degree}$$

(2) Consider an actual heat engine working between the temperatures 500 K and 300 K.

Suppose its efficiency is 20% and it takes 1000 joules of heat from the high temperature reservoir. As the efficiency is 20%.

$$\eta = 1 - \frac{H_2}{H_1}$$

$$\frac{200}{100} = 1 - \frac{H_2}{100}$$

or $$H_2 = 800 \text{ joules}$$

$\therefore$ $$\sum \frac{H}{T} = \frac{H_1}{T_1} + \frac{H_2}{T_2}$$

Here $H_1 = +\ 1000$ joules

$H_2 = -800$ joules (since heat is rejected)

$T_1 = 500$ K

$T_2 = 300$ K

$$\sum \frac{H}{T} = \frac{1000}{500} + \frac{-800}{300}$$

$$= -2/3 \text{ joule/degree}$$

(3) Consider a Carnots reversible engine working between the temperatures 500 K and 300 K. Suppose 1000 joules of heat energy is drawn from the high temperature reservoir.

Here $$\frac{H_1}{T_1} = \frac{H_2}{T_2}$$

$$\frac{1000}{500} = \frac{H_2}{300}$$

or $$H_2 = 600 \text{ joules}$$

$$\sum \frac{H}{T} = \frac{H_1}{T_1} + \frac{H_2}{T_2}$$

Here $H_1 = +\ 1000$ joules

$H_2 = -600$ joules

$T_1 = 500$K

$T_2 = 300$K

$\therefore$ $$\sum \frac{H}{T} = \frac{1000}{500} + \frac{(-600)}{300}$$

or $\sum \frac{H}{T} = 0$

This example shows Σ H/T = 0, only in the limiting case and in no case Σ H/T is greater than zero.

ENTROPY AND THE SECOND LAW OF THERMODYNAMICS

Consider a closed system undergoing a reversible process from state 1 to state 2 along the path A and from state 2 to state 1 along the path B (Fig. 1.33). As this is a reversible cyclic process

$$\oint \frac{\delta H}{T} = 0$$

$$\therefore \qquad \int_{1A}^{2A} \frac{\delta H}{T} + \int_{2B}^{1B} \frac{\delta H}{T} = 0 \qquad ...(i)$$

Now consider the reversible cycle from state 1 to state 2 along the path A and from state 2 to state 1 along the path 0.

For this reversible cyclic process

$$\int_{1A}^{2A} \frac{\delta H}{T} + \int_{2C}^{1C} \frac{\delta H}{T} = 0 \qquad ...(ii)$$

From equations (i) and (ii)

$$\int_{2B}^{1B} \frac{\delta H}{T} + \int_{2C}^{1C} \frac{\delta H}{T} \qquad ...(iii)$$

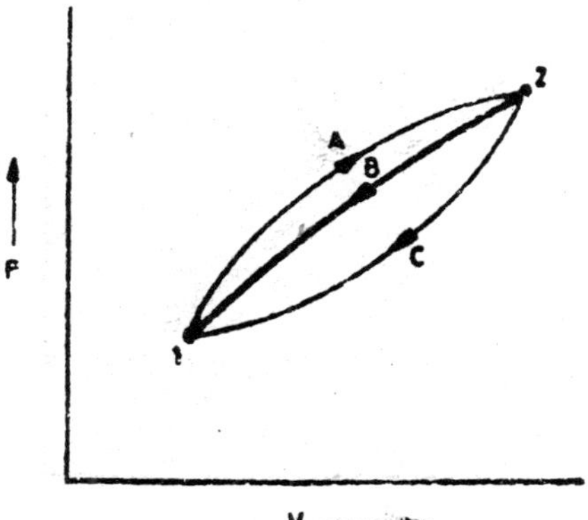

Fig. 1.33

This shows that $\int \delta H/T$ has the same value for all the reversible paths from state 2 to state 1. The quantity $\int \delta H/T$ is independent of the path and is a function of the end states only, therefore it is a property.

This property is called entropy. Entropy is a thermodynamical property and is defined by the relation

$$dS = \frac{\delta H}{T} \qquad \text{...(iv)}$$

or

$$S_2 - S_1 = \int_1^2 \frac{\delta H}{T} \qquad \text{...(v)}$$

The quantity $S_2 - S_1$ represents the change in entropy of the system when it is changed from state 1 to state 2.

ENTROPY CHANGES OF A CLONED SYSTEM DURING AN IRREVERSIBLE PROCESS

Consider a reversible cycle where the state is' changed from 1 to 2 along the path A and 2 to 1 along the path B (Fig. 1.34).

For a reversible cyclic process

$$\oint \delta H = 0$$

$$\int_{1A}^{2A} \frac{\delta H}{T} + \int_{2B}^{1B} \frac{\delta H}{T} = 0$$

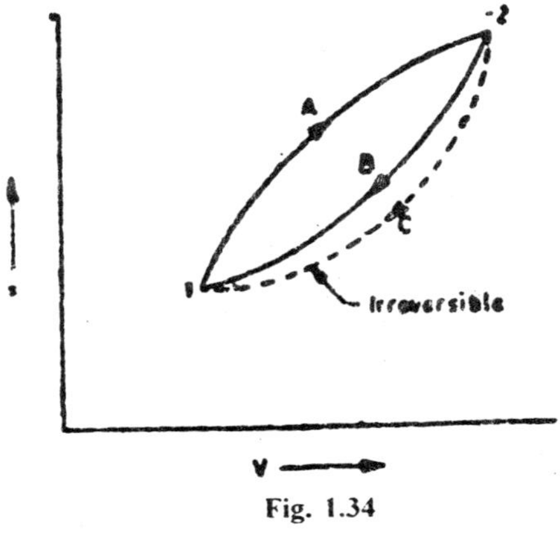

Fig. 1.34

Now consider an irreversible path 0 from state 2 to state 1. Applying Clausius inequality for the cycle of processes A and 0

$$\oint \frac{\delta H}{T} < 0$$

$$\therefore \quad \int_{1A}^{2A} \frac{\delta H}{T} + \int_{2C}^{1C} \frac{\delta H}{T} < 0 \qquad \text{...(ii)}$$

From equations (i) and (ii)

$$\int_{2B}^{1B} \frac{\delta H}{T} - \int_{2C}^{1C} \frac{\delta H}{T} > 0$$

Since path B is reversible and entropy is a property

$$\int_{2B}^{1B} \frac{\delta H}{T} = \int_{2B}^{1B} dS = \int_{2C}^{1C} dS$$

$$\therefore \quad dS > \frac{\delta H}{T} \qquad \text{...(iii)}$$

$$\text{or} \quad S_2 - S_1 > \int_1^2 \delta H \qquad \text{...(iv)}$$

To conclude,

For a reversible process

$$S_2 - S_1 > \int_1^2 \frac{\delta H}{T}$$

Equation (iv) show that the effect of irreversibility is always to increase the entropy of a system.

SOLVED EXAMPLES

Example 1:

Under what conditions does the isothermal expansion of a gas become a free expansion process?

Solution:

The isothermal expansion of a gas becomes a free expansion process only when it expands against a vacuum, *i.e.*, $p_{ext} = 0$. Moreover, the gas must be an ideal gas in which case $\Delta E = 0$ at constant temperature.

Example 2:

Is every adiabatic system isolated? In what ways can the energy of an adiabatic system change?

Solution:

An isolated system is the one in which no interaction with its surroundings takes place. Neither energy nor matter can be transferred to or from it. An adiabatic system involves no exchange of heat from its surroundings, *i.e.* for such a system dq = 0 and, according to the first law of thermodynamics, dE =dw. Thus, the energy of an adiabatic system can be changed by either doing work on the system or by getting work done by the system.

Example 3:

Show that $$C_2 - C_1 = \frac{dL}{dT} - \frac{L}{T}$$

where C_l and C_2 represent the specific heta of a liquid and it saturted vapour and l is the latent heat of the vapour.

Solution:

For a change of state from liquid to vapour,

$$S_2 - S_1 = \frac{L}{T} \quad \text{...(i)}$$

Here S_1 and S_2 are the entropies in the liquid and vapour states respectively.

Differentiating equation (i) with respect to T

$$\frac{dS_2}{dT} - \frac{dS_1}{dT} = - L \cdot \frac{1}{T^2} + \frac{1}{T} \cdot \frac{dL}{dT}$$

$$T\left(\frac{dS_2}{dT}\right) - T\left(\frac{dS_1}{dT}\right) = - \frac{L}{T} + \frac{dL}{dT}$$

$$C_2 - C_1 = \frac{dL}{dT} - \frac{L}{T}$$

This equation is known an Clausius latent heat equation

Example 4:

Calculate under what pressure water would boil at 160°C if the change in specific volume when 1 gram of water is converted into steam is 1676 cc. Given latent heat of vaporisation of steam = 540 cal per gram; J = 4.2 × 10^7 ergs/cal and one atmosphere pressure = 10^6 dynes/cm^2.

Solution:

Here $\delta H = 540 \text{ cal} = 540 \times 4.2 \times 107$ erga

$\delta V = 1676$ cc

$T = 373$ K, and 150°C = 423 K

$\delta T = 423 - 373 = 50$ K

$\delta P = ?$

Applying these values in the Maxwell's thermodynamical relation

$$\left(\frac{\delta H}{\partial V}\right)_T = T\left(\frac{\partial P}{\partial T}\right)_V$$

$$\frac{540 \times 4.2 \times 10^7}{1676} = 373\left(\frac{\partial P}{50}\right)$$

$$\partial P = \frac{540 \times 4.2 \times 10^7 \times 50}{373 \times 1676}$$

$$= 1.814 \times 10^6 \text{ dynes/cm}^2$$

$$= 1.814 \text{ atmospheres}$$

Therefore, the pressure at which water would boil at 150°C

$$= 1.814 + 1.000$$

$$= 2.814 \text{ atmospheres.}$$

Example 5:

Calculate under what pressure ice would freeze at –1°C, if the change in specific volume when 1 gram of water freezes into ice is 0.091 cc.

Given latent heat of fusion of ice = 80 cal/g, J = 4.2 × 10^7 ergs/cal and one atmosphere pressure = 10^6 dynes/cm^3.

Solution:

Here, $\delta H = 80 \text{ cal} + 80 \times 4.2 \times 10^7$ ergs

$\partial V = 0.091$ cc

$T = 273$ K

$\partial T = 273 - 272 = 1$K

$\partial P = ?$

Applying these values in the Maxwell's thcrmodynamical relation,

$$\left(\frac{\delta H}{\partial V}\right)_T = T\left(\frac{\partial P}{\partial T}\right)_V$$

$$\frac{80 \times 4.2 \times 10^7}{0.091} = \frac{273 \times \partial P}{1}$$

$$\partial P = 135.2 \times 10^6 \text{ dyne/cm}^2$$

$$= 135.2 \text{ atmospheres}$$

Therefore, the pressure under which ice would freeze = atmospheric pressure + ∂P = 1 + 135.2 = 136.2 atmospheres.

Example 6:

Calculate the specific heat of saturated steam given that the specific heat of water at 100°C = 1.01 and latent heat of vaporisation decreases with rise in temperature at the rate of 0.64 cal/K. Latent heat of vaporization of steam = 540 cal.

Solution:

We have

$$C_1 = 1.01$$

$$C_2 = ?$$

$$T = 373 \text{ K}$$

$$\frac{dL}{dT} = -0.64 \text{ cal/K}$$

$$C_2 - C_1 = \frac{dL}{dT} - \frac{L}{T}$$

$$C_2 = C_1 + \frac{dL}{dT} - \frac{L}{T}$$

$$= 1.01 + (-0.64) - 540/373$$

$$= -1.077 \text{ cal/g.}$$

It shows that the specific heat of saturated steam is negative.

Example 7:

Calculate the specific heat of saturated steam at 100°C from the following data:

L at 90°C + 545.25 cal

L at 100°C = 539.30 cal

L at 110°C = 533.17 cal

Specific heat of water at 100°C = 1.013 cal/g.

Solution:

Here $\frac{dL}{dT} = \frac{533.17 - 545.25}{20}$

$$= \frac{-12.08}{20} = -0604 \text{ cal/K}$$

$$L = 539.3 \text{ cal}$$

$$T = 373 \text{ K}$$

$$C = 1.013$$

$$C = ?$$

$$C_2 - C_1 = \frac{dL}{dT} - \frac{L}{T}$$

$$C_2 = C_1 + \frac{dL}{dT} - \frac{L}{T}$$

$$C_2 = 1.013 - 0.604 - \frac{539.3}{373}$$

$$C_2 = -1.036 \text{ cal/g.}$$

Example 8:

Using Maxwell's themwdynamical relations, prove that the ratio of the adiabatic to the isochoric pressure coefficient of expansion is equal to

$$\frac{\gamma}{(\gamma - 1)}$$

Solution:

Adiabatic prenxire coefficient of expansion,

$$\beta_S = \frac{1}{P}\left(\frac{\partial P}{\partial T}\right)_S \quad ...(i)$$

Isochoric pressure coefficient of expanison.

$$\beta_V = \frac{1}{P}\left(\frac{\partial P}{\partial T}\right)_V \quad ..(ii)$$

$$\therefore \qquad \frac{\beta_S}{\beta_V} = \frac{\frac{1}{P}\left(\frac{\partial P}{\partial T}\right)_S}{\frac{1}{P}\left(\frac{\partial P}{\partial T}\right)_V} \qquad ...(iii)$$

$$= \frac{\left(\frac{\partial P}{\partial T}\right)_S}{\left(\frac{\partial P}{\partial T}\right)_V}$$

$$= \frac{1}{\left(\frac{\partial T}{\partial P}\right)_S \left(\frac{\partial P}{\partial T}\right)_V}$$

But $\left(\frac{\partial T}{\partial P}\right)_S = \left(\frac{\partial V}{\partial S}\right)_P$ ...(iv)

$$\frac{\beta_S}{\beta_V} = \frac{1}{\left(\frac{\partial V}{\partial S}\right)_P \left(\frac{\partial P}{\partial T}\right)_V} \qquad ...(v)$$

$$= \frac{1}{\left(\frac{\partial V}{\partial T}\right)_P \left(\frac{\partial T}{\partial S}\right)_P \left(\frac{\partial P}{\partial T}\right)_V}$$

$$= \frac{\left(\frac{\partial S}{\partial T}\right)_P}{\left(\frac{\partial V}{\partial T}\right)_P \left(\frac{\partial P}{\partial T}\right)_V}$$

$$= \frac{T\left(\frac{\partial S}{\partial T}\right)_P}{T\left(\frac{\partial V}{\partial T}\right)_P \left(\frac{\partial P}{\partial T}\right)_V}$$

$$= \frac{C_P}{C_P - C_V}$$

or $$\frac{\beta_S}{\beta_V} = \frac{\left(\frac{C_P}{C_V}\right)}{\left(\frac{C_P}{C_V} - 1\right)} = \frac{\gamma}{\gamma - 1} \qquad ...(vi)$$

Example 9(a):

Using Maxwell's thermodynamical relations, show that

$$\left(\frac{\partial C_V}{\partial V}\right) = T\left(\frac{\partial^2 S}{\partial V.\partial T}\right) = T\left(\frac{\partial^2 P}{\partial T^2}\right)_V$$

Solution:

From Maxwell's relations,

$$\left(\frac{\partial S}{\partial V}\right)_T = \left(\frac{\partial P}{\partial T}\right)_V \qquad ...(i)$$

Differentiating equation (i) with respect to temperature,

$$\left(\frac{\partial^2 S}{\partial T.\partial V}\right) = \left(\frac{\partial^2 P}{\partial T^2}\right)_V \qquad ...(ii)$$

But $\qquad C_V = T\left(\frac{\partial S}{\partial T}\right)_V \qquad ...(iii)$

Differentiating equation (iii) with respect to volume,

$$\left(\frac{\partial C_V}{\partial V}\right) = T\left(\frac{\partial^2 S}{\partial T.\partial V}\right) \qquad ...(iv)$$

From equations (ii) and (iv)

$$\left(\frac{\partial C_V}{\partial V}\right) = T\left(\frac{\partial^2 S}{\partial T.\partial V}\right) = T\left(\frac{\partial^2 P}{\partial T^2}\right)_V \qquad ...(v)$$

Example 9(b):

Using Maxwell's thermodynamical relations, show that

$$\left(\frac{\partial C_P}{\partial P}\right) = T\left(\frac{\partial^2 S}{\partial P.\partial T}\right) = -T\left(\frac{\partial^2 V}{\partial T^2}\right)_P$$

Solution:

From Maxwell's relations,

$$\left(\frac{\partial S}{\partial P}\right)_T = -\left(\frac{\partial V}{\partial T}\right)_P \qquad ...(i)$$

Differentiating equation (i) with respect to temperature,

$$\left(\frac{\partial^2 S}{\partial T.\partial P}\right) = -\left(\frac{\partial^2 V}{\partial T^2}\right)_P \qquad ...(ii)$$

But $$C_P = T\left(\frac{\partial S}{\partial T}\right)_P \qquad ...(iii)$$

Differentiating equation (iii) with respect to pressure,

$$\left(\frac{\partial C_P}{\partial P}\right) = T\left(\frac{\partial^2 S}{\partial T.\partial P}\right) \qquad ...(iv)$$

From equations (ii) and (iv)

$$\left(\frac{\partial C_P}{\partial P}\right) = T\left(\frac{\partial^2 S}{\partial T.\partial P}\right) = -T\left(\frac{\partial^2 V}{\partial T^2}\right)_P \qquad ...(v)$$

Example 10:

Using Maxwell's thermodynamical relations, prove that for any substance, the ratio of the adiabatic and isothermal elasticities it equal to the ratio of the two specific heats.

Solution:

From definition,

Isothermal elasticity $E_T = -V\left(\frac{\partial P}{\partial V}\right)_T$

Adiabatic elasticity $E_T = -V\left(\frac{\partial P}{\partial V}\right)_S$

$$\therefore \qquad \frac{E_S}{E_T} = \frac{-V\left(\frac{\partial P}{\partial V}\right)_S}{-V\left(\frac{\partial P}{\partial V}\right)_T}$$

$$= \frac{\left(\frac{\partial P}{\partial V}\right)_S}{\left(\frac{\partial P}{\partial V}\right)_T}$$

$$= \frac{\left(\frac{\partial P}{\partial T}\right)_S\left(\frac{\partial T}{\partial V}\right)_S}{\left(\frac{\partial P}{\partial S}\right)_T\left(\frac{\partial S}{\partial V}\right)_T}$$

$$\frac{E_S}{E_T} = \frac{\left(\frac{\partial S}{\partial P}\right)_T \left(\frac{\partial T}{\partial V}\right)_S}{\left(\frac{\partial T}{\partial P}\right)_S \left(\frac{\partial S}{\partial V}\right)_T} \qquad \text{...(i)}$$

But from the first four Maxwell s equations

$$\left(\frac{\partial S}{\partial P}\right)_T = -\left(\frac{\partial V}{\partial T}\right)_P$$

$$\left(\frac{\partial T}{\partial V}\right)_S = -\left(\frac{\partial P}{\partial S}\right)_V$$

$$\left(\frac{\partial T}{\partial P}\right)_S = \left(\frac{\partial V}{\partial S}\right)_P$$

$$\left(\frac{\partial S}{\partial V}\right)_T = \left(\frac{\partial P}{\partial T}\right)_V$$

∴ Substituting these values in equation (i)

$$\frac{E_S}{E_T} = \frac{\left(\frac{\partial V}{\partial T}\right)_P \left(\frac{\partial P}{\partial S}\right)_V}{\left(\frac{\partial V}{\partial S}\right)_P \left(\frac{\partial P}{\partial T}\right)_V}$$

$$\frac{E_S}{E_T} = \frac{\left(\frac{\partial S}{\partial V}\right)_P \left(\frac{\partial V}{\partial T}\right)_P}{\left(\frac{\partial S}{\partial P}\right)_V \left(\frac{\partial P}{\partial T}\right)_V}$$

$$= \frac{\left(\frac{\partial S}{\partial T}\right)_P}{\left(\frac{\partial S}{\partial T}\right)_V}$$

$$= \frac{\left(\frac{\partial H}{\partial T}\right)_P}{\left(\frac{\partial H}{\partial T}\right)_V}$$

But $\left(\frac{\partial H}{\partial T}\right)_P = C_P$

and $\left(\frac{\partial H}{\partial T}\right)_V = C_V$

$$\therefore \quad \frac{E_S}{E_T} = \frac{C_P}{C_V} = \gamma.$$

Example 11:

Using MavuxIFs thermodynamical relatwns, prove that the ratio of the adiabatic to the isobaric coefficient of expansion is

$$\frac{1}{(1-\gamma)}$$

Solution:

Adiabatic volume coefficient of expansion,

$$\alpha_2 = \frac{1}{V}\left(\frac{\partial V}{\partial T}\right)_S \qquad \text{...(i)}$$

Isobaric volume coefficient of expansion,

$$\alpha_P = \frac{1}{V}\left(\frac{\partial V}{\partial T}\right)_F \qquad \text{...(ii)}$$

$$\therefore \quad \frac{\alpha_S}{\alpha_P} = \frac{\frac{1}{V}\left(\frac{\partial V}{\partial T}\right)_S}{\frac{1}{V}\left(\frac{\partial V}{\partial T}\right)_P} \qquad \text{...(iii)}$$

$$= \frac{\left(\frac{\partial V}{\partial T}\right)_S}{\left(\frac{\partial V}{\partial T}\right)_P} = \frac{1}{\left(\frac{\partial T}{\partial V}\right)_S \left(\frac{\partial V}{\partial T}\right)_P}$$

But $\left(\frac{\partial T}{\partial V}\right)_S = -\left(\frac{\partial P}{\partial S}\right)_V$

$$\therefore \quad \frac{\alpha_S}{\alpha_P} = -\frac{1}{\left(\frac{\partial P}{\partial S}\right)_V \left(\frac{\partial V}{\partial T}\right)_P}$$

$$= \frac{1}{-\left[\left(\frac{\partial P}{\partial T}\right)_V \left(\frac{\partial T}{\partial S}\right)_V \left(\frac{\partial V}{\partial T}\right)_P\right]}$$

$$= \frac{\left(\frac{\partial S}{\partial T}\right)_V}{-\left(\frac{\partial P}{\partial T}\right)_V \left(\frac{\partial V}{\partial T}\right)_P}$$

$$= \frac{T\left(\frac{\partial S}{\partial T}\right)_V}{-T\left(\frac{\partial P}{\partial T}\right)_V \left(\frac{\partial V}{\partial T}\right)_P}$$

But $$C_P - C_V = T\left(\frac{\partial P}{\partial T}\right)_V \left(\frac{\partial V}{\partial T}\right)_P$$

and $$C_V = T\left(\frac{\partial S}{\partial T}\right)_V$$

$\therefore$ $$\frac{\alpha_S}{\alpha_P} = \frac{C_V}{-(C_P - C_V)}$$

or $$\frac{\alpha_S}{\alpha_P} = \frac{1}{1-\left(\frac{C_P}{C_V}\right)}$$

or $$\frac{\alpha_S}{\alpha_P} = \frac{1}{1-\gamma} \qquad ...(iv)$$

Example 12:

Show that for a perfect gas

$$\left(\frac{\partial U}{\partial V}\right)_T = 0$$

Solution:

From the Maxwell's first equation,

$$\left(\frac{\partial S}{\partial V}\right)_T = \left(\frac{\partial P}{\partial T}\right)_V$$

$$\frac{1}{T}\left(\frac{\partial H}{\partial V}\right)_T = \left(\frac{\partial P}{\partial T}\right)_V$$

or $$\left(\frac{\partial H}{\partial V}\right)_T = T\left(\frac{\partial P}{\partial T}\right)_V$$

But $$\delta H = dU + PdV$$

$$\therefore \quad \left(\frac{dU + PdV}{dV}\right) = T\left(\frac{\partial P}{\partial T}\right)_V$$

$$\frac{dU}{dV} + P = T\left(\frac{\partial P}{\partial T}\right)_V$$

$$\left(\frac{dU}{dV}\right)_T = T\left(\frac{\partial P}{\partial T}\right)_V - P$$

But from perfect gas equation,

$$PV = RT$$

$$\therefore \quad \left(\frac{\partial P}{\partial T}\right)_V = \frac{R}{V}$$

$$\left(\frac{\partial U}{\partial V}\right)_T = T\left(\frac{R}{V}\right) - P$$

or $$\left(\frac{\partial U}{\partial V}\right)_T = P - P = 0$$

$$\therefore \quad \left(\frac{\partial U}{\partial V}\right)_T = 0.$$

Example 13:

One mole of a gas is expanded isothermally and reversibly at 27° C form a volume of 5 liters. Calculate q, w, ΔE and ΔH.

Solution:

We know

$$PV = nRT, \quad n = 1$$

State : Initial

$$T_1 = 27 + 273.15 = 300.15 \text{ K}$$

$V_1 = 5$ litres

Final

$T_2 = T_1 = 300.15K$

$V_2 = 10$ litres

(1) Calculation of w :

$$w = \int_{V_1}^{V_2} PdV = \int_{V_1}^{V_2} \frac{RT}{V} dV = RT \ln \frac{V_2}{V_1}$$

$$= 2.303 \times 8.314 \times 300 \log (10/5)$$

$$= 2.303 \times 8.314 \times 300 \times \log^2$$

$$= 2.303 \times 8.314 \times 300 \times 0.3010 \quad [\log 2 = 0.3010]$$

$$w = 1729 \text{ J mol}^{-1}$$

(2) Calculation of ΔE :

$$\Delta E = E_2 - E_1$$

For isothermal-reversible expansion of an ideal gas $E_2 = E_1$ and therefore

$$\Delta E = 0.$$

(3) Calculation of q:

$$q = \Delta E + w \text{ (first law)}$$

$$= 0 + w$$

$$q = w = 1729 \text{ J}$$

(4) Calculation of ΔH

$$\Delta H = \Delta E + \Delta (PV) = \Delta E + \Delta(RT)$$

$$0 + 0 = 0$$

Since $\Delta E = 0$ and $\Delta(RT) = 0$;

R and T being constant

Example 14:

Calculate the minimum work which must be done to compress 1/2 mole of oxygen at 300 k from a pressure of 2 atm to a pressure of 200 atm.

Solution:

As it is required to calculate the minimum work of compression, the change, is reversible, *i.e.*, the gas gets compressed by gradual increase of pressure so that the external pressure becomes only infinitesimally greater than the pressure of the gas, at each stage. Thus

$$w = \text{work done} = \int_{V_1}^{V_2} P\,dV$$

$$= 2.303\, n\, RT \log \frac{V_2}{V_1}$$

$$= 2.303\, nRT \log \frac{p_1}{P_2}$$

given date :

$$P_1 = 2 \text{ atm}$$

$$P_2 = 2 \text{ atm}$$

$$T = 300 \text{ K}$$

$$n = \frac{16}{32} = 0.5 \text{ mole.}$$

On substituting these values in the above equation, we get

$$w = 2.303 \times 0.5 \times 8.314 \times 300 \log \frac{2}{200}$$

$$= -5744 \text{ J.}$$

Example 15:

What will be the work done when 65.38 g of zinc dissolves in hydrochloric acid in case of an open beaker and closed beaker at 300K.

Solution:

The process of dissolution of zinc in hydrochloric acid can be given as

$$Zn(s) + 2HCl\ (aq) = ZnCl_2(aq) + H_2(g)$$

From this equation it is clear that for each gram atom of zinc dissolved we will obtain 1 mole of Hydrogen gas. As a result of liberated gas, on the surrounding atmosphere the work performed will be equal to $P\Delta V$. If the initial volume of the system is neglected in comparison to the total volume of the gas produced and the gas shows ideal behaviour. then the work done in the open beaker is

$$W = P\Delta V \approx PV_{H2}$$

$$= nH2\ RT \qquad [\because T = 300\ k\ R = 8.314\ Jk^{-1}\ mole^{-1}]$$

$$= (1\ mole)\ (8.314\ JK^{-1}\ mol^{-1})\ (300\ K)$$

$$= 2.4942\ kJ.$$

If the reaction takes place in a closed beaker there is change in the volume *i.e.*, $\Delta V = 0$ hence work done is zero.

Example 16:

Calculate the work done when one mole of sulphur dioxide gas expands isothermally and reversibly at 300 k from $2.46 \times 10^{-3}\ m^3$ to $24.6 \times 10^{-3}\ m^3$. Assuming that the gas obeys

(a) ideal gas equation and

(b) van der Waals equation

$$\begin{Bmatrix} a = 0.6799\ nm^4\ mole^{-2} \\ b = 0.564 \times 10^{-3}\ mole^{-1} \end{Bmatrix}$$

Solution:

(a) The reversible work done by 1 mole of gas when it expands form

$$2.64 \times 10^{-3}m^3 \text{ to } 24.6 \times 10^{-3}m^3 = 2.303\ RT \log \frac{V_2}{V_1}$$

$$= (2.303)\ (1\ mole)\ (8.314\ J\ K^{-1}\ mol^{-1})\ (300\ K) \times \log 10$$

$$\left\{\because \log \frac{V_2}{V_1} = \log 10\right\}$$

$$= (2.303)\ (8.314)\ (300\ K)\ \log 10\ J\ mol^{-1}$$

$$= 5744\ J\ mol^{-1}$$

(b) When the gas obeys van der Waal's equation, work done by 1 mole of gas is

$$= 2.303\ RT \log \frac{V_2 - b}{V_1 - b} + a \left\{\frac{1}{V_2} - \frac{1}{V_1}\right\}$$

After substituting the values of various quantities and solving, the work done is

$$= 5794\ J\ mol^{-1} - 252.4\ J\ mol^{-1}$$

$= 5541.6 \text{ J mol}^{-1}$

$= 5.542 \text{ kJ mol}^{-1}$.

Example 17:

Four moles of an ideal gas are held by a piston under 5 atm pressure and at 273.15 K. The pressure is suddenly released to 0.2 atm and the gas is allowed to expand isothermally. Calculate w, q, ΔE and ΔH for the process.

Solution:

As the pressure has been released suddenly, the expansion must be irreversible.

Here n = 4 moles; P_1 = 5 atm; $T_1 = T_2$ = 273.15 K.

(i) Work done irreversibly

$$w = nRT\left\{1 - \frac{P_2}{P_1}\right\}$$

$$= 4 \times 8.314 \times 273.15 \left\{1 - \frac{0.2}{5}\right\}$$

$$= 4 \times 8.314 \times 273.15 \times 0.96$$

$$= 8720 \text{ J.}$$

(ii) As the ideal gas expands isothermally dT = 0 and hence ΔE =0; ΔH = 0.

(iii) First law gives

$$\Delta E = q - w = 0$$

$$\therefore q = w\ 8720 \text{ J.}$$

Example 18:

At low temperature, a nonideal gas follows the relation $PV = RT - a/V$ where $a = 0.3636\ Nm^4\ mole^{-2}$. Calculate the work done by one mole of this gas in expanding form 0.224 litre to 22.4 litre at 400 K. Compare this result with the work done in the corresponding expansion of an ideal gas.

Solution:

For an ideal gas, reversible work done

$$= 2.303\ n\ RT \log \frac{V_2}{V_1}$$

V_1 = 0.224 litres $mole^{-1}$ = 22.4 × 10^{-5} m^3 $mole^{-1}$

P_2 = 22.4 litres $mole^{-1}$ = 22.4 × 10^{-3} m^3 $mole^{-1}$

R = 8.314 J K^{-1} $mole^{-1}$

$$W_{rew} = (2.303)\ (1\text{ mole})\ (8.314\text{ J K}^{-1}\text{ mole}^{-1})\ (400\text{ K}) \times \log \frac{22.4 \times 10^{-3}}{22.4 \times 10^{-5}}$$

$$= (2.303)\ (1\text{ mole})\ (8.314\text{ J K}^{-1}\text{ mole}^{-1})\ (400\text{ K}) \log 100$$

$$= 15320\text{ J mole}^{-1}$$

$$= 15.32\text{ kJ mole}^{-1}.$$

For the non-ideal gas PV = RT – a/V

Therefore, the work done $= \int_{V_1}^{V_2} P\,dV = \int_{V_1}^{V_2} \left\{\frac{RT}{V} - \frac{a}{V_2}\right\} dV$

$$= 2.303\ RT \log \frac{V_2}{V_1} + a\left\{\frac{1}{V_2} - \frac{1}{V_1}\right\}$$

The value of first part is from derived eq. (1) as 15.32 kJ $mole^{-1}$ and of another part can be derived as

$$0.3636\text{ Nm}^4\text{ mole}^{-2} \left\{\frac{1}{22.4 \times 10^{-3}\text{ m}^3\text{ mole}^{-1}} - \frac{1}{22.4 \times 10^{-5}\text{ m}^3\text{ mole}^{-1}}\right\}$$

$$= 1.604\text{ kJ mole}^{-1}.$$

Thus work done = 15.320 k $Joule^{-1}$ – 1.604 k $Joule^{-1}$

$$= 13.716\text{ kJ mole}^{-1}.$$

Example 19:

One mole of a van der Walls's gas is allowed to expand isothermally and reversibly from a volume of 1 litre to 50 litre at 0°C. Calculate w, q, Δ E and Δ H. van der Waal's constants are a = 6.5 atm l^2 mole^{-2} = 0.056 litre mole^{-1} and R = 0.082 l atom deg^{-1} mole^{-1}.

Solution:

Here V_1 = 1 litre,

V_2 = 50 litres, n = 1 mole

$T = 273 + 0 = 273°k,$

$R = 0.082$ l-atm deg^{-1} $mole^{-1}$

$a = 6.5$ atm l^2 $mole^{-2}$,

$b = 0.056$ litre $mole^{-1}$

$$w = 2.303\ nRT\ \log\left(\frac{V_2 - nb}{V_1 - nb}\right) + an^2\left(\frac{1}{V_2} - \frac{1}{V_1}\right)$$

$$= 2.303 \times 1 \times 0.082 + 273\ [\log(50 - 0.056) - \log(1 - 0.056) + 6.5\left(\frac{1}{50} - \frac{1}{1}\right)$$

$= 82.47$ l atm.

$$\Delta E = -an^2\left(\frac{1}{V_2} - \frac{1}{V_1}\right) = 6.5 \times \frac{49}{50}$$

$$q = 2.303nRT\ \log\frac{V_2 - b}{V_1 - b}$$

$= \Delta E + w = 884$ l atm.

Example 20:

The van der Waal's constant a and b for hydrogen in litre atmosphere units are 0.246 and 2.67×10^{-2} respectively. Calculate the inversion temperature of hydrogen.

Solution:

we know $T_i = 2a/Rb$

or $$T_i = \frac{2 \times 0.246}{0.0821 \times 0.0267}$$

$= 224.5°k = (224.5 - 273) = -48.5°C.$

Example 21:

How much heat is required to raise the temperature of 1 mole oxygen from 300K to 1300 K at constant pressure.

$$C_p = 6.095 + 3.325 \times 10^{-3}\ T - 1.017 \times 10^{-6}\ T^2.$$

Solution:

$$H_2 - H_1 \int_{T_1}^{T_2} C_p\ dT$$

$$T_1 = 300 \text{ k}, T_2 = 100 \text{ k}$$

$$\therefore H_{1300} - H_{300} = \int_{300}^{1300} \left(6.095 + 3.253 + 10^{-3}\ T - 1.017 \times 10^{-6}\ T^2\right)$$

[Substituting the value of C_p]

$$\because H_{1300} - H_{300} = 6.095\ (1300 - 300) + \frac{3.253 \times 10^{-3}}{2}$$

$$\times\ [(1300)^2 - (300)^2] - 1/3 \times 1.017 \times 10^{-6} [(1000)^2 - (300)^2]$$

$$= 6095 + 2602.4 - 735.63$$

$$= 7961.77 \text{ cal/mole.}$$

Example 22:

For equation (P _ a/V²) V = RT, prove that (i) dP is an exact differential, (ii) P is a state function and

$$\text{(iii)} \left(\frac{\partial P}{\partial T}\right)_V \left(\frac{\partial T}{\partial V}\right)_P \left(\frac{\partial V}{\partial T}\right)_T + 1 = 0.$$

Solution:

(i) For dP to be an exact differential, it is be proved that

$$\frac{\partial^2 P}{\partial V \partial T} = \frac{\partial^2 P}{\partial T \partial V} \qquad ...(1)$$

$$(P + a/V^2)\ V = RT$$

or
$$P = \frac{RT}{V} - \frac{a}{V^2} \qquad ...(2)$$

When the above equation is differentiated with respect to V at constant temperature T, we obtain

$$\left(\frac{\partial P}{\partial V}\right)_T = -\frac{RT}{V^2} + \frac{2a}{V^3}$$

When the above equation is differentiated with respect to T at constant V, we obtain

$$\frac{\partial^2 P}{\partial T \partial V} = -\frac{RT}{V^2} \qquad ...(3)$$

When equation (2) is differentiated with respect to T at constant volume V, we obtain

$$\left(\frac{\partial P}{\partial T}\right)_V = \frac{R}{V}$$

When the above equation is further differentiated with respect to V at constant T, we obtain

$$\frac{\partial^2 P}{\partial T \partial V} = -\frac{R}{V^2} \qquad ...(4)$$

From equations (3) and (4), we get

$$\frac{\partial^2 P}{\partial T\, \partial V} = \frac{\partial^2 P}{\partial T\, \partial V} = -\frac{R}{V^2} \qquad ...(5)$$

Thus, we have proved condition, (1). This shows that dP is an exact differential.

(ii) In the said question, first of all a change occurs in volume at constant temperature followed by a change in temperature at constant volume, thereby giving the final equation (3).

Again, a change in temperature is considered at constant volume, followed by a change in volume at constant temperature, thereby giving the final equation (4). Both equations (3) and (4) are same, thereby revealing that the final change in P remains the same irrespective of the difference in intermediate changes. Therefore, P is a state function as changes in P have been found to depend upon the intial and final states of the system.

(iii) Equation (2) is as follows :

$$P = \frac{RT}{V} - \frac{a}{V^2}$$

When the above equation is differentiated, we obtain :

$$dP = \frac{R}{V} dT - \frac{RT}{V^2} dV + \frac{2a}{V^3} dV$$

$$= \frac{R}{V} dT - \left(\frac{RT}{V^2} - \frac{2a}{V^3}\right) dV \qquad ...(6)$$

If volume is constant, dV = 0 : equation (6) becomes as follows :

$$dP = \frac{R}{V} dT \text{or} \left(\frac{\partial P}{\partial V}\right)_V = \frac{R}{V} \qquad ...(7)$$

If pressure is constant, dP = 0; equation (6) becomes as follow :

$$\frac{R}{V} dT - \left(\frac{RT}{V^2} - \frac{2a}{V^3}\right) dV = 0$$

or $$\left(\frac{\partial T}{\partial V}\right)_P = \left(\frac{RT}{V^2} - \frac{2a}{V^3}\right) \Big/ \frac{R}{V} \qquad ...(8)$$

If temperature is constant, dT = 0; equation (6) becomes as follows:

$$\left(\frac{\partial T}{\partial V}\right)_T = -\frac{1}{\left(\frac{RT}{V^2} - \frac{2a}{V^3}\right)} \qquad ...(9)$$

On multiplying equations (7), (8) and (9), we obtain

$$\left(\frac{\partial p}{\partial T}\right)_V \left(\frac{\partial T}{\partial V}\right)_P \left(\frac{\partial V}{\partial P}\right)_T = -\frac{R}{V} \times \frac{\left(\frac{RT}{V^2} - \frac{2a}{V^3}\right)}{\left(\frac{RT}{V^2} - \frac{2a}{V^3}\right)} \times \frac{1}{R} = -1$$

or $$\left(\frac{\partial p}{\partial T}\right)_V \left(\frac{\partial T}{\partial V}\right)_P \left(\frac{\partial V}{\partial P}\right)_T + 1 = 0$$

This is cyclic rule.

Example 23:

For an ideal gas PV = RT, prove that dP is an exact differential.

Solution:

We know $$PV = RT$$

or $$P = \frac{RT}{V} \text{ (R is a constant)} \qquad ...(1)$$

On differentiating with respect to T, taking V constant, we obtain

$$\left(\frac{\partial P}{\partial T}\right)_P = \frac{RT}{V} \qquad ...(2)$$

Again, on differentiating with respect to V, we obtain

$$\frac{\partial^2 P}{\partial V \partial T} = -\frac{R}{V^2} \qquad ..(3)$$

On differentiating (1) with respect to volume, taking T constant, we obtain

$$\left(\frac{\partial P}{\partial V}\right)_T = -\frac{RT}{V^2} \qquad ...(4)$$

Again, on differentiating above equation with respect to temperature taking V as constant, we obtain

$$\frac{\partial^2 P}{\partial T \partial V} = -\frac{R}{V^2} \qquad ...(5)$$

From equations (3) and (5), we obtain

$$\frac{\partial^2 P}{\partial T \partial V} = \frac{\partial^2 P}{\partial T \partial V}$$

Thus dP is an exact differential.

Example 24:

For an ideal gas PV = RT, prove that DT is an exact differential.

Solution:

$$PV = RT \qquad ...(1)$$

In order to prove that dT is a perfect differential, we have to prove that

$$\frac{\partial^2 T}{\partial V \partial P} = \frac{\partial^2 T}{\partial P \partial V}$$

On differentiating Eq. (1), we obtain

$$\left(\frac{\partial T}{\partial V}\right)_P = \frac{P}{R}; \text{i.e., } \frac{\partial^2 T}{\partial P \partial V} = \frac{1}{R}$$

Again $$\left(\frac{\partial T}{\partial P}\right)_V = \frac{V}{R}; \text{i.e., } \frac{\partial^2 T}{\partial V \partial P} = \frac{1}{R}$$

Therefore, $$\frac{\partial^2 T}{\partial V \partial P} = \frac{\partial^2 T}{\partial P \partial V}$$

Thus, dT is an exact differential.

Example 25:

Show that PV = nRt, then

(i) $$\frac{\partial^2 P}{\partial n \partial V} = \frac{\partial^2 P}{\partial V \partial n} = -\frac{RT}{V^2}$$

(ii) $$\frac{\partial^2 P}{\partial n \partial T} = \frac{\partial^2 P}{\partial T \partial n} = -\frac{R}{V}$$

(iii) $$\left(\frac{\partial P}{\partial T}\right)_V \left(\frac{\partial T}{\partial V}\right)_P \left(\frac{\partial V}{\partial P}\right)_T = -1$$

Solution:

(i) $\because$ $PV = nRT$

$\therefore$ $$P = \frac{nRT}{V}$$

or $$\frac{\partial P}{\partial V} = \frac{\partial}{\partial V}\left(\frac{nRT}{V}\right)$$ [keeping T as constant]

$$= nRT \frac{\partial}{\partial V}\left(\frac{1}{V}\right) = -\frac{nRT}{V^2}$$

$$\frac{\partial^2 P}{\partial n \partial V} = \frac{\partial}{\partial n}\left(\frac{\partial P}{\partial V}\right)$$

$$= \left(-\frac{nRT}{V^2}\right)$$ [Keeping R, T and V as constant]

$$= -\frac{RT}{V^2} \quad ...(1)$$

Similarly, PV = nRT or $P = \frac{nRT}{V}$

$$\frac{\partial P}{\partial n} = \frac{RT}{V}$$

$$\frac{\partial^2 P}{\partial V \partial N} = \frac{\partial}{\partial V}\left(\frac{RT}{V}\right)$$ [keeping T and R as constant]

$$= -\frac{RT}{V^2} \quad ...(2)$$

From equations (1) and (2), we obtain

$$\frac{\partial^2 P}{\partial n \partial V} = \frac{\partial^2 P}{\partial V \partial n} = -\frac{RT}{V^2}$$

(ii) $$P = \frac{nRT}{V}$$

$$\frac{\partial P}{\partial T} = \frac{\partial}{\partial T}\left(\frac{nRT}{V}\right)$$ [Keeping n and R as constant]

$$= \frac{nR}{V}$$

$$\frac{\partial^2 P}{\partial n \partial T} = \frac{\partial}{\partial n}\left(\frac{nR}{V}\right)$$ [Keeping V and R as constant]

$$= \frac{R}{V} \quad ...(3)$$

Again, $$P = \frac{nRT}{V}$$

$$\frac{\partial P}{\partial n} = \frac{RT}{V}$$ [Keeping RT and V as constant]

$$\frac{\partial^2 P}{\partial T \partial n} = \frac{\partial}{\partial n}\left(\frac{RT}{V}\right)$$ [Keeping RT and V as constant]

or $$\frac{\partial^2 P}{\partial T \partial n} = \frac{R}{V} \qquad ...(4)$$

From equations (3) and (4), we obtain

$$\frac{\partial^2 P}{\partial n \partial T} = \frac{\partial^2 P}{\partial T \partial n} = \frac{R}{V}$$

(iii) Again, $$P = \frac{nRT}{V}$$

$$\left(\frac{\partial P}{\partial T}\right)_V = \frac{nR}{V} \qquad ...(5)$$

Again, $$V = \frac{nRT}{P}$$

$$\left(\frac{\partial V}{\partial P}\right)_T = -\frac{nRT}{P} \qquad ...(6)$$

Again, $$T = \frac{PV}{nR}$$

$$\left(\frac{\partial T}{\partial V}\right)_P = -\frac{P}{nR} \qquad ...(7)$$

On multiplying equations (5), (6), and (7), we obtain

$$\left(\frac{\partial P}{\partial T}\right)_V \left(\frac{\partial T}{\partial V}\right)_P \left(\frac{\partial V}{\partial P}\right)_T = \frac{nR}{V} \times -\frac{nRT}{P^2} \times \frac{P}{nR}$$

$$= -\frac{nRT}{PV} = -1\left[\because 1 = \frac{nRT}{PV}\right]$$

Example 26:

(i) Calculate $\propto$ and β for an ideal gas obeying gas equation PV = RT (for one mole).

Solution:

(i) We know

$$PV = RT$$

On differentiating the above equation, we obtain

$$PdV + VdP = RdT \qquad ...(1)$$

At constant pressure dP = 0, the above equation becomes as follows:

$$\left(\frac{\partial V}{\partial T}\right)_P = \frac{R}{V}$$

or
$$\alpha = \frac{1}{V}\left(\frac{\partial V}{\partial T}\right)_P = \frac{R}{VP} = \frac{1}{T} = T^{-1}$$

At constant temperature dT = 0; equation (1) becomes as follows:

$$\left(\frac{\partial V}{\partial P}\right)_T = -\frac{V}{P}$$

or
$$\beta = -\frac{1}{V}\left(\frac{\partial V}{\partial P}\right)_T = \frac{V}{VP} = \frac{1}{P} = P^{-1}$$

(ii) The van der Waal's equation is as follows :

$$\left(P + \frac{a}{V^2}\right)(v - b) = RT$$

or
$$PV^3 - PbV^2 + aV - ab - RTV^2 = 0 \qquad ...(2)$$

On differentiating the above equation with respect to T at constant pressure, we obtain

$$3PV^2\left(\frac{\partial V}{\partial T}\right)_P - 2PbV\left(\frac{\partial V}{\partial T}\right)_P + a\left(\frac{\partial V}{\partial T}\right)_P$$
$$- 2RTV\left(\frac{\partial V}{\partial T}\right)_P - RV^2 = 0$$

or
$$\left(\frac{\partial V}{\partial T}\right)_P = \frac{RV^2}{3PV^2 - 2PbV + a - 2RTV}$$

$$\alpha = \frac{1}{V}\left(\frac{\partial V}{\partial T}\right)_P$$

$$= \frac{1}{V}\left[\frac{RV^2}{3PV^2 - 2PVb + a - 2RTV}\right]$$

$$= \frac{R}{3PV - 2Pb + \frac{a}{V} - 2RT}$$

But the van der Waal's equation may be put as follows :

$$RT = PV - Pb + \frac{a}{V} - \frac{ab}{V^2}$$

$$\therefore \qquad \alpha = \frac{R}{3PV - 2Pb + \frac{a}{V} - 2\left(PV - Pb + \frac{a}{V} - \frac{ab}{V^2}\right)}$$

$$= R\left[PV - \frac{a}{V} + \frac{2ab}{V^2}\right]^{-1}$$

Again, on differentiating equation (2), with respect to P at constant temperature T, we obtain

$$3PV^2\left(\frac{\partial V}{\partial P}\right)_T + V - 2PbV\left(\frac{\partial V}{\partial P}\right)_T$$

$$- bV^2 + a\left(\frac{\partial V}{\partial P}\right)_T - 2RTV\left(\frac{\partial V}{\partial P}\right)_T = 0$$

$$\left(\frac{\partial V}{\partial P}\right)_T = \frac{V^2(b - V)}{3PV^2 - 2PbV + a - 2RTV}$$

But the van der Waal's equation may be put as follows :

$$RTV = PV^2 + a - PbV - ab/V$$

$$\therefore \left(\frac{\partial V}{\partial P}\right)_T = \frac{V^2(b - V)}{3PV^2 - 2PbV + a - 2\left(PV^2 + a - PbV - \frac{ab}{V}\right)}$$

$$= \frac{b - V}{P - \frac{a}{V^2} + \frac{2ab}{V^3}}$$

Now $\qquad \beta = -\frac{1}{V}\left(\frac{\partial V}{\partial P}\right)_T = -\frac{b - V}{PV - \frac{a}{V} + \frac{2ab}{V^2}}$

$$= -\frac{V - b}{P - \frac{a}{V} + \frac{2ab}{V^2}}$$

Example 27:

For an ideal gas ($PV = nRT$) show that ($1/T$) is an integrating factor for $dw = P\,dV$.

Solution:

$$dw = P\ dV \qquad ..(1)$$

$\because$ $$PV = nRT$$

$\therefore$ $$p\ dV + V\ dP = nR\ dT$$

and $$dV = \frac{nR}{P} dT - \frac{V}{P} dP \qquad ...(2)$$

On substituting the expression for dV in equation (1), we obtain

$$dw = nR\ dT - V\ dP = nR\ dT - \frac{nRT}{P} dP$$

Now $$\frac{\partial}{\partial P}(nR)_T = 0$$

and $$\frac{\partial}{\partial T}\left(-\frac{nRT}{P}\right)_P = -\frac{nR}{P}$$

Hence, dw is inexact differential.

Suppose f = 1/T be an integrating factor. Then

$$f\ .\ dw = \frac{1}{T} nR\, dT - \frac{nR}{P} dP$$

$\therefore$ $$\frac{\partial}{\partial P}\left[\frac{nR}{T}\right]_T = 0$$

and $$\frac{\partial}{\partial T}\left[\frac{nR}{P}\right]_T = 0$$

Thus f. dw$\frac{nR}{T}$dT $-$ $\frac{nR}{P}$dP is an exact differential while 1/T is an integrating factor.

Example 28:

Calculate the maximum work obtainable by (i) the isothermal expansion and (ii) the adiabatic expansion of 2 mol of on ideal gas initially at 25° C form 10 L to 20 L. Assume Cv = (5/2) R.

Solution:

(i) Maximum work is obtained in reversible expansion. Hence

$$w = -\ nRT \ln \frac{V_2}{V_1}$$

$$= -(2 \text{ mol})(8.314 \text{ J K}^{-1} \text{ mol}^{-1})(298 \text{ K})(2.303 \log \frac{20\text{L}}{10\text{L}}$$

$$= -3435 \text{ J}$$

(ii) Firstly, we calculate the final temperature using the expression

$$T_2 V_2^{\gamma-1} = T_1 V_1^{\gamma-1}$$

where $$\gamma = \frac{C_P}{C_V} = \frac{(7/2)R}{(5/2)R} = \frac{7}{5}$$

Hence, $$T_2 = (298\text{K})\left(\frac{10\text{L}}{20\text{L}}\right)^{(7/5)-1}$$

$$= (298 \text{ K})(0.7578) = 225.8 \text{ K}$$

Now $$W_{adi} = \Delta E$$

$$= n\, C_{V,\,m}(T_2 - T_1)$$

$$= (2\text{mol})(2.5 \times 8.314 \text{ JK}^{-1}\text{mol}^{-1})(225.8\text{K} - 298\text{K})$$

$$= -3001 \text{ J.}$$

Example 29:

Show that

$$\left(\frac{\partial \alpha}{\partial P}\right)_T + \left(\frac{\partial \beta}{\partial T}\right)_P = 0$$

where α *and* β *are coefficient of thermal expansion and coefficient of compressibility, respectively.*

Solution:

Since V is a state function, we can write

$$\frac{\partial^2 V}{\partial T\, \partial P} = \frac{\partial^2 V}{\partial P\, \partial T}$$

or $$\frac{\partial}{\partial T}(-V\beta)_P = \frac{\partial}{\partial T}(V\alpha)_T$$

Carrying out the differentiation, we get

$$-\beta\left(\frac{\partial V}{\partial T}\right)_P - V\left(\frac{\partial \beta}{\partial T}\right)_{P'} = \alpha\left(\frac{\partial V}{\partial P}\right)_T + V\left(\frac{\partial \alpha}{\partial P}\right)_T$$

that is $$\left(\frac{\partial \alpha}{\partial P}\right)_T + \left(\frac{\partial \beta}{\partial T}\right)_P = -\frac{\beta}{V}\left(\frac{\partial V}{\partial T}\right)_P - \frac{\alpha}{V}\left(\frac{\partial V}{\partial P}\right)_T$$

$$= -\frac{\beta}{V}(\alpha V) - \frac{\alpha}{V}(-\beta V) = 0$$

Example 30:

Show that Joule Thomson coefficient, μ_{JT} = 0 for an ideal gas. Comment on the liquefaction of an ideal gas.

Solution:

By definition, Joule-Thomson coefficient is defined as

$$\mu_{JT} = \left(\frac{\partial T}{\partial P}\right)_H$$

Using the cyclic rule

$$\left(\frac{\partial T}{\partial P}\right)_H \left(\frac{\partial P}{\partial H}\right)_T \left(\frac{\partial H}{\partial T}\right)_P + 1 = 0$$

we get $$\left(\frac{\partial T}{\partial P}\right)_H = -\frac{1}{\left(\frac{\partial P}{\partial H}\right)_T \left(\frac{\partial H}{\partial T}\right)_P} = -\frac{\left(\frac{\partial H}{\partial P}\right)_T}{C_P}$$

Now using, thermodynamic equation of state

$$\left(\frac{\partial T}{\partial P}\right)_H = V - T\left(\frac{\partial V}{\partial T}\right)_P$$

we get $$\mu_{JT} = \frac{V - T\left(\frac{\partial V}{\partial T}\right)_P}{C_P}$$

Now, for an ideal gas

$$V = \frac{nRT}{P}$$

Hence, $$\left(\frac{\partial V}{\partial T}\right)_P = \frac{nR}{P} = \frac{V}{T}$$

Thus $$\mu_{JT} = \frac{V - T\left(\frac{V}{T}\right)}{C_P} = 0$$

The ideal gas cannot be liquefied as there will not occur any change in temperature when the gas undergoes Joule-Thomson experiment.

Example 31:

Calculate the work down when 50 g of iron dissolves in hydrochloric acid at 25oC in (i) a closed vessel and (ii) an open beaker. (iii) In which case would maximum amount of work be done ?

Solution:

$$\text{Amount of iron} = \frac{50\text{ g}}{55.85\text{ g mol}^{-1}} = \frac{50}{55.85}\text{ mol}$$

(i) In a closed vessel, $\Delta V = 0$. Hence,

$$dw = -PdV = 0$$

that is, no work is involved when iron dissolves in hydrochloric acid in a closed vessel.

(ii) The reaction between iron and hydrochloric acid is

$$Fe + 2HCl \rightarrow FeCl_2 + H_2(g)$$

Thus, the liberated hydrogen gas pushes the atmospheric air and thus involves the work of expansion. In this case, we will have

$$w = -P_{ext}\,\Delta V$$
$$= -P_{ext}\,V_{H2}$$

where V_{H2} is the volume of hydrogen released. According to the ideal gas law, we will have

$$w = -P_{ext}\,(n_{H2}RT/P_{ext})$$
$$= -n_{H2}RT$$
$$= -(50/55.85)\text{ mol }(8.314\text{ J K}^{-1}\text{ mol}^{-1})\text{ }(298\text{ K})$$
$$= -2.2\text{ kJ.}$$

Example 32:

Since $CV = (\partial q/\partial T)\,V$ by definition, one often writes without restriction $dV = C_V dT$. This is generally not true. Explain why.

Solution:

If we take U = f)V, T), then we will have

$$dU = \left(\frac{\partial U}{\partial V}\right)_T dV + \left(\frac{\partial U}{\partial T}\right)_V dT$$

$$= \left(\frac{\partial U}{\partial V}\right)_T \,.\, dV + C_V\, dT$$

Thus, if one writes $dV = C_V\, dT$ without restriction then this statement is not complete. This is applicable for a system in which $(\partial U/\partial V)_T = 0$. An ideal gas is such an example. Alternatively, the system may be undergoing change at constant volume, for which, $(\partial U/\partial V)_T\, dV$ is zero and thus $dV = C_V\, dT$.

Example 33:

Calculate the work done by the system when 2 mol of an ideal gas expand from 0.01 m^3 to 0.1 m^3 at 300 k isothermally :

(i) into a vacuum, and

(ii) reversibly.

Explain how the surroundings can be restored only in one case and not in the other.

Solution:

(i) When the work is done into a vacuum, the work done by the system is zero since P_{opp} in this case is zero.

(ii) For the reversible isothermal expansion work involved is

$$w = -\,nRT \ln \frac{V_2}{V_1}$$

$$= (2)\,(8.314 \times 300\ J) \ln \frac{0.1}{0.01}$$

$$= -\,2 \times 8.314 \times 300 \times 2.303\ J$$

$$= -\,11488\ J = -\,11.488\ kJ.$$

This surroundings are not disturbed when the expansion is done against vacuum. In case of reversible isothermal expansion, heat is absorbed by the system from the surroundings. Now if we carry out reversible isothermal compression of the system till the original state, then the same quantity or heat is released to the surroundings and thus the latter is restored back to the original state. However, in the first case where expansion is done against vacuum, there will be bet heat received by the surroundings during compression. Hence, in this case, it is not restored back to its original state.

Example 34:

Derive $C_{P,m} - C_{V,m} = TV_m \dfrac{\alpha^2}{\beta}$

where α *and* β *are the coefficient of thermal expansion and coefficient of compressibility, respectively.*

Solution:

We start with H = f (T, P) and U = f (T, V) and write their differentials as

$$dH = \left(\frac{\partial H}{\partial T}\right)_P dT + \left(\frac{\partial H}{\partial P}\right)_T dP$$

$$dU = \left(\frac{\partial U}{\partial T}\right)_V dT + \left(\frac{\partial U}{\partial V}\right)_T dV$$

Now since H = U + PV

we have dH = dU + P dV + V dP

$$\text{or} \left(\frac{\partial H}{\partial T}\right)_P dT + \left(\frac{\partial H}{\partial P}\right)_T dP = \left(\frac{\partial U}{\partial T}\right)_V dT + \left(\frac{\partial U}{\partial V}\right)_T dV + P\,dV + V\,dP$$

Dividing by dT, keeping P constant, we get

$$\left(\frac{\partial H}{\partial T}\right)_P = \left(\frac{\partial U}{\partial T}\right)_V + \left(\frac{\partial U}{\partial V}\right)_T \left(\frac{\partial V}{\partial T}\right)_P + P\left(\frac{\partial V}{\partial T}\right)_P$$

Now using the thermodynamic equation of state

$$\left(\frac{\partial U}{\partial V}\right)_T = T\left(\frac{\partial P}{\partial T}\right)_V - P$$

we get
$$\left(\frac{\partial H}{\partial T}\right)_P = \left(\frac{\partial U}{\partial T}\right)_V + T\left(\frac{\partial P}{\partial T}\right)_V \left(\frac{\partial V}{\partial T}\right)_P \qquad ...(1)$$

Now, by definition

$$\alpha = \frac{1}{V}\left(\frac{\partial V}{\partial T}\right)_P \qquad ...(2)$$

$$\beta = -\frac{1}{V}\left(\frac{\partial V}{\partial P}\right)_T \qquad ...(3)$$

Using the cyclic rule

$$\left(\frac{\partial V}{\partial P}\right)_T \left(\frac{\partial P}{\partial T}\right)_V \left(\frac{\partial T}{\partial V}\right)_P + 1 = 0$$

we get $$\left(\frac{\partial V}{\partial P}\right)_T = -\left(\frac{\partial V}{\partial T}\right)_P \left(\frac{\partial T}{\partial P}\right)_V$$

Hence

$$\beta = \frac{1}{V}\left(\frac{\partial V}{\partial T}\right)_P \cdot \left(\frac{\partial T}{\partial P}\right)_V$$

and $$\frac{\alpha}{\beta} = \left(\frac{\partial P}{\partial T}\right)_V$$

Hence, Eq (1) becomes

$$C_{P,m} - C_{V,m} = T\left(\frac{\partial P}{\partial T}\right)_V \left(\frac{\partial V}{\partial T}\right)_P \qquad ...(4)$$

With the use of Eqs. (2) and (4), we get

$$C_{P,m} - C_{V,m} = TV\frac{\alpha^2}{\beta}$$

Example 35:

When a bicycle tyre is inflated with hand pump, the temperature of the air inside increases. Explain.

Solution:

Work done on the system is converted into heat which increases the temperature of air inside the tyre.

Example 36:

Describe a process through with the gas can be restored to its initial state in each of the above cases. Explain how the surroundings can be restored only in one ca. e and not in the other.

Solution:

The gas can be restored to its initial state by compressing it isothermally from 5 dm^3 to 1 dm^3. This may be done reversibly or irreversibly. When the compression is done reversibly, the surroundings in the case of (ii) will be restored whereas in case of (i), it cannot be restored whether the compressions is done reversibly or irreversibly. This is because, while on expansion, surroundings remain unchanged whereas during compression, it has to do work on the system and thus suffers changes.

Example 37:

Can q become a state function ?

Solution:

Heat exchange reversibly at constant volume (or at constant pressure) is equal to the change in internal energy (or enthalpy) of a system. Since the latter is a state function, it follows that in such conditions q also behaves like a state function.

Example 38:

Is the equation PV^γ = constant valid for all processes ? Explain your answer.

Solution:

The expression PV^γ = constant is valid only for adiabatic reversible volume change (*i.e.*, expansion or compression) involving an ideal gas. For adiabatic process, dq = 0.

Hence

$$dU = dw$$

$$C_V dT = - P_{ext}\, dV$$

For revisable process, $P_{ext} = P_{int}$. Now replacing P_{int} = nRT/V and separating the variables followed by integration, we get

$$\frac{Cv}{n}\int\frac{dT}{T} = -R\int\frac{dV}{V}$$

or $$C_{V,m}\ln\frac{T_2}{T_1} = -R\ln\frac{V_2}{V_1}$$

or $$\left(\frac{T_2}{T_1}\right)^{C_{v,m}} = \left(\frac{V_2}{V_1}\right)^{-R}$$

Replacing T_2/T_1 by P_2V_2/P_1V_1 and rearranging, the expression would yield

$$P_2V^\gamma_2 = P_1V^\gamma_1$$

that is $$PV^\gamma = \text{constant}.$$

Example 39:

Two bodies at different temperatures are connected by a wire with infinitesimal thermal conductance so that heat flows infinitely slowly from the hot bodies to the cold body until they are at the same temperature. Is this process reversible? Explain.

Solution:

In a reversible process, at any stage, the external condition responsible for the process to occur differs from the internal condition by an infinitesimal amount. The given transfer of heat is not a reversible process as the two bodies are at different temperatures.

Moreover, the reversible processes are characterized by the fact that when the system is restored to its original state by traversing the forward sequence of steps in the reverse order, then not only the system but also the surroundings are restored to their original states. In the given process, heat flow from a hot body to a cold body does not disturb the surroundings but if we wish to carry out the reverse process, the surroundings will have to do some work. Hence, the surroundings are not brought back to the original state in the reverse process. Thus, the given process is not a reversible one.

Example 40:

How would the energy of an ideal gas change if it is made to expand into vacuum at constant temperature ?

Solution:

For the expansion against vacuum $P_{opp} = 0$

Hence $w = - P_{opp} \Delta V = 0$

Since the expansion is at constant temperature no heat is supplied to the system, *i.e.*, $q = 0$. Now, from the first law of thermodynamics, we can write

$$\Delta E = q + w = 0$$

that is, the energy of an ideal gas does not change if it is made to expand into vacuum at constant temperature. This also follows from the fact that the energy of an ideal gas depends only on temperature and since temperature remains constant, its energy also remains constant.

Example 41:

Four moles of an ideal gas are held by a piston under 5 atm pressure and at 273.15 K. The pressure is suddenly released to 0.2 atm and the gas is allowed to expand isothermally. Calculate w, q, ΔE and ΔH for the process.

Solution:

As the pressure has been released suddenly, the expansion must be irreversible.

Here n = 4 moles; P_1 = 5 atm; $T_1 = T_2$ = 273.15 K.

(i) Work done irreversibly

$$w = nRT\left\{1-\frac{P_2}{P_1}\right\}$$

$$= 4 \times 8.314 \times 273.15 \left\{1-\frac{0.2}{5}\right\}$$

$$= 4 \times 8.314 \times 273.15 \times 0.96$$

$$= 8720 \text{ J.}$$

(ii) As the ideal gas expands isothermally dT = 0 and hence ΔE =0; ΔH = 0.

(iii) First law gives

$$\Delta E = q - w = 0$$

$$\therefore\ q = w\ 8720 \text{ J.}$$

Example 42:

At low temperature, a nonideal gas follows the relation PV = RT − a/V where a = 0.3636 Nm⁴ mole⁻². Calculate the work done by one mole of this gas in expanding form 0.224 litre to 22.4 litre at 400 K. Compare this result with the work done in the corresponding expansion of an ideal gas.

Solution:

For an ideal gas, reversible work done

$$= 2.303\ n\ RT \log \frac{V_2}{V_1}$$

$$V_1 = 0.224 \text{ litres mole}^{-1} = 22.4 \times 10^{-5} \text{ m}^3 \text{ mole}^{-1}$$

$P_2 = 22.4$ litres mole^{-1} = 22.4×10^{-3} m^3 mole^{-1}

R = 8.314 J K^{-1} mole^{-1}

$$W_{rew} = (2.303)\,(1 \text{ mole})\,(8.314 \text{ J K}^{-1} \text{ mole}^{-1})\,(400 \text{ K}) \times \log \frac{22.4 \times 10^{-3}}{22.4 \times 10^{-5}}$$

$$= (2.303)\,(1 \text{ mole})\,(8.314 \text{ J K}^{-1} \text{ mole}^{-1})\,(400 \text{ K}) \log 100$$

$$= 15320 \text{ J mole}^{-1}$$

$$= 15.32 \text{ kJ mole}^{-1}.$$

For the non-ideal gas PV = RT – a/V

$$\text{Therefore, the work done} = \int_{V_1}^{V_2} P\,dV = \int_{V_1}^{V_2} \left\{\frac{RT}{V} - \frac{a}{V_2}\right\} dV$$

$$= 2.303 \text{ RT} \log \frac{V_2}{V_1} + a\left\{\frac{1}{V_2} - \frac{1}{V_1}\right\}$$

The value of first part is from derived eq. (1) as 15.32 kJ mole^{-1} and of another part can be derived as

$$0.3636 \text{ Nm}^4 \text{ mole}^{-2} \left\{\frac{1}{22.4 \times 10^{-3} \text{ m}^3 \text{ mole}^{-1}} - \frac{1}{22.4 \times 10^{-5} \text{ m}^3 \text{ mole}^{-1}}\right\}$$

$$= 1.604 \text{ kJ mole}^{-1}.$$

Thus work done = 15.320 k Joule^{-1} – 1.604 k Joule^{-1}

$$= 13.716 \text{ kJ mole}^{-1}.$$

Example 43:

Under what conditions does the adiabatic expansion of gas become a constant energy process ?

Solution:

If the adiabatic expansions done against a vacuum then in this process energy

On comparing the coefficients in Eqs (1) and (2), we have

$$\left(\frac{\partial E}{\partial T}\right)_V = T \qquad ...(3)$$

and $$\left(\frac{\partial E}{\partial V}\right)_S = -P \qquad ...(4)$$

Eq (4) can be written as

$$dE = T\ dS \qquad ...(5)$$

For a given temperature, the above equation on integration becomes as follows :

$$\int dE = \int TdS + \text{Integration constant}$$

$$E = TS + A \qquad ...(6)$$

or $$E = A - TS$$

where A is an integration constant. It is also known as Helmholtz free energy function.

(d) Enthalpy as a Function of S and P

As H is a function of S and P, we can write

$$H = f\ (S, P)$$

or $$dH = \left(\frac{\partial H}{\partial S}\right)_P dS + \left(\frac{\partial H}{\partial P}\right)_S dP \qquad ...(1)$$

We also know, $dH = T\ dS + V\ dP$ ...(2)

On comparing the coefficients in Eqs (1) and (2), we get

$$\left(\frac{\partial H}{\partial S}\right)_P = T \qquad ...(3)$$

$$\left(\frac{\partial H}{\partial P}\right)_S = V \qquad ...(4)$$

When Eq. (3) is integrated, we get a new function

$$\int dH = \int TdS + \text{constant}$$

$$= \int TdS + G$$

or $$H = TS + G$$

or $$G = H - TS$$

where G is an integration constant and is the same as the Gibbs free energy function.

Example 44:

Two moles of an ideal gas at 300 K expand reversibly and isothermally from 4×10^{-2} m^3 to 8×10^{-2} m^3. Calculate the entropy change for the gas. How would you account for the fact that ΔS is not zero although the process is reversible ?

Solution:

If the process is reversible isothermal it means that $\Delta H = 0$, hence the entropy change is given as follows :

$$\Delta S_{sys} = \frac{Q_{rev}}{T} = \frac{W_{rev}}{T} = nR \ln\frac{V_2}{V_1}$$

$$= (2 \text{ mol})\ (8.314 \text{ JK}^{-1} \text{ mol}^{-1}) \left(2.303 \log \frac{8 \times 10^{-2}}{4 \times 10^{-2}}\right)$$

$$= 2 \times 8.314 \times 2.303 \log 2 \text{ JK}^{-1}$$

$$= 2 \times 8.314 \times 2.303 \times 0.3010 \text{ JK}^{-1}$$

$$= 11.526579 \text{ JK}^{-1}.$$

The total entropy change (system and its surroundings) will be zero for a reversible process.

Example 45:

Calculate the entropy changes involved in the conversion of 1 mole of ice at 0°C and 1 atm to liquid at 0°C and 1 atm [The enthalpy of fusion per mole of ice is 6008 J mol^{-1}].

Solution:

$$H_2O\ (S) \rightarrow H_2O\ (l)$$

$$\Delta S_{fus} = \frac{\Delta H_{fus}}{T_m}$$

$$= \frac{6008 \text{ J mol}^{-1}}{273 \text{ K}}$$

$$= 22.007326 \text{ JK}^{-1}.$$

Example 46:

Calculate the change of entropy for the process

$$H_2O\ (l,\ 373\ K) \rightarrow H_2O\ (v,\ 373\ K)$$

Here $\Delta H_{vap} = 40850\ J\ mol^{-1}$ *at 373 K.*

Solution:

$$\Delta S_{vap} = \frac{\Delta H_{vap}}{T_b}$$

$$= \frac{40850\ J\ mol^{-1}}{373\ K}$$

$$= 109.51742\ JK^{-1}\ mol^{-1}$$

But $\Delta S_{vap} = S\ (vapour) - S\ (liquid)$

$$= 109.5\ JK^{-1}\ mol^{-1}$$

$\therefore$ $S\ (vapour) = S\ (liquid) + 109.5\ JK^{-1}\ mol^{-1}$.

Example 47:

Evaluate the entropy change for the following reversible process.

$$1\ mole\ Sn\ (\alpha,\ 13^oC \rightleftharpoons 1\ mole\ Sn\ (b,\ 13^oC)$$

where $\Delta H_{trans} = 2090\ J\ mol^{-1}$

Solution

$$T_{trans} = 273 + 13 = 286\ K$$

$$\Delta S_{trans} = \frac{\Delta H_{trans}}{T_{trans}}$$

$$= \frac{2090\ J\ mol^{-1}}{286\ K}$$

$$= 7.3076923\ JK^{-1}\ mol^{-1}.$$

Example 48:

Calculate the entropy change when two moles of; an ideal gas expands reversibly from an initial volume of 2 dm³ to a total volume of 20 dm³ at a constant temperature of 298 K.

Solution:

We know, $\Delta S = nR\ \ln\left(\frac{V_2}{V_1}\right)$

$$= 2.303 \text{ nR log} \left(\frac{V_2}{V_1}\right)$$

$$= 2.303 \times 2 \times 8.314 \text{ J JK}^{-1} \text{ mol}^{-1} \log \left(\frac{20\text{dm}^3}{2\text{dm}^3}\right)$$

$$= 2.303 \times 2 \times 8.314 \times \log \text{JK}^{-1} \text{ mol}^{-1}$$

$$= 38.294284 \text{ JK}^{-1} \text{ mol}^{-1}.$$

Example 49:

The mixing of gases is always accompanied by an increase in entropy. Show that in the formation of a binary mixture of two ideal gases the maximum entropy increase results when $X_1 = X_2 = 0.5$.

Solution:

For a binary ;mixture, the entropy per mole of ;the mixture formed is given by

$$\Delta S \text{ mixing} = - R[X_1 \ln X_1 + X_2 \ln X_2]$$

$$= - R[X_1 \ln X_1 + (1 - X_1) \ln (1 - X_1)]$$

For entropy of mixing to be maximum, the first derivative,

$$\frac{\delta(\Delta S \text{mixing})}{\delta X_1}$$

should be zero and the second derivative should be negative. Differentiating, ΔS mixing with respect to X_1 and equating it to zero yields

$$\frac{\delta(\Delta S \text{mixing})}{\delta X_1} = - R\left[\ln X_1 + \frac{X_1}{X_1} + \frac{1 - X_1}{1 - X_1}(-1) + (-1) \ln (1 - X_1)\right]$$

$$= 0$$

$$\ln X_1 + 1 - 1 - \ln (1 - X_1) = 0$$

$$\ln \frac{X_1}{1 - X_1} = 0$$

$$X_1 = 1 - X_1$$

$$X_1 = 1/2.$$

Example 50:

One mole of hydrogen and nine moles of nitrogen are mixed at 291.K and 1 atm pressure. Assuming ideal behaviour for the gases, calculate the entropy of mixing per mole of the mixture formed. Would it make any difference if under similar conditions one mole of hydrogen is mixed with nine moles of oxygen.

Solution:

For ideal gases the entropy of mixing per mole of the mixture is given as follows

$$\Delta S_{mixing} = -R \sum X_i \ln X_i$$

In this case $X_{H2} = 0.1$ and $X_{N2} = 0.9$

$$\Delta Smixing = -R\,[0.1 \ln 0.1 + 0.9 \ln 0.9]$$

$$= -(8.314\ JK^{-1}\ mole^{-1})\ (2.303)\ (0.1)$$

$$[\because \quad R = 8.314\ \ JK^{-1}\ mol^{-1}]$$

$$\left[\log\frac{1}{10} + 9\log\frac{9}{10}\right]$$

$$= 2.704 \quad JK^{-1}\ mol^{-1}$$

When hydrogen is mixed with oxygen, the entropy of mixing would remain unchanged provided oxygen also behaves ideally.

Example 51:

Two moles of an ideal gas are allowed to expand isothermally from 0.04 m³ to 0.4 m³ at 300 K. Calculate the entropy change for the system, surroundings and universe if the expansion is

(i) reversible and

(ii) irreversible against a constant external pressure of 0.2 atm.

Solution:

$$Q_{rev} = W = n\,RT \ln\frac{V_2}{V_1}$$

$$\Delta S_{rev} = \frac{Q_{rev}}{T} = nR \ln\frac{V_2}{V_1}$$

$$= (2\ mol)\ (8.314)\ J\ mol^{-1}\ K^{-1}\ (2.303)\ \log\frac{0.40}{0.04}$$

$= 38.294284\ JK^{-1}$.

The surroundings is losing an exactly equivalent amount of heat and hence its entropy decrease is given as follows :

$$\Delta S_{surr} = \frac{(-Q_{rev})}{T} = -19.14\ JK^{-1}$$

The entropy change of the universe is given as follows :

$$\Delta S_{univ} = \Delta S_{sys} + \Delta S_{surr} = 0$$

(ii) In the irreversible expansion, the entropy change of the system is still the same as in the reversible change, *i.e.*, 19.14 JK^{-1} but heat lost by the surroundings is given by $-P\Delta V$ and consequently the entropy change, if the transfer were reversible, is

$$\Delta S_{surr} = \frac{Q_{surr}}{T} = -\frac{P\Delta V}{T}$$

$$= -\frac{(0.2\,\text{atm.})(0.4 - 0.04\,\text{m}^3)(101325\ \text{Jm}^{-3}\ \text{atm}^{-1})}{300\ \text{K}}$$

$$= -\frac{0.2 \times 0.36 \times 101325}{300}\ JK^{-1}$$

$= 24.318\ JK^{-1}$.

Example 52:

Calculate the entropy change when 1 mole of perfect gas is allowed to expand at 27°C from a volume of 2 litres to a volume of 20 litres against a constant pressure of one atmosphere.

Solution:

We know

$$dS = C_V \frac{dT}{T} + R\frac{dV}{V}$$

By integrating this equation, we get

$$S_2 - S_1 = C_V \ln \frac{T_2}{T_1} + R \ln \frac{V_2}{V_1}$$

At constant temperature,

$$S_2 - S_1 = R \ln \frac{V_2}{V_1}$$

$$= 2.303 \text{ R} \log \frac{V_2}{V_1}$$

$$= 2.303 \times 2 \times \log \frac{20}{2}$$

$$= 2.303 \times 2 \times \log 10$$

$$= 4.606 \text{ cal./ degree/mole.}$$

$$\begin{bmatrix} \because \text{ R} = 2 \text{ cal./degree/mole} \\ V_1 = 2 \text{ litres} \\ V_2 = 20 \text{ litres} \end{bmatrix}$$

Example 53:

The temperature of an ideal monoatomic gas is increased from 546 K to 1638 K. Calculate the pressure change in order that the entropy of the gas remains unchanged in the process

Solution:

The entropy change for the system can be explained by the following relation which is as follows

$$\Delta S_{sys} = nC_P \ln \frac{T_2}{T_1} \text{ nR} \ln \frac{P_2}{P_1}$$

$$\Delta S_{sys} = 0, \text{ thus}$$

$$C_P \ln \frac{T_2}{T_1} = R \ln \frac{P_2}{P_1}$$

$$\frac{5}{2} \text{ R} \log \frac{T_2}{T_1} = \text{R} \log \frac{P_2}{P_1}$$

$$\frac{5}{2} \log \frac{1638 \text{ K}}{546 \text{ K}} = \log \frac{P_2}{P_1}$$

$$\frac{P_2}{P_1} = 15.60$$

Thus in order to make entropy constant, the pressure of the gas must be increased by 15.60 times its initial value.

Example 54:

2 moles of an ideal monoatomic gas ($C_V = 20.91$ J mol^{-1} K^{-1}) are heated from 700 K to 750 K. The volume of the gas changes from 0.08

m^3 to 0.8 m^3. Assuming that the heat capacity remains constant in this temperature range, calculate the entropy change for the system, the surroundings and the universe if the process is carried out (a) reversibly and (b) irreversibly by placing the system in contact with a reservoir at 500 K and allowing the gas to expand against a const. external pressure equal to the final pressure of the gas.

Solution:

For the reversible transformation of an ideal gas the entropy change of the system is given as follows :

$$\Delta S_{system} = nC_V \ln \frac{T_2}{T_1} + nR \ln \frac{V_2}{V_1}$$

$$= (2 \text{ mol})(20.9 \text{ J mol}^{-1} \text{ K}^{-1})(2.303) \log \left.\frac{750}{700}\right)$$

$$+ (2 \text{ mol})(8.314 \text{ J mol}^{-1} \text{ K}^{-1})(2.303) \log \frac{0.80}{0.08}$$

$$= 6.449 + 38.28 = 44.729 \text{ JK}^{-1}.$$

As the process is reversible, the entropy change of the surrounding is as follows.

$$\Delta S_{sur} = -44.729 \text{ JK}^{-1}$$

and the entropy change of the universe is as follows

$$\Delta S_{univ} = \Delta S_{sys} + \Delta S_{surr} = 0$$

(b) In the irreversible transformation the entropy change of the system will be the same. Heat lost by the surrounding is as

$$-Q = \Delta E - W$$

$$\Delta E = -n C_V (750 - 700)$$

and
$$\omega = P_{ext}(V_2 - V_1).$$

Thus according to the final state

$$T_2 = 750 \text{ K}$$

$$V_2 = 0.8 \text{ m}^3$$

and hence the pressure is given at follows

$$P_2 = \frac{nRT_2}{V_2} = \frac{(2 \text{ mol})\left(8.314 \text{ J mol}^{-1} \text{ K}^{-1}\right)(750\text{K})}{\left(0.8 \text{ m}^3\right)}$$

$= 15588.75\ Jm^{-3}$.

Now $P_{ext} = P_2 = 15588.75\ Jm^{-3}$ and hence the heat lost by the surrounding is

$$- Q = - (2\ mol)\ (20.9\ J\ mol^{-1}\ K^{-1})\ (50\ K)$$

$$- (15588.75\ Jm^{-3})\ (0.8\ m^3 - 0.08\ m^3)$$

$$= - 2090\ j - 11223.9$$

$$= 13313.9\ J.$$

Let us assume that this heat is lost reversibly by the surroundings. Its entropy change is given as

$$\Delta S_{surr} = \frac{13313.9\ j}{500\ K} = 26.6278 JK^{-1}$$

and the entropy change of the universe is

$$\Delta S_{univ} = \Delta S_{sys} + \Delta S_{surr}$$

$$= (44.729 - 26.6278)\ JK^{-1}$$

$$= 18.1012\ JK^{-1}.$$

Example 55:

The molar heat capacity at capacity at constant pressure of solid magnesium (0° – 600°C) is expressed by

CP = 6.20 + 1.30 × 10–3 T – 6.80 × 104 T–2

Calculate the increase in entropy when 1 gm atom of metal is heated from 27°C to 127°C at constant pressure.

Solution:

At constant pressure,

$$\Delta S = \int \frac{T_2}{T_1} \frac{C_P}{T} dT$$

$$\therefore \qquad \Delta S = \int_{300}^{400} \frac{\left(6.20 + 1.30 \times 10^{-3}\,T - 6.80 \times 10^4\,T^{-2}\right)dT}{T}$$

$$\int_{300}^{400} 6.20 \frac{dT}{T} + \int_{300}^{400} 1.3 \times 10^{-3} dT - \int_{300}^{400} 6.20 \times 10^4 \frac{dT}{T^3}$$

$$= 6.20 \ln\left[\ln T\right]_{300}^{400} + 1.3 \times 10^{-3} \left[T\right]_{300}^{400} - \frac{6.80 \times 10^4}{-2} \left[\frac{1}{T^2}\right]_{300}^{400}$$

$$= 6.20 \ln \frac{400}{300} + 1.3 \times 10^{-3} \times (400 - 300) + 3.40 \times 10^{4}$$

$$\left[\frac{1}{(400)^2} - \frac{1}{(300)^2}\right]$$

$$= 1.7487 \text{ cal./degree.}$$

Example 56:

Calculate the increase in entropy of three moles of hydrogen as it changes from 300°K atm to 1000°K and 1 atm (C_p = 7 cal./degree/ mole).

Solution:

Entropy change ΔS for n moles

$$= n\, C_P \ln \frac{T_2}{T_1}\, n\, R \ln \frac{P_2}{P_1}$$

$$= 3 \times 7 \times 2.303 \log \frac{1000}{300} - 3 \times 2 \times 2.303 \log \frac{10}{0.1}$$

$$= 25.287996 - 13.818$$

$$= 11.469996 \text{ cal./degree.}$$

Example 57:

A thermostat was maintained at 370.05 K. For nearly an hour 4.2 kJ of heat leaked through the thermostat insulation into a room where the initial temperature of air was 300.05 K. (i) What was the entropy change of the material in the thermostat ? (ii) What was the entropy change of the air in the room? (iii) Was the process spontaneous? (Material in the thermostat is water).

Solution:

(i) Entropy change of the material in the thermostat

$$-\frac{4.2 \text{ kJ}}{370.05\text{K}} = -11.35 \times 10^{3} \text{ kj K}^{-1}$$

(ii) Entropy change of the air in the room

$$= \frac{4.2 \text{ kJ}}{300.05 \text{ K}} = 14.00 \times 10^{3} \text{ kJ K}^{-1}$$

(iii) Now

$$\Delta S_{total} = \Delta S_{thermostat} + \Delta S_{room}$$
$$= (-11.35 + 14.00)\ JK^{-1}$$
$$= 2.65\ J\ K^{-1}$$

Since ΔStotal is positive, the process of leaking is spontaneous.

Example 58:

Derive an expression for the entropy change when a van der Waals gas is heated and expanded simultaneously.

Solution:

Taking S = f(T, V), we get

$$dF = \left(\frac{\partial S}{\partial T}\right)_V dT + \left(\frac{\partial S}{\partial V}\right)_T dV$$

$$= \frac{nC_{V,m}}{T} dT + \left(\frac{\partial P}{\partial T}\right)_V dV$$

Now for van der Waal's gas we have

$$P = \frac{nRT}{V - nb} - \frac{n^2a}{V^2}$$

Therefore $$\left(\frac{\partial P}{\partial T}\right)_V = \frac{nRT}{V - nb}$$

Thus $$dS = \frac{nC_{V,m}}{T} dT + \frac{nR}{V - nb} dV$$

Which on integrating within the limit T_1, V_1 and T_2, V_2 gives

$$\Delta S\ nC_{V,m} \ln \frac{T_2}{T_1} + nR \ln \frac{V_2 - nb}{V_1 - nb}$$

Example 59:

For an adiabatic process, dq = 0, If one were to write

$$\Delta S = \int \frac{dq}{T} = \int \frac{0}{T} = 0$$

Then every adiabatic process would be iso-entropic process. Comment.

Solution:

For an adiabatic process, dq – 0, and according to the first law of thermodynamics, dq = dU – dw

Thus, we will have

$$dU = dw$$

The expression of entropy change will be given as

$$\Delta S = \int \frac{dU - dw}{T}$$

$$= \int \frac{dU}{T} + \int \frac{P_{opp}}{T} dV$$

Now, it is only for reversible process the first integral is equal and opposite sign of the second integral and thus ΔS = 0. For an irreversible process, these two integrals do not have equal magnitude and thus sum is not zero. Hence, ΔS ≠ 0 for an adiabatic irreversible process.

Example 60:

When a system is taken from the state A to the state B, along the path ACB, 80 joules of heat flows into the system, and the system does 30 joules of work (Fig. 1.36).

(a) *Bow much heat flows into the system along the path ADB, if the work done is 10 joules.*

(b) *The system is returned from the state B to the state A along the curved path. The work done on the system is 20 joules. Does the system absorb or liberate heat and how much?*

(c) *If $U_A = 0$, $U_D = 40$ joules, find the heat absorbed in the process AD and DB.*

Solution:

Along the path ACB,

$$HACB = U_B - U_A + W$$

Here $H = +80$ joules

$W = +30$ joules

$\therefore +80 = U_B - U_A + 30$

$U_B - U_A = 80 - 30 = 50$ joules

(a) Along the path ADB,

$$W = +10 \text{ joules}$$

$$H_{ADB} = U_B - U_A + W$$

$$H = 50 + 10 = 60 \text{ joules}$$

(b) For the curved path from B to A,

$$W = -20 \text{ joules}$$

$$H = (U_A - U_B) + W$$

$$= -50 - 20 = -70 \text{ joules}$$

(–ve sign shows that heat is liberated by the system)

(c) $U_A = 0,$

$$U_D = 40 \text{ joules}$$

$$U_B - U_A = 50$$

$\therefore$ $U_B = 50$ joules

In the process ADB, 10 joules of work is done. Work done from 4 to D is +10 joules and from D to B is zero.

For AD,

$$H_{AD} = (U_D - U_A) + W$$

$$= 40 + 10 = 50 \text{ joules}$$

For DB

$$H_{DB} = U_C - U_D + W$$

$$= 50 - 40 + 0 = 10 \text{ joules.}$$

Example 61:

Calculate ΔS, ΔH and ΔU for the process

$$H_2O(l, 20^\circ C, 1 \text{ atm}) \rightarrow H_2O\ (g, 250^\circ C, 1 \text{ atm})$$

Given the following data :

$$C_p\ (l) = 75.6 \text{ J K}^{-1} \text{ mol}^{-1}$$

$$C_p\ (g) = 36.2 \text{ J K}^{-1} \text{ mol}^{-1}$$

ΔH for vaporization of H_2O at $100^\circ C$ and 1 atm is equal to 40.85 k J mol^{-1}.

Solution:

The given process may be replaced by the following processes.

(i) H_2O (l, 20°C, 1 atm) → H_2O (l, 100°C, 1 atm)

(ii) H_2O (l, 100°C, 1 atm) → H_2O (g, 100°C, 1 atm)

(iii) H_2O (g, 100°C, 1 atm) → H_2O (g, 250°C, 1 atm)

Thus we have

$$\Delta S = \Delta S_{(I)} + \Delta S_{(ii)} \Delta S_{(iii)}$$

$$= C_{p,m}(l) \ln \frac{T_2}{T_1} + \frac{\Delta H_{vap}}{T} + C_{p,m}(g) \ln \frac{T_2'}{T_1'}$$

$$= \left(75.6 \ln \frac{373}{293} + \frac{40850}{373} + 36.2 \ln \frac{523}{373}\right) JK^{-1}\ mol^{-1}$$

$$= (18.25 + 109.52 + 12.24)\ J\ K^{-1}\ mol^{-1}$$

$$= 140.01\ J\ K^{-1}\ mol^{-1}$$

$$\Delta H = \Delta H_{(I)} + \Delta H_{(ii)} + \Delta H_{(iii)}$$

$$= C_{p.m}\ (l)\ (T_2 - T_1) + \Delta H_{vap} + C_{pm}(g)\ (T'_2 - T_1)$$

$$= (75.6 \times 80 + 40850 + 36.2 \times 150)\ J\ mol^{-1}$$

$$= 52328\ \ J\ mol^{-1}$$

$$\Delta U = \Delta U_{(I)} + \Delta U_{(ii)} \Delta U_{(iii)}$$

$$= C_{v,m}\ (l)\ (T_2 - T_1) + \Delta U_{vap} + C_{v.m}(g)\ (T'_2 - T'_1)$$

$$= C_{p.m}(l)(T_2 - T_1) + \{\Delta H_{vap} + \Delta_V{}_g RT\} + \{C_{p,m}(g) - R\}(T'_2 - T'_1)$$

$$= [75.6 \times 80 + \{40850 - (8.314)(373)\}$$

$$+ (36.2 - 8.314)(150)]\ J\ mol^{-1}\}$$

$$= (6040 + 37749 + 4183)\ J\ mol^{-1}$$

$$= 47972\ J\ mol^{-1}$$

Example 62:

1 gram molecule of a monoatomic (γ = 5/3) perfect gas at 27°C is adiabatically compressed in a reversible process from an initial pressure of 1 atmosphere to a final pressure of 60 atmospheres. Calculate the resulting difference in temperature.

Solution:

In a reversible adiabatic process

$$\frac{P_1^{\gamma-1}}{T_1^{\gamma}} = \frac{P_2^{\gamma-1}}{T_2^{\gamma}}$$

or $$\left(\frac{P_2}{P_1}\right)^{\gamma-1} = \left(\frac{T_2}{T_1}\right)^{\gamma}$$

Here, $P_2 = 50,$

$P_1 = 1,$

$T_1 = 273 + 27$

$= 300$ K

$T_2 = ?$

$\gamma = 5/3$

$$\therefore \quad (50)^{2/3} = \left(\frac{T_2}{300}\right)^{5/3}$$

$$2/3 \log (50) = 5/3 [\log T_2 - \log 300]$$

$$T_2 = 1{,}434 \text{ K}$$

$$= 1{,}161°\text{C}.$$

Example 63:

A quantity, of dry air at 27°C is compressed (i) slowly and (ii) suddenly to 1/3 of its volume, find the change in temperature in each case, assuming f to be 1.4 for dry air.

Solution:

(1) When the process is slow, the temperature of the system remains constant. Therefore, there is no change in temperature.

(2) When the compression is sudden, the process is adiabatic.

Here $V_1 = V,$

$V_2 = V/3$

$T_1 = 300$ K,

$T_2 = ?$

$\gamma = 1.4$

$$T_2(V_2)^{\gamma-1} = T_1[V_1]^{\gamma-1}$$

$$T_2 = T_1\left[\frac{V_1}{V_2}\right]^{\gamma-1}$$

or $$T_2 = 300\left[\frac{3V}{V}\right]^{\gamma-1}$$

$$= 300\ [3]1.4.1$$

or $$T_2 = 465.5\ K$$

$$= 192.5°C$$

The temperature of air increases by

192.5–27 = 165.5°C or 165.5 K.

Example 64:

A certain mass of gas at NTP is expanded to three times its volume under adiabatic conditions. Calculate the resulting temperature and pressure, γ for the gas is 1.40.

Solution:

(1) Here, $V_1 = V$,

$V_2 = 3V$

$T_1 = 273\ K$

$T_2 = ?$

$$T_1\ V_1^{\gamma-1} = T_2\ V_2^{\gamma-1}$$

or $$T_2 = T_1\left[\frac{V_1}{V_2}\right]^{\gamma-1}$$

$$T_2 = 273\left[\frac{1}{3}\right]^{1.4-1}$$

$$T = 276\ K = -97°C.$$

(2) Here, $V_1 = V$,

$V_2 = 3V$

P_1 = 1 atmosphere,

$$P_2 = ?$$

$$P_1 V_1^{\gamma} = P_2 V_2^{\gamma}$$

$$P_2 = P_1 \left[\frac{V_1}{V_2}\right]^{\gamma}$$

or $$P_2 = 1\left(\frac{1}{3}\right)^{1.4}$$

$$P_2 = 0.2148 \text{ atmosphere.}$$

Example 65:

Find the efficiency of the carnot's engine working between the steam point and the ice point.

Solution:

We have $T_1 = 273 + 100 = 373$ K

$$T_2 = 273 + 0 = 273 \text{ K}$$

$$\eta = 1 - \frac{T_2}{T_1}$$

$$= 1 - \frac{273}{373} = \frac{100}{373}$$

$$\% \text{ efficiency} = \frac{100}{373} \times 100$$

$$= 26.81\%.$$

Example 66:

A motor car tyre has a pressure of 2 atmospheres at the room temperature of 27°C. If the tyre suddenly bursts, find the resulting temperature.

Solution:

Here, $P_1 = 2$ atmospheres

$$T_1 = 273 + 27$$

$$= 300 \text{ K}$$

$$P_2 = 1 \text{ atmosphere}$$

$$T_2 = ?;\ \gamma = 1.4$$

$$\frac{P_1^{\gamma-1}}{T_1^{\gamma}} = \frac{P_2^{\gamma-1}}{T_2^{\gamma}}$$

$$\left(\frac{P_2}{P_1}\right)^{\gamma-1} = \left(\frac{T_2}{T_1}\right)^{\gamma}$$

$$\left(\frac{1}{2}\right)^{0.4} = \left(\frac{T_2}{300}\right)^{1.4}$$

$$0.4 \log (0.5) = 1.4 [\log T_2 - \log 300]$$

$$-0.1204 = 1.4 \log T_2 - 3.4680$$

$$1.4 \log T_2 = 3.4680 - 0.1204$$

$$= 3.3476$$

$$\log T_2 = \frac{3.3476}{1.4}$$

$$= 2.3911$$

$$T_2 = 246.1 \text{ K}$$

$$= -26.9°\text{C}.$$

Example 67:

A quantity of air at 27°C and atmospheric Pressure it suddenly compressed to half its original volume, find the final (i) pressure and (ii) temperature.

Solution:

(i) P_1 – 1 atmosphere; P_2 =?, $\gamma = 1.4$

$$V_1 = V;$$

$$V_2 = V/2$$

During sudden compression, the process is adiabatic

$$P_1V_1^{\gamma} = P_2V_2^{\gamma}$$

$$P_2 = P_1 \left[\frac{V_1}{V_2}\right]^{\gamma}$$

$$= 1[2]^{1/4}$$

$$= 2.636 \text{ atmospheres}$$

(ii) $V_1 = V;$

$V_2 = V/2$

$T_1 = 300\ K;$

$T_2 = ?$

$\gamma = 1.4$

$$T_1(V_1)^{\gamma-1} = T_2\,(V_2)^{\gamma-1}$$

$$T_2 = T_1[2]^{1/4-1}$$

$$= 300[2]^{0.4}$$

$$= 395.9\ K$$

$$= 122.9°C.$$

Example 68:

Air is compressed adiabatically to half its volume. Calculate the change in its temperature.

Solution:

Let the initial temperature be T_1 K and the final temperature

Initial volume $= V_1$

Final volume $= V_2$

$= V_1/2$

During an adiabatic process

$$T_1V_1^{\gamma-1} = T_2V_2^{\gamma-1}$$

$$T_2 = T_1\left[\frac{V_1}{V_2}\right]^{\gamma-1}$$

$$T_2 = T_1[2]^{\gamma-1}$$

But γ for air = 1.40

$$T_2 = T_1[2]^{1.40-1}$$

$$T_2 = T_1[2]^{0.40}$$

$T_2 = 1.319\ T_1$

Change in temperature

$= T_2 - T_1$

$= 1.319\ T_1 - T_1$

$= 1.319\ T_1\ K.$

Example 69:

Find the efficiency of a carnot's engine working between 127°C and 27°C.

Solution:

We have $T_1 = 273 + 127 = 400\ K$

$T_2 = 273 + 27 = 300\ K$

$$\eta = 1 - \frac{T_2}{T_1}$$

$$= 1 - \frac{300}{400} = 0.25$$

% efficiency = 25%.

Example 70:

A carnot's engine whose temperature of the source is 400 K takes 200 calories of heat at this temperature and rejects 150 calories of heat to the sink. What is the temperature of the sink? Also calculate the efficiency of the engine.

Solution:

We have $H_1 = 200$ cal;

$H_2 = 150$ cal

$T_1 = 400$ cal;

$T_2 = ?$

$$\frac{H_1}{T_1} = \frac{H_2}{T_2}$$

$$T_2 = T_2\frac{H_2}{H_1} \times 400 = 300\ K$$

$$\eta = 1 - \frac{T_2}{T_1}$$

$$= 1 - \frac{300}{400} = 0.25$$

% efficiency = 25%.

Example 71:

A Carnot's engine is operated between two reservoirs at temperatures of 450 K and 350 K. If the engine receives 1000 calories of heat from the source in each cycle, calculate the amount of heat rejected to the sink in each cycle. Calculate the efficiency of the engine and the work done by the engine in each cycle. (1 calorie = 4.2 joules).

Solution:

We have $T_1 = 450$ K;

$T_2 = 350$ K

$H_1 = 1000$ cal;

$H_2 = ?$

$$\frac{H_2}{H_1} = \frac{T_2}{T_1}$$

$$H_2 = H_1 \times \frac{T_2}{T_1}$$

$$= \frac{1000 \times 350}{450} = 777.77 \text{ cals}$$

$$\eta = 1 - \frac{T_2}{T_1}$$

$$= 1 - \frac{350}{450} = \frac{100}{450}$$

$$= 0.2222$$

% efficiency = 22.22%.

Work done in each cycle

$$= H_1 - H_2$$

$= 1000 - 777.77$

$= 222.23$ cal

$= 222.23 \times 4.2$ joules

$= 933.33$ Joules.

Example 72:

A carnot engine whose low temperature reservoir is at 7°C has an efficiency of 50%. It is desired to increase the efficiency to 70%. By how many degrees should the temperature of the high temperature reservoir be increased?

Solution:

In the first case

$$\eta = 50\% = 0.5,$$

$$T_2 = 273 + 7 = 280 \text{ K}$$

$$T_1 = ?$$

$$\eta = 1 - \frac{T_2}{T_1}$$

or $$0.5 = 1 - \frac{280}{T_1}$$

or $$T_1 = 560 \text{ K}$$

In the second case

$$\eta' = 70\% = 0.7$$

$$T_2 = 280 \text{ K},$$

$$T_1' = ?$$

$$\eta' = 1 - \frac{T_2}{T_1'}$$

$$0.7 = 1 - \frac{280}{T_1'}$$

or $$T_1' = 840 \text{ K}$$

Increase in temperature $= 840 - 560 = 280$ K.

Example 73:

An inventor claims to have developed an engine working between 600 K and 300 K capable of having an efficiency of 52%, Comment on his claim.

Solution:

The efficiency of a Carnot's engine working between 600 K and 300 K,

$$\eta = 1 - \frac{T_2}{T_1}$$

$$= 1 - \frac{300}{600} = 0.5$$

$$= 50\%$$

The efficiency claimed = η = 52%.

It means that the efficiency of the engine is more than the efficiency of a Carnot's engine working between the same two temperature limits. But, no engine can have an efficiency more than a Carnot's engine, so his claim is invalid.

Example 74:

In a double acting steam engine, the average pressure of steam is 10^5 newtons/metre^2. The length of the stroke if 1 metre and the area of the piston is 0.15 sq metre. Find the power of the engine, if it makes 5 strokes per second.

Solution:

Here P = Wnewtons/metre^2

L = 1 metre

A = 0.15 sq metre

N = 5 strokes/second

$$\text{Power} = \frac{2\,PLAN}{1000}$$

$$\text{Power of the engine} = \frac{2 \times 10^5 \times 1 \times 0.15 \times 5}{1000}$$

$$= 150 \text{ kilowatts.}$$

Example 75:

A carnot's engine working as a refrigerator between 260 k and 300 k receives 500 calories of heat from the reservoir at the lower temperature. Calculate the amount of heat rejected to the reservoir at the higher temperature. Calculate also the amount of work done in each cycle to operate the refrigerator.

Solution:

We have $H_1 = ?$

$$H_2 = 500 \text{ cal}$$

$$T_1 = 300 \text{ K}$$

$$T_2 = 260 \text{ K}$$

$$\frac{H_1}{H_2} = \frac{T_1}{T_2};$$

$$H_1 = H_2 \cdot \frac{T_1}{T_2}$$

$$H_1 = \frac{500 \times 300}{260} = 576.92 \text{ cal}$$

$$W = H_1 - H_2 = 76.92 \text{ cal}$$

$$= 76.92 \times 4.2 \text{ joules}$$

$$= 323.08 \text{ joules.}$$

Example 76:

A carnot's refrigerator takes heat from water at 0°C and discards it to a room at 27°C. 1 kg of water at 0°C is to be changed into ice at 0°C. How many calories of heat are discarded to the room? What is the work done by the refrigerator in this process? What is the coefficient of performance of the machine?

Solution:

We have $H_1 = ?$

$$H_2 = 1000 \times 80 = 80{,}000 \text{ cal}$$

$$T_1 = 300 \text{ K}$$

$$T_2 = 273 \text{ K}$$

(1) $$\frac{H_1}{H_2} = \frac{T_1}{T_2}$$

$$H_1 = \frac{H_2 T_1}{T_2}$$

$$= \frac{80,000 \times 300}{273}$$

$$H_1 = 87,900 \text{ cal.}$$

(2) Work done by the refrigerator

$$= W = J(H_1 - H_2)$$

$$W = 4.2\ (87,900 - 80,000)$$

$$W = 4.2 \times 7900$$

or $$W = 3.183 \times 10^4 \text{ joules}$$

(3) Coefficient of performance,

$$= \frac{H_2}{H_1 - H_2}$$

$$= \frac{80,000}{87,900 - 80,000}$$

$$= \frac{80,000}{7900}$$

$$= 10.13.$$

Example 77:

Calculate the depression in the melting point of ice produced by one atmosphere increase of pressure. Given latent heat of ice = 80 cal per gram and the specific volumes of 1 gram of ice and water at 0°C are 1.091 cm³ and 1.000 cm³ respectively.

Solution:

Here $$L = 80 \text{ cal} = 80 \times 4.2 \times 10^7 \text{ ergs}$$

$$T = 273 \text{ K}$$

$$dP = 1 \text{ atmosphere}$$

$$= 76 \times 13.6 \times 980 \text{ dynes/cm}^2$$

$$V_1 = 1.091 \text{ cm}^3$$

$$V_2 = 1.000 \text{ cm}^3$$

$$\frac{dP}{dT} = \frac{L}{T\ (V_2 - V_1)}$$

$$dT = \frac{dP.T.(V_2 - V_1)}{L}$$

$$= \frac{76 \times 13.6 \times 980 \times 273\ (1 - 1.091)}{80 \times 4.2 \times 10^7}$$

$$= 0.0074 \text{ K.}$$

Therefore, the decrease in the melting point of ice with an increase in pressure of one atmosphere

$$= 0.0074 \text{ K} = 0.0074°\text{C}.$$

Example 78:

Find the increase in the boiling point of water at 100°C when the pressure is increased by one atmosphere. Latent heat of vaporisation of steam is 640 cal/gram and 1 gram of steam occupies a volume of 1677 cm³.

Solution:

We have $dP = 76 \times 13.6 \times 980 \text{ dynes/cm}^2$

$$T = 100 + 273$$

$$= 373 \text{ K}$$

$$L = 540 \times 4.2 \times 10^7 \text{ ergs}$$

$$V_1 = 1.000 \text{ cm}^3$$

$$V_2 = 1677 \text{ cm}^3$$

$$\frac{dP}{dT} = \frac{L}{T(V_2 - V_1)}$$

$$dT = \frac{dP \times T(V_2 - V_1)}{L}$$

$$= \frac{76 \times 13.6 \times 980 \times 373 \times 1676}{540 \times 4.2 \times 10^7}$$

$= 27.92°C.$

Therefore, the increase in the boiling point of water with an increase in pressure of one atmosphere

$= 27.92°C$

$= 27.92\ K.$

Example 79:

Calculate the change in temperature of boiling water when the pressure is increased by 27.12 mm of Hg. The normal boiling point of water at atmospheric pressure is 100°C.

Latent heat of steam $= 537\ cal/g$

and specific volume of steam $= 1674\ cm^3$.

Solution:

We have $dP = 2.712 \times 13.6 \times 980\ dynes/cm^2$

$T = 100 + 273 = 373\ K$

$L = 537 \times 4.2 \times 10^7\ ergs$

$V_1 = 1.000\ cm^3$

$V_2 = 1674\ cm^3$

$$\frac{dP}{dT} = \frac{L}{T(V_2 - V_1)}$$

$$dT = \frac{dP \times T(V_2 - V_1)}{L}$$

$$= \frac{2.712 \times 13.6 \times 980 \times 373 \times 1673}{537 \times 4.2 \times 10^7}$$

$= 1°C$ or $1\ K$.

Example 80:

Calculate the change in the melting point of naphthalene for one atmosphere rise in pressure given that its melting point is 80°C. Latent heat of fusion is 4563 cal/mol and increase in volume on fusion is 18.7 cm^3 *per mol and 1 calorie* $= 4.2 \times 10^7$ *ergs.*

Solution:

We have $\frac{dP}{dT} = \frac{L}{T(V_2 - V_1)}$

$dT = 1$ atmosphere

$= 76 \times 13.6 \times 980$ dynes/cm²

$dT = ?$

$L = 4563$ cal/mol

$= 4563 \times 4.2 \times 10^7$ ergs/mol

$V_2 - V_1 = 18.7$ cm³/mol

$T = 80 + 273$

$= 353$ K

$$dT = \frac{dP.T.(V_2 - V_1)}{L}$$

$$= \frac{76 \times 13.6 \times 980 \times 373 \times 18.7}{4563 \times 4.2 \times 10^7}$$

$= 0.03488$ K.

Therefore, the increase in the melting point of naphthalene with an increase in pressure of one atmosphere

$= 0.03488$ K

$= 0.03488°$C.

Example 81:

Calculate the pressure required to lowe melting point of ice by 0°C. (L = 79.6 cal/g, specific volume of water at 0°C = 1.000 cm² specific volume of ice at 0°C = 1.091 cm³ and 1 atmosphere pressure = 1.013 × 10⁶ dynes/cm²).

Solution:

We have $\frac{dP}{dT} = \frac{L}{T(V_2 - V_1)}$

$dT = -1$ K

$T = 273$ K

$V_2 - V_1 = -0.091$ cm³

$$L = 79.6 \text{ cal/g}$$

$$= 79.6 \times 4.18 \times 10^7 \text{ ergs/g}$$

$$dP = \frac{L.dT}{T(V_2 - V_1)}$$

$$dP = \frac{79.6 \times 4.18 \times 10^7 \times 1}{273 \times 0.091} \text{ dynes/cm}^2$$

or

$$dP = \frac{79.6 \times 4.18 \times 10^7}{273 \times 0.091 \times 1013 \times 10^6} \text{ atmospheres}$$

$$dP = 135.2 \text{ atmospheres}$$

∴ Pressure required

$$= 135.2 + 1$$

$$= 136.2 \text{ atmospheres.}$$

Example 22:

Water boils at a temperature of 101°C at a pressure of 787 mm of Hg. 1 gram of water occupies 1,601 cm³ on evaporation. Calculate the latent heat of steam. J = 4.2 × 10⁷ ergs/cal.

Solution:

We have $\frac{dP}{dT} = \frac{L}{T(V_2 - V_1)}$

$$dP = 787 - 760$$

$$= 27 \text{ mm of Hg}$$

$$= 2.7 \text{ cm of Hg}$$

$$= 2.7 \times 13.6 \times 980 \text{ dynes/cm}^2$$

$$dT = 1°C = 1K$$

$$T = 373 \text{ K}$$

$$V_2 - V_1 = 1{,}601 - 1 = 1{,}600 \text{ cm}^3$$

$$L = ?$$

$$L = \frac{L\,dP\,(V_2 - V_1)}{dT}$$

$$L = \frac{373 \times 2.7 \times 13.6 \times 980 \times 1{,}600}{1} \text{ ergs/g}$$

or $$L = \frac{373 \times 2.7 \times 13.6 \times 980 \times 1{,}600}{4.2 \times 10^7} \text{ cal/g}$$

$$L = 511.3 \text{ cal/g.}$$

Example 83:

When lead is melted at atmospheric pressure, (the melting point is 600 K) the density decreases from 11.01 to 10.66 g/cm³ and the latent heat of fusion is 24.5 J/g. What is the melting point at a pressure of 100 atmospheres?

Solution:

We have $\frac{dP}{dT} = \frac{L}{T(V_2 - V_1)}$

$$dP = 99 \text{ atmospheres}$$

$$= 99 \times 76 \times 13.6 \times 980 \text{ dynes/cm}^2$$

$$L = 24.5 \text{ J/g}$$

$$= 24.5 \times 10^7 \text{ ergs/g}$$

$$V_1 = \frac{1}{11.01} \text{ cm}^3$$

$$V_2 = \frac{1}{10.65} \text{ cm}^3$$

$$V_2 - V_1 = \frac{1}{10.65} - \frac{1}{11.01}$$

$$= \left(\frac{0.36}{10.65 \times 10.01}\right) \text{cm}^3$$

$$dT = \frac{TdP\,(V_2 - V_1)}{L}$$

$$dT = \frac{600 \times 99 \times 76 \times 13.6 \times 980 \times 0.36}{10.65 \times 11.01 \times 24.5 \times 10^7}$$

$$dT = 0.7539 \text{ K}$$

$= 0.7539°C.$

$\therefore$ Melting point of lead at 100 atmospheres pressure

$= 600 + 0.7539$

$= 600.7539\ K.$

Example 84:

Calculate under what pressure water will boil at 120°C. if the change in specific volume when 1 gram of water is converted into steam is 1,676 cm³.

Latent heat of steam

= 540 cal/g

$J = 4.2 \times 10^7$ *ergs/cal*

1 atmosphere pressure

$= 10^6$ *dynes/cm²*.

Solution:

Here $$\frac{dP}{dT} = \frac{L}{T(V_2 - V_1)}$$

$$dT = 120 = 100$$

$$= 20\ K$$

$$T = 373\ K$$

$$(V_2 - V_1) = 1{,}676\ cm^3$$

$$L = 540\ cal/g$$

$$= 540 \times 4.2 \times 10^7\ ergs/g$$

$$dP = ?$$

$$dP = \frac{L.dT}{T(V_2 - V_1)}$$

$$dP = \frac{540 \times 4.2 \times 10^7 \times 20}{373 \times 1{,}676}\ dynes/cm^2$$

$$dP = \frac{540 \times 4.2 \times 10^7 \times 20}{373 \times 1{,}676 \times 10^6}\ atmospheres$$

$$dP = 0.7254 \text{ atmosphere}$$

$$\text{Pressure required} = 1 + 0.7254$$

$$= 1 + 0.7254 \text{ atmospheres.}$$

Example 85:

Calculate the boiling point of benzene under a pressure of 80 cm of mercury. The normal boiling point is 80°C. Latent heat of vaporization is 389 joules/g, density of vapour at the boiling point is 4 g/litre and that of the liquid 0.9 g/cm³.

Solution:

Here $dP = 80 - 76$

$$= 4 \text{ cm of Hg}$$

$$= 4 \times 13.6 \times 980 \text{ dynes/cm}^2$$

$$T = 80°C = 80 + 273$$

$$= 353 \text{ K}$$

$$E = 380 \text{ joules/g}$$

$$= 380 \times 10^7 \text{ ergs/g}$$

$$V_1 = \frac{1}{0.9} = 1.11 \text{ cm}^3$$

$$V_2 = \frac{1,000}{4} = 250 \text{ cm}^3$$

$$\frac{dP}{dT} = \frac{L}{T[V_2 - V_1]}$$

$$dT = \frac{dP \times T[V_2 - V_1]}{L}$$

$$dT = \frac{4 \times 13.6 \times 980 \times 373 \times [250 - 1.11]}{380 \times 10^7}$$

$$= 1.233 \text{ K}$$

$$= 1.233°C.$$

∴ The boiling point of benzene at a pressure of 80 cm of Hg

$$= 80 + 1.233$$

$= 81.233°C.$

Example 86:

Calculate the change in the boiling point of water when the pressure of steam on its surface is increased from 1 atmosphere to 1.10 atmospheres.

Latent heat of water at 100°C

$= 537$ *cal/g*

Volume of one-gram of steam at 100°C

$= 1.676$ *cm*^{3}.

Solution:

We have $dP = 1.10 - 1$

$= 0.10$ atmosphere

$dP = 0.1 \times 76 \times 13.6 \times 980$ dynes/cm^2

$T = 100 + 273$

$= 373$ K

$L = 537$ cals/g

$= 537 \times 4.2 \times 10^7$ergs/g

$V_1 = 1.00$ cm^3

$V_1 = 1.676$ cm^3

$$\frac{dP}{dT} = \frac{L}{T[V_2 - V_1]}$$

$$dT = \frac{dP \times T[V_2 - V_1]}{L}$$

$$dT = \frac{0.1 \times 76 \times 13.6 \times 980 \times 373 \times (1,675)}{537 \times 4.2 \times 10^7}$$

$= 2.792$ K

$= 2.792°C.$

Therefore, the increase in the boiling point of water with an increase of 0.1 atmosphere pressure

$= 2.792$ K

$= 2.792°C.$

Example 87:

Calculate the change in the melting point of ice when it is subjected to a pressure of 100 atmospheres.

Density of ice = 0.917 g/cm³, and

Latent heat of ice = 336 J/g.

Solution:

We have $\frac{dP}{dT} = \frac{L}{T(V_2 - V_1)}$

$$dP = 100 - 1$$

$$= 99 \text{ atmospheres}$$

$$dP = 99 \times 76 \times 13.6 \times 980 \text{ dynes/cm}^2$$

$$L = 336 \text{ J/g}$$

$$= 336 \times 10^7 \text{ ergs/g}$$

$$T = 273\text{K}$$

$$(V_2 - V_1) = 1 - \frac{1}{0.917}$$

$$= -\frac{0.083}{0.917}$$

$$= -0.091 \text{ cm}^3$$

$$\therefore \quad dT = \frac{TdP(V_2 - V_1)}{L}$$

$$= \frac{273 \times 99 \times 76 \times 13.6 \times 980 \times (-0.091)}{336 \times 10^7}$$

$$dT = -0.7326 \text{ K}$$

$$= -0.7326°\text{C}.$$

The decrease in the melting point of ice with a pressure of 100 atmospheres

Example 88:

Calculate the change in entropy when 10 grams of ice at 0°C is converted into water at the same temperature.

Solution:

Heat absorbed by 10 g of ice at 0°C when it is converted into water at 0°C = 10 × 80 = 800 cal

$$\therefore \qquad \delta H = 800 \text{ cal}$$

$$T = 0°C = 273 \text{ K}$$

The gain in entropy

$$dS = \frac{\delta H}{T}$$

$$= \frac{800}{273} = 2.93 \text{ cal/K}.$$

Example 89:

Calculate the change in entropy when 5 kg of water at 100°C is converted into steam at the same temperature.

Solution:

Heat absorbed by 5 kg of water at 100°C when it is converted into steam at 100°C

$$= 5000 \times 540$$

$$= 2700000 \text{ cal}$$

$$SB = 2700000 \text{ cal}$$

The gain in entropy

$$dS = \frac{\delta H}{T}$$

$$= \frac{270000}{373} = 72 \text{ cal/K}.$$

Example 90:

Calculate the increase in entropy when 1 gram of ice at –10°C is Converted into steam at 100°C. Specific heat of ice a 0.5, latent heat of ice = 80 cal/g, latent heat of steam = 540 cal/g.

Solution:

(1) Increase in entropy when the temperature of 1 gram of ice increases from –10°C to 0°C

$$dS = \int_{T_1}^{T_2} \frac{\delta H}{T}$$

$$= ms\int_{T_1}^{T_2} \frac{dT}{T}$$

$$= ms \log_e \frac{T_2}{T_1}$$

$$= ms \times 2.3026 \log_e \frac{T_2}{T_1}$$

$$= 1.0.5 \times 2.3026 \log_{10} \frac{273}{263} = 0.01865 \text{ cal/K.}$$

(2). Increase in entropy when 1 gram of ice at 0°C is converted into water at 0°C.

$$dS = \frac{\delta H}{T}$$

$$= \frac{80}{273} = 0.293 \text{ cal/K}$$

(3) Increase in entropy when the temperature of 1 f of water is raised from 0°C to 100°C.

$$dS = \int_{T_1}^{T_2} \frac{\delta H}{T}$$

$$= ms \times 2.3026 \log_{10} T_2/T_1$$

$$= 1 \times 1 \times 2.3026 \log_{10} 373/273$$

$$= 0.312 \text{ cal/K.}$$

(4) Increase in entropy when 1 g water at 100°C is converted into steam at 100°C

$$dS = \frac{\delta H}{T}$$

$$= \frac{540}{373} = 1.447 \text{ cal/K}$$

Total increase in entropy

$$= 0.01865 + 0.293 + 0.312 + 1.447 = 2.07065 \text{ cal/K.}$$

Example 91:

10 g of steam at 100°C is blown into 90 grams of water at 0°C, contained in a calorimeter of water equivalent 19 grams. The whole of the steam is condensed. Calculate the increase in the entropy of the system.

Solution:

(i) $m_1 = 10g$

$T_1 = 100°C = 373\ K$

$m_2 = 90 + 10 = 100g$

$T_2 = 273\ K$

Let the final temperature be T K

$10 \times 540 + 10(373 - 7) = 100(T - 273)$

$T = 331.2\ K.$

(ii) Change in entropy when the temperature of water and calorimeter rises from 273 K to 331.2 K

$$= \frac{\delta H}{T} = ms \int_{T_2}^{T} \frac{dT}{T}$$

$$= 100 \int_{273}^{331.2} \frac{dT}{T}$$

$$= 100 \times 2.3026 \times \log_{10}\left(\frac{331.2}{273}\right)$$

$$= +19.32\ cal/K.$$

(iii) Change in entropy when 10 grams of steam at 373 K is condensed to water at 373 K

$$= \left(\frac{\delta H}{T}\right) = -\frac{10 \times 540}{273}$$

$$= -14.47 cal/K.$$

(–ve sign indicates decrease in entropy).

(iv) Change in entropy when 10 grams of water at 373 K is cooled to water at 331.2 K

$$= \frac{\delta H}{T} = ms \int_{T_2}^{T} \frac{dT}{T}$$

$$= 10 \times 2.3026 \log_{10}\left(\frac{331.2}{373}\right)$$

$$= -1.188\ cals/K$$

Net change in entropy

$$= 19.32 - 14.47 - 1.188$$

$$= +3.662 \text{ cal/K}.$$

Hence the net increase in the entropy of the system

$$= 3.662 \text{ cal/K}.$$

Example 92:

1 g of water at 20°C is converted into ice at –10°C at constant pressure. Heat capacity for 1 g of water is 4.2 J/g-K and that of ice is 2.1 J/g-K. Beat of fusion of ice at 0°C = 335 J/g. Calculate the total change in the entropy of the system.

Solution:

(i) Change in entropy when the temperature of 1 g of water at 293 K falls to 273 K.

$$dS = \frac{\delta H}{T} = ms \int_{T_1}^{T_2} \frac{dT}{T}$$

$$= 1 \times 4.2 \int_{293}^{273} \frac{dT}{T}$$

$$= 4.2 \times 2.3026 \log_{10} \left(\frac{273}{293}\right)$$

$$= -0.2969 \text{ J/K}.$$

(ii) Change in entropy when 1 g of water at 273 K is converted into ice at 273 K

$$dS = \frac{\delta H}{T} = \frac{-1 \times 335}{273} = -1.227 \text{ J/K}$$

(iii) Change in entropy when the temperature of 1 g of ice at 273 K falls to 263 K

$$dS = \frac{\delta H}{T} = ms \int_{T_1}^{T_2} \frac{dT}{T}$$

$$= 1 \times 2.1 \times 2.3026 \log_{10} \left(\frac{263}{273}\right)$$

$$= -0.07834 \text{ J/K}$$

Total change in entropy of the system

$$= -0.2969 - 1.227 - 0.07834$$

$= -1.60224$ J/K.

Negative sign shows that there is decrease in entropy of the system.

Example 36:

1 kg of wafer of 273 K is brought in contact with a heat reservoir at 873 K:

(1) what is the change in entropy of water when its temperature reaches 873 K?

(2) What is the change in entropy of (i) the reservoir and (ii) the universe.

Solution:

(1) Increase in entropy when the temperature of 1000 g of water is raised from 273 K to 373 K

$$dS = \int_{T_1}^{T_2} \frac{\delta H}{T}$$

$$= ms \times 2.3026 \log_{10} T_2/T_1$$

$$= 1000 \times 1 \times 2.3026 \log_{10} 373/273$$

$$= 312 \text{ cal/K.}$$

(2) (i) Change in entropy of the reservoir,

$$dS = \frac{-\delta H}{T}$$

$$= -\frac{1000 \times 1 \times 100}{372} = -268.1 \text{ cal/K.}$$

Negative sign shows decrease in entropy

(2) (ii) Change in entropy of the universe

$$= 312 - 268.1$$

$$= 43.9 \text{ cal/K.}$$

Therefore, the net increase in entropy of the universe

$$= 43.9 \text{ cal/K.}$$

Example 37:

Deduce Clapeyron's latent heat equation from Maxwell's thermodynamical relations.

Solution:

We have $\left(\frac{\partial H}{\partial V}\right)_T = T\left(\frac{\partial P}{\partial T}\right)_V$ ...(i)

Here $\left(\frac{\partial H}{\partial V}\right)_T$ represents the quantity of heat absorbed per unit increase in volume at constant temperature. This quantity of heat absorbed at constant temperature is the latent heat. If ∂H is the latent heat (L), when a unit mass of the substance changes in volume for V_1 to V_2 at constant temperature, then

$$\partial H = L \quad \text{and} \quad \partial V = V_2 - V_1$$

Substituting these values, in equation (i)

$$\therefore \qquad \left(\frac{L}{V_2 - V_1}\right)_T = T\left(\frac{\partial P}{\partial T}\right)_V$$

$$\text{or} \qquad \frac{L}{V_2 - V_1} = T\frac{dP}{dT}$$

$$\text{or} \qquad \frac{dP}{dT} = \frac{L}{T(V_2 - V_1)} \qquad \text{...(ii)}$$

This is Clapeyron's latent heat equation.

Example 93:

Show that for a homogeneous fluid

$$C_P - C_V = T\left(\frac{\partial P}{\partial T}\right)_V \left(\frac{\partial V}{\partial T}\right)_P$$

Also show that for a perfect gas $C_P - C_V = R$ and for a gas obeying Van der Waah equation

Solution:

We have $\qquad C_P - C_V = R\left(1 + \frac{2a}{RTV}\right)$

Here, $\qquad C_P\left(\frac{\partial H}{\partial T}\right)_P = T\left(\frac{\partial S}{\partial T}\right)_P$

and $\qquad C_V\left(\frac{\partial H}{\partial T}\right)_V = T\left(\frac{\partial S}{\partial T}\right)_V$

Considering S as a function of temperature and volume

$$dS = \left(\frac{\partial S}{\partial T}\right)_V = dT\left(\frac{\partial S}{\partial T}\right)_T dV$$

$$\left(\frac{\partial S}{\partial T}\right)_P = \left(\frac{\partial S}{\partial T}\right)_V \left(\frac{\partial T}{\partial T}\right) + \left(\frac{\partial S}{\partial V}\right)_T \left(\frac{\partial V}{\partial T}\right)_P$$

But from equation (v) [§ 6.52] $\left(\frac{\partial S}{\partial V}\right)_T = \left(\frac{\partial P}{\partial T}\right)_V$

$$T\left(\frac{\partial S}{\partial T}\right)_P = T\left(\frac{\partial S}{\partial T}\right)_V + T\left(\frac{\partial P}{\partial T}\right)_V \left(\frac{\partial V}{\partial T}\right)_P$$

$$C_P = C_V + T\left(\frac{\partial P}{\partial T}\right)_V \left(\frac{\partial V}{\partial T}\right)_P$$

$$\therefore \quad C_P - C_V = T\left(\frac{\partial P}{\partial T}\right)_V \left(\frac{\partial V}{\partial T}\right)_P \quad \text{...(i)}$$

For a Perfect Gas

$$PV = RT$$

$$\therefore \quad \left(\frac{\partial P}{\partial T}\right)_V = \frac{R}{V} \text{ and } \left(\frac{\partial V}{\partial T}\right)_P = \frac{R}{P}$$

But, $C_P - C_V = T\left(\frac{\partial P}{\partial T}\right)_V \left(\frac{\partial V}{\partial T}\right)_P$

$$C_P - C_V = T\left(\frac{R}{V}\right)\left(\frac{R}{P}\right)$$

$$C_P - C_V = \frac{RT^2}{PV} = \frac{R^2T}{RT} = R$$

Hence $\quad C_P - C_V = R$

[R is in heat units]

For a gas obeying Van der Waals equation

$$\left(P + \frac{a}{V^2}\right)(V - b) = RT$$

$$\left(P + \frac{a}{V^2}\right) = \frac{RT}{(V - b)}$$

$$\therefore \qquad \left(\frac{\partial P}{\partial T}\right)_V = \frac{R}{V - b}$$

and $$\left(\frac{-2a}{V^3} + \frac{RT}{(V - b)^2}\right)\left(\frac{\partial V}{\partial T}\right)_P = \frac{R}{V - b}$$

But $$C_P - C_V = T\left(\frac{\partial P}{\partial T}\right)_V \left(\frac{\partial V}{\partial T}\right)_P$$

$$C_P - C_V = \frac{T\left(\frac{R}{V - b}\right)\left(\frac{R}{V - b}\right)}{\left[\frac{RT}{(V - b)^2} - \frac{2a}{V^3}\right]}$$

$$C_P - C_V = \frac{RT\,(V - b)^2}{RT\,(V - b)^2}\left[\frac{R}{1 - \frac{2a(V - b)}{V^3 RT}}\right]$$

Neglecting 6 as compared to V,

$$C_P - C_V = \frac{R}{\left(1 - \frac{2a}{VRT}\right)}$$

Since a is also small as compared to V

$$C_P - C_V = R\left(1 + \frac{2a}{VRT}\right) \qquad \text{...(iii)}$$

[R is in heat units.]

Example 94:

One gram molecule of a gas expands isothermally to four times its volume. Calculate the change in its entropy in terns of the gas constant.

Solution:

Work done $= \int_{V_1}^{V_2} PdV$

But $PV = RT$

or $P = \frac{RT}{V}$

$$W = RT \int_{V_1}^{V_2} \frac{dV}{V}$$

$$= RT \log_e \frac{V_2}{V_1}$$

Here $\frac{V_2}{V_1} = 4$

$$W \doteq RT \times 2.3026 \log_{10}(4)$$

Here, W and R are in the units of work

Gain in entropy = δH/T

$$= \frac{W}{JT} = \frac{RT \times 2.3026 \log_{10} 4}{JT}$$

$$= 1.387 \ R/J \ cal/K.$$

Example 95:

50 grams of water at 0°C if mixed with an equal mass of water at 83°C. Calculate the resultant increase in entropy.

Solution:

(i)m_1 = 50 g; T_1 = 273 K

m_1 = 50 g; T, = 353 K

Let the final temperature of the mixture be T K

$$m_1 \ 8 \times (T - T_1) = m_2 \ s(T_2 - T)$$

$$50 \times 1 \times (T - 273) = 50 \times 1 \times (353 - T)$$

$$T = 310 \ K.$$

(ii) Change in entropy by 50 g of water when its temperature from 273 K to 313 K.

$$= \frac{\delta H}{T}$$

$$= ms \int_{T_1}^{T} \frac{dT}{T}$$

$$= 50 \times 1 \times \log_e \frac{313}{273}$$

$$= 50 \times 2.3026 \times \log_e \frac{313}{273}$$

$$= +6.829 \text{ cal/K.}$$

Here, the +ve sign indicates gain in entropy.

(iii) Change in entropy by 50 g of water when its temperature falls from 353 K to 313 K

$$= \frac{\delta H}{T} = ms \int_{T_2}^{T} \frac{dT}{T}$$

$$= 50 \times 1 \times \log_e \frac{313}{353}$$

$$= 50 \times 2.3026 \times \log_{10} \frac{313}{353}$$

$$= -6.023 \text{ cal/K.}$$

Here, the –ve sign indicates loss in entropy.

Therefore, the total gain in entropy of the system

$$= 6.829 - 6.023$$

$$= 0\ 806 \text{ cal/K.}$$

Example 96:

Derive the specific heat relation or show that

$$C_P - C_V = -T\left(\frac{\partial V}{\partial T}\right)_P^2 \left(\frac{\partial P}{\partial V}\right)_T$$

and $C_P - C_V = -TEa^2V$

where T is the absolute temperature, Sthe bulk modulus of elasticity, a the coefficient of volume expansion and V the specific volume,

Solution:

We have $$C_P\left(\frac{\partial H}{\partial T}\right) = T\left(\frac{\partial S}{\partial T}\right)_P$$

and $$C_V\left(\frac{\partial H}{\partial T}\right)_V = T\left(\frac{\partial S}{\partial T}\right)_V$$

Considering S as a function of temperature and volume,

$$dS \left(\frac{\partial S}{\partial T}\right)_V = dT + \left(\frac{\partial S}{\partial V}\right)_T dV$$

$$\left(\frac{\partial S}{\partial T}\right)_P = \left(\frac{\partial S}{\partial T}\right)_V \left(\frac{\partial T}{\partial T}\right) + \left(\frac{\partial S}{\partial V}\right)_T \left(\frac{\partial V}{\partial T}\right)_P$$

But from equation (v) of article 6.52,

$$\left(\frac{\partial S}{\partial V}\right)_T = \left(\frac{\partial P}{\partial T}\right)_V$$

$$\therefore \quad T\left(\frac{\partial S}{\partial V}\right)_P = T\left(\frac{\partial S}{\partial T}\right)_V + T\left(\frac{\partial P}{\partial T}\right)_V \left(\frac{\partial V}{\partial T}\right)_P$$

$$C_P = C_V + T\left(\frac{\partial P}{\partial T}\right)_V \left(\frac{\partial V}{\partial T}\right)_P \qquad \text{...(i)}$$

Taking the general equation of state for a gas as

$$P = f(V, T)$$

$$C_P = C_V + T\left(\frac{\partial P}{\partial T}\right)_V \left(\frac{\partial V}{\partial T}\right)_P$$

$$\frac{dP}{dT} = \left(\frac{\partial P}{\partial T}\right)_V + \left(\frac{\partial P}{\partial V}\right)_T \left(\frac{\partial V}{\partial T}\right)_P$$

At constant pressure,

$$dP = 0$$

$$\therefore \quad \left(\frac{\partial P}{\partial T}\right)_V = -\left(\frac{\partial P}{\partial V}\right)_T \left(\frac{\partial V}{\partial T}\right)_P$$

Substituting this value in eaquation (i)

$$C_P - C_V = -\left(\frac{\partial P}{\partial V}\right)_T \left(\frac{\partial V}{\partial T}\right)_P^2 \qquad \text{...(ii)}$$

$$C_P - C_V = -T\left(\frac{\partial V}{\partial T}\right)_P^2 \left(\frac{\partial P}{\partial V}\right)_T \qquad \text{...(iii)}$$

But $\quad E = V\left(\frac{\partial P}{\partial V}\right)_T$

and $$\alpha = \frac{1}{V}\left[\frac{\partial V}{\partial T}\right]_P$$

Substituting the values in equation (ii)

$$C_P - C_V = -TEa^2V. \qquad \text{(iv)}$$

Example 97:

Calculate the change in entropy when 50 grams of water at 15°C is mixed with 80 grams of water at 40°C. Specific heat of wetter may be assumed to be equal to 2.

Solution:

(i) $m_1 = 50g$

$T_1 = 15 + 273 = 288$ K

$m_2 = 10$ grams

$T_2 = 40 + 273 = 313$ K.

Let the final temperature be T K.

$$m_1 \times 8 \times (T - T_1) = m_2 \times 8 \times (T_2 - T)$$

$$50 \times 1 \times (T - 288) = 80 \times 1 \times (313 - T)$$

$$T = 303\text{-}4 \text{ K}.$$

(ii) Change in entropy when the temperature of 50 g of water rises from 288 K to 303.4 K

$$= \frac{\delta H}{T} = ms\int_{T_1}^{T}\frac{dT}{T}$$

$$= 50 \times 1 \times 2.3026 \times \log_{10}\frac{303.4}{288}$$

$$= +2.602 \text{ cal/K}.$$

(iii) Change in entropy when the temperature of 80 g of water decreases from 313 K to 303.4 K

$$= \frac{\delta H}{T} = ms\int_{T_2}^{T}\frac{dT}{T}$$

$$= 80 \times 1 \times 2.3026 \times \log_{10}\frac{303.4}{313}$$

$$= -2.487 \text{ cal/K}.$$

Therefore, the net change in the entropy of the system

$= +2.602 - 2.487$

$= +0.115$ cal/K

Hence the net increase in the entropy of the system

$= 0.115$ cal/K.

EXERCISES

1. Explain the terms entropy and isentropics. Show that the entropy of a system tends to a maximum. Represent the Carnot's, cycle on a temperature entropy diagram and prove that its area represents available energy.
2. Derive Clapeyron's latent heat equation.

$$\frac{dP}{dT} = \frac{L}{T(V_2 - V_1)}$$

3. State and prove Carnot's theorem.
4. Define Entropy. What is its physical significance? Show that the entropy of a perfect gas remains constant in a reversible process but increases in an irreversible process.
5. Prove the thermodynamic relation

$$\left(\frac{\partial H}{\partial P}\right)_T = -T\left(\frac{\partial V}{\partial T}\right)_P$$

Hence, show that the increase of pressure heats a body that expands with rise of temperature and cools the one that contracts on heating.

6. State Carnot's theorem. Show how Kelvin used this theorem to define a new scale of temperature which is independent of the nature of the working substance. Compare this temperature scale with the perfect gas scale.
7. Write short notes on:

(i) Adiabatic Process

(ii) Isochoric Process

(iv) Carnot's engine

(v) Carnot's theorem

(vi) Second Law of thermodynamics

(vii) Clement and Desorme'Ls method

8. Describe the absolute scale of temperature. Why is it adopted as the standard scale? What is the meaning of absolute zero on the Kale?

9. Prove that

$$\frac{dL}{dT} - \frac{L}{T} = C_2 - C_1$$

What is the physical significance of negative specific heat?

10. Prove that PV^{γ} = constant in an adiabatic transformation.

11. What do you understand by the absolute scale of temperature? Show that the zero and the size of the degree on this scale and the gas scale are coincident. Is a negative temperature possible on this scale?

12. Explain the concept of entropy. Deduce the expression for the entropy of a monoatomic gas.

13. Derive an expression for the efficiency of a Carnot's engine in terms of the temperatures of the source and the sink Show how an absolute scale of temperature can be defined with the help of the ideal Carnot's engine.

14. Deduce Clausius-Clapeyron's equation.

15. Deduce the Clapeyron's latent heat equation from Maxwell's thermodynamical relations.

16. Deduce Maxwell's thermodynamical relations.

17. Show that for a homogeneous fluid

$$C_P - C_V = T\left(\frac{\partial P}{\partial T}\right)_V\left(\frac{\partial V}{\partial T}\right)_V$$

18. Show from the consideration of Maxwell's thermodynamical relations that

(i) for a perfect gas

$C_P - C_V = R$, and

(ii) for a gas obeying Van der Waals equation

$$C_P - C_V = R\left(1+\frac{2a}{RTV}\right)$$

19. Derive the specific heat relation

$$C_P - C_V = -TE\alpha^2V.$$

20. Calculate the change in entropy when m grams of a liquid of specific heat S is heated from T_1 K to T_2 K and then converted into vapour without raising its temperature. Latent heat of vaporisation at T_2 is L.

21. Show that

$$\frac{\left[\frac{\partial P}{\partial T}\right]_S}{\left[\frac{\partial P}{\partial T}\right]_V} = \frac{\gamma}{\gamma-1}$$

22. What is meant by thermodynamical equilibrium? Discuss the equilibrium between a liquid and its vapour and hence deduce Clausius-Clapeyron's equation.

23. Explain the concepts of reversible and irreversible processes. Obtain an expression for the efficiency of a reversible. Carnot engine with a perfect gas as the working substance. Show that for the same pair of working temperatures, the efficiency of all reversible engines is the same and is the maximum value attainable.

24. Describe with diagrams the working of an Otto engine and deduce an expression for its efficiency.

25. Prove the thermodynamical relation

$$\left(\frac{\partial H}{\partial V}\right)_T = -T\left(\frac{\partial P}{\partial T}\right)_V$$

and hence show that

$$L = T(V_2 - V_1)\left(\frac{dP}{dT}\right)$$

26. State the two laws of thermodynamics and explain their significance. Derive an expression for the efficiency of a Carnot's engine.

27. Define Kelvin's 'absolute or thermodynamic scale of temperature. Show how this scale agrees with that of a perfect gas scale. Is a negative temperature possible on this scale?
28. Derive the relation between volume and pressure of a gas undergoing adiabatic changes.
29. Explain fully what you understand by entropy. Show that the change in entropy of a substance in a cyclic process is zero.
30. Deduce Clapeyron's equation. How does it explain the effect of pressure on:
    (i) the melting point of solids, and
    (ii) the boiling point of liquids.
31. What is a reversible thermodynamic process? Describe a reversible heat engine and find an expression for its efficiency.
32. Derive an expression for the efficiency of an ideal heat engine, working between the temperatures T_1 and T_2K. Prove that the efficiency of a reversible engine is maximum for the given source and sink.
33. Discuss the Second Law of Thermodynamics and the principle of increase of entropy.
34. Deduce the adiabatic equation for an ideal gas and give Clement and Desormes' method for determining γ.
35. State the Second Law of Thermodynamics. Describe Carnot's cycle and deduce the efficiency of an ideal heat engine.
36. Explain what you understand by thermodynamic scale of temperature. Show that it agrees with an ideal gas scale. What is zero on this scale?
37. Write short notes on:
    (a) Fermi Energy
    (b) Planck's radiation law
    (c) Statistical thermodynamics
    (d) Maxwell Boltzmann distribution law
    (e) Fermi-Dirac distribution law
    (f) Bose-Einstein distribution law.

38. Show how the second law of thermodynamics enables us to define a scale of temperature independent of the properties of any working substance. How is the scale realised in practice?

39. Derive Maxwell's thermodynamical equations and show that

$$C_P - C_V = -T\left(\frac{\partial V}{\partial T}\right)_P^2\left(\frac{\partial P}{\partial V}\right)_T$$

40. Describe in detail Clement and Desorme's method of finding the ratio of the two specific heats of air giving the simple theory of the method. What are the objections to the method and what modifications and improvements have been proposed?

41. Establish the relation connecting the temperature and the volume of a gas undergoing adiabatic compression.

42. Establish the latent heat equation,

$$\frac{dL}{dT} - \frac{L}{T} = C_2 - C_1$$

where C_1 and C_2 are the specific heat of the liquid and the saturated vapour respectively.

43. What do you understand by the Kelvin's thermodynamic scale of temperature ? Prove that the ratio of two temperatures on the thermodynamic scale is identical with the ratio of the same two temperatures measured on the perfect gas scale.

44. Describe Carnot's cycle and obtain an expression for the efficiency of an ideal heat engine in terms of temperatures.

45. Derive the relation between the volume and temperature of a perfect gas undergoing adiabatic compression.

46. Explain what you mean by entropy of a substance. Show that for any reversible cyclic change of a system/the total change of entropy is zero. Show that this statement is not true for an irreversible change.

47. Discuss the equilibrium between a liquid and its vapour and hence deduce Clausius-Clapeyron's equation. Explain, how the boiling point of a liquid and the melting point of a solid are affected by change of pressure.

48. Distinguish between isothermal and adiabatic changes. Show that for an adiabatic change in a perfect gas

PV^{γ} = constant.

49. Under suitable conditions the Joule-Thomson effect results in cooling and so does an adiabatic expansion of a gas.

    Distinguish between these two types of cooling.

50. Deduce the following Maxwell's relations

    (i) $\left(\frac{\partial S}{\partial V}\right)_T = \left(\frac{\partial P}{\partial T}\right)_V$

    (ii) $\left(\frac{\partial S}{\partial P}\right)_T = \left(\frac{\partial V}{\partial T}\right)_P$.

51. With the help of appropriate Maxwell's relations, show that for a substance

    $C_P - C_V = -TVE\alpha^2$.

52. State Carnot's theorem and deduce it from the second law of thermodynamics.

53. Write short notes on:

    (a) Steam engine

    (b) Otto cycle

    (c) Entropy is a measure of disorder

    (d) Isothermal Process

54. Derive the Clausius Clapeyron's latent heat equation for first order phase changes.

    $$\frac{dP}{dT} = \frac{L}{T(V_2 - V_1)}.$$

55. Derive Maxwell's first and second thermodynamical relations and deduce the Clausius-Clapeyron's latent heat equation from Maxwell's second relation.

56. Define isothermal and adiabatic transformations. Give examples.

    Obtain equation of state for an ideal gas undergoing (i) an isothermal transformation and (ii) an adiabatic transformation.

57. Dry air at N. T. P. (normal temperature and pressure) is compressed adiabatically to one-third of its original volume. Calculate the resulting pressure. Given that the ratio C_p/C_v of air is 1.40.

58. What is the importance of Clausius Clapeyron latent heat equation? Derive this equation and outline its applications.

59. For a quasi-static adiabatic process of an ideal gas, prove

$$\frac{T}{(P)^{(\gamma-1)/\gamma}} = \text{constant.}$$

60. Define Carnot's cycle. Explain the working of a Carnot's heat engine. Calculate its efficiency when a perfect gas is the working substance.

61. What is meant by the order of a phase change? Discuss it giving examples.

    State and discuss Zeroth law of thermodynamics.

62. State Carnot's Theorem and show that it is a necessary consequence of Second Law of Thermodynamics. Prove that the efficiency of a Carnot engine using an ideal gas as a working substance is $\eta = \dfrac{T_1 - T_2}{T_1}$

63. Derive the following relations:

    (a) $C_P - C_V = -T\left(\dfrac{\partial V}{\partial T}\right)_P^2 \left(\dfrac{\partial P}{\partial V}\right)_T$

    (b) $TdS = C_p dT - T\left(\dfrac{\partial V}{\partial T}\right)_P dP$

    (c) $\dfrac{\left[\dfrac{\partial P}{\partial T}\right]_S}{\left[\dfrac{\partial P}{\partial T}\right]_V} = \dfrac{\gamma}{\gamma - 1}$

64. Write short notes on:

    (i) Ruchhardt's experiment for γ

    (ii) Absolute gas scale

    (iii) Rankine cycle

    (iv) Diesel engine

65. Show that

    (i) $\left(\dfrac{\partial S}{\partial V}\right)_T = \left(\dfrac{\partial P}{\partial T}\right)_V$

(ii) $\left(\frac{\partial H}{\partial V}\right)_T = T\left(\frac{\partial P}{\partial T}\right)_V$

(iii) $\left(\frac{\partial H}{\partial P}\right)_T = -T\left(\frac{\partial V}{\partial T}\right)_P$

(iv) $\left(\frac{\partial T}{\partial V}\right)_S = -T\left(\frac{\partial P}{\partial S}\right)_V$

(v) $\left(\frac{\partial T}{\partial P}\right)_S = T\left(\frac{\partial V}{\partial H}\right)_P$

(vi) $\left(\frac{\partial T}{\partial P}\right)_V\left(\frac{\partial S}{\partial V}\right)_P - \left(\frac{\partial T}{\partial V}\right)_V\left(\frac{\partial S}{\partial P}\right)_V = 1$

and (vii) $\left(\frac{\partial P}{\partial T}\right)_S\left(\frac{\partial V}{\partial S}\right)_T - \left(\frac{\partial P}{\partial S}\right)_V\left(\frac{\partial V}{\partial T}\right)_S = 1$

66. Calculate the temperature at which ice will freeze if the pressure is increased by 135.2 atmospheres. The change in specific volume when 1 gram of water freezes into ice is 0.091 cm^3. One atmospheric pressure = 10^6 dynes/cm^3. Latent heat effusion of ice = 80 cal/g. and J = 4.2×10^7 ergs/cal.

67. Calculate the temperature at which water will boil if the pressure is increased by 1.814 atmospheres. Given that the change in specific volume when one gram of water is converted into steam is 1676 cm^3. Latent heat of vaporization of steam = 540 cal/g. J = 4.2×107 ergs/cal and one atmosphere pressure = 10^{37} dynes/cm^3.

68. Calculate the change in entropy when 20 grams of ice at 0°C is converted into water at the same temperature.

69. Write short notes on:

    (a) Entropy tends to a maximum

    (b) Third Law of Thermodynamics

    (c) Absolute zero temperature

    (d) Entropy of a perfect gas

70. Write short notes on:

    (a) Thermal Equilibrium

(b) Concept of Temperature

(c) Concept of Heat

(d) Zeroth Law in Thermodynamics

(e) Phase changes of the second order.

(f) Temperature Entropy diagram

(g) Thermodynamic system

71. A motor car tyre has a pressure of 3 atmospheres at the room temperature of 27°C. If the tyre suddenly bursts what is the resulting temperature?

72. Calculate the change in entropy when 10 kg. of water at 100°C is converted into steam at the same temperature.

73. Calculate the increase in entropy when 5 g of ice at –10°C is converted into steam at 100°C. Sp. heat of ice = – 0.5; Latent heat of ice = 80 cal/g; Latent heat of steam = 540 cal/g.

74. Two gram molecules of a gas expands isothermally to four times its initial volume. Calculate the change in its entropy in terms of the gas constant.

75. 100 g of water at 0°C is mixed with an equal mass of water at 80°C. Calculate the resultant increase in entropy.

76. A Carnot's engine working as a refrigerator between 250 K and 300 K receives 1000 calories of heat from the reservoir at the lower temperature:

    (i) Calculate the amount of heat rejected to the reservoir at the higher temperature,

    (ii) Calculate also the amount of work done in each cycle to operate the refrigerator.

77. A six faced dice is such that the probability for the number 4 is 1/5. Find the probability that 4 appears 4 times in 10 throws. Find also the ratio of this probability to the same complexion if the dice were normal.

78. You have 400 coins, out of them 20% are prone to 0.6 times head per throw. Find the probability of complexion 200 heads and 200 tails. Is it different from the maximum probability? Why?

79. Calculate the depression in the melting point of ice produced by 2 atmospheres increase of pressure. Given latent heat of

ice = 80 cal/g and the specific volumes of 1 gram of ice and water at 0°C are 1.091 cm^3 and 1.000 cm^3 respectively.

80. Calculate the change in the melting point of naphthalene for 2 atmospheres rise in pressure, given that its melting point is 80°C. Latent heat of fusion is 4563 cal/mol and increase in volume on fusion is 18.7 cm^2/mol. 1 cal = 4.2×10^7 ergs.

81. What do you understand by the internal energy of a system. Slate the first law of thermodynamics and use it to derive a relation between the volume and temperature of a perfect gas undergoing an adiabatic change of state.

82. Calculate the work done in a Carnot's cycle of operations. Deduce the efficiency of a Carnot's engine in terms of the temperatures between which it works.

83. A Carnot's engine is operated between two reservoirs at temperatures of 500 K and 400 K. If the engine receives 2000 calories of heat from the source in each cycle, calculate:

    (a) the amount of heat rejected to the sink in each cycle,

    (b) the efficiency of the engine, and

    (c) the work done by the engine in each cycle in:

        (i) joules,

        (ii) kilo-Watt hours.

84. Find the efficiency of a Carnot's engine working between 227°C and 27°C.

85. A Carnot's engine takes in 1000 kilocalories of heat from a reservoir at 627°C and exhausts it to a sink at 27°C:

    (a) What is its efficiency?

    (b) How much work does it perform? Express it:

        (i) in ergs,

        (ii) kilo-Watt hours,

        (iii) electron volts.

86. A Carnot's engine whose temperature of the source is 400 K takes 500 calories of heat at this temperature and rejects 400 calories of heat to the sink. What is the temperature of the sink? Calculate the efficiency of the engine.

2

STATISTICAI AND IRREVERSIBLE THERMODYNAMICS

INTRODUCTION OF STATISTICAL THERMODYNAMICS

This is a new approach that deals with the applications of statistical mechanics to Thermodynamics. It has been applied successfully to relate the microscopic properties of the individual molecules (moment of inertia, dipole moment, etc.) with macroscopic properties (molar heat capacity, polarization, etc.) of a system having a large number of molecules.

Statistical thermodynamics can be used for systems at equilibrium as well as away from equilibrium. In this chapter, we shall limit our discussion to the equilibrium aspects of the system

Distinction between quantum mechanics, statistical mechanics and statistical thermodynamics. Statistical mechanics acts as a bridge between thermodynamics and quantum mechanics. Quantum mechanics provides information about the energy of the molecular system, statistical mechanics tells us about the possible arrangement of the energy among various molecules of the system and introduces the concept of probability and partition functions. Statistical thermodynamics deals, with the relationships between the probability partition functions and thermodynamic properties. In other words, a physical entity generally manifests itself in :

(i) A Microscopic, and

(ii) A Macroscopic state.

We have dealt with macroscopic or the bulk state of matter in the preceding chapters. The macroscopic variables were pressure, volume, temperature, entropy, etc. The macroscopic variables were related mutually on thermodynamical considerations. Further, we assumed that the number of atoms/molecules in them (microscopic deta ls of a macrosystem) were exorbitantly large $\approx 10^{25}$ m^{-3}. The microscopic systems, on the other hand, have very few particles.

Now, we know that the actual systems, the macro systems, are formed of the microsystems and so there should be a definite relation between the two. Classically, if we want to have a complete description of a system we need to know actual velocity (or momentum), location and mutual interaction (if any, with other particles) of every particle. Since every panicle is described by three positions and three momentum coordinates, hence to describe a macrosystem we need a very large number of data. Further, any change in the parameter of an individual particle should be reflected in the properties of the system as a whole.

This poses a question: How to deal with such a vast data which even a super-computer is not capable to handle, if at all we are able to collect it. If, however, we remember that:

(i) Much of the data and analytical results obtained on micro level are not useful in the study of the macrosystem, and

(ii) The application of classical dynamical principles to a many particle system is theoretically inapplicable, we can easily dispense with the technically impossible and practically useless classical kinetic and thermodynamic methods in favour of new statistical methods.

Statistics is applied only to such systems which contain a large number of identical individuals which may be distinguishable by means of some property. In a statistical method, we study the behaviour of aggregates of particles to calculate the average value without investigating the detailed behaviour of the system and finding there from the value for each individual. Statistically, it is sufficient to know the most probable distribution of particles in different accessible states. This branch of physics has seen its development in the hands of Maxwell, Boltzmann, Gibbs, Fermi-Dirac, Bose-Einstein etc.

In the following sections we will see the importance of the concept of probability in the development of the statistical theory. Hence, we shall first consider some elementary theorems on the calculus of probability. In other words, it refers to a class of events of which the particular event is one member. Mathematically, the probability is defined as: When a certain aspect is possible in a ways and is not possible in b ways, then the probability of occurring the aspect is a/(a + b). (Newton defined probability as the ratio of a certain number of aspects, which were possibly observable, to the total number of aspects included in that class.) Here (a + b) is the total number of aspects each of which has the same chance of occurrence.

Now, as we have shown, if an event can occur in a ways, the probability of occurring of this event is a/(a + b), and similarly, if it fails to occur in b ways, then the probability of its failing is b/(a + b). The sum of the two

$$\frac{a}{a+b} + \frac{b}{a+b} = 1$$

corresponds to the certainty of some event, since the event must occur or fail to occur. If b = 0, the probability of occurrence becomes certain but if a = 0, the probability of its failure is certain.

We may define the probability for a certain event occurring m times in n unrestricted (free) attempts as,

$$P = \lim_{n \to \infty} \frac{m}{n}.$$

In the foregoing discussion we have assumed that every event is equally likely.

Calculation of Probabilities

We can extend the theory of probability in order to include the occurrence of two or more independent events. The combined probability in such cases is given by the product of separate probability of each event. Let us examine some cases:

(i) *Tossing of a coin:* On tossing a single coin, there are two possible aspects that may be presented by a fallen coin, a "head" or a "tail". We may assume here that there is no preference for any particular event, so that after making a large number of throws, the ratio of the number of heads to the number of tails is unity. Thus, for a normal coin the probability of each event is 1/2.

(ii) *Tossing of two unlike coins*: Suppose we toss two coins of different denominations or of different sizes, or of different colours, we have four complexions.

1. $Head_1$ $Head_2$
2. $Head_1$ $Tail_2$
3. $Tail_1$, $Tail_2$
4. $Tail_1$ $Head_2$.

Thus, the probability of any one complexion on a single toss will be 1/4 = 1/2.1/2. Or the composite probability is the product of probability of individual events.

(iii) *Tossing of two similar coins*: If two coins cannot be distinguished from each other, then complexions 2 and 4 of (ii) are indistinguishable whence the probability of one head and one tail is twice than that of two heads or two tails.

(iv) *Tossing of two coins in general*: Let us represent occurrence of heads by A_1, A_2 and the occurrence of tails by B_1, B_2 when two coins are tossed. Then the composite event can be represented by $(A_1 + B_1)(A_2 + B_2) = A_1A_1 + A_1B_2 + A_2B_1 + B B_2$

(v) *Tossing of three unlike coins:* With three unlike coins, we have three distinguishable heads A_1, A_2, A_3 and three distinguishable tails, B_1, B_2, B_3. Here we can have eight equally probable complexions $A_1 A_2 A_3$, $A_1 A_2 B_3$, $A_1 B_2 B_3$, $B_1 A_2 B_3$, $B_1 A_2 B_3$, $B_1 B_2 A_3$ and $B_1 B_2 B_3$ which are really obtained from the product of $(A_1 + B_1)$, $(A_2 + B_2)$, $(A_3 + B_3)$.

(vi) *Tossing of three similar coins:* In this case we have only four probable states with complexions

1. All heads.
2. Two heads and one tail
3. All tails.
4. One head and two tails.

We can tabulate the result as in (iv) for

$(A + B)(A + B)(A + B) = A_3 + 3A^2B + 3AB^2 + B^3$.

(vii) *Tossing of n coins*: Suppose all the coins are different. Then the possible complexions (also known as probability number) will be $(A_1 + B_1)(A_2 + B_2) \ldots\ldots (A_n + B_n)$. And, if the coins are all alike the total number of possible complexions will be

$$(A + B)^n = A^n + {}^nC_1A^{n-1}B + {}^nC_2A^{n-2}B^2 + \ldots {}^nC_rA^{n-r}B^r + \ldots + {}^nC_nB^n$$

or $$= \sum_{r=0}^{r=n} C_r A^{n-r}B^r$$

or, also $$(A + B)^n = \sum_{r=0}^{r=n} C_r A^rB^{n-r}$$

$$\equiv \sum_{r=0}^{r=n} C_r A^{n-r}B^r$$

where $${}^nC_r = \frac{n!}{r!(n-r)!} \equiv \text{Number of events with r heads/tails.}$$

Now, since A and B indicate one event each, the total number of events are $(1 + 1)^n = 2^n = {}^nC_1 + {}^nC_2 + \ldots + {}^nC_n$

∴ The probability of r heads and (n – r) tails to appear is

$$P(r, n-r) = \frac{{}^nC_r}{2^n} = \frac{n!}{r!(n-r)!}\cdot\frac{1}{2^n}$$

Maximum and minimum probability: To find out which of the combination of heads and tails is most likely in a large number of throws of n coins, we have to find the maximum value of ${}^nC_r$. It is known from algebra that the value of ${}^nC_r$ is greatest for r = n/2 when n is even and r = n+1/2 when n is odd.

$$P_{max} = \frac{{}^nC_{n/2}}{2^n} = \frac{n!}{(n/2)!(n/2)}\cdot\frac{1}{2^n}$$

Similarly, the minimum probability, P_{min} obtained for r = 0 or r = n as ${}^nC_n = 1$.

whence $P_{min} = 1/2^n$

(viii) *Tossing of a single coin n times*: When we toss the same coin second, third,... nth time, its behaviour is again unpredictable. It may show a head or a tail each time with 1/2 probability. Hence a single coin tossed n times (and of course, making large number of such attempts, if we want to have satisfactory results) is just equivalent to the case of tossing of n coins as discussed in (vii).

Another equivalent illustration can be: Take 2 boxes, identical in all respects, and throw n balls from a great distance. Assuming that each ball will fall into one or the other box, the distribution of balls in the boxes will be governed by the relation (vii),

(ix) *Tossing of a dice*: If we toss of dice, having six faces, the probability for each face showing up will be 1/6. Since now the total number of aspects is 6 and only one can show up at a time with equal probability. Again, we may take 2, 3,.... n dices and throw them and calculate the composite probability for a certain complexion.

(x) *Tossing of n dices each having m faces*: Here let us assume that dice 1 has faces a_1, a_2, a_3... a_m; dice 2 has faces b_1 b_2 b_3 ... b_m; dice 3 has faces c_1, c_2, c_3 ; etc., then the possible complexions with n dices will be the sum of each aspect

a_1, a_2, a_3... a_m, v_1, b_2, b_3 ... b_m , c_1, c_2, c_3 ... n sets and, if the dice are all alike, we have

$$m_a,\ m_b,\ m_c \ldots \text{ n sets.}$$

If the probability for occurring each of the face is same, *i.e.*, a = b = c... = one aspect, we get total number of possible aspects

$$= m.m.m.... \text{ n times } = m^n$$

One can show that the most probable distribution corresponds to equitable distribution of faces *i.e.*, face 1, face 2, face 3, etc., will appear in equal number. Then all the dices showing face 1 have the probability of only $1/m^n$.

A similar illustration to this is : Take *m identical boxes and throw n* balls onto them from a great distance. We will take up this problem later in more detail. As in actual analysis of physical problems we have a large number of particles which are distributed into a large number of (hypothetical) boxes.

(xi) *Probability with weightage*: So far we have considered the case in which the probability of occurring an event and its failure is the same. But there can be cases where the probability of occurring a particular event is greater than that for any other event.

Let a be the probability of occurring an event and b be the probability of its failure, per trial. Then, if the trial is repeated n times, the probability of r favourable events is

$$a^r.b^{n-r} = a^r (1 - a)^{n-r}$$

But there are ^nC_r ways for r favourable events, therefore, the probability of occurring r events is

$$P(r, n-r) = {}^nC_r\, a^r\, (1-a)^{n-r}$$

Thus, for example, in a dice a = 1/6

$$\therefore \quad P(r, n-r) = {}^nC_r \left(\frac{1}{6}\right)^r \left(\frac{5}{6}\right)^{n-r}$$

But, if certain number, say 3, has a = 2/7 then in n tosses the number 3 will occur r times with a probability.

(xii) *Postulate of equal a priori probability:* It states that all accessible microstates corresponding to a macrostate are equally probable. Thus, the postulate claims that the probability of finding a molecule in one region of phase space is identical with that for any other region of equal volume provided the regions are obeying other conditions of equality (*i.e.*, the regions have extensions of same magnitude and correspond to the same energy). Thus, it follows that the probability of occurrence of a macrostate is proportional to the number of microstates associated with it

i.e., $\quad P_i \propto \Omega_i$

where P_i is the probability and Ω_i is the total number of accessible microstates, in the ith set.

ENSEMBLE METHOD

The *ensemble average* method is superior to the method of *time average*, in determining average value of a physical quantity. So first we recall the characteristics of an ensemble and its way of representation.

1. It is a group of large number of systems.
2. Every member of an ensemble is an exact miniature copy of the system under test.
3. Every member of an ensemble is subjected to the same experimental conditions.
4. There may be three kinds of interactions between the members of the ensemble:

   (a) Thermal-related to T,

   (b) Mechanical-related to V, and

(c) Diffusive-related N or m (*i.e.*, chemical potential).

5. Every member of the ensemble may have a large number of microstates (also called the dynamic state) due to random motion of its particles/molecules/ And when the configuration of the member systems is maintained same in terms of generalised coordinates and momenta, the statistical method is expected to yield quite accurate results.

Ensemble Representation

Ensembles can be represented in a Γ-space by the distribution of its phase-points. Generally, the distribution of phase-points in an ensemble is continuous and can be represented by a density function ρ(p, qt). The number of phase-points in the vicinity of (p, q) in Γ-space is given by ρ (p, q t) dT where d r = dp dq = volume element of Γ- space.

If ρ (p, q t} is known at time t_1, its value can easily be obtained for some other time t_2. Now, from the probability theory

$$d\rho\ (p, q) \propto d\Gamma \qquad \therefore d\rho\ (p, q) = \rho(p, q)d\Gamma$$

Here ρ (p, q) is known as the distribution function. The ensemble average of any function R is then given by

$$\langle R\rangle = \int R\ (p, q)\ \rho(p, q)d\Gamma.$$

Selection of Ensemble

(i) Molecules of real gases are usually formed of 2, 3.... atoms whence the density of phase points is not uniform,

(ii) The density of phase points is non-zero for every range of energy,

(iii) Total number of particles and energy is conserved. Point (i) eliminates use of uniform ensemble. Point (ii) eliminates use of microcanonical ensemble. Point (in) eliminates use of grand canonical ensemble to real gases.

But since the properties of these gases such as N, V, T, ε, H etc., are constant the canonical ensemble finds use in description of real gases for their thermodynamic properties.

STATISTICAL POSTULATES

Following postulates are made for applying the statistical method to physical systems:

(i) Every system has a large number of particles/molecules which are in constant random motion.

(ii) The motion of particles/molecules is described in 2Nf-dimensional phase-space.

(iii) The phase-space is divided into cells.

(iv) Postulate of equal a priori probability holds good.

(v) Probability of a particular configuration is given by the ratio of microstates corresponding to that configuration to total accessible microstates, *i.e.*,

$P_i = \Omega_i/\Sigma\Omega_i$ and the average value of any physical parameter is given by

$$< x > = \Sigma x_i P_i = \frac{\Sigma x_i \Omega_i}{\Sigma \Omega_i}$$

where Qi is the frequency of the configuration.

(vi) The equilibrium state of the system is the state of maximum probability.

(vii) The law of conservation of mass is generally valid whence

$$n_1 + n_2 + n_3 + ... = \Sigma n_i, = N = \text{constant.}$$

(viii) The law of conservation of energy governs the distribution of particles among cells. Thus, if ε_1, ε_2, ε_3 ... denotes energies of each particle in cell 1, 2, 3, etc., then

$$E = \varepsilon_1 n_1, + \varepsilon_2 n_2 + \varepsilon_3 n_3 + ... = \Sigma \varepsilon_i n_i = \text{constant.}$$

(ix) Every point in the phase-space (cell) represents a microstate, the cell volume being h where/is the degree of freedom.

(x) The number of microstates in the energy interval e and $\varepsilon + d\varepsilon$, per unit volume is represented as $\Omega(\varepsilon)$.

(xi) A collection of accessible microstates form a statistical ensemble.

Note: A complexion/configuration/arrangement represents distribution of molecules in different cells, and their form is governed by constraints stated in (vii) and (viii).

ACCESSIBLE MICROSTATES

Let us now count the number of energy states available in a macrosystem. Let E be the total energy of this system which has been divided into small energy intervals δ E so that a sufficient number of quantum stales are available in each interval of δ E. Now, if Ω (E) is the number density of such states in the energy interval E and E + δE then

$$\Omega(E) = \rho(E)\ \delta E \quad \text{...(i)}$$

where ρ (E) is density of states (the number of states in unit energy interval). Thus

$$\Omega(E) \propto .\delta E \quad \text{...(ii)}$$

Let the value of Ω(E) changes with the magnitude of energy interval. Hence we may consider Ω(E) as a smoothly varying function of E.

Again, if ϕ(E) denotes the number of states with energy up to E and ϕ(E + δE) denotes the number of states with energy up to E + δE then

$$\Omega(E) = \phi(E + \delta E) - \phi(E) \equiv \frac{\delta\phi}{\delta E}\delta E \quad \text{...(iii)}$$

Comment on ρ (E). Relations (i) and (ii) (possibly) indicate that ρ(E) is a constant. But it is not so. In fact ρ (E) is an increasing function of E. Let us see how! We know that the total number of microstates is equal to the product of thermodynamic probabilities of different macrostates (composite probability is obtained, always by multiplying probabilities for different complexions), *i.e.*,

$$\Omega = \Omega_1\,\Omega_2\,\Omega_3 \ldots \Omega_i \ldots \Omega_f$$

or

$$\Omega = \prod_i \Omega_i\ (i = 1 \text{ to } f)$$

where f is the degree of freedom.

But Ω_i should be somehow related to E, *i.e.*,

$$\Omega \propto E^a \quad \therefore \Omega \propto E^{fa} \quad \text{...(iv)}$$

usually a ≅ 1/2 and/ranges between 10^{22} and 10^{28}. This suggests that for a certain energy interval δE, ρ(E) increases with the value of E.

STATISTICAL MECHANICS

Statistical Mechanics deals with systems consisting of many particles and the methods employed are to get a collective or macroscopic property of the system without taking into account the individual motion of the particles The word particle is used in a broad sense meaning a fundamental particle *e.g.*, an electron, an atom, a molecule etc. The particle is a well defined and a stable unit of a given physical system. As it is not practically possible to determine the property of each particle individually, a statistical approach is made by using the concept of probability of distribution.

This statistical approach helps in determining the bulk or macroscopic property of the system as a whole. The idea of probability does not imply that the particles move in a random way without obeying the laws. For a many particle system, the statistical analysis is valid regarding the applications of probability distribution of particles.

STATISTICAL EQUILIBRIUM

Consider that a thermodynamical isolated system consists of N particles. The energy states available to the particles are E_1, E_2, E_3 etc. These energy states may be quantized or may be continuous and are due to vibrational and rotational energy of the particles.

Suppose, that at any given instant of time, n_1 particles are in state of energy E_1, n_2, particles with energy state E_2 and so on.

The total number of particles in the system is,

$$N = n_1 + n_2 + n_3 + ... = \sum_i n_i \quad ...(i)$$

Here $i = 1, 2, 3$ etc.

The total energy of the system,

$$U = n_1E_1 + n_2E_2 + n_3E_3 + ...$$

$$U = \sum_i n_i E_i \quad ...(ii)$$

Equation (ii) refers to the total energy of a system in which the particles are non-interacting. Here, the energy of each particle depends only on the coordinates of the particle in the system. For an isolated system, the total energy U is constant.

For isolated system.

$$U = \sum_i n_i E_i = \text{constant} \quad ...(iii)$$

Consider a gas having N molecules at a certain temperature and pressure. Its volume, temperature and pressure are kept constant *i.e.*, the system is isolated. The total energy of this system remains constant. But, the molecules of the gas collide with each other and also with the walls of the container. Consequently, the number of molecules change from one energy state to the other energy state. It means that the value of n_1, n_2, n_3 etc., continuously change. It can be reasonably assumed that for each microscopic State of a system of particles, there is a particular most favoured distribution. When this distribution or partition is reached, the system attains statistical equilibrium. For an isolated system, the values of n_1, n_2, n_3 etc., vary only near the values corresponding to the most probable distribution. Hence, the basic problem in statistical thermodynamics is to obtain the most probable distribution law for a given composition of the system.

In practice, three most probable distribution laws are used. They are:

(i) Maxwell-Boltzmann Distribution Law.

(ii) Fermi-Dirac Distribution Law (Statistics).

(iii) Bose-Einstein Distribution Law (Statistics).

THEOREMS OF PROBABILITY IN STATISTICAL THERMODYNAMICS

The following are the important probability theorems commonly used in statistical thermodynamics:

(1) The number of ways in which N distinguishable particles can he arranged in order is equal to

$$N!$$

(2) The number of different ways in which N particles can be selected from N distinguishable particles irrespective of the order of selection is equal to

$$\frac{N!}{(N-n)!n!}$$

(3) The number of different ways in which n indistinguishable particles can be arranged in g distinguishable states with not more then one particle in each state is equal to

$$\frac{g!}{(g-n)!n!}$$

MAXWELL-BOLTZMANN DISTRIBUTION LAW

Consider a system that contains a large number of particles that are identical and distinguishable. The identical particles refer to the particles having the same structure. The distinction between the particles is due to their energy states at a given instant. Four particles are in energy state E_1, 2 in state E_2, zero in state E_3 and so on. It is assumed that all the energy states are accessible to each particle. Consequently, it can be assumed that the probability of any particular partition is proportional to the number of different ways in which the particles can be distributed in the existing available energy states so as to produce the desired partition.

To obtain the required distribution as the first particle a in state E_1 can be selected in N ways. The second particle b in state E_1 can be selected in (N – 1) ways and so on. Therefore, the total number of ways in which the first four particles in state E_1 can be selected is given by,

$$N(N-1)(N-2)(N-3) = \frac{N!}{(N-4)!}$$

Moreover, the four particles in state E_1 can be arranged in 4! different orders. For example, *abcd, bcda, cdab* and so on. There are 24 ways. But, it is immaterial for these particles to be arranged in any particular order in state E_1, because they are identical. Thus, the total number of *distinguishable* different ways are,

$$\frac{N!}{4!(N-4)!}$$

In general, if the first state consists of n_1 particles, the distinguishable different ways, for arranging n_1 particles in state E_1, are,

$$p_1 = \frac{N!}{n_1!(N-n_1)!} \quad \text{...(i)}$$

For the second state E_2, only $(N - n_1)$ particles are available and n_2 particles are in state E_2. The number of distinguishable different ways are,

$$p_2 = \frac{(N-n_1)!}{n_2!(N-n_1-n_2)!} \quad \text{...(ii)}$$

If this process is continued for all the available states, the total number of distinguishable ways are obtained by multiplying P_1, P_2, P_3 etc.

$$P = p_1 \times p_2 \times p_3 \times \text{......}$$

$$P = \left[\frac{N!}{n_1!(N-n_1)!}\right]\left[\frac{(N-n_1)!}{n_2!(N-n_1-n_2)}\right] \times \text{....}$$

$$P = \frac{N!}{n_1!n_2!n_3!\ldots} \quad \text{...(iii)}$$

The distinguishable ways are,

$$P = \frac{N!}{4!2!0!3!1!} \qquad \text{...(iv)}$$

Here 0! is equal to one.

It has been assumed so far that all the available states have the same probability of occupation by the particles. However, it may happen that the states have different intrinsic probabilities say g_i.

For example, a particular energy state may be favourable with more different angular momentum states than the rest and hence it is more likely to be occupied. Taking into account this intrinsic probability factor, the value of P will be different.

If g_i is the probability of locating a particle in a certain energy state E_i, then the probability of locating 2 particles in the same state is $g_i \times g_i = g^2_i$. For n_i particles, the probability is g_in_i. Hence the total probability for a given distribution is given by

$$P = \frac{N!g_1n_1g_2n_2g_3n_3...}{n_1!n_2!n_3!n_4!...} \qquad \text{...(v)}$$

Here n_1, n_2, n_3 etc., are the number of particles in states E_1, E_2, E_3, etc. and g_1, g_2, g_3 etc., are the intrinsic probabilities for states E_1, E_2, E_3 etc.

If all the particles are further assumed to be indistinguishable *i.e.*, particles in state E, and particles in state E_4 cannot be distinguished, then N! permutations among the particles themselves and occupying the different states result in the same distribution. The probability in this case is given by

$$P = \frac{1}{N!}\left[\frac{N!g_1n_1g_2n_2g_3n_3...}{n_1!n_2!n_3!...}\right]$$

$$\therefore \quad P = \frac{g_1n_1g_2n_2g_3n_3...}{n_1!n_2!n_3!...}$$

$$\therefore \quad P = \prod_i^N \frac{g_1n_1}{n_1!} \qquad \text{...(vi)}$$

Here Π is the product sign (since probability is the product of such distributions.

The most probable distribution can be obtained by evaluating the maximum value of $\log_e$, P in equation (vi). This should also satisfy the two conditions that

$$\sum_i n_i = N \qquad ...(vii)$$

and $$\sum_i n_i E_i = U \qquad ...(vii)$$

According to Stirling's approximation

$$\log_e x! = x \log_e x - x$$

From equation (vi), applying Stirling's approximation, we get

$$\log_e P = \sum_i (n_i \log_e g_i - \log_e n_i!)$$

$$= \sum_i [n_i \log_e g_i - (n_i \log_e n_i - n_i)]$$

$$= \sum_i (n_i \log_e g_i - n_i \log_e n_i + n_i)$$

$$= \sum_i n_i - \sum_i (n_i \log_e n_i - n_i \log_e g_i)$$

$$\log_e P = N \sum_i n_i \log_e \frac{n_i}{g_i} \qquad ...(ix)$$

Differentiating equation (ix)

$$d(\log_e P) = \sum_i (dn_i) \log_e \frac{n_i}{g_i} - \sum_i n_i d\left(\log_e \frac{n_i}{g_i}\right)$$

$$= \sum_i dn_i \log_e \frac{n_i}{g_i} - \sum_i n_i \frac{dn_i}{n_i}$$

$$= \sum_i dn_i \log_e \frac{n_i}{g_i} - \sum_i dn_i$$

But $$\sum_i dn_i = 0.$$

$$\therefore \quad -d(\log_e P) = \sum_i \left[\log_e \left(\frac{n_i}{g_i}\right)\right] dn_i \qquad ...(x)$$

To obtain the maximum value of P,

$$d(\log_e P) = 0$$

$$\therefore \quad \sum_i \log_e \left(\frac{n_i}{g_i}\right) dn_i = 0 \qquad ...(xi)$$

But $\Sigma dn_i = 0$ ...(xii)

and $\Sigma E_i dn_i = 0$ ...(xiii)

Multiplying (xii) by α and (xiii) by β and adding to equation (xi), we get

$$\sum_i \left[\log_e\left(\frac{n_i}{g_i}\right) + \alpha + \beta E_i\right] dn_i = 0$$

The equilibrium distribution is possible if

$$\log_e \frac{n_i}{g_i} + \alpha + \beta\, Ei = 0 \quad ...(xiv)$$

or $$\frac{n_i}{g_i} = e^{-\alpha-\beta Ei}$$

or $$n_i = g_i\, e^{-\alpha-\beta Ei} \quad ...(xv)$$

This gives the maximum probability distribution and a and p are two parameters that depend upon the physical property of the system.

$$N = n_1 + n_2 + n_3 + ...$$

$$N = g_1 e^{-\alpha-\beta E1} + g_1 e^{-\alpha-\beta E2} + ...$$

$$N = e^{-\alpha}[g_1 e^{-\beta E1} + g_2 e^{-\beta E2} + ...]$$

$$N = e^{-\alpha}[\sum_i g_i\, e^{-\beta Ei}]$$

Take $[\sum_i g_i\, e^{-\beta Ei} = Z$ ...(xvi)

Here, Z is called the partition function.

$$N = e^{-\alpha}(Z) \quad ....(xvii)$$

$$e^{-\alpha} = \frac{N}{Z}$$

Substituting this value in equation (vii)

$$n_i = \left(\frac{N}{Z}\right)[g_i e^{-\beta Ei}] \quad ....(xviii)$$

This equation refers to Maxwell-Boltzmann Distribution Law.

MAXWELL-BOLTZMANN DISTRIBUTION IN TERMS OF TEMPERATURE

The total energy of an isolated system is given by

$$U = \sum_i n_i E_i$$

$$U = n_1E_1 + n_2E_2 + n_3E_3 + ...$$

$$U = (g_1e^{-\alpha-\beta E1}) E_1 + (g_2e^{-\alpha-\beta E2}) E_2 + ...$$

$$U = e^{-\alpha}[g_1E_1e^{-\beta E1} + g_2E_2e^{-\beta E2} + ...]$$

But $e^{-\alpha} = \frac{N}{Z}$

$$\therefore \quad U = \frac{N}{Z}[g_1E_1e^{-\beta E1} + g_2E_2e^{-\beta E2} + ...]$$

$$U = \frac{N}{Z}\sum_i g_i E_ie^{-\beta Ei} \qquad ...(i)$$

Here $Z = \sum_i g_i e^{-\beta Ei}$ ...(i)

$$\frac{dZ}{d\beta} = \frac{d}{d\beta}\sum_i g_i e^{-\beta Ei} = -\sum_i g_i E_ie^{-\beta Ei}$$

$$\therefore \quad \sum_i g_i E_ie^{-\beta Ei} = \frac{d}{d\beta}\sum_i g_i E_ie^{-\beta Ei}$$

Substituting this value in equation (i)

$$U = -\frac{N}{Z}\frac{d}{d\beta}\sum_i g_i e^{-\beta Ei}$$

$$U = -\frac{N}{Z}\frac{d}{d\beta}$$

$$U = -N\frac{d}{d\beta}[\log_e Z] \qquad ...(ii)$$

The average energy of a particle is

$$E_{av} = -\frac{U}{N} = -\frac{d}{d\beta}(\log_e Z) \qquad ...(iii)$$

This shows that for a given system, the total energy U, the partition function Z, and the average energy of the particle E_{av}, depend on the parameter β. Therefore, β may be taken to characterise the internal energy of the system and has the units per joule. If T is the temperature in degrees kelvin, then it is more convenient to represent parameter β as

$$\beta = \frac{1}{kT} \text{ or } KT = \frac{1}{\beta} \qquad ...(iv)$$

Here kT has the unit of energy *i.e.*, joule and k is the Boltzmann's constant. Its units are J/K. The value of k is given by

$$k = 1.3805 \times 10^{-23} \text{ J/K}$$

Substituting the value of

$$\beta = \frac{1}{kT}$$

in all the equations, we get

$$Z = \sum_i g_i \, e^{-(E_i/kT)} \qquad \text{...(v)}$$

$$n_i = \frac{N}{Z} \sum_i g_i \, e^{-(E_i/kT)} \qquad \text{...(vi)}$$

This equation represents the Maxwell-Boltzmann distribution law in terms of the temperature of the system.

As $$\beta = \frac{1}{kT}$$

$$d\beta = -\frac{dT}{kT^2}$$

Substituting this value in equation (ii)

$$\therefore \quad U = (kNT^2)\frac{d}{dT}(\log_e Z) \qquad \text{...(vii)}$$

Also, from equation (iii)

$$E_{av} = (kT^2)\frac{d}{dT}(\log_e Z) \qquad \text{...(viii)}$$

Equation (viii) gives the relation between the average energy of the particle and its temperature under equilibrium position. Hence, the temperature of a system in statistical equilibrium is the physical quantity related to the average energy of the particle of the system.

MAXWELL-BOLTZMANN DISTRIBUTION AND IDEAL GAS

Most of the gases obey Maxwell-Boltzmann distribution over a wide range of temperature. Consider a gas having mono-atomic molecules. It is assumed that the gas is ideal and has only kinetic energy of translation. Intermolecular attraction is assumed to be absent. If the kinetic energy is not quantized but considered to possess continuous values of energy, then the partition function Z can be written as

$$Z = \int_0^\infty e^{-(E/kT)}\, g(E)dE$$

Here g_i is replaced by g (E) dE

But $$g(E)dE = \left(\frac{4\pi V(2m^3)^{1/2}}{h^3}\right)E^{1/2}dE$$

Here V is the volume occupied by the gas and h is Planck's constant.

$$Z = \frac{4pV(2m^3)^{1/2}}{h^3}\int_0^\infty E^{1/2}e^{-(E/kT)}dE$$

$$Z = \frac{4\pi V(2m^3)^{1/2}}{h^3}\left[\frac{\sqrt{\pi(kT)^3}}{2}\right]$$

$$Z = \frac{V(2\pi mkT)^{3/2}}{h^3} \quad \text{...(i)}$$

Equation (i) represents the partition function for an ideal mono-atomic gas in terms of the volume and temperature of the gas.

Taking logarithms on both sides

$$\log_e Z = \log_e\left[\frac{(2\pi m)^{3/2} V}{h^3}\right] + \log_e (kT)^{3/2}$$

$$\log_e Z = C + \frac{3}{2}\log_e kT \quad \text{...(ii)}$$

Also $$E_{av} = (kT^2)\frac{d}{dT}(\log_e Z)$$

$$E_{av} = (kT^2)\frac{d}{dT}\left[C + \frac{3}{2}\log_e kT\right]$$

$$= (kT^2)\frac{d}{dT}\left[C + \frac{3}{2}\log_e k + \frac{3}{2}\log_e T\right]$$

$$E_{av} = \frac{3}{2}kT \quad \text{...(iii)}$$

The total energy,

$$U = NE_{av}$$

$$U = N\left(\frac{3}{2}kT\right)$$

$$U = \frac{3}{2}NkT. \qquad ...(iv)$$

Equation (iv) shows that the internal energy of an ideal monoatomic gas depends only on its temperature. The same relation does not however, hold good for real gases. In the case of real gases the internal energy is partly potential and partly kinetic. The total energy depends on the volume of the gas.

INTRODUCTION TO QUANTUM STATISTICS

In Maxwell-Boltzmann distribution, it has been assumed that all the energy levels are accessible to all the particles of the system. However, there may be certain levels prohibited to a certain group of particles. Each energy state is associated with a certain available wave function. The probability of a particular distribution is restricted by the available wave functions of any state. These restrictions are taken into account in quantum statistics. There are two types of quantum statistics

(i) Fermi-Dirac statistics

(ii) Bose-Einstein statistics.

In Fermi-Dirac statistics the particles are assumed to obey Pauli's exclusion principle. They are characterised by antisymmetric wave functions. The particles under, this category are called *fermions*. Protons neutrons and electrons are fermions.

In the case of Bose-Einstein statistics, it is assumed that the particles are not restricted by Pauli's exclusion principle and are characterised by symmetric wave functions. These particles are called *bosons*. It has been experimentally found that all particles having spin zero or integral multiple of 1 are bosons. Helium nuclei and mesons are bosons.

In both the kinds of quantum statistics, the particles are identical and indistinguishable. At high temperature and low pressure, all the three statistics give practically the same result.

FERMI-DIRAC DISTRIBUTION LAW

Consider a system consisting of a large number of particles. It is assumed:

(i) The particles are *identical* and *indistinguishable*, and

(ii) The particles obey exclusion principle. It means that no two particles can have the same dynamical state and the wave function of the whole system must be antisymmetric. The particle satisfying these conditions are called *fermions*. In general, all fundamental particles with spin are fermions.

In quantum statistics the intrinsic probability g_i is governed by the different quantum states relating to a given energy *i.e.*, the degeneracy of the energy state. Each quantum state corresponds to a particle wave function. The Wave functions are determined by each of the possible arrangements of quantum number corresponding to a given energy level. For particles with spin 1/2, in the absence of magnetic forces, each of the particle may be in the energy states with spin +1/2 or −1/2. Hence the intrinsic probability g_i in this case is 2. For motion in a central field, the energy of the particle is independent of the orientation of the orbital angular momentum Due to this, a degeneracy of $(2l + 1)$ is introduced and it is the value of g for that particular energy state. If the particles possess spin, the total degeneracy = $2(2l + 1)$. As no two particles can be in the same energy state having the same quantum number, the instrinsic probabilities g_i's give the maximum number of particles that can be accommodated in a particular energy level without violating the exclusion principle *i.e.*,

$$n_i \leq g_i$$

It means that the n_i value for a given distribution does not exceed the corresponding value of g_i.

Let n_i, be the number of particles for energy level E_i The first particle can be placed in any one of the available g_i states *i.e.*, this particle can be assigned to any of the gi sets of quantum numbers. Thus, the first particle can be distributed in g_i different ways. Similarly, the second particle can be arranged in $(g_i - 1)$ different ways and the process continues.

Thus, the total number of different ways of arranging n_i particles among the available g_i states with energy level E_i is

$$= g_i(g_i - 1)(g_i - 2) ......[g_i - (n_i - 1)]$$

$$= \frac{g_i!}{(g_i - n_i)!} \qquad ...(i)$$

Further, if the particles are taken to be indistinguishable, it will not be possible to detect any difference when n_i particles are reshuffled into different states occupied by them in the energy level E_i. Therefore, the total number of different and distinguishable ways is,

$$= \frac{g_i!}{n_i!(g_i - n_i)!} \qquad \text{...(ii)}$$

Therefore, the total number of different and distinguishable ways of getting the distribution n_1, n_2, n_3, etc., among the various energy levels, E_1, E_2, E_3...,etc.. can be obtained by multiplying the various factors.

$$\therefore \qquad P = \frac{g_1!}{n_1!(g_1 - n_1)!} \cdot \frac{g_{2i}!}{n_2!(g_2 - n_2)!} \ldots$$

$$P = \prod_i \frac{g_i!}{n_i!(g_i - n_i)!} \qquad \text{...(iii)}$$

The most probable distribution can by obtained by evaluating the maximum value of $\log_e$, P in equation (iii).

This should also satisfy the condition that

$$\sum_i n_i = N$$

and $$\sum_i n_i E_i = U.$$

According to Stirling's approximation

$$\log_e x! = x \log_e x - x$$

From equation (iii), applying Stirling's approximation,

$$\log_e P = \sum_i [(g_i \log_e g_i - g_i) - (n_i \log_e n_i - n_i)$$
$$- [(g_i - n_i) \log_e (g_i - n_i) - (g_i - n_i)]$$

$$\log_e P = \sum_i [g_i \log_e g_i - n_i - \log_e n_i - (g_i - n_i)$$
$$\log_e (g_i - n_i)] \qquad \text{....(iv)}$$

Differentiating equation (iv)

$$-d(\log_e P) = \sum_i [\log_e n_i - \log_e (g_i - n_i)] dn_i$$

To obtain the maximum value of P,

$$d(\log_e P) = 0$$

$$\therefore \qquad \sum_i [\log_e n_i - \log_e (g_i - n_i)] dn_i = 0 \qquad \text{...(v)}$$

But $\sum_i dn_i = 0$ ...(vi)

and $\sum_i E_i dn_i = 0$ ...(vii)

Multiplying (vi) by α and (vii) by β and adding to equation (v), we get

$$\sum_i [\log_e n_i - \log_e (g_i - n_1) + \alpha + \beta E_i] dn_i = 0$$

The equilibrium distribution is possible if

$$\therefore \quad \log_e n_i - \log_e (g_i - n_1) + \alpha + \beta E_i = 0 \qquad ...(viii)$$

$$\log_e \left(\frac{n_i}{g_i - n_i} \right) = -\alpha + \beta E_i$$

$$\frac{n_i}{g_i - n_i} = e^{-\alpha - \beta Ei}$$

$$\frac{g_i - n_i}{n_i} = e^{\alpha + \beta Fi}$$

$$\frac{g_i}{n_i} - 1 = e^{\alpha + \beta Ei}$$

$$\frac{g_i}{n_i} = (e^{\alpha + \beta Ei}) + 1$$

$$n_i = \left(\frac{g_i}{e^{\alpha + \beta E_i}} \right) + 1 \qquad ...(ix)$$

Equation (ix) represents the Fermi-Dirac distribution law. The parameter has the same role as in the case of Maxwell-Boltzmann distribution law *i.e.*, for the system consisting of fermions in statistical equilibrium.

$$\beta = \frac{1}{kT}$$

$$\therefore \quad n_i = \frac{g_i}{[e^{(\alpha + E_i/kT)}] + 1}$$

In most cases the value of a is negative and is taken to be equal to

$$\frac{-E_F}{kT}$$

$$n_i = \frac{g_i}{\left[e^{(E_i - E_F)/kT}\right] + 1}$$

The value of E_F is positive and is independent of temperature.

For $T = 0$, all the energy states are fully occupied and $n_i = g_i$ All the states with $E > E_F$, are empty *i.e.*, $n_i = 0$.

$$\left[e^{(E_i - E_F)/kT}\right] = \begin{cases} 0 \text{ for } E_i - E_F < 0 \\ \infty \text{ for } E_i - E_F > 0 \end{cases}$$

Limit T → 0

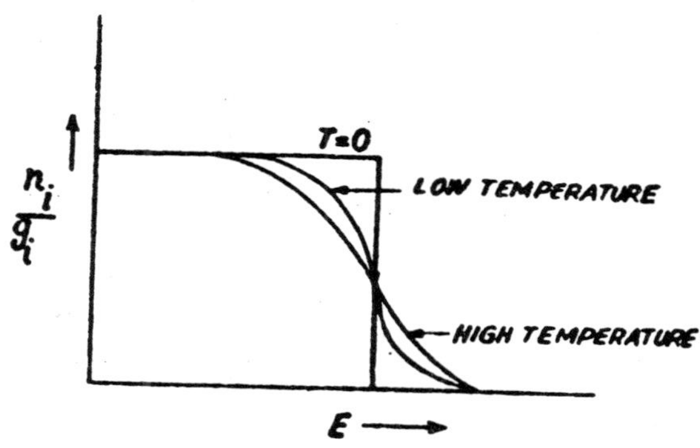

Fig. 2.1

In the case of Fermi-Dirac statistics, the accumulation of particles at the ground level is not allowed and at temperature $T = 0$, the particles occupy the lowest energy levels upto E_F. Here, the energy E_F gives the indication of the maximum energy of the fermions in the system. By is also called Fermi energy. For higher temperatures, the particles, occupy higher energy states greater than E_F. The curves (Fig. 2.1) indicate that only those fermions with energies close to E_F can move into unoccupied higher energy states. If $k\theta_F = E_F$, the temperature θ_F is called the Fermi temperature.

ELECTRON GAS

Electrons in a metal belong to a most characteristic system of fermions because electrons obey the exclusion principle. For electrons in a metal, the energy levels are grouped in bands. Practically at all temperatures, the lower level energy bands are filled with electrons. The upper level energy bands are only partially filled with electrons. The distribution of electrons is to be considered only in the upper bands called the conduction band.

The zero energy level is taken at the lowest level of the conduction band. It is also assumed that the electrons have free movement within the conductor, provided the energy associated with the electrons is of the order of upper level energy bands. As the energy of the electron in the conduction band is continuous, the term g_i is replaced by g(E) dE. Here dn electrons have energy in the range E and E + dE. According to Fermi-Dirac distribution law

$$n_i = \frac{g_i}{\left[e^{(E_i - E_F)/kT}\right] + 1} \qquad ...(i)$$

Substituting the value of g_i = g (E) dB in equation (i) and replacing n_i by dn

$$dn = \frac{g(E)dE}{\left[e^{(E_i - E_F)/kT}\right] + 1}$$

As an electron has the spin ±1/2, the total number of states in the sphere is twice. $V/(2\pi)^3$ refers to the translational states per unit volume in the Fermi space Fermi sphere of radius kF has the total number of particles accommodated,

$$n = \frac{2\left[\frac{V}{(2\pi)^3}\right]\left(\frac{4}{3}\pi(kF)^3\right)}{\left[e^{(E_i - E_F)/kT}\right] + 1}$$

Here $$E = \frac{p^2}{2m} \frac{\left(\frac{h}{2\pi}\right)^2 (kF)^2}{2m}$$

$$\therefore \quad kF = \frac{p}{h/2\pi} = \frac{2\pi p}{h}$$

$$\therefore \quad n = \frac{2\left[\frac{V}{(2\pi)^3}\right]\left(\frac{4}{3}\pi\left(\frac{2\pi p}{h}\right)^3\right)}{\left[e^{(E_i - E_F)/kT}\right] + 1}$$

But $p = (2mE)^{1/2}$

$$\therefore \quad n = \frac{2\left[\frac{V}{(2\pi)^3}\right]\left[\left(\frac{4}{3}\pi\left(\frac{2\pi p}{h}\right)^3(2mE)^{3/2}\right)\right]}{\left[e^{(E_i - E_F)/kT)}\right]+1}$$

$$n = \frac{\left(\frac{8\pi V}{(3h^3}\right)(2m)((2m)^{1/2}E^{3/2}}{\left[e^{(E_i - E_F)/kT)}\right]+1}$$

Differentiating

$$dn = \frac{\left(\frac{8\pi V}{(3h^3}\right)(2m)((2m)^{1/2} \times \frac{3}{2}E^{1/2}dE}{\left[e^{(E_i - E_F)/kT)}\right]+1}$$

$$\frac{dn}{dE} = \frac{\left[\frac{8\pi V(2m^3)^{1/2}}{(3h^3}\right]E^{1/2}}{\left[e^{(E_i - E_F)/kT)}\right]+1} \quad \text{...(ii)}$$

Equation (ii) represents the energy distribution for free electrons. This is also called Fermi-Dirac formula of free fermions.

At $\quad T = 0K,$

$$p = (2m\ E_F)^{1/2} \quad \text{...(iii)}$$

and $$N = \left(\frac{2V}{h^3}\right)\left(\frac{4}{3}\pi p^3\right)$$

or $$P = \left(\frac{3Nh^3}{8\pi V}\right)^{1/3} \quad \text{...(iv)}$$

Equating (iii) and (iv)

$$(2mE_F)^{1/2} = \left(\frac{3Nh^3}{8\pi V}\right)^{1/3}$$

Squaring

$$2mE_F)^{1/2} = \left(\frac{3Nh^3}{8\pi V}\right)^{2/3}$$

or $$E_F = \frac{h^2}{8m}\left(\frac{3N}{\pi V}\right)^{2/3} \qquad ...(v)$$

Knowing the value of N/V *i.e.*, the number of free electrons per unit volume, the Fermi energy for electrons in a metal can be obtained.

For silver, the value $\frac{N}{V}$

$= 5.86 \times 10^{28}$ electrons/m^3

$$\therefore \quad E_F = \left(\frac{(6.624\times10^{-34})^2}{8\times9\times10^{-31}}\right)\left(\frac{3\times5.86\times10^{28}}{3.14}\right)^{2/3}$$

$$E_F = 9 \times 10^{-19} J.$$

But $$1 eV = 1.6 \times 10^{-19} J$$

$$\therefore \quad E_F = \frac{9\times10^{-19}}{1.6\times10^{-19}}$$

$$E_F = 5.625 \text{ eV}.$$

It means that the maximum kinetic energy of free electrons in silver at absolute zero temperature is 5.6 eV.

The Fermi temperature θ_F is given by

$$\theta_F = \frac{E_F}{k}$$

As E_F practically independent of temperature, the value θ_F is fixed for a given metal. The values of θ_F and E_F are given in the following table.

Metals	*E_F (electron volts)*	*θ_F(K)*
Potassium	2.14	2.4×10^4
Sodium	312	3.7×10^4
Lithium	4.72	6.5×10^4
Silver	5.51	6.4×10^4
Gold	5.64	6.4×10^4
Copper	7.04	8.2×10^4

BOSE-EINSTEIN DISTRIBUTION LAW

Bose-Einstein distribution is applied to systems composed of identical and indistinguishable particles that are not restricted by the exclusion principle. In such systems, there is no limit to the number of particles occupying a particular quantum state. These particles are called *bosons*. Their spin is zero or 1. Mesons and helium nuclei are examples of bosons.

In the case of Bose-Einstein statistics the values of g refer to degeneracy of each energy level. Suppose, that n_i particles are arranged in a row and distributed among g_i quantum states with $(g_i - 1)$ partitions in between.

The total number of possible arrangements of particles and partitions is equal to the total number of permutations of $(n_i + g_i - 1)$ objects in a row. Therefore the total possible ways of arranging n_i particles with $g_i - 1$ partitions

$$= (n_i + g_i - 1)!$$

As the particles are identical and indistinguishable the possible number of distinct arrangements

$$= \frac{(n_i + g_i - 1)!}{n_i!(g_i - 1)!}$$

The total number of distinguishable and distinct ways of arranging N particles in all the available energy states is given by

$$P = \frac{(n_1 + g_1 - 1)!}{n_1!(g_1 - 1)!} \times \frac{(n_2 + g_2 - 1)!}{n_2!(g_2 - 1)!} \times \ldots$$

$$P = \prod_i \frac{(n_i + g_i - 1)!}{n_i!(g_i - 1)!} \qquad \ldots(i)$$

The most probable distribution can be obtained by finding the maximum value of $\log_e$, P.

According to Stirling's approximation

$$\log_e x! = x \log_e x - x$$

Also $\quad \sum_i n_i = N \qquad \ldots(ii)$

and $\quad \sum_i n_i E_i = U \qquad \ldots(iii)$

From equation (i), applying Stirling's approximation

$$\log_e P = \sum_i [\log_e (n_i + g_i - 1) - \log_e n_i ! \log_e (g_i - 1)!]$$

$$\log_e P = \sum_i [(n_i + g_i - 1)\log_e(n_i + g_i - 1) - (n_i + g_i - 1)$$

$$- (n_i \log_e n_i - n_i) - (g_i - 1)\log_e(g_i - 1) - (g_i - 1)]$$

$$\log_e P = \sum_i [(n_i + g_i - 1)\log_e(n_i + g_i - 1)$$

$$- n_i \log_e - n_i - (g_i - 1)\log_e(g_i - 1)] \quad ...(iv)$$

The maximum value of P is obtained by taking

$$d(\log_e P) = 0.$$

Differentiating equation P.

$$d(\log_e P) = \sum_i [\log_e(n_i + g_i - 1)\, dn_i - \log_e n_i - dn_i] = 0$$

$$\therefore \quad -d(\log_e P) = \sum_i [-\log_e(n_i + g_i - 1)\, dn_i + \log_e n_i dn_i] = 0$$

or

$$\sum_i [-\log_e(n_i + g_i - 1) + \log_e n_i] dn_i = 0 \quad ...(v)$$

As the total number of particles and total energy are constants, we have,

$$\sum_i dn_i = 0 \quad ...(vi)$$

$$\sum_i E_i dn_i = 0 \quad ...(vii)$$

Multiplying (vi) by α and equation (vii) by β and adding to equation (v), we get

$$\sum_i [-\log_e(n_i + g_i - 1) + \log_e n_i + \alpha + \beta E_i] dn_i = 0$$

$$\therefore \quad -\log_e(n_i + g_i - 1) + \log_e n_i + \alpha + \beta E_i = 0$$

Taking $n_i + g_i$ very large as compared to 1, the quantity 1 can be neglected.

$$\therefore \quad -\log_e(n_i + g_i) + \log_e n_i + \alpha + \beta E_i = 0$$

$$\log_e\left(\frac{n_i}{ng_i + g_i}\right) = -\alpha - \beta E_i$$

$$\frac{n_i}{n_i + g_i} = e^{-\alpha - \beta Ei}$$

$$\frac{n_i + g_i}{n_i} = e^{\alpha + \beta Ei}$$

$$1 + \frac{g_i}{n_i} = e^{\alpha + \beta Ei}$$

$$\frac{g_i}{n_i} = (e^{\alpha + \beta Ei}) - 1$$

$$n_i = \left(\frac{g_i}{e^{\alpha + \beta E_i}}\right) - 1 \qquad \text{...(viii)}$$

Equation (ix) represents the Bose-Einstein distribution law.

Taking $\beta = \dfrac{1}{kT}$

$$\therefore \qquad n_i = \frac{g_i}{[e^{(\alpha + E_i/kT)}] - 1}$$

The value of the constant a is governed by the equation $\Sigma n_i = N$. As n_i cannot be negative, α must always have a positive value. The distribution of the particles for different energy levels is shown in Fig. 2.2 for low and high temperatures.

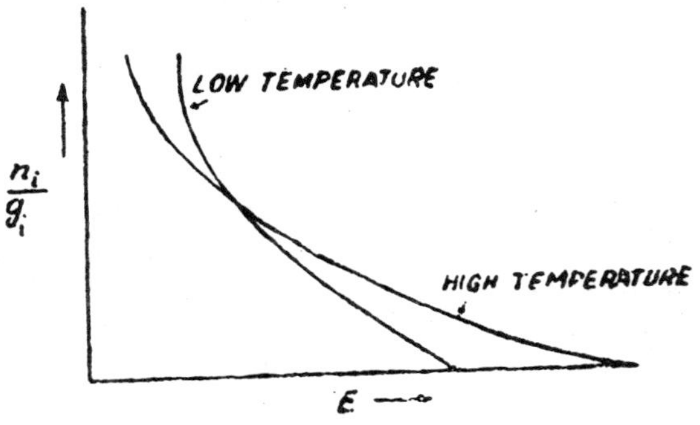

Fig. 2.2

The Bose-Einstein distribution has more emphasis on the lower energy levels.

SOME USEFUL DEFINITIONS

It would be appropriate to discuss, at some length, the physical entities involved, in understanding the statistical problems.

A Physical Quantity

Essentially, we have two kinds of physical quantities (a) the intensive quantities that do not depend on the mass of the system, *e.g.*, P and T, and (b) the extensive quantities which depend on the mass of system, *e.g.*, S, V, E, etc.

System

It is a finite region in the space where the experimental body is kept. It Is obligatory for the system to have a finite mass. The system can be a closed one (may have a real physical boundary) or may have an imaginary boundary in space. Hence it can be penetrable or Impenetrable to the transport of energy. The properties of the particles in the system define the properties of the system.

Microstate

Each macrostate can have several microstates associated with it. Microstate is that state of the system where the individuality of the particles is not ignored. Hence the microstates are affected by change in position, momentum, energy (and mutual interaction) of individual particles. These states, however, cannot be identified by any physical experiment. Following table will help in understanding the difference between macro and microstates. We take two boxes A and B and four distinguishable particles a, b, c, d, and investigate their distribution.

It is evident from part B of the table that when the individuality of the particles is ignored, there remains no difference between the number of macrostates and associated microstates. By definition, given above, such a distribution will not give statistical probability or correct probable distribution (last column). Another illustration for the above table is to distribute 4 distinct books on 2 shelves. We have a total of 16 distributions as in part A of the table but if we distribute 4 identical books on same 2 shelves we have only 5 arrangements.

From the table, we see that for the most probable distribution (2, 2) we have 6 microstates. In other words, the macro distribution is most probable when number of microstates involved is maximum. In actual physical problems, we deal with extremely large number of particles as $\approx 10 m^{-3}$ whence the number of microstates can be unimaginably large.

Macrostate

It is that state of the system which can be perceived by experiments. It is an isolated state of the system (not influenced by external agencies) and can be defined by certain value of pressure P, temperature T, and volume V. A macrostate can also be defined in terms of its microstructure, *e.g.*, by the specification of number of molecules (or phase-points in each cell of the phase space). Let us consider the distribution of 8 particles in two boxes. We can have (0, 8), (1, 7), (2, 6)... (7, 1) and (8, 0) distributions. These 9 distributions form 9 macrostates. Here we may note that a macrostate does not distinguish individuality of particles. Hence, for n particles we have (n + 1) macrostates when the distribution of particles is restricted in 2 boxes. This number will increase if the number of boxes is increased.

Phase Space

In order to specify the state of the gas from the molecular point of view, we shall know the position and momentum of each of its molecules, *i.e.*, we must specify six quantities x, y, z. p_x, p_y, p_z for each of the molecules. In three-dimensional space, we can easily consider an element of volume dx dy dz. Similarly, we can plot momentum components p_x, p_y and p_z in three mutually perpendicular directions and again consider three-dimensional volume. In other words, let us consider a particle with only a motion of translation. Then, classically we need three positional and three momentum coordinates to describe its state, (see point P in Fig. 2.3). Just as the space is represented by a three dimensional positional coordinate system, we can also represent momentum space by a three-dimensional momentum coordinate system. The state of the system then can be defined by six-dimensional positional-space and momentum space (phase) system. The two spaces together, defined by 6-dimensional (3 space and 3 momentum) hypothetical coordinate systems, is called phase space. Phase-space is purely a mathematical concept and cannot be depicted by a diagram like Fig. 2.3. So, phase-space is just a hypothetical space occupied by an infinite set of such six coordinate points.

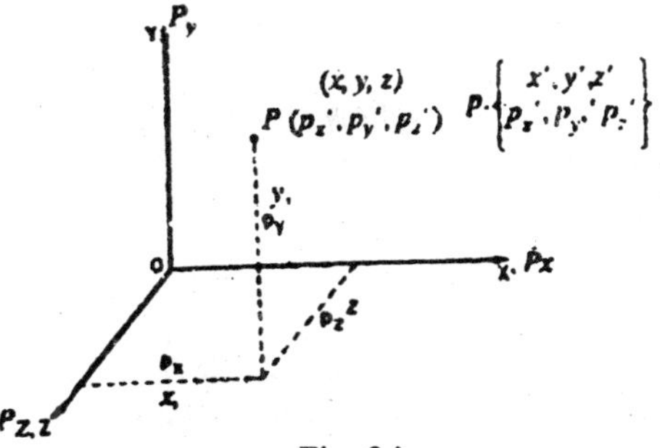

Fig. 2.1.

With the passage of time the point P (known as phase-point) traces out a certain trajectory known as phase-path. As the position and momentum, in translated motion, change with lime, the phase-path may be quite complicated. Such 6-dimensional (6-d) phase space is also known as the μ-space. A large number of 6-d cells, each with a volume of $d\tau = (dx\, dy\, dz)\, (dp_x\, dp_y\, dp_z) = dV.\, dp$, together form the μ-space.

Let us now pass on to a many particle system. Let the system has N particles. Then, to define their state we need 3N positional and 3N momentum coordinates in a 6-d phase-space. We can consider this problem in another way:

A single point in 3-d space represents 3 coordinates; in 6-d space represents 6 coordinates; in n-d space represents n coordinates. Hence in 6N-d space a single point corresponds to 6N coordinates. If N be the number of molecules in a kilogram-mole (or a Mole), the 6N-dimensional phase-space is called r-space (or y-space). We can generalise this representation by assuming that the system has N particles each having f degrees of freedom the Γ- space will then be 2Nf dimensional, having Nf positional coordinates (q_i, i = 1 to Nf) and Nf momentum coordinates (P_i, i = 1 to Nf).

Phase-cells

The concept of phase space enables us to understand the state of micro particles -A their position and energy. When a particle changes its momentum and position with time, there will be infinite points in the phase-space which will express the state of this moving particle. Again in a finite volume of phase space, we have infinite microstates available for the particle. Hence, we can divide the whole of the phase space into finite sized small cells. The volume of the cell, however, cannot indefinitely be small.

Accessible Microstates

Those microstates which follow stipulated conditions (like number of particles is conserved, energy is conserved, system as finite extension) are called the accessible microstates.

The State of Equilibrium

It is the steady state of an isolated system where the values of P, V and T do not change with the passage of time. In such systems, no energy is given to or taken out of it. In statistical terms, equilibrium state corresponds to that macrostate which has maximum microstates. One must, however, remember that an isolated system, in equilibrium, is equally likely to be in any of its accessible microstate.

Events

When an operation is performed or is allowed to take place, the occurrence of certain complexion, configuration or arrangement of the system, at one such trial is called an event. When number of trials is increased the probability of certain event may increase.

STATISTICS APPLIED TO MOLECULES

Let us consider a monatomic perfect gas. The state of each molecule of the gas in the μ-space is represented by a point (and by a cell in quantum mechanical terms). But, since the gas molecules are in constant motion, their state will be changing continuously in space and, due to collisions (and also mutual interactions), there is a change .in momentum state also. The trajectory of such a molecule (see Fig. 2.4) is given by a constant energy surface given by

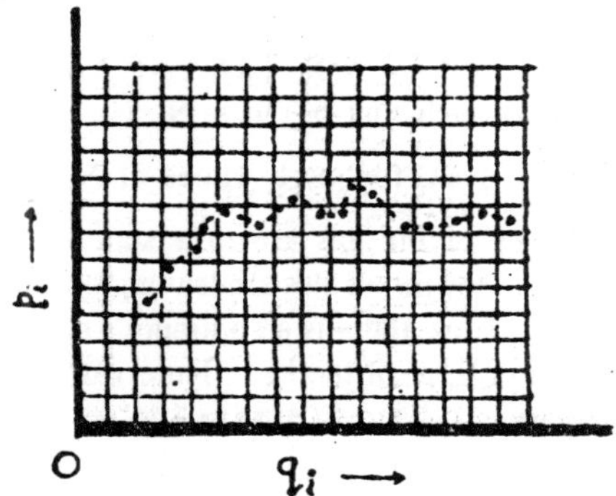

Fig. 2.4

$$E = \frac{p_x^2 + p_y^2 + p_z^2}{2m} = V(q_x, q_y, q_z)$$

The real gas molecules, however, are endowed with mutual interactions in addition to usual collisions, hence their state is better represented by a point in y-space. The rate of change of its state, then, depends on the quantum of interactions. The path of representative point in y-space is given by the relation

$$E = \sum_i T_i + \sum_i V_i + \sum_{i,j}{}' U_{ij}$$

where T_i, V_i and U_{ij} refer to kinetic energy, potential energy and energy of interaction of ith particle. The prime on the summation sign suggests that i = j is not allowed (which would mean self-interaction).

With this background and remembering that the number of molecules is very large in a macrosystem, we now proceed to investigate the distribution details.

CHARACTERISTIC FEATURES OF MACROSCOPIC SYSTEMS

Let us now discuss some of the characteristic features of the macrosystems. In doing so we will assume that it has a large number of microscopic particles.

Fluctuation

Let the isolated system has N molecules of a perfect gas and that it was left to itself for quite some time so that it is in equilibrium. Further, also consider that the system has been partitioned into two identical (also equal) parts by an imaginary wall, each part A and B has n and n molecules respectively such that n + n = N.

Now, as we have seen, for large values of N, $n \cong n^1 = N/2$

But the molecules of the gas are in a state of constant random motion. So that some of the molecules are leaving portion A and moving into B and vice-versa. Thus, there is a continuous change in the number of molecules in each portion of the box. Time variation of this change is known as fluctuation.

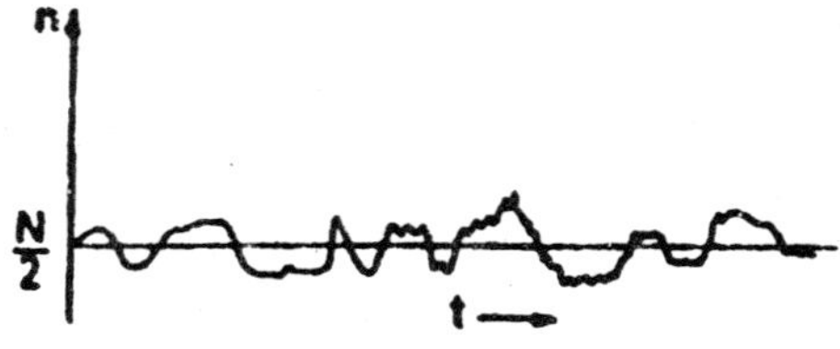

Fig. 2.5

Fig. 2.5 shows the state of normal fluctuation of an isolated system. Usually, N/2 – n is only a small number. For large deviation, the number of microstates (and hence the probability) reduce drastically. The number of microstates for different values of N and N/2 – n. For the sake of simplicity the deviation N/2– n is represented as a fraction of total number of particles. Value of R ($\cong P_x/P_{max}$) is also shown to arrive at qualitative results;

In actual physical problems the number of molecules are $\sim 10^{24} m^{-3}$ whence even 0.01% deviation also becomes quite improbable. This is the reason for quick diffusion and most equitable distribution of air molecules in the available space.

Equilibrium State of the System

The macrostate of a gas at a given instant is obtained from the distribution of molecules at that instant. But, if the macrostate of the multimolecular system does not change with time, the isolated system is said to be in equilibrium. Statistically, in the equilibrium state, the probability of the isolated system being in different accessible states does not vary with time. It may be noted that every system has an inherent tendency to approach equilibrium. If, anyhow, a situation (like point t_1 in Fig. 2.6) is created so that the system goes into a higher fluctuation state (lower probability), the motion of the molecules will set in such a way as to bring the system back into normal fluctuation state, with

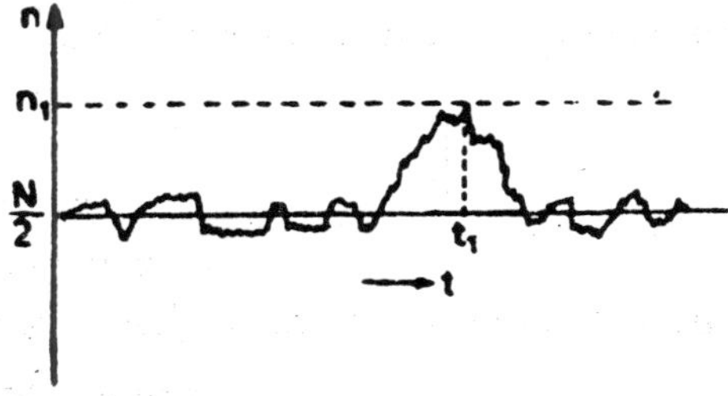

Fig. 2.6

the passage of time. The time taken by the system to attain normal state from its disturbed (excited) state is called the relaxation *time of decay*. It is very easy to perturb the normal state of the system by external effects (by pressure/wind; diffusion of perfume is one such example). But the system will again tend to attain uniform distribution/most probable distribution. To check whether the macrostate is in equilibrium we plot fluctuation versus time curve for a certain period τ. The experiment is repeated again and again. If the curves agree macrostate will be in equilibrium state. In other words, the time average of number of molecules in certain region of space at equilibrium

$$\overline{n(t)} = \frac{1}{\tau}\int_t^{t+\tau} n(t)dt$$

GIBBS ENSEMBLE

The concept of ensemble was put forth by Gibbs in 1902. In his view, it was a mathematical device which provided us with an opportunity to follow a probabilistic approach in defining the state of the system at a given time. Consider a system A such that a number of similar observations can be taken on it. Further, we assume that the system undergoes exactly similar changes in its state during each observation, *i.e.*, after every set of operations, the system returns back to its initial state (*i.e.*, the system is perfectly reversible). If this be the case, we can define the state of the system in terms of its statistical probability. But this is not practically feasible as:

(i) The number of molecules/particles in the system are so large that it is not possible to have the macrostate exactly the same as it was during the preceding observation,

(ii) Each macrostate has several microstates. We cannot ascertain their identity,

(iii) Each observation may take quite a long time whence for applying statistics, several observations may need several thousand years,

(iv) To manage and process a large number of data, over years together is not possible,

(v) The system may not show reversibility to different operations.

Ensemble was a satisfactory solution to it. An ensemble is a group of N_T identical systems. These N_T systems have the same configuration, energy and accessible states. In other words, the ensemble has N_T isolated systems each of which are exact copies of the experimental system A Thus, we have a large number of systems that behave exactly in the same manner during a set of operations as the system A Then, if N_r systems out of N_T systems produce a particular result r, we have

$$P_r = N_r/N_T$$

as the probability for that result.

If we want to measure a particular property, say x, of the system

$$< x > = \frac{n_1x_1 + n_2x_2 + \dots + n_rx_r +}{n_1 + n_2 + \dots + n_r +}$$

or $$< x > = \frac{n_1x_1}{N_T} + \frac{n_2x_2}{N_T} + ... \qquad \because \Sigma n_i = N_T$$

or $$= P_1x_1 + P_2x_2 + ...P_rx_r + ...$$

i.e., $$= \Sigma P_r x_r$$

where x_r is the property of rth group of N_r similar systems and P_r is the probability for that result.

In this unique way Gibbs replaced the method of time averages (observations made on the same system at different times to obtain average) by ensemble average as shown above. The main advantage of the ensemble method is "the observations on all systems can be taken simultaneously under similar conditions", *e.g.*, test of quality of soaps of different brands will be quicker by millions of users.

SOME WELL-KNOWN ENSEMBLES

It would be appropriate to classify the ensembles according of their dependency on macroparameters. Since an ensemble is an assembly of macroscopically identical but mutually independent systems, a change in macroparameter (like volume, pressure, energy, number of molecules, etc.,) may lead to another set of systems:

Canonical Ensemble

In this ensemble all its members are identical and remain in thermal equilibrium with the source (*i.e.*, members of the ensemble can exchange thermal energy with the reservoir). Thus all the members of a canonical ensemble have the same number of particles N, volume V and are at the same temperature T. A canonical ensemble. Its members are shown separated by impermeable but conducting rigid, walls and they are in thermal contact with the source. Gibbs gave a relation,

$$\rho(\varepsilon) = Ae^{-\varepsilon\tau}$$

for density of its phase points. A and T in the relation are constants. The ensemble can be viewed physically as a freezer containing water filled metal-ice cube tray.

Grand Canonical Ensemble

The members of this ensemble can interact thermally, mechanically and also diffusively with each other and with the reservoir. Hence they are at the same temperature of same volume and at same chemical potential such an ensemble. Each member here is separated by flexible, permeable and conducting walls, which help exchange mass and energy between its members and with the surroundings. The constituent molecules in the member systems are thus of different kinds (different chemical species). The density of phase points in such ensemble is

$$\rho(N) = e^{(\Omega+N\mu-\varepsilon)/\tau}$$

where, Ω, μ and τ are constants. A grain of sugar in boiling water can best be viewed as a grand canonical ensemble.

Uniform Ensemble

Those ensembles which have same density in phase space, are called *uniform ensembles.*

Hence, if ΔN represents the number of system, in volume element $d\Gamma$ we have, for a uniform ensemble,

$$\lim_{d\Gamma \to 0} \frac{1}{d\Gamma} \frac{\Delta N}{N} = \text{constant}$$

Microcanonical Ensemble

In these ensembles the energy of their member systems remain constant, *i.e.*, they do not interact with each other or with the surroundings. Thus, they are free from external effects. The ensemble is thus conceptually an idealised one and can be represented by a function that depends only on the energy. An ensemble, here ε and V are constant. Every member is separated from the other by rigid, impermeable and insulated walls. The density of phase points within each member system is uniform and is zero at the walls. Physically, we may view the microcanonical ensemble as a perfect insulating enclosure encompassing several isolated systems. It is suitable for ideal gases.

SOLAR CONSTANT

The sun is the source of heat radiations and it emits heat radiations in all directions. The earth receives only a fraction of the energy emitted by the sun. The atmosphere also absorbs a part of the heat radiations and air, clouds, dust particles etc., in the atmosphere scatter the heat and light radiations falling on them. From the quantity of heat radiations received by the earth, it is possible to estimate the temperature of the sun. Therefore, to determine the value of a constant, called solar constant, certain ideal conditions are taken into consideration.

Solar Constant

It is the amount of heat energy (radiation) absorbed per minute by one sq cm of a perfectly black body surface placed at a mean distance of the earth from the sun, in the absence of the atmosphere, the surface being held perpendicular to the sun's rays.

The instruments used to measure the solar constant are called *pyrheliometers*. The heat energy absorbed by a known area in a fixed time is found with the help of the pyrheliometers. To eliminate the effects of absorption by the atmosphere, the value of the solar constant is found at various altitudes of the sun on the same day under similar sky conditions. If S is the observed solar constant, S_0 the true solar constant and Z the altitude (angular elevation) of the sun, then

$$S = S_0 \, a^{\sec z} \qquad \text{...(i)}$$

$$\log S = \log S_0 + \sec Z \log a \qquad \text{...(ii)}$$

Here a is a constant.

A graph is plotted between log S along the y-axis and sec Z along the x-axis. The graph is a straight line. Produce the graph to meet the y-axis. The intercept on the y-axis gives log S_0. From the value of log S_0, the value of S_0 the solar constant can be calculated. The value obtained varies between 1.90 and 2.60 calories per sq cm per minute.

TEMPERATURE OF THE SUN

The sun consists of a central hot pardon surrounded by the photosphere. The central portion has a temperature of the order of 10^7 K. The photosphere has a temperature of about 6000 K. This temperature is also called the effective temperature of the sun. Considering the sun as a perfect black body radiator, the temperature of the sun can be calculated.

Let the mean distance of the sun from the earth be R and S the solar constant. Then, the total amount' of heat energy received by the sphere of radius R in one minute = $4\pi R^2S$.

If r is the radius of the sun, then the amount of heat energy radiated by 1 sq cm surface of the sun in one minute

$$E = \frac{4\pi R^2 S}{4\pi r^2} = \left(\frac{R}{r}\right)^2 \times S$$

Taking $R = 148.48 \times 10^7$ km

$r = 6.928 \times 10^6$ km

The mean value of

$S = 1.94$ cals per cm^2 per minute.

$$E = \left(\frac{148.48 \times 10^7}{6.928 \times 10^5}\right) \times \frac{1.94}{60} \text{ cal per second} \quad ...(i)$$

Also $E = \sigma T^4$

But $\sigma = 5.75 \times 10^{-5}$ ergs per cm^2 per second

$$= \frac{5.75 \times 10^{-5}}{4.2 \times 10^7} \text{ cal per cm}^2 \text{ per second}$$

$$E = \frac{5.75 \times 10^{-5}}{4.2 \times 10^7} . T^4 \quad ...(ii)$$

Equating (i) and (ii)

$$\left(\frac{5.75 \times 10^{-5}}{4.2 \times 10^7}\right) T^4 = \left(\frac{148.48 \times 10^7}{6.928 \times 10^5}\right) \times \frac{1.94}{60}$$

$$T = 5730 \text{ K.} \quad ...(iii)$$

This temperature gives the effective temperature of the sun acting as a black body radiator. The actual temperature of the sun is higher than this value. The temperature of the sun is usually taken as 6000 K.

Temperature of the sun can also be calculated from Wien's displacement law,

$$\lambda_{max} T = 0.2892$$

The wavelength of the radiations for which the energy is maximum in the spectrum is 4900×10^{-8} cm.

Substituting the value of λ_m, the value of T comes out to be 5902 K. This value is in agreement with the accepted value. Hence, the effective temperature of the sun (photosphere) is about 6000 K.

INTRODUCTION OF STEFAN'S LAW

The experimental study of the rate of emission of heat energy by a hot body by Tyndall helped Stefan (in 1879) to enunciate the law called Stefan's law in 1884, Boltzmann gave a theoretical proof of Stefan's law on the basis of thermodynamics. Therefore, this law is also called Stefan-Boltzmann law.

According to this law, *the rate of emission of radiant energy by unit area of a perfectly black body it directly proportional to the fourth power of its absolute temperature*

$$R \propto T^4$$

or $$R = \sigma T^4 \quad ...(i)$$

where a is called Stefan's constant. If the body is not perfectly black and its emissivity or relative emittance is e, then

$$R = e\sigma T^4 \quad ...(ii)$$

Hence e varies between zero and one, depending on the nature of the surface. For a perfectly black body e = 1. The law is not only true for emission but also for absorption of radiant energy. The hot body will continue emitting heat upto zero degree absolute temperature, if the temperature of the surroundings is zero degree absolute. But, in actual practice, the hot body is surrounded by a wall at some lower temperature. Due to this the body is continuously emitting and absorbing the heat radiations. When the body has the same temperature as that of the surroundings, the rate of emission and absorption are equal.

Hence, if a perfectly black body at temperature T_1 is surrounded by a wall (surroundings) at a temperature T_2 the net rate of loss (or gain) of heat energy per unit area of the surface is given by,

$$R \propto (T_1^4 - T_2^4)$$

$$R = \sigma(T_1^4 - T_2^4) \quad ...(iii)$$

If the body has an emissivity e,

then $$R = e\sigma(T_1^4 - T_2^4) \quad ...(iv)$$

MATHEMATICAL DERIVATION OF STEFAN'S LAW

The fact that blade body radiations exert pressure similar to a gas, helps in applying thermodynamics to heat radiations.

Let ψ be the energy density of radiations inside a uniform temperature enclosure at temperature T. P is the pressure and V is the volume.

Applying the first law of thermodynamics

$$\delta H = dU + P.dV \quad ...(i)$$

Applying thermodynamical relation

$$\left(\frac{\partial H}{\partial V}\right)_r = \left(\frac{\partial P}{\partial T}\right)_v \quad ...(ii)$$

$$\left(\frac{\partial U + P\partial V}{\partial V}\right)_r = T\left(\frac{\partial P}{\partial T}\right)_v$$

$$\left(\frac{\partial U}{\partial V}\right)_r = T\left(\frac{\partial P}{\partial T}\right)_v = P \quad ...(iii)$$

Now $U = V\psi$

and $P = \frac{\psi}{3}$

or $\left[\frac{\partial U}{\partial V}\right]_r = \psi$

Here ψ is a function of temperature alone.

Substituting these values in equation (iii),

$$\psi = \frac{T}{3}\frac{d\psi}{dT} - \frac{\psi}{3}$$

$$\frac{4\psi}{3} = \frac{T}{3}\frac{d\psi}{dT}$$

or $\frac{d\psi}{\psi} = 4\frac{dT}{T}$

Integrating, $\log \psi = 4 \log T + \text{constant}$

or $\psi = KT^4$ ...(iv)

Here K is a constant

Also the total rate of emission per unit area of a black body is proportional to the energy density.

$\therefore$ $R \propto \psi \propto T^4$

$\therefore$ $R = \sigma T^4$ ...(v)

where σ is Stefan's constant.

The value of Stefan's constant in C.G.S. system is 5.672×10^{-5} C.G.S. units and in M.K.S. system it is 5.672×10^{-8} M.K.S. units.

DERIVATION OF NEWTON'S LAW OF COOLING FROM STEFAN'S LAW

Stefan's law is applicable for all temperatures of a hot body. But Newton's Law is applicable when the difference of temperature between the hot body and the surrounding is small. Consider a hot body at a temperature T_1 placed in a uniform temperature enclosure at T_1. According to Stefan's law,

$$R = e\sigma(T_1^4 - T_1^4) \qquad \text{...(i)}$$

Here e is the emissitivity of the surface of the hot body

$$R = e\sigma(T_1 - T_2)\,(T_1^3 + T_1^2 T_2 + T_1 T_2^2 + T_2^3)$$

As $(T_1 - T_2)$ is small, T_1 can be taken approximately equal to T_2.

Then,
$$R = e\sigma(T_1 - T_2)\,(T_2^3 + T_2^3 + T_2^3 + T_2^3)$$

$$R = 4e\sigma T_2^3((T_1 - T_2)$$

Taking $4e\sigma T_2^3 = k$

$$R = k(T_1 - T_2)$$

or
$$R \propto (T_1 - T_2). \qquad \text{...(ii)}$$

This equation represents Newton's law of cooling and is true when the difference of temperature is small.

EXPERIMENTAL VERIFICATION OF STEFAN'S LAW

In 1897, Lummer and Pringsheim experimentally verified Stefan's law over a wide range of temperature (100°C to 1,300°C).

The apparatus consisted of a black body C. For temperatures between 200°C and 600°C, a hollow copper sphere coated inside with platinum black was used. The fused nitrates of sodium and potassium having a melting point of 219°C were used as the bath surrounding the black body. For temperature between 900°C and 1,300°C, an iron cylinder coated inside with platinum black was used as a black body and it was enclosed in a double walled gas furnace.

A thermocouple T was used as a thermometer. A bolometer B was used to measure the intensity of the emitted heat radiations. S_1, S_2 and S_3 were the water-cooling shutters. Another black body A at 100°C was used to standardize the bolometer. The double walled vessel of the black body A contained boiling water at 100°C. The bolometer B was allowed to face the opening of the black body A and the shutter S_3 raised. The deflections in the galvanometer of the bolometer at various distances were noted and it was found that the deflection was inversely proportional to the square of the distance between the bolometer and the opening of the black body A. Thus, the deflection in the galvanometer was proportional to the intensity of heat radiations.

The shutter S_3 was closed and the bolometer B was allowed to face the opening of the black body C. The shutters of S_1 and S_2 were raised. The bath surrounding the black body was maintained at a constant temperature and the maximum deflection produced in the galvanometer of the bolometer was noted. Thus at various constant temperatures of the black body, corresponding to constant deflections (in the galvanometer of the bolometer) were observed. Then the data was reduced to a common arbitrary unit in terms of the total radiations from the black body A at 100°C.

Let θ be the deflection in the galvanometer, T_1 the temperature of the black body and T_2, the temperature at the entrance of the bolometer. It was found that

$$\theta \propto (T_1^4 - T_2^4)$$

But $$\theta \propto R$$

∴ $$\theta \propto (T_1^4 - T_2^4)$$

This verifies Stefan's law.

Recently Coblentz has verified Stefan's law more accurately. He took an electrically heated black body whose temperature was measured by an accurate thermocouple. An absolute bolometer was used to measure the amount of heat radiations emitted by the black body. He was able to show the correctness of Stefan's law experimentally up to 1,600°C.

THERMODYNAMIC POTENTIAL OR GIBBS FUNCTION

The Gibbs function G of a system is given by,

$$G = U - TS + PV$$

Consider a system that can do other forms of work, in addition to P.dV work, *e.g.*, a voltaric cell. In the case of a voltaic cell, the electrical work is –E.dl. Similarly for a magnetic material, the magnetic work is –m.dH. In general, the work will be given by P.dV plus a sum of terms each being the product of intensive variable (such as P, E or m) and the differential of an extensive variable (such as dV, dI and dH). In the case of a voltaic cell, the intensive variable is S and differential of extensive variable is dI.

Suppose, in general, in addition to PdV the intensive variable is y and differential of extensive variable is dx. The work done for any reversible process,

$$\delta W = PdV + ydx$$

$$W = \int_{V_1}^{V_2} PdV + \int_{x_1}^{x_2} ydx$$

Take $\int_{x_1}^{x_2} ydx = A$

Consider a process where the system works at constant pressure P_0 and the change in volume is $(V_2 - V_1)$

$$\therefore \quad \int_{V_1}^{V_2} PdV = P_0 [V_2 - V_1]$$

$$\therefore \quad W = P_0[V_2 - V_1] + A \qquad \text{...(i)}$$

For a system that exchanges heat with a reservoir temperature

$$W < (U_1 - U_2) - T_0 (S_1 - S_2) \qquad \text{...(ii)}$$

$$P_0[V_2 - V_1] + A < (U_1 - U_2) - T_0 (S_1 - S_2)$$

or
$$A < (U_1 - U_2) - T_0 (S_1 - S_2) + P_0[V_1 - V_2] \qquad \text{.. (iii)}$$

Consider a specific process, where the initial and the final states of the system and the surroundings are at the same temperature (T_0) and pressure (P_0)

$$To = T \text{ and } P_0 = P$$

From equation (iii)

$$A_{P,T} < (U_1 - U_2)_{P,T} - T(S_1 - S_2)_{P,T} + P[V_1 - V_2]_{P,T} \qquad \text{...(iv)}$$

But, for the Gibbs function,

$$G = U - TS + PV \qquad \text{...(v)}$$

Therefore, for two equilibrium states at the same pressure and temperature,

$$[G_1 - G_2)_{P,T} = (U_1 - U_2)_{P,T} - T[S_1 - S_2]_{P,T} + P[V_1 - V_2]_{P,T} \qquad \text{...(vi)}$$

From equations (iv) and (vi)

$$A_{P,T} < (G_1 - G_2)_{P,T} \qquad \text{(vii)}$$

Thus, the difference between Gribbs function of a system between two equilibrium states sets the maximum limit to the work in addition to PdV work, provided the initial and the final states are at the same pressure and temperature and the system exchanges heat with a single heat reservoir. The work done will be maximum when the process is reversible. The process in this case will be isothermal–isobaric. If the process is irreversible, work done will be less than the maximum.

PHOTON GAS

The interaction of electromagnetic radiations with matter, led to the idea that electromagnetic radiations are composed of discrete energy particles called photons. Each photon has an energy hν and momentum h/λ. Here ν is the frequency and λ is the wavelength of the radiations. The electromagnetic radiations trapped in a cavity and in thermal equilibrium with the walls of the cavity are termed as black body radiations. In the equilibrium condition, the black body radiations can be considered as the *photon gas*. It is assumed that the photons do not interact among themselves. The photons interact only with-the atoms of the walls of the cavity. It is further assumed that the photons are indistinguishable and many photons can have the same energy. Photons are taken as bosons and they obey Bose-Einstein statistics.

As the photons can either be emitted or absorbed by the atoms of the walls of the cavity, the number of photons is not constant *i.e.*, the condition $\sum_i dn_i = 0$ is no longer valid.

Due to this reason the value of α is equal to zero in the Bose-Einstein distribution law.

$$n_i = \frac{g_i}{[e^{(\alpha + E_i/kT)}] - 1} \quad \text{...(i)}$$

Here $\alpha = 0$

$$\therefore \quad n_i = \frac{g_i}{[e^{E_i/kT}] - 1} \quad \text{...(ii)}$$

In case, the cavity is large as compared to the wavelength of the radiations, the energy spectrum of the photons is taken to be continuous. In this case, the energy difference between successive allowed energy value is very small. Thus, replacing g_i by g(E) dE, and n_i by dn

$$dn = \frac{g(E)dE}{\left(e^{E/kT)}\right) - 1} \qquad ...(iii)$$

As the energy of a photon, E = hν, the value of g(E) dE can be taken equal to g (ν) dν. The factor g(ν) dν corresponds to the number of oscillatory modes in the frequency range dν and relating to the energy range dE.

The number of states in a black body radiation in the frequency range ν and ν + dν can be obtained by calculating the spherical volume bound by the spheres of radii $\frac{h(\nu + d\nu)}{c}$ and $\frac{h\nu}{c}$

The volume of the spherical shell

$$= \frac{4}{3}\pi\frac{h^3}{c^3}(\nu + d\nu)^3 - \frac{4}{3}\pi\frac{h^3}{c^3}\nu^3$$

$$= \frac{4}{3}\pi\frac{h^3}{c^3}[\nu^3 + 3\nu^2 d\nu + ... - \nu^3]$$

$$= \frac{4}{3}\pi\frac{h^3}{c^3} \times 3\nu^2 d\nu$$

$$= 4\pi \frac{h^3}{c^3} \nu^2 d\nu \qquad ...(iv)$$

The phase space has volume V = h^3 and there are two states of polarization for the radiation. The number of states in the black body radiation in the frequency range ν and ν + dν is given by

$$g(\nu)d\nu = \frac{8\pi\nu}{c^3}\nu^2 d\nu \qquad ...(v)$$

$$dn = \left(\frac{8\pi V\nu^2 d\nu}{c^3}\right)\frac{1}{\left(e^{h\nu/kT}\right) - 1} \qquad ...(vi)$$

For dn photons in the frequency range ν + dν and ν, the energy is equal to (hν) dn and the energy per unit volume

$$= \frac{(h\nu)dn}{V}$$

Therefore, the energy density distribution for black body radiation is given by

$$E(\nu) = \frac{(h\nu)dn}{V.d\nu} \qquad ...(vii)$$

Substituting the value of dn from equation (vi), we get

$$E(\nu) = \frac{8\pi h\nu^2 d\nu.h\nu}{c^3 V.d\nu\left[\left(e^{h\nu/kT}\right)-1\right]}$$

$$E(\nu) = \left(\frac{8\pi h\nu^3}{c^3}\right)\left[\frac{1}{\left(e^{h\nu/kT}\right)-1}\right]^{d\nu} \qquad ...(viii)$$

Equation (viii) represents Planck's radiation law for black body radiations.

From equation (viii)

$$E(\nu)d\nu = \frac{8\pi h\nu^3}{c^3}\left[\frac{1}{\left(e^{h\nu/kE}\right)-1}\right]^{d\nu}$$

But $\nu = \frac{c}{\lambda}$

or $d\nu = -\frac{c}{\lambda^2}d\lambda$

Neglecting the negative sign, we get

$$\therefore \quad E(\lambda)d\lambda = \frac{8\pi h\nu^3}{c^3} \times \frac{c}{\lambda^2}\left[\frac{1}{\left(e^{h\nu/kT}\right)-1}\right]^{d\lambda}$$

or
$$E(\lambda) = \frac{8\pi hc}{\lambda^5} \times \frac{c}{\lambda^2}\left[\frac{1}{\left(e^{h\nu/kT}\right)-1}\right] \qquad ...(ix)$$

This gives the energy density for wavelength λ in the spectrum of the black body. Both the equations (viii) and (ix) represent Planck's radiation law for black body radiation.

IRREVERSIBLE THERMODYNAMICS

Introduction : Classical thermodynamics is concerned with the detailed study of the systems which are in equilibrium. However, many transport processes (involving flow of different types of quantities) may take place in the system which may be irreversible and the system may not be in equilibrium with respect to these quantities. A few examples of such transport phenomena include flow (conduction) of heal along a metal bar whose ends are kept at a fixed but at different temperatures, the development of heat when an electric current flows through a metallic conductor, diffusion of a solid or a fluid across a concentration gradient, etc.

The branch of science dealing with the study of thermodynamic properties of the systems which are not in equilibrium and Involve transport processes which are irreversible is termed as Non-equilibrium or Irreversible thermodynamics or Thermodynamics for Irreversible processes.

In order to develop the general theory for the irreversible processes, some additional postulates (assumptions) have to be introduced- These postulates are solely applicable only when the system is "not too far" from equilibrium *i.e.* to the states which are close to equilibrium. Hence, irreversible thermodynamics is applicable to those systems which are not too far from equilibrium.

POSTULATE (ASSUMPTION) OF LOCAL EQUILIBRIUM

In order to understand this postulate suppose the system is divided into a number of small volume elements (called cells or sub-systems). Every cell will have a fixed volume V. It is further assumed that at any instant of time, the subsystem has an internal energy U and contains m_i mass units of the molecular species i. At equilibrium, temperature T, pressure P. partial specific Gibb's function ($\mu_i = (\partial G/\partial m_i)_{T, P}$ and entropy S of a subsystem are well defined parameters and because V is constant, these parameters are solely determined by U and m_i for the subsystem (note that here μ_i stands for the chemical potential per unit mass whereas ordinarily this symbol represents the chemical potential per mole).

If equilibrium does not exist, it becomes necessary to redefine the temperature, pressure; partial specific Gibbs function and entropy. It is assumed that

"*Temperature (T), pressure (P), partial specific Gibbs function (G) and entropy S for a cell in a non-equilibrium state depend upon the internal energy (U) and the mass units (mi) of the molecular species i exactly in the same manner as in an equilibrium situation. In other words, each cell of a system in non-equilibrium is treated exactly in the*

same manner (statistically as well as thermodynamically) as if equilibrium exists in each of these cells".

This is termed as the assumption of local equilibrium.

ENTROPY PRODUCTION

The entropy of an isolated system in equilibrium is maximum. Hence, if such a system is not in equilibrium, the entropy will increase but may not decrease *i.e.*, equilibrium lies in the direction of increasing entropy. This is termed "entropy production.

The concept of entropy production in an irreversible process may be understood in a simple manner as follows. It is known that

$$dS \geq \frac{dQ}{T}$$

or which can be rearranged in the form

$$dS - \frac{dQ}{T} \geq 0$$

The quantity on the left is greater than or equal to zero. So we may write

$$dS - \frac{dQ}{T} = d\sigma \qquad ...(1)$$

where, $d\sigma$ will be either zero or positive.

If it is assumed that the system is in contact with a reservoir at T, and a quantity of heat dQ flows into the system, then a quantity, –dQ, flows in the reservoir. If the quantity, dQ, is transferred reversibly to the reservoir, then the entropy change of the reservoir is

$$dS = -\frac{dQ}{T} \qquad ...(2)$$

so that the Eq. (1) can be written as

$$dS + dS_{res} = d\sigma \qquad ...(3)$$

The quantity $d\sigma$ refers to the entropy increase of the system plus that of the surroundings the reservoir) The $d\sigma$ is called the *entropy production* of the process. For an irreversible process entropy production is positive while for a reversible process, the entropy production is zero.

Let us now derive the exact expressions for the entropy production accompanying the flow of heat or flow of matter (which are irreversible processes) for the systems not in equilibrium but very close to the equilibrium.

(a) *Entropy Production in Heat Flow* : Suppose our system is having a metal rod. Consider two regions of the metal rod maintained at different temperatures T_1 and T_2 *i.e.*, each region is isothermal. This can be achieved by allowing the heat to enter one region and leave the other region at the same rate.

If δq_1 refers to the amount of heat that enters the region at T_1 per unit time and δq_2 is the amount of heat that leaves the region at T_2 per unit time, then

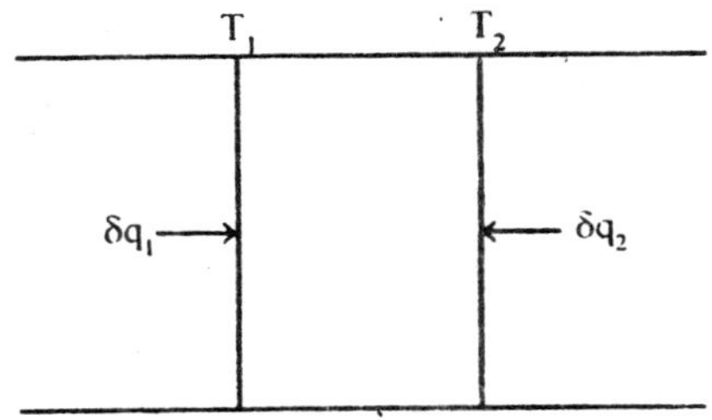

Fig. 2.7 : Heat flow along a metal rod.

Entropy change in region 1 = $\dfrac{\delta q_1}{T_1}$

and entropy change in region 2 = $\dfrac{\delta q_2}{T_2}$

But as each of the regions 1 and 2 is isothermal, therefore we must have

$$\delta q_1 = -\delta q_2 \qquad \text{...(4)}$$

∴ Net entropy change accompanying the irreverible flow of heat will be given be

$$dS_{irr} = \delta q_2 \left(\frac{1}{T_2} - \frac{1}{T_1} \right) = \delta q_2 \frac{T_1 - T_2}{T_1 T_2} \qquad \text{...(5)}$$

The irreversible entropy increase (dS_{irr}) must, of course, be positive, Hence $T_2 < T_1$ which has been found to be in agreement with the well known direction of spontaneous heat flow.

If the temperature difference is infinitesimal (so that $T_1 - T_2 = dT$ and $T_1 = T_2 = T$ say so that $T_1 T_2 = T_2$), the above equation becomes

$$dS_{irr} = \delta q \frac{dT}{T^2} \qquad ...(6)$$

which can be written in the form

$$dS_{irr} = d\ q\ d(1/T) \qquad ...(7)$$

(b) *Entropy Production in Matter Flow* : Consider the flow of δn moles of some components of the matter (or of electricity) from one region of temperature T_1. where the chemical potential is μ_1, to a second region where the temperature is T_2 and the chemical potential is μ_2.

When matter (fluid) flows from a cooler region to the hotter region, not only the het content of the substance increases say be dH per mole (or represented as $\overline{H}$) but also a heat effect takes place when the fluid enters the surface of the barrier and passes into the interior. This may be thought of as primarily the heat of solution. This quantity is called the heat of transfer and is written as Q* per mole.

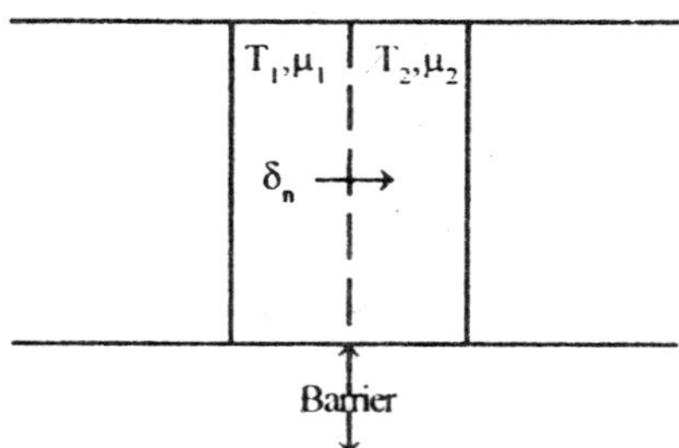

Fig. 2.8 : Flow of matter from one region to another.

Now the partial molal entropy of a system (entropy per mole) having molal enthalpy $\overline{H}$ and chemical potential μ and maintained at temperature T is given by

$$\overline{S} = \frac{\overline{H}}{T} - \frac{\mu}{T} \qquad ...(8)$$

Taking that het of transfer (Q*) also into consideration the above equation becomes

$$\overline{S} = \frac{\left(\overline{H} + Q^*\right)}{T} - \frac{\mu}{T} \qquad ...(9)$$

According to first law of thermodynamics, the sum $\overline{H}$ + Q* must be same whether we are considering region 1 or region 2.

Thus the partial molal entropy of region 1 is

$$\overline{S}_1 = \frac{(\overline{H}+Q^*)}{T_1} - \frac{\mu_1}{T_2} \qquad ..(10)$$

and the partial molal entropy of region 2 is

$$\overline{S}_2 = \frac{(\overline{H}+Q^*)}{T_2} - \frac{\mu_2}{T_2} \qquad ..(11)$$

∴ Increase of entropy per mole transfer of matter from region 1 to region 2 will be

$$\overline{dS} = \overline{S}_2 - \overline{S}_1 = \left(\frac{\mu_1}{T_1} - \frac{\mu_2}{T_2}\right) + (\overline{H}+Q^*)\left(\frac{1}{T_2} - \frac{1}{T_1}\right) \qquad ...(12)$$

∴ Entropy increase for the transfer of δn moles will be given by

$$dS_{irr} = \delta n\left[\left(\frac{\mu_1}{T_1} - \frac{\mu_2}{T_2}\right) + (\overline{H}+Q^*)\left(\frac{1}{T_2} - \frac{1}{T_1}\right)\right] \qquad ...(13)$$

or for infinitesimal differences, as before, we can write

$$dS_{irr} = \delta n\left[-d\left(\frac{\mu}{T}\right) + (\overline{H}+Q^*)\, d\left(\frac{1}{T}\right)\right]$$

If $T_2 = T_1$, the second term in eqn. (13) and hence in eqn. (14) drops out. This explains why the heat of transfer never needs to be considered in isothermal problems.

FORCES AND FLUXES

The irreversible thermodynamics is different from the classical thermodynamics in the sense that in the latter when the system s in equilibrium the parameters like temperature, chemical potential, etc. are same at each point of the system whereas in the former, these parameters may increases or decrease from point in the system (say longitudinally *e.g.*, in a metal rod). Thus gradients exist in the system which result in the flow of some kind or the other. For example temperature gradient results in the flow of heat, gradient of chemical potential results in the flow of matter and so on. The gradients such as temperature gradients ; chemical potential gradients etc. is called the driving force whereas the flow of energy. matter etc. (in calories/sec or moles/sec) that takes place due to the gradient is called the *flux*. Thus, the force and flux have a cause-effect relationship *i.e.*, force is the cause and flux is the effect.

Similarly, when a potential difference exists at the end of a conductor, a current flows so the that potential difference is the force and flow of current is the flux. Again a reaction takes place when Gibb's free energy change (ΔG) is negative. Thus Gibb's free energy chargė is the driving force and rate of flow of reaction (or also called the 'affinity' of the reaction) is called the flux of the reaction.

In general, force is represented by X and the flux by J. The two are related to each other by the relation

$$J = LX \qquad ...(1)$$

where L is the coefficient not depending upon X or J. These coefficients in different relationships are known as phenomenological coefficients and the equations are known as phenomenological equations of thermodynamics.

The equation as given above is the generalisation of the single-flux equations of motion *i.e.*, involving only one type of flow by a particular type of force.

However, if a number of processes occur simultaneously, each force X_i gives rise to the flux J_i. The force and its corresponding flux are called conjugate parameters. Further, a particular type of flux may take place as a result of two or more forces. For example, flow of heat or flow of electricity is dependent on the gradient of electric potential as well as that of temperature. Thus the heat flux (J_i) which will be due to the force of temperature gradient (represented be X_u) and due to the force of electric potential gradient (represented by X_e) will be given by

$$J_u = L_{uu}X_u + L_{ue}X_e \qquad ...(2)$$

L_{uu} and L_{ue} are the phenomenological coefficients of X_u and X_e. They provide a numerical measure of the extent to which the particular driving force contributes to the flux under consideration. The first subscript attached to L represents the nature of the flux while the second signifies the nature of the contributing force.

Analogous to equation (2), the flux of the flow of electricity (J_e) will be given by

$$J_e = L_{eu}X_u + L_{ee}X_e \qquad ...(3)$$

In general, if n processes occur simultaneously, the associated fluxes J_i are linearly dependent on the conjugate forces X_i. *i.e.*

$$J_i = \sum_{j=1}^{n} L_{ij} X_j \qquad ...(4)$$

where $i = 1, 2, ... n.$

Further, it can be shown that when n forces X_i give rise to n fluxes J_i, the entropy production is

$$\sigma = \sum_i J_i X_i \qquad ...(5)$$

i.e., entropy production in the sum of products of forces and fluxes.

ONSAGAR RELATIONS AND APPLICATIONS

Introduction : The three laws of thermodynamics have been used to describe fully the thermodynamics of reversible processes like the dielectric polarisation of a crystal by an electric field etc. However, these three laws furnish only qualitative explanation for the irreversible processes such as that flow (effect) because of temperature gradient (cause), current flow (effect) because of potential difference (cause), etc. Further, onsagar derived certain relations which are able to describe the quantitative aspects of such irreversible processes. Thus. Onsagar relations are applied to study the thermodynamics of irreversible process.

Onsagar Relations

The thermodynamics of irreversible processes has been based on the following two concepts :

1. Linear Law

This law holds only when system under study is close to equilibrium *i.e.*, only removed slightly from equilibrium. Some examples of this law are Ohm's law between electric current and potential gradient, Fourier's law between heat flow and temperature gradient etc. The causes which give rise to irreversible process)*e.g*., temperature gradient, potential difference, etc.) are termed as driving forces (denoted by X) and the effects produced (*e.g.*, flow of heat, flow of current, etc.) are flux (denoted by J). Thus, the linear relations, near the equilibrium have been of the following type :

$$J_i = \sum_{k=1}^{n} L_{ik} X_k \quad (i = 1, 2, ... n) \qquad ...(1)$$

In the above linear relations, the fluxes are proportional to the forces. Relations of this type (Eq. (1)] are termed as phenomenological relations and the coefficients L_{ik} are termed as phenomenological coefficients. The coefficients L_{ik} may denote heat conductivity or electrical conductivity, etc., where are coefficients L_{ik} $(i \neq k)$ may denote the interference of two irreversible processes i and k, e., thermal conduction and diffusion.

2. Onsagar Reciprocal Relations

These are also relations on which thermodynamical of irreversible processes is based. Onsagar gave the following fundamental theorem pertaining to such irreversible processes:

If one makes a 'proper choice' of the fluxes J_i and X_i, the matrix of phenomenological coefficients L_{ik} would be symmetric, i.e,

$$L_{ik} = L_{ik} \; (i_i \; k = 1, 2, \ldots n) \qquad \ldots(2)$$

These identities are termed as Onsagar reciprocal relations. The notion of proper choice of fluxes and forces may be explained as follows.

If the state of the system (local temperature, pressure etc.) may be described by a number of parameters $A_1, A_2, \ldots A_n$ with their equilibrium values $\overset{\circ}{A}_1, \overset{\circ}{A}_2, \ldots \overset{\circ}{A}_n,$ then deviation of state parameters from their equilibrium values is termed as state variable, $\propto$. Hence

$$\propto_i = A_i - \overset{\circ}{A}_1 \qquad (i = 1, 2, \ldots n)$$

Now, we will define the proper choice of fluxes and forces as the time derivative of the state variable $\propto_i$:

$$J_i = \propto_i (i = 1, \ldots n) \qquad \ldots(3)$$

and the following combination of the state variables $\propto_i$:

$$X_i = \frac{\partial}{\partial \alpha_i} (\Delta S) \; (i = 1, 2, \ldots n) \qquad \ldots(4)$$

where, ΔS represents the deviation of the entropy from the equilibrium value.

As entropy gets increased in irreversible process, this change in entropy ΔS from the equilibrium value can be put as a function of the state variables, *i.e.*,

$$\Delta S = \frac{\partial}{\partial \alpha_1} (\Delta S) \alpha_i + \frac{\partial(\Delta S)}{\partial \alpha_2} \alpha_2 + \ldots$$

$$= \sum_i \alpha_i \frac{\partial(\Delta S)}{\partial \alpha_2} \quad \ldots(5)$$

$$= \sum_i J_i X_i, \quad \text{[Using Eqs. (3) and (4)]}$$

In order to illustrate the above derived quantities *e.g.*, fluxes and forces, we will consider a system which is composed of two parts, both enclosed within the same rigid adiabatic enclosure. Suppose the two parts are at uniform temperatures T_1 and T_2. if dQ represents the amount of heat flow from part at temperature T_2 to that at T_1 then increase in enthalpy of the system would be given as follows :

$$dS = dQ \left[\frac{1}{T_1} - \frac{1}{T_2} \right] = dQ. \frac{T_2 - T_1}{T_1 T_2}$$

$$= dQ. \frac{\Delta T}{T^2},$$

where $T_2 - T_1 = \Delta T$

and $T = \sqrt{(T_1 T_2)}$.

Hence rate of entropy production would be as follows :

$$\dot{S} = \dot{Q} \frac{\Delta T}{T^2} \quad \ldots(6)$$

As heat flow, called flux, denoted by Q occurs due to temperature gradient, called force denoted by ΔT, we can put

$$\dot{Q} = J_i \text{ and } \frac{\Delta T}{T^2} = X_i \quad \ldots(7)$$

so that eq. (6) would becomes as follows :

This is thus as eq. (5)

On putting relations (7) in eq. (1) we obtain

$$\dot{Q} = L \frac{\Delta T}{T^2}$$

This is nothing but is Newton's law of cooling.

Proof of Onsagar Reciprocal Relations

In order to develop the proof of Onsagar reciprocal relations, we will consider an adiabatically isolated system which is represented by microcanonical ensemble. The developing of the theory of onsagar relations is based on the assumption that the rate at which a macroscopic irreversible process is occurring remains the same as the average rate of decay or regression of the statistical fluctuations in the state of the system. Hence, we shall discuss it in two parts :

Step (i) : Fluctuations of an Isolated System

First of all we will find out the statistical mechanics of fluctuations of a system which remain isolated for a sufficient length to ensure thermodynamic equilibrium. Suppose the state variable is

$$\alpha_i = A_i - \overset{\circ}{A}_i$$

where is same as sated earlier.

The deviation of the entropy from its equilibrium value due to fluctuations α_i is denoted by ΔS and is given as follows :

$$\Delta S = -\frac{1}{2}\sum_{i,\,k=1}^{n}\left(\frac{\partial^2(\Delta S)}{\partial\alpha_i\,\partial\alpha_k}\right)_0 \alpha_i\,\alpha_k \qquad ...(1)$$

where, suffix 0 denotes the values of these derivatives at equilibrium. Therms liners in α_i's have been excluded as in equilibrium entropy is having maximum value and the state variables are zero. It is possible to further put the above relation in the form

$$\Delta S = -\frac{1}{2}\sum g_{ik}\,\alpha_i\alpha_k \qquad ...(2)$$

Hence $$X_i = \frac{\partial}{\partial\alpha_i}(\Delta S) = -\sum_k g_{ik}\,\alpha_k \qquad ...(3)$$

We know, $$\Delta S = -\sum\alpha_i\,g_{ik}\,\alpha_k$$

$$= \sum_i J_i\,X_i \qquad ...(4)$$

From Einstein's fluctuations theory, it is known that the probability P of fluctuations $d\alpha_1$, $d\alpha_2$, ... is proportional to exp. $(\Delta S/k)$, where k refers to the Boltzmann's constant. Thus, the probability of finding a state in which the values of α_i lie between μi, and $\mu i + d\alpha_i$ may be given as follows:

$$P\,d\alpha_1 \ldots d\alpha_n = \frac{\exp.\left(\Delta S/k\right),\ d\alpha_1 \ldots d\alpha_n}{\int \ldots \int \exp.\left(\Delta S/k\right),\ d\alpha_1 \ldots d\alpha_n} \quad \ldots(5)$$

with normalisation condition given as follows :

$$\int \ldots \int d\alpha_1 \ldots d\alpha_n = 1 \quad \ldots(6)$$

Now an attempt is made to find the average

$$\overline{\alpha_i X_J} \equiv \int \ldots \int \alpha_i X_J \, d\alpha_1 \ldots d\alpha_n \quad \ldots(7)$$

In eqns. (3) and (5) are used, it can be shown that

$$X_J = \frac{\partial(\Delta S)}{\partial \alpha_j} = \frac{\partial}{\partial \alpha_j}(k \log P)$$

$$= k \frac{\partial}{\partial \alpha_j}(\log P)$$

If this value is put in Eq. (7), we obtain

$$\overline{\alpha_i X_j} = k \int \ldots \int \alpha_i \frac{\partial(\log P)}{\partial \alpha_j}.\ P\,d\alpha_1 \ldots d\alpha_n$$

$$= k \int \ldots \int \alpha_i \frac{\partial(\log P)}{\partial \alpha_j}.\ P\,d\alpha_j\,d\alpha_1 \ldots d\alpha_{j-1,}\,d\alpha_{j+1,} \ldots, d\alpha_n$$

$$= k \int \ldots \int d\alpha_1 \ldots d\alpha_{j-1,}\ d\alpha_{j+1} \ldots d\alpha_n \int \alpha_i \frac{\partial(\log P)}{\partial \alpha_j}.\ P\,d\alpha_j$$

$$= k \int \ldots \int d\alpha_1 \ldots d\alpha_{j-1,}\ d\alpha_{j+1} \ldots d\alpha_n \int \alpha_i \frac{\partial P}{\partial \alpha_j}.d\alpha_j \quad \ldots(8)$$

By carrying out integration by parts, it can be shown that

$$\int_{-\infty}^{+\infty} \alpha_i \frac{\partial P}{\partial \alpha_j}\, d\alpha_j = \left[\alpha_i P\right]_{-\infty}^{+\infty} - \int_{-\infty}^{+\infty} \alpha_i \frac{\partial \alpha_i}{\partial \alpha_j} P\, d\alpha_j$$

The first term would be zero as probability of fluctuations would be zero at $\alpha_i = \pm\, \infty$. Hence,

$$\int_{-\infty}^{\infty} \alpha_i \frac{\partial P}{\partial \alpha_j}\, d\alpha_j - \int_{-\infty}^{+\infty} \delta_{ij}\, P\, d\alpha_j.$$

where $\delta_{ij} = \dfrac{\partial \alpha_i}{\partial \alpha_j} = 0$ if $i \neq j$

$= 1$ if $i = j$

If this term is substituted in Eq. (8), we obtain

$$\overline{\alpha_i X_j} = -k \int \ldots \int d\alpha_i \ldots d\alpha_{j-1}, d\alpha_{j+1} \ldots d\alpha_n \int P\,\delta_{ij}\, d\alpha_j$$

$$= -k \int \ldots \int P\, d\alpha_1 \ldots d\alpha_n\, \delta_{ij}.$$

$$= k\,\delta_{ij}, \;(i, j = 1, \ldots n) \qquad \ldots(9)$$

on using the normalisation condition (6).

In combination with the result of step (ii), Eq. (9) can be used to arrive at Onsagar relation.

Step (ii):

This step is involving the concept of microscopic reversibility which means the invariance of equations of motion of individual particles with time reversal. *i.e.*, $t \to -t$. Now we will denote these values by $\alpha_i(t)$ and $\alpha_j(t + \pi)$. The average of their product after a long lapse of time may be put as follows :

$$\overline{\alpha_i(t)\,\alpha_j(t+\pi)} = \lim_{\pi \to \infty \pi} \frac{1}{\pi} \int_0^{\pi} \alpha_i(t)\,\alpha_j(t+\pi)\,dt \qquad \ldots(10)$$

This, for one single system (subensemble) would be equal to the average over a microcanonical ensemble which is obtained by using the probability function eq. (6).

Further the average value of the product $\alpha_i(t)\,\alpha_j(t+\pi)$ is different from the average of product given in eq. (10) merely by the substitution $t \to -t$. Thus the microscopic reversibility may be put by the relation.

$$\overline{\alpha_i(t)\,\alpha_j(t+\pi)} = \overline{\alpha_j(t)\,\alpha_i(t+\pi)} \qquad \ldots(11)$$

On subtracting $\overline{\alpha_i(t)\,\alpha_j(t)}$ from both sides and dividing by π, we obtain

$$\overline{\alpha_i(t)\frac{[\alpha_j(t+\pi) - \alpha_j(t)]}{\pi}} = \overline{\alpha_j(t)\frac{[\alpha_i(t+\pi) - \alpha_i(t)]}{\pi}}.$$

This, when $\pi \to 0$, gives

$$\overline{\alpha_i(t)\,\alpha_j(t)} = \overline{\alpha_j(t)\,\alpha_i(t)} \qquad \ldots(12)$$

Further, it was assumed by Onsagar that on the average the decay or regression of a fluctuation would follow the linear relations of the form

$$\alpha_i = \sum_k L_{ik} X_k$$

This when substituted in eq. (12) yields

$$\overline{\sum_k \alpha_i L_{ik} X_k} = \overline{\sum_k \alpha_j L_{ik} X_k}$$

The above expression on rearrangement yields

$$\overline{\sum_k L_{ik} \alpha_i X_k} = \overline{\sum_k L_{ik} \alpha_j X_k} \qquad ...(13)$$

On combining the result of the above tow steps by using Eqs. (9) and (13), we get

$$-k \sum_k \delta_{ik} L_{jk} = -k \sum_k \delta_{jk} L_{ik}$$

But $\delta_{ij} = 0$ for $i \neq j$, we get

$$L_{ji} = L_{ij} \qquad ...(14)$$

This is the Onsagar relation.

Application of Onsagar Relation

We will make an attempt to obtain relations that are used describe the thermodynamics of any irreversible process. First of all we will calculate entropy production ΔS and then we will calculate proper fluxes and forces.

We will assume an adiabatically isolated system which is composed of two vessels I and II maintained at temperatures T and T + ΔT. Now a hole is drilled between the two vessels for combination. This will cause thermal flow and mass with interference between the two.

Suppose V is the volume of two vassals. Now U, M and S donate the energy, mass and entropy respectively corresponding to each of the vessels in the state of thermodynamic equilibrium. Further as U and M obey simple conservation laws, they can be chosen as state variables $\propto_i$.

Now the variation of ΔS_I of entropy I is given as follows:

$$\Delta S_I = \left(\frac{\partial S}{\partial U}\right)_M \Delta U + \left(\frac{\partial S}{\partial M}\right)_U \Delta M + \frac{1}{2}\left\{\frac{\partial^2 S}{\partial U^2}\right\}_M$$

$$(\Delta U)^2 + \frac{\partial^2 S}{\partial U\,\partial M} \Delta U\,\Delta M + \frac{1}{2}\left(\frac{\partial^2 S}{\partial M^2}\right)_U (\Delta M)^2 \qquad ...(1)$$

Further it is also possible to write a similar expression for chamber II. From conservation laws, we have

$$(\Delta U)_I = -(\Delta U)_{II};\ (\Delta M)_I = -(\Delta M)_{II}$$

The total entropy variation of the whole system may be given as follows.

$$2\Delta S = (\Delta S)_I + (\Delta S)_{II}$$

or

$$\Delta S = \frac{1}{2}\left(\frac{\partial^2 S}{\partial U}\right)_M (\Delta U)^2 + \frac{\partial^2 S}{\partial U\,\partial M}\Delta U\,\Delta M + \frac{1}{2}\left(\frac{\partial^2 S}{\partial M^2}\right)_U (\Delta M)^2 \quad ...(2)$$

On taking the time derivative, we obtain

$$\Delta S = \left\{\frac{\partial^2 S}{\partial U^2}\right\}_M \Delta U\,\Delta U + \frac{\partial^2 S}{\partial U\,\partial M}\Delta U\,\Delta M + \frac{\partial^2 S}{\partial U\,\partial M}\Delta U\,\Delta M + \left(\frac{\partial^2 S}{\partial M^2}\right)\Delta M\,\Delta M$$

$$= \Delta U\left[\left\{\frac{\partial^2 S}{\partial U^2}\right\}_M \partial U + \frac{\partial^2 S}{\partial U\,\partial M}\Delta M\right] + \Delta M\left[\left\{\frac{\partial^2 S}{\partial M^2}\right\}_U \partial M + \frac{\partial^2 S}{\partial U\,\partial M}\Delta U\right] \quad ...(3)$$

We have now arrived at the expression of entropy production. Now we will make an attempt to specify the fluxes and forces As there are two flows, there would be two fluxes J_U and J_M denoting energy flow and mass flow respectively. Similarly there are two forces, X_U and X_M.

As fluxes are the time derivative of state variable α_i, in this case we have

$$\left.\begin{aligned} J_U &= \Delta U \\ J_M &= \Delta M \end{aligned}\right\} \quad ...(4)$$

Also the corresponding forces are given as follows :

$$\left.\begin{aligned} X_U &= \Delta\left[\frac{\partial S}{\partial U}\right]_M = \left[\frac{\partial^2 S}{\partial U^2}\right]_M \Delta U + \left[\frac{\partial^2 S}{\partial U\,\partial M}\right]\Delta M \\ X_M &= \Delta\left[\frac{\partial S}{\partial M}\right]_U = \left[\frac{\partial^2 S}{\partial M^2}\right]_U \Delta M + \left[\frac{\partial^2 S}{\partial M\,\partial U}\right]\Delta U \end{aligned}\right\} \quad ...(5)$$

If we substitute Eqs. (4) and (5) in (3), we get

$$\Delta S = J_U X_U + J_M X_M \qquad ...(6)$$

The linear relation may be put as follows.

$$\left.\begin{aligned} J_M &= L_{11} X_M + L_{12} X_U \\ J_u &= L_{21} X_M + L_{22} X_u \end{aligned}\right\} \qquad ...(7)$$

and from Onsagar relation, we have

$$L_{12} = L_{21} \qquad ...(8)$$

Eqs. (5) and (7) have been the general expressions for forces and fluxes in the present case. For a simple system at constant volume, we have

$$T\, dS = dU - \mu\, dM \qquad ...(9)$$

where μ is the chemical potential per unit mass. From this relation, we have

$$\left(\frac{\partial}{\partial U}\right)_M = \frac{1}{T} \text{ since } dM = 0 \text{ and } \left(\frac{\partial}{\partial M}\right)_U = -\frac{\mu}{T} \text{ since } dU = 0$$

so that $X_U = \Delta\left(\frac{\partial S}{\partial U}\right)_M = \Delta \frac{1}{T} = -\frac{\Delta T}{T^2}$ ...(10)

and $X_M = \Delta\left(\frac{\partial S}{\partial M}\right)_U = \Delta\left(-\frac{\mu}{T}\right) = -\Delta\left(\frac{\mu}{T}\right)$

or $= -\left(\frac{\Delta\mu}{T} - \frac{\mu}{T^2}\Delta T\right)$ ...(11)

∵ $\mu = u + pv - Ts = h\ \ Ts,$

so that $\Delta m = \Delta u + p\,\Delta v + v\,\Delta p - T\,\Delta s - s\,\Delta T = v\,\Delta p - s\,\Delta T,$

Other changes being zero. Putting it in eq. (11) we obtain

$$X_M = -\left(\frac{v\,\Delta p - s\,\Delta T}{T} - \frac{\mu}{T^2}\Delta T\right) = -v\frac{\Delta p}{T} + \frac{\Delta T}{T}\left(s + \frac{\mu}{T}\right)$$

$$= -v\frac{\Delta p}{T} + \frac{\Delta T}{T}\left(s + \frac{u + pv - Ts}{T}\right) = -v\frac{\Delta p}{T} + \frac{\Delta T}{T}\left(\frac{u + pv}{T}\right)$$

$$= -v\frac{\Delta T}{T} + \frac{h\,\Delta T}{T^2} \qquad ...(12)$$

If Eqs. (12) and (10) are substituted in Eq. (7) we obtain

and

$$\left.\begin{aligned} J_M &= -\frac{L_{11} v}{T} \Delta p + \frac{L_{11} h - L_{12}}{T^2} \Delta T \\ J_U &= -\frac{L_{21} v}{T} \Delta p + \frac{L_{21} h - L_{22}}{T^2} \Delta T \end{aligned}\right\} \quad ...(13)$$

In the stationary state mass flow would be zero and we can put $J_M = 0$ so that we get

$$0 = -\frac{L_{11} v}{T} \Delta p + \frac{L_{11} h - L_{12}}{T^2} \Delta T$$

or

$$\left(\frac{\Delta p}{\Delta T}\right)_{JM} = 0 = \frac{L_{11} h - L_{12}}{L_{11} vT} \quad ...(14)$$

Eq. (14) gives theorem-molecular pressure difference. It is possible to observe the difference of the two effects, namely thermal flow and mass flow by maintaining a certain pressure difference between the two values and a uniform temperature throughout the system. Then the matter would be flowing (mass flow) from one vessel to another associated with thermal energy flow (that is proportional to the flow of matter). Such an effect is tamed as thermomechanical effect and is given as follows :

$$\left(\frac{J_U}{J_M}\right) \Delta = 0 = \frac{L_{21}}{L_{11}} = Q^* \quad ...(15)$$

On substituting Eq. (15) in Eq. (14), we get

$$\left(\frac{\Delta p}{\Delta T}\right)_{JM} = 0 = \frac{h - (L_{21}/L_{11})}{vT} = \frac{h - Q^*}{vT} \quad ...(16)$$

Eq. (15) connects the two effects.

WIENER-KHINTCHINE THEOREM

This theorem is concerned with a random process.

A random process may be defined as a process in which a variable y is not dependent in a completely definite way on the independent time variable t. Two important characteristics of a random process are as follows :

(i) The power spectrum of the process, and

(ii) The correlation function of the process.

The Wiener-Khintchine theorem gives a relationship between these two characteristics, (i) and (ii).

We will now consider a periodic variable y (t) which could be expanded in Fourier series in the interval $0 < t < T$ as given below :

$$y(t) = \alpha_o + \sum_{n=1}^{\infty} \alpha_n \cos(2\pi f_n t) + \sum_{n=1}^{\infty} b_n \sin(2\pi f_n t). \quad ...(1)$$

In the above equation $f_n = n/T$, time period $T = 1/f_o$; f_u = fundamental frequency and $f_n = nf_o$.

Hence we assume that $<y(t)> = 0$. Where the angular parentheses , > denotes time average. As the average is regarded to be zero, there will be no constant term in Fourier series. Under this condition, we get

$$y(t) = \sum_{n=1}^{\infty} \{\alpha_n \cos(2\pi f_n t) + b_n \sin(2\pi f_n t)\} \quad ...(2)$$

Here $$a_n = \frac{2}{T} \int_o^T y(t) \cos(2\pi f_n t) dt \quad ...93)$$

and $$b_n = \frac{2}{T} \int_o^T y(t) \sin(2\pi f_n t) dt$$

Before we derive the theorem, we will prove that the ensemble average of the time average power dissipation $\overline{\langle P_n \rangle}$ associated with n^{th} components of y (t) has been equal to the square of standard deviation σ_n, *i.e.*,

$$\overline{\langle P_n \rangle} = \sigma_n^2. \quad ...(4)$$

The power in the nth component may be given as follows :

$$P_n = \{a_n \cos(2\pi f_n t) + b_n \sin(2\pi f_n t)\}^2 \quad ...(5)$$

The time average of P_n may be given as follows :

$$<P_n> = \frac{1}{2} < a_n^2 > + \frac{1}{2} < b_n^2 > = < a_n^2 + b_n^2 > \frac{1}{2}$$

because $<\cos^2(2\pi f_n t)> = \frac{1}{2}$, $<\sin^2(2\pi f_u t)> = \frac{1}{2}$

and $<\cos(2\pi f_n t). \sin(2\pi f_n t)> = 0$

Now we regard the ensemble average (which is an average over a large set of independent records for random process) which is denoted here by a over the quantity. We get

$$\overline{a_n} = 0, \overline{b_n} = 0, \overline{a_n \ b_m} = 0 \qquad ...(6)$$

$$\overline{a_n \ a_m} = \overline{b_n \ b_m} = \sigma_n^{\ 2} \delta_{nm}$$

where σ_n refers to standard deviation.

Now $\overline{\langle P_n \rangle} = \overline{\{a_n \cos(2\pi f_n t) + b_n \sin(2\pi f_n t)\}^2}$

$$= \sigma_n^{\ 2}\{\cos^2(2\pi f_n t) + \sin^2(2\pi f_n t)\}$$

$$= \sigma_n^{\ 2}$$

$\therefore$ $\overline{\langle P_n \rangle} = \sigma_n^{\ 2}.$ ...(7)

Power Spectrum

One can define the power spectrum or spectral density W (f) of random process as the ensemble average of the time average of power dissipation per unit frequency bandwidth. If we select a frequency bandwidth Δf_n equal to the separation between two adjacent frequencies that is

$$\Delta f_n = f_{n+1} - f_n = \frac{n+1}{T} - \frac{n}{T} = \frac{1}{T},$$

We get $W(f_n)\Delta f_n = \overline{\langle \rho_n \rangle} = \sigma_n^{\ 2}$ ...(8)

It can be proved that

$$\overline{y^2(t)} = \sum_n \sigma_n^{\ 2}$$

or $\overline{y^2(t)} = \sum_n W(f_n) = \int_0^\infty W(f)\,df$ ...(9)

The integral of the power spectrum over all frequencies provides the ensemble average total power, which is assumed to be independent of time, so we talk of it simply as the average total power.

Correlation Function

The correlation function may be defined as follows :

$$K(\pi) = \langle y(t)\, y(t + \pi)\rangle$$

Without altering the result let us take an ensemble average of the time average $\langle y(t)\, y(t + \pi)\rangle$.

So that,

$$K(\pi) = \overline{\langle y(t)\, y\,(t + \pi)\rangle}$$

$$\therefore \quad K(\pi) = \overline{\Big\langle \sum_{n,\,m} \big[a_n \cos(2\pi\; f_n t)\, b_n \cos(2\pi\, f_n t)\big]\big[a_n \cos 2\pi\; f_m(t + \pi)\big]}$$

$$\overline{+\; b_m\; \sin 2\pi\; f_m\;(t + \pi)\big]\Big\rangle}$$

$$= \frac{1}{2}\sum_n \overline{\left(a_n^{\;2} + b_n^{\;2}\right)} \cos\,(2\pi\; f_n\; \pi) = \sum_n \sigma_n^{\;2} \cos\,(2\pi\; f\; \pi) df$$

$$= \int_0^{\infty} W\,(f) \cos\,(2\pi\, f\; \pi)\; df$$

Hence $\quad K\,(\pi) = \int_0^{\infty} W\,(f) \cos\,(2\pi\, f\; \pi)\; df$ ...(10)

or $\quad W\,(f) = 4\int_0^{\infty} K\,(\pi) \cos\,(2\pi\, f\; \pi)\; d\pi$

(Using Fourier transform) ...(11)

Equations (10) and (11) are termed as Wiener-Khintchine theorem.

LINEAR LAWS

There are a number of simple transport processes in which some physical quantity such as mass or energy or momentum or electrical charge is transported from one region of a system to another. For example :

(i) Heat flows from one end to another of a metal rod if the two ends are at different temperatures.

(ii) Electrical charge flows from one end of a wire to another if the two ends have a potential difference.

(iii) Mass flows from one part of the system to another if a concentration gradient exists.

(iv) A gas or a liquid flows from one region to another if a pressure difference exists, and so on,

In all cases of flow, the amount of the physical quantity transported in unit time through a unit area perpendicular to the direction of flow (called the *flux*) is proportional to the gradient of some other physical quantity such as temperature or pressure or electrical potential, choosing the x-axis as the direction of flow, the general law for transport is

$$J_X = -B\frac{\partial Y}{\partial x} \quad ...(1)$$

where, J_x is the flux (*i.e.*, the amount of the quantity transported per cm^2 per sec) – B is the proportionality constant, and ($\delta Y/\delta x$) is the gradient of Y in the direction of flow; Y may be any of the quantities like temperature, electrical potential, pressure etc. Since flow occurs in a particular direction, it is a vector quantity.

For the examples mentioned above, the individual equations for the flow in the x-direction are as follows :

Heat flow, $J_X = -kT\frac{\partial T}{\partial x}$ (Fourier law) ...(2)

Electrical current, $J_X = -k\frac{\partial V}{\partial x}$ (Ohm's law) ...(3)

Fluid flow, $J_X = -C\frac{\partial p}{\partial x}$ (Poiseuille's law) ...(4)

Diffusion , $J_X = -D\frac{\partial c}{\partial x}$ (Fick's law) ...(5)

In the equations given above

Kp is the thermal conductivity coefficient

K is the electrical conductivity

C is the frictional coefficient related to viscosity

and D is the diffusion coefficient.

The various laws as stated above in which the flux is proportional to the gradient of some force are called *linear laws*. These are in fact, equivalent to the equations J = LX.

STATIONARY STATES

In thermodynamics, quite often we study systems in a state called the 'stationary state' as it can be readily subjected to mathematical analysis in a number of situations of practical importance.

A system is said to be in a stationary state if its macroscopic properties such as temperature, pressure, composition and entropy do not change with time inspite of the possible occurrence of irreversible processes. Of the macroscopic properties, the intensive ones though unchanged in time, will generally still vary from point to point in the system.

The concept of a stationary state is illustrated by the following examples :

(i) If heat is added at a constant rate to one end of a metal bar and withdrawn at an equal rate from its other end, the temperature at each point of the bar approaches a time independent value. All the same, the temperature varies along the length of the bar and entropy is produced continuously as a result of heat conduction.

(ii) Consider a metal rod between whose ends there is a potential difference ΔV. An electric current flows though the rod. Suppose that the rod is placed along its length in contract with a heat reservoir at the temperature T, and that the rate of heat flow out of each element into the reservoir is equal to the rare at which the electrical work is done on the element. All the properties of the rod (temperature, internal energy, entropy etc.) then remain Constant with time inspite of the irreversible generation of heat (due to flow of electric current).

The stationary states may be classified into the following two classes :

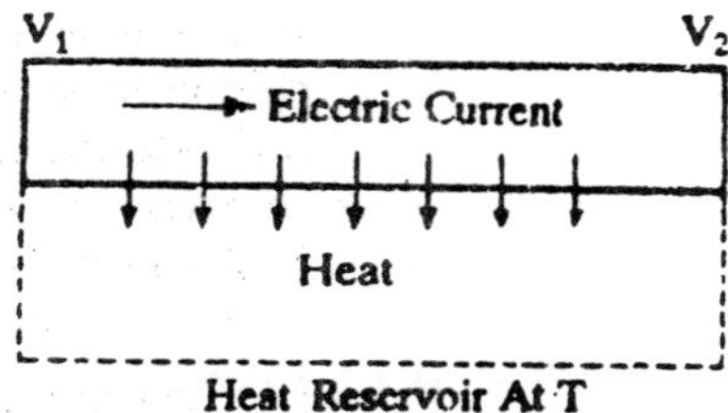

Fig. 2.9 : Understanding the stationary state of an irreversible process.

(i) Equilibrium stationary states *i.e.*, the stationary states attained in a system in equilibrium.

(ii) Non-equilibrium stationary states *i.e.*, the stationary states attained in a system not in equilibrium.

The two differ mainly in the fact that in the former, the value of any intensive property not only remains constant with time but also has the same value at every point whereas in the latter, the value of any intensive property though remains constant with time at any point but differs from point to point and thus a continuous inflow of energy or matter and energy is required from the surroundings to the system. Thus, whereas equilibrium stationary states can be attained only in an isolated system (or a system in contact with a uniform environment), the non-equilibrium stationary states can be attained in open systems.

Another method of classifying stationary states is in the following manner :

Consider a system characterised by n independent forces X_1. X_2..., X_3, and let a number k of them, say X_1, X_2..., X_k, be kept at fixed values through the operation of external constraints. E is then found empirically that the system will sooner or later reach a stage where the remaining forces, X_{k+i}, X_{k+2}...X_n, will also remain constant with the passage of time. In the end, therefore, all the forces X_i. and as a result, all the fluxes J_i (depending linearly on the forces) become independent of time. The stationary state attained by this method is called the *stationary state of order k.*

In the special case, when no forces X_i are held fixed (k = 0). The system will continue till it reaches a stage when all the fluxes, and consequently all the forces, have vanished. Thus, the stationary state of zero order is identical with the state of thermostatic equilibrium.

The theory of stationary states related to open system has applications of considerable importance to living phenomena (biological systems). It has been suggested that if the living organisms and cells are treated as open systems, the basic biological phenomena such as metabolism and growth can be easily explained.

SOLVED EXAMPLES

Example 1:

The molar heat capacity at capacity at constant pressure of solid magnesium (0° – 600°C) is expressed by

$$CP = 6.20 + 1.30 \times 10 - 3\ T - 6.80 \times 104\ T - 2$$

Calculate the increase in entropy when 1 gm atom of metal is heated from 27°C to 127°C at constant pressure.

Solution:

At constant pressure,

$$\Delta S = \int_{T_1}^{T_2} \frac{C_P}{T} dT$$

$$\therefore \quad \Delta S = \int_{300}^{400} \frac{\left(6.20 + 1.30 \times 10^{-3}\, T - 6.80 \times 10^{4}\, T^{-2}\right) dT}{T}$$

$$\int_{300}^{400} 6.20 \frac{dT}{T} + \int_{300}^{400} 1.3 \times 10^{-3} dT - \int_{300}^{400} 6.20 \times 10^{4} \frac{dT}{T^3}$$

$$= 6.20 \ln\left[\ln T\right]_{300}^{400} + 1.3 \times 10^{-3} \left[T\right]_{300}^{400} - \frac{6.80 \times 10^{4}}{-2}\left[\frac{1}{T^2}\right]_{300}^{400}$$

$$= 6.20 \ln \frac{400}{300} + 1.3 \times 10^{-3} \times (400 - 300) + 3.40 \times 10^{4}$$

$$\left[\frac{1}{(400)^2} - \frac{1}{(300)^2}\right]$$

$$= 1.7487 \text{ cal./degree.}$$

Example 2:

Calculate the increase in entropy of three moles of hydrogen as it changes from 300°K atm to 1000°K and 1 atm (C_p = 7 cal./degree/ mole).

Solution:

Entropy change ΔS for n moles

$$= n\, C_P \ln \frac{T_2}{T_1}\; n\, R \ln \frac{P_2}{P_1}$$

$$= 3 \times 7 \times 2.303 \log \frac{1000}{300} - 3 \times 2 \times 2.303 \log \frac{10}{0.1}$$

$$= 25.287996 - 13.818$$

$$= 11.469996 \text{ cal./degree.}$$

Example 3:

A thermostat was maintained at 370.05 K. For nearly an hour 4.2 kJ of heat leaked through the thermostat insulation into a room where the initial temperature of air was 300.05 K.

(i) What was the entropy change of the material in the thermostat?

(ii) What was the entropy change of the air in the room ?

(iii) Was the process spontaneous? (Material in the thermostat is water).

Solution:

(i) Entropy change of the material in the thermostat

$$-\frac{4.2\ \text{kJ}}{370.05\text{K}} = -11.35\times 10^{3}\ \text{kj K}^{-1}$$

(ii) Entropy change of the air in the room

$$= \frac{4.2\ \text{kJ}}{300.05\ \text{K}} = 14.00\times 10^{3}\ \text{kJ K}^{-1}$$

(iii) Now

$$\Delta S_{total} = \Delta S_{thermostat} + \Delta S_{room}$$

$$= (-11.35 + 14.00)\ \text{JK}^{-1}$$

$$= 2.65\ \text{J K}^{-1}$$

Since ΔStotal is positive, the process of leaking is spontaneous.

Example 4:

Calculate ΔS, ΔH and ΔU for the process

$$H_2O(l,\ 20^{\circ}C,\ 1\ atm \rightarrow H_2O\ (g,\ 250^{\circ}C,\ 1\ atm)$$

Given the following data :

$$C_p\ (l) = 75.6\ J\ K^{-1}\ mol^{-1}$$

$$C_p\ (g) = 36.2\ J\ K^{-1}\ mol^{-1}$$

ΔH for vaporization of H_2O at 100°C and 1 atm is equal to 40.85 k J mol^{-1}

Solution:

The given process may be replaced by the following processes.

(i) H_2O (l, 20°C, 1 atm) → H_2O (l, 100°C, 1 atm)

(ii) H_2O (l, 100°C, 1 atm) → H_2O (g, 100°C, 1 atm)

(iii) H_2O (g, 100°C, 1 atm) → H_2O (g, 250°C, 1 atm)

Thus we have

$$\Delta S = \Delta S_{(i)} + \Delta S_{(ii)}\ \Delta S_{(iii)}$$

$$= C_{p,m}(l)\ \ln\frac{T_2}{T_1} + \frac{\Delta H_{vap}}{T} + C_{p,m}(g)\ \ln\frac{T_2'}{T_1'}$$

$$= \left(75.6 \ln \frac{373}{293} + \frac{40850}{373} + 36.2 \ln \frac{523}{373}\right) \text{JK}^{-1}\ \text{mol}^{-1}$$

$$= (18.25 + 109.52 + 12.24)\ \text{J K}^{-1}\ \text{mol}^{-1}$$

$$= 140.01\ \text{J K}^{-1}\ \text{mol}^{-1}$$

$$\Delta H = \Delta H_{(i)} + \Delta H_{(ii)} + \Delta H_{(iii)}$$

$$= C_{p.m}\ (l)\ (T_2 - T_1) + \Delta H_{vap} + C_{pm}(g)\ (T'_2 - T'_1)$$

$$= (75.6 \times 80 + 40850 + 36.2 \times 150)\ \text{J mol}^{-1}$$

$$= 52328\ \ \text{J mol}^{-1}$$

$$\Delta U = \Delta U_{(i)} + \Delta U_{(ii)}\ \Delta U_{(iii)}$$

$$= C_{v.m}\ (l)\ (T_2 - T_1) + \Delta U_{vap} + C_{v.m}(g)\ (T'_2 - T'_1)$$

$$= C_{p.m}(l)(T_2 - T_1) + \{\Delta H_{vap} + \Delta_{V|g}RT\} + \{C_{p.m}(g) - R\}(T'_2 - T'_1)$$

$$= [75.6 \times 80 + \{40850 - (8.314)\ (373)\}$$

$$+ (36.2 - 8.314)\ (150)]\ \text{J mol}^{-1}\}$$

$$= (6040 + 37749 + 4183)\ \text{J mol}^{-1}$$

$$= 47972\ \text{J mol}^{-1}$$

Example 5:

For N = 400, find the ratios of the probabilities for (300, 100) and (200, 200) distribution in two identical boxes.

Solution:

We have

$$P(300, 100) = \frac{400!}{300!\ 100!} \frac{1}{2^{400}}$$

$$P(200, 200) = \frac{400!}{200!\ 200!} \frac{1}{2^{400}}$$

$$\frac{P(300, 100)}{P(200, 200)} = \frac{200!\ 200}{300!\ 100!} \cong 10^{-5}$$

Example 6:

Eight similar coins are tossed, find the probability of three heads and t tails.

Solution:

We know $$P(3, 5) = \frac{^8C_3}{2^8} = \frac{8\times7\times6}{3\times2\times1\times2^8}$$

or $$P(3, 5) = \frac{7}{32}$$

Example 7:

A system consists of 6000 particles distributed in three energy states with equal spacing. The energy of the three states are $E_{1'} = 0$, $E_{2'} = x$ and $E_3 = 2x$. All the three slates have the same intrinsic probability g. At a certain instant there are 3000 particles in lower level, 2500 in the middle level and 500 in the upper level. Compare the relative probabilities with the distribution obtained, by the transfer of one particle from the middle to the lower level and one particle from the middle to the upper level and the original distribution.

Solution:

Let P_1 and P_2 be the probabilities in the two cases

In the first case,

$$N = 6000,$$

$$n_1 = 3000,$$

$$n_2 = 2500,$$

$$n_3 = 500.$$

$$P_1 = \frac{g^N}{n_1!n_2!n_3!}$$

$$P_1 = \frac{g^{6000}}{3000!2500!500!} \quad ...(i)$$

In the second case

$$N = 6000,$$

$$n_1 = 3001,$$

$$n_2 = 2498,$$

$$n_3 = 501.$$

$$P_1 = \frac{g^N}{n_1!n_2!n_3!}$$

$$P_1 = \frac{g^{6000}}{3001!2498!501!}$$

Dividing (ii) by (i)

$$\frac{P_2}{P_1} = \frac{3000!2500!500!}{3001!2498!501!}$$

$$\frac{P_2}{P_1} = \frac{2500 \times 2499!}{3001 \times 501!}$$

$$\frac{P_2}{P_1} = 4.157$$

$$\approx 4.2.$$

It means the transfer of one particle from the middle to the upper and one particle from the middle to the lower state has changed the probability by a factor 4.2. This shows that both these distributions are not near the equilibrium state.

Example 8:

At low temperature, a nonideal gas follows the relation $PV = RT - a/V$ where $a = 0.3636$ Nm^4 $mole^{-2}$. Calculate the work done by one mole of this gas in expanding form 0.224 litre to 22.4 litre at 400 K. Compare this result with the work done in the corresponding expansion of an ideal gas.

Solution:

For an ideal gas, reversible work done

$$= 2.303 \text{ n RT log } \frac{V_2}{V_1}$$

V_1 = 0.224 litres $mole^{-1}$ = 22.4 × 10^{-5} m^3 $mole^{-1}$

P_2 = 22.4 litres $mole^{-1}$ = 22.4 × 10^{-3} m^3 $mole^{-1}$

R = 8.314 J K^{-1} $mole^{-1}$

$$W_{rew} = (2.303)\ (1 \text{ mole})\ (8.314 \text{ J } K^{-1} \text{ mole}^{-1})\ (400 \text{ K}) \times \log \frac{22.4 \times 10^{-3}}{22.4 \times 10^{-5}}$$

$$= (2.303)\ (1 \text{ mole})\ (8.314 \text{ J } K^{-1} \text{ mole}^{-1})\ (400 \text{ K}) \log 100$$

$$= 15320 \text{ J mole}^{-1}$$

$= 15.32 \text{ kJ mole}^{-1}$.

For the non-ideal gas PV = RT – a/V

Therefore, the work done $= \int_{V_1}^{V_2} P\,dV = \int_{V_1}^{V_2} \left\{ \frac{RT}{V} - \frac{a}{V_2} \right\} dV$

$$= 2.303 \text{ RT} \log \frac{V_2}{V_1} + a\left\{ \frac{1}{V_2} - \frac{1}{V_1} \right\}$$

The value of first part is from derived eq. (1) as $15.32 \text{ kJ mole}^{-1}$ and of another part can be derived as

$$0.3636 \text{ Nm}^4 \text{ mole}^{-2} \left\{ \frac{1}{22.4 \times 10^{-3} \text{ m}^3 \text{ mole}^{-1}} - \frac{1}{22.4 \times 10^{-5} \text{ m}^3 \text{ mole}^{-1}} \right\}$$

$= 1.604 \text{ kJ mole}^{-1}$.

Thus work done $= 15.320 \text{ k Joule}^{-1} - 1.604 \text{ k Joule}^{-1}$

$= 13.716 \text{ kJ mole}^{-1}$.

Example 9:

What will be the work done when 65.38 g of zinc dissolves in hydrochloric acid in case of an open beaker and closed beaker at 300K.

Solution:

The process of dissolution of zinc in hydrochloric acid can be given as

$$Zn(s) + 2HCl\ (aq) = ZnCl_2(aq) + H_2(g)$$

From this equation it is clear that for each gram atom of zinc dissolved we will obtain 1 mole of Hydrogen gas. As a result of liberated gas, on the surrounding atmosphere the work performed will be equal to PΔV. If the initial volume of the system is neglected in comparison to the total volume of the gas produced and the gas shows ideal behaviour, then the work done in the open beaker is

$$W = P\Delta V \approx PV_{H2}$$

$= nH2\ RT \qquad [\because T = 300 \text{ k } R = 8.314 \text{ Jk}^{-1} \text{ mole}^{-1}]$

$= (1 \text{ mole}) (8.314 \text{ JK}^{-1} \text{ mol}^{-1}) (300 \text{ K})$

$= 2.4942 \text{ kJ}$.

If the reaction takes place in a closed beaker there is change in the volume *i.e.*, $\Delta V = 0$ hence work done is zero.

Example 10:

Calculate the work done when one mole of sulphur dioxide gas expands isothermally and reversibly at 300 k from 2.46 × 10 ³ m³ to 24.6 × 10 ³ m³. Assuming that the gas obeys

(a) ideal gas equation and

(b) van der Waals equation

$$\left\{\begin{matrix} a = 0.6799 \text{ nm}^4 \text{ mole}^{-2} \\ b = 0.564 \quad 10^{-3} \text{ mole}^{-1} \end{matrix}\right\}$$

Solution:

(a) The reversible work done by 1 mole of gas when it expands form

$$2.64 \times 10^{-3}\text{m}^3 \text{ to } 24.6 \times 10^{-3}\text{m}^3 = 2.303 \text{ RT} \log \frac{V_2}{V_1}$$

$$= (2.303)\ (1 \text{ mole})\ (8.314 \text{ J K}^{-1} \text{ mol}^{-1})\ (300 \text{ K}) \times \log 10$$

$$\left\{\because \log \frac{V_2}{V_1} = \log 10\right\}$$

$$= (2.303)\ \ (8.314)\ (300 \text{ K})\ \ \log 10 \text{ J mol}^{-1}$$

$$= 5744 \text{ J mol}^{-1}$$

(b) When the gas obeys van der Waal's equation, work done by 1 mole of gas is

$$= 2.303 \text{ RT} \log \frac{V_2 - b}{V_1 - b} + a\left\{\frac{1}{V_2} - \frac{1}{V_1}\right\}$$

After substituting the values of various quantities and solving, the work done is

$$= 5794 \text{ J mol}^{-1} - 252.4 \text{ J mol}^{-1}$$

$$= 5541.6 \text{ J mol}^{-1}$$

$$= 5.542 \text{ kJ mol}^{-1}.$$

Example 11:

One mole of a van der Walls's gas is allowed to expand isothermally and reversibly from a volume of 1 litre to 50 litre at 0°C. Calculate w, *q, Δ E and Δ H. van der Waal's constants are a = 6.5atm l^2mole^{-2} = 0.056 litre mole^{-1} and R = 0.082 l atom deg^{-1} mole^{-1}.*

Solution:

Here $V_1 = 1$ litre,

$V_2 = 50$ litres, n = 1 mole

$T = 273 + 0 = 273°k$,

R = 0.082 l-atm deg^{-1} mole^{-1}

a = 6.5 atm l^2 mole^{-2},

b = 0.056 litre mole^{-1}

$$w = 2.303 \text{ nRT} \log\left(\frac{V_2 - nb}{V_1 - nb}\right) + an^2\left(\frac{1}{V_2} - \frac{1}{V_1}\right)$$

$$= 2.303 \times 1 \times 0.082 + 273 \, [\log(50 - 0.056) - \log(1 - 0.056)$$

$$+ 6.5\left(\frac{1}{50} - \frac{1}{1}\right)$$

$= 82.47$ l atm.

$$\Delta E = -an^2\left(\frac{1}{V_2} - \frac{1}{V_1}\right) = 6.5 \times \frac{49}{50}$$

$$q = 2.303\text{nRT} \log \frac{V_2 - b}{V_1 - b}$$

$= \Delta E + w =$ **884** l atm.

Example 12:

The van der Waal's constant a and b for hydrogen in litre atmosphere units are 0.246 and 2.67 × 10^{-2} respectively. Calculate the inversion temperature of hydrogen.

Solution:

we know $T_i = 2a/Rb$

or $$T_i = \frac{2 \times 0.246}{0.0821 \times 0.0267}$$

$= 224.5°k = (224.5 - 273) = -48.5°C.$

Example 13:

How much heat is required to raise the temperature of 1 mole oxygen from 300K to 1300 K at constant pressure.

$$C_p = 6.095 + 3.325 \times 10^{3} T - 1.017 \times 10^{6} T^2$$

Solution:

$$H_2 - H_1 \int_{T_t}^{T_2} C_p \, dT$$

$$T_1 = 300 \text{ k}, T_2 = 100 \text{ k}$$

$$\therefore H_{1300} - H_{300} = \int_{300}^{1300} \left(6.095 + 3.253 + 10^{-3} T - 1.017 \times 10^{-6} T^2\right)$$

[Substituting the value of C_p]

$$\because H_{1300} - H_{300} = 6.095 (1300 - 300) + \frac{3.253 \times 10^{-3}}{2}$$

$$\times [(1300)^2 - (300)^2] - 1/3 \times 1.017 \times 10^{-6} [(1000)^2 - (300)^2]$$

$$= 6095 + 2602.4 - 735.63$$

$$= 7961.77 \text{ cal/mole.}$$

Example 14:

For equation $(P \_ a/V^2) V = RT$, prove that (i) dP is an exact differential, (ii) P is a state function and

$$\text{(iii)} \left(\frac{\partial P}{\partial T}\right)_V \left(\frac{\partial T}{\partial V}\right)_P \left(\frac{\partial V}{\partial T}\right)_T + 1 = 0.$$

Solution:

(i) For dP to be an exact differential, it is be proved that

$$\frac{\partial^2 P}{\partial V \partial T} = \frac{\partial^2 P}{\partial T \partial V} \qquad ...(1)$$

$$(P + a/V^2) V = RT$$

or

$$P = \frac{RT}{V} - \frac{a}{V^2} \qquad ..(2)$$

When the above equation is differentiated with respect to V at constant temperature T, we obtain

$$\left(\frac{\partial r}{\partial V}\right)_T = -\frac{RT}{V^2} + \frac{2a}{V^3}$$

When the above equation is differentiated with respect to T at constant V, we obtain

$$\frac{\partial^2 P}{\partial T \partial V} = -\frac{RT}{V^2} \qquad ..(3)$$

When equation (2) is differentiated with respect to T at constant volume V, we obtain

$$\left(\frac{\partial P}{\partial T}\right)_V = \frac{R}{V}$$

When the above equation is further differentiated with respect to V at constant T, we obtain

$$\frac{\partial^2 P}{\partial T \partial V} = -\frac{R}{V^2} \qquad ...(4)$$

From equations (3) and (4), we get

$$\frac{\partial^2 P}{\partial T\ \partial V} = \frac{\partial^2 P}{\partial T\ \partial V} = -\frac{R}{V^2} \qquad ...(5)$$

Thus, we have proved condition, (1). This shows that dP is an exact differential.

(ii) In the said question, first of all a change occurs in volume at constant temperature followed by a change in temperature at constant volume, thereby giving the final equation (3).

Again, a change in temperature is considered at constant volume, followed by a change in volume at constant temperature, thereby giving the final equation (4). Both equations (3) and (4) are same, thereby revealing that the final change in P remains the same irrespective of the difference in intermediate changes. Therefore, P is a state function as changes in P have been found to depend upon the intial and final states of the system.

(iii) Equation (2) is as follows :

$$P = \frac{RT}{V} - \frac{a}{V^2}$$

When the above equation is differentiated, we obtain :

$$dP = \frac{R}{V}\,dT - \frac{RT}{V^2}\,dV + \frac{2a}{V^3}\,dV$$

$$= \frac{R}{V}\,dT - \left(\frac{RT}{V^2} - \frac{2a}{V^3}\right)dV \qquad ...(6)$$

If volume is constant, dV = 0 : equation (6) becomes as follows :

$$dP = \frac{R}{V}\,dT \text{ or } \left(\frac{\partial P}{\partial V}\right)_V = \frac{R}{V} \quad ...(7)$$

If pressure is constant, dP = 0; equation (6) becomes as follow :

$$\frac{R}{V}\,dT - \left(\frac{RT}{V^2} - \frac{2a}{V^3}\right)dV = 0$$

or

$$\left(\frac{\partial T}{\partial V}\right)_P = \left(\frac{RT}{V^2} - \frac{2a}{V^3}\right)\Big/\frac{R}{V} \quad ...(8)$$

If temperature is constant, dT = 0; equation (6) becomes as follows:

$$\left(\frac{\partial T}{\partial V}\right)_T = -\frac{1}{\left(\frac{RT}{V^2} - \frac{2a}{V^3}\right)} \quad ...(9)$$

On multiplying equations (7), (8) and (9), we obtain

$$\left(\frac{\partial p}{\partial T}\right)_V\left(\frac{\partial T}{\partial V}\right)_P\left(\frac{\partial V}{\partial P}\right)_T = -\frac{R}{V}\times\frac{\left(\frac{RT}{V^2} - \frac{2a}{V^3}\right)}{\left(\frac{RT}{V^2} - \frac{2a}{V^3}\right)}\times\frac{1}{R} = -1$$

or

$$\left(\frac{\partial p}{\partial T}\right)_V\left(\frac{\partial T}{\partial V}\right)_P\left(\frac{\partial V}{\partial P}\right)_T + 1 = 0$$

This is cyclic rule.

Example 15:

For an ideal gas PV = RT, prove that dP is an exact differential.

Solution:

We know $PV = RT$

or

$$P = \frac{RT}{V} \text{ (R is a constant)} \quad ...(1)$$

On differentiating with respect to T, taking V constant, we obtain

$$\left(\frac{\partial P}{\partial T}\right)_P = \frac{RT}{V} \quad ...(2)$$

Again, on differentiating with respect to V, we obtain

$$\frac{\partial^2 P}{\partial V \partial T} = -\frac{R}{V^2} \quad ..(3)$$

On differentiating (1) with respect to volume, taking T constant, we obtain

$$\left(\frac{\partial P}{\partial V}\right)_T = -\frac{RT}{V^2} \qquad ...(4)$$

Again, on differentiating above equation with respect to temperature taking V as constant, we obtain

$$\frac{\partial^2 P}{\partial T \partial V} = -\frac{R}{V^2} \qquad ...(5)$$

From equations (3) and (5), we obtain

$$\frac{\partial^2 P}{\partial T \partial V} = \frac{\partial^2 P}{\partial T \partial V}$$

Thus dP is an exact differential.

Example 16:

For an ideal gas PV = RT, prove that DT is an exact differential.

Solution:

$$PV = RT \qquad ...(1)$$

In order to prove that dT is a perfect differential, we have to prove that

$$\frac{\partial^2 T}{\partial V \partial P} = \frac{\partial^2 T}{\partial P \partial V}$$

On differentiating Eq. (1), we obtain

$$\left(\frac{\partial T}{\partial V}\right)_P = \frac{P}{R}; \text{i.e., } \frac{\partial^2 T}{\partial P \partial V} = \frac{1}{R}$$

Again $$\left(\frac{\partial T}{\partial P}\right)_V = \frac{V}{R}; \text{i.e., } \frac{\partial^2 T}{\partial V \partial P} = \frac{1}{R}$$

Therefore, $$\frac{\partial^2 T}{\partial V \partial P} = \frac{\partial^2 T}{\partial P \partial V}$$

Thus, dT is an exact differential.

Example 17:

Show that PV = nRt, then

(i) $$\frac{\partial^2 P}{\partial n \partial V} = \frac{\partial^2 P}{\partial V \partial n} = -\frac{RT}{V^2}$$

(ii) $\frac{\partial^2 P}{\partial n \partial T} = \frac{\partial^2 P}{\partial T \partial n} = -\frac{R}{V}$

(iii) $\left(\frac{\partial P}{\partial T}\right)_V \left(\frac{\partial T}{\partial V}\right)_P \left(\frac{\partial V}{\partial P}\right)_T = -1$

Solution:

(i) $\because$ $PV = nRT$

$\therefore$ $P = \frac{nRT}{V}$

or $\frac{\partial P}{\partial V} = \frac{\partial}{\partial V}\left(\frac{nRT}{V}\right)$ [keeping T as constant]

$= nRT \frac{\partial}{\partial V}\left(\frac{1}{V}\right) = -\frac{nRT}{V^2}$

$\frac{\partial^2 P}{\partial n \partial V} = \frac{\partial}{\partial n}\left(\frac{\partial P}{\partial V}\right)$

$= \left(-\frac{nRT}{V^2}\right)$ [Keeping R, T and V as constant]

$= -\frac{RT}{V^2}$ ...(1)

Similarly, $PV = nRT$ or $P = \frac{nRT}{V}$

$\frac{\partial P}{\partial n} = \frac{RT}{V}$

$\frac{\partial^2 P}{\partial V \partial N} = \frac{\partial}{\partial V}\left(\frac{RT}{V}\right)$ [keeping T and R as constant]

$= -\frac{RT}{V^2}$ ...(2)

From equations (1) and (2), we obtain

$$\frac{\partial^2 P}{\partial n \partial V} = \frac{\partial^2 P}{\partial V \partial n} = -\frac{RT}{V^2}$$

(ii) $P = \frac{nRT}{V}$

$\frac{\partial P}{\partial T} = \frac{\partial}{\partial T}\left(\frac{nRT}{V}\right)$ [Keeping n and R as constant]

$$= \frac{nR}{V}$$

$$\frac{\partial^2 P}{\partial n \partial T} = \frac{\partial}{\partial n}\left(\frac{nR}{V}\right) \text{[Keeping V and R as constant]}$$

$$= \frac{R}{V} \qquad ...(3)$$

Again, $P = \frac{nRT}{V}$

$$\frac{\partial P}{\partial n} = \frac{RT}{V} \qquad \text{[Keeping RT and V as constant]}$$

$$\frac{\partial^2 P}{\partial T \partial n} = \frac{\partial}{\partial n}\left(\frac{RT}{V}\right) \qquad \text{[Keeping RT and V as constant]}$$

or $$\frac{\partial^2 P}{\partial T \partial n} = \frac{R}{V} \qquad ...(4)$$

From equations (3) and (4), we obtain

$$\frac{\partial^2 P}{\partial n \partial T} = \frac{\partial^2 P}{\partial T \partial n} = \frac{R}{V}$$

(iii) Again, $P = \frac{nRT}{V}$

$$\left(\frac{\partial P}{\partial T}\right)_V = \frac{nR}{V} \qquad ...(5)$$

Again, $V = \frac{nRT}{P}$

$$\left(\frac{\partial V}{\partial P}\right)_T = -\frac{nRT}{P} \qquad ...(6)$$

Again, $T = \frac{PV}{nR}$

$$\left(\frac{\partial T}{\partial V}\right)_P = -\frac{P}{nR} \qquad ...(7)$$

On multiplying equations (5), (6), and (7), we obtain

$$\left(\frac{\partial P}{\partial T}\right)_V \left(\frac{\partial T}{\partial V}\right)_P \left(\frac{\partial V}{\partial P}\right)_T = \frac{nR}{V} \times -\frac{nRT}{P^2} \times \frac{P}{nR}$$

$$= -\frac{nRT}{PV} = -1 \left[\because 1 = \frac{nRT}{PV}\right]$$

Example 18:

(i) Calculate α and β for an ideal gas obeying gas equation $PV = RT$ (for one mole). (ii) The van der Waal's equation is as follows:

Solution:

(i) We know

$$PV = RT$$

On differentiating the above equation, we obtain

$$PdV + VdP = RdT \qquad ...(1)$$

At constant pressure dP = 0, the above equation becomes as follows:

$$\left(\frac{\partial V}{\partial T}\right)_P = \frac{R}{V}$$

or $$\alpha = \frac{1}{V}\left(\frac{\partial V}{\partial T}\right)_P = \frac{R}{VP} = \frac{1}{T} = T^{-1}$$

At constant temperature dT = 0; equation (1) becomes as follows:

$$\left(\frac{\partial V}{\partial P}\right)_T = -\frac{V}{P}$$

or $$\beta = -\frac{1}{V}\left(\frac{\partial V}{\partial P}\right)_T = \frac{V}{VP} = \frac{1}{P} = P^{-1}$$

(ii) $$\left(P + \frac{a}{V^2}\right)(v - b) = RT$$

or $$PV^3 - PbV^2 + aV - ab - RTV^2 = 0 \qquad ...(2)$$

On differentiating the above equation with respect to T at constant pressure, we obtain

$$3\,PV^2\left(\frac{\partial V}{\partial T}\right)_P - 2PbV\left(\frac{\partial V}{\partial T}\right)_P + a\left(\frac{\partial V}{\partial T}\right)_P - 2RTV\left(\frac{\partial V}{\partial T}\right)_P - RV^2 = 0$$

or $$\left(\frac{\partial V}{\partial T}\right)_P = \frac{RV^2}{3PV^2 - 2PbV + a - 2RTV}$$

$$\alpha = \frac{1}{V}\left(\frac{\partial V}{\partial T}\right)_P$$

$$= \frac{1}{V}\left[\frac{RV^2}{3PV^2 - 2PVb + a - 2RTV}\right]$$

$$= \frac{R}{3PV - 2Pb + \frac{a}{V} - 2RT}$$

But the van der Waal's equation may be put as follows :

$$RT = PV - Pb + \frac{a}{V} - \frac{ab}{V^2}$$

$$\therefore \qquad \alpha = \frac{R}{3PV - 2Pb + \frac{a}{V} - 2\left(PV - Pb + \frac{a}{V} - \frac{ab}{V^2}\right)}$$

$$= R\left[PV - \frac{a}{V} + \frac{2ab}{V^2}\right]^{-1}$$

Again, on differentiating equation (2), with respect to P at constant temperature T, we obtain

$$3PV^2\left(\frac{\partial V}{\partial P}\right)_T + V \quad - 2PbV\left(\frac{\partial V}{\partial P}\right)_T$$

$$- bV^2 + a\left(\frac{\partial V}{\partial P}\right)_T - 2RTV\left(\frac{\partial V}{\partial P}\right)_T = 0$$

$$\left(\frac{\partial V}{\partial P}\right)_T = \frac{V^2(b - V)}{3PV^2 - 2PbV + a - 2RTV}$$

But the van der Waal's equation may be put as follows :

$$RTV = PV^2 + a - PbV - ab/V$$

$$\therefore \left(\frac{\partial V}{\partial P}\right)_T = \frac{V^2(b - V)}{3PV^2 - 2PbV + a - 2\left(PV^2 + a - PbV - \frac{ab}{V}\right)}$$

$$= \frac{b - V}{P - \frac{a}{V^2} + \frac{2ab}{V^3}}$$

Now $\qquad \beta = -\frac{1}{V}\left(\frac{\partial V}{\partial P}\right)_T = -\frac{b - V}{PV - \frac{a}{V} + \frac{2ab}{V^2}}$

$$= -\frac{V-b}{P-\frac{a}{V}+\frac{2ab}{V^2}}$$

Example 19:

For an ideal gas (PV = nRT) show that (1/T) is an integrating factor for dw = P dV

Solution:

$$dw = P\ dV \qquad ...(1)$$

$\because$ $$PV = nRT$$

$\therefore$ $$p\ dV + V\ dP = nR\ dT$$

and $$dV = \frac{nR}{P}dT - \frac{V}{P}dP \qquad ...(2)$$

On substituting the expression for dV in equation (1), we obtain

$$dw = nR\ dT - V\ dP = nR\ dT - \frac{nRT}{P}dP$$

Now $$\frac{\partial}{\partial P}(nR)_T = 0$$

and $$\frac{\partial}{\partial T}\left(-\frac{nRT}{P}\right)_P = -\frac{nR}{P}$$

Hence, dw is inexact differential.

Suppose f = 1/T be an integrating factor. Then

$$f\ \ dw = \frac{1}{T}nR\,dT - \frac{nR}{P}dP$$

$\therefore$ $$\frac{\partial}{\partial P}\left[\frac{nR}{T}\right]_T = 0$$

and $$\frac{\partial}{\partial T}\left[\frac{nR}{P}\right]_T = 0$$

Thus f. dw$\frac{nR}{T}dT - \frac{nR}{P}dP$ is an exact differential while 1/T is an integrating factor.

Example 20:

The opposite faces of a metal plate of 0.2 cm thickness an at a difference of temperature of 109°C and the area of the plate is 200 sq cm. Find the quantity of heat that will flow through the plate in one minute if K = 0.2 CGS units.

Solution:

Here,

$$K = 0.2$$

$$A = 200 \text{ sq cm}$$

$$d = 0.2 \text{ cm}$$

$$(\theta_1 - \theta_2) = 100°C$$

$$t = 60s$$

$$Q = \frac{KA(\theta_1 - \theta_2)t}{d}$$

$$= \frac{0.2 \times 200 \times 100 \times 60}{0.2}$$

$$= 12 \times 10^5 \text{ cal.}$$

Example 21:

A bar of length 30 cm and uniform area of cross-section 5 cm² consists of two halves AB of copper and BC of iron welded together at B. The end A is maintained at 200°C and the end C at 0°C. The sides of the bar are thermally insulated. Find the rate of flow of heat along the bar when the steady state is reached. Thermal conductivity of copper if 0.9 and thermal conductivity of iron is 0.12 CGS units.

Solution:

Suppose the temperature at the interface. B is θ after the steady state is reached.

$$\therefore \quad \frac{K_1A(200-\theta)}{d} = \frac{K_2A(\theta-0)}{d}$$

$$0.9(200 - \theta) = 0.12\,\theta$$

$$\theta = 176.5°C.$$

After the steady state is reached, the rate of flow of heat is the same in both the bars.

$$\therefore \quad Q = \frac{K_1A(\theta-0)}{d}$$

$$Q = \frac{0.9 \times 5 \times (200 - 176.5)}{15}$$

$$Q = 7.05 \text{ cal/s.}$$

Example 22:

An ice box is built of wood 1.76 cm thick, lined inside with cork 3 cm thick. If the temperature of the inner surface of the cork is 0°C and that of the outer surface of wood is 12°C, what is the temperature of the interface ? The thermal conductivity of wood and cork are 0.0006 and 0.00012 CGS units respectively.

Solution:

Suppose the temperature of the interface is θ after the steady state is reached

$$\therefore \quad \frac{K_1A(12-\theta)}{d_1} = \frac{K_2A(\theta-0)}{d_2}$$

Here
$$K_1 = 0.0006,$$
$$K_2 = 0.00012$$
$$d_1 = 1.75 \text{ cm},$$
$$d_2 = 3 \text{ cm}$$

$$\frac{0.0006(12-\theta)}{1.75} = \frac{0.00012(\theta)}{3}$$

$$\theta = 10.74°\text{C}.$$

Example 23:

Find the time in which a layer of ice 3 cm thick on the surface of a pond will increase its thickness by 1 mm when the temperature of the surrounding air is –20°C.

Thermal conductivity of ice = 0.005

Latent heat of ice = 80 cal/g

Density of ice at 0°C = 0.91 g/cm³.

Solution:

$$\int dt = \frac{\rho L}{K\theta}\int x dx$$

$$t = \frac{\rho L}{2K\theta}[x_2^2 - x_1^2]$$

Here,
$$\rho = 0.91 \text{ g/cm}^3$$
$$L = 80 \text{ cal/g}$$

$$K = 0.005$$

$$\theta = 20^{o}C$$

$$x_1 = 3 \text{ cm}$$

$$x_2 = 3.1 \text{ cm}$$

$$t = \frac{0.91 \times 80}{2 \times 0.005 \times 20} [(3.1)^2 - (3)^2]$$

$$= 222.04 \text{ s}$$

$= 3$ min 42 s approximately.

Example 24:

Calculate the work down when 50 g of iron dissolves in hydrochloric acid at 25oC in :

(i) A closed vessel, and

(ii) An open beaker.

(iii) In which case would maximum amount of work be done ?

Solution:

$$\text{Amount of iron} = \frac{50 \text{ g}}{55.85 \text{ g mol}^{-1}} = \frac{50}{55.85} \text{ mol}$$

(i) In a closed vessel, $\Delta V = 0$. Hence,

$$dw = - PdV = 0$$

that is, no work is involved when iron dissolves in hydrochloric acid in a closed vessel.

(ii) The reaction between iron and hydrochloric acid is

$$Fe + 2HCl \rightarrow FeCl_2 + H_2(g)$$

Thus, the liberated hydrogen gas pushes the atmospheric air and thus involves the work of expansion. In this case, we will have

$$w = - P_{ext} \Delta V$$

$$= - P_{ext} V_{H2}$$

where V_{H2} is the volume of hydrogen released. According to the ideal gas law, we will have

$$w = - P_{ext} (n_{H2}RT/P_{ext})$$

$$= - n_{H_2}RT$$

$$= - (50/55.85) \text{ mol } (8.314 \text{ J K}^{-1} \text{ mol}^{-1}) (298 \text{ K})$$

$$= - 2.2 \text{ kJ}.$$

Example 25:

Since $C_V = (\partial q/\partial T)_V$ by definition, one often writes without restriction $dV = C_V dT$. This is generally not true. Explain why.

Solution:

If we take U = f)V, T), then we will have

$$dU = \left(\frac{\partial U}{\partial V}\right)_T dV + \left(\frac{\partial U}{\partial T}\right)_V dT$$

$$= \left(\frac{\partial U}{\partial V}\right)_T . dV + C_V \, dT$$

Thus, if one writes $dV = C_V \, dT$ without restriction then this statement is not complete. This is applicable for a system in which $(\partial U/\partial V)_T = 0$. An ideal gas is such an example. Alternatively, the system may be undergoing change at constant volume, for which, $(\partial U/\partial V)_T \, dV$ is zero and thus $dV = C_V \, dT$.

Example 26:

Calculate the work done by the system when 2 mol of an ideal gas expand from 0.01 m^3 to 0.1 m^3 at 300 k isothermally :

(i) Into a vacuum, and

(ii) Reversibly.

Explain how the surroundings can be restored only in one case and not in the other.

Solution:

(i) When the work is done into a vacuum, the work done by the system is zero since P_{opp} in this case is zero.

(ii) For the reversible isothermal expansion work involvec is

$$w = - nRT \ln \frac{V_2}{V_1}$$

$$= (2) (8.314 \times 300 \text{ J}) \ln \frac{0.1}{0.01}$$

$$= -2 \times 8.314 \times 300 \times 2.303 \text{ J}$$

$$= -11488 \text{ J} = -11.488 \text{ kJ}.$$

This surroundings are not disturbed when the expansion is done against vacuum. In case of reversible isothermal expansion, heat is absorbed by the system from the surroundings.

Now, if we carry out reversible isothermal compression of the system till the original state, then the same quantity or heat is released to the surroundings and thus the latter is restored back to the original state.

However, in the first case where expansion is done against vacuum, there will be bet heat received by the surroundings during compression. Hence, in this case, it is not restored back to its original state.

Example 27:

Derive $C_{P,m} - C_{V,m} = TV_m \dfrac{\alpha^2}{\beta}$

where α *and* β *are the coefficient of thermal expansion and coefficient of compressibility, respectively.*

Solution:

We start with H = f (T, P) and U = f (T, V) and write their differentials as

$$dH = \left(\frac{\partial H}{\partial T}\right)_P dT + \left(\frac{\partial H}{\partial P}\right)_T dP$$

$$dU = \left(\frac{\partial U}{\partial T}\right)_V dT + \left(\frac{\partial U}{\partial V}\right)_T dV$$

Now since H = U + PV

we have dH = dU + P dV + V dP

$$\text{or} \left(\frac{\partial H}{\partial T}\right)_P dT + \left(\frac{\partial H}{\partial P}\right)_T dP = \left(\frac{\partial U}{\partial T}\right)_V dT + \left(\frac{\partial U}{\partial V}\right)_T dV + P\,dV + V\,dP$$

Dividing by dT, keeping P constant, we get

$$\left(\frac{\partial H}{\partial T}\right)_P = \left(\frac{\partial U}{\partial T}\right)_V + \left(\frac{\partial U}{\partial V}\right)_T \left(\frac{\partial V}{\partial T}\right)_P + P\left(\frac{\partial V}{\partial T}\right)_P$$

Now using the thermodynamic equation of state

$$\left(\frac{\partial U}{\partial V}\right)_T = T\left(\frac{\partial P}{\partial T}\right)_V - P$$

we get $$\left(\frac{\partial H}{\partial T}\right)_P = \left(\frac{\partial U}{\partial T}\right)_V + T\left(\frac{\partial P}{\partial T}\right)_V\left(\frac{\partial V}{\partial T}\right)_P \quad ...(1)$$

Now, by definition

$$\alpha = \frac{1}{V}\left(\frac{\partial V}{\partial T}\right)_P \quad ...(2)$$

$$\beta = -\frac{1}{V}\left(\frac{\partial V}{\partial P}\right)_T \quad ...(3)$$

Using the cyclic rule

$$\left(\frac{\partial V}{\partial P}\right)_T\left(\frac{\partial P}{\partial T}\right)_V\left(\frac{\partial T}{\partial V}\right)_P + 1 = 0$$

we get $$\left(\frac{\partial V}{\partial P}\right)_T = -\left(\frac{\partial V}{\partial T}\right)_P\left(\frac{\partial T}{\partial P}\right)_V$$

Hence $$\beta = \frac{1}{V}\left(\frac{\partial V}{\partial T}\right)_P \cdot \left(\frac{\partial T}{\partial P}\right)_V$$

and $$\frac{\alpha}{\beta} = \left(\frac{\partial P}{\partial T}\right)_V$$

Hence, Eq (1) becomes

$$C_{P,m} - C_{V,m} = T\left(\frac{\partial P}{\partial T}\right)_V\left(\frac{\partial V}{\partial T}\right)_P \quad ...(4)$$

With the use of Eqs. (2) and (4), we get

$$C_{P,m} - C_{V,m} = TV\,\frac{\alpha^2}{\beta}$$

Example 28:

When a bicycle tyre is inflated with hand pump, the temperature of the air inside increases. Explain.

Solution:

Work done on the system is converted into heat which increases the temperature of air inside the tyre.

Example 29:

Two large closely spaced concentric spheres (both are black body radiators) are maintained, at temperatures of 200 K and 300 K *respectively. The space in between the two spheres is evacuated. Calculate the net rate of energy transfer between the two spheres. (σ = 5.672 × 10^{-8} M.K.S. units).*

Solution:

Here $T_1 = 300$ K

$T_2 = 200$ K

$\sigma = 5.672 \times 10^{-8}$ M.K.S. units

$R = \sigma(T_1^4 - T_2^4)$

$= 5.672 \times 10^{-8}[(300)^4 - (200)^4]$

$R = 368.69$ watts/m^2.

Example 30:

Calculate the radiant emittance of a black body at a temperature of (i) 400 K (ii) 4000 K. (σ = 5.672 × 10^{-8} M.K.S. units).

Solution:

Here $T = \sigma T^4$

(i) $R = 5.672 \times 10^{-8} [400]^4$

$= 1452$ watt/m^2.

(ii) $R = 5.672 \times 10^{-8}(4000)^4 = 1452 \times 10^4$ watts/m^2

$= 14520$ kilo-watts/m^2.

Example 31:

The relative emittance of tungsten is approximately 0.35. A tungsten sphere of surface area 10^{-8} sq metres is suspended inside a large evacuated enclosure whose walls are at 300 K. What power input is required to maintain the sphere at a temperature of 3000 K? The conduction of heat along the supports can be neglected. (σ = 5.672 × 10^{-8} M.K.S. units).

Solution:

Here $R = \sigma A e[T^4 - T_0^4]$

$A = 10^{-3}$ sq meters

$e = 0.35$

$\sigma = 5.672 \times 10^{-8}$ M.K.S. units

$R = 5.672 \times 10^{-8} \times 10^{-3} \times 0.35[(3000)] \quad (300)^4]$

$= 1609$ watts

The power input $= 1609$ watts.

Example 32:

An aluminium foil of relative emittance 0.1 is placed in between two concentric spheres at temperatures 300 K and 200 K respectively. Calculate the temperature of the foil after the steady state is reached. Assume that the spheres are perfect black body radiators. Also calculate the rate of energy transfer between one of the spheres and the foil. ($\sigma = 5.672 \times 10^{8}$ M.K.S. units).

Solution:

Here $T_1 = 300$ K

$T_2 = 200$ K

$e = 0.1$

$\sigma = 5.672 \times 10^{-8}$ M.K.S. units.

(i) Let x be the temperature of the foil. After the steady-state is reached,

$$e\sigma(T_1^4 - x^4) = e\sigma(x^4 - T_2^4)$$

or $[(300)^4 - x^4] = [x - 200)^4]$

$$x^4 = 48.5 \times 10^8$$

$$x = 263.8 \text{ K}$$

(ii) $R = e\sigma(T_1^4 - x^4)$

$$R = 0.1 \times 5.672 \times 10^{-8}[(300)^4 - (263.8)^4]$$

$$R = 18.5 \text{ watt/m}^2.$$

Example 33:

Calculate the energy radiated per minute from the filament of an incandescent lamp at 2000 K, if the surface area is 5.0×10^{5} sq metres and its relative emittance is 0.85.

Solution:

$$E = Ae\ \sigma t\ (T^4)$$

$$A = 5 \times 10^{-5} m^2$$

$$e = 0.85$$

$$\sigma = 5.672 \times 10^{-8} \text{ M.K.S. units.}$$

$$t = 60s$$

$$T = 2000 \text{ K}$$

$$E = 5 \times 10^{-6} \times 0.85 \times 5.672 \times 10^{-8} \times 60 \times (2000)^4$$

$$E = 2315 \text{ joules.}$$

Example 34:

An iron furnace radiates 1.53 × 10^5 calories per hour through an opening of cross-section 10^{-4} sq metre. If the relative emittance of the furnace is 0.80, calculate the temperature of the furnace. (Given σ = 1.36 × 10^{-8} cal/m^2-s-K^4).

Solution:

$$E = Ae\ \sigma\ f(T^4)$$

$$E = 1.53 \times 10^5 \text{ calories}$$

$$A = 10^{-4} m^2;\ e = 0.80$$

$$t = 3600 \text{ s};\ T = ?$$

$$T^4 = \frac{E}{Ae\sigma t}$$

$$T = \left(\frac{E}{Ae\sigma t}\right)^{1/4}$$

$$= \left(\frac{1.53\times10^5}{10^{-4}\times0.80\times1.36\times10^{-8}\times3600}\right)^{1/4}$$

$$T = 2500 \text{ K.}$$

Example 35:

Calculate the black body temperature of the sun from the following data.

Solution:

Stefan's constant $= 1.37 \times 10^{-12}$ cal/cm^2/s

Solar constant $= 2.3$ cal/cm^2/minute

Radius of the sun $= 7 \times 10^{10}$ cm.

Distance between the sun and the earth

$= 1.5 \times 10^{13}$cm

$$E = \frac{4\pi R^2 S}{4\pi r^2} = \left(\frac{R}{r}\right)^2 .S$$

Here $R = 1.5 \times 10^{13}$cm

$r = 7 \times 10^{10}$cm

$S = 2.3$ cal/cm^2/minute

$$E = \left[\frac{1.5 \times 10^{13}}{7 \times 10^{10}}\right]^2 \times \frac{2.3}{60} \text{cal / s} \quad ...(i)$$

$$1.37 \times 10^{-12} \times T^4 = \left[\frac{1.5 \times 10^{13}}{7 \times 10^{10}}\right]^2 \times \frac{2.3}{60}$$

$$E = \sigma T^4 \quad ...(ii)$$

Equating (i) and (ii)

$T = 5987$K.

Example 37:

In an Ingen-hausz experiment, wax melted over 10 cm of copper rod and over 4 cm of iron rod. What is the conductivity of iron when the conductivity of copper is 0.90?

Solution:

Here, $l_1 = 10$cm

$l_2 = 4$cm

$K_1 = 0.90$

$K_2 = ?$

$$\frac{K_2}{K_1} = \frac{l_2^2}{l_1^2}$$

$$K_2 = \frac{l_2^2}{l_1^2} \times K_1$$

$$= \frac{16}{100} \times 0.90$$

$$K_2 = 0.144.$$

Example 37:

How much time will it take for a layer of ice of thickness 10 cm to increase by 5 cm on the surface of a pond when the temperature of the surroundings is –10°C?

Solution:

$$K = 0.005$$

$$L = 80 \text{ cal/g}$$

$$p = 0.90 \text{ g/cm}^3$$

Here $\int dt = \frac{\rho L}{K\theta} \int x dx$

$$t = \frac{\rho L}{2K\theta}[x_2^2 - x_1^2]$$

Here $x_1 = 10$ cm,

$$x_2 = 15 \text{ cm}$$

$$t = \frac{0.90 \times 80}{2 \times 0.005 \times 10}[(15)^2 - (10)^2]$$

$$= 9 \times 10^4 \text{s} = 25 \text{ hours.}$$

Example 38:

Calculate the maximum work obtainable by (i) the isothermal expansion and (ii) the adiabatic expansion of 2 mol of on ideal gas initially at 25° C form 10 L to 20 L. Assume Cv = (5/2) R.

Solution:

(i) Maximum work is obtained in reversible expansion. Hence

$$w = -nRT \ln \frac{V_2}{V_1}$$

$$= -(2\ \text{mol})(8.314\ \text{J K}^{-1}\ \text{mol}^{-1})(298\ \text{K})(2.303 \log \frac{20\text{L}}{10\text{L}}$$

$$= -3435\ J$$

(ii) Firstly, we calculate the final temperature using the expression

$$T_2 V_2^{\gamma-1} = T_1 V_1^{\gamma-1}$$

where $\gamma = \frac{C_P}{C_V} = \frac{(7/2)R}{(5/2)R} = \frac{7}{5}$

Hence, $T_2 = (298\text{K})\left(\frac{10\text{L}}{20\text{L}}\right)^{(7/5)-1}$

$$= (298\ \text{K})(0.7578) = 225.8\ \text{K}$$

Now $W_{adi} = \Delta E$

$$= n\, C_{V,}\, m(T_2 - T_1)$$

$$= (2\text{mol})(2.5 \times 8.314\ \text{JK}^{-1}\text{mol}^{-1})(225.8\text{K} - 298\text{K})$$

$$= -3001\ \text{J}.$$

Example 39:

Show that

$$\left(\frac{\partial \alpha}{\partial P}\right)_T + \left(\frac{\partial \beta}{\partial T}\right)_P = 0$$

where α and β are coefficient of thermal expansion and coefficient of compressibility, respectively.

Solution:

Since V is a state function, we can write

$$\frac{\partial^2 V}{\partial T\, \partial P} = \frac{\partial^2 V}{\partial P\, \partial T}$$

or $\frac{\partial}{\partial T}(-V\beta)_P = \frac{\partial}{\partial T}(V\alpha)_T$

Carrying out the differentiation, we get

$$-\beta\left(\frac{\partial V}{\partial T}\right)_P - V\left(\frac{\partial \beta}{\partial T}\right)_P = \alpha\left(\frac{\partial V}{\partial P}\right)_T + V\left(\frac{\partial \alpha}{\partial P}\right)_T$$

that is $$\left(\frac{\partial \alpha}{\partial P}\right)_T + \left(\frac{\partial \beta}{\partial T}\right)_P = -\frac{\beta}{V}\left(\frac{\partial V}{\partial T}\right)_P - \frac{\alpha}{V}\left(\frac{\partial V}{\partial P}\right)_T$$

$$= -\frac{\beta}{V}(\alpha V) - \frac{\alpha}{V}(-\beta V) = 0$$

Example 40:

Show that Joule Thomson coefficient, μ_{JT} = 0 for an ideal gas. Comment on the liquefaction of an ideal gas.

Solution:

By definition, Joule-Thomson coefficient is defined as

$$\mu_{JT} = \left(\frac{\partial T}{\partial P}\right)_H$$

Using the cyclic rule

$$\left(\frac{\partial T}{\partial P}\right)_H \left(\frac{\partial P}{\partial H}\right)_T \left(\frac{\partial H}{\partial T}\right)_P + 1 = 0$$

we get $$\left(\frac{\partial T}{\partial P}\right)_H = -\frac{1}{\left(\frac{\partial P}{\partial H}\right)_T \left(\frac{\partial H}{\partial T}\right)_P} = -\frac{\left(\frac{\partial H}{\partial P}\right)_T}{C_P}$$

Now using, thermodynamic equation of state

$$\left(\frac{\partial T}{\partial P}\right)_H = V - T\left(\frac{\partial V}{\partial T}\right)_P$$

we get $$\mu_{JT} = \frac{V - T\left(\frac{\partial V}{\partial T}\right)_P}{C_P}$$

Now, for an ideal gas

$$V = \frac{nRT}{P}$$

Hence, $$\left(\frac{\partial V}{\partial T}\right)_P = \frac{nR}{P} = \frac{V}{T}$$

Thus $$\mu_{JT} = \frac{V - T\left(\frac{V}{T}\right)}{C_P} = 0$$

The ideal gas cannot be liquefied as there will not occur any change in temperature when the gas undergoes Joule-Thomson experiment.

EXERCISES

1. Distinguish between Classical Statistics, Fermi-Dirac Statistics and Bose-Einstein Statistics.
2. Calculate the change in entropy when 100 g of water at 15°C is mixed with 160 g of water at 40°C. Specific heat of water may be assumed as equal to I.
3. Calculate the change in the melting point of wax for a pressure of 50 atmospheres from the following data. Melting point of wax = 64°C. Specific volume of solid at 64°C = 1.161 and that of the liquid at 64°C = 1.166. Latent heat = 97 cal/g.
4. Calculate the change in temperature of the boiling point of water due to a change of pressure of 1 cm of Hg. L = 536 cal/g. Volume of 1g of water at 100°C = 1 cc and volume of 1 g of saturated steam at 100°C == 1600 cc.

6. Calculate the pressure required to make ice freeze at –1°C. Change in specific volume when one gram of water freezes into ice is equal to 0.091 cm^3. J = 4.2 × 10^7 ergs/ad. One atmosphere = 10^6 dynes/cm^2. Latent heat of ice = 80 cal/g.

6. Calculate the change in entropy when one gram of ice is mixed with 2 millilitres of water at 55°C. Assume that the specific heat and the specific gravity of water remain constant (*i.e.*, equal to 1 in both the cases) between 0°C and 55°C. Latent heat of ice = 80 cal/g.

7. A quantity of air (γ = 1.4) at 27°C is compressed suddenly to 1/4 of its original volume. Find the final temperature.
8. A quantity of air at 27°C and atmospheric pressure is suddenly compressed to 1/5 of its original volume. Find:

   (i) the final pressure, and

   (ii) the final temperature.
9. Find the efficiency of the Carnot's engine working between 150°C and 50°C.
10. Derive Planck's radiation law for the black body radiation.

11. Define entropy. What is its physical significance? Show that the entropy remains constant in a reversible process. What happens in case the process is an irreversible one?
12. A system consists of 8000 particles distributed in three energy states with equal spacing. The energy of the three states are $E_1 = 0$, $E_2 = x$. $E_3 = 2x$. All the three states have the same intrinsic probability g. At a certain instant, there are 4000 particles in the lower level, 3000 particles in the middle level and 1000 particles in the upper level. Compare the relative probabilities with the distribution obtained by the transfer of one particle from middle to the lower level and one particle from the middle to the upper level and the original distribution.
13. Enunciate the second law of thermodynamics. Define a temperature scale without making use of the peculiarities of any selected thermometric substance. Show that Kelvin's work scale is such a scale and that the ratio of the two temperatures as measured on the Kelvin scale is identical with the ratio of the same two temperatures on a perfect gas scale.
14. State the first law of thermodynamics and use it to derive a relation between pressure and temperature of a perfect gas undergoing an adiabatic change.
15. Establish the distribution law of Maxwell and Boltzmann.
16. Discuss the free electron gas model for metals. Obtain the distribution law for the electron gas in a metal at absolute zero.
17. Comment "Uncertainty principle leads to statistical results."
18. Write short notes on: Entropy and probability, canonical ensemble, phase-space, macro and microstates, distribution of N molecules in m cells, degeneracy, quantum states.
19. Distinguish between classical and quantum "statistics,
20. Explain what you understand by the term statistical equilibrium?
21. Discuss Maxwell-Boltzmann distribution law and cerive the relation.
22. On the basis of Maxwell-Boltzmann statistics show that the temperature of a system in statistical equilibrium is related to average energy of the particles of the system.

23. Applying Maxwell-Boltzmann distribution law, show that the internal energy of an ideal mono-atomic gas depends only on its temperature.

24. Write short notes on:

 (a) Electron gas

 (b) Photon gas

 (c) Phase space

 (d) Quantum statistics

 (e) Statistical equilibrium

 (e) Fermi temperature.

25. Explain what you mean by entropy of a substance. Show that the entropy remains constant in a reversible process but increases in an irreversible process.

26. Prove that $\frac{E_S}{E_T} = \gamma$.

27. State the first law of thermodynamics. Express it mathematically and explain its physical significance.

28. If N = 300, find the ratio of the distribution 10% off from maximum probable, to the most probable one.

29. Deduce the first latent heat equation. Discuss how the boiling point of a liquid and the melting point of a solid are affected by change of pressure.

30. Define entropy. State and prove the principle of increase of entropy.

31. Define work scale of temperature. Show that the ideal gas scale and the work scale are identical.

32. Show that

$$\left(\frac{\partial P}{\partial T}\right)_V \left(\frac{\partial V}{\partial T}\right)_V$$ is independent of the path for a reversible change.

33. Calculate the number of quantum states available to a proton inside a nucleus ($r = 10^{-14}$m) whose momentum does not exceed 10^{-19} kg m.s^{-1}

34. An oven is at 600 K. Calculate the probability for 3 photons to be in a quantum state of energy 0.2 eV. Assume chemical potential of photon to be zero.
35. Deduce Clausius-Clapeyron's equation and discuss the effect of change of pressure on the melting and boiling points of a substance.
36. Deduce the Clausius-Clapeyron's equation for the change of equilibrium pressure of two phases with temperature.
37. Show that as the molecules become numerous the deviation from most probable distribution is very rare.
38. How will you use statistical mechanics in deriving a relation for magnetisation in terms of temperature and external magnetic field B.

35. Describe Partington's method for the determination of the ratio of the two specific heats of a gas.
36. What are isothermal and adiabatic changes? Derive the equation PV^{γ} = constant, for an ideal gas.
37. What is meant by a reversible process? Describe Carnot's cycle and show that all reversible engines working between the same two temperatures have the same efficiency.
39. Obtain an expression for Bose-Einstein distribution law.
40. What is the principle of equal a priori probability (Write statistical postulates.
41. Find the increase in the boiling point of water at 100°C when the pressure is increased by 2 atmospheres. Latent heat of vaporisation of steam is 540 cal/g and 1 g of steam occupies 1677cm^3 volume.
42. Explain the statistical significance of entropy and prove that

$$S = k \log W.$$

43. What is Gibbs ensemble? Differentiate between different types of ensembles.
44. What are the fundamental postulates of statistical mechanics? Obtain an expression for the number of states for a macroscopic system.